# Business

## Book 1

2nd Edition





David Dooley • Rob Dransfield
John Goymer • Philip Guy
Catherine Richards

www.heinemann.co.uk
✓ Free online support
✓ Useful weblinks
✓ 24 hour online ordering

01865 888058

Heinemann is an imprint of Pearson Education Limited, a company incorporated in England and Wales, having its registered office at Edinburgh Gate, Harlow, Essex, CM20 2JE. Registered company number: 872828

www.heinemann.co.uk
Heinemann is a registered trademark of Pearson Education Ltd.



First published 2007

12 11 10 09
10 9 8 7 6

British Library Cataloguing in Publication Data is available from the British Library on request.

ISBN 978 0 435465 44 5



Edited by Linda Mellor
Designed by Pentacor Big Ltd
Typeset by Tech-Set Ltd
Original illustrations © Pearson Education Limited 2007
Illustrated by Tek-Art Ltd
Cover design by Wooden Ark
Picture research by Helen Reilly
Cover photo © Getty
Printed and bound in China (SWTC/06)

**Websites**
The websites used in this book were correct and up-to-date at the time of publication. It is essential for tutors to preview each website before using it in class so as to ensure that the URL is still accurate, relevant and appropriate. We suggest that tutors bookmark useful websites and consider enabling students to access them through the school/college intranet.

# Contents

# Acknowledgements


The author and publisher are grateful to all those who have given permission to reproduce material. Every effort has been made to contact copyright holders of material reproduced in this book. Any omissions will be rectified in subsequent printings if notice is given to the publishers.

## Photo acknowledgements

Atlas Copco – pages 76, 234, 374
AMT Coffee Ltd – page 59
Arnost Design Ltd – pages 111, 173, 177, 238–239, 280–281, 289, 298
B&Q – page 101
Corbis – Case study icon of Atomium, Brussels; and Thinking point icon of Kuwait Towers
Corbis/David Reed – page 224
Corbis/Helen King – page 338
Corbis/Jon Sparks – page 130
Digital Vision – pages 98–99
Dreamstime /Simon Schmidt – Practice point icon of Arche de la Défense, Paris
Fotolia/andrsr – page 430
Fotolia/Marcin Balcerzak – page 349
Fotolia/Martin Purmensky – page 352
Fotolia/tmcnem – pages 328–329
Getty Images – page 261
Getty Images/Iconica – page 389
Getty Images/PhotoDisc – pages 58–59, 190, 203, 144–145; and End of unit test icon of Radcliffe Camera, Oxford
Liam Halpin – page 245
Harcourt Ltd/Peter Evans – Outcome activity icon of Battersea Power Station, London
Innocent Smoothies – page 3
istock/Loren Radis – page 129
istock/bulent ince – page 129
istock/Diane Diederich – page 157
istock/Lisa FX Photograph – page 440
istock/Marcin Palko – pages 198–199
istock/mddphoto – pages 2–3
istock/Joris van Caspel – pages 368–369
istock/Rafa Irusta – pages 400–401
istock/Sean Locke – page 284
istock/Sue Colvil – Consider this icon of Burj al Arab hotel, Dubai
istock/The Image Area – page 369
istock/absolut_100 – page 61
JoinRed.com – page 8
Lloyds – page 74
Marks & Spencers – page 269
The National Lottery – page 304
OXFAM – page 17
Photos.com – Remember icon of Capitol Hill, Washington DC
Dan Raistrick – page 331
Rex Features Ltd/IPC Magazines: *Chat* – page 43
The Rugby Football Union – pages 209, 387
Skoda – page 246
Sony – pages 48, 406, 414
Topfoto – page 50
Tesco – page 21
Unilever – page 252
Virgin – page 68

## Text acknowledgements

Advertising Standards Authority – page 110
Amazon.com Inc – page 434 (courtesy of Amazon.com Inc and its affiliates. All rights reserved)
Bells Fish and Chips – page 427
BRAD – page 268
BT plc – page 355 (© BT plc)
ClickZ.com – pages 410, 412, 421, 422
Co-op Bank – page 410
Copernic Public Relations – page 423
Direct Marketing Association – page 110
Electricnews.net, for extract from article 'Yahoo! now bigger than Google', Tuesday 9th August 2005 – page 428
Experian, for M&S Mosaic – page 125
Fast Track 100 Ltd – page 27
Google Inc – pages 184, 402 (© Google Inc)
Health and Safety Executive – page 68
HSBC – page 419
IMRG – page 257
Innocent Smoothies – page 38
Ivor Solutions Ltd – pages 443, 444
Newspaper Association of America – page 424 (All rights reserved)
Next – page 409
NI Syndication – page 51
The Register – pages 408, 435, 438
RS Components – page 408
Scottish Enterprise Network – page 407
Solent University – page 63
Sony Computer Entertainment Europe – page 205
Tesco Stores Ltd – page 437
UK Banners – page 428
The Whale Rescue Team – page 394 (reprinted with permission of the author Peter Wallerstein)
Woolley & Co Solicitors – page 447
Yahoo! Inc – pages 65, 436 (Yahoo! and the Yahoo! logo are trademarks of Yahoo! Inc)
Yell Ltd – page 425

Crown copyright material is reproduced under Class Licence No. C01W0000141 with the permission of the Controller of HMSO and the Queen's Printer in Scotland – pages 193, 292

BTEC National Business courses have been designed to be as practical as possible and allow you to get a good job with an employer or give you skills to enable you to progress on to university. Throughout your course you need to organise yourself, produce assignments and work with others – all using business-related materials. This book contains lots of very useful information with up-to-date real-world business scenarios to help you to become more aware of the business world around you.

## Background to the BTEC National Business Qualifications

There are different types of BTEC National Business qualification that you may be studying – it could be a BTEC National Award that requires you to study 6 units, a BTEC National Certificate with 12 units or a BTEC National Diploma with 18 units. You may also have the chance to specialise, for example in Finance or Human Resources. Whichever qualification you are doing, you will find this book an invaluable companion to your study.

A BTEC National is a coursework-based qualification that requires a lot of time and hard work to achieve, but at the end of it you will have skills and ideas that will make you an asset to any business. Assessors will be checking that your work meets national standards throughout the year, and your work may be looked at by an external verifier as well.

You can access any extra information that you might need about BTEC National Qualifications at their website www.edexcel.org.uk.

## About this book

This book is divided into 10 chapters covering all the core units and some specialist units. Each chapter represents a different unit. If you are following the BTEC National Certificate general pathway you will find enough information in this book to guide you to achieving the qualification at this level.

The 10 Units covered within the book are:

| | |
|---|---|
| Unit 1 | Exploring Business Activity |
| Unit 2 | Investigating Business Resources |
| Unit 3 | Introduction to Marketing |
| Unit 4 | Effective People, Communication and Information |
| Unit 5 | Introduction to Accounting |
| Unit 9 | Exploring Creative Product Promotion |
| Unit 10 | Introduction to Marketing Research |
| Unit 13 | Investigating Recruitment and Selection |
| Unit 19 | Exploring Team Development |
| Unit 29 | Introduction to the Internet and E-Business |

This book can be used in lots of different ways. You may wish to use it as a classroom-based resource by completing activities in class and sharing your ideas with your fellow learners, or you may also wish to use it to help you stay focused and ahead within your learning. What is important is for you to make maximum use of the material provided in order for you to achieve success within your BTEC National Business course.

This book has been endorsed by Edexcel, which means that it has been through a rigorous quality assurance programme to ensure that it is a suitable companion to the specification for both teachers and students.

## What's in a Unit?

There are several new features in this book, designed to guide you towards success on your BTEC National course and help you achieve the best grade possible.

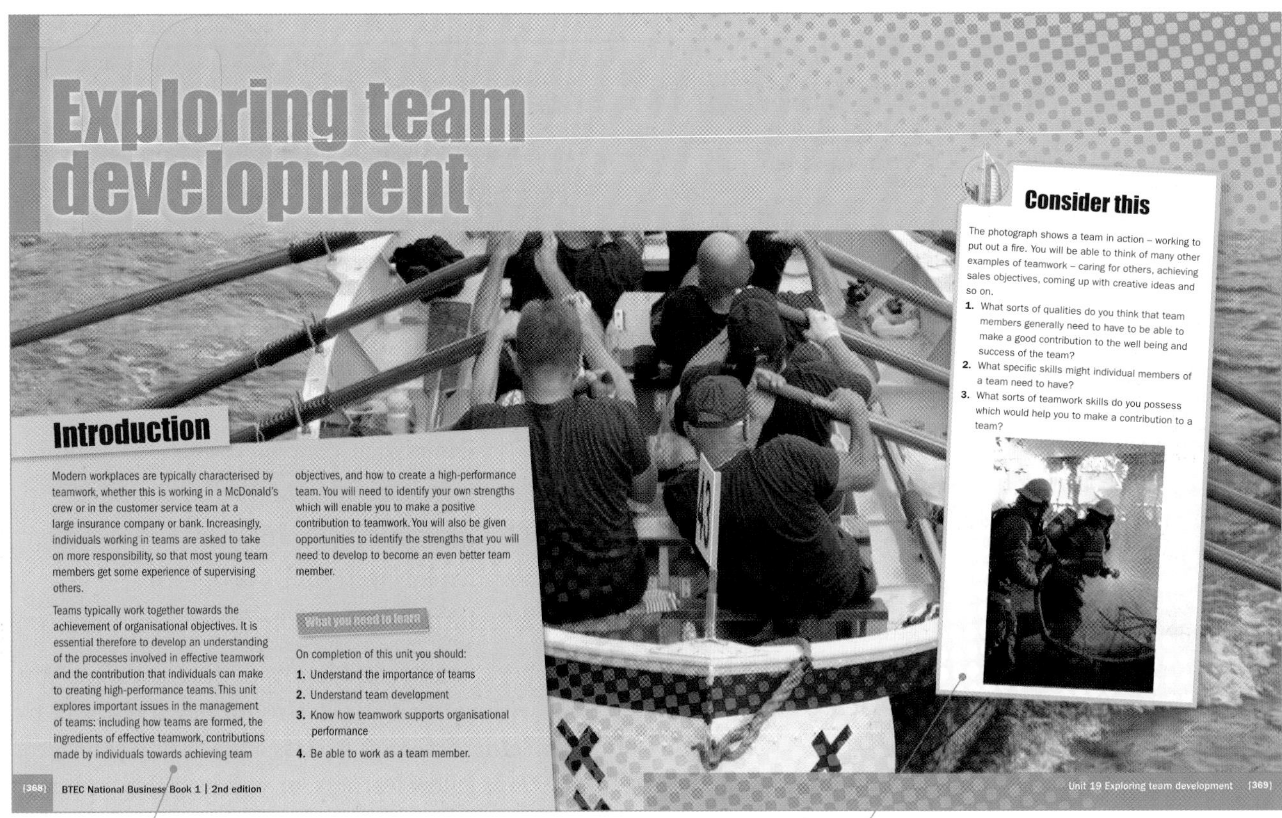

# Exploring team development

## Introduction

Modern workplaces are typically characterised by teamwork, whether this is working in a McDonald's crew or in the customer service team at a large insurance company or bank. Increasingly, individuals working in teams are asked to take on more responsibility, so that most young team members get some experience of supervising others.

Teams typically work together towards the achievement of organisational objectives. It is essential therefore to develop an understanding of the processes involved in effective teamwork and the contribution that individuals can make to creating high-performance teams. This unit explores important issues in the management of teams: including how teams are formed, the ingredients of effective teamwork, contributions made by individuals towards achieving team objectives, and how to create a high-performance team. You will need to identify your own strengths which will enable you to make a positive contribution to teamwork. You will also be given opportunities to identify the strengths that you will need to develop to become an even better team member.

### What you need to learn

On completion of this unit you should:

1. Understand the importance of teams
2. Understand team development
3. Know how teamwork supports organisational performance
4. Be able to work as a team member.

### Consider this

The photograph shows a team in action – working to put out a fire. You will be able to think of many other examples of teamwork – caring for others, achieving sales objectives, coming up with creative ideas and so on.

1. What sorts of qualities do you think that team members generally need to have to be able to make a good contribution to the well being and success of the team?
2. What specific skills might individual members of a team need to have?
3. What sorts of teamwork skills do you possess which would help you to make a contribution to a team?

[368] BTEC National Business Book 1 | 2nd edition

Unit 19 Exploring team development [369]

### ■ Introduction

Each chapter has an introduction to the unit, breaking it down into relevant areas that relate directly back to the specification (syllabus). This gives you an overall idea of what is covered in the unit.

### ■ Consider this

An activity is provided at the start of each unit – this is designed to get you to consider the broad issues that relate to that unit's business area.

## ■ Thinking points

These activities are designed to help you reflect and build on your skills, and should help you when completing your assessed coursework. They will help you to broaden your knowledge and demonstrate your ability within business.

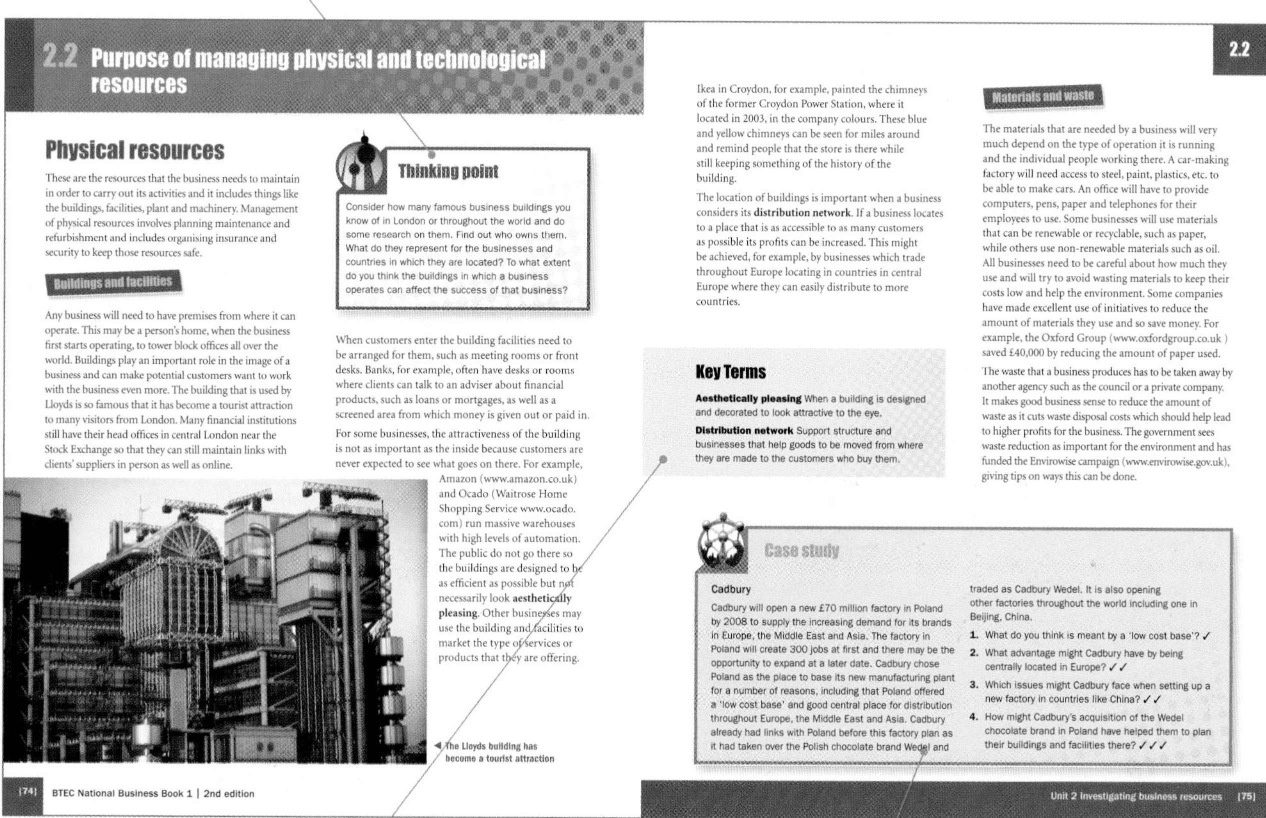



### 2.2 Purpose of managing physical and technological resources

#### Physical resources

These are the resources that the business needs to maintain in order to carry out its activities and it includes things like the buildings, facilities, plant and machinery. Management of physical resources involves planning maintenance and refurbishment and includes organising insurance and security to keep those resources safe.

**Buildings and facilities**

Any business will need to have premises from where it can operate. This may be a person's home, when the business first starts operating, to tower block offices all over the world. Buildings play an important role in the image of a business and can make potential customers want to work with the business even more. The building that is used by Lloyds is so famous that it has become a tourist attraction to many visitors from London. Many financial institutions still have their head offices in central London near the Stock Exchange so that they can still maintain links with clients' suppliers in person as well as online.

**Thinking point**

Consider how many famous business buildings you know of in London or throughout the world and do some research on them. Find out who owns them. What do they represent for the businesses and countries in which they are located? To what extent do you think the buildings in which a business operates can affect the success of that business?

When customers enter the building facilities need to be arranged for them, such as meeting rooms or front desks. Banks, for example, often have desks or rooms where clients can talk to an adviser about financial products, such as loans or mortgages, as well as a screened area from which money is given out or paid in.

For some businesses, the attractiveness of the building is not as important as the inside because customers are never expected to see what goes on there. For example, Amazon (www.amazon.co.uk) and Ocado (Waitrose Home Shopping Service www.ocado.com) run massive warehouses with high levels of automation. The public do not go there so the buildings are designed to be as efficient as possible but not necessarily look **aesthetically pleasing**. Other businesses may use the building and facilities to market the type of services or products that they are offering.

◄ The Lloyds building has become a tourist attraction

Ikea in Croydon, for example, painted the chimneys of the former Croydon Power Station, where it located in 2003, in the company colours. These blue and yellow chimneys can be seen for miles around and remind people that the store is there while still keeping something of the history of the building.

The location of buildings is important when a business considers its **distribution network**. If a business locates to a place that is as accessible to as many customers as possible its profits can be increased. This might be achieved, for example, by businesses which trade throughout Europe locating in countries in central Europe where they can easily distribute to more countries.

**Key Terms**

**Aesthetically pleasing** When a building is designed and decorated to look attractive to the eye.

**Distribution network** Support structure and businesses that help goods to be moved from where they are made to the customers who buy them.

**Materials and waste**

The materials that are needed by a business will very much depend on the type of operation it is running and the individual people working there. A car-making factory will need access to steel, paint, plastics, etc. to be able to make cars. An office will have to provide computers, pens, paper and telephones for their employees to use. Some businesses will use materials that can be renewable or recyclable, such as paper, while others use non-renewable materials such as oil. All businesses need to be careful about how much they use and will try to avoid wasting materials to keep their costs low and help the environment. Some companies have made excellent use of initiatives to reduce the amount of materials they use and so save money. For example, the Oxford Group (www.oxfordgroup.co.uk) saved £40,000 by reducing the amount of paper used.

The waste that a business produces has to be taken away by another agency such as the council or a private company. It makes good business sense to reduce the amount of waste as it cuts waste disposal costs which should help lead to higher profits for the business. The government sees waste reduction as important for the environment and has funded the Envirowise campaign (www.envirowise.gov.uk), giving tips on ways this can be done.

**Case study**

**Cadbury**

Cadbury will open a new £70 million factory in Poland by 2008 to supply the increasing demand for its brands in Europe, the Middle East and Asia. The factory in Poland will create 300 jobs at first and there may be the opportunity to expand at a later date. Cadbury chose Poland as the place to base its new manufacturing plant for a number of reasons, including that Poland offered a 'low cost base' and good central place for distribution throughout Europe, the Middle East and Asia. Cadbury already had links with Poland before this factory plan as it had taken over the Polish chocolate brand Wedel and traded as Cadbury Wedel. It is also opening other factories throughout the world including one in Beijing, China.

1. What do you think is meant by a 'low cost base'? ✓
2. What advantage might Cadbury have by being centrally located in Europe? ✓✓
3. Which issues might Cadbury face when setting up a new factory in countries like China? ✓✓
4. How might Cadbury's acquisition of the Wedel chocolate brand in Poland have helped them to plan their buildings and facilities there? ✓✓✓

|74| BTEC National Business Book 1 | 2nd edition

Unit 2 Investigating business resources |75|

## ■ Key Terms

Throughout each chapter there are explanations of important concepts as they occur.

## ■ Case studies

The most up-to-date Case studies have been selected to increase your knowledge and awareness of current business trends and activities. Questions at the end of each Case study are graded in difficulty, with one tick being the easiest and three ticks being the hardest. Case studies give you the opportunity to work on your skills before you complete your assessed outcome activities.

## Outcome activities

Outcome activities are given within each chapter. These activities are taken directly from the unit performance criteria. That means that by completing these activities you will produce coursework that can be assessed as part of your BTEC National qualification.

To help you think about the level of qualification that you are working towards, each Outcome activity is clearly marked with Pass, Merit and Distinction icons, mapped to the unit grading criteria.

To achieve a Pass for a unit, you will need to complete all the Pass Outcome activities in that chapter. There will be different numbers of activities depending on the size and type of unit that you are studying. To achieve a Merit in a unit you will need to achieve all of the Pass *and* Merit Outcome activities. Finally, to achieve a Distinction you will need to achieve all of the Pass *and* Merit *and* Distinction Outcome activities in that unit.

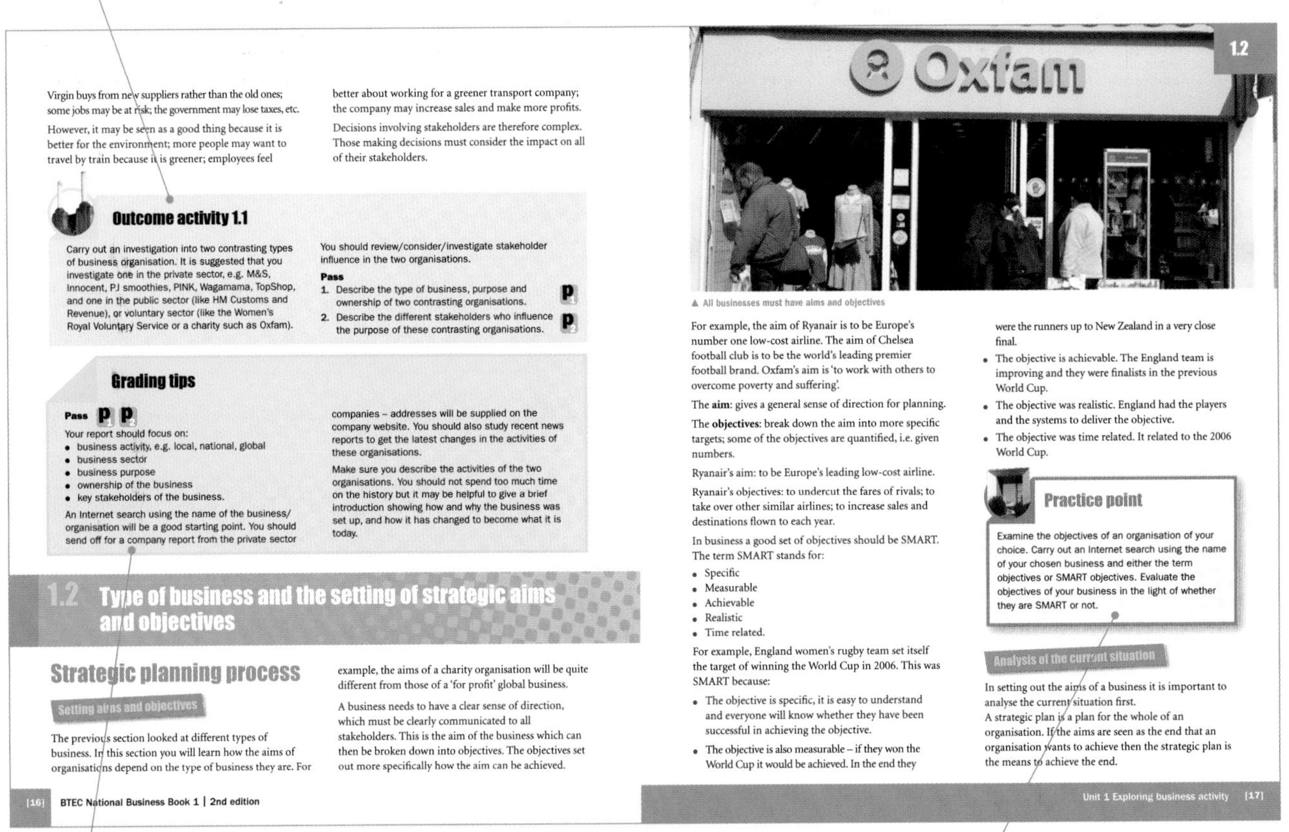
Virgin buys from new suppliers rather than the old ones; some jobs may be at risk; the government may lose taxes, etc.

However, it may be seen as a good thing because it is better for the environment; more people may want to travel by train because it is greener; employees feel better about working for a greener transport company; the company may increase sales and make more profits.

Decisions involving stakeholders are therefore complex. Those making decisions must consider the impact on all of their stakeholders.

**Outcome activity 1.1**

Carry out an investigation into two contrasting types of business organisation. It is suggested that you investigate one in the private sector, e.g. M&S, Innocent, PJ smoothies, PINK, Wagamama, TopShop, and one in the public sector (like HM Customs and Revenue), or voluntary sector (like the Women's Royal Voluntary Service or a charity such as Oxfam).

You should review/consider/investigate stakeholder influence in the two organisations.

**Pass**

1. Describe the type of business, purpose and ownership of two contrasting organisations. P1
2. Describe the different stakeholders who influence the purpose of these contrasting organisations. P2

**Grading tips**

**Pass** P1 P2

Your report should focus on:

- business activity, e.g. local, national, global
- business sector
- business purpose
- ownership of the business
- key stakeholders of the business.

An Internet search using the name of the business/organisation will be a good starting point. You should send off for a company report from the private sector companies – addresses will be supplied on the company website. You should also study recent news reports to get the latest changes in the activities of these organisations.

Make sure you describe the activities of the two organisations. You should not spend too much time on the history but it may be helpful to give a brief introduction showing how and why the business was set up, and how it has changed to become what it is today.

**1.2 Type of business and the setting of strategic aims and objectives**

**Strategic planning process**

**Setting aims and objectives**

The previous section looked at different types of business. In this section you will learn how the aims of organisations depend on the type of business they are. For example, the aims of a charity organisation will be quite different from those of a 'for profit' global business.

A business needs to have a clear sense of direction, which must be clearly communicated to all stakeholders. This is the aim of the business which can then be broken down into objectives. The objectives set out more specifically how the aim can be achieved.

[16] BTEC National Business Book 1 | 2nd edition

1.2


▲ All businesses must have aims and objectives

For example, the aim of Ryanair is to be Europe's number one low-cost airline. The aim of Chelsea football club is to be the world's leading premier football brand. Oxfam's aim is 'to work with others to overcome poverty and suffering'.

The **aim**: gives a general sense of direction for planning.

The **objectives**: break down the aim into more specific targets; some of the objectives are quantified, i.e. given numbers.

Ryanair's aim: to be Europe's leading low-cost airline.

Ryanair's objectives: to undercut the fares of rivals; to take over other similar airlines; to increase sales and destinations flown to each year.

In business a good set of objectives should be SMART. The term SMART stands for:

- Specific
- Measurable
- Achievable
- Realistic
- Time related.

For example, England women's rugby team set itself the target of winning the World Cup in 2006. This was SMART because:

- The objective is specific, it is easy to understand and everyone will know whether they have been successful in achieving the objective.
- The objective is also measurable – if they won the World Cup it would be achieved. In the end they were the runners up to New Zealand in a very close final.
- The objective is achievable. The England team is improving and they were finalists in the previous World Cup.
- The objective was realistic. England had the players and the systems to deliver the objective.
- The objective was time related. It related to the 2006 World Cup.

**Practice point**

Examine the objectives of an organisation of your choice. Carry out an Internet search using the name of your chosen business and either the term objectives or SMART objectives. Evaluate the objectives of your business in the light of whether they are SMART or not.

**Analysis of the current situation**

In setting out the aims of a business it is important to analyse the current situation first.

A strategic plan is a plan for the whole of an organisation. If the aims are seen as the end that an organisation wants to achieve then the strategic plan is the means to achieve the end.

Unit 1 Exploring business activity [17]

## Practice points

These activities are a bit more practical and may involve producing a poster, writing a letter or working out calculations. They allow you to continue to develop your skills and practice theoretical concepts.

## Grading tips

Each Outcome activity comes with grading tips to give you extra guidance about what you need to do to achieve the individual criteria.

## ■ End of unit tests

At the end of each chapter, there is a test with questions that check your understanding of that unit's content. You may choose to complete the test before you decide to start work on the outcome activities.

## ■ Resources

A list of useful resources – such as books, magazines or journal articles and website addresses is given at the end of each chapter. This provides you with the opportunity to do further research and gain understanding of the area that you are studying. This is particularly useful if you are aiming for Merit or Distinction level work.

## ■ Grading criteria grids

Each unit ends with a grading criteria grid, an easy-to-use reference to how that chapter's outcome activities are mapped to specific grading criteria.

## ■ Glossary

Finally at the end of the book there is a glossary of terms. This contains all the Key Terms that you will have come across within the book. They have been put into alphabetical order in one place so that if a Key Term has been used in more than one Unit but not explained in both chapters you can still easily access its meaning.

We have written this book with the aim of bringing the course to life with topical case studies and activities to interest and inspire you. We wish you luck with your course and hope you enjoy it.

Catherine Richards, David Dooley, Rob Dransfield, John Goymer and Philip Guy

# Exploring business activity

## Introduction

You will already have quite a good idea of what some leading businesses do. As customers, you will have bought goods directly or indirectly from some of the UK's best known companies such as Boots, M&S, and Virgin. You may also have worked part time for a business and so have an 'inside view'.

This unit allows you to explore a wide range of business activities. You will develop an insight into what the owners and other influential figures in a business are trying to achieve. You will also consider how organisations are 'organised' – for example, the way they are divided into specialist sections and how these sections fit together.

Businesses are affected by different events in the world around them – the business environment. You will be expected to investigate this environment.

### What you need to learn

On completion of this unit you should:

1. Understand the different types of business activity and ownership
2. Understand how the type of business influences the setting of strategic aims and objectives
3. Understand functional activities and organisational structure
4. Know how external factors in the business environment impact on organisations.

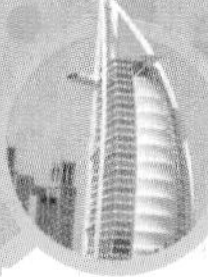

## Consider this

1. Carry out an Internet search for www.innocentdrinks.co.uk and read about how the founders of Innocent decided to set up and go into business. The story is an interesting one so tell a friend about it.
2. Try to find out about the origins of another well-known company that has grown to become a national name.

In this unit we introduce a range of businesses like Innocent, which is widely regarded to be a 'cool brand'. Innocent focuses on making drinks that taste good and are good for you, with ingredients that are 100% natural. Innocent is currently the number one smoothie brand in the UK, with a market share of 62%. More than 6000 retailers in the UK, Ireland, France, Holland and Belgium now stock Innocent drinks.

To find out more about cool brands visit www.superbrands.com/uk.

## Types of business activity

Business activity typically involves one person or organisation providing a product or service which they supply to someone else. Usually this involves payment. Think of the things that you might have needed or wanted this week. For example:

| Product or service required | Want or need that it satisfies |
|---|---|
| to buy or rent a DVD | for entertainment |
| to purchase a sandwich | because you were hungry |
| to have a tooth filled | because a filling had come out that was causing pain |
| to have a haircut | because you wanted to look more attractive |

You can see how business activity helps you to meet these requirements and various businesses have been set up to do this. So:

- a video shop – supplies customers with DVDs to buy or rent
- a bakery or supermarket – sells sandwiches
- a dentist – carries out dental work for customers
- a hair salon – washes, cuts, colours and styles hair.

### Thinking point

Make a list of ten businesses that you are likely to visit this week. In each case state what the business is, and what the activity will be that the business will carry out to meet your need or requirement.

### Local, national, international and global business

A new business that sets up in your town is a local business. However, one day it may set up outlets in other parts of Britain so that it becomes a national business. Soon after, it might start to sell its products overseas – becoming an international business. Finally, it may produce goods and develop selling outlets across the globe – by which time it will be a global business. Toni and Guy is an example of a business that has expanded very quickly.

### Case study

**Toni and Guy**

The Toni and Guy chain, started by the Mascolo family, was originally a simple local family business. Now it has almost 500 salons spread across the globe, many of which are on a **franchise** basis. In addition to this, the chain sells a range of hair care and styling products worth hundreds of millions of pounds each year. The latest part of the **strategy** has been the setting up of a website to market these products.

The business started with the father, Francesco, who emigrated from Italy to England in the 1950s. He taught his five sons the hairdressing trade. The eldest two, Toni and Guy, set up their own salon which created the world's best known brand in hairdressing. A third brother, Bruno, set up a Toni and Guy salon in the United States in the 1980s. The chain is now owned by four of the brothers.

Anthony (Toni) sets the trends in London for the other salons to follow. Each year he creates a hair collection with a range of haircuts. The methods involved in creating these haircuts are then taught to the hairdressers who work in the various salons.

Toni sees his styles as adapting to fashion and popular culture. He believes that we see hair as an accessory to fashion. However, the styles are not bizarre or extreme. Toni believes that hairstyles should be practical.

1. At what point did Toni and Guy become an international business? ✓
2. What benefits do you think that businesses like Toni and Guy gain from becoming national rather than local businesses? ✓✓
3. What difficulties might arise from becoming an international business? ✓✓✓
4. How might the website help the business to succeed globally? ✓✓✓

## Key Terms

**Franchise** Granting another individual or business the right to set up or trade using your name, and to provide the service that you provide or the product that you supply.

**Strategy** The business plan.

Marks & Spencer and the Body Shop are good examples of British organisations that started off as small local businesses. Both then went on to become national, international and global businesses. However, both have also faced difficulties – particularly in developing an international presence.

### Public and private businesses

You also need to know the difference between a public sector and a private business. Public sector businesses are those that have been set up or taken over by the government. Private businesses are owned by private citizens. In most countries the majority of businesses are owned by private individuals.

For example, the mobile phone company Vodafone is owned by shareholders. You or I can buy shares in Vodafone. A well-known example of a shareholder is Roman Abramovich, the Russian who owns most of the shares in Chelsea football club. Abramovich also has shares in many Russian companies, including one of Russia's major oil companies. However, until the 1990s nearly all of the businesses in Russia were owned by the government – they were public sector businesses.

Today most people recognise that businesses are run better when they are privately owned. Private owners risk their own money so are determined for their business to succeed.

In the UK there are very few public businesses left. Most businesses have been **privatised**.

Examples of public sector businesses today include:

- Her Majesty's Customs and Revenue – collecting your taxes.
- National Archives – the body responsible for looking after government records and records from the courts of law.

Examples of private businesses include: Virgin, Intel, Tesco, Cadbury-Schweppes and LastMinute.com.

## Key Term

**Privatisation** Transferring the ownership of a business from the government to private owners.

## Thinking point

What do you think would be the advantages and disadvantages of top football teams, such as Arsenal men's or women's football teams, being owned by the government rather than by private shareholders?

## Remember

Public sector organisations are those owned by the government for the people. Private sector businesses are owned by private owners and shareholders like you and me.

### Not-for-profit/voluntary businessess

Not all businesses are set up to make a profit. For example, a voluntary organisation works on quite different lines. It is a 'not-for-profit' organisation. It is set up, organised, staffed and run by people who are working purely on a voluntary basis, usually for a 'good cause'. Examples of voluntary organisations are the Women's Royal Voluntary Service (WRVS) and Voluntary Service Overseas (VSO).

## Case study

**VSO**

VSO is an example of a 'not-for-profit' global organisation. It is a UK-based organisation that seeks to match volunteers with volunteer projects in areas of the world that need help. For example, a volunteer might teach English to children in an African country, or teach them how to use computers. Many volunteers are young people, but in addition volunteers include older people with specialist skills who can make a real difference to the lives of people in need.

1. Why do you think that voluntary organisations work on a 'not-for-profit' basis? ✓
2. To what extent would you say that it is important for voluntary organisations to be businesslike? ✓✓
3. What sorts of people are most likely to work for voluntary organisations and why? ✓✓
4. Check out the VSO website and set out four examples of ways in which VSO can be said to operate in a businesslike way. ✓✓✓

## Sectors of business – primary, secondary and tertiary

Most of you will have tasted an orange-flavoured smoothie. Oranges typically grow in a Mediterranean-type climate in countries like Spain, Morocco, or Israel. When the oranges are ripe they are transported to market. They may then be sold as fruit or processed into orange juice.

Today we are increasingly aware of the importance of healthy diets. Orange juice can contribute to this by providing a rich source of vitamin C. Over the last five years smoothies – which are a blend of real fruit – have become very popular. The supply of smoothies provides a good illustration of the three sectors of business.

The **primary** stage is concerned with extracting the primary products of nature. Oranges are a primary product. They are grown on trees by orange farmers.

The second stage of producing a smoothie is to remove the skin and pips and to blend the oranges with other fruit. Bottling the finished smoothie is part of this **secondary** process.

Bringing you your finished smoothie involves the **tertiary** business sector. Tertiary activities involve providing services – both to businesses and to consumers. Examples of services involved in providing smoothies include:

- transporting the oranges and the finished smoothies
- selling the smoothies in a shop or supermarket
- advertising the smoothies
- providing insurance services to the transport, **manufacturing** and **retailing** companies.

## Key Terms

**Primary sector** Extracting raw products from nature.

**Secondary sector** Transforming those raw products into finished and part finished goods.

**Tertiary sector** Providing services to individuals and businesses.

**Manufacturing** Making things (in the secondary sector).

**Retailing** Selling things in small quantities (shops in the tertiary sector).

## Practice point

Classify the following list into primary, secondary and tertiary sector businesses:

- a mining company
- an advertising agency
- a canning factory
- an oyster gathering business
- a building company
- a fishing business
- a business that makes fish fingers
- an insurance business
- a web page design business
- a newspaper publishing company
- a newspaper delivery business
- a forestry business
- a furniture manufacturer
- a second-hand furniture shop
- a car manufacturer
- a car insurer.

### Remember

Most people in Britain today are involved in the service sector of the economy. It makes sense. If you think about it, most of the people you know will work in services.

# Business purposes

## Reasons why businesses exist

In September 2006, the rock memorabilia auction house Cooper Owen joined the Alternative Investment Market (AIM). By joining AIM Cooper Owen was able to sell its shares to people who want to buy shares. AIM is similar to the Stock Exchange but for smaller companies. Cooper Owen raised almost £2 million from selling shares on AIM, so enabling it to expand.

Cooper Owen auctions off all sorts of rock memorabilia such as:

- a gold-plated guitar owned by Frank Zappa
- John Lennon T-shirts
- an acoustic guitar on which Paul McCartney learned his first chords.

Cooper Owen is already very well known as an **auction** business in Britain. It now wants to expand by buying similar businesses overseas and also to expand into sports memorabilia. The company has an Internet shop and a private auction business.

So what is the purpose of Cooper Owen? At one level its purpose is to sell memorabilia belonging to sellers to buyers. However, another very important business purpose is to make a **profit**. Paul McCartney's guitar was sold for more than £100,000. From this sale Cooper Owen would take a commission which might be as much as 15 per cent of the sale price, i.e. £15,000.

However, this £15,000 would not all be profit because Cooper Owen needs to cover its costs. These costs would include printing catalogues to advertise the items for sale, paying salaries to staff and everyday running costs like paying the phone and electricity bills of the business.

As with many businesses, Cooper Owen's purpose is to make a profit. It is able to make a profit because people are willing to pay for the service it offers.

### Key Terms

**Auction** Selling items to the highest bidder.

**Profit** Difference between money coming in (revenue) and costs paid out.

## Supplying products and services for profit

Where there is a demand for a product, there will be businesses set up to meet that demand. This is illustrated by the growth of the private charter airline business. Over the last few years this industry has expanded enormously. This is because business executives are determined to avoid the nightmare delays involved in conventional flying which result from terror alerts.

Charter airlines have had a surge in bookings from business travellers who are willing to pay thousands of pounds for the luxury of turning up at an airport just 20 minutes before the flight departs and who want the reassurance of knowing who their fellow passengers are. Business flyers, unhappy at the delays and cancellations that have caused chaos at Heathrow, are choosing private flights that depart from smaller airports like Stansted and Manchester. Rising demand has enabled charter airlines to raise their prices. Higher prices in this instance lead to higher profits.

## Supplying at cost and below cost

Businesses do not always seek to sell their products for a profit. Sometimes they are willing to do so 'at cost'. Supplying at cost occurs when the money received from selling a product is equal to the cost of supplying that product. For example, the England Netball Association may offer schools low cost seats at an England netball fixture to increase interest in the sport. They may have worked out that the cost to the Netball Association of each spectator at a match is £5. This cost might include the cost of lighting and heating in the stadium, payments to stewards, etc.

In some cases businesses are willing to supply products at below the cost of production. This might be because the business is trying to generate interest in a new product. Initially they sell it at below cost price. Once the buying public is aware of the product it will be possible to raise the price so that profits can be made.

## Key Terms

**Fixed costs** Costs which the firm has to pay, regardless of how much they make or sell. For example, the sandwich shops would have to pay out rent, rates and electricity charges whatever their level of sales.

**Average cost per item** The typical cost of making or selling an item. These costs are separate from overheads.

## Practice point

There are three shops selling sandwiches in your town. Superior Sandwiches has **fixed costs** of £1000 per month. They sell sandwiches at an average price of £1. The **average cost** of making each sandwich (bread, ingredients and labour) is 50p. They sell 2000 sandwiches a month.

Excellent Sandwiches has fixed costs of £800 per month. They also sell sandwiches at an average price of £1. Their average cost of making each sandwich is 40p. They sell 1000 sandwiches a month.

Top of the Market Sandwiches has fixed costs of £1000 per month. They sell sandwiches at an average price of £2. Their average cost of making each sandwich is 60p. They sell 900 sandwiches a month.

Which of these businesses is selling at cost? Which is making a profit? Which is selling below cost?

What could the firm that is selling at cost do to make a profit?

## Case study

### RED

In 2006 a charitable initiative called RED was set up. Initially five companies were involved with the scheme but it was hoped that more would become involved. The first companies were Gap, Converse, Emporio Armani, American Express and Motorola. These companies launched special lines of RED products, donating a percentage of their profits to the Global Fund to Fight Aids, Tuberculosis and Malaria. The aim of the project is to provide a stream of funds from consumers. The first six months of running the project raised £5 million for the fund.

Creating this scheme enables consumers to contribute directly to a good cause – if they have a credit card they can have a RED one, if they have a mobile phone they can use a RED one, they can wear a RED T-shirt etc.

One of the first activities was for the designer Roland Mouret to design a collection for Gap for RED. This is a collection of ten dresses priced between £45 and £78. Half the profits from each dress go to the Global Fund.

1. Are firms who are part of the RED scheme supplying for profit, at cost or below cost? ✓
2. What are the benefits to businesses that join the RED scheme? ✓✓
3. What would be the dangers to a business of supplying items 'below cost'? ✓✓
4. How might businesses be able to supply items to the market 'below cost'? ✓✓✓

## Supplying products and services to customers

The supply of a product is the quantity that a supplier is willing to provide at different prices. Typically suppliers will supply more at higher than at lower prices.

For example, a charter airline might run six planes a day between Stansted and Paris when business passengers are prepared to pay £200 each for the return journey. However, if business passengers are willing to pay £300 each then the airline might buy more planes and run nine planes a day. At £400 each they might run twelve planes. Supply can then be illustrated on a supply curve as shown below.

Supplying goods and services to the market involves organising people and other resources to make products available.

Some products will be supplied directly to consumers – for example, Sainsbury's organises the supply of groceries, including tinned, chilled, frozen and fresh produce. To get these goods to us Sainsbury's has to organise a supply chain of activities. Sainsbury's supply chain is organised through a computer ordering system that tells them how much is in stock and when new orders should be made.

▼ A supply curve

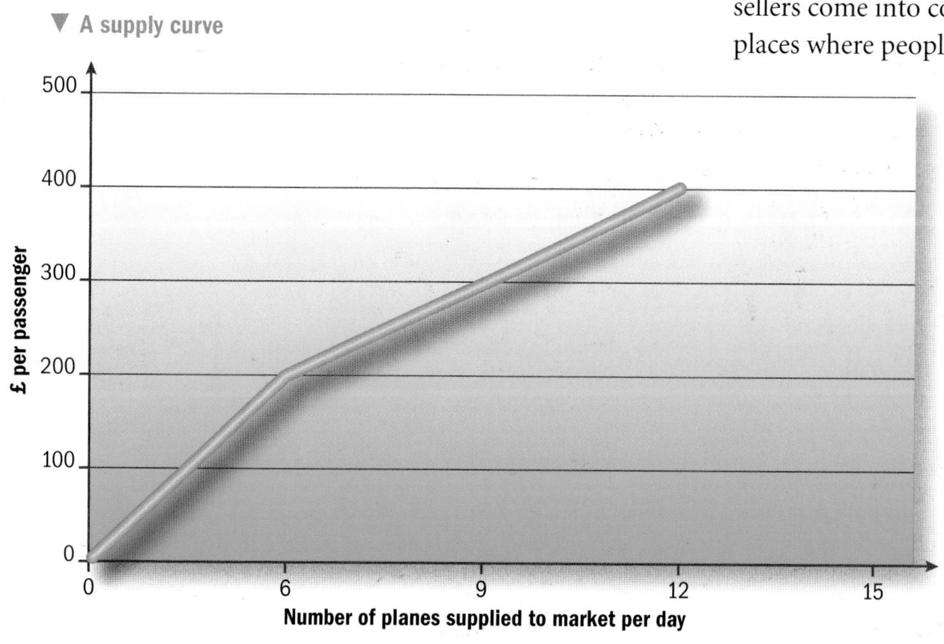


## Supplying products and services to businesses and government agencies

Some products are supplied by businesses to other businesses. For example, builder's merchants supply builders with bricks, cement, tools and equipment. Other products are supplied by businesses to the government. For example, private refuse collecting firms will take away your bins and other forms of rubbish. The local council will pay them to do this. Of course the local council raises its funds for this and other purposes by charging taxes.

| | | |
|---|---|---|
| **B2C** | Businesses that supply direct to consumers | E.g. a supermarket, cinema, or newsagent |
| **B2B** | Businesses that supply to other businesses | E.g. a builder's merchants, a factory machinery supplier |
| **B2G** | Businesses that supply goods or services to and for government | E.g. a publishing company that supplies documentation for Her Majesty's Customs and Revenue, a television production company that provides a documentary for the BBC, etc. |

## Supplying in response to demand

A market exists in any situation in which buyers and sellers come into contact. Markets range from physical places where people exchange goods and services to 'virtual' markets where trade is carried out over the Internet and other forms of electronic communication. In a local market local traders and customers come into contact. For example, you can buy a bunch of bananas from a fruit stall in your local market.

Nowadays electronic trading is becoming more and more popular. Trading through a website provides a good example of electronic trading. For example, you could put your coat up for sale by subscribing to e-Bay.

Your coat would then be bought by the highest bidder. If not many people bid then you would say that demand is low. If lots of people bid then demand is high.

Patterns of demand change regularly. They change because customers' wants and expectations change and because new products enter the market. As new products enter markets the demand for old ones often declines. For example, this is illustrated by the market for television sets and their associated gadgets. Black and white TV sets were replaced by colour sets. Today many people opt for plasma screens and HD TV. VHS video formats have been replaced by DVD formats, but these may soon be replaced by another type of disk.

### Remember

Supply is the quantity of a product that suppliers will make available to the market at different prices. Demand is the quantity that buyers will be willing and able to buy at different prices.

## Business owners

In the public sector, businesses are owned by the government or agencies appointed by the government to provide a service. In the private sector, businesses are owned by individuals. An individual owner is typically a single owner or a group of partners, or the owners will be shareholders. In the voluntary sector organisations typically have groups of trustees responsible for overseeing the work of the organisation.

| Private sector | Public sector | Voluntary sector |
|---|---|---|
| Owned by individuals or shareholders | Owned by government | Supervised by trustees |
| Profit is often the major driving force | Has wider objectives than profit – often has wider social service aims | Usually set up to provide a service to the wider community |

### Case study

**The white carrot**

Most people associate carrots with the colour orange. However, before the sixteenth century carrots came in many colours; this was before the Dutch bred the orange carrots that have become so popular.

Now this might change. The supermarket Asda has bought in substantial quantities of Satin White carrots. This is a new 'snowy white' variety that has been bred by growers in Yorkshire. The white carrot is regarded to be sweeter and juicier than the orange type. The white variety has a smoother flavour than the orange version and a higher level of other naturally-occurring compounds called phytochemicals, which give the root vegetable a rich taste.

Asda and other sellers hope that interest in the white carrot will help to increase the popularity of carrots.

1. What is likely to happen to the price of white carrots if they prove to be popular? ✓
2. If the demand for white carrots continues to increase, what is likely to be the impact on their supply? ✓
3. Give other examples of situations in which increased demand has impacted on the supply of a product. Explain what the impact was. ✓✓
4. How are demand and supply inter-related in the marketplace? ✓✓✓

## Private sector organisations

The owners of a business are the people to whom the business belongs. For example, Fred's corner store may be owned by Fred on his own – he is a sole trader. In contrast, the solicitors Makepeace, Patel and Amin would be a partnership.

Sole trader and partnership businesses are not only owned by the owners, they are also controlled by them. Control refers to decision making. Fred makes his own decisions about what he sells, who he employs and when he opens and shuts his shop.

In companies, however, there is a distinction between the ownership and the control of the business. Companies are owned by shareholders but it is often directors or managers who make decisions and hence control the business.

Shareholders are people who put the capital (funds) into a business. They receive a reward for the risk they take in the form of a return called a dividend paid out on company profits.

## Sole traders

A sole trader business is owned and controlled by one person. It is the most common type of business and is found in a wide range of activities (e.g. window cleaning, plumbing, electrical work, busking). No complicated work is required to set up a sole trader business. Decisions can be made quickly and close contact can be kept with customers and employees. All profits go to the sole trader, who also has the satisfaction of building up his or her own business.

But there are disadvantages. As a sole trader you have to make all the decisions yourself, and you may have to work long hours. (Then what happens if you are ill or want a holiday?) Another disadvantage is that you don't have the legal protection of limited liability. What this means is that should the business run up debts these become the responsibility of the business owner. The debts are unlimited and the owner may be forced to sell their house and other personal possessions to pay off their business debts.

The sole trader typically provides much of their own finance, although they may also borrow from a bank, or friends. As a sole trader you need to be a jack-of-all-trades, and just because you are a good hairdresser does not necessarily mean that you have a head for business!

## Partnerships

A partnership is usually formed by signing a Deed of Partnership with the paperwork being supervised by a solicitor. Partnerships are typically found in professional work, e.g. a medical or dental practice, a group of accountants or solicitors. People in business partnerships can share skills and the workload, and it may be easier to raise the capital needed.

For example, a group of vets is able to pool knowledge about different diseases and groups of animals, and two or three vets working together may be able to operate a 24-hour service. When one of the vets is ill or goes on holiday, the business can cope.

The Deed of Partnership sets out how profits will be shared and the different responsibilities and payments to partners.

The main disadvantages of partnerships are that people can fall out ('she doesn't work as hard as me!'), ordinary partnerships don't have limited liability and partnerships can rarely borrow or raise large amounts of capital. Business decisions may be more difficult to make (and slower) because of the need to consult all the partners. There may be disagreements about how things should be done. A further disadvantage is that profits will be shared.

A new type of business was created in Britain in 2003. This is the 'limited liability partnership'. This type of partnership exists in businesses like accounting and the law where there are hundreds of partners. This is to protect individual partners should another partner's actions cause the partnership trouble. For example, it would be unfair for accountancy partners to be liable for irregularities in auditing accounts by one of their colleagues.

## Public and private limited companies

A limited company has to be registered before it can start to operate, but once all the paperwork is completed and approved the limited company becomes recognised as a legal body. The owners of the limited company are its shareholders. They elect directors to represent their interests. A managing director is the senior director on the Board. The Board consists of executive directors who make the major policy decisions about the business. The Board will also have some non-executive directors in its membership. Non-executives are there to provide specialist advice and because of their links with other businesses.

It is the shareholders who choose the Board of Directors.

Shareholders are able to have a say about the way the limited company is run when they attend an Annual General Meeting each year. At this AGM highlights of the Annual Report will be presented to shareholders as well as the annual accounts. At this meeting the shareholders are able to question company policy; they can vote out the directors and take actions such as refusing to approve pay rises to directors.

Shareholders put funds into a limited company by buying shares. New shares are often sold in face values of £1 per share, but this is not always the case. Some shareholders will only have a few hundred pounds' worth of shares, whereas others may have thousands or millions of pounds' worth.

There are two main types of limited company:

- **Private limited companies** tend to be smaller than public ones (discussed below) and are often family businesses. There must be at least two shareholders but there is no maximum number. Shares in private limited companies cannot be traded on the Stock Exchange, and often shares can only be bought with the permission of the Board of Directors.
  Private limited companies may find it possible to raise more cash (by selling shares) than unlimited-liability businesses. The shareholders can also have the protection of limited liability.
- A **public limited company** has its shares bought and sold on the Stock Exchange. The main advantage of being a public limited company is that large amounts of capital can be raised very quickly. One disadvantage is that control of a business can be lost by the original shareholders if large quantities of shares are purchased as part of a 'takeover bid'. It is also costly to have shares quoted on the Stock Exchange.

### Practice point

The following task should be based on research carried out in your local town supported by knowledge that students in your group acquire from work experience and part-time jobs.

Make a study of a sole trader, partnership, private limited company and public limited company. Who owns these businesses? How much capital does each have? (If you can't find out the exact sum, give a breakdown of the main forms of capital it relies on, e.g. *x* per cent owner's capital, *y* per cent borrowings, etc.) What are the advantages and disadvantages of this organisational form for this particular business organisation? As a group you could present the work as a newspaper feature using a desktop publishing package. The title of the feature could be 'Some interesting businesses in our local area'.

## Franchises

Franchising is an attractive option for those looking for a ready-made business opportunity. The franchisor has already established a brand and a business model. The franchisee then has to put money and effort behind their side of the operation to reap the rewards. The franchisor grants the right to the franchisee to use their trading name in a particular area. They will often supply products, business systems and 'know how' to the franchisee. The franchisee usually pays a fixed sum to have the franchise, followed by regular payments. In 2006 franchising generated £10 billion of sales in the UK and nearly 400,000 people operated franchises.

Today there are more than 33,000 franchise operations in Britain. They are not all connected with fast food or shoe repair. Opportunities are available in diet and fitness, home improvements and even in education and childcare.

A franchise is not a form of business ownership. Someone with a franchise can set up their own business as a sole trader, partnership or company. However, whatever form of ownership they have for their business they must agree a contract with the franchisor which governs the terms of the franchise.

### Practice point

Carry out an Internet search using the terms 'franchise opportunities' and UK. Find out about a particular franchise business. What is the business idea? How does the franchisor help the franchisee? How much does it cost to take out the franchise? What percentage of the profits does the franchisee have to give to the franchisor?

## Public sector business

Public sector organisations are owned by the government. There are government departments and government agencies. A government department like the Department for Customs and Revenue operates on behalf of the government and is staffed by civil servants, known as customs and revenue officers. Their job is to collect income tax and other taxes on behalf of the government, to collect repayments on student loans, and to make payments known as tax credits. Rather than seeking to make a profit they will want to collect taxes efficiently and make sure that taxpayers get a fair deal.

Government agencies are more independent than government departments. These are bodies that have been set up by the government to take responsibility for a particular activity. For example, the Child Protection Agency is a government-funded body responsible for looking after the rights of children. Although it is funded by government and accountable to government it has considerable freedom to manage its own affairs. These bodies are set up with tight guidelines but in the interest of fairness they need to be seen to operate in an independent way.

Local government is an important branch of government activity. Local councils are responsible for supervising and, in a small number of cases, owning local services. Local councils cover specific areas of the country. What is your local council? In their specific area, the local authority will give contracts to private companies to run certain services such as managing refuse collection. It is the job of the council to oversee the efficient running of these services. Local councils also own and supervise the collection of rents and repairs to social housing. They manage local parks, leisure centres and swimming pools, street lighting and other essential activities.

## Worker co-operatives

A worker co-operative is a body that is owned by its members – the people that work for it. A worker co-operative has limited liability. To become a member of a worker co-operative an employee would have to buy a share in the organisation. Each member has one vote in making decisions. This type of business is democratic and prevents one or a few individuals gaining control. Members receive a share of the profits of the business in the form of a dividend. When they leave the co-operative they can take their funds back. The basic principle behind a worker co-operative is that those who do the work should get the rewards. They tend to be small-scale local enterprises.

## Charitable trusts

A charity is an organisation that is set up to raise funds and support other people or a good cause. The business objective of charities is to create a surplus to use for helping others. A surplus occurs when the revenue (money coming into the charity) is greater than the costs of running the charity.

The management of charity work is overseen by a group of trustees, who are volunteers with a reputation as responsible citizens. Many will have a range of experience in both charity and business activities. Charities have to register as such and must produce annual accounts that are available to be viewed.

Most charity organisations start out when someone recognises the need for such an organisation. For example, the charity Shelter was set up in 1966 to help the many homeless people on the streets. The Toybox Charity was founded in 1991 by the Dyason family, who were horrified by a television documentary showing the plight of some of the 250,000 children orphaned by civil war in Guatemala. The charity grew into a comprehensive rescue plan for children who live in the streets in Guatemala City.

Charities employ paid managers and workers (unlike voluntary organisations, which rely on the goodwill of their staff).

## Key stakeholders

In 1988 the giant Swiss global company Nestlé took over the UK company Rowntree Macintosh. Rowntree's of York was famous for producing confectionery such as Smarties, Quality Street and a range of other leading brands. In September 2006 Nestlé announced that it would be losing 645 jobs at its York plant and that a number of brands would be cut back. No longer will Smarties be made in York but in Hamburg.

Which individuals and groups do you think will be affected by this decision – for better or worse?

People who have an interest in the decisions that businesses make are called stakeholders. Most decisions affect a number of stakeholders.

The illustration below shows a number of stakeholders in Nestlé's decision to pull out of York.

You can see from the Smarties example that stakeholders' interests are intertwined. Sometimes a decision is good for a range of stakeholders. Sometimes a decision is good for some stakeholders and bad for others.

The key stakeholders in a business are:

1. **Customers**. They want a company to produce high quality, value for money products. Customers often identify with the brands they buy. For example, car purchasers want their car to be the best available within a particular bracket. They like to see improvements that give them better value for money.

**Remember**

A stakeholder is someone who has an interest in how an organisation is run and the decisions it makes.

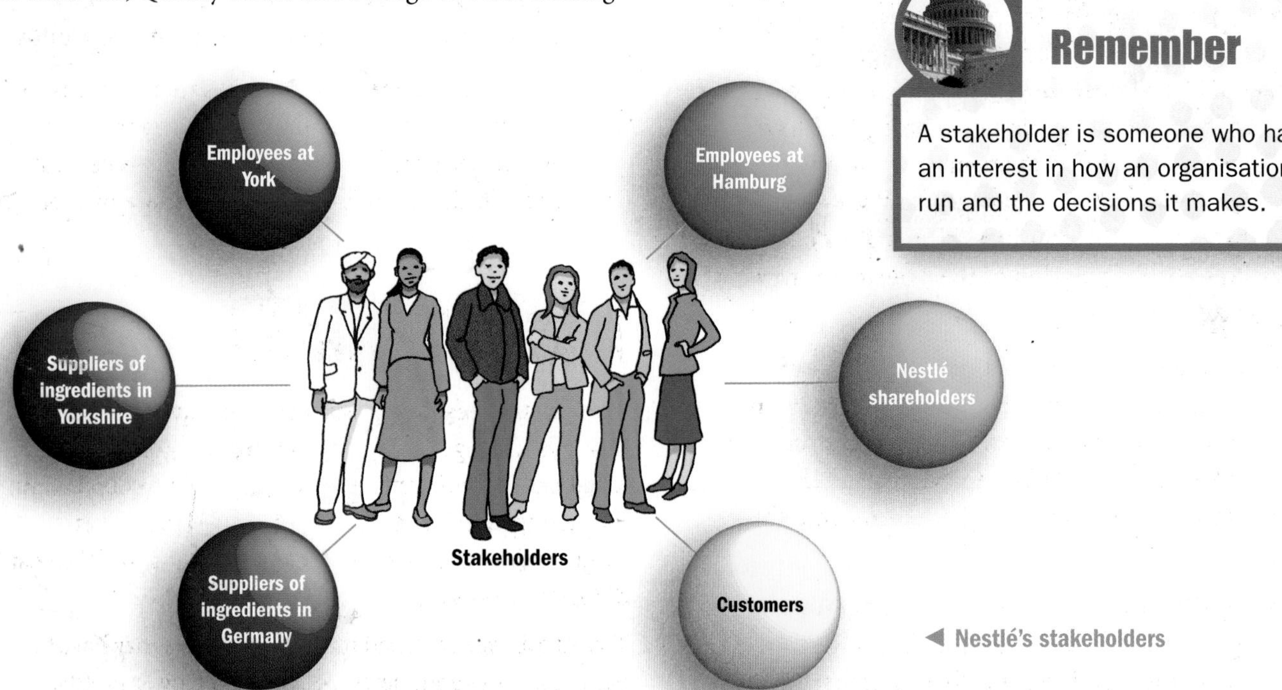


◀ Nestlé's stakeholders

## Practice point

In each of the following instances explain what the conflict of interest might be between the two stakeholder groups indicated.

| Decision | Stakeholder group 1 | Stakeholder group 2 | Conflict of interest |
|---|---|---|---|
| To give employees a wage rise | Shareholders | Employees | ? |
| To open a new pipeline to an oil field | Shareholders | People who live close to the pipeline | |
| To raise the price of a product | Shareholders | Customers | |
| To close down a factory | Shareholders | Employees | |

2. **Employees**. Their stake is that the company provides them with a livelihood. They seek security of employment, promotion opportunities, and good rates of reward. They also want to work for a company that they are proud of.
3. **Suppliers** want steady orders and prompt payment. They also want to feel valued by the company that they supply.
4. **Owners**. This may be a single owner in a sole trader business or the partners in a partnership. In a company it would be the shareholders. Owners are often regarded to be the most important stakeholders because they might have put a good part of their life into setting up a business. They see themselves as being the principal risk takers. Owners like to see their share of profit increasing, and the value of their business rising. They also want to see the reputation of their business grow over time.
5. **Pressure groups** seek to exert pressure on business decision making. Examples of pressure groups are Greenpeace and Friends of the Earth, which see themselves as defending the environment. They will try to press environmental concerns onto the business.
6. **Trade unions** represent the interests of groups of employees. They seek to secure higher wages and better working conditions for their members.
7. **Employer associations** are the employer's equivalent of the trade unions. These bodies represent the interests of groups of employers. For example there are employers' associations representing the interests of employers in specific industries.
8. **Local and national communities.** The actions of business can have a dramatic effect on communities. For example, the oil giant Shell has built vast pipelines in Nigeria. These pipelines run through the lands of various tribal people. The pipelines can be very dangerous and cause local pollution. Community leaders therefore represent important interest groups.
9. **Governments**. The government wants business to be successful – to create jobs and to pay taxes. It wants to see prosperous businesses that take a full responsibility in looking after the welfare of society.

### Links and interdependencies

A business needs to take account of the interests of all of its stakeholder groupings. These interests are all linked together. The various interest groups are interdependent. For example, if Richard Branson decides to run his Virgin trains using greener fuels, this means that the cost of journeys on Virgin trains increases . . .

This may be seen as a bad thing as customers may have to pay higher fares and shareholders may get lower profits;

Virgin buys from new suppliers rather than the old ones; some jobs may be at risk; the government may lose taxes, etc.

However, it may be seen as a good thing because it is better for the environment; more people may want to travel by train because it is greener; employees feel better about working for a greener transport company; the company may increase sales and make more profits.

Decisions involving stakeholders are therefore complex. Those making decisions must consider the impact on all of their stakeholders.

## Outcome activity 1.1

Carry out an investigation into two contrasting types of business organisation. It is suggested that you investigate one in the private sector, e.g. M&S, Innocent, PJ smoothies, PINK, Wagamama, TopShop, and one in the public sector (like HM Customs and Revenue), or voluntary sector (like the Women's Royal Voluntary Service or a charity such as Oxfam).

You should review/consider/investigate stakeholder influence in the two organisations.

**Pass**

1. Describe the type of business, purpose and ownership of two contrasting organisations. 
2. Describe the different stakeholders who influence the purpose of these contrasting organisations. 

## Grading tips

**Pass**  

Your report should focus on:

- business activity, e.g. local, national, global
- business sector
- business purpose
- ownership of the business
- key stakeholders of the business.

An Internet search using the name of the business/organisation will be a good starting point. You should send off for a company report from the private sector companies – addresses will be supplied on the company website. You should also study recent news reports to get the latest changes in the activities of these organisations.

Make sure you describe the activities of the two organisations. You should not spend too much time on the history but it may be helpful to give a brief introduction showing how and why the business was set up, and how it has changed to become what it is today.

# 1.2 Type of business and the setting of strategic aims and objectives

## Strategic planning process

### Setting aims and objectives

The previous section looked at different types of business. In this section you will learn how the aims of organisations depend on the type of business they are. For example, the aims of a charity organisation will be quite different from those of a 'for profit' global business.

A business needs to have a clear sense of direction, which must be clearly communicated to all stakeholders. This is the aim of the business which can then be broken down into objectives. The objectives set out more specifically how the aim can be achieved.

▲ All businesses must have aims and objectives

For example, the aim of Ryanair is to be Europe's number one low-cost airline. The aim of Chelsea football club is to be the world's leading premier football brand. Oxfam's aim is 'to work with others to overcome poverty and suffering'.

The **aim**: gives a general sense of direction for planning.

The **objectives**: break down the aim into more specific targets; some of the objectives are quantified, i.e. given numbers.

Ryanair's aim: to be Europe's leading low-cost airline.

Ryanair's objectives: to undercut the fares of rivals; to take over other similar airlines; to increase sales and destinations flown to each year.

In business a good set of objectives should be SMART. The term SMART stands for:

- Specific
- Measurable
- Achievable
- Realistic
- Time related.

For example, England women's rugby team set itself the target of winning the World Cup in 2006. This was SMART because:

- The objective is specific, it is easy to understand and everyone will know whether they have been successful in achieving the objective.
- The objective is also measurable – if they won the World Cup it would be achieved. In the end they were the runners up to New Zealand in a very close final.
- The objective is achievable. The England team is improving and they were finalists in the previous World Cup.
- The objective was realistic. England had the players and the systems to deliver the objective.
- The objective was time related. It related to the 2006 World Cup.

### Practice point

Examine the objectives of an organisation of your choice. Carry out an Internet search using the name of your chosen business and either the term objectives or SMART objectives. Evaluate the objectives of your business in the light of whether they are SMART or not.

## Analysis of the current situation

In setting out the aims of a business it is important to analyse the current situation first.

A strategic plan is a plan for the whole of an organisation. If the aims are seen as the end that an organisation wants to achieve then the strategic plan is the means to achieve the end.

## Case study

### Thorntons

Like many confectionery businesses Thornton's has recently seen a dip in its profits. For example, in the first half of 2006 Thornton's experienced a 36% fall in profits. The reaction of the company was to cut costs wherever possible. At the same time it has started to place more emphasis on a new range of organic chocolate products. It is also looking to emphasise the possible health benefits of some products, such as high level of antioxidants in dark chocolate. Despite bad results Thornton's is opening ten new stores and spending £1m on refurbishing 367 stores.

1. What happened to Thornton's profits in the first half of 2006? ✓
2. Why do you think this was? How might this information affect the aims and objectives that Thornton's establishes for itself? ✓ ✓
3. Do you think that it is wise to focus on new product areas? ✓ ✓
4. Does it make sense to be opening new stores? Explain your answer. ✓ ✓ ✓

## Quantitative and qualitative analysis

Before creating a detailed plan it is essential to carry out quantitative and qualitative analysis of the current situation.

A **quantitative analysis** is one that is based on numbers.

A **qualitative analysis** is more about feelings and instincts about trends that are taking place. A qualitative analysis is more emotional.

Both types of analysis are important in creating a plan.

The types of things that are worth studying through quantitative analysis include:

- What is happening to sales – are they rising or falling?
- How do sales compare with this time last year?
- How much of the overall market do we have, i.e. what is our market share?
- How do our prices compare with those of rivals?
- What percentage of our customers are satisfied with us and our products?
- What is happening to profits – are they rising or falling?
- How do profits compare with this time last year?
- What is happening to our costs?

Quantitative analysis helps us to make an appropriate plan. For example, if our costs are lower than those of rivals we can undercut their prices, or make more profits from the same volume of sales.

If we are selling more than rivals are, we could set ourselves the aim of retaining market leadership.

If our customers are satisfied then we can focus on customer satisfaction to beat competitors.

Quantitative analysis also helps us to measure what is happening outside our business. For example, if interest rates are rising we know that costs are likely to rise if we have borrowed money. If business is bad in the economy as a whole – as measured by general consumer spending – then we might expect our own sales to fall in the near future.

Qualitative analysis provides more 'emotional' information. Qualitative analysis can be gained from asking questions and discussing issues with various groups. For example, we could interview small groups of customers to find out what they think of our company or products. How do customers view us compared with the competition? We can talk to employees and pressure groups to find out what they think of us.

### Planning strategies

In the section above you were given some information about Thornton's. The quantitative information about profits might suggest that the company should be wary about expanding at this time. Qualitative information about growing customer preference for organic products might suggest that they expand their organic lines. Perhaps Thornton's could seek to gain market leadership in the more healthy type of chocolate market.

Organisations need to develop plans to take them forward into the future – maybe for five years or more. The plan should set out where the organisation wants to go – the aims and objectives, and details of how they will achieve these aims; this is referred to as the strategy.

A well thought-out strategy should be:

- acceptable to the various stakeholder groups. For example, it will be acceptable to shareholders if it is likely to achieve profits, and acceptable to employees if it will keep their jobs and wages secure
- realistic, i.e. possible to put into practice given the resources of the business.

So what sorts of strategies are different types of organisations likely to employ?

## Public and voluntary sector strategies

In the public and voluntary sector the emphasis is most likely to be on providing a good service.

### Public sector service provisions

Primary health care trusts have been set up to meet the needs of local populations for health care. For example, if you have an accident at home, in work or at school or college you would expect to get medical care and attention at the Accident and Emergency department of your local hospital. You would be surprised if the hospital staff said to you, 'We can only treat you if you pay £100 because we have to make a profit on the service we offer.' Primary health care trusts work on a different basis to this.

The trust receives funds from government and is then expected to manage these funds efficiently to meet government targets. Targets relate to such things as managing waiting lists so that patients do not have to wait too long for treatment. The Trusts are managed by professional managers who seek to cut out waste and to make sure that priority is given to the most important health needs. As a result, when you go to A&E one factor determining how quickly you will be treated is the urgency of your case. Primary health care trusts are thus designed to seek to give the maximum service given the resources available.

### Voluntary sector services

In the voluntary sector too the emphasis in the aims and strategies of organisations is on providing service. For example, the St John Ambulance Service is a voluntary organisation designed to provide medical support to the public at times of need. It plays a particularly important role in training volunteers to give first aid, and provides volunteers for a range of public events, e.g. at sporting events. St John's raises money through a range of fundraising activities. This money can then be used to provide training, and pay for the maintenance of ambulances and other public services.

#### Practice point

Carry out an Internet search using the term 'voluntary service' coupled with 'UK'. This will enable you to find a range of sites involved in voluntary service. Focus on a specific voluntary service. Find out how it is funded and what the current aims and strategy of the organisation is.

#### Remember

Voluntary service organisations are staffed by unpaid volunteers.

## Service level agreement

An important aim of public sector organisations is to meet the terms of required service level agreements. These agreements are made between a provider of a service and those providing the funds or with responsibility for initially setting up the body.

In creating a service level agreement it is important to establish certain standards that need to be met. We have already seen this in the case of primary health care, relating to the length of patient waiting lists and the time taken for a patient to be treated.

## Quality assurance

The term quality refers to something or somebody doing what is expected of them. For example, your local council is responsible for making sure that your bins are emptied. They hire contractors to do this. The contractor has a service level agreement with the local council. They are expected to meet standards of punctuality and cleanliness. They provide a quality service if they turn up on time and do exactly what is expected of them in a friendly and cheerful way.

Your local council has a responsibility for checking that these standards are met. If they are not they can take the contract away from the contractor.

Quality assurance is the process of checking that the contractor is meeting the service level agreement. An inspector at your local council will make checks. Some of these will be quantitative, e.g. a survey of householders to find out satisfaction levels. Others will be qualitative, e.g. based on a public meeting at which residents are able to express their views.

If public services are to give customers good service then it is essential to have quality assurance procedures in place.

## Provision at or below cost

There is less pressure on public sector and voluntary organisations to provide goods and services at a profit. This is because the government, rather than a private owner, is the key stakeholder in the organisation. Because the government represents the community it is more concerned with making sure that there is a high return to society. For example, health and social services provide home nursing to the elderly and sick at below cost price. They do this because these are people in need. In addition these people may have paid taxes for many years. So the government will provide many services and products at below cost to certain groups.

## Case study

### The Audit Commission

An 'audit' is a formal examination of a set of accounts to see that they are true and fair. In the public sector, where public money has been raised from taxes and other sources, it is essential to check that it is being used properly.

The Audit Commission is an independent public body that seeks to make sure that public money in areas such as housing, health, and the fire and rescue services is used properly. Although the body is independent it is accountable to the Office of the Deputy Prime Minister.

Auditors working for the Audit Commission must make sure that bodies such as Primary Health Care Trusts are using money wisely and honestly. They must check that there is no fraud or that money is not being used for purposes other than it should be. An audit therefore identifies areas of concern and reports the issues, which results in greater efficiency, and higher levels of public service.

1. Why is it important to have service level agreements? ✓
2. How does it help those providing services to have service level agreements? ✓✓
3. How does it help customers when there are service level agreements? ✓✓
4. What is the role of the Audit Commission in making sure that the public gets the service it deserves? How could this role be enhanced? ✓✓✓

Examples include:

- free bus and rail passes
- free eye testing and prescriptions
- free hospital treatment.

Although the government provides these and many other items at cost or below cost level, this does not mean that it does not operate in a businesslike way. Service level agreements and quality assurance activities are designed to make sure that public servants make best use of public money. Bodies like the Audit Commission are forever seeking to cut out waste and poor use of resources.

# Private sector strategies

Private sector businesses have quite different strategic aims and objectives. A major reason for this is that their most influential stakeholders are their owners.

The next section examines a number of strategies that are employed by businesses in the private sector. They are:

- profit maximisation
- survival
- sales maximisation
- break-even
- increasing revenue and cutting costs
- meeting the needs of the market
- outshining the competition.

## Profit maximisation

Many people believe that the main objective of businesses is to maximise the profits they make. Although businesses probably seek to achieve high profits in the longer term, they may have different short-term objectives. For example, in order to gain market leadership a business may have to invest heavily in the short period so that short-term profits fall. By sacrificing short-term profit maximising, a business can secure long-term profit growth.

| | Private sector | Public sector |
|---|---|---|
| Who are the key stakeholders? | Owners/shareholders | Government and user groups |
| What are the main aims and objectives? | To make high sales and profits and to dominate the market | To give high levels of service |
| What are the main strategies? | Being competitive to win market share, sales and profit | To guarantee high levels of service |

## Case study

### Tesco

Tesco is widely regarded to be Britain's most successful retailer in recent years. Not only is Tesco the number one supermarket by sales, but it is also highly profitable. Tesco's new online service with home deliveries of a range of items in addition to groceries gives the chain the opportunity to expand still further.

As a result Tesco's profits have continued to grow. This is illustrated by the table below showing profits from Tesco's day-to-day operations in the UK.

| Year | 2000 (£m) | 2001 (£m) | 2002 (£m) | 2003 (£m) | 2004 (£m) |
|---|---|---|---|---|---|
| Tesco operating profit (UK) | 993 | 1100 | 1213 | 1297 | 1526 |

1. Explain what the table shows you about Tesco's profitability. ✓
2. Why does Tesco need to make this profit? ✓✓
3. What do you think that Tesco does with this profit? ✓✓
4. How could Tesco have made its profit higher during the period shown? Why might it have been happy not to maximise its profit in this period? ✓✓✓

## Sales maximisation

Another strategy that private sector firms can implement is to maximise sales. There are two ways of measuring sales:

1. Sales volume – the number of items sold.
2. Sales value – the money received from making sales. This is also called **sales revenue.**

### Key Terms

**Sales revenue** Number of sales multiplied by average price per item sold.

You might think that it would be better to maximise profits than to maximise sales, but this is not necessarily so. When you increase sales then you are taking sales away from competitors. This means that they have a smaller share of the market. If you have 51% of the market then the most your nearest rival can have is 49%.

The biggest companies have all sorts of advantages over smaller ones. For example, suppliers prefer to deal with larger businesses because they make larger orders. Bigger businesses can win bigger discounts.

Sales maximisation is thus seen as a better strategy than profit maximisation in the short period. Sales maximisation will win you profits in the future as well as today.

### Key Terms

**Turnover** This is another term describing sales revenue.

## Survival

Walk down any high street and you will find a selection of businesses that have been there a long time – they have survived. Some of the survivors, like Marks & Spencer or WH Smith, may have seen better days. At one time it would have been unthinkable that Marks & Spencer would have to struggle to survive. Up until the 1990s Marks & Spencer went from strength to strength and represented the very best of British quality. It was said that you could walk into any room where people were gathered together and know with certainty that the majority of women would be wearing Marks & Spencer underwear.

## Case study

### The growth of Tesco's sales

In business there is a saying that if you can win the lion's share of the market – then the profits will fall. Tesco today dominates the groceries market in the UK. The following table shows the growth of Tesco's sales and the growth of its profits over a five-year period.

| Year | 2000 (£m) | 2001 (£m) | 2002 (£m) | 2003 (£m) | 2004 (£m) |
|---|---|---|---|---|---|
| UK Turnover | 16,808 | 18,203 | 19,821 | 21,309 | 24,760 |
| UK Profit | 993 | 1100 | 1213 | 1297 | 1526 |

1. Describe what has happened to Tesco's **turnover** over the period shown. ✓
2. When examining profitability it is useful to calculate profitability as a percentage of sales revenue. To do this you do the calculation:

$$\frac{\text{Turnover}}{\text{Profit}} \times \frac{100}{1}$$

This is called profit margin. It shows how much operating profit Tesco made for each £1 of sales. Do this calculation for each of the five years shown above. ✓✓

3. What has happened to Tesco's profit margin over the five years shown? ✓✓
4. What do these figures tell you about how successful Tesco has been in achieving its objective of increasing profitability? ✓✓✓

However, by the 1990s many other new stores were springing up and there was a rapid change in consumers' tastes and the desire to become more fashionable. M&S was left behind and its profits started to suffer. Fortunately M&S woke up to the problem in time. In recent years it has completely revamped many of its stores and employed 'state of the art' designers to make its clothing desirable (for example the Per Una range has been particularly successful). However, today M&S is engaged in a real battle for survival in an intensely competitive marketplace. For example, in recent times Asda has started selling cut-price school uniforms to threaten M&S's hold in this area.

M&S has had to change in a number of ways in order to survive. For example, it has changed the name to M&S because very few people use the term Marks and Spencer, has created new attractive store layouts and carried out some successful advertising.

## Breaking even

Any business that fails to cover its costs will find itself going down a slippery slope. Breaking even is therefore an important business objective, and one that is essential to ensure survival at least in the short term.

Let's look at break even by examining how a fictional business (Café Smoothie) can break even.

Café Smoothie sells luxury smoothies, which cost £2 to produce. The costs that go directly into producing each luxury smoothie include:

- raw materials – the plastic bottle and label, the fruit mix
- staff wages – which are based on how many smoothies they make.

The smoothie drinks are sold for £3 each. On the face of it, it seems that the business is making a profit of £1 on each smoothie sold (£3 minus £2).

However, we haven't accounted for all the costs yet, only for what are called **variable costs** – how much it costs directly to produce each smoothie. These are called variable costs because they vary directly with the number of items produced or sold: one smoothie costs £2, two smoothies cost £4, three smoothies cost £6 and so on.

However, we haven't included the fixed costs, which are the costs of running the business – regardless of how many smoothies are produced.

### Remember

The break-even point is the point at which the business exactly covers all of its costs with its revenues.

### Key Terms

**Variable cost** A cost that increases with the level of output or sales, e.g. the cost of ingredients in producing smoothies.

These fixed costs include the rent of the premises on which the smoothies are made, local business taxes, fuel bills, insurance, the manager's salary, and so on.

Let's say that these fixed costs add up to exactly £20,000 per year. The business has to sell enough smoothies to cover these fixed costs too, or it will make a loss.

As we saw above, every smoothie sold brings in (or contributes) £1 towards covering the fixed costs. This £1 **contribution** comes from the sale price of £3 less the variable cost per smoothie of £2.

The business therefore has to sell 20,000 smoothies per year to cover all of its fixed costs (£20,000 divided by 1 = 20,000 smoothies).

If the business is open for 50 weeks in the year (being closed for two weeks' holiday) this means that 400 smoothies will need to be sold each week (20,000 divided by 50 weeks). As long as Café Smoothie sells 400 smoothies on average each week, it will be safe!

## Key Terms

**Contribution** The financial contribution that each unit of an item sold makes towards paying off the fixed costs of a business. For example if the variable cost of producing a biro is 10p and the biro is sold for 40p, each biro is contributing 30p (revenue minus variable cost = 40 – 10 = 30).

## Remember

Break-even analysis can be converted into a formula or rule that goes like this:

Break-even sales = fixed cost divided by contribution

Another way of expressing this is:

Break-even sales = overhead divided by contribution

In this case:

$$\text{Break-even} = \frac{£20{,}000}{(£3 - £2 = £1)}$$

= 20,000 smoothies

Let's try these calculations again with a different business example. Imagine you run a hairdressing salon and charge £15 on average for each haircut. If the cost per haircut in terms of staff wages and materials is £5 and annual fixed costs are £50,000, how many haircuts do you need to do each year in order to cover your total costs and break even?

**Answer**: overheads divided by contribution

$$= \frac{£50{,}000}{£10} = 5{,}000 \text{ per year}$$

If we assume again that your business operates for 50 weeks a year, then you need to provide 5000 divided by 50 = 100 haircuts each week (on average) to break even.

## Practice point

Use the break-even formula to work out the weekly break-even sales for the following examples, assuming each business operates for 50 weeks per year. You may need to use a calculator. There are three key pieces of information we will be using: fixed costs, variable costs per unit and sales price per unit.

1. A taxi driver charges an average of £10 per trip, with a cost per trip of £5 and has fixed costs of £25,000 per year.
2. A beauty salon charges an average of £12.50 per visit, with a cost per visit of £5 and has fixed costs of £100,000 per year.
3. A recording studio charges £25 per studio hour, with a variable cost of £7.50 per studio hour and fixed costs of £50,000 per year.

The information can be summarised in the following table:

| Business | Average charge or sale price | Cost per unit | Fixed cost | Break-even sales level |
|---|---|---|---|---|
| Taxi driver | £10 | £5 | £25,000 | |
| Beauty salon | £12.50 | £5 | £100,000 | |
| Recording studio | £25 | £7.50 | £50,000 | |

### Increasing revenue and cutting costs

Of course breaking even is not a suitable long-term objective for a business. Typically when a business calculates its break-even point it will be looking beyond this to identify how much profit it can generate.

The two main ways to increase profit are to increase sales revenue and to lower costs. These are the main strategies that businesses will pursue in order to raise profit margins.

## How can you increase sales revenue?

One way of raising revenue is to raise your price. However, this might be dangerous because if you raise prices then customers may switch to buying from rivals.

An alternative is to lower prices. However, when you lower prices then you need to make more sales to cover the loss in sales revenue per unit.

Other ways of raising sales revenue include:
- improving your product
- spending more on advertising your product.

However, these last two suggestions may lead to an increase in costs. Rising costs are not a problem if they lead to greater than proportional increases in sales. For example, if you spend £5000 on an advertising campaign which then leads to a doubling of sales from £500,000 to £1 million then this should be considered worthwhile.

However, problems arise when costs are rising while sales are stagnant or falling. At these times businesses will seek to cut costs. In cutting costs it is always important to differentiate between those costs that result from inefficiency and those costs that encourage greater efficiency.

## How can you cut your costs?

There are many costs that can be cut. For example:
- overmanning – e.g. two people doing work that could be done by one person
- unnecessary costs – e.g. lighting and heating left on when it is not required
- wasteful use of other resources.

### Case study

**Laloo turns round the fortunes of India's railways**

The politician and entrepreneur Laloo Prasad Yadav is well known for having turned round the fortunes of India's railways. Laloo is a popular figure in India who one day hopes to become Prime Minister. He comes from the Indian state of Bihar. His well-known catch phrase is 'as long as there is aloo (potato) in your samosa, there'll be Laloo in Bihar.' In July 2001 an expert declared that India's railway network was on the edge of fatal bankruptcy. By 2006 this position had been turned round and railways have become the second largest cash generator in India's public sector.

The turnaround was a result of the ideas of Laloo Yadav, who took over the running of the railways in 2004.

In 2001 the cost of running the railway was 107% of revenue (a loss-making position).

'Laloo' (as he is popularly known) changed this round. So in 2005 costs had been cut to 84% of revenues (a surplus position) and in 2006 costs were 78% of revenues. How did Laloo turn the position round?

Instead of raising fares, he cut them. This led to much higher occupancy rates on trains – in other words there are fewer unfilled seats. At the same time Laloo lengthened the trains. Because each train pulls more carriages the cost per passenger has fallen. Laloo has also increased the speed of trains – the target is that they run at 100km per hour (twice the current speed).

On the freight side Laloo introduced 'round the clock' loading seven days a week (rather than five). This has increased the freight carrying capacity of the railways by 25%.

1. How has Laloo increased the revenues of Indian railways? ✓
2. How has he lowered the costs of the railways? ✓✓
3. How have these two effects led to the creation of a surplus made by the railways? ✓✓
4. Are there any dangers that you can see in this strategy? ✓✓✓

## Marketing

We have already seen that businesses who win market share are likely to succeed. The best way of winning market share is to find out what your customers want and then to give it to them. The process of identifying and then meeting customer requirements is called marketing. For example, research carried out by M&S showed it that people use the term M&S rather than Marks and Spencer. This helped the firm to rebrand itself under the new name. Other market research carried out by M&S showed that in the 1990s the public found M&S clothes to be dull and uninspiring. M&S brought in a range of designers to produce the sorts of goods that the public were looking for.

### Thinking point

Can you think of other businesses that have recently changed their image or changed their products so as to give the market what it wants?

### Case study

**Tesco's market share**

The following table shows the market share of leading supermarkets in 2003 and 2004.

| Supermarket | Market share 2003 | Market share 2004 | Market share 2005 |
|---|---|---|---|
| Tesco | 26.8% | 28% | 30.6% |
| Asda | 17.0% | 16.9% | 16.5% |
| Sainsbury's | 15.9% | 15.3% | 15.9% |
| Morrisons | 14.5% | 13.6% | 11.3% |

1. Which supermarket is the market leader? ✓
2. What does the table indicate about how Tesco has been able to increase its market share? ✓✓
3. What strategies do you think Tesco should employ to increase its market share? ✓✓✓
4. What could other chains do to fight back? ✓✓✓

## Competitors

Businesses today operate in competitive local, national, international and global markets. Businesses need to be aware of what competitors are doing. They must make sure that they are seen as market leaders rather than market followers. Being first to market is important. In business we talk about 'first mover advantage'. The firm that comes up and delivers new ideas before rivals steals a march on them.

A great example of this is the newspaper industry. Newspapers know that their business is news. They want the stories before their rivals. Newspapers therefore continually seek to gain exclusive rights to stories about what the famous and infamous are getting up to. The same principle applies to any type of business, whether it is a confectionery company seeking to be the first and best into organic chocolate, the yoghurt company providing probiotic yoghurt or the sports television channel offering exclusive viewing of premium events.

# Growth

Growth is an important objective of modern business. The business that fails to grow finds that it is dwarfed by a rival who then steals all the advantages that come from size. Today we see this in all walks of business:

- large publishers taking over smaller publishing companies
- big banks taking over smaller (and not so small) banks
- telecommunications companies seeking to swallow up other telecom providers.

Growth takes a number of forms, as we shall see in the last part of this unit. Businesses can grow by ploughing back their own profit into expanding their company. Alternatively they may take over another company.

## Profit, sales and market share

There are three key ways of measuring the growth of a business. These are:

1. Growth of profit. This can be measured in terms of the size of the profit, e.g. a growth from £1 million to £2 million in a year. Alternatively it can be growth

of the profit margin, e.g. from 10p for every £1 of sales to 15p for every £1 of sales.

2. Growth of sales. This can be measured by the growth in the volume or value of sales. For example, going from 1000 sales per year to 1500 sales per year would be by volume. Going from £100,000 to £150,000 is measuring the growth by value.

3. Growth of market share. This is measured in terms of the percentage of the market that a particular firm controls.

On 24 September 2006 *The Sunday Times* Tech Track 100 printed a list of Britain's fastest growing private technology companies by sales growth. Some details of the top ten of these are shown in the table below.

| Rank | Name | Activity | Location | % increase in annual sales | 2005 sales £000s | 2003 sales £000s | In profit? | Staff 2005 | Founded | Features |
|---|---|---|---|---|---|---|---|---|---|---|
| 1 | Gamesys | Gaming website operator | London | 301.48 | 9454 | 587 | Yes | 51 | 2001 | Claims to pay out more than £1m a day in prize money |
| 2 | Apertio | Mobile telecoms software developer | Bristol | 299.50 | 8509 | 533 | No | 158 | 2002 | Raised £17m, the second largest British technology investment in 2005 |
| 3= | Pulsic | Silicon chip software developer | Bristol | 272.31 | 3009 | 217 | No | 29 | 2000 | Claims its automation software reduces chip design time by more than 90% |
| 3= | The Search Works | Search engine advertiser | London | 272.31 | 18,576 | 1340 | No | 53 | 1999 | Helps likes of Comet boost its Internet search rankings |
| 5 | Redtray | E-learning software developer | London | 253.19 | 4478 | 359 | Yes | 30 | 2002 | Acquiring three firms in two years helped sales grow more than tenfold |
| 6 | ITM Soil | Soil testing equipment | Sussex | 249.32 | 4637 | 380 | Yes | 58 | 1999 | Technology used in construction projects such as Heathrow's Terminal Five |
| 7 | Mobile Fun | Online retailer | Birmingham | 237.83 | 7525 | 659 | Yes | 50 | 2000 | Founded by graduate software developer when he was only 21 |
| 8 | Vivo Technologies | Communication accessories provider | London | 204.30 | 3903 | 422 | Yes | 7 | 2002 | Integrates GPS technology into mounts for pocket PCs |
| 9 | Assima | E-learning software publisher | London | 195.02 | 5669 | 651 | Yes | 85 | 2002 | Four years after being set up company is interested in Stock Exchange flotation |
| 10 | Latitude | Digital marketing agency | Warrington | 191.42 | 18,748 | 2208 | Yes | 52 | 2001 | Reports its clients spend £1m a month advertising on Google |

(*Source:* Compiled by Fast Track 100 Ltd. Reprinted with permission)

## Practice point

Carry out some Internet-based research to gain figures for a company of your choice in recent times. What has happened to the growth of the profit, sales and market share of the business? Carry out searches such as putting in the name of the company, the term profit and the year you want to investigate.

## Outcome activity 1.2

You have been investigating the different types of business activity and ownership. Now you need to investigate and analyse how the type of business and different stakeholders influence the setting of strategic aims and objectives.

**Pass**

Outline the rationale of the strategic aims and objectives of two contrasting organisations. 

**Merit**

Explain the points of view from different stakeholders seeking to influence the strategic aims and objectives of your two contrasting organisations. 

## Grading tips

**Pass** 

Show in two contrasting organisations what the key strategies are. Clearly these will be different in different sectors. For example, if your private sector organisation is seeking to become the market leader, by increasing sales so as to increase profit, explain how it is doing this. You will need to research the aims and purposes of the organisation and the strategic plans. You should be able to access these by carrying out Internet searches using search terms such as Manchester United (the name of the organisation) and business aims and strategies. You should get a clear overview of what the aims are from company reports. Similarly if you are investigating a charity, voluntary service or government department look for details in their most recent report.

**Merit** 

If you want to achieve a higher grade, make sure that you set out clearly what the different types of organisations are seeking to achieve – their objectives. Show how each of the separate stakeholder groups will have sought to influence the objectives. Suggest ways in which the interests of these stakeholders might be similar or whether they could clash.

# 1.3 Functional activities and organisational structure

## Organisational structures

The structure is the shape of an organisation. Organisations create the structure that enables them to best meet the needs of their stakeholders. For example, an important part of the structure of a public limited company is the place of the Board of Directors at the top. Giving high priority to the Board means that the interests of the owners (the shareholders) are given priority.

In the modern world customers are very important. The organisational structure therefore needs to be organised so that there are clear links to customers – for example, the organisation may give priority to the position of customer service managers.

## Organisation charts

The shape/structure of the organisation is best revealed by examining the organisational chart. The chart shows the main parts of the organisation, and the relationship between the various parts.

For example, the illustration below shows the structure of a manufacturing company making office furniture. Note that important parts of the structure are the production department and the sales department selling direct to other businesses.

## Purposes

When you look at an organisational chart it should give you a clear picture of what the relevant sections of the organisation are and who reports to whom.

When we refer to line management we are talking about a person who is directly responsible for somebody else. For example, the production manager reports to the general manager. The production supervisors report to the production manager. The production supervisors supervise the work of the production workers.

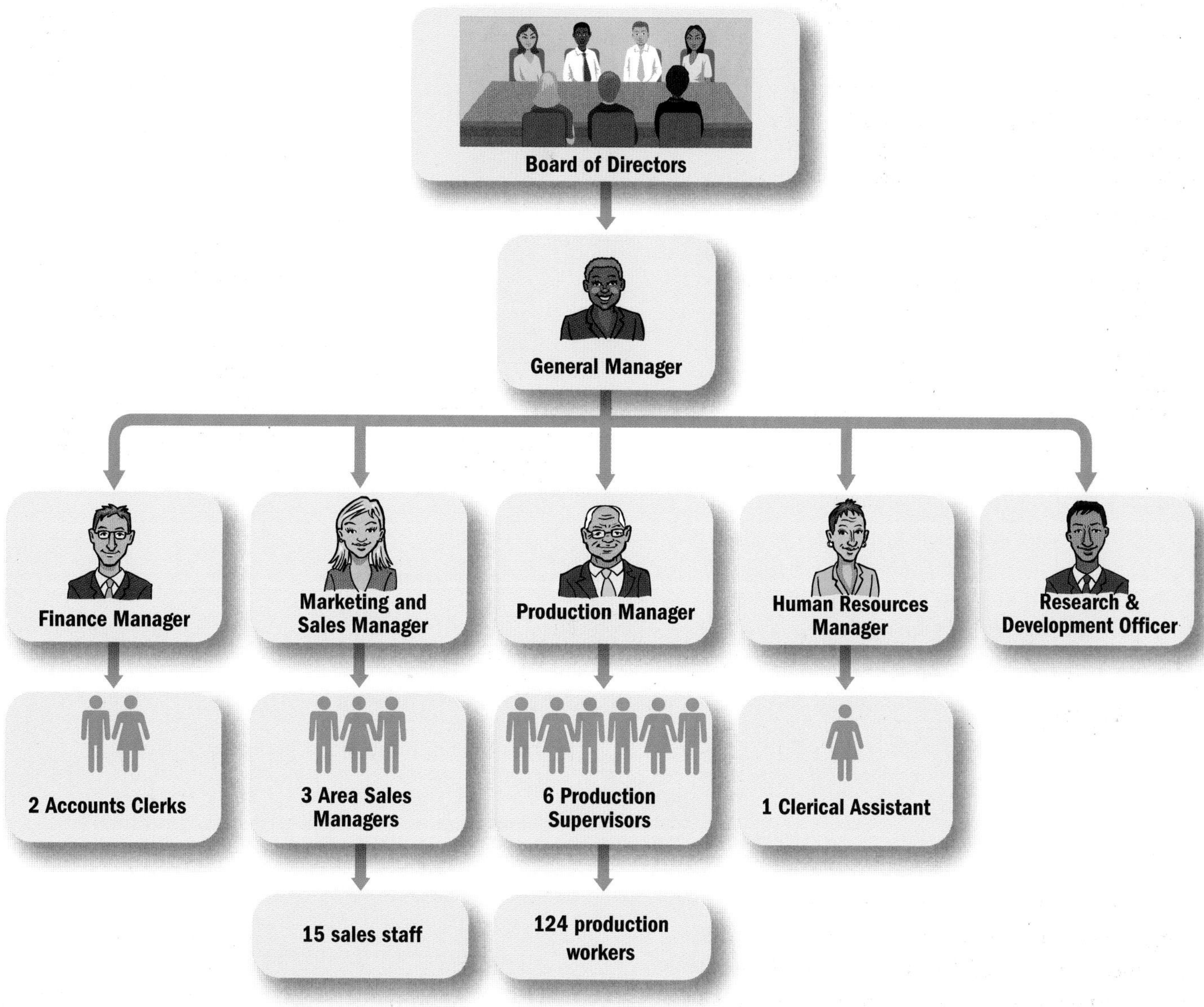


▲ Organisational chart for a manufacturing company

## Practice point

Create an organisational chart for an organisation that you are familiar with. It should show the key areas of the organisation, and who is responsible for whom.

### Division of work

The structure must show clearly how work will be divided up in an organisation. For example:

- who is responsible for dealing with customer complaints
- who is responsible for dealing with the payment of wages
- who should be responsible for making sure that the IT systems in an organisation are working smoothly.

## Practice point

Choose an organisation that you are familiar with, such as your college/school, or place where you have part-time employment. Work out a list of questions about the organisation – each question should start out with 'who should be responsible for?' When you have created a list of about twenty questions, draw up an organisational chart which would help to divide up work so that people are responsible for each of these areas.

### Span of control

The span of control is the number of people that individuals are responsible for in an organisation. The wider the span of control, the greater the number of people for whom the individual is responsible. The manager who tries to supervise too many people may be so overworked that his or her staff are unable to perform their duties effectively. On the other hand, if a manager has too few people to supervise, his or her time may be wasted, for example in explaining things to a single individual.

### Levels of hierarchy

Levels of hierarchy relate to the number of levels within an organisation. A tall organisation is one in which there are lots of levels within the hierarchy. Communication will always be a problem within a hierarchy. Another problem of tall organisations is that those at lower levels tend to be given little responsibility – they are always having to get permission from someone higher up.

## Practice point

Look at the company structure below for a tomato ketchup bottling factory:

- Managing Director
- Finance Director – Accounts administrator – Assistant accounts administrator – Accounts clerk – Accounts junior
- Production Director – 345 Production operatives
- Marketing Director – Sales Manager – 34 Marketing and sales team members.

What key weaknesses can you see in the structure?

### Division of work

There are a number of ways of structuring an organisation:

- **Functional** – is probably the most common way of grouping employees. Functional organisation means that the business is divided into specialisms, such as sales and production. Descriptions of major functions are given in the section below.
- **Geographic** – this is common when an organisation is a national, international or global business. For

example, the company may have a Europe, North American and Asian division. These divisions will report to Head Office.

- **By product or service** – an organisation can be divided up according to the products supplied (e.g. in a supermarket into breakfast cereals, fruit and vegetables, toiletries) or the service (such as your local council's division into environmental services, parks, housing, etc.).
- **By customer** – often businesses are divided into areas that deal with different types of customers. For example, in banking there may be a department that deals specifically with business customers, and another with the general public. This is sometimes referred to as wholesale and retail banking.
- **By process or equipment** – this is common practice in manufacturing in which a work area may be divided up into different types of machinery and activity. For example, in a printing company one department may be responsible for printing business catalogues, and another for magazines.
- **Matrix structures.** A popular form of organisation structure today is the matrix which involves people working together on projects working as a team. A person working on a project may be accountable to more than one team leader – the team leader of the department in which they work, and the project team leader.

The following grid shows a situation in which Min Patel is working both on project 1 in a cross-functional team as well as in his own department (production).
Of course, we can add many more dimensions to the matrix structure according to the number of projects an individual is working on.

| | Production | Finance | Marketing | Administration |
|---|---|---|---|---|
| Project manager for project 1 | Min Patel | | | |
| Project manager for project 2 | | | | |
| Project manager for project 3 | | | | |

# Functional activities

The following section describes the key functions of a modern business. Businesses are commonly organised in departments carrying out these key functions.

## Finance

Finance department functions include:

- keeping records of financial activity
- providing managers with information and helping to create financial plans.

The chief accountant supervises the work of the accounts department. The managers of an organisation need to be constantly aware of the financial state of the business and the financial implications of any decisions they want to make. Computers speed up the work of finance – shared databases and spreadsheet information will be available to managers and others.
Accounts may be subdivided into two sections:

- **Financial accounting** is responsible for keeping records of financial events as they occur – e.g. the sale of a car in a car salesroom. Records need to be kept of both cash and credit transactions. This section will produce the annual accounts and keep VAT records.
- **Management accounting** analyses current figures and makes predictions about the future. Their work is to supply information that helps managers to make decisions. This includes working out the costs of various activities, such as producing various items. Management accountants set out budgets which are plans set out in numbers. The work of management accountants helps the business to make decisions for the future, based on predictions of past figures.

## Human resource management

Human resource managers are responsible for all aspects of people management in an organisation. The type of work covered in the human resource function might include the following:

- policy making role – creating major policies about people in the organisation

- welfare role – concerned with looking after people and their needs
- supportive role – helping other functional managers to develop their work, such as helping them to recruit new staff
- bargaining and negotiating role – acting as an intermediary between different groups, e.g. trade unions and managers
- administrative role – paying wages and supervising health and safety requirements
- educational and development role – helping to train and develop employees.

## Research and development

Also known as R&D, this department investigates new products and processes and then seeks to develop them into the finished article.

R&D plays a major role in competitive organisations. For example, car manufacturers today are researching environmentally friendly cars that run on biofuels (vegetable fuels), electricity, solar power and other sources of energy. Food manufacturers are continually striving to develop healthier foods. The R&D department of some organisations is extremely large, for example in large pharmaceutical companies like Astra Zeneca and Glaxo, where they are continually searching for better treatments for cancer and a range of other medical areas. In other organisations R&D will be relatively small or non-existent.

## Production

Production organises:

- who makes the goods
- how the goods are made
- when the goods are made.

The production director of a company is responsible for making sure raw materials are processed into finished goods well. He or she must make sure work is carried out to an appropriate standard, and must supervise work activity.

Production management is often referred to as 'operations management'. It involves the activities necessary to produce a good or service of the right quality that satisfies a customer and it usually employs the largest amount of capital and other resources.

Production managers will decide how goods will be produced, i.e. the methods of production. They will also be responsible for working out who does what and when. This involves creating schedules of hours when employees will carry out particular tasks. The production manager will typically have production supervisors working under them. In large factories it is a tough job because the production manager will often have quite a large span of control. This is why it is so important to create work systems so that everyone knows what they should be doing.

## Service delivery

In the modern workplace, many operations are no longer concerned with old-fashioned manufacturing. Many modern operations are concerned with dealing with customers (such as greeting people as they enter a supermarket, dealing with customer queries over the telephone in telephone banking and insurance, etc.).

Customers are the most important people for any organisation. Organisations are therefore developing relationships with customers through the quality of customer service they provide.

Many organisations therefore have a functional department called customer service. This has a number of functions, such as:

- dealing with customers
- handling customer complaints
- making sure customers are getting good service
- training staff to work with customers, e.g. face to face or by phone or email.

## Marketing

The marketing function is responsible for identifying, anticipating and satisfying customer requirements profitably. Marketing is concerned with identifying the needs and wants of customers. This involves carrying out market research to find out which types of customer make up a particular market, what they want, where they want it, how they like it and at what price. In any type of business there should always be very close cooperation between the marketing and the production planning department. This is so that the wishes of customers can closely be tied in with product development.

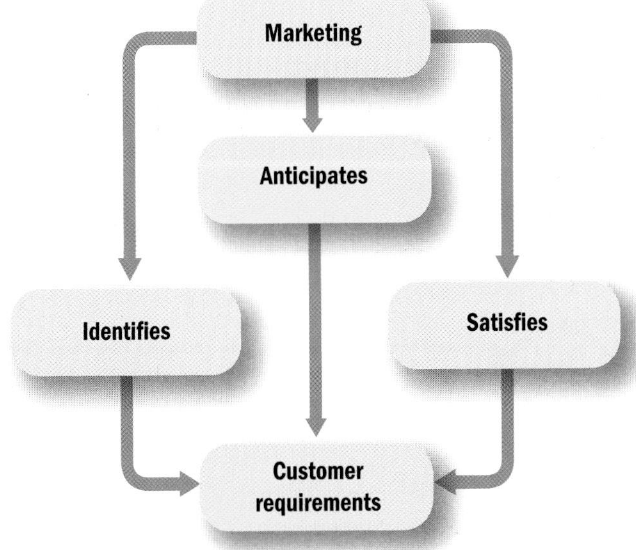


▲ The role of marketing

An important part of marketing will be organising market research. Marketers will have an important say in deciding:

- the **products** that the company produces
- the **prices** charged
- the **promotions** designed to encourage customers
- the **place** where goods will be sold.

These are called the four Ps of marketing.

## Sales

This department is responsible for the process of getting customers to buy what the company produces. It liaises closely with the marketing department. The main responsibility of the sales department is to create orders for goods and services. The size of this department and how it operates will vary. For example, some organisations employ a large sales force on a regional basis, e.g. businesses selling photocopiers or cars. Other organisations depend on advertising to stimulate sales and only employ a small sales team.

## Procurement

Procurement is very important. It is concerned with obtaining important resources, such as raw materials and office supplies, to keep the organisation running smoothly. In procurement it is important to develop lists of suppliers on a database. It is then necessary to keep records of how reliable and how competitive are the prices charged by these suppliers. When procurement works well, other functions should never be short of supplies.

## Information technology services

IT services:

- support other business functions
- provide specialist IT support
- manage computer functions.

The IT manager is there to exploit IT in the organisation and provide the guidance, support and expertise necessary to accomplish this. IT specialists play an important role across the organisation in creating and maintaining systems and helping in the training of other staff to use IT applications. Whereas many other functional departments may work in their own specialist areas, IT specialists work horizontally across the organisation. For example, IT specialists may help others to set up and use applications, such as databases, and at other times will be there to trouble shoot computer-related problems. IT plays a significant role in protecting systems against **viruses** and computer **hacking**.

## Key Terms

**Virus** Program that enters a computer network and sets out to destroy all or part of the files contained in it.

**Hacking** Breaking into a computer system and trying to access data illegally.

### Customer service call centre

A customer service call centre consists primarily of:

- call centre employees
- computer databases and other data sources
- telephone networks.

A call centre is a specialist unit within an organisation which is designed to receive and make telephone calls to customers. Call centre operatives work with a computer screen giving them access to lots of data, such as customer details, payment systems, and details of company products and services. The centre is overseen by a call centre manager, and typically call centre employees will work in teams. A team leader is able to listen into the calls being made and has details about such things as how long an individual employee is spending on answering each call.

Call centres are highly structured parts of the organisation. Each employee is given training and has clear details and guidelines on how to answer calls. Call centres are thus based on a very top-down approach.

### Management information systems

A management information system (MIS) is designed to provide managers with relevant and necessary information. A management information system is a large, usually computerised, databank to which managers have access. It is made up of a number of files consisting of key data which are regularly updated.

Armed with this data, managers are able to keep up to date and on top of all current developments in the business environment and in business activities. Managers are able to have a much clearer understanding of how businesses are developing and to have a clearer understanding of the effects of the decisions they make.

Today, systems designers create systems which are designed specifically to meet the needs of managers in specific companies and specific management roles.

### Logistics

Logistics involves organising the delivery of goods by a business and various materials and products around an organisation.

The role of logistics is to make sure that various products and processes run smoothly in an organisation. Key elements of logistics are transport and postal services. Distribution managers will plan routes and deliveries of finished and semi-finished goods. The post room will be responsible for getting the mail out efficiently and collecting and making various deliveries within the business.

### Managing the functions in small and micro-businesses

In the descriptions above we outlined twelve major functions within an organisation. It makes sense for large companies, like Tesco, Shell or Virgin, to have staff specialising in many if not all of these functions. But

## Remember

Functions are the specialist areas that a business is divided into, like marketing and finance.

what about small and micro-businesses that employ just one or two people?

Just because a business is small doesn't mean that it shouldn't have specialists. It is not possible for one or two people to handle all of the important functions listed above. Specialists may need to be hired to manage important activities, such as marketing or IT. Small businesses also contract out some of their functions. For example, they might pay an accountant to produce the annual accounts – paying them for just a few days work. In the same way, a small business might pay an advertising agency to organise an advertising campaign for them.

## Relationships between functional activities

One criticism made of some organisations is that they 'work in silos'. A silo is a tall container. If you imagine an organisation made up of a lot of silos – then you would see a situation in which there would be poor communication.

In modern business practice it is important to break down these silos so that the various parts of the organisation work together.

### Flow of work

Managing the flow of work between the functions of an organisation is important. For example, in organising an advertising campaign for a new product, specialist input might need to come from different sources.

Marketing may need to explain what their market research indicated that customers' needs and expectations were.

Production might need to explain how the product works and what key features have been built into it.

Sales may need to explain the key selling messages they are trying to get over.

You can thus see a flow of work as shown:

Marketing input leading to Production input leading to Sales input leading to Advertising input.

Of course, when the advertising department has created a campaign then the proposal has to be sent back to each of these functions to see whether they feel that it is appropriate.

All sorts of work will need to flow around the functions of an organisation. For example, policies and

◄ Communication is poor in organisations where staff 'work in silos'

documents provided by the various functions will need to be presented to Quality Control to check that the documentation meets the company quality standards.

## Independencies

In modern organisations it is important to break down silos. This is often achieved by organising employees into cross-functional teams. This approach is widely used in managing projects. For example, when doing research and bringing out a new product it makes sense to have a team consisting of:

- production specialists to put forward ideas about how the product can be made
- marketing specialists who identify what sorts of products are desired by customers
- financial specialists who can carry out costings and set out the financial implications of a particular project.
- quality specialists who emphasise quality related issues
- human resource specialists who can add inputs about work-related issues
- ICT specialists who can draw out the ICT implications of the project.

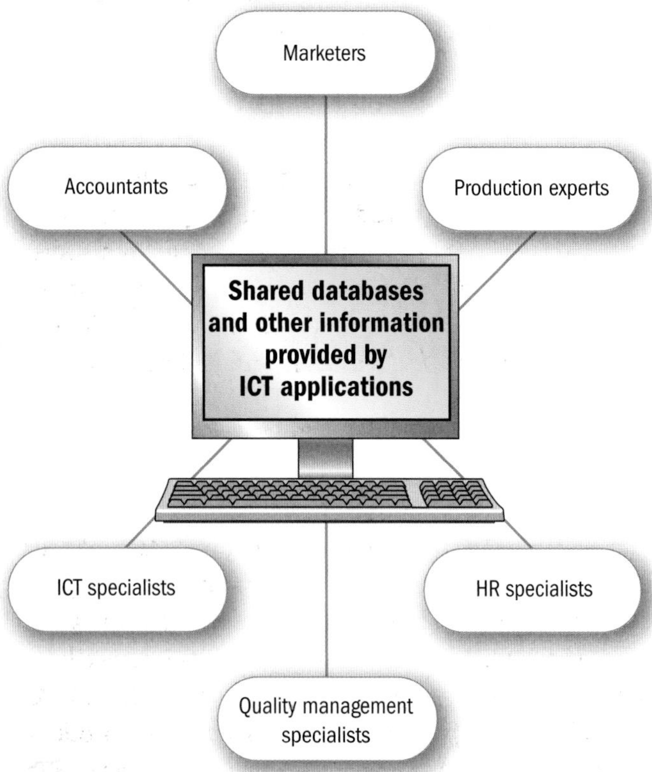


▲ A modern cross-functional team

In modern project management ICT can be used so that the team can share ideas and communicate with each other. They will have access to team databases, and other shared information sources. Sometimes teams don't have to physically get together in the same location. They can communicate using electronic links. This is often the case when the specialists live and work in different countries. Where the team just meets electronically we refer to this as a 'virtual team'.

Teams will get together to discuss issues. Sometimes they will be split into smaller sub-teams to tackle key aspects of the project. For example, accounts and production may get together to tackle the costings.

## Outsourcing of functions

Modern organisations have two main types of activities:

1. Core activities, which are the things that the business does particularly well. Businesses earn the bulk of their revenue and profit from core activities.
2. Non-core activities, which are the things that the business needs to do/or needs someone else to do for them but which are not at the heart of the business.

Until the 1990s large businesses tended to do both core and non-core activities themselves. However, from the 1990s onwards businesses realised that they could be more competitive if they **outsourced** non-core activities.

### Key Terms

**Outsourcing** Paying for outside contractors to do some of the work rather than doing it yourself. You buy in services from outside sources.

## Case study

**Outsourcing at Shell**

Until about 20 years ago Shell – one of the world's leading oil and gas companies – had a massive organisational structure. Most of the activities in which the company was involved were carried out by divisions of Shell.

However, this changed from the 1980s onwards when Shell realised that it was more effective to contract out non-core activities. Instead of running all its operations the organisation contracts others to do some of the work for it. Shell sets tough standards for these suppliers, and can always take the contract away.

An example of this is contracting out photography work to other firms. Until the 1990s Shell had its own photography department. These were full-time Shell employees. Today, Shell has a small number of photographers but typically contracts out the work to private agencies. This cuts back on Shell's costs. The organisation doesn't need to pay contractors 365 days a year or provide office space for the photographers. Another example of contracting out involves maintenance work on oil rigs, where much of the work is now carried out by private contractors.

1. What do you understand by the term outsourcing? ✓
2. How does outsourcing operate in the case of Shell? Can you give other examples of activities that Shell is likely to outsource? ✓✓
3. Why don't firms outsource all of their activities? ✓✓
4. What are the disadvantages of outsourcing? ✓✓✓

Examples of activities that companies outsource today include call centre work, administration, delivery and production.

## Call centre work

Many large businesses outsource call centre work to private call centres. The company will establish the routines and patterns of work that it wants the call centre to do for it and will establish minimum standards for the call centre to meet. The call centre will then be responsible for handling the work on behalf of the company. Call centres can carry out a range of activities, from handling consumer complaints to selling products. Increasingly now call centre work is being outsourced overseas to countries where labour costs are lower but where ICT skills are high.

## Administration

Aspects of administration are also outsourced. For example, a company may outsource work involving the photocopying of materials, the word processing of documents, the maintenance of databases, etc.

Companies can also outsource work involving the setting up and maintaining of websites.

## Delivery

Companies may outsource work which involves the delivery of company products, or packing and storing products. Rather than a company having the problems of owning a fleet of lorries and vans itself it can cut its costs by outsourcing. The costs which are cut include the costs of purchasing, insuring and maintaining vehicles.

## Production

Many companies also outsource the production of their goods. They can then concentrate on core activities such as selling, advertising and marketing products. For example, the food sold in M&S stores is typically produced by firms who are contracted to work for M&S – producing recipe dishes and a range of other products for the company. M&S can then concentrate on what it does best – retailing the products.

## Case study

### Innocent

Innocent is one of Britain's best known companies. The company produces smoothies (pulped fruit drinks with no additives). It was set up by Adam Balon, Richard Reed and Jon Wright (who are still only in their thirties). In 2006 it had a turnover of £70m. Innocent Smoothies are free of concentrates and preservatives and are sold in eco-friendly bottles and supermarket tetrapaks. It is a company that has captured the public's imagination – because it gives away 10% of its profits (to causes such as the Rainforest Alliance), has no chief executive, and constantly seeks to find out the views of customers. The business operates with 100 staff from a warehouse base in west London.

Innocent does not own any juicing facilities. It contracts out the work of producing the smoothies to five secret sites in Britain. Once sales build in Europe it plans to sign similar outsourcing contracts on the Continent.

1. What would you say is the core activity of Innocent? ✓
2. Why do you think it outsources production? ✓✓
3. What are the possible drawbacks of outsourcing production? ✓✓
4. Do you think that the benefits outweigh the drawbacks? ✓✓✓

### Supply chain

The supply chain for a product consists of all the stages involved in bringing a product from the raw material stage to the point at which the product is made available to consumers in the shops. Outsourcing the supply chain involves outsourcing all or some of the activities involved in extracting raw materials, transporting them, organising the logistics, making final products, and then distributing them to the end customer.

# Factors influencing organisational structure

What factors affect the structure that an organisation chooses to adopt? Key factors are:

- size
- business environment
- strategic plans.

### Size

The larger the organisation is, the more formal the structure tends to become, in order to coordinate larger numbers of workers, departments, and/or diversity of products or services.

Differentiation establishes individual tasks and jobs, whilst integration links and coordinates all these individual tasks and jobs.

Most large global organisations have very clear structures setting out responsibilities. For example, an international company may have the following structure:

▲ Geographical divisions in a large company

Each of these regional areas may then be broken down into functional specialisms.

In contrast, smaller organisations may have a much looser structure in which the responsibility for managing functional specialisms may be shared. Individuals may have more than one specialism. Of course, this can be a problem in that it may lead to lack of clarity about who is responsible for what.

## Business environment

The business environment is a major determinant of organisational structure. The business environment consists of all those factors which lie outside the business.

There are major differences between:

- **competitive and non-competitive environments.** In competitive environments it is very important that businesses are able to make quick decisions to outsmart the competition. There is less pressure in non-competitive environments.
- **static and dynamic environments.** Static environments are ones in which there is little need to change. For example, sales may have peaked and remain constant over a period of time. The organisation may therefore feel little need to restructure. In contrast, in dynamic environments the pace of change may be rapid. Structures are required which can enable rapid change. It is suggested that flexible teamwork structures are more beneficial in dynamic environments. Team members can be encouraged to come up with ideas for themselves rather than being told what to do. Self-managing teams are ones in which the team manages itself and in which decisions are made independently by the team.

Much emphasis is placed on work teams in modern business; the idea being that a large number of people can carry out a variety of activities working in small groups and using skills which complement those of the others. This moves business away from the traditional hierarchal structure that existed in a lot of businesses until the 1990s.

Today we talk about 'customer-facing teams'. A customer-facing team is one in which employees who work directly with customers (by phone, face to face, and by email or website links) are organised into small teams. These team members have considerable powers of decision making.

Customer-facing teams operate in a range of industries from insurance and banking to retail and leisure centres.

## Strategic plans

The type of organisational structure also depends on business plans. For example, organisations that seek to become more market oriented will develop structures that place an emphasis on marketing and customer focus. Companies that seek to develop internationally will develop structures that allow geographical specialisation.

If the strategy is one of market leadership, then companies will expand their presence in new sectors of market growth. If the strategy relates to increasing sales then the number of sales people is likely to increase.

### Outcome activity 1.3

To achieve the outcome here you will need to show that you understand functional activities and organisational structure.

**Pass**

Describe the functional activities and their interdependencies in two contrasting organisations.

**Merit**

Compare the factors which influence the development of the internal structures and functional activities of two contrasting organisations.

## Grading tips

**Pass** P4

To gain a pass you will need to describe the functional activities and their interdependencies (how they fit together) in two organisations. Use the same two organisations that you have been looking at for your assignment work so far on this unit, and draw charts and diagrams which show their functional activities. Explain in detail what each of the functions involves. Show how the functions fit together, e.g. the relationship between marketing and customer service, or how the call centre fits into the overall structure of the organisation.

Draw a clear and well-labelled diagram of your organisation. Use lines and arrows to join up the various positions in the company. Then describe clearly what each of the functions involves and how they fit together.

**Merit** M2

To gain a merit you will need to compare the factors which influenced the development of the internal structures and functional activities of these organisations. Why do they have different structures? How does the structure relate to the particular sector (private/public/voluntary or charity) that the organisation is in?

You may want to evaluate how effective the organisational structure is (does it work well or could it be improved?). If the organisations do not already provide organisational charts themselves you could construct one of your own from research about the organisation on its website and in documents. Perhaps you could write to the organisation asking them for a copy of an organisational chart.

# 1.4 Impact of external factors in the business environment on organisations

There is a simple rhyme which goes:

> Environment to each must be
> All there is that isn't me.

You can see therefore that the business environment consists of all those things outside the business. The business needs to keep a watchful eye on the environment because it is continually changing.

Key elements in the environment are:

1. Competition. Rival companies are continually changing what they have to offer. They may lower prices, bring out new products, engage in exciting new advertising campaigns, and a range of other activities.
2. Political factors. The action of government affects business and other organisations. Governments are continually changing the rules and the laws that affect business. This is illustrated by the way in which government rules affect schools. Simon Jenkins in an article in *The Sunday Times*, on 24 September 2006 illustrates this well when he wrote: 'This government tries to keep control of every school. Since coming to office its education department has issued 500 **regulations**, 350 policy targets, 175 efficiency targets, 700 notes of guidance, 17 plans and 26 separate incentive grant streams.'
3. Economic factors. The economy consists of businesses, individuals and government. The international economy consists of the economies of all the countries in the world. The economy consists of many markets – the market for goods, the market for services and the market for money are key parts of this. These markets determine the price that business has to pay for its resources such as labour, and raw materials. Businesses are continually affected by changes in the economy.

4. Social factors. Society is made up of all the people in a given area. It is important to be able to find out what the main trends are that are happening in society because these trends affect business. For example, changes in age patterns, such as the increasing numbers of older people in the population, determine which goods are popular. Then there are social trends which are affected by fashion – for example this year some goods will be 'in', whereas next year nobody or very few people will want to buy them.
5. Technological factors result from the development of new techniques, i.e. new types of products and new processes to make products. For example, recent years have seen a massive change in information technology which has transformed the way we run our lives. For example, today more than 90% of young people possess a mobile phone.

## Key Term

**Government regulations** Rules set out by government that businesses need to abide by.

# Political factors

## National and international law

Government creates laws that affect business. There are many laws (referred to as legislation) that affect a business or industry. Businesses are affected by laws at a number of levels.

Local laws affect local businesses. For example, local traffic laws determine which roads lorries and vans are allowed to travel on when making deliveries. Parking regulations determine when and where goods vehicles are allowed to load and unload. These local laws will be created by local councils and enforced by local officials.

Parliament creates national laws – such as Acts of Parliament and rules and regulations. Examples of national laws are those such as extending licensing hours, or banning smoking in public places. These laws affect businesses such as pubs, brewers and cigarette companies.

International laws are created by international bodies. In particular Britain is affected by European Union laws. Today the European Union courts are increasingly important in making judgements which apply across the union. European Union laws are regarded as having supremacy over national laws.

## Case study

### Nightclubs affected by new regulations

At the end of 2006 many British nightclubs were reporting falling profit figures. Some nightclubs, such as Entrepreneurial Leisure which owned Heaven and Hell nightclubs, and Barvest which ran Po Na Na, both got into serious financial difficulty.

Nightclub owners blamed government regulation for their difficulties. In November 2005 licensing laws were relaxed so that pub opening hours were extended. At the same time worries about 'binge drinking' frightened away some people from visiting town centres.

These factors affected patterns of when and where people drink. A survey of 18- to 35-year-olds by CGA-Centro, the market research group, found that 65% went out later since the new rules were brought in, often after 11pm. A lot of 18- to 35-year-olds prefer to drink at home or in pubs. They are less willing to pay entry fees into nightclubs. All this means that nightclubs fill up later with people who have less to spend.

1. Identify one political factor mentioned above that has affected business. ✓
2. Identify one social factor that has affected business. ✓
3. Is it possible to separate social and political factors or should they be seen as closely related? ✓✓
4. How might night clubs respond to the political and social factors mentioned above? ✓✓✓

There are two main types of rules that the European Union (EU) makes:

| Type of rule | Description | Example |
|---|---|---|
| Regulations | These are directly binding on member states. National legislation is not required to put them in place. Regulations therefore provide the most powerful element of EU law making. | The European Design Regulation applies to individuals and business and involves creating a system of Community Patents whereby designers can protect their ideas through a single EU-wide patent system. |
| Directives | These bind member states to the objectives to be achieved within a certain time limit, but leave national authorities to decide on how to implement them. Directives have to be implemented in national legislation. | The Directive on Privacy and Electronic Communication recognises that the development of new advanced digital technologies requires the protection of personal data and the privacy of the user. |

Legislation is very complex and can cover thousands of pages of complicated text. Here we describe just a few examples of laws:

### Employment legislation

Employment legislation consists of UK and EU regulations and directives that concern employers and employees.

The EU has passed a number of employment directives, including:

- The Equal Treatment Directive 1975 sets out that there should be no discrimination on grounds of sex, nor by reference to marital or family status, in access to employment, training, working conditions, promotion or dismissal.
- The Equal Pay Directive 1975 states that all discrimination on the grounds of sex in respect to pay should be eliminated.
- The EU Employment Directive 2000 required member states to implement laws prohibiting discrimination on grounds of sexual orientation and religious discrimination by the end of 2003. Legislation on age discrimination came into force from October 2006.
- The EU Race Directive 1976 (Amended 2003) is concerned with principles of equal treatment of people, irrespective of their racial or ethnic background.

The Working Time Directive (1993) sets out that:

- there should be a minimum rest period of 11 consecutive hours for every 24-hour period
- there should be a rest break if the working day is longer than 6 hours
- there should be a minimum rest period of one day per 7-day period
- there should be a minimum of 4 weeks' paid annual leave
- there should be an average of no more than 8 hours work per night in a 24-hour period.

The government's new age discrimination laws (2006) give individuals important new rights, extend existing rights and remove traditional barriers. These laws will help ensure that people are no longer denied jobs or harassed because of their age, and in most cases, workers of all ages will have an equal chance of training and promotion.

The current upper age limit for unfair dismissal and redundancy rights has been removed. This means that older workers get the same rights to claim unfair dismissal – or to receive a redundancy payment – as younger workers. Employees have a legal right to request working beyond compulsory retirement, which employers have a 'duty to consider'. Employees must also give workers at least six months' notice of their retirement date.

## Contract of employment

In addition to employment legislation, employees have rights under their contract of employment. An employment contract is a legal agreement between an employer and an employee, setting out the terms on which one agrees to employ the other. An employment contract will deal with many issues, including the employee's job description and duties, hours of work, pay, holiday and sick leave.

A contract should include the following items:

- names of employer and employee
- job title or job description
- date employment started, the place of work and the address of the employer
- amount of pay and how often it will be paid
- hours of work
- holiday pay entitlement
- sick pay arrangements
- pension arrangements
- notice periods
- for temporary jobs, the date employment will cease
- disciplinary rules.

### Remember

A contract of employment is a legal agreement between the employer and the employee setting out a range of work-related details.

Other important employment legislation includes equal pay laws, whereby employers must give women and men equal treatment in the terms and conditions of their employment contracts.

The national minimum wage is an important part of UK government and EU policy to provide employees with decent minimum standards and fairness in the workplace. It applies to nearly all workers and sets hourly rates below which pay must not be allowed to fall. It helps businesses by ensuring companies will be able to compete on the basis of quality of the goods and services they provide and not on low prices based on low rates of pay. The rates set are based on the recommendations of the independent Low Pay Commission.

The national minimum wage protects all workers ▶

### Practice point

Carry out an Internet search putting in the terms 'minimum wage' and the year in which you do your search. This should give you the latest figures for the minimum wage.

## Consumer rights

Businesses must make sure that their goods and services meet general safety requirements. They must make sure that everyone on their premises is safe. In addition, they must ensure that what they offer the customer is accurately described and that the claims they make about their products are true.

Consumer legislation provides real challenges for business:

- Compliance costs money. Making sure that you keep within the law is a costly business, but is well worth it in the long run in order to maintain a reputation.
- Consumer legislation helps to further inform consumers about their rights. This leads to ever-increasing pressures on business to operate in a safe and reliable way.
- Businesses must invest in training staff to comply with relevant consumer protection laws.
- Failure to act as a consumer champion can lead to a loss of competitive edge over rivals.

It is helpful to examine in brief some of the most important pieces of legislation involving consumers. To find out more about these laws carry out an Internet search using a search which includes the name of the relevant piece of legislation.

## Sale of Goods Act 1979

This was amended by the Sale and Supply of Goods Act 1994 and sets out that goods must be:

- of satisfactory quality – i.e. free from significant faults
- fit for purpose – they should do what they are supposed to do
- as described by the seller or on the package.

These laws also relate to the supply of services, for example by a hairdresser or cleaner. A service should be carried out:

- with reasonable care and skill
- within a reasonable time
- at a reasonable charge, if no price has been fixed in advance.

## Sale and Supply of Goods to Consumers Act 2002

This Act sets out that:

- for the first six months after purchase/delivery, the burden of proof when reporting faulty goods is reversed in the consumer's favour
- guarantees offered by manufacturers or retailers must be legally binding, and written in plain language.

## Trade Descriptions Act 1968

This makes it a criminal act for a trader to describe goods falsely.

## Consumer Credit Act 1974 (updated 2005)

The 1974 and 2005 Acts relate to agreements made between a 'debtor' and a 'creditor'. The Acts:

- regulate the formation, terms and enforcement of credit agreements
- require those giving credit to be licensed
- set out that advertisements for credit must show the true cost of the credit agreement
- set out restrictions on doorstep selling
- set out that those taking out credit must be informed about:
  - the total charge for credit, e.g. £1000 over two years
  - the Annual Percentage Rate of charge (APR), e.g. 20% APR
  - the price at which the goods can be bought for cash
  - state that all credit agreements must be in writing and the customer must be given a copy
- set out 'cooling off' periods in which the customer can withdraw from the agreement.

The 2005 Act sets rules for businesses providing credit card services, hire purchase agreements and loan deals. This affects all retailers that offer their customers credit terms.

## Environmental issues

The environment has become a major issue. Businesses need to show that they are aware of green issues if they are to keep various stakeholder groups happy, including:

- customers – who may want to buy green products
- employees – who may not want to work for a company with a poor environmental record
- shareholders – who may only want to invest in green businesses
- pressure groups – like Friends of the Earth and Greenpeace.

Businesses like Tesco have gained a competitive edge over rivals by taking initiatives such as offering a green tray for consumers to carry their shopping in, having environmentally friendly shopping bags, selling a wide range of organic products, etc.

The government has introduced a range of regulations that affect businesses. These include the following:

Pollution Prevention and Control (1996) is a legal set of rules for controlling pollution resulting from some industrial activities. Businesses are required to use the Best Available Techniques (BAT) to control pollution.

The European Union's Pollution and Prevention Controls cover emissions to air, water and land. Companies must apply for permits to create pollution.

The EU Directive on Packaging and Packaging Waste (1994, amended 2004) sets targets for waste recovery and recycling. Businesses that handle packaging are required to recover and recycle given amounts.

The Hazardous Wastes Directive (1998) deals with how dangerous wastes should be managed. They must be stored in special containers.

The Producer Responsibility (Packaging Waste) Regulations (1994, amended 2004) limits the amount of waste that businesses can use and create. Businesses must make sure that they minimise the waste and packaging they use.

Other environmental regulations relate to how asbestos is disposed of, and restrictions on how hazardous substances are stored.

The Waste Electronic and Electrical Equipment Directive implemented in 2004 requires computers to be disposed of in a safe way. Computers contain small amounts of dangerous chemicals such as cadmium.

### Thinking point

How are environmental regulations likely to affect business costs?

## Fraud

Fraud costs the UK economy up to an estimated £14bn a year (2006). Although there is an increased amount of fraud which takes place as a result of cybercriminals hacking into company databases, the majority of fraud takes place within companies. It is estimated that much of this fraud may take place with the collusion of senior managers and members of Boards of directors.

Typical examples of company fraud include:

- stealing company assets
- directors making the profits look better than they are so that they can take more out of the company in profit share schemes
- employees and suppliers altering invoices – for example adding goods bought for private consumption to a company invoice
- forging signatures on company cheques
- stealing cash and equipment.

The banking group HBOS carried out a survey which showed that nearly half of all companies with more than 36 employees had been hit by fraud.

The problem is that many companies don't have effective fraud controls. This means that they are prey to the harmful actions of unscrupulous people.

### Real lives

**Rogue Trader**

You may have seen the film 'Rogue Trader'. It is based on the story of a young employee, Nick Leeson, who was working for one of this country's best known investment banks – Barings. His job was to make investments for the bank in overseas markets. At first he was very successful, and the bank put more and more trust in him. However, unfortunately he made some bad investment decisions and lost a lot of money. To try to cover it up he risked more and more of the bank's money. All this time Leeson was not being checked up on. He created more and more debts for Barings so that eventually the bank collapsed and had to be sold for £1.

1. Were Leeson's actions fraudulent in your view? ✓
2. Who was responsible for the problem – Leeson or his superiors? ✓ ✓
3. What should businesses be doing to prevent fraud taking place? ✓ ✓
4. Taking one other example of fraud explain what checks a business could make to prevent this fraud. ✓ ✓ ✓

### Government taxes and subsidies

Government actions have a direct impact on business. Each week the government creates new regulations about health and safety at work, employment rights, consumer protection, fraud, e-commerce and many other areas of business life.

Another major area of government activity comes in the form of taxes and subsidies.

The government taxes various activities:

- to raise revenue for government spending
- to discourage certain activities such as the creation of pollution.

Tax involves taking money away from a business or individual. For example, income tax is paid at a given rate (e.g. 30%) on income earned above a certain level. In addition, employers are expected to pay other tax-based costs such as National Insurance contributions. This is a contribution that the employer makes to covering provision for the state pension, sickness, unemployment and other benefits for individual workers.

Another major form of tax is Value Added Tax (VAT). This is a tax on spending. Providers of goods and services pay a tax to the government on the value they have added to the goods they provide for you. They then pass this tax on to you. For example, when you have your car serviced you will see VAT added on to your bill.

By levying income tax the government is able to pay for the services it provides such as spending money on schools, hospitals and the police.

Taxation directly affects business. When the government raises taxes this immediately raises costs to business. For example if the government increased VAT by 2% then businesses would have to buy raw materials, machinery and equipment which is 2% more expensive.

Another form of tax that directly affects business is Corporation Tax. This is a tax on company profits. Businesses are not happy when this is raised because it immediately eats into their profits.

The opposite of a tax is a subsidy. Here the government gives money to producers to support their activities.

The government subsidises certain activities to encourage them. For example, in this country the film industry is subsidised by the government. British film companies with budgets up to £20 million for a film are entitled to £4 million a film. The British film industry is regarded to be very important and the government wants to give priority to it.

Other examples of government subsidies are subsidies to farmers through European Union farm support. Farming is thought to be very important because it provides us with our food supplies.

## Economic factors

The economy has a major effect on business. For example, if consumers spend more then businesses will receive more revenue. If the government raises taxes then this raises business costs.

Businesses therefore need to be very aware of what is going on in the economy. They need to know about all sorts of economic variables such as what is happening to key costs such as wages and energy prices.

### Pay levels

Wages typically account for 70% of the costs of running a business. Controlling costs is therefore essential. For example, two or three years ago lots of football clubs in this country got into trouble because they let their wage bills rise too high. One exception is Manchester United which seeks to keep its wage bill at less than 50% of revenue. But Manchester United is the exception.

### Cost of credit

Much business activity is funded by **credit**. For example:

- businesses often buy machinery and equipment through some form of borrowing arrangement
- businesses buy supplies and raw materials on credit terms.

### Key Terms

**Credit** Involves receiving a good or service now and paying for some or all of it over a period of time.

## Case study

### Wage demands at BT

In the spring of 2005, the telecoms giant BT was facing demands from its employees' trade union that would have added more than £300m to its payroll costs. The Communications Workers Union demanded an 8% pay rise for BT's 100,000 staff.

BT felt that this figure was unrealistic and only offered 2%. However, the Communications Workers Union stated that this was too little. They said their demand was realistic because BT had made profits of £1.09 billion in the previous six months. The Union said that it was only fair that the employees should share in the profits.

In the end a settlement was agreed between the figure demanded and the figure offered.

1. Why do you think that BT would be reluctant to offer 8%? ✓
2. Do you think the union was justified in demanding 8%? ✓✓
3. What do you think the effect on ongoing company profits will be of allowing high wage increases? ✓✓
4. Do you think that there would be a knock-on effect on other businesses from allowing high pay increases? Explain how this effect would work. ✓✓✓

The interest rate is the cost of borrowing money. When someone lends you money they will want to be paid back with interest because they are sacrificing their ability to use that money. Businesses must be careful not to borrow more than they can afford because interest repayments can rise, causing a drain on the business.

A driving force in determining interest rates is the Bank of England's base lending rate. This is the rate at which the Bank of England is prepared to lend money to financial institutions like banks. They will therefore set their own interest rates based on this. The Bank of England's rate is determined by the Monetary Policy Committee, made up of the Chair of the Bank of England and a panel of independent experts. They raise or lower rates according to whether they think people in this country are borrowing and spending too much money or not.

Businesses must be aware of the current interest rate and likely changes, for the following reasons:

- Rising interest rates add to business costs. If a business has borrowed £100,000 for one year at 2.5 per cent – then it will only have to pay back £102,500 (£2500 in interest). However, if the rate is 5 per cent then the interest repayment will be £5000.
- Rising interest rates also choke off consumer expenditure. When interest rates rise consumers will borrow less so that demand for the outputs of business will fall. A dramatic fall in sales can hit a business hard.

## Practice point

Read the minutes of the Monetary Policy Committee on www.bankofengland.co.uk/publications/minutes.

Find out how interest rates have changed over the last 12 months, and list any predictions for future changes. How would this information help you to advise a business that was thinking about borrowing more money to expand?

## Competitive pressures

Competition is one of the biggest influences on business.

Businesses compete through:

1. Prices – higher or lower than rivals.
2. Differentiating their product.

There are many different ways to beat the competition. One of the current trends in competitive strategy is to be the greenest in the business. The table on page 48 illustrates competitive strategy in green supermarkets.

| Tesco | Asda | J Sainsbury | Wm Morrison | Waitrose |
|---|---|---|---|---|
| Cutting carrier bags. Between 2006 and 2008 will reduce numbers given out by 25%. Is cutting deliveries to stores to cut congestion. Introducing regional counters in stores to promote local produce. | Plans to have no waste going to landfill sites by 2010. Has invested £40m on new recycling facilities at distribution centres. Introducing biodegradable packaging on organic food. | All ready meals to move to compostable packaging by end of 2007. Installing state-of-the-art recycling centres in many stores. Carbon emissions from its sites reduced by 20% since 2000. | Introducing recyclable packaging for some own-brand products. Highest proportion of seasonal UK vegetables of any UK supermarket. 72% of all store-generated waste is recycled. | Trying out scheme to allow local suppliers to deliver goods directly to stores. No GM ingredients in any own-branded food products. |

## Globalisation

One of the major changes to affect British business since 2000 has been the impact of globalisation.

Globalisation involves the creation of global markets. Key aspects of globalisation include:

- Huge economies like China and India entering the marketplace. These economies are very competitive. For example, if you have bought a cheap T-shirt lately then there is a good chance that it was made in China. The fact that these huge economies are able to produce large quantities of products at very low costs makes life very difficult for UK-based competitors.
- The creation of global brands – people round the world instantly recognise global brands like Magnum ice cream, Apple iPod, Nokia phones, and Coca-Cola.
- Sony has been creating cult electronic products since the 1950s. Today the same innovative approach that developed the transistor radio and Walkman Personal Stereo continues to give Sony the lead in the new digital entertainment world. Sony's BRAVIA range of flat screen products leads the way in high definition entertainment and in digital imaging. Cyber-shot cameras have redefined digital photography with Real Imaging Processors and advanced CCD chip technology. Sony's music, movies, game and online businesses are also global leaders.
- The creation of global products and global marketing. The same products and marketing and advertising campaigns can be used worldwide. This significantly lowers costs. For example, a Christmas advert for Coca-Cola can be shown on television in hundreds of countries.
- The creation of almost instant communications. Transport links move goods and people around the world within hours. Information and communications technologies enable instant link-ups between people on opposite sides of the world.

▲ Sony is a good example of a global brand

Each of these factors has led to a reduction in the costs of products. This forces businesses to become competitive. Large British-based companies like Cadbury-Schweppes (producing confectionery), Vodafone, and Shell need to engage in global strategies if they are to compete with overseas rivals.

Of course, businesses should also see globalisation as an opportunity. A UK company can expand quickly by producing goods and services that are wanted by consumers across the world.

## Labour supply and demand

We saw earlier in this unit that markets are made up of suppliers – those prepared to supply a good or service – and 'demanders' – those wishing to buy a product or service. In the labour market the service that is being traded is manual and intellectual labour – 'brawn power and brain power'. Today there is more and more emphasis on 'intellectual intelligence'. New knowledge workers, such as those working in IT, can receive high salaries. It is also argued that 'emotional intelligence' is in short supply. Emotional intelligence involves the ability to get on with customers. This is very important in people who interact with customers directly, e.g. service and telesales workers.

The marketplace brings together suppliers of labour (employees) with labour to sell and consumers of labour (employers) wanting to buy intellectual, physical and emotional labour.

In the case of the market for labour, supply consists of employees and potential employees who are prepared to work for a business. **Demand** consists of a firm's wants and need for employees to work for them.

## Key Terms

**Demand** exists when consumers have wants and needs backed up by the purchasing power to buy the products they desire.

When labour is in short supply then wages are likely to rise. In contrast if there are more people looking for jobs than there are jobs available – then wages will fall. The number of workers in the UK earning above average salaries has been increasing. About half a million people earn at least £100,000 before tax – about 400,000 of these are men.

In 2004 the European Union was extended to include 10 new countries including Poland. People from these new EU countries are now able to work in Britain. This has increased our labour force by almost half a million people with a beneficial effect for business of bringing down wages. At the same time employers have access to a wider pool of skilled and unskilled labour.

### Energy prices

Energy prices are important costs for many businesses. This is particularly true of manufacturing companies where power is needed to run machinery. However, it is also important for service industries, like insurance, which rely on computer networks and in which heating and lighting costs for the offices in which employees work can be a substantial cost.

Since October 2003 there have been substantial increases in energy prices in this country. The effect on organisations is shown in the following table:

| |
|---|
| 70% average gas price increases for the chemical industry between 2004 and 2006 |
| 40–50% average gas and electricity price increases in the retail sector over the same period |
| £41 million increase in NHS gas bill between November 2003 and November 2004 |
| £100 million combined increase in local government gas and electricity bills in 2004 |

Reasons for this include:

- the decline in gas supplies in the North Sea
- the soaring price of oil owing to diminishing supplies and because of instability in oil-producing parts of the world such as Iraq
- lack of storage capacity for gas in this country. This means that we have to buy in gas at inflated prices from Continental Europe.

## Case study

### The plastics industry in the UK

There are 200,000 jobs in the UK plastics industry. Companies in this sector have seen average rises of nearly 60% for gas and electricity in 2004 and 2005. As these increases are higher than those of their mainland European competitors, and as mainland Europe is the major trading partner for the industry, these rises have devastating potential for the industry in the UK.

1. What other industries apart from plastics are likely to be hit hard by rising energy costs? ✓
2. How will the rising energy costs affect the prices business can charge for plastic products? ✓✓
3. What will be the impact on the competitiveness of the UK plastics industry? ✓✓✓
4. Which business stakeholders are likely to suffer and how as a result of these rising costs? ✓✓✓

# Social factors

Changes in the population structure of society and changing patterns of social behaviour also affect business.

### Ageing population

The number of older people in Britain is increasing fast. Statisticians predict that during the next century there will be a substantial increase in those living to be over 100. According to recent estimates, the number of people over 60 could rise by 40% in the next 30 years.

In 1995 there were less than 9 million people over 65 – by 2030 there may be about 13 million.

People tend to work and save when they are young and live off the proceeds when they retire. Wealth peaks at retirement age and then begins to fall. People have different patterns of saving and spending at different times in their lives.

As the population ages then we may see more people spending the proceeds of their previous earnings. They are also likely to have different spending patterns to the young. For example, there will be greater demand for stair lifts, anti-ageing creams, botox injections, and world cruises. New businesses will spring up to cater for the needs of the elderly and e-commerce will be a particularly useful vehicle for selling directly into the homes of this group. There will be a profound impact for the pharmaceutical and health industries which will need to expand to meet the needs of an ageing population.

Another major impact on business may be increased labour shortages. Small businesses in particular may be forced to raise wages to attract labour. As the percentage of the elderly rises in the population the government may be forced to increase taxes and National Insurance contributions to support the elderly population.

**Thinking point**

Identify three business opportunities that might develop as a result of the ageing of the population.

### Hosting of major sporting or cultural events

Another way in which a business can capture public attention and thus enhance its position in society is through hosting important cultural and sporting events. This is why companies like Coca-Cola seek to sponsor the World Cup and other football events. According to this thinking, football is the world game and Coca-Cola is the world drink.

Companies compete with each other to gain exclusive rights to sponsor events such as the London Promenade Concerts or the British Grand Prix.

### Celebrity culture

Today a lot of people want to be celebrities. If they can't be celebrities they want to live like celebrities. We are obsessed by celebrity, giving rise to a host of magazines such as *Hello* and *OK* which chart the life and lifestyles of celebrities.

From a business point of view celebrities help to create demand for products. Celebrities create social trends

▲ Kate Moss exemplifies our modern celebrity culture

– whether it is Madonna wearing a kabbala bracelet or Victoria Beckham putting extensions in her hair.

Kate Moss exemplifies the celebrity process. In 2006 she earned an estimated £30m from lucrative contracts with Rimmel, Stella McCartney and Agent Provocateur. Kate Moss is regarded by many to be 'cool' because of her lifestyle which is regarded to involve beauty, danger and taste. These characteristics which she is supposed to represent enable her picture to be used to sell anything from eye shadow to mobile phones.

Of course, it doesn't always work like this. Sometimes celebrities can have an adverse effect on a brand. Nothing kills clothing like the wrong celebrity wearing it.

### Thinking point

Can you think of a situation in which celebrities have helped to make a particular well-known brand appear uncool? Remember how negative tabloid press comments – connected with her drug use – damaged the prestige of Kate Moss so that H&M dropped her from their advertising campaign.

## Technological factors

We live in an age of technological advance. Indeed one boast of many advertisers is that their product includes more technology than their rivals. For example, you can see this in the way Nike advertises its trainers.

The Internet has changed the way in which businesses do business. It is a global network linking millions of computers across the world. Any individual or organisation can link to this network using a telephone line or cable connection.

Today it is essential for a business to have a good website that is easy to navigate (find your way around) and which is attractive and appealing to use. Increasingly, the Internet has come to be accepted as a way of making purchases. This is illustrated by the following table showing shoppers using the Internet to buy presents at Christmas:

| Year | % of shoppers |
|---|---|
| 1998 | 2 |
| 1999 | 8 |
| 2000 | 11 |
| 2001 | 12 |
| 2002 | 22 |
| 2003 | 29 |
| 2004 | 32 |
| 2005 | 51 |

### Case study

**Kate Moss from top model to Topshop**

'What do you do the morning after you have celebrated the most unlikely coup in high-street fashion?

If you are the boss, you usually put your feet up. If you are the new hire you are usually in the office at 8am sharp.

But on Friday morning Kate Moss was nowhere to be seen at Topshop's central London office. Instead, her boss, Sir Philip Green, was running his fingers along rack after rack of £15.99 V-neck sweaters. "I've spent all morning approving next season's knitwear," he said wearily.

Moss, the world's most famous model, is the only person in fashion who gets to tell the pugnacious Green what to do.

Under the terms of the deal she signed last week to design a clothing range for one of Britain's most successful high-street retailers, she chooses her own hours, her own ad campaigns, enjoys an almost limitless budget and has approval for all designs and merchandise.'

(Source: John Arlidge *The Sunday Times Business* 24 September 2006)

1. Why do you think Topshop were so keen to sign Kate Moss? ✓
2. Why have they given her so much freedom? ✓✓
3. Do you think the cost to them will be worth the rewards that ensue? ✓✓✓
4. How do you think celebrity can make a brand cool? ✓✓✓

### Broadband and telephony developments

To access the Internet individuals need to have an ISP (Internet Service Provider). Today large numbers of people prefer to use broadband services which give much quicker and more reliable access to the Internet than dial-up services.

Previously, computer users who wanted to connect to the Internet had to use a dial-up modem. There were disadvantages to this; for example, unless you had a separate telephone line, when someone was using the Internet in your house then you wouldn't be able to use the phone at the same time, and it was also quite slow.

Broadband has changed all this. Broadband services provided by telephone and cable companies allow home users and small businesses to have always-on access to the Internet, which was previously something only large businesses could afford. The same phone line can be used for broadband as is used for the telephone and they can both be used at the same time, with no interference.

Broadband has also brought high-speed Internet to small businesses and home users, enabling them to transfer large amounts of data very quickly. This has provided many cost benefits to business, as well as opening up many more business opportunities, in terms of what can be delivered via the Internet and what consumers expect from the Internet.

## How do external factors impact on organisations?

So far we have built a picture of a very complex and rapidly changing business environment. So how do political, social, economic and technological factors affect business?

### Creation of new organisations

These changes provide an opportunity for new organisations to set up. For example, because of environmental legislation a range of new organisations has been created which clear up pollution and process waste for other businesses.

Changing social trends provide opportunities for lots of new companies to set up. For example, one of the reasons that Innocent has been so successful is because a lot of people today are moving to healthier diets. Jamie Oliver's championing of healthy eating has led to a substantial decrease in the sale of products like chips, pizza and drinks like cola and lemonade. This provides an opportunity for new 'healthy living' businesses to enter the market.

Young people have a particularly important role in the success of new products. Many young people are particularly knowledgeable about new technologies. They are not easily convinced by the advertising hype that is associated with new products. They are more interested in word of mouth – what other young people say about products. For example, this has led to the success of new products such as the iPod, Motorola's V3 Razr phone and Sony's PlayStation.

### Winding up existing organisations

On the downside we see that adverse environmental factors can lead to businesses running into difficulty. At the start of this section we saw that changes in the legal and social environment have led to a number of nightclubs winding up. This is where a business has to close down and often has its assets sold off to pay its debts.

### Take-overs and mergers

Another way that businesses respond to changes in the environment is through take-overs and mergers. These enable businesses to grow in size and to cut out weaker parts of an organisation in order to focus on the stronger elements.

If a business wishes to **take over** another business it will set out to purchase more than 50% of the shares. As soon as the investing business has a 50% share plus one share it is in control. It can make all the decisions as it cannot be outvoted by the other shareholders.

The business that has acquired the shares is known as the holding company. The business whose shares have been acquired is known as the subsidiary company.

A **merger** occurs when two businesses combine to form a single company. A merger is very similar to a take-over except the existing shareholders of both businesses retain a share interest in the new business.

An **acquisition** occurs where one business gains control of part of another business. A business may be prepared to sell off one of its divisions which it no longer wishes to keep.

Mergers and take-overs occur for a number of reasons, such as:

- because there is too much supply in the market relative to demand, a firm may take over part of a rival in order to reduce supply to the market
- to move into new markets. A firm may take over another business to get access to new markets, perhaps in other countries
- to acquire new technologies. A quick way of developing new technologies is to take over businesses which have developed new technologies
- to acquire dynamic brands. Businesses whose own brands are not particularly dynamic may buy up smaller businesses with more dynamic brands.

## Revision of strategic plans

Business plans should not be regarded as set in stone. The intelligent business continually changes its plans. It is essential to continually keep in tune with what is happening in your business environment and to adjust your plans to keep in touch with what is happening in the wider environment.

For example, in September 2006 Richard Branson announced that his Virgin trains and planes would invest in new and more environmentally friendly fuels. He was responding to green pressure groups and the green consumer movement.

## Impact on stakeholders

Stakeholders are affected by external changes, and so what they expect of their business has changed. We can see this, for example, in growing environmental awareness and health consciousness.

Today:

- Customers want healthier, more environmentally friendly products.
- Pressure groups are more influential and know how to use the media to get their point across to organisations.
- The government is more aware of its responsibility for the environment and the health of the nation and therefore exerts pressure on business through regulation.
- Shareholders know that their business will only be profitable if customers are convinced that their business is environmentally friendly and health conscious.
- Employees are most likely to work for companies with good environmental and health records.

You can see therefore that stakeholders will have a major influence on the types of strategies that businesses adopt. The attitudes of stakeholders are shaped by the political, social, economic, and technological environment.

## Functional activity changes

Businesses change their shape to take account of changes in their environment. For example, during the 1980s and much of the 90s M&S did not put much emphasis on marketing. The company thought it knew what it was customers wanted. However, they were in for a rude awakening when customers took their shopping elsewhere. Today this has changed. M&S is now a market-driven organisation, listening carefully to its customers.

In the modern world some functions of a business have become particularly important:

- customer service – because of the recognition of the importance of customers
- marketing – to find out what customers want
- human resources – people that work for organisations need to feel that they are valued if they are to be motivated. Human resource management has thus grown in importance
- information and communications technology – because of the growth of the Internet, broadband and associated technologies
- call centres – as a means of outsourcing work.

You can therefore see that modern organisations are vastly different from the organisations of the past.

## Outcome activity 1.4

The final part of your outcome activity requires you to show how external factors in the business environment impact on the business. You will explore a range of political, social, economic and technological factors that affect business. Remember that while some of these factors apply to all businesses, some may be specific to your business. For example, the ageing population affects all businesses. However, it affects some organisations more than others. Although demographics may have little effect on a modern hairstyling company like Toni and Guy, it may have a big effect on a charity for the elderly such as Age Concern.

**Pass**

Describe how three external factors are impacting upon the business activities of your selected organisations and their stakeholders. 

**Merit**

Analyse how these external factors have impacted on the two contrasting organisations. 

**Distinction**

Evaluate how external factors, over a specified future period (e.g. the coming year) may impact on the business activities, strategy, internal structures, functional activities and stakeholders of a specified organisation. 

## Grading tips

**Pass** P5

It is important that you focus on factors which specifically affect your organisations. Examine changes in laws and regulations; examine changes in the economy, such as interest rates, pay, and energy costs; examine social trends and how technology specifically affects your organisation.

Carry out Internet searches using search terms such as 'UK interest rates' and the year you are investigating. You may speculate about wage rates, for example putting in terms such as 'UK wage rates' 'rising', etc. This will provide you with a wealth of information about the business environment. Additionally a company or organisational report will give a good overview of what is happening in the environment.

**Merit** 

Instead of just saying that wages have risen and by how much, you will need to look at how these wage increases have increased costs – what have been the implications for prices and the competitiveness of the organisation – whether it has led to job cuts, etc.

**Distinction** 

The key word here is 'evaluate' – you will need to analyse the various impacts in relation to activities, strategy, internal structures, functional activities and stakeholders, and then make a judgement, supported by reasons, about how important these are likely to be to the organisations concerned.

## End of unit test

1. Classify the following according to whether they are in (a) the public sector, (b) the voluntary sector, or (c) the private sector:
   - Manchester United PLC
   - The BBC
   - Oxfam
   - Amnesty International
   - Mars (confectionery)
   - Dr Martens
   - gaydar.co.uk
   - ChildLine
   - Bank of England
   - local councils
   - McDonald's
   - the armed forces
   - Orange
2. What is meant by the term 'supply'? Why does supply need to be market led?
3. Who owns public sector businesses? Who owns private sector businesses?
4. List three groups of important stakeholders in a PLC, and explain what their stake is in the company. Explain how the interests of these stakeholder groups might conflict in some situations.
5. What does the term 'service level agreement' mean?
6. One of the objectives of private sector businesses is to maximise sales. Describe two other objectives that they might have.
7. If a business has fixed costs of £100,000, sells its products at £10 each and has variable costs of £5, what is:
   a. contribution per unit?
   b. the break-even level of sales?
8. What are the advantages to business structure of having narrow rather than wider spans of control?
9. Identify three major functions of a business that involve communicating with customers. Describe the role of each function. Explain any links between these functions.
10. How might a matrix structure help the smooth running of project work in a business?
11. Explain how the purpose of a private sector business might be different from that of a public sector business. Use examples.
12. Describe three ways of measuring the growth of a business. Which of these methods of growth do you think is most helpful in measuring the growth of a new business?
13. Describe the key differences between procurement and logistics as business functions.
14. How do changes in interest rates affect businesses? Illustrate your answer by reference to a specific business.
15. How could a new technological development be seen as both a threat and an opportunity to an existing business?

# Resources

If you want to find out about the origins of some of the UK's most exciting enterprises try starting an Internet search with the name of one of the UK's most enterprising people of recent years, such as:

Lakshmi Mittal
Anita Roddick
Richard Branson
Martha Lane Fox
Reuben Singh
Toni Mascolo

To find out more about a specific organisation try one of the following:

www.innocentdrinks.co.uk – Innocent smoothies brand

www.marksandspencer.com – M&S

www.gaydar.co.uk – an alternative gay enterprise

www.toniguy.com – Toni and Guy chain of hairstylists

www.easyjet.com – Easyjet low-cost airline

www.amazon.com – Amazon

www.lastminute.com – last-minute travel and entertainment

www.tesco.com – Tesco online

www.iron-directory.com – a new UK-based site selling iron products tipped to be a giant of the future

www.thomaspink.co.uk – selling a range of shirts from central London

Another useful resource is:

www.tt100.biz – a specialist site providing business case studies about well-known UK and overseas businesses. Search the website index to find cases about stakeholders, business ownership, business organisation and environmental influences.

# Books

Dransfield R. and Needham, D. 2006 *Applied Business*, Harcourt Education

These texts look at popular businesses:

Bevan, J. 2002 *The Rise and Fall of Marks and Spencer*, Profile Books
Creaton, S. 2005 *Ryanair: How a Small Irish Airline Conquered Europe*, Aurum Press
Jones, L. 2005 *easyJet: The Story of England's Biggest Low-Cost Airline*, Aurum Press
Roddick, A. 2005 *Business as Unusual: My Entrepreneurial Journey*, Anita Roddick Books

| Grading criteria | Outcome activity | Page number |
|---|---|---|
| To achieve a pass grade the evidence must show that the learner is able to: | | |
| P1 Describe the type of business, purpose and ownership of two contrasting organisations | 1.1 | 16 |
| P2 Describe the different stakeholders who influence the purpose of two contrasting organisations | 1.1 | 16 |
| P3 Outline the rationale of the strategic aims and objectives of two contrasting organisations | 1.2 | 28 |
| P4 Describe the functional activities and their interdependencies in two contrasting organisations | 1.3 | 39 |
| P5 Describe how three external factors are impacting upon the business activities of the selected organisations and their stakeholders | 1.4 | 54 |
| To achieve a merit grade the evidence must show that, in addition to the pass criteria, the learner is able to: | | |
| M1 Explain the points of view from different stakeholders seeking to influence the strategic aims and objectives of two contrasting organisations | 1.2 | 28 |
| M2 Compare the factors which influence the development of the internal structures and functional activities of two contrasting organisations | 1.3 | 39 |
| M3 Analyse how external factors have impacted on the two contrasting organisations | 1.4 | 54 |
| To achieve a distinction grade the evidence must show that, in addition to the pass and merit criteria, the learner is able to: | | |
| D1 Evaluate how external factors, over a specified future period, may impact on the business activities, strategy, internal structures, functional activities and stakeholders of a specified organisation | 1.4 | 54 |

# 2 Investigating business resources

## Introduction

You may have noticed – through work experience or a part-time job – the different types of resources that businesses use to perform effectively. These resources come from four different areas: human, physical, technological and financial. Human resources are anything that relates to people in the business, e.g. staff, managers, etc. Physical resources are those that are physically used by the business, e.g. land, raw materials, buildings or equipment. Technological resources are those that make use of IT or technology, e.g. computers, software or systems. Financial resources relate to any aspects of the business relating to money, such as cash, money owed to the business or by the business.

It is essential for any business to control, manage and make the best use of these resources in order to achieve the best possible results. This unit will help you to investigate these different types of business resources by looking at how they are managed, what they are used for, how they can be sourced and finally the way in which data can be used to see if they are being used to their full potential.

It starts by investigating human resources and the way that people are recruited and allocated to different departments and teams. It then goes on to consider the use of technology within the workplace and its many issues and benefits, including legal requirements to protect business ideas. Finance represents a huge area of resource management and you will learn how financial statements and budgeting are used. You will also be shown how to take those financial statements and be able to view trends or changes by applying accounting ratios to compare business performance with others in its market.

### What you need to learn

On completion of this unit you should:

1. Know how human resources are managed
2. Understand the purpose of managing physical and technological resources
3. Understand how to access sources of finance
4. Be able to demonstrate the ability to interpret financial statements.

## Consider this

Using the four categories – human, physical, technological and financial – produce a mind map of the different resources you think would be needed to start up and run a new coffee shop in your area.

Using your list draw a line with a scale of 1 to 6 and label it 1 'essential for this business' and 6 'not essential for this business'.

| 1 | 2 | 3 | 4 | 5 | 6 |
|---|---|---|---|---|---|
| Essential | | | | | Not essential |

Now write your list of resources onto cards, one for each. Place your cards underneath the scale at a number that reflects how essential they are to the business.

When you have completed this activity, look at the work of others in your group:

- Were there common resources and were they given the same rating?
- What makes a resource essential and what influences that judgement?
- Are there any other factors you should take into account when considering the provision of resources?

# 2.1 How human resources are managed

Managing human resources is carried out in two main ways. First, it is important for organisations to recruit the right people, monitor them and then decide how they can best be used. Then resources have to be provided for these employees in order to maintain an effective business operation.

## Human resources

Employees are the human resource in businesses that need careful management. Unlike financial or physical resources, humans need to be dealt with sensitively. If a machine is no longer useful it could be thrown away or replaced. Humans cannot be treated in the same way because they are protected by legislation so it is important to recruit, employ and treat them appropriately.

More information on human resources can be found in Unit 4 Effective People, Communication and Information.

### Staffing to meet changing business demands

Suitably qualified staff may be recruited or trained within the organisation to have the right level of skills when they first join the business. The level and type of staffing also needs to change to keep up with the changing demands of the business, and this is likely to affect the number of employees needed and the skills that those workers need to have.

Many businesses keep a Human Resource Information System (HRIS) that stores computerised records of the training and experience that employees have to help them to be able to plan for the future. This information can help them to plan to expand or reduce (contract) the number of employees that they need. It can also help them plan for the future – this is known as succession planning. A junior employee may receive management training to prepare them to take over the running of a team or department. Businesses that plan well are less likely to have problems as their needs change. You will study technological change in more detail later in this unit. Many businesses are changing the way that they trade and are making greater use of online methods of dealing with customers. This means that employees need to be able to carry out different tasks and so need training to be able to do this. A prime example of a change in staffing levels is the move to self-service checkouts in supermarkets.

In July 2006 it was estimated that 1.5 million customers scanned their own shopping within Tesco stores at self-service checkouts and there are plans to increase the number of checkouts provided. British Airways has expanded its provision of self-service check-in facilities so that customers can choose their own seat and print boarding cards before they arrive at the airport. Both changes mean that fewer employees are needed and that the type of skills that existing staff need must change, so they can deal with more technical enquiries relating to the use of the systems, or other problems that a customer may have, rather than being skilled in the processing of the transaction. These are just two of the many organisations that need to change their staffing to meet business needs.

### Coordination of team resources to meet targets

As well as making sure that individual employees are managed within the organisation, it is essential that resources are used effectively within teams to meet company targets that are set. You may have heard the expression 'there is no I in team' or 'the sum is only as good as the total of all the parts'. Both these expressions emphasise the need for team resources to be co-ordinated. The resources might be skills within the team, experience or even financial resources that will help the team to achieve what it needs to. As looking after teams might be a very involved process, some organisations may appoint team leaders to help managers to look after team members on a day-to-day basis, with the manager only overseeing the whole process.

Coordination of team resources may also involve deciding which members of the team can use training resources to improve the performance of the team and how this training can then be shared. As long as the team is working together in a coordinated way then targets should be met.

## Monitoring of team performance

Coordinating a team is likely to mean that a company knows what employees should be doing to work towards their targets; but it is also essential to monitor the team's performance to make sure that they *are* actually making progress. One way to measure performance is for the business to monitor how closely the targets have been met. This might involve measuring sales figures, seeing how much the team has spent (under or over budget) or even considering the number of customer complaints during a given time period. Regular meetings by the team can give an indication of how the team members are feeling about their targets and if all is going well. Individual and team appraisals may be carried out to see what can be done to improve the way the team works together and mind mapping suggestions can give the team themselves the opportunity to suggest how things can be improved.

Managing team working means that a set of individuals need to be monitored rather than one person. It needs to be done carefully to make sure that all the team are performing equally and that no one is being lazy or working too hard. Sometimes managers give their employees incentives such as a bonus or prize for achieving good results in a team. This helps to reward hard working teams. The same is true of badly performing teams: managers would need to follow the disciplinary procedures to deal with a team that gets poor results or may even have to break up the team altogether.

### Remember

The performance monitoring of teams is very complicated and needs to be done carefully to make sure everyone is working to the same level.

### Case study

**Purbeck Ice Cream**

Purbeck Ice Cream is an award-winning producer of different ice creams, ranging from more traditional flavours like Vanilla Bean to more unusual ones such as Cracked Black Pepper or Chilli.

Peter and Hazel Hartle, who own the company, suggest that one of the reasons it is so successful is because of the team-working ethos that they employ. Although the business is quite small (fewer than 15 employees), by encouraging employees to work more closely together and through careful monitoring the team has been able to become stronger as individuals have developed themselves and taken on new skills to improve the team as a whole.

The team still needs to be coordinated into relevant areas to ensure that progress is being made to the right level in every part of the business, such as production, marketing and administration. It is also essential, however, to ensure that everyone is involved in making plans for the future. Working in this way has certainly helped Purbeck Ice Cream move from a small enterprise to one that now supplies supermarket chains all over Dorset and even distributes its award-winning products to wine bars and top hotels in London.

1. How has team working helped Purbeck Ice Cream to be a success? ✓
2. What might the possible disadvantages of close team working be to a small organisation like Purbeck Ice Cream? ✓✓
3. Discuss the view that team working and the monitoring of team performance is less important in a smaller organisation than a larger one. ✓✓✓

## Case study

### Call centres

Many modern call centres (where people are employed to answer the telephone and give customer service) use team working. Targets are set for teams and charts show how well the team is doing each day. At the end of the week a prize or bonus is given for the team that deals with the most calls.

1. Why might call centres want to use team working? ✓
2. In a small group, produce a list of advantages to a call centre of working in teams. Are there any possible problems that might result? ✓✓
3. Produce a complete guide to office team working giving tips for best practice in team working. ✓✓✓

Many modern call centres have decided to relocate to other countries around the world. India has become a popular choice. In the UK, call centre workers are paid between £12,500 and £15,000 per year but in India a person doing the same job may only be paid £2000 per year.

4. Do some research into the advantages and disadvantages of moving a call centre to India from the UK. What are the implications for team working? ✓✓✓

## Liaison with other departments

Large organisations may have hundreds of different teams working across the organisation and unless each is able to work with other departments and coordinate as a whole organisation there will be conflict or unsatisfactory performance. Organisations may be responsible for different functions within the business, such as finance, marketing or human resources, and each will need to work with the others to ensure the smooth running of the business. One way to make sure that employees work together effectively between departments is to have cross-functional teams. This means that members who are working at the same level in the organisation are taken from each department so that they can work together to understand what each part of the business does. These teams don't have to meet physically – sometimes organisations choose to use virtual cross-functional teams where employees meet over the Internet by using technology such as web conferencing. This type of team structure is already being used by a number of different large organisations including British Airways and IBM.

## Establishment of professional culture

Part of the management of human resources concerns teaching employees about how the business operates – its professional culture; for example the level of formality it uses and the way that managers and staff deal with each other.

You will already have noticed differences in formality at social events you have been to, such as weddings or parties, or the different way that teachers speak to you if you have moved from school to college. The language and the way you address people is different depending on where you are and the same is true of business. Some businesses are very formal and managers will refer to each other using their title, such as Mr, Mrs or Dr. Other organisations will only use first names. Professional culture may also relate to the unwritten expectations that an employer might have of its employees, such as whether or not people are expected to stay late in the office on a Friday or can go home early.

The same differences also occur within organisations when comparing work and personal lives. Some organisations make sure that people's home lives and work lives are completely separate. This may include only having social activities for staff members and not families, or discouraging relationships between employees.

## Case study

### Solent University

Solent University has devised a policy to help employees understand when personal relationships are acceptable and when they might cause problems. This makes it very clear for everyone what is acceptable behaviour.

1. Give two reasons why Solent may have chosen to write a policy to deal with personal relationships at work. ✓
2. What are the advantages and disadvantages of having such a policy? ✓✓
3. Justify whether or not you agree with the use of such policies in the workplace. ✓✓✓

**Responsibility – Personnel Service (Policy number P-26)**

1. This policy applies to all staff of the University. It provides guidance about personal relationships between staff, and students and staff and suppliers. The guidelines are designed to protect the interests of staff, students and the University ensuring that staff do not compromise their professionalism or find themselves open to allegations that they have done so.
2. Personal relationships include:
   - immediate family relationships
   - sexual relationships
   - very close friendships
   - business, commercial and financial relationships.
3. If you are unsure about whether you should declare a personal relationship, you are urged to seek guidance in confidence, from the Director of Personnel, a senior member of the Personnel Service or your union representative.
4. It is not intended that personal relationships should be discouraged, however it is your responsibility to declare one should there be a conflict of interest.
5. Examples of relationships which may involve a conflict of interest:
   relationship between a line manager and member of staff for whom he/she is responsible.
   relationship between interview panel member and applicant for post.
   relationship between member of staff and student, particularly where there is involvement in assessment or recording of marks.
   relationship between staff and suppliers, or goods and services to the University.
6. Should you declare a personal relationship and it is thought that a potential conflict of interest arises, arrangements will be made to re-organise the work of both parties.
7. It is hoped that staff will understand the need to adhere to the policy. Should it be shown that unfair advantage has been secured by either party through the existence of an undeclared personal relationship, disciplinary action may be taken.

(*Source:* by kind permission of Solent University)

## Thinking point

Carry out research into the effect of the Human Rights Act on written policies regarding relationships at work. Consider the challenge of maintaining an individual's privacy against the rights of the business to guard itself against any detrimental effects.

Other organisations may differ and may allow activities or relationships to be brought into the organisation. An example of this is public house management where job vacancies are often advertised as for 'couples' rather than single people.

Managing different formalities and work/personal life activities is just one part of managing human resources in the workplace. The whole process is complex and it can be hard for management to be objective (i.e. acting without taking their own personal influence into account).

As well as taking into account personal relationships at work, it is also necessary to make it clear to employees whether or not they are allowed to work outside the organisation in a second job or do another job in the evening. Taking on a second job is known as 'moonlighting'. Some employers are happy to allow their staff to take on another job in a non-related capacity, for example an office worker working in a bar. Other employers may choose to ban such practices by writing express terms in their contract that require employees to ask permission before taking a second job. This helps to protect an employer from having employees taking business from them in the evening or not being able to cope with their usual working hours due to tiredness.

### Remember

Making sure that employees are clear about what is expected of them at work helps to avoid problems such as inappropriate relationships.

## Provision of appropriate incentives

To manage human resources effectively managers may decide to use **incentives** to encourage employees to work harder or to produce work of a higher quality.

### Key Terms

**Incentive** Something that is used to encourage people to work harder.

There are many different incentives that can be used in the workplace by employers. At school or college you may have noticed your teachers using incentives, such as allowing you to finish the lesson five minutes early if you have worked particularly hard, or giving prizes at the end of the year. Employers are the same; they need to think of different ways to encourage their employees to work harder. Some of the main ways of rewarding employees like this can be seen in the table below.

| Type of incentive | Description |
|---|---|
| Performance-related pay | This is when an employee receives extra money for working harder, either as a one-off payment such as a bonus, or an increase in their salary. In sixth form colleges performance-related pay is given to teachers who, amongst other things, help their students to get good results. |
| Share schemes | This is when employees are offered shares in the company, either free or at a reduced rate depending on company performance and how long they have worked there. |
| Profit-sharing | Employees are given a share of the profits of the business as a bonus to their salary, depending on how long they have worked there and the level of their job. |
| Desirable treats | Some organisations choose not to use pay as an incentive for employees but use treats to encourage staff to work harder. These treats might be anything from a voucher for a weekend in a health spa to being given a microwave or television. The treats may be awarded after appraisals or given on a points system so that employees can keep earning points to work towards the treat of their choice. |
| Working hours or home-work balance | Employees with families or other outside commitments may prefer to have time off in lieu rather than extra money or treats. Some organisations use this to provide incentives by offering time off for good performance, e.g. being able to leave early on certain days or taking extra holidays. |
| Social events | Providing an office party or trip to a sports game can also be a way of providing incentives for employees. As they can be used with whole departments these events can increase morale in the workplace and then lead to even more work being completed. |
| Useful benefits | Additional incentives include other benefits that employees might find useful but are not considered treats. These might include free pension funds, insurance payments, discounts at retailers, free gym membership or free parking. All of these benefits can save the employee money. |

It is most important that the incentives offered by an organisation are appropriate for the employees involved because if employees are not convinced that they are worth working for they won't work harder to get them. To help make sure this doesn't happen employers can provide a package of different incentives that employees can choose from; that way they can decide what they want to work towards. Employers must also be careful, when offering any incentives, to find out whether or not employees will need to pay tax on these benefits to the Inland Revenue.

## Encouragement of creativity and initiative

Businesses that are able to change quickly and can be adaptable to customer needs are more likely to be successful. This is now even more important because the Internet allows businesses to compete all over the world. Two ways for businesses to become more adaptable include being more creative and showing initiative. This means that organisations allow their employees to develop new ideas and solutions so that they can get better and better.

It is sometimes more difficult to develop new ideas quickly in larger organisations because so many of people are involved in the decision making. Some business people believe that smaller businesses find it easier to adapt and that in future there will be more businesses but they will be smaller. Sometimes businesses start out small and become much larger by being creative and using initiative. One well-known example is Yahoo.

### Real lives

**Yahoo!**

Yahoo! was set up in the mid-1990s by two university students in the US. Their creativity and initiative led them to change their hobby – a guide to the World Wide Web – into a huge money-making corporation that now trades all over the world.

'Yahoo! is also the most recognized and valuable Internet brand globally, reaching over 237 million unique users in 25 countries and 13 languages.' (www.yahoo.com)

In less than ten years two students changed their hobby into a multi-million dollar business that is now one of the largest navigational tools for use around the web. This transformation happened because the founders David Filo and Jerry Yang had both the creativity and initiative to think that their idea could be made into a successful business.

1. What is meant by creativity at Yahoo!? ✓
2. Name three advantages and disadvantages for Yahoo! of needing to show initiative in a fast moving technological market. ✓✓
3. 'Some people think that business success involves creativity, initiative and some luck.' Discuss this statement by giving reasons to support and disagree with it. Give your final judgement on how true you think it is. ✓✓✓

## Outsourcing versus in-house

Organisations can either make use of their own services (**in-house**) or those services of external agencies (**outsourcing**) doing work for them. You will need to be aware of the differences between these different options and the issues and benefits associated with each.

### Key Terms

**Outsourcing** When a company pays another one to have part or all of some work done.

**In-house** Employees within the organisation carry out the work.

It may be more expensive to employ people within an organisation to undertake project work or provide maintenance than to ask another company to do this work. This is because the business will need to recruit these people, employ them on a contract and pay them for a given time, and provide them with benefits and office space or equipment. Outsourcing pushes all those issues across to the outsourcing company in exchange for a fee. Another reason that companies may outsource is if they do not have the expertise in their employees in-house and it would cost a lot of money to train or employ someone. Using another company to do this work means they can use workers as and when they are needed, rather than employing people permanently.

Outsourcing can be used in many different ways to manage human resources for everything from recruiting employees in the first place to having cleaners brought in to keep the workplace clean and tidy.

There are many advantages and disadvantages to outsourcing rather than working in-house, so it is important to consider the reasons why outsourcing might be used and the length of the project involved. If outsourcing is used carefully it can be an effective way of working for a business, but it could result in it costing the business more than if it had done the work itself.

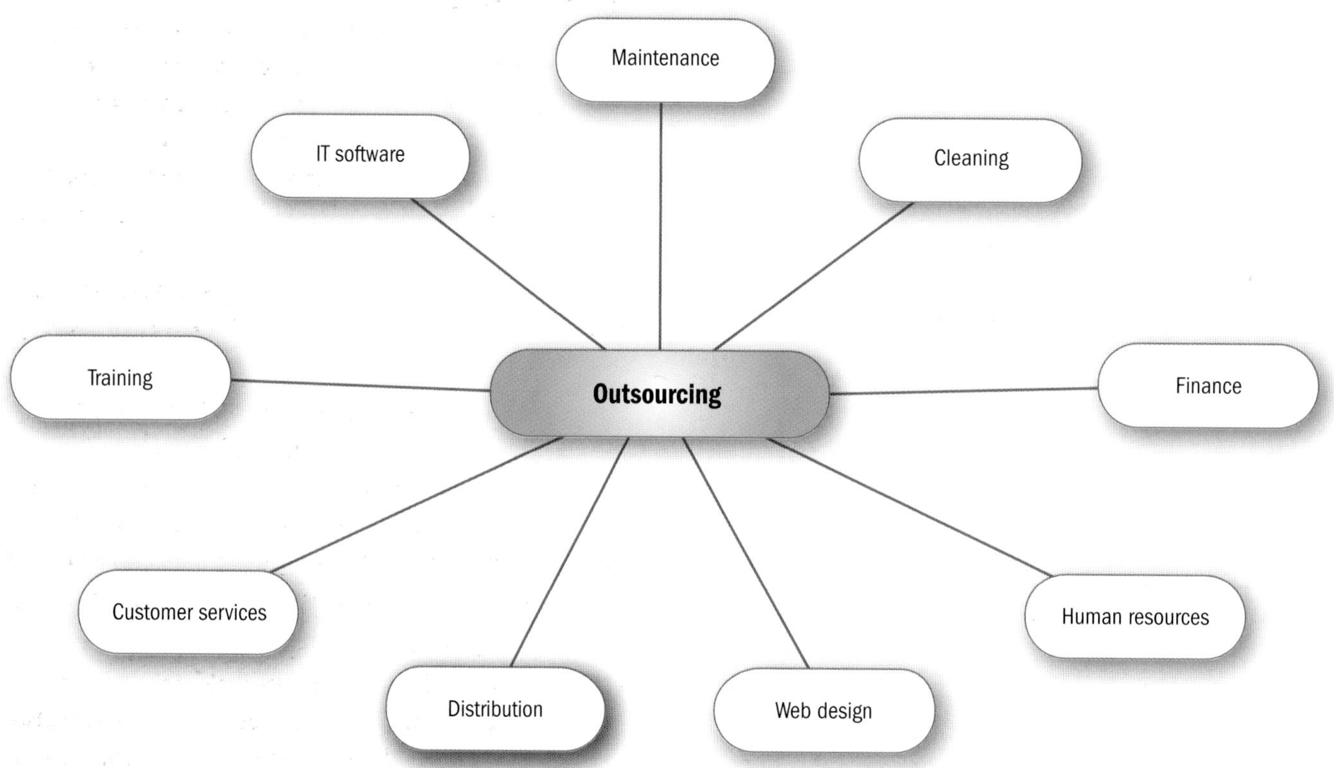


▲ Different ways outsourcing can be used

| Advantages | Disadvantages |
|---|---|
| • The company or individuals, e.g. contractors/consultants, can be employed only when needed making outsourcing potentially cost-effective and able to be reduced or increased more easily.<br>• It may be cheaper to get another organisation to do the work as they are specialists in this area and can achieve **economies of scale** through their contacts or they may employ staff in countries where wages are lower.<br>• It may reduce management and coordination costs as the company only gets the final results and doesn't need to keep checking on progress every day.<br>• By asking another company to concentrate on one aspect of the business, e.g. new IT software rather than it doing it by themselves, the company is able to concentrate on the core business rather than be distracted by the IT project.<br>• The quality that could be produced by the outsourcing company may be higher than doing the work in-house. | • It may be difficult to find a suitable company that can do the work required.<br>• The outsourcing company may use the ideas provided with another rival company or confidential information may be accessed (but it may be possible to put a confidentiality clause into an outsourcing contract).<br>• It may be difficult to manage or coordinate the project when it is done by another company.<br>• There may be additional or hidden costs that are difficult to predict so the project may become expensive without the company being able to keep control of it.<br>• The business that is doing the work for the company may go out of business and the work is lost.<br>• Employees within the company may feel upset if jobs are lost and training is reduced, so they may become demotivated. |

## Key Terms

**Economies of scale** The cost to do a job or make a product reduces as more are made, for example through bulk buying or expertise within the company.

# Maintenance of operation

Maintaining business operations is critical for any organisation. Unless the business can carry out its day-to-day activities efficiently it will lose customers or clients. Resources need to be available for employees and there needs to be sufficient employees to use those resources to provide good service.

## Adequate resources to meet tasks

### Staffing

It is essential to make sure there are sufficient resources. If there are not enough staff working, tasks cannot be done. A restaurant without a chef, waiting staff or kitchen assistants cannot operate effectively and may end up with complaints from customers. Therefore all businesses need to manage their human resources carefully. They need to make sure that there are enough staff, that the staff have adequate skills to carry out their jobs and that the staff are working to the best of their ability.

It is a careful balancing act to ensure that there are enough employees. Too many staff will cost a business a lot of money and potentially damage profits and too few staff could damage the reputation of a business and so also damage profits. Staffing may need to change according to the seasons so there may need to be a mixture of permanent and temporary staff to meet different levels of demand in the winter compared to the summer. Holiday company Pontin's employs 300 permanent staff and then takes on another 1600 temporary staff during the spring and summer months. The company encourages temporary staff to keep returning to work for it by offering good training and other incentives. This helps to avoid the costs of having to recruit new staff each year.

In other organisations, such as the NHS, there will be clear guidance for minimum staff levels based on ratios. There may, for example, need to be one nurse for five patients on one ward or one nurse per patient on another. Getting the right number of staff for each ward is essential for the effective operation of that hospital.

The skills of those staff employed are also critical. There is no point having staff available if they are not qualified to do the jobs that are needed. There may also be a problem due to skills shortages in different sectors which can prevent work from being carried out.

## Case study

### Virgin Trains

In October 2005 Virgin Cross Country Trains suffered as a result of not having enough trained drivers to operate new full-speed tilting trains. The new trains needed drivers to undergo specialist training in order to operate them at full speed. Without this training Virgin did not have adequate human resource to operate its business to its maximum efficiently.

The effect of this lack of human resources was that train journeys were longer than they were expected to be. It affected the aim of Virgin Cross Country Trains as a business in that journey times were longer leading to less efficiency and potential customer dissatisfaction. When an organisation decides to achieve the aim of a better service, or greater customer satisfaction, it needs to make sure that adequate numbers of appropriately trained staff are provided to make it happen.

1. What was the consequence of inadequate numbers of trained staff for Virgin Trains? ✓
2. What effect might the lack of appropriate staff have had on the efficiency and reputation of Virgin Trains? ✓✓
3. Make a judgement about whether or not you think this situation could have been avoided. ✓✓✓

You have already learned that it is important to have the right number of properly trained staff. Employees also need the resources to do their jobs in order to allow the business to operate effectively. You will learn more about the physical, technological and financial resources that are needed later on in this unit but initially it is important to consider four resources that are needed by workers to make sure that the business operates successfully:

- equipment
- working capital
- facilities
- administration.

## Equipment

This is important in order for employees to be able to carry out their daily duties. Equipment might take the form of machinery, or consumables that are part of their everyday work, or could be as simple as the uniform that they need to wear. For some jobs, equipment is required by law. Employees working in the print room of an organisation might need to wear ear defenders to protect their hearing under the Health and Safety at Work Act. Those working in a factory may need to wear eye shields to protect themselves while they are working. A lack of equipment could mean employees are unable to do their jobs effectively, but also that the organisation is breaking the law because they have a duty of care to their employees. Therefore some equipment must be provided free of charge if needed.

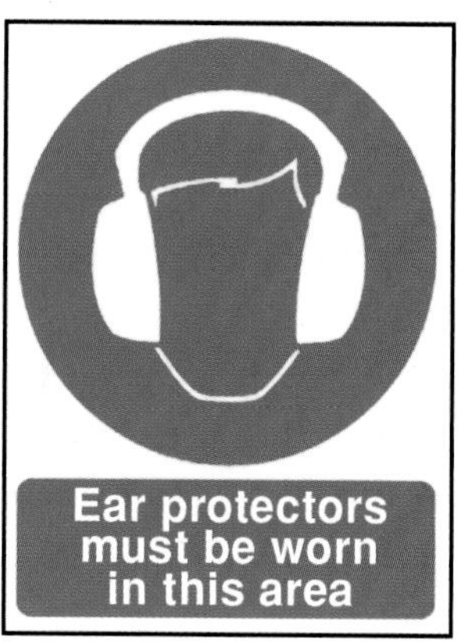


▲ Equipment is essential to running a business and may be required by law

## Practice point

Complete the table below, considering the different types of equipment that may be needed by employees doing the following jobs. Note the consequences for the employee or organisation if they do not have access to that equipment.

| Type of job | Equipment needed | Consequences for the organisation and employee of no equipment |
|---|---|---|
| Fire fighter | | |
| IT maintenance worker | | |
| Accountant | | |
| Travel agent | | |
| Online retailer | | |

Opportunity cost means the cost to a business by going for one option rather than another, for example by spending money on equipment there may be less money to employ staff. Consider the opportunity costs to a business that needs to pay for expensive equipment and the possible effects on staffing levels or morale. How can businesses maintain both staff and equipment effectively? What might the consequences be if they are unable to do this? You may wish to consider the NHS for this.

## Working capital

This is a form of resource – the day-to-day money needed to pay the bills for the business to remain trading. Working capital is the difference between the current assets that the business possesses and its current liabilities (the debts that must be paid in the short term). It is important to estimate how much working capital is needed by the business in order to make sure it can continue trading. Working capital is calculated by the following formula:

working capital = current assets – current liabilities

Working capital needs careful management within a business – too much working capital will mean that the business has lots of cash available that is not being best used. This is an interest cost to the business as this money could have gained interest from alternative investments. On the other hand, not enough working capital in the business means that your business won't be able to pay its bills and may become insolvent.

Factors that influence how much working capital your business has include:

- the level of sales – high sales means that money needs to be available to buy more supplies or stock
- trade credit – the time offered by suppliers to pay for purchases, e.g. one month or two months, and whether or not that payback is with or without interest
- payment time – how long it takes to get payment from customers
- the level of inflation in the economy, i.e. if levels are high then working capital needs to be higher to allow for price and wage increases.

Ensuring the business has enough working capital is essential as it will be needed to pay staff and keep the business running.

## Facilities

Facilities are essential for the operation of any business. Facilities can be anything from the provision of buildings and equipment to services that are offered for staff to support them at work or places for customers to access. Like equipment, some facilities are required to be offered by law for staff, for example employers must provide:

- toilet and washing facilities
- access to drinking water
- a rest area or room for breaks
- facilities for preparing or obtaining a hot drink.

You will learn more about facilities within this unit when you consider physical resources on page 74.

## Administration

Administration is needed within an organisation to make sure that everything runs smoothly. It is the process whereby resources are controlled and managed through the use of systems or processes that help to keep everyone organised. Administration covers a number of different areas, as you can see in the diagram below. It is important for the smooth running of the business that administration is carried out effectively.

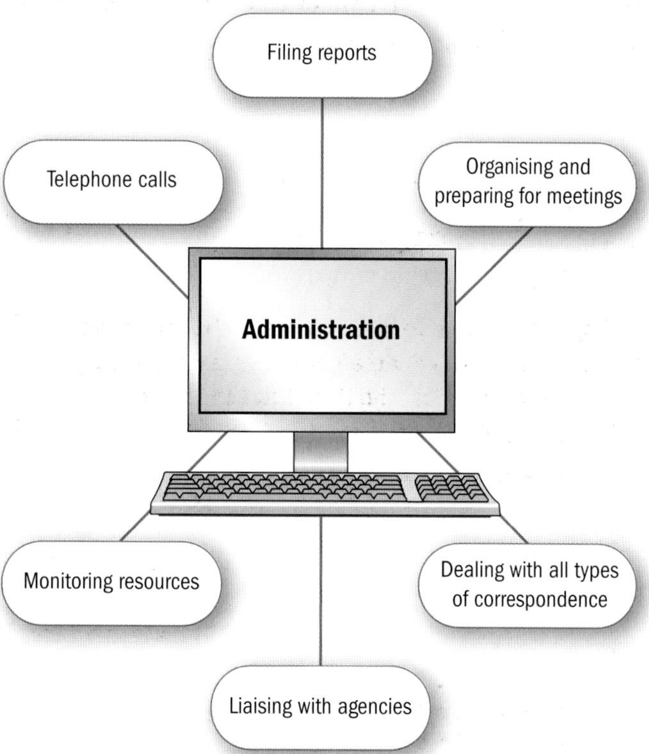


▲ **Different aspects of administration**

The level and type of administration that will be needed will depend on the type of organisation that you are studying. Large organisations may have specific departments that work on part of the administration process whereas in smaller organisations one individual might have responsibility for a number of different aspects.

## Monitoring

Monitoring takes place in two main ways within a business: formal monitoring, when managers are checking or watching the employee in some way, and informal monitoring, whereby they are making subtle judgements about how an employee is fitting in to the workplace or noticing if that employee may have some kind of problem.

Some organisations will have very strict monitoring policies so that employees are monitored at all times throughout their working day, for example in customer service/call centres where employees are constantly dealing with customer enquiries. Supervisors in this case often listen in to calls to monitor customer service or have calls recorded so that they can be checked at a later date. Managers will often monitor emails that have been sent or have CCTV showing employees at the workplace. Employers have to make employees aware that monitoring is taking place.

### ■ Formal monitoring

Formal monitoring may also be necessary in order to comply with the law; for example, the Data Protection Act 1998 forces employers to ensure that personal information is protected and is only accessed if necessary. Some employers also carry out drug and health tests as part of monitoring in the workplace; for example, hospitals may test their medical workers for diseases like tuberculosis so they do not pass them on to patients, or organisations that require employees to use machinery may test for drugs.

Staff may also be monitored to see how often they are absent, for example through sickness, how often they are late, how much work they produce during a day or even how often they leave and need to be replaced. Calculations can be used to monitor trends in sickness or absence, as follows:

Absence measurement (%)

$$\frac{\text{Hours of absence}}{\text{Hours of total time}} \times 100$$

Sickness measurement (%)

$$\frac{\text{Hours of sickness}}{\text{Hours of total time}} \times 100$$

By monitoring the rate of absence or sickness, organisations can identify areas where there might be a problem and take action to solve it. You can find out how to monitor staff however on page 148 of Unit 4.

The best way to ensure that formal monitoring is conducted properly is to have a formal monitoring policy that can be used by managers, and that employees are aware of, in order to make sure that everyone knows what is happening.

## Informal monitoring

This is a much less scientific approach to monitoring and needs extra care and attention in order that the manager does not intrude too much on an employee's privacy. All monitoring may feel uncomfortable for an employee (you will know yourself how it feels to be monitored by invigilators in examinations), so it is important that employees feel happy with it and know why it is happening. Informal monitoring may be used to help managers assist their employees in ways to improve or at review times during the year.

Some kind of monitoring has always existed within the workplace but it is essential that it is very carefully carried out, whether formal or informal. This is because by being intrusive an employer may breach the Human Rights Act 2000. Changes in technology have made monitoring seem much more menacing in some organisations, where all email exchanges and Internet access are logged, but it is important for managers to make sure that employees understand when and why they are being monitored.

Another type of monitoring that can be used within organisations is known as 'workforce optimisation'. By thinking of human resources like any other type of resource businesses are able to consider when employees are most productive, when they might be wasting time and how they can be made more efficient. By analysing what employees actually do – and when – businesses are able to employ more staff at peak times and fewer when it is quieter.

**Remember**

Employees must be made aware of the fact if they are going to be monitored or the organisation may break the law under the Data Protection Act or Human Rights Act.

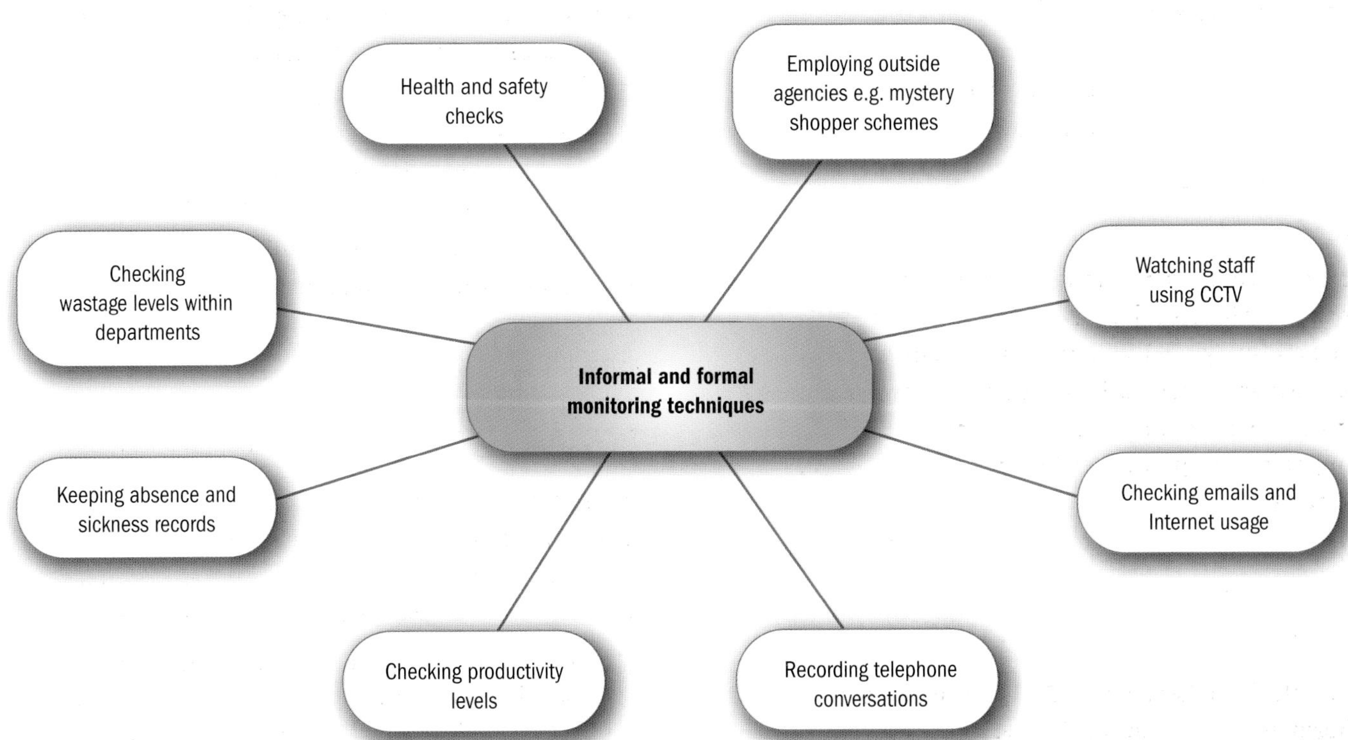


▲ **Different types of informal and formal monitoring that may be used within the workplace**

## Case study

### Workforce optimisation in supermarket retailing

Somerfield has used 'workforce optimisation' techniques and the use of technology to work out that up to 30% of staff time was being wasted in its supermarkets. It did this by looking at when stores were busy and when they were quieter. Obviously a quiet store is not making good use of its human resources, as employees may not have anything to do.

By using IT systems, Somerfield was able to work out when different stores were busy and when they were quiet and it found that there were huge differences. Stores nearer universities were busier at night and those nearer towns or cities were busier in the evening when people were coming home from work. By looking at these patterns Somerfield is able to employ more people with the right skills in stores near universities during the night and fewer people during the morning. This means that it can save money on staffing costs during the day and also be more efficient at times when more workers are needed.

The IT system that Somerfield used can work out the human resources that are needed to satisfy demand, but it is also able to monitor the hours employees work and when they are absent due to illness or personal reasons. By the end of 2007, it is expected that all stores will be working using this system.

1. What is meant by workforce optimisation? ✓
2. How can workforce optimisation help a retailer like Somerfield? ✓
3. What might be the issues for staff working within such a system – both positive and negative? ✓✓
4. Judge how important you think workforce optimisation is likely to be for all retailers in the future, taking into account other influences such as the increase in online shopping. ✓✓✓

What other industries may decide to use workforce optimisation? Consider issues such as levels of demand, skill shortages or unpredictable levels of demand.

## Troubleshooting and problem solving

As you have already learned, monitoring is an essential part of maintaining an effective business. Without such monitoring a business may not even know there is a problem. Troubleshooting and problem solving are a result of monitoring as they show areas of a business where there are problems and then how they can be worked on.

Trouble shooting and problem solving are important but extremely diverse activities because of the very nature of the words 'trouble' or 'problem'. They will vary from one organisation to another and something that is a problem for one manager may not be for another. The extent to which troubleshooting and problem-solving skills are needed will depend on the size of the organisation and the skills and competence of the managers involved.

Managers may:

- look for problems
- solve problems as they happen.

Looking for problems is a **proactive** approach. It means the organisation is constantly looking for ways to improve its business and by solving smaller issues hopes to avoid big problems altogether. This is known as **continuous improvement** or **kaizen**. These processes require everyone in the organisation to seek to make improvements in some small way so that the quality of the product or service is continually being improved. The extent to which this can happen effectively will depend on the culture and resources within the organisation.

### Key Terms

**Proactive** When someone is seeking out problems or issues and trying to resolve them before they are actually formally presented to them.

**Continuous improvement (kaizen)** The ability across the organisation to make improvements to the way things are done, including working practices and customer service. Each employee is responsible for their own small set of changes that builds up a culture of improvement.

Solving problems as they arise, in order of how urgent they are, may also be used by some organisations. For example, a restaurant manager may have a number of problems to deal with but the issue of someone ringing in that they are unwell and can't work would be dealt with first as it is more important than another problem such as the food order for next week. If a manager has too many problems in one go, and keeps having to deal with one after another, it is known as 'fire fighting' as it is like trying to put out a fire in that new flames appear as quickly as the ones you have just put out. Working in an environment where fire fighting is a common management technique for problem solving can be very stressful and tiring.

## Case study

### The Hongwa Clothing Factory in North Shanghai

During August 2005 there was a crisis amongst clothing retailers and manufacturers. EU quota limits for clothing had been taken away some years before and then were reintroduced during 2005. This meant that orders for clothing from China were stopped at ports and not allowed entry to the European Union if they were over the specified import limit. The reality of this happening was that clothing became stranded at UK ports whilst waiting for clearance into the UK. In order to help solve the problem the Hongwa factory, at first, cleverly switched production of garments as the quota for trousers was reached first whilst the quota for jackets and shirts was still not met. The alternative for the company was to switch production to clothing for the Chinese market or to make workers redundant. The EU quota limit was imposed to try to protect clothing manufacturers in Spain and Italy but UK retailers of the Chinese garments risked having their profit margins reduced as the clothing was much cheaper to buy in from China than Europe. The final solution to the crisis was to allow the imports waiting at port locations to be allowed into the EU and to count them against the 2006 quota limits as some form of compromise. While this did alleviate some of the problems for retailers for 2005, the problem was moved into 2006 as limits were certain to be reached again.

1. How did EU quotas outside its control affect production at the Hongwa Factory? ✓
2. How did the Hongwa Factory sort out its problems? ✓
3. Using information from the case study and relevant newspaper articles (related to Chinese EU trade tariffs), to what extent do you think problems with tariffs could have been avoided for both EU retailers and Chinese manufacturers? ✓✓✓

## Outcome activity 2.1

**Pass**

Write a report describing how human resources are managed in a selected organisation that you know well. 

## Grading tips 

To do this you will need to address the following:

- Consider how organisations recruit staff and retain the right people, including the skills that are needed, and the documents used to recruit those people, including the job description and contract of employment.
- You should describe the use of teams and how teams are monitored within the organisation.
- Consider what kind of culture this business has and what kind of incentives, resources and facilities are given to staff on a day-to-day basis.

# 2.2 Purpose of managing physical and technological resources

## Physical resources

These are the resources that the business needs to maintain in order to carry out its activities and it includes things like the buildings, facilities, plant and machinery. Management of physical resources involves planning maintenance and refurbishment and includes organising insurance and security to keep those resources safe.

### Buildings and facilities

Any business will need to have premises from where it can operate. This may be a person's home, when the business first starts operating, to tower block offices all over the world. Buildings play an important role in the image of a business and can make potential customers want to work with the business even more. The building that is used by Lloyds is so famous that it has become a tourist attraction to many visitors from London. Many financial institutions still have their head offices in central London near the Stock Exchange so that they can still maintain links with clients' suppliers in person as well as online.

◄ The Lloyds building has become a tourist attraction

#### Thinking point

Consider how many famous business buildings you know of in London or throughout the world and do some research on them. Find out who owns them. What do they represent for the businesses and countries in which they are located? To what extent do you think the buildings in which a business operates can affect the success of that business?

When customers enter the building facilities need to be arranged for them, such as meeting rooms or front desks. Banks, for example, often have desks or rooms where clients can talk to an adviser about financial products, such as loans or mortgages, as well as a screened area from which money is given out or paid in.

For some businesses, the attractiveness of the building is not as important as the inside because customers are never expected to see what goes on there. For example, Amazon (www.amazon.co.uk) and Ocado (Waitrose Home Shopping Service www.ocado.com) run massive warehouses with high levels of automation. The public do not go there so the buildings are designed to be as efficient as possible but not necessarily look **aesthetically pleasing.** Other businesses may use the building and facilities to market the type of services or products that they are offering.

Ikea in Croydon, for example, painted the chimneys of the former Croydon Power Station, where it located in 2003, in the company colours. These blue and yellow chimneys can be seen for miles around and remind people that the store is there while still keeping something of the history of the building.

The location of buildings is important when a business considers its **distribution network**. If a business locates to a place that is as accessible to as many customers as possible its profits can be increased. This might be achieved, for example, by businesses which trade throughout Europe locating in countries in central Europe where they can easily distribute to more countries.

## Key Terms

**Aesthetically pleasing** When a building is designed and decorated to look attractive to the eye.

**Distribution network** Support structure and businesses that help goods to be moved from where they are made to the customers who buy them.

## Materials and waste

The materials that are needed by a business will very much depend on the type of operation it is running and the individual people working there. A car-making factory will need access to steel, paint, plastics, etc. to be able to make cars. An office will have to provide computers, pens, paper and telephones for their employees to use. Some businesses will use materials that can be renewable or recyclable, such as paper, while others use non-renewable materials such as oil. All businesses need to be careful about how much they use and will try to avoid wasting materials to keep their costs low and help the environment. Some companies have made excellent use of initiatives to reduce the amount of materials they use and so save money. For example, the Oxford Group (www.oxfordgroup.co.uk ) saved £40,000 by reducing the amount of paper used.

The waste that a business produces has to be taken away by another agency such as the council or a private company. It makes good business sense to reduce the amount of waste as it cuts waste disposal costs which should help lead to higher profits for the business. The government sees waste reduction as important for the environment and has funded the Envirowise campaign (www.envirowise.gov.uk), giving tips on ways this can be done.

## Case study

### Cadbury

Cadbury will open a new £70 million factory in Poland by 2008 to supply the increasing demand for its brands in Europe, the Middle East and Asia. The factory in Poland will create 300 jobs at first and there may be the opportunity to expand at a later date. Cadbury chose Poland as the place to base its new manufacturing plant for a number of reasons, including that Poland offered a 'low cost base' and good central place for distribution throughout Europe, the Middle East and Asia. Cadbury already had links with Poland before this factory plan as it had taken over the Polish chocolate brand Wedel and traded as Cadbury Wedel. It is also opening other factories throughout the world including one in Beijing, China.

1. What do you think is meant by a 'low cost base'? ✓
2. What advantage might Cadbury have by being centrally located in Europe? ✓✓
3. Which issues might Cadbury face when setting up a new factory in countries like China? ✓✓
4. How might Cadbury's acquisition of the Wedel chocolate brand in Poland have helped them to plan their buildings and facilities there? ✓✓✓

## Practice point

Using the website www.envirowise.gov.uk to help you, produce an information pack on ways that businesses of your choice could reduce the amount of materials needed and waste produced. Include the following:

- 10 tips for waste reduction for that business.
- Issues that the business may face when trying to reduce waste.
- Judge the impact on the business of not reducing waste in the future.
- Judge the impact on other stakeholders, such as local residents and the environment, of that business not reducing waste in the future.

### Plant and machinery

Like materials and buildings, each business has specific requirements for the type of **plant** and machinery that it might need. A business may spend thousands of pounds on its factory and machinery by buying everything that is needed. For other businesses it may be easier and more cost effective to **lease** what is needed.

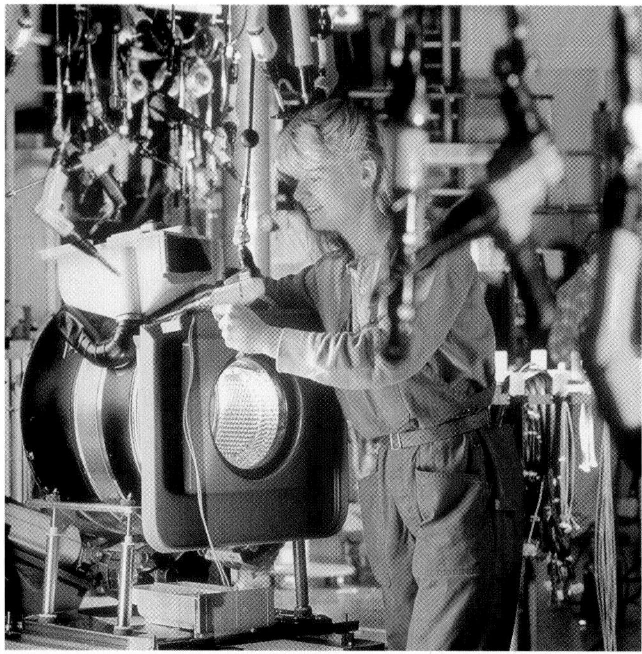

▲ Plant and machinery is especially important for manufacturing

## Key Terms

**Plant** The factory or base where the machinery is located; may also refer to mobile machinery and equipment.

**Leasing** Paying to use a factory or machine for an agreed amount of time.

## Practice point

Complete the table below using 3 contrasting businesses near you.

| Name of business | Type of business | Location of buildings | Plant and machinery used | Costs of buildings and plant/machinery (Low or High) |
|---|---|---|---|---|
| | | | | |
| | | | | |
| | | | | |

1. What do you notice about the different requirements for buildings and plant of each business?
2. How might these different costs affect the pricing and profits of the different businesses?
3. To what extent might buildings and plant/ machinery enhance the image of the business?
4. 'High investment in plant and machinery is the most important factor affecting the success of a manufacturing business.' Discuss this view.

### Equipment including IT

Equipment is essential for a business to operate smoothly. For example, your teacher is unable to work effectively without a board marker or access to the register to check who is present. Equipment is critical for profit and not-for-profit organisations alike.

In some types of organisations, lack of equipment means that a job or service cannot be carried out. A hospital without trolleys or wheelchairs is unable to move patients. A catering business without access to mixers and ovens is unable to produce food. Many organisations include IT within their list of essential equipment as both **hardware** and **software** are becoming essential pieces of kit.

## Key Terms

**Hardware** The physical parts of an IT system such as the keyboard or screen.

**Software** The packages that make the computer work, e.g. Microsoft Windows or Vista, or applications packages to be used on the computer such as Microsoft Word or Excel.

Some traditional businesses have also taken to using IT to help support and enhance their methods of working. Cows in the UK and Australia are, in some cases, doing self-milking and research is being conducted by the University of Nottingham into the benefits of using more technology on the farm. This means they choose when to be milked and robots conduct the process. This may seem like a crazy idea but it has been found to lead to happier cows and an increase in the amount of milk that they produce.

## Planned maintenance and refurbishment

All buildings, plant and machinery require regular maintenance and updating. Even factories that work using **flow production** 24 hours a day have to allow time to check that machines are working properly and make minor adjustments to them if necessary. If this maintenance does not take place machines may break down, stopping production and leading to a loss of profits. Building maintenance such as regular cleaning and painting, is also needed to keep buildings in good order, clean and safe.

## Key Terms

**Flow production** Manufacturing where goods move through a continuous line of different stages until the goods are finished, e.g. canned foods.

Refurbishment is when a business gives a new look to its offices or stores. It can help keep staff and customers happy. A good working environment is likely to make staff happier, work harder and stay with the company longer. Refurbishment can help the environment if the new resources are eco-friendly or energy saving, such as installing solar panels, and this can give a good image for the company as well as saving energy and therefore reducing costs.

▲ Technological milking means happy cows!

## Case study

### Eco Schools and Colleges

One way that schools and colleges can work to improve the quality of buildings and the effect on the environment for pupils and teaching staff is by becoming an Eco School or College.

The individual school or college registers for the programme and refurbishments are made to be environmentally friendly, for example by using energy-saving bulbs and water-reducing solutions.

The benefits of maintaining and introducing eco-friendly techniques into education include saving money, helping the local area and community and raising achievement. An environmentally friendly school or college is likely to lead to happier pupils and therefore increased achievement.

The Eco School scheme itself requires the school or college to undertake an audit and then put into place an action plan of things that can be done to make changes.

Using the Eco Schools website (www.ecoschools.org.uk) conduct research into the Eco Schools programme.

1. What is the programme trying to achieve? ✓
2. Outline the advantages and disadvantages to schools and colleges of belonging to such a scheme when conducting maintenance and refurbishments to their buildings? ✓✓
3. To what extent do you believe that all organisations should be encouraged to join such an eco programme? ✓✓✓

Consider the issues and benefits for your school or college of adopting a scheme like Eco Schools. What would the impact be on the local community? What are the implications of not adopting an eco approach?

### Emergency provision

The Health and Safety at Work Act 1974 requires organisations to draw up policies and provisions for what should happen in the event of an emergency within a building. This means that evacuation training must be given to employees and clear instructions provided about what you should do in the event of a fire or other incident within the building. The organisation must also provide other equipment within the building, including fire alarms to detect fire, fire escapes for use in high buildings and fire extinguishers. Regular audits of health and safety provision must take place so that any new equipment can be provided. It is not just the employer's responsibility to ensure that the building is safe, employees must also inform their employer about any hazards that exist so that they can be corrected. Employers also have a duty of care towards any customers or visitors who come into the workplace so this is a high priority for any organisation.

### Insurance

All buildings owned or leased by businesses must have insurance. If the business owns the building it will arrange this cover itself but if the building is leased it is often arranged with the landlord. A fee is paid each month and then protection is given to the business in the event that something happens to or within the building such as:

- a flood, fire, earthquake or storm that damages the building and stock
- damage to any equipment
- theft from the building
- vandalism
- leaking pipes
- collision by vehicles.

The type of insurance coverage and the amount of money paid will depend on the individual policy that the business takes out. The business is also required to have some other types of insurance.

**Employers' liability insurance** is compulsory by law. It provides insurance in case employers have to pay any employee or their family as a result of accidental death, bodily injury or disease as a result of an individual's employment.

**Public liability insurance** must be paid by employers to cover any payments to the public for injuries suffered or property damaged.

There are also other types of insurance that businesses can take out, including product liability insurance, professional indemnity insurance and so on. Choosing the right policy for the organisation can be complicated and specialist advice may be required.

### Security

▲ Working with the police helps to reduce business crime

The building must be made secure and looked after, even when employees have gone home. Some businesses will employ full-time security staff to do this and they patrol the building, sometimes using dogs to help them. Other organisations will use security cameras and alarms which are linked to police stations. There are now many schemes for businesses including 'Beating Business Crime' (in Warwickshire, for example) and the national 'Business Watch', working with the police. These organisations give help and advice on how to keep buildings and stock secure, such as installing safe letter boxes, fitting appropriate doors and only holding a limited amount of cash or stock within the building.

## Technological resources

Technological resources are more than just equipment. Computer hardware, such as a modem and monitor, is a physical resource and is treated as such. Technological resources in this instance are things like software, music or text. These resources are owned, like physical resources, and have to be managed in the same way. Technological resources can be considered in four main areas: intellectual property, accumulated experience and skill, software licensing and patents and copyright.

### Intellectual property

Intellectual property rights allow people to own ideas and have rights concerning what happens to these ideas, including how often they are used, what they are associated with and if they have permission to be copied. There are considered to be five different types of intellectual property, as shown in the table below.

All of these different types of communication are covered within copyright and patenting law and have to be protected like any other. You will learn more about patenting and copyright on page 80.

### Accumulated experience and skill

Accumulated experience means experience gained over a number of years when a person has come across lots of different issues to do with the job. This can mean it protects the business by keeping people in their jobs – so that the level of experience in the business can grow. Experienced employees are more likely to be able to do a good job in an organisation and should be managed carefully. Sometimes this might mean paying people more or giving them special conditions.

It is important to build up a person's skills but organisations have to be careful not to create a situation where, for example, only one person can operate a piece of machinery or fix a software programme. If that person then leaves the organisation it is difficult to maintain that resource and the business may not

| Designs | Drawings | Text | Music | Video |
|---|---|---|---|---|
| Covers the features or decoration of products such as colours, lines, materials, shape or texture | Covers the drawings of a product including the drawing of a patent | Covers the actual style and content of text that is used including data written on websites | Covers the use of music for public or private performances and its copying | Covers the use of video clips within websites or whole films and the protection against copying or performances in public places |

▲ Different types of intellectual property

function effectively. Organisations have to make sure that there is backup available for specialist employees dealing with such resources and that training is **cascaded**. This means that others receive training on how to look after that resource.

## Key Terms

**Cascading training** The process when someone gives training to others. They pass on skills that they might have gained from doing the job or after completing a training course.

### Software licences

Many businesses invest a lot of money into software and its use within the working day. Sometimes **bespoke** software will be designed for a business or they will use someone else's software and pay a licence fee to use it.

## Key Terms

**Bespoke** When something is specially made for an individual or organisation.

The computers that you use when you are completing your BTEC National course which have Word or Excel on them are licensed to Microsoft, so money has to be paid to Microsoft to use that software. Licences may allow the software to be installed on one computer, a limited number of computers or even a whole site so that everyone can use the software. The licence may also allow employees to have the software installed on laptops or at home. Universities often use 'chest licences' so that teachers and students can gain access to cheaper licences for educational purposes.

If businesses do not buy a licence or are 'under-licensed' (meaning that they run software on a higher number of computers than they have a licence for), they are breaking the law. Sometimes businesses may find themselves in the opposite position where they are over licensing. This may be because a number of different departments have bought software individually. By applying for a whole site licence they may be able to save money. Businesses should therefore carry out a software audit where each computer is checked for software and a central database kept by the IT department.

▲ Conducting a software audit can prevent licensing problems

### Patents and copyright

It can be difficult and costly for businesses to protect technological resources. Legislation can help to protect these resources but it is sometimes difficult to prove if someone has taken your idea and used it. Patents and copyright are two areas of intellectual property law.

| Patents | Copyright |
|---|---|
| Protection for inventions or new and improved products that can be made by industry | Protects the use of literary or artistic material. This includes songs, software, multimedia and films |

It was reported by the Alliance Against Counterfeiting and Piracy (www.aacp.co.uk) that UK industry lost £10 billion due to counterfeiting and piracy in 2002, of which £400 million was lost by the video industry (www.fact-uk.org.uk – Federation Against Copyright Theft).

A patent gives an inventor the legal rights to stop someone else copying or using part of their invention without their permission. This helps to ensure that new ideas can be given time to be developed and manufactured once the idea has been registered with the UK Patent Office (www.patent.gov.uk/patent.htm).

## Real lives

### The Baby Dream Machine and Hushbye Baby Rocker

Barry Haigh came up with a design for a machine to rock babies to sleep. It works by placing the pram or pushchair on a motorised device that rocks to soothe the baby. Barry applied for a patent to protect the idea in the UK. Along with his friend, Graham Whitby, they were able to set up the Baby Dream Machine Company and start manufacturing their products in Hungary. The company has sold more than a thousand of their machines, including sales in Israel and South Africa. The patent has helped to protect the invention in Europe. The product sells in the UK for £79.99.

Meanwhile, in Australia, Newton McMahon was designing an automatic baby rocker that works with prams, pushchairs or even cots. His device also includes a micro-motion device that checks whether or not the baby is breathing and alerts the carer if they are not. This product, called the Hushbye Baby Rocker, is similar to the Baby Dream Machine.

Sometimes within patenting law it is difficult to prove whether or not something is similar to another product. A patent taken out in the UK will also only provide protection within the UK unless the inventor has taken out an International Patent to protect it throughout the world. Patents are not free in the UK; the first stages of applying for a patent cost at least £200 and the licence has to be reviewed every year. It usually takes between 2 and 3 years to grant a patent and during this time the invention is not protected.

1. What is meant by a patent and what is its purpose? ✓
2. What are the limitations of a patent? ✓✓
3. To what extent has online shopping and international purchasing habits by UK citizens limited the effectiveness of UK patenting law? ✓✓✓

## Outcome activity 2.2

**Pass**

Prepare a presentation using software such as PowerPoint or overhead transparencies to describe the main physical and technological resources that need to be considered by the selected business that you chose for Outcome Activity 2.1. P2

**Merit**

Assess how managing the human, physical and technological resources that you have researched so far can improve the performance of your chosen organisation.

## Grading tips

**Pass** 

You should make sure you cover the following points within your presentation:

- Physical resources including buildings, facilities, materials, waste, plant, machinery and equipment, including how emergency provision is covered and issues such as insurance and security.
- Technological resources including issues surrounding intellectual property, skills, software and copyright/patenting.

**Merit** 

You will need to expand on the work you produced earlier by going into more detail about how managing the resources you have described will help the organisation to perform better. You should also consider any limitations that might be placed on managers working with these resources.

For merit work you should make sure you provide enough detail and consider the approaches needed for different types of resources, including which are the most and least important for the business. (You should do this separately from your presentation.)

# 2.3 Access sources of finance

There are two main ways that businesses can access financial resources: from within the business (internal source) or from outside the business (external source).

## Internal sources

Internal sources of finance can be from savings or profits. The owner of a business often has to use their own personal savings to start the business, particularly if they are a new sole trader, i.e. a person who owns and runs their own business. This is because banks may not be willing to take a risk and invest in them. Savings are a good source of finance for a business as interest does not need to be paid to someone else while the money is being used and the business remains totally in the control of the owner.

Once a business is operating it may be able to use the money that it makes as profits to invest back in the business. Investing money back into the business means that even greater potential profits may be made in the future. The amount of profit to be invested back in the business – or in new businesses – will depend on how much profit the owners want to keep for themselves against how much they want the business to expand. For some businesses it is not possible to use capital from profits, for example if they are a charity or not-for-profit organisation.

## External sources

There are a number of different external sources that can be used to fund a business. Some of these are outlined in the table below.

| | |
|---|---|
| **Banks** | Banks are able to offer loans, business accounts, commercial mortgages and overdraft facilities based on the business plan. Interest is payable based on the predicted risk. Some security will need to be provided, e.g. assets such as a house. |
| **Building societies** | Building societies are also able to offer loans, business accounts, commercial mortgages and overdraft facilities based on the business plan. Interest is payable based on the risk of the venture. Some security will need to be provided, e.g. assets such as a house. |
| **Hire purchase** | Hire purchase means that resources can be used by the business while they are being paid for. Until the last payment is made on the agreement the goods are not owned by the business and if payments are not made the finance company can take them back. |
| **Leasing** | Leasing means that a business can make use of resources and pay to use them every month. The business does not own the goods at the end of the lease. Leasing is often used by companies for vehicles. |
| **Venture capitalists** | These are people who invest in new sometimes risky ventures, usually in return for share of the ownership. The business investors on television programmes like 'Dragon's Den' are venture capitalists. |
| **Factoring** | Debt factoring is another method of gaining additional sources of finance. This means that the business sells its debts to another company and receives some of the money immediately. The debt factoring company collects the debts and takes a percentage cut for this service. |
| **Share issues** | Issuing shares is a good way for many companies to raise finance. Small businesses will issue shares when they move from being a sole trader/partnership to become limited (Ltd). The shares are not offered publicly but business contacts, friends or family can buy them. Limited companies are then able to sell shares on the Stock Exchange if they become public limited companies (Plc). This is known as floating on the Stock Exchange. Sometimes large public limited companies will have a new share issue as well when they want to invest in a large project and these are also floated on the Stock Exchange. |
| **Friends or family** | Money from friends and family may either be invested in the business in exchange for Ltd shares or paid back as a loan - often at a lower rate than would be payable to a bank or other lender. |
| **Government grants and Prince's Trust loans and grants** | These are available from the EU, national and local government. A grant is money that is given to an entrepreneur that doesn't have to be paid back and the amount will depend on where it is coming from. For more information see www.businesslink.gov.uk. Businesses run by people between the age of 18 and 30 can apply for low interest loans from the Prince's Trust (www.princes-trust.org.uk). |

▲ External sources of finance

### Real lives

**Le Beanock**

Le Beanock was a concept invented by Tracie Herrtage. The beanock itself is a form of hanging bean bag that is suspended from the ceiling of an apartment and this is where it gets its name from, Le Beanock (half bean bag and half hammock). Five wealthy entrepreneurs and venture capitalists were invited to invest in new ideas and Tracie's idea was selected to be supported. Two of the venture capitalists invested in her project in exchange for a part share of the business and also a part share of any profits made. More information about Le Beanock can be found at www.lebeanock.com.

1. What does a venture capitalist do? ✓
2. What are the advantages for Tracie Herrtage of having investment from venture capitalists? ✓✓
3. What are the disadvantages for Tracie of having investment from a venture capitalist? ✓✓
4. What other issues should Tracie take into account before deciding whether to fund her business in this way? ✓✓✓

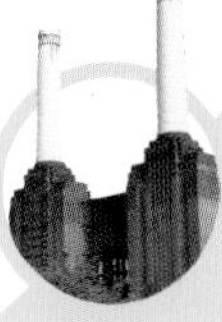

### Outcome activity 2.3

**Pass**

Kalpesh Parmar is thinking of setting up his own music mixing business. He needs more information about where to access funds to help him get his business off the ground. Produce an information pack for him describing where he can obtain different sources of finance. P3

### Grading tips

**Pass** 

You should make sure you include as many sources as possible. Include relevant details about each method, including why they might be suitable for Kalpesh to use.

# 2.4 Interpret financial statements

As part of your understanding of resources you will need to be able to use financial statements and work out how a business is managing financial resources in three main ways: costs and budgets, financial statements and basic ratios.

## Costs and budgets

The management of costs is a very important aspect of managing financial resources. If costs are not managed effectively, it can lead to profits being damaged and the business potentially unable to pay its expenses. Keeping within a budget, increasing income in order to cope with change and making sure that working capital is available and money set aside for emergencies is all part of the balancing exercise.

### Costs managed to budget

There are two main types of costs that you will need to learn about: fixed costs and variable costs.

## Fixed and variable costs

Fixed costs are costs that do not change regardless of the number of goods that are sold or services that are offered. These costs include rent, insurance, salaries. Whether the business makes 100 or 10,000 products, these costs must be paid.

Variable costs are costs that change according to output. These costs change directly according to how many products are made; for example, a business producing footballs will have varying requirements for amounts of leather, rubber, thread and valves, depending on how many footballs it makes.

### Practice point

**Fixed or variable?**

The Herb Pots is a small business growing culinary herbs that are sold in hand painted clay pots. The business is run from a unit rented on a local farm. Each pot is hand painted by local people in their spare time. They are paid £2 per pot. The clay is ordered when it reaches a minimum level and is dependent on the sales made that month. Electricity and gas is paid monthly. The Herb Pots has a website that advertises its products and a web master is paid monthly to maintain the site and process the orders. The herbs are bought in bulk and grown at the back of the unit until they are ready to be planted in the completed pots. Orders are received by email and by phone.

What are the fixed costs that the Herb Pots must pay? What are the variable costs that the Herb Pots must pay? Can you think of any additional costs which may be incurred that are not included above?

## Break-even point

Businesses can use the calculations that they make of fixed costs, variable costs and sales to work out the point at which their costs equal their sales. This point is known as break-even and shows how many products they need to produce and sell, or services they need to offer, to get to the point where they are neither making a profit or a loss.

The break-even point (BEP) can be worked out as follows:

$$\text{BEP} = \frac{\text{Fixed costs}}{\text{Unit contribution (selling price} - \text{variable cost per unit)}}$$

Calculating break-even allows a business to work out how many products it needs to sell before it can actually start to make a profit.

The margin of safety (MOS) can also be calculated in order to allow the business to work out the amount of units by which sales can fall before the business starts to make a loss and is calculated with the following formula

$$\text{MOS} = \text{actual sales in units} - \text{BEP in units}$$

A break-even chart enables a business to identify the following:

- BEP in sales units and sales revenue
- MOS
- amount of profit or loss made at different levels of sales
- the effect of changes in fixed costs, variable costs and selling prices.

The chart on page 85 displays the revenue and costs at future levels of output. The chart enables the user to identify the break-even point.

Using a break-even chart it is also possible to work out the contribution that a product or service makes to fixed costs. This is worked out in the following way:

$$\text{Unit contribution} = \text{selling price} - \text{variable cost}$$

This is useful as it allows individual products or services to be viewed in terms of how much they contribute towards overall overhead costs, or indeed if they have a negative contribution and might be losing the business money.

Profit can also be worked out by multiplying the margin of safety by unit contribution. This is useful when comparing different products or services within the business.

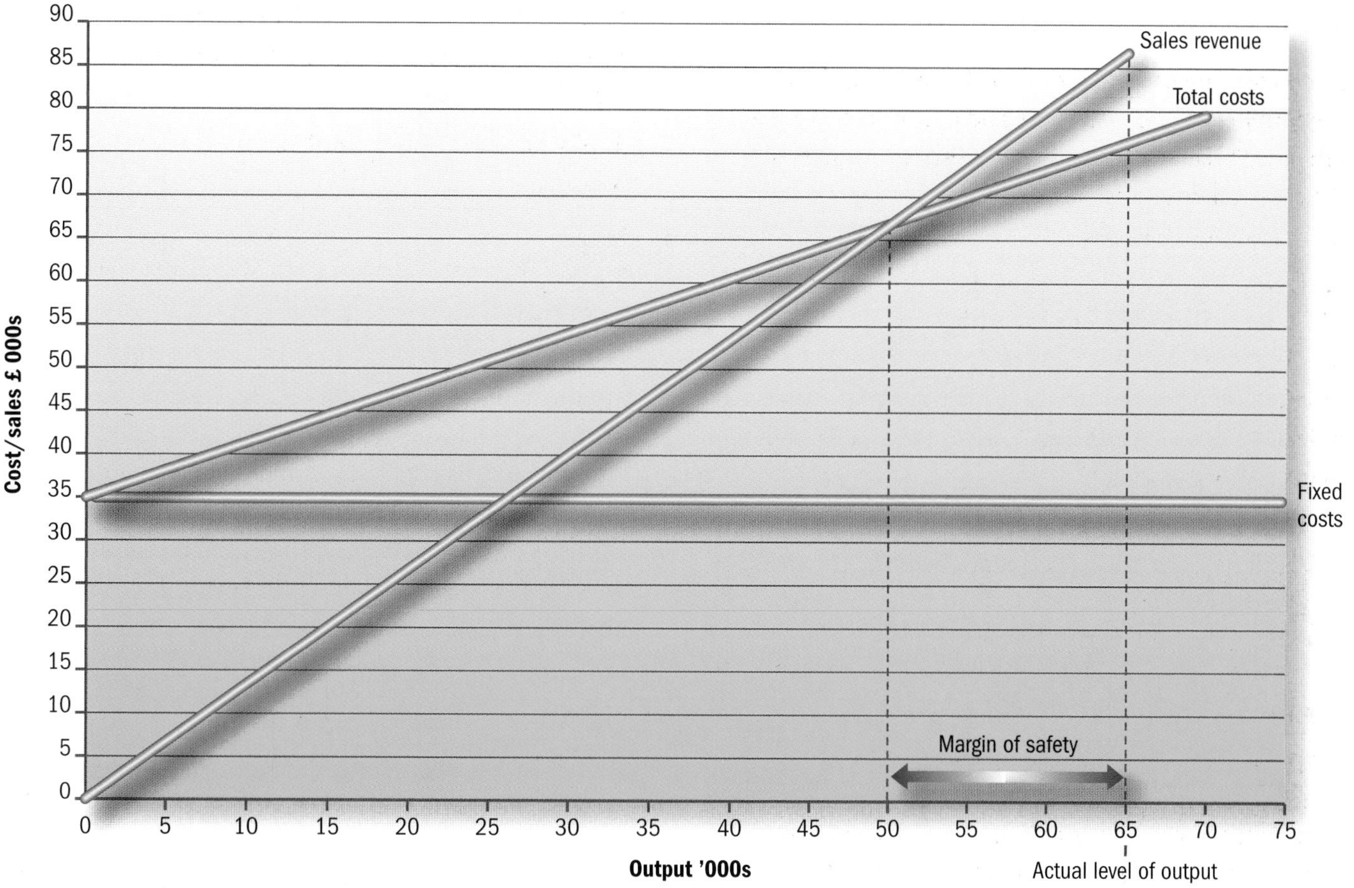


▲ **Break-even chart**

There are some benefits and limitations of break-even that you should be aware of and these are shown in the table below.

| Benefits of break-even | Limitations of break-even |
|---|---|
| 1. It can provide very quick results for display either by hand or on a computer.<br>2. It can be used to help investors decide whether or not to invest in a small business.<br>3. It allows small businesses to forecast what might happen to their business if sales go down or costs go up.<br>4. It is easy to apply with a minimum amount of training needed. | 1. It can oversimplify the situation in terms of pricing as often businesses will offer different prices to different customers, e.g. discounts or trade prices.<br>2. It is only useful for a short amount of time as both costs and prices may be changing rapidly.<br>3. It is only as useful as the data that is put into it in terms of future costs and sales.<br>4. It does not take into account economies of scale whereby as more products are made the cost per unit starts to reduce.<br>5. It may be difficult to use if the business sells a range of different products that cover the fixed costs in differing amounts.<br>6. It needs to be supported with relevant market research and economic predictions in order to be useful. |

## Practice point

**Deluxe Car Wash Services**

Produce a break-even chart and check your workings using the break-even formula for the following car wash business:

Car wash price = £12.50 per car
Overhead costs = £175 per week
Labour costs per wash = £4.50 per car
Materials and water cost = £1.00 per car

- Make sure you label your graph in full and include the break-even formula to show you are right.
- Deluxe Car Wash Services averaged 30 cars per week during July – work out the margin of safety.
- How much profit would Deluxe Car Wash Services make if they did 20 car washes during one week and what recommendations would you make to the company about this?

## Monitoring budgets and variances

Once the business has worked out its break-even point it knows the levels which it must reach or keep to in order to become profitable. To make sure that the business reaches these levels it must set budgets and monitor its progress towards those budgets.

Budgeting is a difficult process because it seeks to give a guide to how much the business thinks it will spend in a given area in the future. Some businesses will choose to use zero budgeting. This is when departments are given no budget but they have to ask their managers for money based on what they believe they will need for that year. Allocated budgeting is the opposite; this is when money is allocated for a budget and divided according to how many departments and people are working there. The budget is usually set at the start of the financial year and the business must ensure each month that it is sticking to its predictions. If sales are higher than budgeted this is likely to be positive for the business, but if costs are higher this could lead to lower profits or even problems with paying their expenses.

Measuring the difference between what is budgeted and the actual costs or sales revenue that has been received is known as variance analysis. If the result is better than expected, e.g. sales revenues are higher or costs are lower, this variance is known as Favourable (F). If sales are lower or costs higher than expected, this variance is known as Adverse (A). Monitoring the variances is really important as if they are noticed early enough the business can make changes to put the business back on track.

### Income increased to budget

A budget provides a business with a good outlook and structure for future plans. Income represents a key area of budgeting as without income there is no money to work with in the future and therefore no funds. Sometimes it is necessary to increase the amount of income that is available to budget with. This can be done by selling more products or raising prices. If costs are higher than expected, and income is not increased, profits may be affected. A business with an adequate budget, which it does not exceed, should be able to keep paying its expenses (bills) and therefore continue trading. Any excess money that is left over can be kept and used in case of an unexpected situation. This is known as a contingency fund.

### Bidding to increase future resources

Sometimes businesses realise that they do not have enough money available in their budgets to, for example, expand or buy new equipment. Therefore they may choose to bid for additional funding through a capital grant or ask others to invest in the business. This type of budget funding is particularly important for organisations that work within the public sector as they are often funded on a short-term basis and a bit is put in to pay for resources, e.g. wages for employees. A business may also choose to increase future resources by asking others to invest in the business. This means that the business owner(s) gets the use of the money invested and in return offers a percentage stake in the business. A private limited or public limited company may choose to do this by offering shares.

Other businesses do not have investment from large organisations or do not want another big company to be involved. They need to raise money in other ways so may choose to go to their bank for a loan or may try to

## Case study

### Variance analysis

'Hair to Wear Ltd' is a company that specialises in making hair extensions delivered to hairdressing salons. Below is the budget for November, December and January.

| Budget for 'Hair to Wear' Ltd | | | |
|---|---|---|---|
| | Nov £ | Dec £ | Jan £ |
| Materials | 300 | 300 | 200 |
| Petrol | 200 | 200 | 200 |
| Wages | 800 | 800 | 800 |
| Advertising | 200 | 200 | 200 |
| Insurance | 300 | 300 | 300 |
| Factory Rental | 400 | 400 | 400 |
| Bank Loan Payment | 350 | 350 | 350 |
| Van Payment | 250 | 250 | 250 |
| Total | 2800 | 2800 | 2700 |

The actual costs for November, December and January are given as follows:
Materials were £200, £300 and £250.
Petrol costs were £100, £150 and £100.
Wages were as expected.
Advertising was £250 every month.
Insurance was more expensive than predicted at £400 per month.
The factory rental was reduced by 50% for January only.
The bank loan payment was £375 every month.
The van repayment was £230 per month.

1. Calculate the variances against the actual costs using the information above. ✓
2. What recommendations would you make to 'Hair to Wear' based on the variance analysis that you have just conducted? ✓✓
3. Discuss the usefulness of variance analysis to a company like 'Hair to Wear'. ✓✓✓

raise finance by getting a grant. Grants can be given to businesses by national or local government agencies for many different reasons, including where the business is located, how big the business is or if the business is in an industry that has problems. The most common organisations to receive grants currently are those in farming, manufacturing or tourism.

## Practice point

Organisations like the Prince's Trust (www.princes-trust.org.uk) give out grants to young people to help them set up in business. Using websites like this, carry out some research into three different types of grant that are available to people starting up in business. Compare the different types of grants by considering their advantages and disadvantages. Judge how effective you think grants are compared to loans for a new small business.

## Provision of appropriate liquidity/working capital

As discussed above, working capital is the day-to-day money needed to pay the bills and so the business can remain trading. It is the difference between the current assets (cash plus debtors due to settle their accounts plus stock) that the business has and its current liabilities (the debts that must be paid in the short term).

The table below shows some figures for Bob's Construction Ltd.

| | Current Assets £ | Current Liabilities £ |
|---|---|---|
| Cash | 4000 | |
| Debtors (people that owe you money) | 500 | |
| Stock | 100 | |
| Creditors (people that you owe money to) | | 1600 |
| Bank overdraft | | 2000 |
| Total | 4600 | 3600 |

The working capital figure for Bob's business would be £4600 – £3600 = £1000.

Working capital is extremely important to businesses because it puts them into a position where they can pay their bills. Large businesses may make things more difficult for smaller businesses by negotiating long payment periods so if a small business is, for example, offering a window cleaning service to a large company, that company may negotiate payment after 14 days which means that costs will be incurred at least two weeks before payment is received. It is quite common for debtors to fail to settle invoices within the time negotiated so there needs to be extremely careful cash flow management. The measurement that shows how easily a business can turn its assets into cash to pay its debts is known as **liquidity**. The higher the level of liquidity, the easier it is for the business to access extra funds and so be able to pay off any debts that it has.

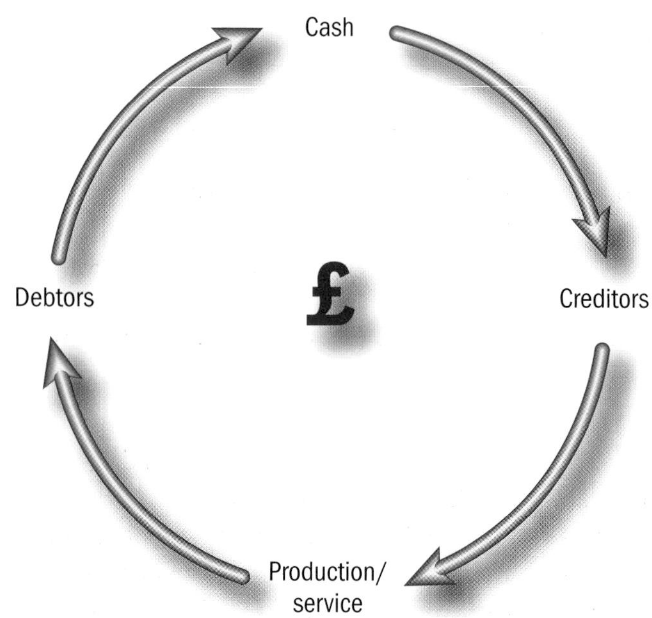


▲ **Negotiating payment deals can increase working capital**

## Practice point

| Brains Pet Food Ltd | | Kipper Fish Snax Ltd | |
|---|---|---|---|
| | £ | | £ |
| Bank | 200 | Bank | 500 |
| Creditors | 400 | Creditors | 200 |
| Loan from bank | 2000 | Loan from bank | 750 |
| Debtors | 750 | Debtors | 300 |
| Stock | 600 | Stock | 1000 |
| Cash | 300 | Cash | 250 |

Work out the working capital figure for each business. What does this figure show for each one?

What recommendations would you make for each business?

## Key Terms

**Liquidity** The ability of a business to change its assets or stock into cash to be able to pay its bills.

## Thinking point

Speed Ferries was introduced in May 2004 as a new concept in low-cost ferry services. Its services are up to 50% cheaper than other operators. In 2005 it won the 'Best European Crossing Operator' Award at the Telegraph Travel Awards and after 18 months had captured 12% of the market.

Using the information provided and the company's website (www.speedferries.org) consider the issues that a business, starting up with high fixed costs and investment needed, may have regarding its cash flow, working capital and liquidity position. Think about external forces such as the weather and competitor behaviour to evaluate Speed Ferries and its approach to these issues.

## Provision of appropriate reserves to address emergencies/crises

Businesses, like the rest of us, have to make sure that they keep some money back at the end of every month in case an emergency should happen. This ensures that if they do have problems, such as an unexpected expense, or there is a downturn in their market due to world events or a natural disaster, they have enough funds to continue in business.

Some analysts recommend that reserves should be maintained which will allow the business to continue for at least three months in the event of an emergency. It is also important for businesses to have some reserves in the early stages of their budget planning as it may be difficult to make accurate budget predictions and costs, and income calculations may need to be adjusted. An emergency budget will keep extra funds to allow for additional expenses.

## Outcome activity 2.4

**Pass**

You have been asked by a local enterprise group to write a detailed newspaper article for their next publication. The title is 'Why costs and budgets need to be controlled.'

**Merit**

To provide more detail for the group you should also analyse the reasons why costs and budgets need to be controlled and provide detailed explanations of the problems that can occur if they are left unmonitored.

**Distinction**

Having read your first draft the group would like you to evaluate how managing resources and controlling budgets can improve the performance of a business.

## Grading tips

**Pass** 

You should include as many references to real business situations as you can to illustrate your points and make sure you include detailed descriptions of the use of:

- different types of costs
- break-even
- budgeting
- variance analysis
- bidding for resources
- reserves.

**Merit**

You should give the advantages and disadvantages associated with controlling costs and budgets, including examples from the business world that you have read about as part of your course. You could also consider issues such as how variable costs could be reduced and so make savings for the organisation.

Make sure you include detailed reasoning and explanation for merit level work. You should make clear reference to businesses that you have researched and it is recommended that you include a bibliography with your work.

**Distinction** 

Using all your notes to date, provide detailed judgements about the implications of resourcing and budgetary control on a business. How important is such management to a business? When might it not be important? Which other factors do you need to take into account?

At distinction level you should bring together all of the work that you have produced so far for Outcomes 2.1, 2.2, 2.3 and 2.4 to provide a conclusion which can be argued or justified, making sure you include suitable business examples.

# Financial statements

Financial statements allow businesses to measure their financial resources. Public limited companies (Plcs) must publish their accounts so that investors can see how well they are doing and judge whether or not to buy their shares on the Stock Exchange. The two main types of financial statement you need to learn about are the profit and loss account and the balance sheet.

## Profit and loss account

The profit and loss account is a useful tool as it shows how much has been made at the end of a financial year and therefore can help a bank or other lender to decide whether or not it is worth the risk to invest in your business. For smaller businesses, such as private limited companies (Ltd) and sole traders, it is useful to be able to see how much profit has been made at the end of the year. Often businesses will use projected profit and loss accounts to help them to plan their finances and this can help with budget setting.

A very simplified version of a profit and loss account is shown below to help you understand. This business is a consultancy offering business services.

**Shannon Coleman Business Services**
**Profit and Loss Account for the year ended April**

| | | £ |
|---|---|---|
| Sales | | 19,500 |
| Less expenses: | | |
| Overheads | 10,660 | |
| Labour | 7020 | 17,680 |
| Net profit before tax | | 1820 |

This is a very simple version of a service-based profit and loss account, showing you how sales are shown and then expenses deducted giving the net profit left over.

Khalida's Fashions Ltd shows another example below; this one also shows stock and gives a gross profit figure. Gross profit is when the cost of the sales has been taken away from the sales figure. Expenses are then deducted to get the net profit figure. You will learn more about using gross and net profit calculations to check the financial health of a business in this unit on page 92.

**Khalida's Fashions Ltd**
**Profit and Loss Account for the year ended**

| | | £ |
|---|---|---|
| Sales | | 150,000 |
| Less cost of sales | | |
| Opening stock | 5000 | |
| Purchases | 51,000 | |
| Less closing stock | 6000 | 50,000 |
| Gross Profit | | 100,000 |
| Less expenses | | |
| Rent & business rates | 15,600 | |
| Advertising | 2000 | |
| Wages & salaries | 28,000 | |
| Administration | 1000 | |
| Insurance | 2000 | |
| Interest on loans | 2100 | |
| Telephone | 600 | |
| Accountancy Fees | 900 | |
| Legal Fees | 1000 | |
| Bank charges | 400 | |
| Depreciation | 500 | |
| Repairs & maintenance | 300 | |
| Heat & light | 600 | |
| Miscellaneous | 300 | |
| | | 55,300 |
| Net profit before tax | | 44,700 |

Profit and loss accounts produced by large public limited companies can be extremely complicated and make use of many different accounting principles but it is worth remembering that a profit and loss account is there to show the business, and people that are interested in it, how much profit it is able to generate. The higher the profitability of a business the better performance that business has had. Tesco plc in 2005 made profits of more than £2 billion. This shows how effectively it had performed in that year to be able to make such large profits.

## Balance sheet

The balance sheet is important because it gives a snapshot showing assets (things a business owns), liabilities (debts a business owes) and equity (the amount invested in the business). Fixed assets are assets that are owned and expected to be retained for one year or more, e.g. land, buildings, vehicles or equipment. Current assets are those that can be converted into cash more easily and are only retained for a short time. Producing a balance sheet is important as it shows how the business is financed, through the investor's own money or through loans from other people known as creditors. Because the balance sheet shows the assets of the business, it also allows the investor to get a snapshot of how much the business is actually worth. The balance sheet below is a simplified version for a limited company. A balance sheet must balance! Here this is shown with the figure £93,000.

**Better Books Ltd**
**Start Up Balance Sheet**

| | | | £ |
|---|---|---|---|
| Fixed Assets | | | |
| Shop Premises | | | 75,000 |
| Fixtures and fittings | | | 5000 |
| | | | 80,000 |
| Current Assets | | | |
| Stock | | 15,000 | |
| Bank | | 3000 | |
| Cash | | 2000 | |
| | | 20,000 | |
| Less current liabilities | | | |
| Creditors | 7000 | 7000 | |
| Working capital | | | 13,000 |
| Total assets less current liabilities | | | 93,000 |
| Financed by | | | |
| Long-term liabilities | | | |
| Bank Loan | 10,000 | | |
| Mortgage | 60,000 | 70,000 | |
| Capital and reserves | | | |
| Capital | | 23,000 | |
| Capital employed | | | 93,000 |

## Remember

The profit and loss account gives investors an insight into the financial *performance* of a business. The balance sheet provides insight into the financial *position* of a business.

# Basic ratios

One of the ways a business can measure how it is doing is through ratio analysis. Ratios can help the business to see how it is doing now and allow it to see how it compares to last year or the year before and against other competitors. For these ratios to be useful they should be compared over time to see if there are any trends and also between businesses within the same industry (i.e. competitors).

### To determine solvency

## Key Terms

**Solvency** An organisation is able to pay its expenses as it has money available within the business.

Businesses can use ratios to work out their **solvency** by using the current ratio and acid test ratio. These ratios allow businesses and potential investors to see how well they are able to meet their liabilities.

$$\text{Current ratio} = \frac{\text{current assets}}{\text{current liabilities}}$$

This ratio shows how many assets a business has compared to liabilities, in other words how easily it would be able to pay its creditors. If the figure is just over 1 then the organisation may be in a difficult position for payment as its current assets would be virtually equal to its liabilities. It is considered good practice to have a figure of between 1.5 and 2, so that the business can be sure it can pay its liabilities easily. A figure higher than 2 would not be good as the money should be placed elsewhere to improve the business.

$$\text{Acid Test Ratio} = \frac{\text{current assets-stock}}{\text{current liabilities}}$$

This ratio shows the assets compared to liabilities like the current ratio, but by taking out the stock figure from the current assets it shows how well a business can meet its liabilities without having to sell stock. Again, the figure should be higher than 1 but not higher than 2 as shown above.

## Case study

### Current and acid test ratios

Compare the following two businesses using both the current and acid test ratios. They are both in the confectionery industry and the figures are taken from their annual accounts as at the end of April 2004.

| Delicious Delights Ltd | | Scrumptious Toffees Ltd | |
|---|---|---|---|
| Bank | £200 | Bank | £500 |
| Creditors | £400 | Creditors | £200 |
| Loan from bank | £2000 | Loan from bank | £750 |
| Debtors | £750 | Debtors | £300 |
| Stock | £600 | Stock | £1000 |
| Cash | £30 | Cash | £250 |

For each business, work out which are the current assets and current liabilities.

1. Calculate the current ratio and acid test ratio for each business. ✓
2. How do the ratios compare? What difference does stock make to their ability to pay their liabilities? ✓✓
3. Make recommendations to each business about what they could do to improve their positions in the future. ✓✓✓
4. Research into other examples of businesses within the confectionery industry, such as Cadbury Schweppes, Masterfoods or Nestlé, and by using their company reports and accounts compare their current and acid test ratios. ✓✓✓

## To determine profitability

Ratios can also show how profitable a business really is – either as a snapshot or over time. There are three ways of working out how profitable a business really is: **gross profit** percentage, **net profit** percentage and return on capital employed.

### ■ Gross profit percentage

This calculation shows gross profit as a percentage of the turnover (sales and any other income that a business gets). For example, if the gross profit is £1000 and the turnover of the business is £2000 the gross profit percentage would be:

$$\frac{£1000}{£2000} \times 100 = 50\%$$

Gross profit percentage is also sometimes called gross profit margin and the calculation shows how well the business is managing its purchases of stock. A high gross profit percentage shows the business is doing well as it is controlling the cost of its purchases.

## Key Terms

**Gross profit** The profit made by the business just taking into account direct purchases that the business made to get the goods to the customer, e.g. stock. It does not take into account other running costs of the business such as rent or staff wages.

**Net profit** The gross profit less the other costs of the business that are needed to run it, e.g. rent or staff wages.

### ■ Net profit percentage

This calculation takes the idea of profitability one stage further by actually considering the profit as a percentage of turnover after all the other expenses have been taken out. It is worked out as follows:

$$\frac{\text{Net profit}}{\text{Turnover}} \times 100 = \text{Net profit percentage}$$

This shows the profit that the business has made before tax has been taken off. This calculation shows how well the business manages its other expenses, especially

## Case study

### Gross and net profit

The following three businesses all sell shoes – Shooz is run online and Footwear and Boots and All are both run from the high street. The only variable costs that all three shops have are for the footwear themselves (stock).

| | Shooz £ | Footwear £ | Boots and All £ |
|---|---|---|---|
| Fixed costs (operating costs) | 500 | 600 | 800 |
| Variable costs (stock) | 300 | 400 | 600 |
| Revenue (sales) | 900 | 1200 | 1000 |

Using the figures provided in the table, work out the gross profit and net profit percentages for each business.

1. Which one has the best gross profit percentage? ✓
2. Which one has the best net profit percentage? ✓
3. Which business do you think is performing the best? Give reasons for your justification. ✓✓
4. 'Gross profit is less important than net profit.' Give a judgement about this view using real examples of companies you have studied to illustrate your thinking. ✓✓✓

when it is compared to the gross profit percentage. If a business has a high gross profit percentage but a low net profit percentage its operating costs (i.e. day-to-day running costs such as wages, rent and insurance) are too high as they are taking out too much profit from the business. Sometimes it is possible to have a business where the gross profit percentage is good but the net profit percentage might be extremely low or even show a loss. This means that action to reduce operating costs must be put in place.

## Return on capital employed (ROCE)

This is the final calculation that a business might use to judge profitability. It is worked out by considering the net profit as a percentage of the capital employed by that business. The reason this ratio is useful is because it shows the amount of money an investor is receiving back on their capital as a percentage. This means they can compare the percentage received against what they would have received if they had put the money into the bank.

$$\frac{\text{Net profit}}{\text{Capital employed (including shareholder funds)}} \times 100 = \text{ROCE (\%)}$$

If the interest rate at the bank is higher than that shown in the ROCE, it would make more sense for the investors to put their money there.

## To determine performance

The final set of ratios that a business might want to use are those that determine performance and these show the stock turnover, debtor's collection period and asset turnover.

### Stock turnover

There are two main ways to work out this ratio and they show how quickly the business has sold its stock. This is a useful way of measuring efficiency as the faster the stock is turned over the more likely the business is to be efficient. This is also extremely important if the goods that are being sold are **perishable**.

### Key Terms

**Perishable** Goods that are perishable are likely to spoil or go off, for example food items with limited dates on them.

The calculation for stock turnover can be shown either as a percentage or in days. Both show how quickly that stock is turned around and therefore how effective the stock control system is.

For stock turnover (in number of times):

$$\frac{\text{Cost of sales}}{\textbf{Average stock} \text{ (number of times)}}$$

= stock turnover

For stock turnover shown in days:

$$\frac{\text{Average stock}}{\text{Cost of sales}} \times 365$$

= stock turnover (days)

## Key Terms

**Average stock** This is opening stock plus closing stock divided by two.

**Debtors** People that owe the business money for goods or services they have received.

▼ **Stock must be turned over quickly to help efficiency, especially if it is perishable**

## ■ Debtor's collection period

$$\frac{\text{Debtors}}{\text{Credit sales}} \times 365 = \text{total number of days it takes debtors to pay}$$

The debtor's collection period looks at the link between the number of **debtors** and how long on average it takes the business to collect its debts. The fewer the number of days, the better credit control the business has because it collects what is owed to it more quickly. If information about credit sales is not available the calculation can still be worked out by using the total sales figure.

## ■ Asset turnover

The final ratio that can help to work out the performance of a business is asset turnover. This ratio looks at the sales as a percentage of the total assets that a business owns.

$$\frac{\text{Sales}}{\text{Total assets}} = \text{asset turnover}$$

By dividing the sales by the total assets, the business is able to work out how many pounds it earns for every pound invested in total assets. The example below is given to demonstrate this.

$$\frac{30{,}000}{10{,}000} = 3 \text{ times}$$

This means for every £1 of assets the business was able to generate £3 worth of sales.

The asset turnover ratio can also be broken down further into:

$$\frac{\text{Sales}}{\text{Fixed assets}} \text{ and } \frac{\text{Sales}}{\text{Current assets}}$$

The fixed asset turnover ratio can show how much money has been invested in land and buildings so if the business is investing a lot in recent months this is likely to be lower. Current assets such as stock, debtors or cash can be used within the current asset turnover calculation to see how many sales are generated per pound of current assets.

Asset-based ratio analysis can be very useful to businesses looking at trends in their performance to see how well they are making use of assets that they own. It is also important to consider the industry that the business is working in to be able to tell how well it is doing. Some industries require a lot of investment in assets, for example an engineering works or manufacturing plant. For others the investment might be relatively low, for example an online business operating from home using a website. It is important to make comparisons about asset turnover with relevant competitors and look at trends to see how well the business is doing.

## Outcome activity 2.5

Your tutor will give you a set of accounts including the profit and loss account and balance sheet to work with for this outcome activity.

**Pass**

1. Interpret the contents of a given profit and loss account and balance sheet. 
2. Illustrate the financial state of a given business by showing examples of accounting ratios. 

**Merit**

Using your notes from P5 and P6 to help you, interpret the contents of a given profit and loss account and balance sheet and describe in detail how accounting ratios can be used to monitor the financial state of the organisation. 

**Distinction**

You should now evaluate how useful accounting ratios are as a means of monitoring business health in this organisation and give examples to show your understanding.

## Grading tips

**Pass**  

Within your account you should comment on the content of each statement and the purpose of each element.

You should include ratios for:

- Solvency
- Profitability (if applicable to the business)
- ROCE
- Performance indicators.

**Merit** 

You should include plenty of detail within your answers, explaining how these statements are useful and any limitations that you may feel about their usefulness.

**Distinction** 

To achieve a full distinction you should provide clear judgements linked to evidence and examples making specific reference to the business you are studying. This task should be like a conclusion for the tasks above but also take into account other issues that might be outside an organisation's control, such as world events or changes in the economy.

## End of unit test

1. What is meant by performance-related pay?
2. How might outsourcing benefit a business organisation?
3. Name three disadvantages of outsourcing.
4. What is meant by working capital?
5. What is meant by absence measurement and how is it calculated?
6. What is the difference between informal and formal monitoring?
7. Name three areas that need to be considered by businesses when considering intellectual property.
8. What is meant by bespoke software?
9. What is the difference between patenting and copyright?
10. Name three sources of finance available to a business.
11. Describe the elements contained within a balance sheet and a profit and loss account.
12. To what extent do ratios help a business to consider their financial health?

# Resources

www.acas.org.uk – The Advisory, Conciliation and Arbitration Service

www.adviceguide.org.uk – Citizens Advice Bureau with guides to the workplace

www.businesslink.gov.uk – Business Link Advice for businesses

www.cbi.org.uk – Confederation of Business and Industry

www.cipd.co.uk – Chartered Institute of Personnel and Development

www.coachingnetwork.org.uk – Useful tips

www.dti.gov.uk – Department of Trade and Industry on coaching and mentoring

www.investorsinpeople.co.uk – Investors in People website

www.managementqualifications.co.uk – Management Qualifications website giving advice

www.mindtools.com – Tools that can be used to help managers

www.mybusiness.co.uk – My Business provides information on management issues for small businesses including resources

www.personneltoday.co.uk – Personnel Today human resource information provider (UK)

www.statistics.gov.uk – National Statistics published by the government

www.envirowise.gov.uk – Government funded campaign giving practical environment support to businesses.

www.compactlaw.co.uk/free_legal_articles/health_and_safety.html – Compact Law website including information about health and safety and intellectual property

http://www.patent.gov.uk/patent.htm – The Patent Office

www.fact-uk.org.uk – Federation Against Copyright Theft

www.aacp.org.uk – Alliance Against IP Theft

# Books

Alred, A., Garvey, B. and Smith, R. 2006 *The Mentoring Pocket Book,* Management Pocket Books

Bartol, K. and Martin, D. 1997 *Management,* McGraw-Hill

Chaffey, D. 2002 *E-Commerce and E-Business Management,* Pearson Education

Gillespie, A. 2002 *Business in Action,* Hodder & Stoughton

Kirton, M. (ed.) 1989 *Adaptors and Innovators: Styles of Creativity and Problem-Solving,* Routledge

Parsloe, E. and Wray, M. 2000 *Coaching and Mentoring,* Kogan Page

Harvey-Jones, John 2003 *Making It Happen: Reflections on Leadership,* Profile Business

Martin, M. and Jackson, T. 2002 *Personnel Practice (People and Organizations),* Chartered Institute of Personnel and Development (CIPD)

# Journals

*Business Review*
*Personnel Management*

| Grading criteria | Outcome activity | Page number |
|---|---|---|
| To achieve a pass grade the evidence must show that the learner is able to: | | |
| P1 Describe how a selected business manages its human resources | 2.1 | 73 |
| P2 Describe the main physical and technological resources that need to be considered in the running of a selected organisation | 2.2 | 81 |
| P3 Describe where sources of finance can be obtained for starting up a selected business | 2.3 | 83 |
| P4 Give the reasons why costs and budgets need to be controlled | 2.4 | 89 |
| P5 Interpret the contents of a given profit and loss account and balance sheet | 2.5 | 95 |
| P6 Illustrate the financial state of a given business by showing examples of accounting ratios | 2.5 | 95 |
| To achieve a merit grade the evidence must show that, in addition to the pass criteria, the learner is able to: | | |
| M1 Assess how managing human, physical and technological resources can improve the performance of a selected organisation | 2.2 | 81 |
| M2 Analyse the reasons why costs and budgets need to be controlled and explain in detail problems that can arise if they are left unmonitored | 2.4 | 89 |
| M3 Interpret the contents of a given profit and loss account and balance sheet and explain in detail how accounting ratios can be used to monitor the financial state of the organisation | 2.5 | 95 |
| To achieve a distinction grade the evidence must show that, in addition to the pass and merit criteria, the learner is able to: | | |
| D1 Evaluate how managing resources and controlling budgets can improve the performance of a business | 2.4 | 89 |
| D2 Evaluate the adequacy of accounting ratios as a means of monitoring business health in a selected organisation, using examples | 2.5 | 95 |

# Introduction to marketing

## Introduction

This unit will show you that marketing is at the heart of every organisation's activity, including voluntary bodies such as charities and public institutions like universities. At the centre of marketing is the customer. The unit introduces you to the tools and techniques used by marketing managers to ensure the organisation achieves its overall objectives by meeting the customer's needs and expectations.

Marketing operates in ever-changing circumstances which are often outside the control of the organisation. You will have the opportunity to consider the analytical techniques used by an organisation to identify these factors and the range of appropriate actions available to ensure the long-term profitability of the organisation.

Making successful marketing decisions using analytical techniques can be greatly improved with good quality marketing information, usually provided by effective marketing research. You will have the chance, in this unit, to explore how the information is acquired, and then used by organisations to increase demand for their products, sometimes using new developments such as Internet marketing and relationship marketing.

### What you need to learn

On completion of this unit you should:

1. Understand the key concepts and principles of marketing and their application in the business environment
2. Know how and why marketing research is conducted by organisations
3. Understand how marketing information is used by organisations
4. Understand how marketing techniques are used to increase demand for products (goods and services).

## Consider this

Marketing is often considered to be simply advertising, whereas it really involves a great many activities such as developing new products, setting prices and training people to deal with customers effectively. Keep a diary for a few days, noting down all the activities that organisations seem to be undertaking which you believe are related to marketing. What conclusions can you draw about the work of a marketing team?

Marketing is also associated mainly with large companies. Using your diary information, classify the organisations you observed into local, national, international, public (such as the police), government departments (such as schools) and volunteer (such as Oxfam). Which organisations are not involved in marketing?

Not so long ago organisations found it difficult to discover marketing research information. Think of a market in which you have an interest, perhaps Personal Digital Assistants (PDAs) and do an Internet search to understand how much data is now there for the marketing manager to consider.

It is probably true that organisations which react effectively to developments outside their business survive and remain profitable in the long term. Kodak has had to transform its business to cope with the digital age, whereas it had been world famous for producing film.

Marketing is both challenging and rewarding because it requires scientific and creative skills. Collecting the information is a scientific activity and developing solutions requires creative skills. This is your opportunity to develop those essential skills.

Marketing should be at the heart of any organisation. Modern marketing is about identifying ever-changing customer needs in a global market and continually creating products that satisfy those needs. Many organisations have adopted this concept as the philosophy that drives all of their business functions.

# Principles of marketing

## Overall concept

The marketing concept directs organisations to focus on customers. A company that follows the marketing concept puts the customer at the centre of all its business decision making and planning and not just the marketing team's decision making and planning. An organisation with this approach is said to be marketing-orientated. You are, however, likely to come across organisations that have other types of orientation such as production, product or sales.

The differences between the various orientations are outlined below:

The **production concept** concentrates on production and distribution economies. This in turn is based on the notion that customers will choose lower priced products that are readily available. This perhaps applies to builders when they are buying concrete.

The **selling concept** is based on the notion that customers need to be persuaded to buy through aggressive selling and promotion. There are regular reports in the news about electricity and gas companies whose sales people have used selling tactics with these characteristics.

The **product concept** has been adopted by organisations which believe that their product is the most innovative in the market, is of top quality and brimming with special features. This perhaps describes some electrical manufacturers that offer products with plenty of features which the customer perhaps never really uses.

The **marketing concept** is based on the idea that organisations can best meet their objectives by concentrating on customer needs and satisfying those needs better than competitors.

Organisations do not always adopt the marketing concept in the beginning but find they evolve towards the concept as they seek to survive and remain profitable in the long term. For example, a business might successfully establish itself through a new invention but over time the appeal of the product falls and it consequently has to adopt the marketing concept to create and develop other products with a market appeal.

The marketing concept seems a sensible path to follow but you might be surprised that many organisations experience considerable difficulty trying to sustain their commitment to the customer. Look out for examples of business practices which are designed for the organisation's convenience rather than the customer.

### Practice point

Working with a friend, draw up a list of organisations which you think do *not* put customers at the centre of their business. Then try to decide which orientation best describes their approach to business.

### Take it further

Choose three of the organisations you have considered and explain why you have decided they approach business in a particular way. Do you think they are right to choose that approach?

## Marketing definitions

Marketing plays an important part in ensuring the products that customers want are readily available. The Chartered Institute of Marketing's definition provides a clear picture of the activities involved in marketing.

Marketing is:

> The management process responsible for identifying, anticipating and satisfying customer requirements profitably.

It is a management activity because it requires continuous information gathering, analysis and then evaluation in order to make decisions. The information collected should help an organisation identify customer requirements.

But it is not sufficient to find out what consumers are thinking and doing now; it is necessary to consider what might happen in the future. Future consumer tastes and preferences need to be anticipated; sometimes businesses can even create them – they use marketing to create needs where none existed.

Once consumer needs have been identified the organisation still has to satisfy these needs successfully. Designing the right product to satisfy such needs may not prove so easy.

It is essential to do all this and make a profit to invest in new products, advertising campaigns and provide a reward for investors or, in the case of public or voluntary organisations, to fund continued and improved services.

Marketing puts consumers at the centre of everything an organisation undertakes and is the link between producer and customer.

## Marketing principles

These are the underlying goals of marketing:

- **Understanding consumer needs**. Markets change rapidly and so it is essential that organisations constantly look for new product and market opportunities. Plenty of organisations have failed to appreciate the importance of this principle and have found themselves operating in declining markets, e.g. CDs, and/or competing against organisations with superior products, e.g. MP3 players.
- **Keeping ahead of competition.** Increased competition can have a dramatic impact on an organisation. For example, a competitor might start offering delivery in three days, whereas previously the best performance in the market might have been seven days. Customers might immediately switch to the faster service.
- **Communicating effectively with consumers.** Even the best product, effectively distributed at the right price to the target market, may experience poor sales if the promotional support is ineffective. In many markets where competition is intense, high levels of promotional support are a necessity if an organisation is to succeed.
- **Utilising new technology.** This is an area that has been gaining in importance in recent years. The ability to book flight tickets over the Internet with companies such as easyJet, is changing how the airline industry works. The use of technology is now considered by many marketing managers as a key marketing principle. Marketing should seek to exploit its potential.

## Marketing functions

Marketing functions are the broad areas of marketing that contribute towards the achievement of the marketing principles.

- **Establish a distinctive identity for a product or organisation**. There are very few unique products nowadays, so organisations develop brands to give

▼ Establishing a distinctive identity is essential

them a distinct image in the market. A brand can be a name, a symbol or a design used to identify a product and make it different from its competitors. The Nike 'tick' or 'swoosh' is instantly recognisable across the world. Other organisations seek to create a **corporate image** in the market. Corporate image means the characteristics an organisation wishes to establish for itself in the minds of the public. For example, B&Q supports local community groups by providing employee action teams to help renovate and decorate community amenities to enhance its image of being a caring and responsible organisation.

- **Plan, coordinate and monitor the marketing mix.** An organisation has to allocate resources between the ingredients of the **marketing mix**: either between the 4Ps, product, place, price and promotion, for goods, or the 7Ps, product, place, price, promotion, people, processes and physical evidence (**extended marketing mix**) for services. Products need to be replaced by new improved versions, which can require high spending on development. It may be necessary to offer discounts to customers to encourage them to buy, and the resulting loss of income has to be considered. To encourage retailers to stock a product, producers may have to provide display units – and these are always expensive. An organisation has to invest in promotion. The effectiveness of the marketing mix chosen needs to be monitored and changed if the expected results are not forthcoming.

## Key Terms

**Corporate image** The characteristics an organisation seeks to establish for itself in the minds of the public.
**Marketing mix** The combination of product, price, place (sometimes called distribution), promotion, people, processes and physical evidence offered by an organisation to potential consumers.
**Extended marketing mix** The normal elements of product, price, promotion, packaging and place plus another 3Ps (often referred to as the 7Ps) associated with marketing services: people, process and physical evidence.

- **Coordinate marketing activities effectively.** The decision by the marketing team to launch a new product usually has implications for many other departments in an organisation. Any new product launch is likely to involve the design department in completing the design on time. The distribution department needs to be made aware of the nature of the product to ensure it can be stored and delivered successfully. The sales team must be briefed about the product's features and benefits and any special launch promotions. While all these groups have to be kept informed about developments, their activities also need to be coordinated. For example, the production unit has to ensure stock has been produced to coincide with the sales team obtaining orders.

### Thinking point

Many departments within an organisation have to be coordinated by the marketing team. This is also true of contacts outside the organisation. Produce a list of those outside contacts, such as the advertising agency, before indicating why they would need to be informed about a new product launch.

- **Manage changes in technology, competition and consumer tastes.** Marketers have a variety of analytical techniques to manage change. All the techniques taken together are generally called a 'situational analysis' or 'marketing audit'. They are discussed later in the unit (see page 126).

## Marketing objectives (SMART)

The most effective marketing objectives should be SMART – specific, measurable, achievable, realistic and time related, for example 'to achieve a 5% market share in the French market within 18 months'. This objective is **specific** in that it details exactly what has to be done. It is **measurable** because a market share requirement is included. The objective would be **achievable** if everybody in the organisation accepted the aim. It would be **realistic** if it was calculated that it was possible to attain. It is **timetabled**, as the length of time given to achieve the objective is stated.

## Marketing activities

Marketing activities are the detailed actions that have to be undertaken to achieve the objectives. These are the day-to-day jobs which personnel in the marketing team are likely to be doing:

- conducting marketing research into new product concepts or promotional ideas
- implementing promotional campaigns by producing TV commercials, booking airtime with satellite television broadcasters
- calculating new prices when implementing a price increase.

For every marketing objective a marketing plan is written. These plans determine exactly which marketing activities should be undertaken. The plans are also important for controlling and evaluating the work of the marketing team.

## Link between organisational objectives and marketing objectives

It is important that the marketing objectives and plans support the overall business objectives, in order that the organisation has a common purpose. The overall objectives of the business should have a strong influence on the marketing objectives and plans. The transformation of corporate objectives into marketing activity is shown in the table below:

| Planning level | Content |
|---|---|
| Corporate mission statement | Overall vision, e.g. to be the market leader |
| Corporate objectives (overall business objectives) | What has to be achieved to deliver the vision, e.g. to achieve a market share of 35% |
| Marketing objectives | Marketing contribution to the corporate objectives, e.g. launch six new products into our main markets |
| Marketing plan | Marketing tactics to be used, e.g. promote on national TV throughout year |

## Case study

### Jaguar left in the slow lane

New cars take a long time to develop and Jaguars take longer than most. The current XJ has many excellent technical features, is reliable and is finished to a high quality standard. But is its improved speed and economy, much better than its German competitors, hidden to the customer because of its old fashioned looks? The new XK has the same problem. This has resulted in annual sales of about 90,000 against targets approaching 200,000.

To compound the problem Jaguar had not anticipated the popularity of diesel engines for premier cars, unlike the more marketing aware BMW company. By the time an appropriate diesel engine was available the product had failed to impress its really important American customers.

The arrival of the new S-Type and rival to the BMW 5-series did not help. The prestige brand found itself subject to its new owner's production techniques. The 'Ford way' saw mass produced, cheap looking, poor quality cars.

Having resolved the diesel engine issue, and returned the brand's production to the quality standard required, the company needs an exceptional restyling to generate a dramatic image change and restore its former glories.

1. Explain the key words in the Chartered Institute of Marketing's definition of marketing. ✓
2. Describe the main marketing principles, functions and activities. ✓✓
3. Explain Jaguar's orientation to its business. ✓✓
4. Recommend another orientation Jaguar could adopt and the benefits of such an approach. ✓✓✓

Once a marketing plan is written it not only influences the day-to-day activity within a marketing team, but it is also used to monitor and evaluate activity.

## Use of marketing principles

There is such a variety of organisations in the business world that it means marketing managers find themselves working in many different environments. It is likely that each type of environment will emphasise different aspects of the four marketing principles, as can be seen in the table below.

## Planning, control and evaluation processes

Not too many years ago marketing was characterised by a lack of structured planning. Marketing managers often acted on a hunch or intuition. Different marketing activities in different parts of the organisation were often uncoordinated. Sometimes, for example, the sales function and the marketing function would be pulling in different directions. While the marketing team might be trying to improve profit margins, the sales team could be giving away ever-increasing discounts. Similarly, the important

| Organisation | Understanding consumer trends | Keeping ahead of competition | Communicating effectively with consumers | Using new technology |
|---|---|---|---|---|
| Retailer, e.g. Next | New product range every season reflecting latest fashion developments such as new colours. | Fashion retailing has many participants. Currently Primark is securing market share; previously it was Matalan. | Uses all the available communication methods but especially important is the Next Directory catalogue. | Uses website. |
| Public, e.g. University | Review courses being offered annually to satisfy student requirements such as course with year placements in organisations. | With the expansion of places in Higher Education a significant number of universities need to attract students to survive. Some are already offering lower tuition fees than the national standard of £3000. | Becoming more adventurous in their approach. Prospectus, open days, personalised letters and the website are universally used – some utilising TV and sponsorship, e.g. Huddersfield Giants RLFC sponsored by local university | Apart from website, communicates with potential students by email and text message. Many have also developed courses so students can acquire new technology skills, e.g. courses about e-commerce. |
| Government department, e.g. Ofsted – inspector of schools | Respond to requirements of government. For example, reporting on successful introduction of citizenship into the curriculum. | This government agency does not have any competition. It is accountable and scrutinised by a parliamentary committee. | Only required for information purposes. Has a website and publishes individual school inspection reports and an annual review. | Has a website. |
| Voluntary, e.g. charity such as Oxfam | Focus on areas requiring urgent help, such as some areas of Africa. Encourage donations by identifying new 'giving trends', e.g. buying gifts such as goats for communities using a catalogue. | A large number of charities are competing for donations from supporters. They need to be seen to be providing appropriate help effectively while spending only a small part of their donations received on administration and marketing. | Uses many traditional promotional techniques to obtain donations and keep donors updated on the success of aid effort, e.g. direct mail letters, newsletters and website. | Uses website to obtain donations and report on success of projects. Donors can now text donations to some charities. |

▲ Aspects of the four marketing principles

coordinating role of marketing was often neglected. Increasingly, however, marketing is now characterised by much more structured marketing planning using a variety of powerful and sometimes sophisticated planning tools and techniques. The reasons for this move towards a planning culture are numerous, but some of the more important reasons for this are:

- an ever changing and more competitive marketing environment
- higher levels of investment required to develop new products and markets
- better trained marketing managers using more sophisticated and powerful planning tools
- recognition of the need for improved coordination and integration of marketing with other company functions.

The benefits of adopting a marketing planning culture include:

- more structured analysis of the marketing environment
- objectives and plans based on exploiting company strengths and marketing assets
- an awareness of the key marketing trends and possible future developments
- proactive rather than reactive approach to marketing activities
- an increased customer focus and customer orientation
- integrated marketing programmes involving the entire organisation.

The process of monitoring involves comparing actual performance against required performance objectives and taking any necessary action to correct differences. The monitoring process uses the original marketing objectives and plans. Without monitoring it is impossible to assess the extent to which the marketing objectives are likely to be achieved. Given the potentially large costs and use of resources in implementing the marketing plan, it would be inadvisable not to assess how well these resources are being used.

At the end of the planning cycle the plans and results have to be evaluated. The business environment changes, customers change, competitors change, even the company itself can change over time. This means that marketing needs to reflect and cope with these changes. Without evaluation there is the danger that marketing principles, functions and activities become outdated and no longer fit the market situation. The final section of this unit has a step-by-step diagram of this planning process – see page 140.

## Development of e-marketing

The emergence of e-marketing is beginning to fundamentally change the nature of marketing. Detailed below are some of the developments which are contributing to this changing nature:

- The collection of marketing research information can be easily undertaken through Internet surveys and the use of search engines like Google to identify sources of relevant information.
- The construction of sophisticated databases for use, not simply to mail people more junk mail, but to analyse consumer behaviour and generate more effective marketing communication material. For example, the online retailer Amazon automatically suggests new book titles that customers might like to consider based on previous purchases.
- New methods of promotion are available, such as banner advertising, affiliate programmes (having links from other sites), optimising positions on search engine results, identifying and submitting entries to Internet directories.
- Organisations can become marketing orientated through being more responsive and flexible. Email allows better access to key managers for customers to express views and pass on comments. Website technology allows customers to personalise the product they want more effectively, such as looking at combinations of furniture and fabrics when redesigning a room.
- Details of consumers can be collected cost effectively, by asking online shoppers to register if they want some extra information from the site or by using loyalty card data. Organisations have not spent millions of pounds developing loyalty cards, such as Boots' Advantage Card or the Tesco Clubcard, simply to give consumers additional discounts. The prime motivation is to collect consumer data to develop their business.

## Thinking point

The developments in e-marketing are also shaping the markets of the future. For example, more and more customers are shopping from home over the Internet – even buying their regular groceries from retailers such as Sainsbury's and Tesco. In what other ways are markets changing because of the influences of e-marketing?

# Marketing mix

Once the marketing objectives have been agreed, marketing plans must be developed to achieve goals. The marketing mix provides an excellent framework for developing marketing plans. The marketing mix for physical goods is generally accepted to be made up of four parts (the 4Ps), namely: product, price, promotion and place. With services an additional three elements are included: people, processes and physical evidence; this gives us the 7Ps.

### Product

Product means the combination of goods and services that are offered to the target consumer. For example, Apple offers a range of iPod products along with the iTunes service. The two aspects together make up the product being offered to the consumer.

### Price

Price is the amount of money consumers have to pay to acquire the product. This can vary considerably. For example, the store PC World offers discounts and credit terms which all combine to alter the price individual consumers pay for a laptop.

▲ The marketing mix – 'a new improved recipe'

### Place

Place describes where and how the consumer can obtain the product. Tesco has stores all over the country but place does not have to be a physical location. Nowadays consumers can buy such products as insurance, holidays and books over the telephone, via the Internet or through their TV remote control. Producers have to carefully choose the best method to ensure consumers can find their product in an appropriate place when they decide to make a purchase.

### Promotion

Promotion describes the activities undertaken to ensure the consumer knows about the product and its capabilities. It usually combines advertising, sales promotion, public relations and personal selling. These terms are explained in Unit 9 Exploring Creative Product Promotion.

### People

A major factor in how the customer perceives the service and the degree of satisfaction received by the customer is determined by the person actually providing the service. Often the extent to which a customer is happy with the service is due to the attitude, skills and appearance of the people the customer comes in contact with. In some cases the customer will purchase a service primarily because of the people they deal with. It is crucial to have the right people delivering a service, because often a service is only delivered once. You cannot ask the customer to call back so a hair stylist can have another go at providing a decent haircut – it is simply too late.

Organisations must therefore invest in training such as understanding company policies on delivery, appearance such as uniforms and selling skills such as describing product benefits.

## Processes

The systems employed by an organisation must be customer-friendly. These systems include all the processes which might involve the customer from handling the delivery of a product, ordering an out-of-stock item, accepting the return of a faulty product, undertaking a repair and dealing with a complaint.

It happens too frequently that customers are required to complete complicated forms if they want to make a complaint, wait weeks for an estimate for a repair or make numerous phone calls to negotiate compensation when something goes seriously wrong. You have probably experienced such annoying situations yourself.

## Physical evidence

This describes those factors that can help to shape the customer's perception and image of the service being provided. For example, you have probably noticed that many hotels provide writing paper, pens, entertainment and information in their rooms. This is designed to convey an image of caring and quality. Fast food restaurants like to pay attention to the décor and how it is furnished. Shopping centres such as the Metro Centre near Gateshead strive to create a special atmosphere for shoppers. At garages, when car owners take their car to be serviced they may be met by a receptionist wearing a smart uniform in an area with comfortable seats and tables with complimentary drinks available, Internet access points and magazines and newspapers to browse through to complete that special atmosphere.

It is now increasingly recognised that all products have a service component and indeed for many physical products the service element can be the most important aspect of customer choice. Because of this, some parts of the service marketing mix are being applied to physical products.

For each part of the marketing mix the marketing manager needs to develop plans. For example, they must consider what prices they will charge and what should be provided in terms of a uniform and training for people who meet customers.

## Blending the elements of the marketing mix

The secret of success lies in blending the elements of the marketing mix effectively, as each individual product requires a different blend. Ice cream producers need to ensure their product tastes pleasant but the most important marketing mix elements are probably place and promotion. People who want ice creams need to find them in a variety of convenient locations, such as local shops and station kiosks. They are unlikely to search extensively to find their preferred ice cream if it is not there but will choose an alternative. Promotion is used to make a particular ice cream stand out from the crowd. The successful launch of Magnum Gold was mainly due to widespread distribution and high profile advertising.

### Practice point

Describe the marketing mix of an organisation selling consumer products such as cars, a public organisation like a school or college and a charity such as Cancer Research.

### Take it further

Compare the marketing mix for each of the three organisations – highlighting and justifying the parts of the mix which are especially important for each organisation. Discuss any changes you might make to the present marketing mix for the organisations investigated.

# Limitations and constraints on marketing

Marketing managers are encouraged to act responsibly through a number of constraints. There are some laws which have to be observed, although generally marketing 'polices itself' through Codes of Practice published and monitored by organisations such as the Advertising Standards Authority. In addition, professional behaviour is encouraged by pressure groups (such as Greenpeace and the Consumers' Association) and consumerist activity (such as TV programmes like *Watchdog*).

**Common law** and **statutory law** protects the consumer and ensures marketing is carried out in a responsible manner.

## Key Terms

**Common law** Developed through the courts, this is based on previous decisions. Precedent, as it is called, requires the courts to follow past decisions in cases with similar facts and covering the same points of law.

**Statutory law** This is created when Parliament passes new legislation through an Act of Parliament.

## Legislation

The makers and suppliers of products owe a 'duty of care' to consumers. If a customer feels that a product is in some way harmful, they can bring a claim against the producer. Different Acts of Parliament have been passed which have strengthened consumer protection.

### Sale of Goods Act 1979

This Act was amended by the Sale and Supply of Goods Act 1994 and the Sale and Supply of Goods to Consumers Regulations 2002. Under this legislation goods bought from a trader should be:

- of satisfactory quality
- fit for any particular purpose made known to the seller
- as described.

Satisfactory quality means that the goods would meet the standard a reasonable person would regard as satisfactory, taking into account the description of the goods and the price. The quality of the goods includes their state and condition including their appearance and finish, freedom from minor defects, safety and durability. They should also be fit for all purposes for which goods of that kind are commonly supplied. A consumer's rights under this Act are against the person who sold the goods and not the manufacturer.

From 31 March 2003 consumers have had more rights under the Sale and Supply of Goods to Consumers Regulations 2002. If a product that was faulty at the time of sale is returned to the retailer, you are legally entitled to a full refund, a reasonable amount of compensation or a repair or replacement product.

**Guarantees**: where goods are offered with a consumer guarantee, the consumer can request that the guarantee be made available in writing and should give details of how to make a claim under the guarantee.

### Trade Descriptions Act 1968

This prohibits false or misleading statements about products. The Act is designed to ensure that the quantity or size of a good is correctly described including:

- the way they were made or processed (such as hand made)
- what they are made of (such as plastic)
- their fitness for the purpose for which they were intended including strength, performance and behaviour (such as unbreakable)
- any physical characteristics they possess (e.g. fitted with disc brakes)
- a statement that the goods have been tested and/or approved (this is usually to British Standards)
- where they were made (such as made in China)
- when they were made
- information about their history (such as reconditioned).

### Consumer Credit Act 2006

This aims to protect the rights of consumers when they purchase goods on credit. All traders who make such agreements must obtain a licence from the Office of Fair Trading. The Act lays down rules covering:

- The form and content of agreements – customers must have a full understanding of the agreement with terms and conditions clearly stated within any literature.
- The method of calculating the Annual Percentage Rate (APR) of the Total Charge for Credit.
- The procedures to be adopted in the event of default, termination and early settlement.
- The provision of annual statements on credit agreements to borrowers.
- The provision of arrears notices and information sheets for borrowers.
- Guidelines for lenders about 'extortionate credit bargains' to prevent borrowers being charged excessive amounts.

## Data Protection Act 1998

This Act has assumed greater significance to consumers as marketers have increasingly been using direct mail techniques to communicate with them. The information stored by marketers on electronic databases must be:

- obtained fairly and lawfully
- used only for the purposes stated during collection
- adequate, relevant and not excessive in relation to the intended use
- accurate and where necessary kept up to date
- not kept for longer than necessary
- protected from unauthorised use
- available for inspection and correction by the individual
- subject to procedures to prevent unlawful processing, accidental loss, destruction and damage to personal data
- protected from transfer to an area outside the European Economic Area (EEA), unless adequate protection exists for that data in the area.

A new act gives consumers greater control on how the data can be used. It is now illegal to telephone or fax a business or person who has registered with the Telephone Preference Service (TPS). Consumers supplying personal details through electronic commerce must now give permission for their details to be passed to other interested parties.

## Voluntary constraints

Voluntary Codes of Practice are statements by a committee or organisation about methods of working recommended as 'good practice' for the firms and individuals within an industry. Organisations who 'volunteer' to abide by the codes are allowed to display symbols showing customers that they participate in such schemes. The codes normally have no legal backing but use other ways of encouraging compliance. An example of an organisation that publishes and administers a Code of Practice would be the Advertising Standards Authority (www.asa.org.uk).

The ASA is responsible for all advertisements and promotions across all media, including new advertising media such as SMS messaging and email promotions. Their advertising standards do not currently apply to websites. The rules governing this type of activity are contained in two Codes of Practice: the British Code of Advertising, Sales Promotion and Direct Marketing (CAP Code) for non-broadcast advertisers, and the BCAP Code which covers TV and radio. Headline claims, terms and conditions, small print, pricing claims, special offers and comparisons are just some of the areas covered by the advertising codes. There is a range of measures the ASA can use to deal with problematic advertisers, including agreeing to approve an advertisement before publication or broadcast, referring the matter to the Office of Fair Trading under the Control of Misleading Advertisements Regulation or asking media owners to remove the adverts from their schedules.

The ASA protects the consumer by helping advertisers, agencies and the media to produce advertisements that will not mislead or offend consumers. The basic principles are the advertisements should be:

- legal, decent, honest and truthful
- prepared with a sense of responsibility to the consumer and society
- in line with the principles of fair competition generally accepted in business.

Just one complaint can trigger an investigation, although a large number of complaints does not necessarily mean an organisation will have to withdraw an advertisement. KFC's Zinger Crunch Salad TV commercial generated a record number of complaints because people were concerned that the call centre staff were shown talking with their mouths full which would encourage bad manners. Interestingly the ASA did not object to the advertisement, because it suggested that table manners are taught over a period of time and were unlikely to be compromised by a single advertisement.

Marketing managers operate in an environment where the boundaries of acceptability are shifting all the time. Changes in public policy (such as concerns about binge drinking), technological developments (such as spam email promotions) and public opinion (such as concerns about obesity) all impact on what is judged as the acceptable content of advertisements.

## Practice point

Using the checklists provided for each Act and the Argos catalogue, decide whether Argos is following the rules. Find some catalogue descriptions of the toys it sells and consider how well they conform to the Trade Descriptions Act. Then look at the CAP Code in respect of children and discuss how closely they adhere to the guidelines. The website www.asa.org.uk is a useful resource.

## Take it further

How effective do you think Codes of Practice are compared with legislation to encourage acceptable behaviour?

Write a toy description for the Argos catalogue which fulfils the requirements of the Trade Descriptions Act and the ASA Code of Advertising Practice.

## Direct Marketing Association (DMA)

The DMA is concerned with all forms of direct response marketing, e.g. email marketing and direct mailshots. It protects consumers from inappropriate, unethical behaviour by unscrupulous or ignorant businesses and promotes best practice through codes of conduct. In addition to the general code of practice the association has developed others, including the Code of Practice for eCommerce; for Electronic Communications to Children On Line; for SMS Marketing and for Email Marketing.

Most people in the UK have bought a product or service using direct marketing methods. However, despite its proven use and success, a proportion of consumers still do not welcome direct mail, telephone or fax offers. To assist them, the DMA administers a group of preference services that allow consumers to register their details, free of charge, to stop unsolicited sales and marketing communications by telephone, fax, mail and email.

▲ The logos of the ASA and DMA

## Pressure groups and consumerism

Pressure groups are organisations formed by people with a common interest who join together in order to further that interest. Pressure groups watch organisations and influence how they act. They can be extremely effective in changing organisational behaviour. Examples are shown in the table below.

| Pressure group | Example of concerns |
|---|---|
| Drinkaware (www.drinakaware.co.uk) | Reducing the amount and impact of excessive drinking. Encouraging drinks companies to include on labels acceptable consumption quantities. |
| Confederation of British Industry (www.cbi.org.uk) | CBI promotes business interests and encourages good business practices. |
| Amnesty International (www.amnesty.org.uk) | Exposes businesses that are using unacceptable trading methods, such as the store Zara which was allegedly buying shoes from Portuguese producers who were using child labour. |
| Citizens Advice (www.adviceguide.org.uk) | Publishes many fact sheets explaining consumer rights. |

▲ Consumer rights

Consumerism can be defined as a 'social movement seeking to augment the rights of buyers in relation to sellers'. Advocates of consumerism argue that consumers have four main rights as shown in the illustration above.

Before the 1960s, consumers had few rights and had to rely on their own vigilance and common sense. The phrase 'Let the buyer beware' summed up the position; manufacturers and suppliers of goods and services had considerably more power than consumers.

While some businesses may view consumerism as a threat, more enlightened organisations recognise it as an opportunity to identify and respond to changing consumer needs and wants.

▲ No organisation would voluntarily put warnings of this nature on their product

| Organisation/activity | Nature of activity |
| --- | --- |
| *Watchdog, Rogue Traders* | Exposing on national television traders using unacceptable trading practices. |
| Consumers' Association (www.which.net) | Publishes product reports, *Which?* magazine and fact sheets reviewing business practices and informing people of their rights. |
| Office of Fair Trading (www.oft.gov.uk) | Helps to make markets work effectively because when businesses are in open, fair and vigorous competition consumers have genuine power. Ensures consumer legislation and regulations are enforced and that action is taken against unfair traders. |

## Practice point

You can now consider the impact of pressure groups. A pressure group concerned with the general rights of consumers is the Consumers' Association – which produces a magazine called *Which?*. Using the Internet site www.which.net look at the rights consumers can expect from an organisation. Consider whether you believe an organisation like Argos is providing those rights.

## Take it further

Have you any ideas about additional rights which might benefit consumers?

What might be the key points in a Code of Practice concerning sending promotional SMS messages?

### Acceptable language

This is a subjective area but the rules that tend to govern whether certain words are acceptable are based on the target audience for the marketing activity. Images and words that are relevant to the product being advertised are likely to be accepted, but may be rejected when they are unrelated to the product. For example, Wonderbra's bold approach with 'Hello boys' was acceptable, while other advertisers using a similar approach have been asked to withdraw their adverts. Humour can often help to mitigate offence, but if pushed too far the joke may become offensive. Blasphemy – treating something sacred with irreverence – is likely to cause offence and alienate customers.

Adverts which use text messaging language are probably not seen as acceptable by some people, but if the advert is targeted at young adults it probably would be acceptable. You might also be surprised to learn that exaggerations and obvious untruths are permitted – for example, an estate agent could feature Hampton Court on a leaflet because the public are unlikely to believe that it is for sale.

## Outcome activity 3.1

### The great cider revival

Not so long ago, it was the height of cool among the nation's younger drinkers to insert a wedge of lime into the top of their Mexican lager. These days, accessorizing your beer with citrus fruit is passé. The latest summer trend has been to drink cider over ice from a pint glass.

Magners Cider developed its entire marketing campaign around the concept of pouring cider from a bottle into a pint glass filled with ice cubes. It led to market growth of 7% in volume and 13% in terms of value over the previous year.

While the hot summer stimulated demand the product was portrayed successfully as a premium high quality product competing with premium lagers such as Stella Artois. This change has been expensive to achieve with spending on marketing of over £20m. Producers hope that the fashion will not simply fade away but that the drink will maintain its appeal and become what the industry calls a 'repertoire' drink.

There has also been a lot of product innovation in the category with the creation of organic ciders and single-variety (made from one apple) ciders mirroring recent wine developments.

The new drinks have been developed at the expense of alcopops and other 'ready-to-drink' brands such as Smirnoff Ice. Drinkers aged in their mid-twenties (sometimes called the maturing alcopop generation) have rejected alcopops that came in bright green or blue colours and are now preferring to drink a natural product like cider. It is hoped our emerging preference to drink colder drinks, following a similar trend in America, will also help sustain its appeal.

**Pass**

1. Describe the concept and principles of marketing. **P1**
2. Describe how the key concepts and principles of marketing have been applied by Jaguar Cars and Magners Cider. **P2**

**Merit**

Compare the effectiveness of the concepts and principles applied to the marketing of the products of Jaguar Cars and Magners Cider. 

**Distinction**

Evaluate the concepts and principles applied to the marketing of products by Jaguar Cars and Magners Cider and make recommendations for improvement. 

## Grading tips

**Pass** 

'Describe' here means to write about the characteristics of the marketing mix, the limitations and constraints on marketing and all aspects covered by the principles of marketing. You should describe the marketing mix for both Jaguar Cars and Magners Cider, show how they have followed the principles of marketing and then finish with a section devoted to how they have been encouraged to act responsibly when marketing their products.

**Merit**

Consider producing a table showing how Jaguar Cars and Magners Cider have reacted to the concepts and principles of marketing. Highlight the ones you think significantly helped each organisation to be effective and comment about the ones you think perhaps made a lesser contribution.

| Principles/ concepts | Jaguar Cars | Magners Cider |
|---|---|---|
| Marketing mix | | |
| Product | Plenty of new products which are technically excellent but lack modern styling | A product which has capitalised on hot summer and emerging trend for 'iced' drinks |

**Distinction** 

You need to make a series of judgements as to how well the concepts and principles of marketing were applied by Jaguar Cars and Magners Cider. The content of the merit task should help considerably. This evaluation should reveal areas for improvement; use these findings to generate a series of recommendations. Show the benefits of any changes you propose.

# 3.2 How and why marketing research is conducted by organisations

## Marketing research

Marketing research aims to help organisations make effective decisions by providing information that can inform the decision-making process. Research provides information about customers, competitors and the overall market environment, as shown in the table on the following page.

▼ Information obtained through market research

| Marketing research theme | Provides information on |
| --- | --- |
| Customers | Consumer trends that can be used for forecasting future customer needs and preferences (such as colours), lifestyle (such as eating out) and aspirations (such as career plans). |
| Competitors | Comparison of products, prices, distribution methods and promotional methods.<br>Profit and overall financial position.<br>Likely reaction to competition – how they will respond if another company increases advertising. |
| Market environment | Market size and market shares.<br>Economic influences (such as expected performance of economy).<br>Social influences (such as increasing number of people over 65 years old).<br>Technological influences (such as impact of the Internet). |

## Primary and secondary research

The two methods of research are known as **primary** and **secondary research**. Organisations should undertake secondary research first because this is research that is already available (in libraries or in existing reports) and is consequently cheaper and quicker to obtain than primary research. Secondary research makes use of research already carried out by somebody else for some other marketing project. Both types of research can be **internal** (information held inside an organisation) or **external** (information that is outside an organisation, such as government statistics).

### Key Terms

**Primary research** Carried out to find new information required for a marketing research project, which has never previously been collected.

**Secondary research** Makes use of work already carried out by someone else for some other marketing project or other purpose.

Primary research is usually carried out to answer questions that are beyond the scope of the secondary research currently available. For example, an organisation wishing to gauge reaction to a new advertising idea is unlikely to find the answer in research already available.

## Qualitative and quantitative research

Primary and secondary research can be either qualitative or quantitative in its nature. **Quantitative research** produces numbers and figures – such as the number and percentage of consumers who are aware of a particular service. Quantitative research can therefore be used to:

- measure product sales week by week
- track prices across a variety of retailers and brands
- estimate market shares of competing brands
- estimate market and segment sizes.

**Qualitative research** provides data on why people buy – what motivates them to buy – or their impression of products, services or advertisements. Qualitative research can be used to:

- investigate customer attitudes towards an organisation
- ascertain consumer reactions to changes in price
- ascertain information about consumer preferences, lifestyles and aspirations.

### Key Terms

**Internal research data** This is secondary information held inside an organisation, such as sales records and customer complaint reports.

**External research data** This is secondary data that is available outside an organisation, such as government statistics.

**Quantitative research** Produces numbers and figures, such as the number and percentage of consumers who are aware of a brand.

**Qualitative research** Provides information of a qualitative nature, such as about why people buy, what motivates them to buy or their impression of, for example, products and advertisements.

### Uses and limitations

Secondary research sources, in particular, are widely used as they tend to be widely available and are cheaper than carrying out primary research. However, there can be some problems with this type of information:

- The information may not be detailed enough to help organisations make decisions about their own operations. Reports tend to be about an industry as a whole rather than a particular sector.
- The information may have been collected to promote the status of an industry and the figures may be inaccurate.
- Markets change rapidly and the information may be quickly out of date.
- The method in which the research was gathered may not be reliable.

Nevertheless, secondary research can be useful in providing a comprehensive insight into a market in terms of size, segments and trends.

## Primary research

### Methods and purposes

Primary research is carried out to answer questions that are beyond the scope of the secondary research currently available. A variety of methods are available to a marketing manager considering doing some primary marketing research.

| Primary research method | Characteristics |
|---|---|
| Observation | Useful when a topic first needs to be explored, for example how children play with a new toy. There is no communication between the researcher and the people being observed.<br>This method also includes the 'mystery shopper' concept where a researcher visits a store acting as a consumer to obtain facts about perhaps customer service and selling techniques. They can be used to assess performance of own products/stores as well as competition. |
| Experimentation | Researchers use it to try to identify the impact of a change in something such as price or packaging format while keeping everything else the same. Usually undertaken in an artificial environment such as a special store which is not used by everyday shoppers. |
| Surveys | Use questionnaires to collect data by face-to-face interviews, using the post, email, telephone or Internet. Used to obtain data about attitudes, awareness, motivations and lifestyle. Easy to administer but **respondents** may be unwilling or unable to answer questions. Can be used to gather data on own organisation as well as competitors. Need to ask a significant number of people (more than 1000) before conclusions about overall market environment can be drawn. |
| E-marketing | Nowadays websites can reveal plenty of useful research information, for example which products are being viewed by surfers and from where (such as Germany). Much consumer information can be obtained when surfers are asked to register to access special areas on a site. If they then buy something a record of interests can be collected with some sites making suggestions about other potential purchases.<br>In a similar way, loyalty cards issued by organisations like Tesco (Club Card) and Debenhams (Nectar) enable organisations to gather a vast amount of data about customers. These organisations have been prepared to invest heavily in these cards not to give consumers more discounts, but to obtain vital marketing data. |
| Focus groups | An interview conducted by a researcher among a small group of consumers in an unstructured and natural manner. Good for gaining insights as people feel sufficiently relaxed to discuss their feelings. Mainly used to gauge reactions to new products, advertising ideas and the overall image of an organisation. Can be used to assess competitor activity – but not enough people involved for conclusions to be drawn about the overall market. |
| Panels | Consists of a number of consumers who have agreed to provide data over an extended time period (such as three months). Very useful for obtaining overall market environment data, such as market share of major brands, while it can also identify changes brought about by more advertising or lower sales promotion activity. |
| Field trials | Similar to experimentation except carried out under actual market conditions – for example in a proper store. They tend to be used when a long time period is required (such as assessing consumer views on a washing machine after a prolonged period of use). Can be used to ascertain performance of competitive products. |

▲ Experimentation cannot explain consumer reaction

## Key Terms

**Respondent** A person who is asked and agrees to participate in a marketing research project.

### Practice point

You need to investigate the market for MP3 players. Taking each primary research technique in turn, describe whether it would provide data about consumers, competitors and the overall market environment.

## Accessability, fitness for purpose, validity, cost, time and reliability

Knowing the strengths and limitations of the various marketing research methods is very important for marketing managers. They have to pick the right one for the issues being investigated. The factors which determine the suitability of a method are accessibility, fitness for purpose, validity, cost, time and reliability. Check these key aspects in the table on page 117.

Organisations have to select the methods that will provide the data they need. The costs will prevent them using all of the different methods while some will not produce the information they are seeking. All these methods are considered in more detail in Unit 10 Introduction to Market Research.

### Take it further

Depending on your decisions, give an example of the sort of information you might obtain from each technique about consumers, competitors and the overall market environment.

Which methods would you choose to use first given the opportunity? Justify your recommendation(s).

▼ Suitability of marketing research methods

| Suitability factors | Key characteristics |
|---|---|
| Accessibility | Not every method is available to all organisations. Postal and email surveys are something all managers can consider using. But the accessibility of methods which require investment in technology (such as observation) and special facilities (such as a laboratory store) can only be considered by large, wealthy organisations. |
| Fit for purpose | Each marketing research method has strengths and limitations in terms of the type of data it can collect. Face-to-face personal interviews and focus groups are excellent for gathering qualitative information. But they are not 'fit for the purpose' of obtaining quantitative data. That type of data would normally be collected using consumer panels or surveys. A focus group would be a good way of investigating the type of facilities required for a leisure centre whereas a postal survey would be sufficient to ascertain whether staff were courteous to customers. (See Unit 10 Introduction to Market Research for a review of the various methods.) |
| Validity | Researchers must ensure the data is valid. Respondents can sometimes provide a seemingly sensible answer without understanding the question; the answer under such circumstances would be considered invalid. Do you consider inflation to be too high? This can produce a sensible answer without the respondent understanding the term inflation. Questions have to be constructed carefully to reduce the possibility of invalid answers. Methods which record actual behaviour such as observation, website statistics and panel data naturally produce valid answers. Focus groups and personal interviews which can explore a topic in depth are also considered to produce consistently valid results. |
| Cost | Organisations need to make sure the research they undertake is not determined by cost but by the information required. A postal survey might be appropriate to find out how well staff at a leisure centre are treating customers. But personal interviews or focus groups might be a more effective way to investigate which new facilities should be built.<br>Field trials, experimentation and personal interviews are generally expensive because of the time and effort needed to find people who are willing to participate, and then to organise their attendance at a venue.<br>Methods that require significant investment in technology, such as loyalty cards, e-marketing and observation, can be costly options for organisations. |
| Time | Telephone interviews, web statistics and loyalty cards can collect information quickly and produce virtually instantaneous results. Personal interviews can take much longer to organise, especially when home interviews have to be completed. Postal, email and Internet surveys can take a long time to be returned by respondents.<br>Observation, personal interviews and focus group data take time to be analysed – tapes have to be viewed or listened to, perhaps several times, before the key issues begin to emerge from the opinions expressed.<br>Sometimes there is not enough time to complete the preferred research. For example, if field trials and consumer panels are to be genuinely effective they need plenty of time to operate so that patterns, issues and changes over time can emerge. Production deadlines may not always allow these techniques to be used. |
| Reliability | Researchers need to satisfy themselves that the data is reliable. If they ask the same question to the same person on different occasions and received the same answer then the response is considered reliable. This can be a limitation of surveys where perhaps people are not concentrating, are in a hurry when completing the survey or simply do not care what answers they give.<br>Focus groups and personal interviews can give differing results when a topic is being explored. When this happens, further interviews or focus groups are undertaken until a common view begins to emerge. |

## Thinking point

You have decided to conduct some primary research among your fellow students about a new course your school or college may offer next year. You are uncertain whether to use focus groups or personal face-to-face interviews to gather the data. Using the table above as a checklist, make a recommendation about the best method to use.

## Types of sampling and accuracy

Research involving everybody in the population is called a census. This is seldom possible because of the expense. Consequently, samples are used; in marketing terms this means using a small number of individuals to gain an insight into the views of the whole group. The two ways of selecting respondents are **probability** and **non-probability sampling.** Five probability sampling techniques – random sampling, systematic sampling, stratified sampling, cluster sampling and

## Key Terms

**Probability sampling** This means that everybody in the population has the same chance of being selected, just as in the Lottery draw every ball has an equal chance of being selected at any time. This requires everybody in the population to be known and allocated a number.

**Non-probability sampling** This relies on the judgement of the researcher in terms of selecting respondents.

multi-stage sampling – are discussed in detail in Unit 10 Introduction to Market Research. Commonly used non-probability techniques include convenience sampling, judgement sampling and quota sampling. They are all discussed in more detail in Unit 10.

| Probability sampling | Non-probability sampling |
|---|---|
| Results can be projected to represent the total population.<br>Results are clear and not in doubt.<br>Researchers can be sure of obtaining information from a representative group of the population being investigated.<br>Respondent selection and sample design significantly increase the cost and time. | Cost is significantly lower than probability sampling.<br>Sample sizes tend to be smaller.<br>Researchers can target important respondents.<br>The results reveal likely views.<br>Researcher does not know how representative the sample is of the population being investigated. |

Errors can occur in the sampling process that affect the overall results of the research project:

- A low response rate may mean that the final sample is unrepresentative of the whole population.
- Respondents might give the answer that they feel will please the researcher.
- Inappropriate answers might be given because the respondent is tired, does not fully understand the question or simply cannot remember something accurately.
- Respondents usually feel they should give a socially acceptable answer to sensitive or potentially embarrassing questions.
- In some way the interviewer might influence the answer, record the answer incorrectly or falsify the response.

## Planning the marketing research, defining objectives and identifying needs

Professionally organised research projects will follow a particular planning cycle. To ensure effective research is undertaken an organisation should do the following:

- Define the objectives and identify the information it needs. It is important that the researcher defines the requirements of the research effectively. Defining the problem too narrowly will mean vital data is missed. Defining the problem too broadly will mean time and resources will be wasted gathering unwanted information.
- Design an appropriate research plan. This is a complex area and involves several major considerations, including whether to undertake primary and/or secondary research, the selection of an appropriate research technique (such as a survey), and the type of sampling plan required (such as random sampling).
- Consider how to collect the data. The researcher must be quite sure what information needs collecting and what the organisation already possesses.
- Analyse and interpret the data effectively. Information analysis usually involves taking the information from a variety of sources and drawing relevant conclusions before arriving at appropriate recommendations.
- Plan for the effective presentation of the findings. Information has no value unless it helps managers to make better decisions. This may involve a presentation to senior managers or preparation of a PowerPoint presentation for email circulation.

## Sources of bias

Bias is defined as the difference between the answer obtained from respondents and the truth. The ordering of potential responses in a multiple-choice question is important as it can influence a respondent's choice, especially when they are slightly unsure of the answer. Research has shown that respondents are more likely to choose answers at the beginning or end of a list rather than in the middle. To reduce the impact of this, interviewers are asked to rotate the sequence of questions.

Questions that may reveal the respondent in a poor light should be avoided, as many people will give the answer that they think will gain approval rather than the truthful answer. It is important that the researchers are well trained, otherwise the way they ask the question may encourage a certain answer. They must be people who can record answers correctly, while they should not feel they can falsify an answer if perhaps they hold strong views on the matter themselves.

### Electronic data collection

Organisations which ask web surfers to register to browse a website or which collect information during a purchase can gather very detailed information. Loyalty cards perform this function for some retailers. The information can be used to create sophisticated databases that can be used for a number or purposes:

- identifying an organisation's best customers
- sending direct mail letters and email newsletters about products that might interest a customer
- recognising customers who have just bought a product and contacting them to reinforce the good sense of such a purchase
- cross-selling related and complementary products
- providing a personalised customer service.

**Thinking point**

Your school or college wants to construct a database to help it identify the needs of its students. Draw up a list of the information which it might be useful to have on the database. For six items on your list describe how the school might use the data to improve life in the school or college.

### Data analysis

A 'data warehouse' is a storage area able to hold vast amounts of data from a variety of sources. The storage is organised to make it easy to find and use the data. It can be updated using the scanning of barcodes at checkouts and loyalty card data.

Data mining is the technique which describes the process of exploring these large amounts of data, with the objective of discovering hidden relationships or patterns which provide an insight into customer behaviour. For example, there is the well-known story of how Wal-Mart noticed a relationship between the sales of nappies (diapers in the USA) and beer in their American stores. On investigation they found that men on their way home from work were stopping to buy diapers and treating themselves for helping the mother by purchasing some beer for the forthcoming evening. So Wal-Mart began to display beer near the diapers to further encourage the indulgence.

**Thinking point**

Schools and colleges nowadays issue students with ID cards which could be used to collect valuable data. What sort of data could be collected by the school or college?

If you were in charge of marketing at the school or college how might the data be useful?

Organisations are obliged to treat all personal and sensitive information about customers as private and confidential. They should not disclose the information to a third party (such as an associated business) without the written consent of the customer.

Under the Data Protection Act 1998, individuals have a right to see personal information held about them on an organisation's records. The organisation can charge the customer a fee to disclose the information.

## Secondary research

Secondary research is research that has already been carried out by somebody else for some other reason or marketing project.

### Importance

Secondary research is important because it:

- may answer some of the organisation's research needs quickly and inexpensively, for example market share of major competitors

- could assist in the design of a primary research project, for example identify what type of people to interview
- should enable researchers to interpret primary research data better because secondary research is excellent at providing background information
- could provide a source of comparative data to help validate primary data results
- may provide data that cannot be collected in any other way, such as information on government spending.

## Sources of data and information – internal and external

Secondary research can be obtained from a variety of internal and external sources. There is a large amount of secondary data available to the marketing researcher, although only a very small proportion of the existing data may be useful for any one project. Marketing researchers should know where to obtain relevant internal and external information. Internal secondary data is produced by an organisation during its day-to-day activities:

- EPOS (electronic point of sale) systems used by retailers to record, for example, sales by store and product
- loyalty scheme records of purchases by individual customers
- sales by sales person, region and even country
- website statistics showing what surfers are looking at
- e-transaction records show what surfers have bought
- accounting records about how much customers have spent or owe
- reports from sales people about market developments.

In many cases internal research data may be collected in an unorganised way with managers having little idea about what is actually available.

External secondary data refers to information that comes from a wide variety of sources outside an organisation. Some of the more useful external sources of secondary research are described below.

## News reports

News reports are a source of very useful data.

- Newspapers produce country and industry reports on a regular basis as well as having articles about products, markets and consumer trends.
- Magazines such as *The Economist* contain plenty of useful marketing information.
- TV and radio current affairs and news programmes are useful, especially those on Radio 4.
- The Consumers' Association – publishers of *Which?* – can be a valuable source of information.

◀ Secondary research should be relevant

## Practice point

You will be surprised how much marketing information appears in the national newspapers in a fortnight. Choose an industry and produce a booklet from the relevant articles you spot over a period of two weeks.

## Take it further

Summarise each report in a short sentence and then indicate whether it provides information about consumers, competitors or the overall market environment.

Comment on the effectiveness of this simple method of acquiring marketing research data.

### Trade journals

These are magazines which are aimed at certain industry sectors, such as *Marketing Week*. They can contain useful industry information in terms of buying trends and new technical developments.

### Market analyses (including online sources) from specialist agencies

Market research companies produce reports on the market and products and then offer them to organisations with an interest in that particular sector – producers, retailers and suppliers. The reports are expensive to buy. The market leading companies are Mintel, Dun & Bradstreet and DataStream. They can be accessed online.

Mintel produces a wide variety of reports covering market size, market segments, main brands, levels of advertising expenditure, factors determining market growth and future forecasts. They are also available online at www.mintel.com.

Dun & Bradstreet (http://dbuk.dnb.com) publishes, for example, comprehensive financial reports on companies and on the trading prospects in a particular industry. Other Dun & Bradstreet reports, using the name MarketLine, can be accessed online from http://dbic.datamonitor.com on industries, companies and countries.

Thomson Financial (www.thomson.com) produces DataStream, a valuable source of current financial data including stock market share prices, historical economic data, future economic forecasts and exchange rate information.

### Government statistics

These are principally supplied by National Statistics, Eurostat (the statistical office of the European Union) and the OECD (Organisation for Economic Co-operation and Development).

- National Statistics Family Expenditure Survey – details how families spend their money.
- National Statistics Social Trends paints a broad picture of Britain and how it is changing.

A fuller range of secondary research sources is discussed in Unit 10 Introduction to Market Research.

## Practice point

Look at the contents of the Family Expenditure Survey or Social Trends and note the topic areas it covers.

## Take it further

For each information area comment on whether it contains valuable data on consumers, competitors and the overall market.

Identify some markets where this information may be particularly valuable, explaining your reasons.

## Outcome activity 3.2

Ahmed, a business student, has carried out some research into Magners' primary and secondary research methods. He has come up with the following initial results:

**Pass**

Describe how marketing research information is likely to be used by Magners Cider to understand the behaviour of customers, competitors and market environment. P3

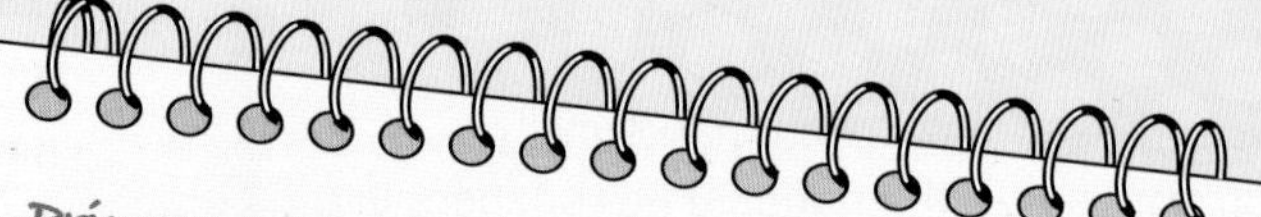

**Primary Research**

- Focus groups with young adults aged 20-25 – four groups comprising eight participants.
- A panel of 20 young adults aged 20-25 completing a diary of their drinking habits over a three-month period.

**Secondary Research**

- A review of the Family Expenditure Survey.
- Purchase the latest Mintel report on the alcoholic drinks market.
- Summary from the ONS publication Social Trends about aspects of British society likely to have an impact on the alcoholic drinks market.

## Grading tips

**Pass** 

Consider the likely topics that would have been discussed in the focus group. Think about what information the consumer panel might reveal about this market.

Look at a copy of the Family Expenditure Survey, Social Trends and a Mintel report.

Produce a table summarising and organising the information you have acquired using the classifications of consumer, competitors and market environment.

| Research method | Information obtained about customers, competitors and the market environment |
|---|---|
| Focus groups | Customers<br>· Would now drink cider instead of alcopops<br>· Cold drinks 'over ice' now very much enjoyed<br>Competitors<br>· Seems a product similar in image to Stella Artois |

# Using marketing research

Marketing information aims to help an organisation make effective marketing decisions that ultimately enable the organisation to achieve its objectives. It provides information about consumers, competitors, different sorts of markets (such as business to business and business to consumer) and developments within markets (such as new tastes) that require a reaction. This information is then used to develop new products, devise promotional campaigns, pricing policies and select places where the product can be bought by customers.

## Key themes and business objectives

Key marketing research themes are highlighted below.

## Competitors' activities

It is also vital that organisations take into account the activity of competitors when developing marketing activities. The acquisition of competitive information can be very useful to an organisation. A straightforward way of investigating the activity of competitors is to look at four aspects – financial, organisational, production and product, and marketing. It is a genuine marketing research activity. The table below shows how an organisation might use the acquired data.

| Competitor profile | Information gained | Possible use of information |
|---|---|---|
| Organisational | Sort of new people being recruited | Suggest new international markets are being targeted. |
| Production and product | Acquisition of new machines | Particular type of new product being developed. |
| Marketing | Best-selling products | Guide new product development plans. |
| Financial | Profit being generated | Show ability to invest in new products and/or promotional activity.<br>Indicate how much prices could be reduced to maintain sales. |

### Thinking point

Complete a competitor survey of your college or school, using where relevant the framework illustrated above. Some of the points that you may include could be courses offered, impact of marketing to potential students and their parents and people who have been recruited recently. Then draw up a list of conclusions about the school which your local competitor might well discover if they did a similar exercise.

## Understanding customers' lifestyles, preferences and aspirations

Different marketing research methods, such as focus groups and personal face-to-face interviews, can be used to establish the lifestyles, preferences and aspirations of customers. Such methods can help an organisation assess a new 'fitness' product in a variety of practical ways, as illustrated on page 124.

| Lifestyle | • How it would contribute to their lifestyle? (improve fitness)<br>• What might be the extent of that contribution? (daily or weekly) |
|---|---|
| Preferences | • Whether they like to pay by debit or credit card<br>• When they like to receive deliveries – in the evening or at weekends |
| Aspirations | • What might be their planned next step? (run in half marathon)<br>• Have they a long-term objective? (run the London Marathon) |

◀ Assesing a new 'fitness' product

Within markets not all groups are the same – they do not have the same tastes or want the same things. It's helpful to think of a market as an orange. It appears to be a single entity, yet when you peel off the skin you find that it's made up of a number of segments – each of which exists within the whole. The segments in an orange are more or less identical, but in markets they are different in terms of size and character.

Sophisticated segmentation techniques combine marketing research from many sources to identify classifications of neighbourhoods or segments. The assumption is that people who live in a particular neighbourhood will have similar lifestyles, preferences and aspirations and will react to marketing activity in the same way.

A neighbourhood type or segment is a unique group of customers who share common characteristics and which makes them different from other groups. Different segments may have different needs; they may require different versions of the product and may pay different prices; they may buy in different places and they may be reached by different media.

## ■ Classifications

Two neighbourhood classifications are commonly used by organisations – ACORN and MOSIAC. ACORN (www.caci.co.uk) is A Classification Of Residential Neighbourhoods, using predominantly census data. It has identified 54 neighbourhood types, an example of one is detailed below.

The other classification is MOSAIC (www.experian.com) which combines, among other sources, census information, credit history, share ownership and postcode data to identify household types. The case study on page 125 incorporates a MOSIAC profile.

Organisations find neighbourhood analysis useful for a variety of purposes. The table below ranks the uses to which they put this data.

| Application of geodemographic data | Rank (most frequent first) |
|---|---|
| Targeting direct mail letters | 1 |
| Market segmentation identification | 2 |
| Customer database building | 3 |
| Selecting appropriate media | 4 |
| New store location analysis | 5 |
| Sales force organisation | 6 |

Further approaches to segmentation are discussed in the final section of this unit.

## Segment, target and position using the 4Cs

Once the characteristics of the segments which interest an organisation have been established, then marketing research can help establish the type of marketing activities appropriate for each segment.

| ACORN category | ACORN group | ACORN types | Statistics |
|---|---|---|---|
| Expanding (B) | Affluent executives living in family housing; well-off workers living in family housing. | Affluent working families with mortgages<br>Affluent working couples with mortgages in new homes<br>Home owners with no children<br>Families with mortgage and young children | Number – 6.5 million or 11.8% of the population. |

## Case study

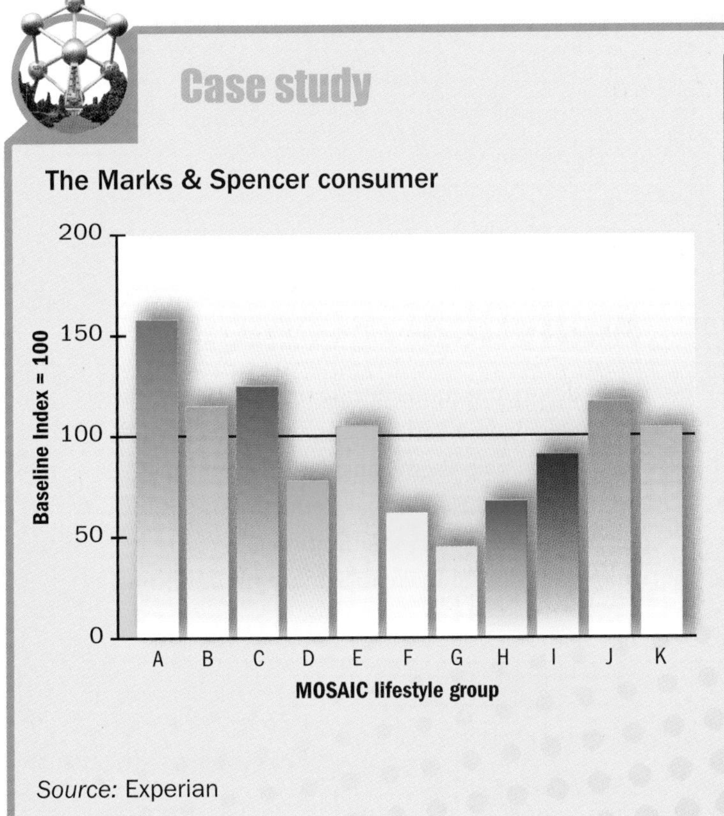


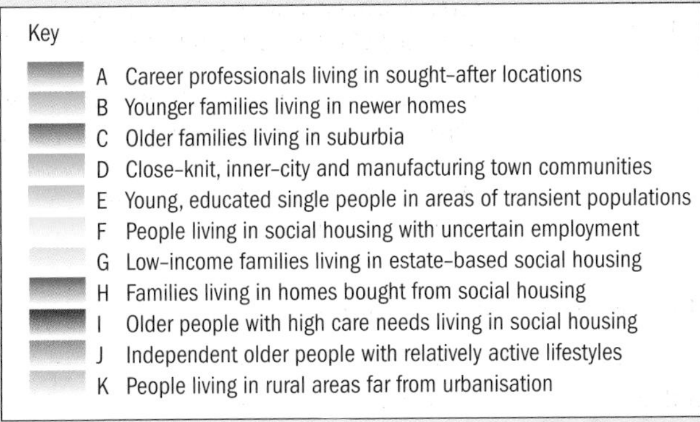


The profile of Marks & Spencer customers shows that career professionals and older families living in suburbia are most likely to shop at Marks & Spencer but families living in social housing or those with uncertain employment tend to shop elsewhere.

1. What sort of products might this information about lifestyle encourage Marks & Spencer to stock? ✓
2. If Marks & Spencer were considering a new store format and style, what sort of consumer would you recommend it targets? ✓✓

▼ **Market research helps establish appropriate marketing activities**

| | |
|---|---|
| **Segmentation** | Segmentation techniques such as ACORN and MOSIAC use marketing research to help identify groups of consumers who will respond to marketing activity in the same way. |
| **Targeting** | Research can then help select the groups whose needs and wants can be best met by the organisation. |
| **Positioning** | Research can help discover why customers are likely to buy a product (because it is exciting) – enabling organisations to develop brands, products and promotional activity which is going to generate a positive response. |

Traditionally this has concentrated on producing an appropriate marketing mix, utilising – increasingly nowadays – the 7Ps, which were discussed earlier in the unit. Marketing research would help make decisions about, for example, product features, acceptable prices and designing customer friendly processes. Another approach to developing marketing plans is to use the customer-focused 4Cs (choice, cost, convenience, communication). This approach possibly requires a greater contribution from marketing research. Look below at the sort of information required to produce effective marketing approaches to these two wine buying groups using the 4Cs:

| Customer focus | Busy professionals | Retired professionals |
|---|---|---|
| Choice (product) | Adequate – but not too many to consider. | Wide variety of choice in terms of grape choice, country of origin and packaging. |
| Cost (price) | Above the average – considered a worthwhile investment. Positioned as a reward for hard work. | Prepared to buy at a variety of prices – but always pleased to find a lower cost, 'value for money' wine. Positioned as 'makes life worth living'. |
| Convenience (place) | No time to browse – would typically buy from the Internet or by direct mail. | Buys from supermarkets, wine clubs and specialist wine merchants. |
| Communication (promotion) | Uses 'wine experts' on websites. | Consults magazines, wine books, and food experts. |

### Decision-making units

A decision-making unit (DMU) comprises all the individuals and groups who participate in the purchasing decision process, for example in a business. A typical DMU could include the following groups:

- Users, who will be interested in the benefits the product offers, such as increased production rates or reduced waste.
- Buyers or purchasing officers, who will be concerned about easy purchasing arrangements and delivery dates.
- Influencers, who are individuals whose opinion may be sought about a product or organisation. They will probably be influenced themselves by brand and company reputation.
- Deciders, such as managing directors, who will probably be most concerned with the overall cost of the product and whether the organisation can afford it.
- Gatekeepers, who may deny potential users information for a variety of reasons, including safety concerns or financial considerations. They can prevent sellers reaching the key decision makers.
- Specifiers, who are people who decide on the detailed specification of the product to be purchased. They may well want technical information about such things as component performance and material characteristics.

Marketing research can help identify and understand these groups.

### Environment

The environment consists of many influences that are beyond the power of organisations to shape and control but which have an impact on them. Marketers use an analytical technique called PESTLE (political, economic, social and cultural, technological, legal and environmental) to investigate the external environment in which an organisation is operating. Organisations need to be sensitive to what is happening in their outside environment, while also employing people who are marketing-orientated and consequently prepared to plan and implement activity to ensure the organisation will be successful in the future. Marketing research has a key role in gathering data from the outside environment for managers to consider. The case study on page 127 is an excellent example of how social change is affecting a market.

## Analytical techniques

How do organisations decide on the way forward? Marketers have a variety of analytical techniques available to help them consider their options. Marketing information is used to make effective use of the analytical techniques which an organisation can use to identify the changes it should make to achieve its ambitions.

### Situation analysis

All the techniques taken together are generally called a 'situational analysis' or 'marketing audit'. Some of the most frequently used are discussed in this section. The marketing research themes are the source of much of the data used by these analytical techniques.

### Product life cycle and product portfolio analysis

Product portfolio analysis is a tool for assessing the potential of a firm's products or business. It helps management decide which of its current products should receive more or less investment to ensure the business achieves its objectives. The two techniques commonly used by organisations are the product life cycle (PLC) concept and the BCG (Boston Consulting Group) matrix.

The idea that all products have a pattern to their lives lies behind the product life cycle concept. It suggests that a new product enters a life cycle once it is launched on the market.

In the **introductory stage** a product takes time to find acceptance by purchasers and there is slow growth in sales. Only a few organisations are likely to be operating in the market, each experiencing high costs because output is low. They may charge high prices to

## Case study

### The baby boomers

It is perhaps surprising that organisations are focusing on baby goods because the UK population is ageing rapidly. The last census recorded for the first time that there are more people aged over 65 than under 16. But the same factors that are behind the ageing population partly explain the level of interest in baby goods.

First-time parents are getting older. The average age of a woman becoming a mother in 1975 was 24; in 2005 it was 27. It means that women having children are more financially independent and they have more money to spend on their babies.

At Mothercare, for example, the range of pushchairs which the stores carry runs from an entry level model costing £30 right up to luxury brands, such as the Bugaboo, with the most expensive retailing at £700.

With grandparents living longer and having more money to spend on grandchildren, and families having fewer children, more money is being spent on each newborn child than in previous generations. For each birth in Britain in 2000, some £1200 was spent on baby products. In 2009 it will be closer to £1600.

Another factor behind this growth is the increase in the divorce rate. With mothers and fathers living part, there has been an inevitable doubling-up in spending as both households have to get the right equipment for the baby.

Britain is not the only country where more and more money is being spent on babies. Countries with rapidly developing economies, such as China and India, have a growing middle class that is splashing out on baby products. Annual spending on baby products in emerging markets is forecast to grow about 10% a year.

1. Explain why the market for baby products in the UK is growing. ✓
2. Apart from products directly related to the birth of babies, what other products are likely to benefit from this demographic change? ✓✓
3. What types of product are likely to benefit from the ageing population of the UK? ✓✓
4. If you were a producer of baby products, what sort of future plans might you be considering to develop the business? ✓✓✓

cover development and the initial promotional costs, but even then profitability may be difficult to achieve. Promotion concentrates on telling consumers what the product does.

If the product achieves market acceptance then sales grow rapidly. In this **growth stage** profits begin to materialise as higher production levels reduce unit costs. However, the growing market attracts competition and soon producers have to invest in building a brand image, product improvements and sales promotions to obtain a dominant market position.

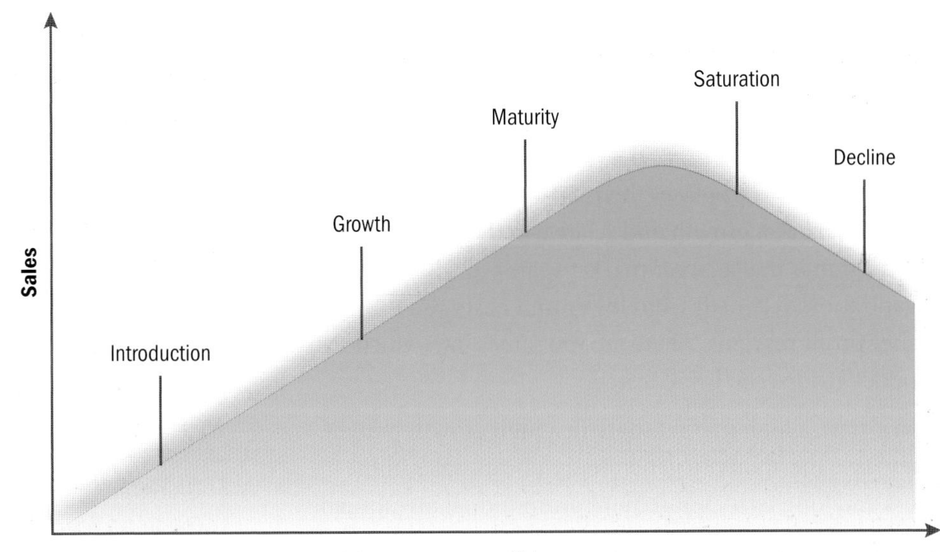


▲ Product life cycle

The **maturity stage** follows when a product experiences stable sales. This is generally the longest period of a successful product's life. But eventually sales fall and the market finds itself with too many producers who begin to suffer poor sales and falling profits. Some leave the market, while others employ strategies to extend the life of the product.

Most products reach the **saturation stage** when sales begin to fall. During this period, some brands will leave the market.

Products reach a stage of **decline** when sales fall significantly. Organisations progressively abandon the market, sometimes leaving a few producers who are able to trade profitably on low sales totals.

Organisations use the product life cycle to devise new product plans. An organisation will look to introduce new products to coincide with the decline of the established ones.

## Remember

Marketing information aims to help an organisation make effective marketing decisions so that the organisation can achieve its objectives. It is used to develop, for example, new products, promotional campaigns, pricing policies and places where the product can be bought by customers.

The BCG matrix identifies the product groups of an organisation and places them on a matrix that considers market growth and relative market share. The assumption is that a larger market share will enable an organisation to benefit from lower unit costs and thus higher profit margins. There are four areas into which product groups can be allocated.

**'Stars'** have a high market share in a high growth market. They have the ability to generate significant sales in the short and long term, but require promotional investment to maintain their market position.

**'Question marks'** have a low market share in a market that is growing rapidly. The low market share normally

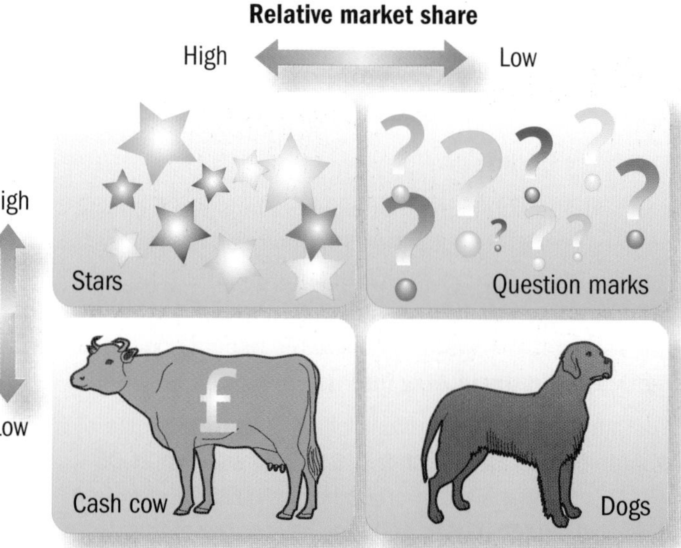


▲ The Boston Consulting Group matrix

indicates that competition is strong. If the market looks to have long-term potential, the organisation needs to decide whether to invest heavily in building market share. If the growth in the market is unlikely to continue, or the investment requirement is substantial, the organisation should consider abandoning the product.

**'Cash cows'** have a high market share in a market showing little growth. These products are generally well established with plenty of loyal customers. The product development costs are typically low and the marketing campaign is well established. The cash cows will normally make a substantial contribution to overall profitability. They finance the investment needed to maintain the high market share of stars and to develop 'question marks'.

**'Dogs'** are products experiencing little growth with a low market share. Organisations must consider whether to abandon the area and in the short term 'harvest' the product by raising prices or delete the item from the product range altogether.

## Practice point

Using the product range of a well-known organisation (such as Sony) classify its products (such as Walkman) as stars, question marks, cash cows or dogs. Position them all on a BCG matrix.

▲ Did Dixons use the product life cycle or the BCG matrix to make the decision to stop selling these products?

## Take it further

Explain the usefulness of the product life cycle and product portfolio analysis techniques to organisations like Sony.

The product life cycle and product portfolio analysis techniques have been found to be very useful for organisations but also have their limitations, as outlined in the table below.

## PESTLE analysis

Marketers use PESTLE analysis (political, economic, social, technological, legal, and environmental) to investigate the outside environment in which an organisation is operating.

**Political** factors affect the activity of business. Political developments are generally out of the control of an organisation, but it needs to forecast and anticipate change and then react accordingly. The development of the European Union has provided both opportunities and threats to British organisations. Its recent enlargement meant the market for British products expanded by 45 million customers. In contrast, Polish companies have a 60 million-customer British market to approach.

**Economic** influences look at how the performance of the economy impacts on organisations. All economies go through cycles of prosperity (high levels of demand, employment and income), recession (falling demand, employment and income) and recovery (gradual improvement in production levels, lowering unemployment and increasing incomes). The business cycle is especially important because of its direct effect on consumer and business spending. During times of prosperity, both consumers and business customers buy more goods and services.

The **social** environment describes the characteristics of society, the people who live in that society and their values and beliefs. The first area of study tends to focus on the population – demographics – revealing

| Limitations of BCG matrix | Limitations of product life cycle |
|---|---|
| • Difficult, time-consuming and costly to implement.<br>• Assumes high profits are generated by acquiring high market share in growth markets – not always the case.<br>• Needs good marketing research information – market share and market growth data. A surprisingly large number of companies will be uncertain about this information.<br>• Difficult to judge when product has entered a new category. When does a 'question mark' become a 'star'?<br>• Oversimplifies complex market situations and does not help 'future' planning. | • Can only record past events – difficult to predict when a stage will end or begin; not helpful for predicting the future.<br>• Suggests that products all follow similar pattern – but products are less predictable.<br>• No timescale can reliably be attributed to the product life cycle.<br>• Managers must be careful that predictions do not become self-fulfilling by deciding a product is in decline and just letting its sales fall.<br>• Does not recognise that product life cycles are becoming shorter. |

information about size, gender, ethnic groups, income levels, educational attainment, occupations and family structure. The information is very useful to marketers in predicting the size of markets for many products from holidays to pencils.

Many **technological** developments affect organisations. Growing ownership of computers and the influence of the Internet is allowing people to buy virtually anything without leaving their homes. Mobile phones are being used for advertisements. Downloading music from the Internet is having a dramatic affect on CD sales.

The **legal** climate constantly changes as the government introduces new laws through Parliament. For example, the law governing gaming has recently changed. Super casinos will be constructed and they will be allowed to promote themselves with new members able to play immediately rather than wait 24 hours as at present.

▲ Blackpool was unsuccessful in its bid to become a super casino

**Environmental** factors can also affect an organisation. Businesses have to consider, for example, packaging their products in recyclable materials rather than using substances such as polystyrene, and also how to cut down on their own waste materials. Environmental concerns are becoming increasingly important.

### Practice point

In the UK there are always changes taking place that will impact on businesses. Develop a list of five or six that might have an impact on a school or college.

### Take it further

Draw six equal-sized boxes on a sheet of A4 paper, label them – political, economic, social, technological, legal, environment – and allocate your ideas and any others that emerge into the relevant box. It is not necessary to have something in every box – it is the identification of the key issues which is important. Then consider how useful this sort of analysis might be to a school or college.

## Competitor and competition analysis

One of the most interesting approaches to examining competition was presented by Michael Porter in his book *Competitive strategy: Techniques for analysing industries and competitors* (1980, Free Press). Porter argued that the most important factors determining the performance of an organisation were the features of the industry in which it was trading. He identified five forces which he felt determined the level of competition and consequently profitability.

Porter assumed that profits are high when competition is low. The five forces are:

- **Rivalry amongst existing competitors**: this is the most obvious form of competition, the head-to-head rivalry between firms offering similar products

and selling them in the same markets. Rivalry can be intense and cut-throat, or it may be governed by unwritten agreements that help the industry to avoid the damage that excessive price cutting, advertising and promotional expenses can inflict on profits.

- **Threat of entry**: if it is easy to start a business in an industry, as soon as profits look attractive, new firms will arrive. Industries are relatively easy to enter if there are no large start-up costs, patents or copyrights. You probably notice new hairdressing salons opening up all the time. This is because it is relatively easy to start such a business. However, we do not see new accountants opening offices so often because they have to qualify over many years to become a chartered accountant. This reduces the number of people able to establish such a business.
- **Threat of substitutes**: a substitute is something that meets the same needs as another product. For example, a recyclable cardboard carton may become more attractive to producers than polystyrene packaging. A substitute may be quite different in some respects, but provide the same benefits to consumers. If the substitute becomes more attractive in terms of price, performance or both, then buyers will be tempted to move their custom.
- **Power of buyers**: powerful buyers can bargain away potential profits. They can cause firms to undercut each other to gain the buyer's business and they can use their power to extract other benefits – such as quality improvements or credit terms. Buyers tend to be powerful when there are relatively few of them buying a large proportion of the total output. A good example is how some clothing brands, like George (Asda), can obtain low prices from the many textile producers around the world.
- **Power of suppliers**: in a similar way, suppliers of resources which are vital to an industry can extract high prices from their customer. Such suppliers would include organisations supplying raw materials, power, skilled labour and components.

This analysis helps marketers to understand the markets they are operating in, but it also helps them understand the strategy which another organisation, such as a competitor, might be following. It then becomes much easier to anticipate their actions and behaviour.

## Practice point

Porter's Five Forces analysis helps marketing managers to assess the amount of competition and to understand the factors producing it. Simply answer yes or no to the questions below. They are all about the clothing retailers. If your answers are predominantly 'yes', the market is probably very competitive. If you answer 'no', the likelihood is that competition is low key.

- Is the market declining in terms of unit sales or value?
- Are there a significant number of clothing retailers?
- Is the number of clothing retailers in the market increasing?
- Do customers tend to show loyalty to a particular retailer?
- Could the retailers easily serve more customers?
- Could the clothing retailers convert their stores quickly and inexpensively to serve another market (such as a sandwich bar or coffee house)?

## Local, national and global marketplace

In some situations it might prove useful to consider developments in local, national and global marketplaces, as shown in the table below. International developments can have a significant impact on national and local markets.

## SWOT analysis – strengths, weaknesses, opportunities and threats

A common approach is to use SWOT analysis (strengths, weaknesses, opportunities, threats) to draw together all the evidence from the various analytical techniques used. It is a way of producing a summary which then provides the basis for developing marketing objectives or aims and ultimately strategies or plans. Strengths, weaknesses, opportunities and threats analysis provides a framework within which marketers can identify significant developments in the markets.

- **Strengths** refer to the internal features of an organisation which provide a competitive advantage. An example could be a well-regarded brand name which is easily recalled by consumers.
- **Weaknesses** are internal aspects of the organisation which may not stand comparison with competition or are not performing effectively. An example might be the inability to have key-selling items constantly in stock.
- **Opportunities** focus on events and developments external to an organisation. The growing use and acceptance of the Internet to sell products will present some companies with the chance to increase profits by selling directly to consumers. The rapid emergence of iTunes has shown the potential of the Internet to create new sorts of businesses and alter the way markets operate.
- **Threats** are developments external to the organisation which potentially could damage overall performance. These threats can originate from new laws, changes in government policy or social developments such as the trend towards healthier diets.

A SWOT analysis is a summary of all the information collected during the situational analysis.

## Diversification

Once an organisation has produced its situational analysis, using a variety of analytical techniques, and it has developed its marketing objectives and plans, it is possible these do not then meet the aims of the organisation's overall objectives. For example, the sales expected to be achieved are not sufficient.

The original plans may therefore have to be revised – sometimes several times. This can be a dangerous process because some changes bring with them a greater risk of failure. If an organisation decides that the only way forward is the development of completely new products for markets in which it has little experience, then the chances of success are low. This business

| Market | Developments | Consequences |
|---|---|---|
| Global | Global communication news programmes and the Internet have forced international companies to launch new products across major world markets simultaneously. | Demand can be very large very quickly, straining distribution systems. Promotional activity has to be coordinated to begin in all markets at the same time. |
| National | Companies have to organise the launch of a new product to coincide with launches elsewhere in the world. | Companies have to use the brand name and in many instances the promotional approach adopted across the other major markets. Products such as Cif (formerly Jif) have had their name changed to follow the approach used in other international markets. Brand names used in individual markets, such as Vauxhall – Opel elsewhere in Europe – have been declining. |
| Local | The brand names have to be promoted locally. | Stores have to alter signs and replace display units. |

▲ Developments in local, national and global marketplaces

strategy is called diversification. It may be the only route to the sales which the organisation's overall business objectives demand.

It is usually considered better for an organisation to adopt a market development strategy where it launches its established products into new markets (such as Russia) or a product development strategy where it designs new products for its existing customers. Both these strategies have lower risks associated with them.

The strategy associated with the lowest level of risk is market penetration, where the organisation decides it can sell more of its existing products to its existing customers.

## Implications of social and technological change

Organisations can be forced to change their plans for any number of reasons, but nowadays the most likely reasons will be to do with social and technological developments. Detailed below are some examples of such changes and their implications for businesses.

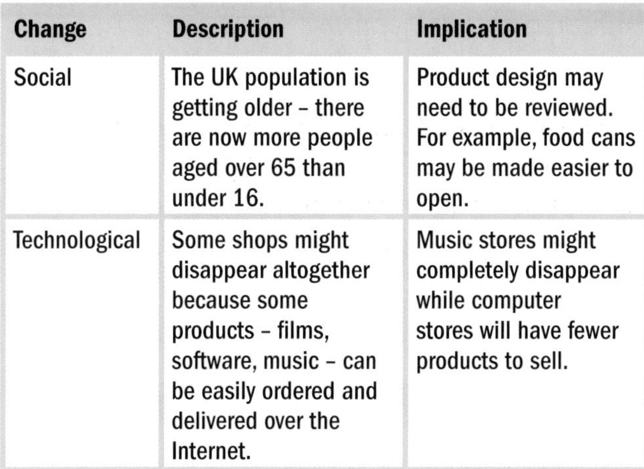

| Change | Description | Implication |
|---|---|---|
| Social | The UK population is getting older – there are now more people aged over 65 than under 16. | Product design may need to be reviewed. For example, food cans may be made easier to open. |
| Technological | Some shops might disappear altogether because some products – films, software, music – can be easily ordered and delivered over the Internet. | Music stores might completely disappear while computer stores will have fewer products to sell. |

### Thinking point

Draw up a list of three social and three technological changes currently affecting Britain. Then consider the impact the changes might have for the marketing mix being used by organisations.

## Outcome activity 3.3

**Pass**

Apply two analytical techniques – product life cycle, BCG matrix – to Magners Cider. 

**Merit**

Compare the analytical techniques used in supporting the marketing decisions made by Magners Cider. 

## Grading tips

**Pass** 

Draw individual product life cycles for Magners Cider, Smirnoff Ice, Strongbow Cider and Reef. Then take those same products and put them onto a BCG matrix.

**Merit** 

Produce a table like the one below highlighting the strengths and limitations of the techniques you chose. Then comment and explain which technique possibly provoides Magners with the most valuable marketing information.

| Product life cycle | |
|---|---|
| **Strengths** | **Limitations** |
| • Suggests type of marketing which should be undertaken, such as brand building in growth stage. | • Difficult to predict when a product is entering a new stage. |

A marketing research-led situational analysis should lead to some marketing objectives which generate plans involving marketing techniques to increase the demand for products. These techniques are discussed in this section.

## Market segmentation and targeting

### Importance

Segmentation allows organisations to develop products and plans which fit the needs of customers more effectively, thus increasing overall demand. Once the segments in a market have been discovered, the next step is to identify ones where the needs and wants of the consumer can be met by the organisation. An organisation may not have the resources to target every segment, or it may feel its expertise and resources are relevant to one or two of the segments.

#### Remember

Segmentation techniques divide a market into groups that share the same characteristics. Different segments require different marketing approaches.

The final step is positioning, which takes into account the perception customers have about a product. The secret of success is to match the motive customers have for buying an item with the perception they have of it. If customers are buying clothes to show they are professional executives they might choose Next, whereas others who may want to be seen as fashionable might pick Zara. The perceptions a customer has of a product can be shaped by intelligent deployment of the marketing mix. This is the art of positioning.

### Basis for segmentation – geographic, demographic, psychographic and lifestyle

The skill of the marketing manager is to segment their market to discover factors which enable them to develop effective marketing plans.

**Geographic segmentation** is used when the needs and behaviour of potential customers in the USA differ from those in, for example, Russia.

**Demographic segmentation** uses population factors such as age, gender, family or social groupings to identify and describe segments. An interesting example would be the 'family life cycle' which looks at age, marital status, career status (income) and the presence or absence of children, and identifies various stages through which many households progress. The top table opposite shows a fairly traditional life cycle and the particular products and services which could be marketed at certain stages in the life cycle of families.

Neighbourhood analysis is a particularly effective method of segmenting a market in the UK. Two popular methods – ACORN and MOSIAC – were discussed earlier in this unit on page 124.

**Psychographic** or **lifestyle segmentation** seeks to classify people according to their values, opinions, personality characteristics and interests. Lifestyle segmentation deals with the person as opposed to the product, and attempts to discover the lifestyle patterns shared by groups of customers. This offers an insight into their preferences for various products and services. Marketing managers can target products and promotions at particular lifestyle groups.

Lifestyle data can be used to place customers in various lifestyle categories which can be targeted appropriately. See the lower table opposite – perhaps you can identify yourself somewhere in the categories?

| Stage | Description | Consumer interests |
|---|---|---|
| Bachelor | Independent. Young. Early stage of career and earnings. | Clothing. Car. Travel. Eating and drinking out. Entertainment. |
| Newly wed | Two incomes. Relative independence. Present and future orientated. | Furnishing. Travel. Clothing. Durables. Appeal to togetherness. |
| Full nest 1 | Youngest child under 6 years. One/one and half incomes. Future orientated. | Goods and services geared to child. Family-orientated products. Practicality of items and appeal to economy important. |
| Full nest 2 | Youngest child over 6 years. One and half to two incomes. Future orientated. | Savings, home, education. Children-orientated items. Family vacations. Appeal to comfort and luxuries. |
| Full nest 3 | Youngest child at home but independent. High income level. Thoughts of retirement. | Education. Expensive durables for children. Replacement and improvement of parental consumer durables such as TV. Appeal to comfort and luxury. |
| Empty nest 1 | No children at home. Independent. Good income. Thoughts of retirement and self. | Retirement home. Travel. Entertainment. Luxuries. Appeal to self-gratification. |
| Empty nest 2 | Retirement. Limited income. Present orientated. | Travel. Recreation. Health-related products and services. Little interest in luxury. Appeal to comfort. |
| Sole survivor 1 | Only one spouse alive. Good income. Employed. Present orientated. | Immersion in jobs and friends. Travel. Entertainment. Clothing. Health. |
| Sole survivor 2 | Only one spouse alive. Limited income. Retired. | Travel. Entertainment. Health-related items. Appeal to economy and social activity. |

▲ Traditional life cycle

▼ Lifestyle segmentation

| Lifestyle | Characteristics |
|---|---|
| Self-explorers | Motivated by self-expression (singing, acting) and self-realisation (drawing, painting, writing, learning new skills). |
| Social resistors | Caring group concerned with fairness and social values, often appearing intolerant and moralistic. Member of pressure groups such as Greenpeace. |
| Experimentalists | Highly individualistic, motivated by fast moving enjoyment (such as F1 racing). Materialistic and pro-technology – for example, use Blackberry. |
| Conspicuous consumers | Materialistic and pushy. Motivated by acquisition, competition and getting ahead. Career minded. Concerned about law and order being upheld. |
| Belongers | Seek a quiet life, are conservative (dislike change) and rule followers (pay taxes). |
| Survivors | Strongly class conscious and community spirited (organise and support local events). |
| Aimless | Live from day to day and includes the young, unemployed and old. |

▲ Which lifestyle categories would these people fall into?

When the segments in a market are successfully identified, products and marketing activities can be better designed to genuinely match their needs – so increasing overall demand.

### Key Terms

**B2B** Business-to-business markets.

**B2C** Business-to-consumer markets.

## Design of marketing mix to satisfy needs of target group

Segmentation demands that the marketing mix ingredients must be modified according to the segment being targeted. This can best be illustrated through an example, as detailed in the table on page 137, with a holiday and events organisation selling to **B2B** and **B2C** markets.

### Remember

The original marketing mix contained 4Ps – product, place, promotion and price. The 7Ps, sometimes called the extended marketing mix, is the combination of product, price, promotion, place, people, processes and physical evidence offered by an organisation to potential customers.

| Marketing mix | B2C | B2B |
|---|---|---|
| Product | Enjoy cultural holidays to destinations such as Italy and Egypt. | Short breaks to help team build or rewards for achieving objective (such as sales target), such as skiing and snowboarding in Alps or Pyrenees. |
| Price | Prepared to pay above average for a holiday with a guide and suitable programme. | Happy to pay premium price for holiday which includes events especially devised to meet aims of organisation. |
| Place | Explore the Internet for 'interesting' locations and book through specialist travel agents. | Book through sales executive who might visit organisation to discuss requirements and obtain booking. |
| Promotion | Articles in magazines, detailed websites about destinations, brochures and direct mail letters. | Advertisements in trade journals, attend special 'event' exhibitions, sales executives contact organisations. |
| Processes | Book on website or over the telephone by credit or debit card. All travel documents organised such as visas and insurance. | Sales executive deals with everything. Organisation has an appointed person to deal with customer. |
| People | Knowledgeable staff who have a genuine interest in the destinations themselves. | Effective interpersonal, administrative and negotiator skills. |
| Physical evidence | Provide comprehensive itinerary, guide books and T-shirt. | Everything provided for event – all things pre-booked, fully detailed itinerary. |

▲ Modifying the marketing mix according to segment

## Practice point

Part-time and full-time students possibly need different marketing mixes to attract them to study. Design a marketing mix – using the 7Ps – for each group.

## Take it further

Decide whether segmentation is appropriate for organisations with such customers. Discuss whether another approach to segmentation might be more worthwhile, such as one based on demographics.

## Greater individualisation afforded by e-business and e-marketing

E-commerce is the online version of a business process or commercial activity that is already available offline, for example buying from a supermarket over the Internet instead of physically going to the store. This is opposed to e-business, which is an entirely new business method that could not exist without the capabilities of the Internet. Developments in e-business and e-marketing are enabling some organisations to deliver individual marketing mixes to customers – sometimes called micro-marketing. This is a more advanced technique than segmentation.

Powerful databases are now able to undertake micro-marketing functions:

- Match new products and new offers to customers who are likely to be interested. For example, Amazon notes the books customers have previously bought and alerts them when similar titles are published.
- Strengthening customer loyalty through, for example, reminders about key events. Websites ask surfers to register and access special information areas. This can involve giving some key details, including areas of interest, which are then used to communicate with that customer. This is called 'permission marketing' and is considered a more effective way to deal with a customer because they have actively asked you to send them certain sorts of information to which they are more likely to respond. As a consequence the messages sent are individualised for that customer.

- Re-activating customer purchasing by providing something special to regain a customer. Databases can be used to send out materials just before a lapsed customer is about to purchase that product, such as insurance, once again.

### Thinking point

Micro-marketing can only be successfully undertaken if consumers are prepared to release information about themselves. Would you be prepared to give organisations possibly confidential information about yourself? Explain your viewpoint to somebody who perhaps thinks differently to you.

## Branding

It is now recognised that brands are among the most important influences on buying decisions and customer choice, and can increase demand for products considerably.

### Importance in influencing buyer behaviour

Brands represent one of the most important and powerful ways for an organisation to create and maintain a distinctive and advantageous image for its products. They can have physical (such as the Adidas three stripes) as well as emotional characteristics (Nike's association with successful sports people). They can increase demand for products in two ways:

- Because markets are now characterised by a wealth of alternative products, the task of choosing between competing products has simply become too difficult, time-consuming and expensive for most buyers. In addition, the customer is subjected to an enormous variety of competing advertising claims and selling messages. Reputable brands allow the customer to choose with confidence and reduce the risks associated with choice.
- Brands are strongly associated with and bought for emotional, psychological and status reasons as well as for functional (what they actually do) reasons. Most watches tell the time accurately, so why do some people choose to pay more for a Rotary or Tag Hauer watch? The emotional factors associated with brand values reflect the fact that in many societies customers have moved from merely buying products and services to fulfil basic physical needs and requirements, to buying products to satisfy higher needs such as feeling good about oneself.

### Brand building and positioning

A brand is a name, term, sign, symbol or design intended to identify the product of a seller and to differentiate it from competitors. Successfully establishing, building and supporting a brand is not an easy process and will often require considerable skill, investment and patience on the part of the organisation.

Key steps in building and positioning a brand:

- Establish target market and customer needs.
- Determine the brand values to be established in response to those needs.
- Ensure that brand values are communicated to customers.
- Ensure that brand values can be justified and defended.
- Monitor changes in organisation and competitor brand positions and update brands as appropriate.

### Brand extension

Brand extension is the introduction of such developments as new flavours and packaging sizes to capitalise on existing brand loyalty. Recent examples include the introduction of Persil washing-up liquid and Mars ice cream. New additions to the product range are beneficial for two reasons:

- They require a lower level of marketing investment because the brand is already familiar to customers.
- The extension of the brand presents less risk to customers who might be worried about trying something new. This is particularly important in consumer durables involving a relatively large investment, such as a stereo system.

## Practice point

Make up a list of products which Kellogg's, Mercedes and Burger King could brand to develop their businesses. What would be the benefits of branding such products in this way?

### Take it further

What might be the problems associated with such a strategy? How would you assess the risks involved?

## Practice point

Schools and colleges rarely keep in touch with their past students. What might they actually do to maintain such contacts?

### Take it further

If a college adopted a 'relationship marketing' approach to these students what might be the benefits? Do you think it would be a worthwhile investment in terms of time and resources?

# Relationship marketing

Relationship marketing is focused on maximising the lifetime value of desirable customers and segments.

Relationship marketing can be defined as the identifying, establishing, maintaining, enhancing and – where necessary – terminating the relationship with customers at a profit. Relationship marketing aims to bring together customer service, the concept of a quality organisation and the marketing function in a particular approach to the customer. Its focus is on maintaining and enhancing customer relationships. The table on page 140 helps to identify the distinguishing features of this approach.

▲ A lifetime of loans?

| Transactional approach (buying from Argos) | • Focus more on single transaction<br>• Emphasis on product features<br>• Some emphasis on customer service<br>• Limited customer commitment<br>• Little customer contact – but when it occurs there is the expectancy of a sale<br>• Quality concentrated on product |
|---|---|
| Relationship marketing approach (being a car dealership customer) | • Focus more on customer retention<br>• Emphasis on product benefits<br>• High emphasis on customer service<br>• Higher customer commitment<br>• Regular customer contact – without expecting a sale immediately<br>• Quality concern of all employees, especially ones which impact on customer buying experience |

# Planning, control and evaluation processes

How does a marketing manager go about creating plans to increase demand? Such a plan is the concluding part of the planning process. They are likely to follow a process similar to the diagram.

The nature of the monitoring process was described in the first section of this unit (see page 105).

Normally an organisation would evaluate annually the actual overall performance of their plans against the targets and objectives originally set at the beginning of the year. It should then evaluate why some things seemed to work very well (such as magazine advertising, for example) while other aspects (such as that few retailers used the point-of-sale material available) perhaps failed to live up to expectations. The results of this evaluation should then be taken into account when the new planning cycle starts and the new objectives and plans are prepared for the next trading year.

It is the outcome of the planning, monitoring and evaluation process which is really important and that outcome is the marketing plan. The marketing plan is the action plan for the marketing team over the planning period.

**PLANNING PROCESS**

↓

**Formulation of overall business objectives (such as 'to improve profit margins by 5% over the next 12 months')**

↓

**Conduct a marketing research-based situational analysis using a range of analytical techniques (using product life cycle, BCG matrix, PESTLE analysis, Porter's Five Forces analysis)**

↓

**Complete audit by classifying the important findings into a SWOT analysis (internal strengths and weaknesses; external opportunities and threats)**

↓

**Set marketing objectives based on principles and functions of marketing (such as launching a new drug to help heart attack victims)**

↓

**Write marketing plans determining strategy and marketing activities to be undertaken (using marketing mix framework – 7Ps or 4Cs)**

↓

**Design marketing tactics (such as targeting segments, branding and/or relationship marketing)**

↓

**Implement plans (activate promotional activity)**

↓

**Monitor and evaluate (check progress and take action, such as employ more sales people if objectives look as if they may not be achieved)**

▲ Market planning process model

# Outcome activity 3.4

Ahmed has carried out some further research into Magners' marketing mix and has come up with the following results:

**Pass**

Describe how marketing techniques – branding, segmentation – are used by Magners Cider to increase demand for its product. **p5**

**Merit**

Explain the marketing techniques used by Magners Cider and analyse why these techniques have been chosen. **m3**

**Distinction**

Evaluate the marketing techniques, research and analysis used by Magners Cider and make original recommendations for improvement. **d2**

## Magners Original Irish Cider – Marketing Plan

| | |
|---|---|
| Marketing objective | To make this Irish cider a 'repertoire' drink. |
| Segmentation/brand | The drink for young adults aged 20-25 with a 'mature intellectual appeal'. |
| Product | Naturalness, tradition, heritage and craft have always been the strength of this crisp, refreshing drink. Still uses the handcrafted oak vats & presses made over 50 years ago. Fermentation takes eight weeks, providing the distinctive taste. Product in growth stage of product life cycle and just emerged as a BCG 'star' product. |
| Price | Premium priced in similar fashion to Stella Artois. |
| Place | Can be purchased at bars/clubs, off licences, supermarkets and convenience stores. |
| Promotion | National TV showing the iconic Magners pint bottle being served over mounds of fresh ice. Promotion reminds customers that the quality and craftsmanship of the brand takes 'time'. Promotion emphasises this through the slogans 'all in its own good time' and, more recently, 'time dedicated to you'.<br><br>Sponsors London Wasps, Edinburgh Gunners and the Magners Rugby Union League. Also in partnership with the Scottish Golf Union as sponsors of the Scottish Golfers Championship.<br><br>Also sponsors the Edinburgh Fringe Festival venue boards and maps, a festival which attracts 1.5 million visitors annually. |
| People | No investment in bar, off licence or supermarket staff. |
| Processes | Not appropriate |
| Physical evidence | No budget allocated to this aspect of the marketing mix. |

## Grading tips

**Pass** 

Describe the method Magners has chosen to segment the market and then, using the 7Ps as a framework, note the approach the company has taken towards the segment. Include the description about what the Magners brand means to its customers in the product section.

**Merit** 

Explain segmentation, targeting and positioning, branding and market planning and how they influence the marketing mix. Include the benefits to Magners Cider of using these techniques.

**Distinction** 

Identify areas where Magners Cider is perhaps not generating any or enough marketing information. You should then recommend some marketing research methods which would provide the information required. Clearly show the scope of the additional information, using the classifications: consumers, competitors and market environment. Conclude by explaining why it would be useful to Magners Cider.

Decide whether the limitations of the techniques used mean they are not very useful for Magners Cider. You might decide that one or more of the other techniques – PESTLE analysis, Porter's Five Forces – is more useful to the organisation. Whatever your decision you will have to support your recommendations with the benefits that will flow from your view. It is a possibility that applying PESTLE analysis and Porter's Five Forces to Magners Cider will provide you with ideas to help you formulate some recommendations.

Finally, discuss whether the techniques being used by Magners Cider are going to increase demand for its product. This should highlight where improvements can be made. Remember to clearly indicate the benefits to Magners Cider of any proposed improvements such as the use of relationship marketing to increase demand.

## End of unit test

1. Give your own definition of marketing.
2. What are the three Ps closely associated with marketing services?
3. What are the advantages of Codes of Practice?
4. Name three Codes of Practice published by the Direct Marketing Association
5. List six primary research methods.
6. What sort of information does quantitative research reveal?
7. Name three sources of secondary research.
8. Describe three groups you would expect to find in a DMU.
9. What does the acronym PESTLE describe?
10. Name each of Porter's Five Forces.
11. Explain what a 'cash cow' is in the Boston Consulting Group matrix.
12. What are the characteristics of a market segment?
13. Describe the two reasons for the rising importance of brands.
14. Note five distinguishing characteristics of relationship marketing.
15. Draw a flow diagram to illustrate the marketing planning process.

# Resources

www.adassoc.org.uk – The Advertising Association

www.asa.org.uk – Advertising Standards Authority

www.cim.co.uk – The Chartered Institute of Marketing

www.mintel.com – Mintel

www.thomson.com – DataStream

http://dbuk.dnb.com – Dun & Bradstreet

www.the-dma.org – Direct Mail Association

www.which.net – Consumers' Association publishers of *Which?*

www.statistics.gov.uk – National Statistics

www.oecd.org – Organisation for Economic Co-operation and Development.

www.europa.eu.int/comm/eurostat/ – European Union Statistical Office

# Books


Ali, M. 2006 *Practical Marketing and Public Relations for the Small Business*, Kogan Page

Smith, C. and Hiam, A. 2006 *Marketing for Dummies*, Wiley


| Grading criteria | Outcome activity | Page number |
|---|---|---|
| To achieve a pass grade the evidence must show that the learner is able to: | | |
| **P1** Describe the concept and principles of marketing | 3.1 | 112 |
| **P2** Describe how the concept and principles are applied to the marketing of products in two organisations | 3.1 | 112 |
| **P3** Describe how marketing research information is used by one of the organisations to understand the behaviour of customers, competitors and market environment | 3.2 | 122 |
| **P4** Apply two analytical techniques to a selected product (goods or services) offered by a selected organisation | 3.3 | 133 |
| **P5** Describe how marketing techniques are used by one organisation to increase demand for a selected product (goods or services) | 3.4 | 141 |
| To achieve a merit grade the evidence must show that, in addition to the pass criteria, the learner is able to: | | |
| **M1** Compare the effectiveness of the concepts and principles applied to the marketing of products by the two chosen organisations | 3.1 | 112 |
| **M2** Compare the analytical techniques used in supporting the marketing decisions of a selected business or product | 3.3 | 133 |
| **M3** Explain the marketing techniques used by a selected organisation and analyse why these techniques might have been chosen | 3.4 | 141 |
| To achieve a distinction grade the evidence must show that, in addition to the pass and merit criteria, the learner is able to: | | |
| **D1** Evaluate the concepts and principles applied to the marketing of products by a selected organisation and make recommendations for improvement | 3.1 | 112 |
| **D2** Evaluate the marketing techniques, research and analysis used by a selected organisation and make original recommendations for improvement | 3.4 | 141 |

# Effective people, communication and information

## Introduction

This unit considers three of the most important elements that make up any successful business:

- People – the staff who work for an organisation are its most important resource. If people do their jobs well the business may succeed, however if the wrong people are employed or not trained properly then even an organisation with an excellent product or service will struggle to survive.
- Communication – one of the most important skills needed by all employees is effective communication with customers and colleagues. The ability to build positive relationships and engage effectively with customers is a powerful influence on an organisation's success.
- Information – managers have to make decisions about the direction of the business; however, the quality of those decisions is often dependent on the quality of information that they receive. Gathering accurate and timely information is therefore also crucial for the business.

This could be one of the most important units you study throughout this course!

### What you need to learn

On completion of this unit you should:

1. Understand the importance of employing suitable people
2. Know how to communicate using appropriate methods
3. Understand different types of information and how it can be processed
4. Be able to present information effectively.

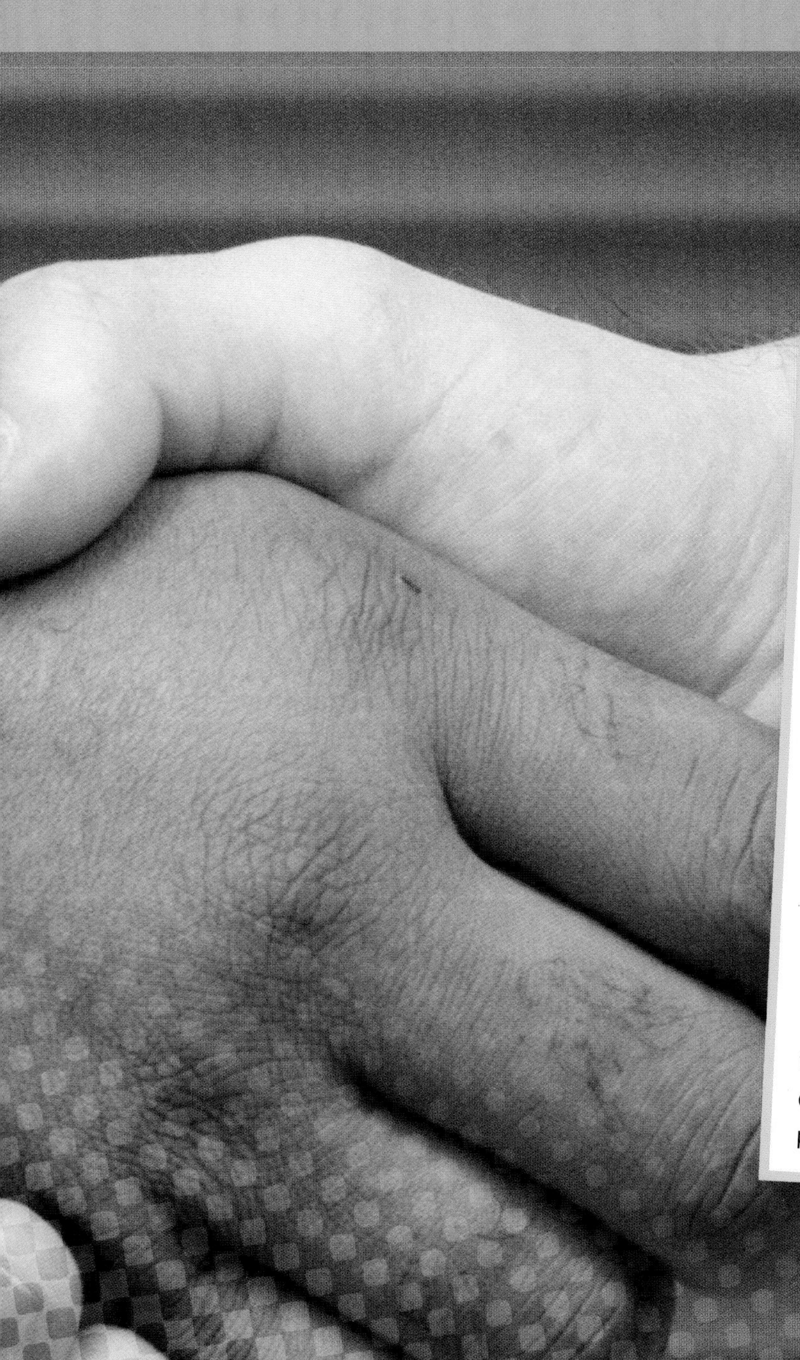

## Consider this

As human beings we are communicating all of the time. Every message we convey gives an impression of us. What messages do these extracts convey to you?

> I don't think I take the beef as seriously as they do, because I don't consider them artists. They can't do anything to me. What can they do to me? They have no credibility, no respect, no talent, they have nothing. All they can do is diss me vocally, they can't diss me lyrically.
> Eminem – Rapper. (Source: *www.eminem.net*)

How does he seem to you?
What about this message?

> LO Patrick, I hOp U R weL. R U frE 2 MEt 2nt @ 7pm n d pub? I hOp so az we nEd 2 TLK bout gigs 4 d B&.
> c U s%n.
> D

A translation of this is: 'Hello Patrick, I hope you are well. Are you free to meet tonight at 7pm in the pub? I hope so as we need to talk about gigs for the band. See you soon. David.'

How does this writer seem to you? How appropriate would this be in a business context?

In business we often only get one chance to convince our audience. This unit is all about creating positive impressions with our audience by presenting information in a professional manner.

# 4.1 Importance of employing suitable people

Recruiting staff can be a time-consuming and expensive activity; it is therefore vital to get it right first time whenever possible. For a start it is essential to be clear about the type of person who is needed; in this unit we will examine some of the key attributes that make a person useful to a company and therefore more employable.

### Key Terms

**Recruitment** Taking on employees.

## Human resources

### Recruitment and retention

Finding suitable staff to work within the organisation is critical as without the right people the right business decisions are unlikely to be made. There are many different ways that businesses can attract workers. Traditional methods to make people aware of job vacancies now have to compete with Internet-based methods of **recruitment**. The table below shows you different types of traditional and online methods of recruitment that can be used by organisations to get the best people to work for them.

New members of staff can be found through using internal recruitment (selecting from people who already work for the organisation) or through external recruitment (bringing in new staff). There are strong arguments for recruiting internally if possible, as the managers already know what such people are capable of and the employees already know a lot about the business and so may need less training than a new member of staff. When recruiting externally managers have to make decisions based on very limited information and therefore there is more risk involved. However, it is not often possible to recruit internally and sometimes managers are keen to get new people into the business in order to bring fresh ideas and approaches into the company; in such circumstances it is important to approach recruitment in a very systematic way to ensure the best chance of getting the right person for the job.

Recruitment online is much faster than previous methods of recruitment and has a number of benefits over using paper. For example, it is possible to monitor how many people have gone on to a website to look at a job (a web counter can help to do this because it counts the number of people that visit that page). The business can see how many of those people then go on to apply for the job so they can monitor whether or not this method of recruitment is the best way for them to choose to encourage people to work for them. By using online application forms, data supplied by applicants can be put straight into computer software.

| Traditional methods | Internet-based methods |
|---|---|
| Newspaper advertisement | Online application form |
| Paper-based curriculum vitae | Online curriculum vitae |
| Letter | Email |
| Word of mouth | Web advertisement |
| Paper-based application form | Web page with curriculum vitae details |
| Careers fair | Web page with job board |
| Poster | Web page pop-up |

▲ Traditional versus online methods of recruitment

Recruitment is an expensive process for any organisation and some organisations prefer to use an agency to do part of their recruitment process. Organisations like http://fish4.co.uk/jobs are able to advertise vacancies throughout the world. This may be an advantage for larger organisations that are able to recruit from the UK or worldwide. For other organisations the web may not be the best place to advertise a job. If they are a small local firm looking for employees they may find dealing with a large number of applications from abroad very difficult to cope with.

Consider some of the issues relating to the use of online recruitment: for example, equality of access by all potential candidates, authenticity of applications and worldwide advertising for a business specialising in IT software design making or a manufacturer of handmade pots. With the increasing use of IT within industry, how important are innovations in online recruitment?

The table below gives an overview of the recruitment process.

## Practice point

Innovations Ltd is a small IT specialist organisation thinking about using online recruitment.

1. Using research from the web (a useful website list is provided below) and classroom-based resources produce a mind map in pairs showing the advantages or disadvantages of using online recruitment.

   www.oneclickhr.com

   www.stirlingjobs.co.uk

   www.onrec.com
2. Discuss your results with other members of your class.
3. Produce a written report giving a judgement about the importance of choosing the right method of recruitment for a business like Innovations Ltd to help it manage its resources.

| | |
|---|---|
| **1. Job analysis is carried out** | The process where an employer examines what the business requires from a current job. This could be done by observing someone on the job, through questioning the current jobholder or by interviewing the appropriate supervisor/manager. |
| **2. A job description is prepared** | A list of the working conditions for the job, e.g. pay, hours and duties. |
| **3. A person specification is prepared** | A list of attributes needed by a person to perform a job, such as personality type, abilities or experience. |
| **4. Plans are made for advertising the job** | This could be done internally within the business or externally through newspapers, journals or job centres. |
| **5. Advertisements are placed** | According to plans made. |
| **6. Applicants are short-listed** | A small number of applicants will be selected to proceed; this will be done by comparing the data on the applications to the person specification. |
| **7. References are requested** | These will usually include the applicant's current or most recent employer, but the opinions of other professional persons may be sought. Some organisations will do this after the successful candidate has been offered the job. |
| **8. Candidates are invited for interviews and/or selection tests** | A combination of interviews and tests may be used to assess the candidate's suitability for the job. |
| **9. Data obtained from interviews is compared to person specification** | This should enable an objective decision to be made. |
| **10. Successful candidate is offered the job** | Following the appointment it would be useful to evaluate the process to see how successful it was in selecting a good candidate. |

▲ The recruitment process

After advertising, selecting candidates is not a straightforward process either. Some organisations prefer to test their candidates before selecting them for interview and may use online psychometric tests. These are tests that aim to measure the intelligence or personality type of candidates usually using questionnaires. You can learn more about the use of these tests and how to select candidates in Unit 13 Investigating Recruitment and Selection.

There is also more detail about the recruitment process in Unit 13.

▼ Psychometric tests aim to measure intelligence and personality types

## Retention

Keeping staff is also extremely important. This is known as staff **retention**. When a business has spent a lot of time and effort recruiting staff it needs to make sure that they are going to stay with the organisation and work to the best of their ability. If an employee joins a business and then decides to leave quickly the business will have to pay recruitment costs again and retrain another member of staff. This costs a lot of money so it will want to avoid this. It can also leave other workers in the business feeling fed up and unhappy if they have to do extra work until a new employee is appointed again. Businesses can use measurements to work out how long staff are staying with them and work out targets to maintain or improve the trend. The key measurement that can be used is known as staff turnover. This is where the number of staff leaving during a year is worked out as a percentage of all the staff employed in that year.

$$\frac{\text{Number of staff leaving in a year}}{\text{Average number of staff employed in that year}} \times 100$$

This helps the business to be able to monitor trends to see how many employees are leaving, if there is a potential problem with their human resources and what could be done about it.

### Key Terms

**Retention** Keeping employees at the workplace for as long as possible to benefit from their experience.

### Thinking point

Recruitment is expensive and very time-consuming and therefore sometimes managers are tempted to take short cuts with the process. What are the potential problems with this?

### Suitably skilled staff

Crucial to ensuring that the best staff are recruited and retained is making sure that potential employees have the right qualities and skills. Managers will look for people who have:

- a range of employability skills
- good personal skills
- effective communication skills.

Each of these areas is examined in detail later in this unit.

However, having suitably skilled staff is not just about recruiting new people; it is also important to make sure that employees already working for the organisation are continually trained and updated. It is crucial that they are given new skills to cope with changes in their jobs or the way that the work is completed. Without suitably

## Case study

### Matfen Hall

Matfen Hall is a large country house hotel located just outside of Newcastle. It was voted 'Large Hotel of the Year in 2006' in the Enjoy England Awards for Excellence. Its staff turnover in 2006 was around 8%. This figure is very low for the hotel and catering industry where turnover figures can be as high as 50%.

Matfen Hall has been able to achieve this low turnover figure through a number of different initiatives. The hotel works with colleges and schools in the area to recruit local staff to work there. Within 174 full- and part-time staff employed, 20 staff in March 2006 were Polish. These employees are given English lessons each week to help them to improve their communication skills. Support is also given to employees who are living away from home in the hotel accommodation for the first time.

Of course, winning awards, and the hotel has won many, helps to make Matfen Hall a good place to work and encourages people to stay there. This is because its reputation is good so people feel proud to work there. If staff are happy working at the hotel they are more likely to make the guests happy so they come back again or tell their friends about the good time they have had. Employees receive extra benefits such as special rates on rooms for them to use and their opinions are also listened to for how improvements can be made to the hotel.

For more information about the hotel access www.matfenhall.com.

1. How many employees left Matfen Hall in 2006? ✓
2. Why might staff turnover be high in the hotel and catering industries? ✓
2. Outline the advantages and disadvantages of two of the different initiatives that Matfen Hall has used to help keep staff turnover low. ✓✓
2. Make a judgement about how important it is to keep staff turnover as low as possible in a customer service industry like hotels and catering. ✓✓✓

skilled workers a business cannot operate; it will need to get additional help or will lose money if it cannot carry out its day-to-day business. There are three main elements to making sure a business has suitably skilled employees: attracting the right people in the first place, training staff while in work and educating potential workers so that they leave college or university with the right level of skills. All three elements are essential to ensure that businesses are able to make use of suitably skilled staff.

## Case study

### Skills and training needs

The 2020 Vision for Skills Report, produced by the TUC in 2006, suggested that in the previous year over a third of employers admitted to not providing training at all and 40% of the workforce (approximately 8 million employees) have not received any training in the past year.

The Ready, Willing and Able TUC report (also 2006) revealed over one million 50–65-year-old workers who wanted to work but couldn't get jobs because employers would not recruit older workers or retain the ones they had by investing in training or making minor adjustments for people with disabilities.

1. What might the impact of this lack of training have on the UK workforce and the ability of a business to find suitability qualified staff? ✓
2. Why is it so important to encourage all employers to provide training for their workforce? ✓✓
3. To what extent are employers, rather than the government, responsible for providing skills and training? ✓✓✓

### Remember

Recruiting and keeping the right staff in the first place can save significant amounts of money in the long term.

A number of important documents are used during the recruitment process. Three of the most important ones are considered here: contracts of employment, job descriptions and person specifications. More information about job descriptions and contracts of employment is found in Unit 13 Investigating Recruitment and Selection.

### Contracts of employment

The main rights and duties of both employers and employees will be found in the contract of employment. These rights are specified in the terms of the contract. The contract of employment exists to protect both the employer and the employee so that each party to the contract knows what is expected of them. The Employment Rights Act 1996 states that all employees should receive a written contract of employment within eight weeks of the start of their employment. The terms of employment should include:

- the names of the employer and employee
- the job title or job description
- the date employment commenced, the place of work and the address of the employer
- the amount of pay and how often payments will be made
- hours of work
- holiday pay entitlement
- sick pay arrangements
- pension arrangements
- notice periods
- for temporary jobs, the date employment will cease
- grievance and appeal arrangements
- disciplinary rules, although these are now covered by the Employment Act 2002 and all organisations should abide by this.

### Job description

This is a document that gives full details of the job that needs to be filled. It is used by potential applicants who wish to know exactly what will be expected of them in the new job, but it will also be used by the managers of the organisation who will refer to the **job description** when preparing the person specification. An example of a job description can be seen in Unit 13 on page 340.

### Key Terms

**Job description** This is the list of working conditions related to the job, for example pay, hours and duties.

### Person specification

This document identifies the skills, experiences and personality traits that will be needed to do the job well. Managers will compare candidates against this document during the selection process to find the applicant who fits the requirements most closely. There are more details and an example of a person specification in Unit 13 on page 341.

## Employability skills

Each job requires the person doing it to possess a range of specialist skills. However, there is also a set of skills that are useful to a wide variety of careers and are therefore transferable between jobs. These are known as **employability skills** and they are essential to be able to work effectively in a modern workplace. Two of the most important sets of transferable employability skills are personal skills and communication skills, and we consider those later in this unit; but first we will look at some of the most important specific skills and abilities that would appeal to specific employers.

Some skills are required for a range of different jobs ▶

## Key Terms

**Employability skills** A range of skills that will allow a person to perform different jobs well.

### Suitable qualifications

Different jobs require different types of qualification. Some employers will be happy to take on applicants with GCSE qualifications, although others may require more specific skills such as NVQ qualifications. For professional careers such as accountancy, marketing and human resources, employers will often look for candidates with problem-solving and critical skills and so will often need candidates with at least A-level or BTEC National qualifications. For professional careers that lead to management roles, higher education qualifications such as HNDs or degrees are often required, as those job holders will need to be educated to a high level in order to be able to cope with the demands of such work. To be useful to an employer, therefore, it is important that you have the correct level of qualifications and in the right subjects too. The good news is that the BTEC National Business is a good start towards a wide range of professional jobs, so you are already making one positive step towards a rewarding career!

### Thinking point

Visit your school or college library and obtain a copy of one local paper and a professional journal. Find advertisements for a range of six different jobs, at least three of which should be for professional roles such as managers, accountants or trainers. Try to find at least two jobs that might be of interest to you in the future. Make detailed notes about the qualifications that each of the jobs requires.

> **Take it further**
>
> Explain why each of the qualifications required for the professional jobs is necessary in order to do that job well.

### Experience in similar role or the same industry

If you can show that you have done similar work before, for another company, this should indicate that you can do it again for a new organisation. Therefore, when applying for a job, you should think carefully about any previous experience that might show how you already have some of the skills required to be successful in the new role. If you have already worked in that industry you should make this fact very clear in your letter of application or CV as such experience is likely to be valued by the prospective employer.

### Knowledge of products/services

Product knowledge is vital, especially if you intend to work in a customer service role, so you will improve your chances of obtaining a job if you can demonstrate a sound understanding of the products or services that a business delivers. This may require some research prior to an interview, but time spent on the organisation's website will certainly give you an advantage over other candidates.

### Effectiveness in meeting personal and team/departmental targets

Meeting targets is vital for business success, and individual employees must be able to meet targets too. Therefore if you can demonstrate an ability to hit targets and meet deadlines, this is likely to make you stand out at interview. If you have worked to targets in previous jobs you should be able to explain in your letter of application or interview how successful you have been in this area previously. Completing the BTEC National Business course successfully will require you to meet many deadlines and targets, which you will also be able to emphasise to a prospective employer.

### Ability to observe and raise professional standards of production/service delivery

An employee who is able to work consistently to the standards required by the organisation will be valued by the organisation; one who seeks to improve standards by suggesting and implementing better ways of doing the job is even more useful. Candidates who can describe or demonstrate how they have done this in previous posts will undoubtedly improve their chances of being employed.

## Personal skills

Certain skills will be beneficial regardless of the job or career that you pursue and these transferable personal skills make a candidate attractive to a new employer.

### Hardworking and patient

Someone who gets lots of work done is bound to be valued, whereas those employees who spend too much time talking, answering their mobile phones or surfing the Internet during working hours will not make a good impression. So take care to manage the distractions of modern life. Patience is also required in many jobs, especially if you are dealing with members of the public!

### Good interpersonal skills

**Interpersonal skills** enable us to get on with other people, promote positive relationships in the workplace and so enable the job to be done better or more efficiently. Some people are naturally good at getting on with others and encouraging colleagues, but it is possible to learn good interpersonal skills. If you think your skills might be lacking in this area it would be worth working on them; such abilities will make you

## Thinking point

With a partner you should consider jobs listed in the following table. If you were looking to employ a new person to perform these roles what special skills would you need them to have? Complete the table with the specific skills you would look for under each of the headings we have discussed to answer this task.

| | Qualifications | Experience | Knowledge of products/ services | Effectiveness in meeting personal and team or departmental targets | Ability to observe and raise professional standards | Other specific skills |
|---|---|---|---|---|---|---|
| Supervisor in a bank | | | | | | |
| Playgroup worker | | | | | | |
| Leader of a team of accountants | | | | | | |
| Manager of a football club | | | | | | |
| McDonald's crew member | | | | | | |

more employable and will also enable you to do a better job of work. Some interpersonal skills are very simple, such as smiling. A cheerful smile can break down barriers and encourage someone to listen and talk to you, so remembering to smile is a good start to improving your interpersonal skills.

## Key Terms

**Interpersonal skills** Skills that enable us to get on with other people and promote positive relationships in the workplace.

There are some other important areas to consider.

### ■ Communication skills

Being able to communicate effectively is a vital interpersonal skill and is discussed at length in the next section in this unit.

### ■ Listening

Are you good at listening? Many people think they are good listeners but not many are. Before reading on, have a go at the practice point on page 154.

What the activity should have illustrated to you is that listening is not as easy as it sounds. Most people only listen passively; in other words they hear the words being spoken but they do not think about what is being said, and consequently they do not remember what is said. Listening should be an active process: as you hear someone speaking you should be thinking about what is being said. Question it in your mind; does it sound reasonable? Pick out the main points and try to summarise them in your own mind. Most importantly you should concentrate on the words being spoken and try to put other thoughts and distractions from your mind.

### ■ Politeness

People appreciate politeness and you are much more likely to build positive relationships by avoiding rudeness or being abrupt with them.

### ■ Patience

Be patient when dealing with others and they are more likely to respond positively to you. However, in an

## Practice point

Get together with a group of six or seven friends and sit in a circle facing each other. One person should hold a tennis ball; no one in the group is allowed to speak unless they are holding the ball. At the start of the activity the person holding the ball begins to talk about what they enjoy doing in their spare time. After talking for a minute or so the speaker throws the ball randomly to another person in the circle. The person who receives the ball must then start talking by repeating the last two sentences that the previous person spoke; they can then go on to speak about what they like doing in their spare time. After a minute or so of talking about themselves they then throw the ball randomly to another group member. The activity continues until everyone has had a turn; the ball should end up with the person who started the activity.

At the end of the activity you should rate each other on your success in remembering and repeating what the person previous to you in the circle said.

Who was best?

Which members of the group did less well?

Why does the best person think they were good at listening and remembering?

What could the less successful people do to improve their skills in this area?

age of 'instant gratification' we can be encouraged to want and expect things immediately: movies delivered to our living rooms at the touch of an interactive TV button; Internet pages that appear instantaneously over broadband connections; downloading songs in seconds to avoid the delay of having to go to a shop to purchase them; pre-orders of new DVDs so that we get them on the morning of the day they are released. Patience may no longer be a virtue; but in many jobs it can be essential.

Being patient with people is not always easy, and it is undoubtedly easier with some people than with others. Patience is an important skill for a businessperson in more than one context. Rushed decisions are rarely the best ones; it is usually much better to consider options and potential consequences before making decisions. Once decisions are made, good methodical planning is more likely to lead to success than rushing headlong at an idea; it is better to lay good foundations before you build a house – it's less likely to fall down! All of this takes patience, and it is equally true when dealing with people. Consider the possible consequences of your actions before you say or do something; weigh up the best way to approach someone and avoid acting on impulse until you are experienced with your interpersonal skills.

### ■ Building trust

Trust is an important element of productive relationships but will not appear quickly or easily. You will build the trust of your colleagues if you appear to be fair when dealing with them, if you avoid talking about other people behind their backs and if you do your best to keep your promises.

### ■ Empathising with people

When we empathise with others we understand their problems, opinions and feelings and we can imagine what it would be like to be in their position. This is not easy for most people as we are naturally very much involved in our own lives and experiences. It can be difficult to forget our own problems and put ourselves in another person's shoes. However, a sense of **empathy** will enable us to build trust in our working relationships. Good listening skills will enable us to become more empathetic towards others.

## Key Terms

**Empathy** Understand the problems, opinions and feelings of other people, imagining clearly what it would be like to be in their position.

## Avoiding conflict

Conflict can be very destructive in a work environment so taking steps to avoid it (or positively to resolve conflict) is a useful skill. We can do this by being respectful to others, respecting differences in other people, thinking carefully before we speak (so many conflicts have been caused by ill-advised, hasty and confrontational comments), being patient and empathising with others.

## Accepting responsibility

We all make mistakes so we should all be prepared to accept responsibility for those errors when they occur. People who continually make excuses for their shortcomings or, worse still, blame others in the organisation, will not build up positive working relationships.

## Cooperating with others

Line managers will expect you to cooperate with their ideas and wishes, but you should also work cooperatively with other colleagues wherever possible.

## Don't moan!

No one likes to listen to a moaner; being positive is far more likely to build your friendships and working relationships.

### Able to work as part of a team

Interpersonal skills will be crucial to your ability to work effectively in a team of people, but a range of other skills and considerations will also be important. These are discussed at length in Unit 19 Exploring Team Development.

### Negotiation

Another useful skill for an employee is the ability to negotiate effectively. Negotiating involves discussing a topic in order to produce some agreement or common ground. At the start of negotiations the parties involved usually have quite different opinions on what should happen, so the art of negotiation is in finding common ground that both parties can agree upon – making it a 'win–win' situation. Negotiation is the process of seeking agreement and can therefore be useful for resolving conflicts between members of staff, agreeing personal or departmental targets, agreeing budget allocations and interviewing, especially for new staff members. It can also be personally useful for negotiating pay rises or better working conditions.

### Interview skills

Interviewing skills can be useful in a number of contexts. Being able to interview customers or clients effectively to encourage sales or improve customer relationships will be useful to many organisations. In addition it will be an asset to effectively identify the best candidates when interviewing potential new employees or deal with appraisal situations for current members of staff.

# Communication skills

### Formal and informal communication

There is a wide range of communication going on within all organisations, some of these are formal and some informal.

## Formal communications – use of appropriate language

Examples of formal communication include board meetings, letters, formal reports and presentations. We describe these as formal methods because when using them we have to use specific formats and follow acceptable rules and conventions. Business letters, for example, always follow a particular structure (you can see an example of this on page 167) and so do business meetings. The type of language used is also formal; it is very important to avoid using slang words or colloquialisms – standard English must be used and it is important to avoid slipping into 'text speak' or the common abbreviations used in personal emails.

## Practice point

You should do this activity with someone who knows you reasonably well. The aim is to consider how good you are at using the key interpersonal skills that have been discussed previously. First you should make two copies of the table below; you and your partner should have one each. Remember that you should try to be as honest as you can with each other.

Fold here

| Name: | | |
|---|---|---|
| | **How I see myself** | **How I see you** |
| Good communicator | 1 2 3 4 5 6 7 8 9 10 | 1 2 3 4 5 6 7 8 9 10 |
| Good listener | 1 2 3 4 5 6 7 8 9 10 | 1 2 3 4 5 6 7 8 9 10 |
| Polite | 1 2 3 4 5 6 7 8 9 10 | 1 2 3 4 5 6 7 8 9 10 |
| Patient | 1 2 3 4 5 6 7 8 9 10 | 1 2 3 4 5 6 7 8 9 10 |
| Trustworthy | 1 2 3 4 5 6 7 8 9 10 | 1 2 3 4 5 6 7 8 9 10 |
| Empathetic | 1 2 3 4 5 6 7 8 9 10 | 1 2 3 4 5 6 7 8 9 10 |
| Avoids conflict | 1 2 3 4 5 6 7 8 9 10 | 1 2 3 4 5 6 7 8 9 10 |
| Accepts responsibility | 1 2 3 4 5 6 7 8 9 10 | 1 2 3 4 5 6 7 8 9 10 |
| Cooperative | 1 2 3 4 5 6 7 8 9 10 | 1 2 3 4 5 6 7 8 9 10 |
| Avoids moaning | 1 2 3 4 5 6 7 8 9 10 | 1 2 3 4 5 6 7 8 9 10 |

**Step 1** Sit separately so that you cannot see what each other is writing. At the top of your sheet you should write the name of your partner; your partner should put your name on their sheet. You should now rate your partner under each of the headings down the right side of the page, giving a mark out of 10 by ringing the appropriate numbers under the How I see you column. Assume that 1 is a low rating and 10 a high rating, e.g. 10 in the first row would mean that you were a very good communicator, but 1 would mean you need to improve a lot in this skill.

**Step 2** When you have finished Step 1 you should fold the paper backwards along the line indicated so that your partner cannot see what you have written; your partner should do the same with their sheet about you. Swap sheets and then rate yourself under the same headings.

**Step 3** When you have both finished open up your sheet and compare how closely you and your partner agreed about your interpersonal skills. Things to look at are: headings where you have put a similar score to your partner (within 2 marks) means you have a good estimation of your skills in this area. Headings where your scores differ by more than two points show that you have either under-rated or over-rated your skills in this area. Headings with low scores will be areas for you to work on in order to improve your interpersonal skills.

**Step 4** You should now draw up your own action plan in order to improve your interpersonal skills. You can use the following template to help with this:

| Skill to improve | What I will try to do to improve this skill | How I will judge my success in improving this skill | Review date | Further action required following review |
|---|---|---|---|---|
| | | | | |
| | | | | |
| | | | | |
| | | | | |

## Informal communications

Informal communications do not follow any prescribed conventions or formats and often happen spontaneously, such as conversations and most (but not all) emails and text messages.

▲ Professional communication skills are essential

### Non-verbal/verbal communication methods

Business communications can be divided into non-verbal and verbal methods of communicating.

## Non-verbal communication methods

These generally involve written communication, either on paper or screen-based. Common methods are letters, memos, reports, invoices, flow charts, publicity material, email, text messaging and web pages; all of these are discussed at length later in this unit.

## Verbal communication methods

Commonly used verbal methods of communication (those using the human voice) are presentations, interviews, meetings, telephone calls and video conferencing. We shall be looking at effective presentation and verbal skills later in this unit.

### Listening

This is an important communication skill, which was examined earlier in this unit.

### Presentation skills

There are few professional business people who will not have to make presentations at some point in their careers, whether this is delivering the results of research into new products, pitching for customers or explaining ideas to members of staff. Presentational skills are therefore vital.

Unfortunately many people are very apprehensive about making presentations. The best way to calm those nerves is to be adequately prepared and to follow a few simple rules when constructing your presentation.

### Thinking point

This activity should be done in groups of four. Your task is to consider presenters that you have seen in action. These might have been teachers who have taught you at school, TV presenters, actors performing on stage or even visiting speakers at your school or college. Think carefully about both the good and bad presenters that you have experienced and draw up a list of techniques that contribute to a good presentation. You should also make notes about errors that should be avoided when presenting. Make notes of good and bad points for presenters on flip chart paper.

### Take it further

Prepare a short presentation to deliver your group's findings to the rest of the class. Try to use some of the good techniques that you have identified and try to avoid the pitfalls that you have listed.

It is very important to give a presentation structure; like an essay it should have a beginning, a middle and an end, and it must also be prepared carefully. Here are some tips for preparation and a structure.

### ■ Set your objectives

Decide on the main message that you want your audience to receive, or what you want them to do following your presentation. Summarise those aims in a few short sentences as this will help you to stay focused during your preparations. You might consider outlining those aims to your audience during the introduction to your talk.

### ■ Consider your audience

You will need to adapt your delivery to the people you are delivering to. This is discussed in detail in Section 2 of this unit, 'Commmunicating using appropriate methods'.

### ■ Structure your presentation

Your structure should follow the following sequence:

1. Introduction: say who you are and what you are hoping to do in your talk.
2. Signpost: give a list of the stages in your talk that will follow so the audience knows what to expect.
3. Main body: deliver the main facts in a logical order.
4. Conclusion: you should summarise or recap the main points; list these visually as well as orally to give maximum impact. If you want your audience to do something with the information you have delivered you should tell them at this stage.
5. Invite questions: ask your audience to put questions to you about anything in your talk.

Most importantly, you must ensure that you rehearse your presentation well beforehand to eliminate any potential errors and stumbling blocks.

### ■ Visual aids

**Visual aids** are useful for several reasons: they can help your audience to understand what you are saying, they can add impact to your talk and they can also act as a useful prop if you are nervous when delivering your presentation. However, you also have to be careful with visual aids. Some students spend so much time preparing stunning visual aids that they forget to deliver the key messages.

## Key Terms

**Visual aids** Pictures, charts, video, PowerPoint slides and other visual materials used in a presentation to aid understanding.

## Remember

The most important part of your talk is the message you are trying to deliver not the medium you are using to deliver it!

You should consider using a variety of visual aids. **PowerPoint** is an excellent tool but try using others too in order to make an impact on your audience. For example:

- flip charts
- overhead projectors
- handouts
- models
- physical examples
- demonstrations
- role plays
- video.

You will find tips on using some of these methods in the last part of this unit (see page 189, 'Presenting information effectively').

## Key Terms

**PowerPoint** Applications software produced by Microsoft that allows you to produce professional and versatile slides for display using a computer during a presentation.

### ■ Use of cue cards

Cue cards are a useful tool to help you to remember where you are in a presentation and what comes next. They are simply a pile of small cards (about playing card size) that you hold in your hand while you talk. Written on each card is a few short words to remind you of what comes next; you glance down to see your reminder, and then while talking you move the top card to the bottom of the pack so the next reminder is ready for you. Cue cards can help you to appear fluent and unflustered; they should give you confidence, but try to avoid dropping them!

## Eye contact

It is good practice to make eye contact with people while you talk. In fact, you should try to make contact with as many members of the audience as you can during your presentation. Eye contact is important for several reasons:

- A speaker who does not look at the audience but continually looks at their feet or out of the window gives the impression that they are not happy to be doing the presentation. That may be true, but it is not the impression you want to give. Being prepared to make eye contact gives the impression that you are confident and well prepared (even if you aren't!) and therefore gives the audience confidence in you.
- It helps you to establish some rapport with your audience.
- It allows you to check whether your audience is listening or not. If you achieve little eye contact you may have lost them.
- It should help to give you feedback about your audience's reactions to what you are saying.

## Facial expressiveness

Your face is an important part of your communication. We all have control over the words that we speak; however we are not always aware of the messages our faces are delivering as many expressions are involuntary. Open and smiling expressions are more likely to encourage effective communications than puzzled, miserable or angry expressions; this is certainly true when making presentations, so try to be aware of what your face is doing, and think about the messages it is giving. Try videoing yourself making a short presentation and then look carefully at the expressions on your face on the video. You might be alarmed by what you see but it should help you to think about what your facial expressions say when you speak.

## Use appropriate professional language

Don't forget that a presentation requires you to use a formal style of language. As you would for business letters, avoid using slang words or colloquialisms, and particularly look out for words that your audience may find offensive. Even the mildest swear word is strictly unacceptable in a business context, so be careful; it is very easy for such language to slip out, especially if you are used to speaking that way with friends.

### Remember

You need to create a positive impression with your audience, and in the working world you will not gain new customers if your use of language is unprofessional.

### Body language

We may talk with our mouths but our bodies are communicating messages to those around us all the time. In the same way that our faces can give clues about our inner thoughts, the rest of our body is doing likewise to a skilled communicator. The degree of eye contact we make and our facial expressions are good examples of our bodies conveying messages; but someone trained in observing **body language** can pick up many other messages too.

▲ **What can these people's body language tell us about them?**

## Key Terms

**Body language** Gestures, expressions and movements that a person subconsciously uses to communicate.

### ■ Intention movements

These are certain involuntary gestures that people perform which can indicate their intentions. Obvious examples are people in an audience who are shuffling in their seats or people in a meeting who are drumming their fingers on the desk. These gestures indicate impatience and a desire to leave the room. You might see someone sitting down who is clasping both knees with their hands, and this can indicate that the person is about to get up and leave.

Sometimes in a meeting you may witness someone leaning forward slightly and possibly raising a hand or finger slightly. This indicates that the person is keen to speak or make a suggestion, and a skilled chairperson should look for such gestures and invite the person to make their point.

## Key Terms

**Intention movements** Involuntary gestures that indicate people's intentions.

### ■ Displacement activities

**Displacement activities** are movements that indicate a degree of nervousness in a person. You can observe these movements in places like hospital waiting rooms; people fiddle with watchstraps, continually take sips from a cup of coffee or even sit smoothing their clothes. Sometimes people will keep checking the contents of their bags or pockets, or sit polishing their glasses. All of these movements say, 'I don't want to be here but I haven't a choice.' The inner tension in the person is released to an extent by the displacement activity and a skilled observer can use this information to recognise when someone is ill at ease. Since communication is likely to be more effective if the participants are relaxed, steps can be taken to try to bring this about.

### ■ Self-touching and defensive postures

Self-touching movements are rooted in early childhood. Children will often hide behind their mother for protection; when we get older we do not have this option but sometimes we inadvertently replace this urge with self-touching movements that are an attempt to comfort ourselves. Stroking your hair or face, crossing your arms and even crossing your legs are attempts to throw up protective barriers; if you are talking to someone who adopts this posture you should get the message that they feel threatened by you.

## Key Terms

**Displacement activities** Involuntary movements that indicate a degree of nervousness in a person.

## Practice point

Go to a crowded place where people meet and talk, such as your college refectory or school dinner hall. Sit apart and out of earshot of what people are saying and observe the gestures and body positions people are adopting. See if you can draw any conclusions about the state of mind of the people you observe. If you are brave you might ask them afterwards what they were feeling to see how accurate you were.

## Take it further

The next time you have to visit the doctor or the dentist, observe the postures adopted by people in the waiting room. Don't speak to them as people in this situation are likely to find that intrusive.

## Adapting communication techniques to audience requirements

It would be wrong to think that the same delivery techniques work with different audiences. The skilled presenter will adapt the presentation to suit the people listening. This topic is discussed in detail later in this unit, see page 162 'Audience requirements'.

## Checking audience understanding

Communicating is all about ensuring that your message is understood by those receiving it, so a good communicator will try to check whether this has happened. With written communication you might only be able to invite the reader to reply with queries; however if you are presenting to an audience there are several ways that you could check that understanding has taken place. Most obviously you could ask them to put questions to you at the end of your presentation, but there are other ways. You could ask them one or two key questions to check that the most important messages have been received, or you could hand round a short set of written (possibly multiple-choice) questions for the audience to answer, again focusing on the key messages of your talk.

### Thinking point

With a partner you should try to think of as many methods of checking that your audience has understood your main messages as you can and list them. When you have thought of at least five methods discuss them together to come up with your preferred method. Be prepared to explain your favourite idea to the rest of the class.

## Seeking clarification

It is also important in any communication to ensure that you have understood correctly. A good communicator will always respond and seek clarification if there is any element of doubt. Don't be afraid to do this as it is not a sign of weakness; it simply indicates that you want to be clear that you understand. Your teachers would prefer you to ask questions in a lesson to avoid any confusion, and a business presenter will feel the same.

## Responsiveness

Skilled communicators will always be able to respond to the needs of their audience. Sometimes those needs are obvious, for example when someone asks a question it is clear that they need more explanation; however sometimes they are less obvious. Displacement activities and intention movements were discussed earlier in this section, look out for these when you are talking or presenting as responding positively and appropriately to them will improve your communications.

## Inviting commitment to shared goals

Skilled business communicators can get the audience on their side and encourage them to support the goals of the department or company. Much business communication, especially from managers, is about trying to get staff to help, lead or support planned projects; so the ability to win people over is valuable. To be effective in this way you will need:

- good interpersonal skills
- the ability to explain clearly
- to be honest
- to explain clearly how what you propose will benefit your audience (if they can see no benefit they are unlikely to respond)
- a persuasive manner.

## Outcome activity 4.1

**Pass** P1

You have recently set up your small business and now need to recruit some staff. Unfortunately you are unsure how to go about finding new staff, what documentation is required and how to keep the staff once you have taken them on. You decide to do some research on local business to help formulate your ideas.

To answer this task you will therefore need to interview the manager of a local business. This could be a firm that you work for, a shop that you visit regularly or even a family business. Your interview should find out the following:

- The recruitment process the business uses, i.e. who does what and in what order. If the firm has a written recruitment policy ask if it would be acceptable for you to see a copy.
- What steps the manager of the business takes to ensure that they retain good staff.
- You should try to obtain examples of job descriptions and person specifications that the business has used along with any other recruitment documents.

You should now write a detailed description of the recruitment and retention process and recruitment documentation used in your selected organisation. You should do this in the form of a series of guidance notes that can be referred to whenever new staff are required.

## Grading tips

**Pass** P1

Make sure you write a list of questions to ask before you conduct the interview. Ask your tutor to check these before you go.

Your guide can be any form you choose, such as a leaflet or a booklet. You might like to use a DTP program to help produce a professional document.

# 4.2 Communicate using appropriate methods

A professional business person will be able to adapt the content of the communication to suit the different people receiving the information, whether this is written or oral. It is essential to understand the needs of the reader, or to obtain some idea of the make up of an audience before you prepare your communication, as you may need to make some significant changes to ensure that your audience gets your message. If you are preparing a presentation, for example, you need to know beforehand about the people likely to be in the audience. This means that you can cater for the needs of everyone, including, for instance, someone who is partially sighted.

## Audience requirements

We will now look at some of the reasons why changes might be necessary and how you might cater for the individual needs of your readers or audience.

▲ Know your audience

## Age and attention span

Most younger people can only concentrate for shorter periods of time, while older people and those who are more highly educated are usually better able to listen to a presentation or read (a report, for example) for extended periods. It is helpful for any audience if you build variety into your communication, but it is even more crucial for the young or the less well educated. Younger people also respond well to visual stimuli, such as pictures, video and models; therefore web-based communication methods or PowerPoint presentations can work well for such an audience. If you are doing a verbal presentation, the key is to change style during the presentation, maybe start with a visual stimulus to attract attention, then talk formally for a few minutes, follow that with an activity, more talk, a video, etc.

## Use of examples – age, gender and ethnicity

A good way to help your audience understand your message is to give examples to illustrate your explanations, but you may need to adapt these to take account of your audience. Use examples that draw on the lives of your listeners, or reflect their experiences and interests. It is preferable to use examples drawn from different ethnic backgrounds and which draw from the experiences of both men and women in positive ways.

## Special needs of audience – accessibility

You should consider the need to adapt your written communications or presentation materials to make them more **accessible** to your audience. Large font sizes can help the partially sighted; so bear this in mind for handouts and PowerPoint presentations as well as formal written communication methods. Some visually impaired students also find certain

### Key Terms

**Accessibility** Methods used to make business communications (and all aspects of everyday life) accessible to people with disabilities.

colour combinations, such as green and yellow, to be problematic, so these should be avoided. There are several points to consider when producing web-based communications, (for more details see page 187, 'Adherence to legislation – w3c').

There are different issues to consider when preparing verbal presentations; for example, some individuals may have special needs that you should be aware of. You may need to adapt the environment so that students with special needs sit in appropriate positions in the room. People with hearing difficulties who lip read, for example, would not want you to be standing in front of a window as they would only see you silhouetted – which makes lip reading very difficult. You should also ensure that you stand facing a lip reader at all times to give them maximum opportunity to receive your message.

If you have audience members with mobility problems, such as wheelchair users, the layout of the room should be considered. Wide aisles may be needed for access, and you should remove one or two chairs from an aisle so that the wheelchair user can be in the main body of the audience.

If your presentation is to involve any sort of group activity you might also consider grouping people so that a person with special needs works with cooperative group members.

### Readability

You may need to adapt the language that you use to suit your audience. Younger, less intellectually developed or industrially inexperienced people may prefer you to use simple language rather than jargon, whereas an older or more professional audience would expect you to use technical terms and phrases.

### Interest

You might need to know how interested your reader or audience actually is in the topic you are to communicate about. If they are already keen to hear what you have to say, then you don't need to work too hard, but sometimes audiences will need to be won over.

One of the key methods here is to get to the point quickly, and explain how the topic is relevant to your reader or audience. Variety can also help with maintaining interest, as can a little humour on occasions. There are very few instances when humour is appropriate for a professional business document (except maybe in advertisements or some other marketing communications); however, a good joke at the start of a presentation is a great way of engaging your audience and getting them on your side. But you do have to be careful how you use humour: if you crack a joke and nobody even smiles you will wish you hadn't got up that morning! A joke which is badly received, simply because it is unfunny or worse still offensive, can leave you flustered and with a lot of ground to make up – so if you are in any doubt at all, don't do it. However, if you can deliver a joke well, there is no better way of relaxing and engaging the interest of your audience.

### Legibility

A document that is legible is one that is easy for your audience to read. There are several factors that combine to make a document legible to the reader.

- **White space** – do not cram pages full of text. This is intimidating to the reader and immediately becomes a barrier to the message getting through.
- **Font** – some are much easier to read than others. Times New Roman, Tahoma and Arial are often the easiest to read.
- **Font size** – small font sizes can reduce **legibility**; size 12 is a good standard to use. However, there are times when this needs to be changed. PowerPoint and overhead transparencies, for example, benefit from larger font sizes, such as a minimum of 18 point; 24 point is even better. This will look too large on screen while you are preparing the slides, but will look good when projected.

#### Key Terms

**Legibility** How easy a document is for your audience to read, its 'readability'.

- **Colour contrast** – dark text on light backgrounds (or vice versa) works best for most people, but this is especially true of a reader who is visually impaired; black and white is often the best choice.
- **Line spacing** – This is the gap between lines of text. Double line spacing can often be easier to read.

## Practice point

Legibility is a particular problem on web pages; some are much easier to read than others. Visit a variety of web pages and identify which are easiest to read. You should look carefully at the design of each of the pages you visit and identify the features that make the pages easy or hard to read.

Prepare a short presentation for your class. Explain the good and bad techniques you have identified by showing the relevant websites to the class.

## Take it further

Visit the website: www.webstyleguide.com/type/legible.html. Using the site make a full list of the key design features that will make your web-based documents more legible.

## Distraction avoidance

If your message is to get through it is important that the people in your audience is not distracted; this is especially true during oral presentations. Therefore you will need to make sure that others know that you are not to be disturbed; have another person ready to greet late-comers outside the room and avoid them entering the room inappropriately while you are talking; and make sure that all mobile phones are switched off before you begin – including your own!

## Business and industry-related experience and knowledge

Inexperienced people will need the basics explained first. If you miss this out they will not get anything from your communication. However, if you labour your way through the basics of a topic when you are writing or speaking to experienced business people you will come over as patronising and they are unlikely to listen. By the time you get to the main point, they will already have switched off.

The overall message then is simple: *know your audience*!

▲ **Don't let a mobile phone ruin your presentation!**

## Case study

### Fujax UK

You work for Fujax UK, manufacturers of photographic equipment, and you are preparing a presentation to deliver to the Board of Directors about the latest high specification camera that is about to be launched. The presentation will cover both the features and technical details of the new model and the promotional plan for its launch. The Board of Directors has also asked you to present the same information to the workforce later in the day. The workforce consists of people aged from 16 to 60 and includes one lady who is profoundly deaf.

1. Outline in general terms the types of adaptation you would include to ensure that the second presentation goes as well as the first. ✓
2. Produce a handout summarising the main points of the presentation. You should make sure that this handout is as accessible for as many different types of person as possible. ✓✓
3. Produce a series of bullet points to justify each of the techniques that you have used in preparing your handout. These points should explain why the techniques are useful and what type of person would most benefit from each of the techniques used. ✓✓✓

# Methods of written communication

Today there are many ways of communicating in business situations – written and verbal, electronic and non-electronic. The diagram below shows methods you could choose from.

## Letter

Although they might be seen as relatively 'old-fashioned', vast numbers of letters are still sent by organisations every day. This is not only because they are simple and quick to produce, but they also provide a written record of correspondence that can be useful in the event of a dispute. On the following page is an example of a business letter style.

It may look old-fashioned to you, but it is the style that businesses will expect to receive so you should adopt this style for all letters you write during your BTEC National course. Remember that your writing style gives messages about you and about your organisation, so you must take steps to make a good impression. The following guidelines will help you.

### Structure

Good business letters should follow a certain structure:

1. Introduction – say what the letter is about and why you are writing.
2. Details – the main body of the letter should contain the information you wish to convey to your reader.
3. The next step – tell your reader what they should do next in response to your letter.

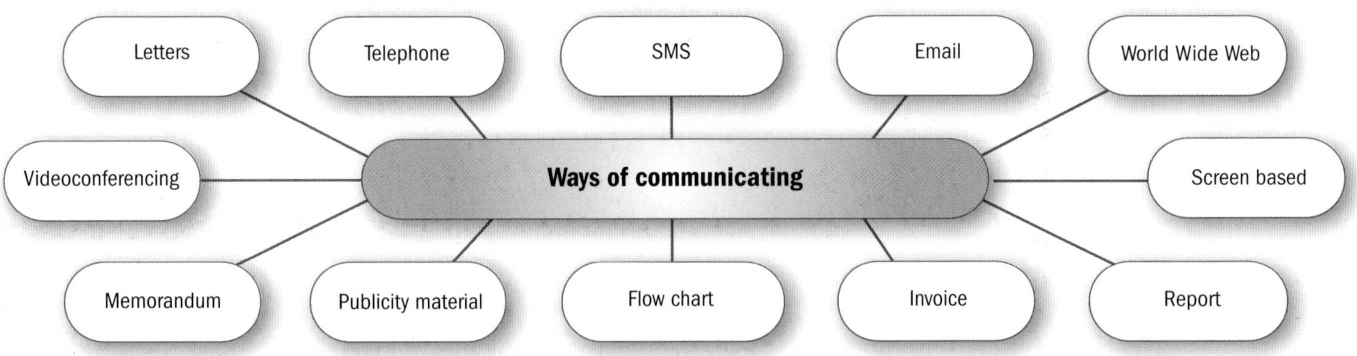

This is the address of the company sending the letter

Reference details: first two letters are initials of person signing the letter, the second two are those of the administrator who typed it

The address of the person and company receiving the letter

All business letters must have a title

Use 'sincerely' if you address the letter to a named person, use 'faithfully' if you don't know the person's name

Name and designation of the person signing

'Enc' indicates that there is a document attached to the letter

**E Turner PLC**

**Head Office**
**35 Robyn Street**
**Carlisle**
**Cumbria**
**CA1 5DT**

Our Ref: FB/PT

21 March 2007

Miss M Byte
Manager
Marshalls Micros Ltd
Marshall House
Adwick-Le-Street
Doncaster
South Yorkshire
DN14 8TY

Dear Miss Byte

**Enquiry for Quotation**

Further to our telephone conversation on 19 March, I have pleasure in enclosing our quotation for supply of 125 motherboards and PC power supplies about which you enquired.

I trust that this quotation meets your requirements, but should you need any further information please do not hesitate to contact me. If you wish to place an order, please telephone our order line 01302 558930 and quote the reference number on the attached quotation form.

Thank you very much for your enquiry. I look forward to hearing from you again soon.

Yours sincerely
E Turner PLC

*Frances Billinghurst*

Frances Billinghurst
Sales Manager

Enc

▲ **A business letter**

## ■ Style

Remember that when you write a business letter you are not writing to your best friend! You will not write in the same way that you speak, as we are all lazy with our conversational English; instead you have to be formal and correct. Good punctuation will help your reader to understand the points you are making. If you know that you are weak in this area speak to your teacher or lecturer to arrange some extra help. Get your spelling right! The spell check on your computer will help, but make sure that you have a UK English dictionary installed not an American one or you will get American spelling creeping into your work.

You should always write in sentences – but they don't need to be long sentences. Some students think that business communications should be full of long-winded sentences because they sound more important or professional. This is a mistake. Simple is usually best. The important thing is to get the message through to your reader. Long sentences can often confuse, so keep it short and don't use 20 words when 10 would do. Use proper English and avoid colloquialisms and slang words.

Under no circumstances should you use text speak or email style abbreviations in your business letters. Your tone should be professional and objective, not chatty, casual or over-friendly. Hence:

'We deeply regret the impolite treatment that you received today in our store. I can assure you that prompt steps are being taken to ensure that this does not happen again'

is better than:

'Sorry about the mix-up, don't worry, I'm sorting it.'

## ■ Draft it first

Don't expect to be able to write a good letter first time without any revisions. You should read and re-read your letters to ensure that they make sense. Better still, get a friend to read it for a more objective opinion. You should avoid irrelevance and stick to the point; a long-winded letter is likely to end up in the bin. Also, don't rely on the computer to pick up all of your grammatical errors; a 'grammar-check' is no substitute for a critical re-reading.

## ■ Always be helpful

You've heard the maxim that 'the customer is always right'. It is true and your job is to help at all times, even when you think that the customer is mistaken or rude.

Therefore you must remember to be apologetic if you are replying to a complaint letter. You must always start with an apology, even when you feel that your organisation is not in the wrong. (Don't try to argue back – this is not professional and not helpful!) Sympathise with the customer and state how you are going to sort things out.

### Practice point

Your assistant has drafted the content of a letter for you in reply to a complaint received by your organisation this morning. Examine the draft carefully. It has a number of errors contained in it. Pick out and correct all of the mistakes and then type up the letter that you would send back to the customer. Assume that you work for E Turner PLC, Head Office, 35 Robyn Street, Carlisle, Cumbria, CA1 5DT. You will be replying to Miss M Byte, Manager, Marshalls Micros Ltd, Marshall House, Adwick-Le-Street, Doncaster, South Yorkshire, DN14 8TY. She has written to complain that you have not delivered a consignment of PC components that she ordered last week (she was promised delivery the following day), and she also has not received an invoice for some goods that she ordered this day last month. Her letter suggests that she would like some compensation for your errors. Miss Byte is a long-standing customer who places a lot of valuable orders with your firm.

Dear Mrs Byte

Complaint

I really cannot except that we didn't deliver the goods you ordered on time. I have checked the delivery records myself and we definititely sent them to you, Perhaps u should of looked more carefully in your post room. We didn't send you an invoise for the goods you ordered last munth, but it'll be with you expeditiously.

Yours faithfully

E Turner plc

## Practice point

Your name is Annabelle Fryer and you work as Store Manager at BrillBurger Ltd, a franchised fast food store in Wolverhampton. You have today received the letter of complaint below.

Your task is to write a reply to this letter. Use this structure to help you when replying to letters of complaint:

- Start with a statement of regret. Acknowledge receipt of the letter of complaint, show that you understand the problem and apologise for the distress caused.
- Explain how the problem arose. This should be done following investigation into the incident.
- State the action you are taking to resolve the problem.
- Conclude by restating your apology and a statement that you hope to retain the goodwill of the customer.

76 Hardknott Close
Wolverhampton
WV3 5TR

14 July 2007

Miss A Fryer
Restaurant Manager
BrillBurger
41 Main Street
Wolverhampton
WV1 7YT

Dear Miss Fryer

Last Saturday I entered your store at around 1.30pm and purchased one of your Bumper Burger Meal Deals for myself and my five-year-old daughter. Imagine my horror when halfway through our meal my daughter found a fried snail in her meal! When we had calmed down we approached a member of your counter staff who told me that you were unavailable. He was rather off-hand with me and seemed to find the incident amusing. He offered me my money back but I was so upset by his manner that I left the store without the money and feeling very offended at the way I had been treated.

My daughter was very upset by the whole incident and, despite being a regular customer of yours over the last few years, I feel it is unlikely that we will want to come back to your restaurant.

I am writing to you to let you know how angry and disappointed I feel and to ask you what you are going to do about this distressing incident.

Yours sincerely

C Read

Mr C Read

▲ **A letter of complaint**

## Memorandum

A memorandum is an internal form of communication and is intended for relatively short messages between members of staff. Unlike a letter, there is no complimentary close and memos are not normally signed unless they are being used to authorise payments. Memos always have a title and it is common to use simple bullet points in the main text. Here is an example of a typical memorandum:

**MEMORANDUM**

To: H Jackson
From: J Leadbetter
Date: 20 October 2007
Subject: Training Programme

Further to our recent conversation, I can now confirm that the details of the training programme for new recruits have been finalised. We will need you to give an introductory talk to the new staff as follows:

- 10 am 29 October
- 3 pm 31 October
- 10 am 17 November.

I should be grateful if you would confirm your availability as soon as possible. Please let me know if you will need any supporting equipment during your talks.

### Practice point

Write a memo to your manager requesting two new members of staff for your department. Explain why this is necessary and outline the skills the new staff will need. You should invent the details yourself.

## Fax

Fax is short for facsimile machine; such machines use telephone lines to send pictures and documents. The telephone number of the receiving fax is input into the sending machine and the document is then fed into the machine; the machine scans the document and sends it to the receiving machine that then prints it out. Faxes are used by organisations that need to send copies of documents quickly to clients or business colleagues although email attachments are beginning to take the place of many fax transmissions. Faxes are normally sent with a cover sheet that includes the following details:

- the date the fax is sent
- the number of pages sent
- who the document is being sent to
- who is sending the document
- any message the sender wished to give to the receiver.

## Report

A report is a very commonly used style of written communication in business. It is a formal reply to a task that has been set or investigations that an employee has undertaken. For example, your manager might ask you to investigate the efficiency levels in the production department and to make some recommendations for improvements. This is a complex investigation and might require you to gather a lot of information before you can make any suggestions. You might need to:

- observe what happens on the factory floor
- interview staff members
- discuss matters with supervisors
- gather the thoughts of senior managers
- investigate new technologies that have become available
- visit different companies to observe different management techniques or working practices.

Once you have acquired the information you might present the results to your manager in the form of a business report, as follows. Note that a report always carries the same seven sections:

1.0 Terms of reference
2.0 Procedure
3.0 Findings
4.0 Conclusion
5.0 Recommendations
Bibliography
Appendices

When compiling reports you should pay careful attention to the layout and the numbering system. Professional business reports can be many pages long, so the numbering of sections and sub-sections is important so that it is easy to refer to parts of the report during discussions.

The person who will receive the report

The introduction. You should say what you are doing and why

The steps you took to gather the information

This is the longest report section. It includes all of the information and opinions that you have gathered

This should refer back to your Terms of Reference. What is the answer to the task that you have been set?

What you think should happen as a result of your findings

List your sources of information. You should use the Havard Referencing System

Any attached documents referred to in the text should be included at the back of your report

**CONFIDENTIAL**

For: A Bailey, Production Director — Ref:PG

From: P Guy, Production Manager — Date: 18 October 2007

**REPORT ON THE EFFICIENCY OF THE PRODUCTION LINE AT PHIL'S ELECTRICALS**

1.0 TERMS OF REFERENCE

On 3 September you asked me to investigate production line efficiency on the shop floor. I was asked to comment on the current systems used, the mood amongst the production team and any recent developments that might help to improve performance.

2.0 PROCEDURE

In order to obtain the relevant information and opinions, I followed the following procedures:

2.1 Observations were made on various occasions on the factory floor.
2.2 Interviews were conducted with staff members on the production line.
2.3 Extensive discussions were conducted with production line supervisors.
2.4 Those senior managers with experience of the production function were interviewed.
2.5 New technologies were evaluated off site.
2.6 Visits were conducted to RTK PLC and Middletons Ltd (Stockport).

3.0 FINDINGS

3.1 The mood of the staff of the production line is generally good, the managerial style used by the supervisors seems to suit the nature of the staff employed, however . . . .

3.2 Procedures implemented in the department work adequately well but many of them have not been reviewed for some considerable time . . . . . . .

3.3 . . . . . . . . . . . .

3.4 . . . . . . . . . . . .

4.0 CONCLUSIONS

It is clear that the general management of the production function at the company is effective, however . . . . . . . . . .

5.0 RECOMMENDATIONS

As a result of my investigations, I recommend that the Board of Directors give active consideration to the following:

5.1 The introduction of JIT procedures would undoubtedly improve the efficiency of production . . . . . . . . . .

5.2 A variety of new technologies have become available in recent years, and the following seem to be the best of those available . . . . . . . . . .

BIBLIOGRAPHY

MOYLES, P.C. AND GREW, P., 2001. *Production Techniques.* 2nd ed. London: Heinemann.
TURNER, E., 2003. *Management of Production,* 7 (4), 17-25.
*Guide to Production.* Nottingham Trent University. Available from: http://www.ntu.ac.uk/library/

APPENDICES

▲ **A business report**

## Practice point

You are to carry out an investigation into the quality of food and service in your school or college canteen. You should use a range of primary sources for your investigation, including interviews and observations (plus any others you would like to include). You should then write a report detailing your findings; don't forget the conclusion and your recommendations for improvement.

## Invoice

An **invoice** is a document produced by a business that is selling goods or services on credit, and it is normally produced by the sales department when the goods are dispatched to the buyer. It is intended to confirm the details of the goods purchased and the details of payment that is required, both the total amount and the date when payment is required. Invoices are usually kept for a period of at least six years as they may be needed as evidence of a contract between the business and the customer if any legal action should be taken over the goods sold. Below is an example of a typical invoice.

▼ **An invoice is a demand for payment**

**PHIL'S ELECTRICALS LTD**
27 Maybank Road Cheltenham Gloucestershire GL43 8TR

**Date/Tax Point**
3 November 2007

Tel: 0202 459876
Fax: 0202 459878

To: Purchasing Department
Old College Newark

VAT Reg. No.
275 230097

**INVOICE No.**
1045

Order Number: 67

| **Quantity** | **Catalogue Number** | **Description** | **Unit Price £** | **Total Price £** |
|---|---|---|---|---|
| 15 | PE7/679 | 10m Extension Cables | £3.99 | £59.85 |
| 12 | PE7/491 | Hitachi Microwave Ovens | £39.99 | £479.88 |
| 2 | PE7/398 | Dyson Vacuum Cleaners | £249.98 | £499.96 |
| | | | | £1039.69 |
| | | | Less Trade Discount @ 10% | £103.97 |
| | | | Total (Excluding VAT) | £935.72 |
| | | | Add VAT @ 17.5% | £163.75 |
| | | | **Total Due** | £1099.47 |

Terms: Net 30 days
Carriage Paid
E & OE

Annotations:
- The company selling the goods
- The date the sale was made
- The company buying the goods
- Each invoice has a unique number
- Unit Price x Quanitity
- Good customers may qualify for discount
- Payment is expected in 30 days. Cost of delivery has been paid by the supplier

## Key Terms

**Invoice** A demand for payment sent to the customer once the goods (or services) have been sent to the customer.

## Flow charts

**Flow charts** are a useful way of illustrating a process that takes a number of logical steps and requires decisions to be taken along the way. In a flow chart an oval represents the start or end of the chart, oblong boxes contain instructions and diamonds contain decisions. Here is an example of a simple flow chart to follow if your TV is not working.

TV not working
Is TV plugged in? — No → Plug in and switch on
Yes
Is fuse OK? — No → Replace fuse → Plug in and switch on
Yes
Call engineer

A flow chart shows different stages and decisions to be made ▶

## Key Terms

**Flow chart** Diagram illustrating a process that involves a number of steps and a series of decisions.

## Practice point

Draw a flow chart for a student trying to decide which method of transport to use to get home from school or college at the end of the day. Assume the choice is between walking, cycling, catching the bus and getting a lift from a parent after they finish work.

## Publicity material

There are many forms of **publicity materials** used by different organisations, and although they vary greatly they all carry certain essential qualities. They:

- are attractive to the eye
- are informative
- enhance the **corporate image** of the organisation.

## Key Terms

**Publicity material** Publications produced by an organisation that are intended to attract attention and promote sales.

**Corporate image** The characteristics an organisation seeks to establish for itself in the minds of the public, for example it might want to be seen as caring, innovative or trustworthy.

The level of detail given varies. While posters and stickers carry only minimal information (but enough to attract attention), brochures and websites can carry much more for the customer to read.

▼ Publicity material is intended to be attractive and informative

## Practice point

Assume that you are starting up one of the following businesses:

- CD/DVD shop
- mobile phone store
- sandwich shop
- newsagent.

Produce two items of publicity material to support the launch of your chosen new business.

### Take it further

Produce a written explanation of the content of the publicity materials that you have designed. Give a full justification of the content of your publicity materials and the design elements that you have used. Explain ways that your designs could be improved if you had more money or resources.

## Screen-based communication

Communication in business increasingly uses technology and much of this is based around screens. Computer screens are used for email and Internet communications; mobile phone screens are used for text messaging; and TV screens have been used for advertising for many years but communication through TV sets is becoming increasingly interactive with new digital technology. Display screens on railway stations and in airport lounges provide information about journeys and even bank cash machines offer new products and services while we withdraw our cash. Electronic and screen-based communication is clearly the way of the future.

## Email

Email is a powerful communication method for modern organisations. It is quick, easy to use and very cheap, costing far less than a letter or telephone call. Emails can be with a customer almost instantly, and they give both parties a written copy of the message, which is useful for reference. Because emails are received digitally they are also easy to store.

Many email users use abbreviated words in emails, but it is considered bad practice to do this with an email to a client or another business. You must remember to consider the impression you create when sending an email message. However, emails can be a relatively informal means of communication, so it is not unusual to receive business emails that are written in a less formal and quite friendly tone.

## Practice point

Ask for the email address of your tutor and send them an email. You should outline what you see as the main benefits of using email over other forms of business communication. You should also give details of the email provider company that you use and explain why you chose that particular company.

### Take it further

Evaluate in detail the service that you receive from your chosen mail provider.

## SMS (Short Message Service)

SMS, more commonly referred to as 'text messaging', is available between mobile phones and is now being used in many creative ways by organisations. Here are a few examples:

- Short messages can be sent between employees, as a replacement for memos and email.
- Travelling members of staff, such as sales people, can be kept up to date with important developments.

- Many businesses now accept orders via text message, payment for the orders may be made by charging the customer's mobile phone account.
- Travel companies deliver information to passengers about when buses are due or flights are delayed.
- Companies deliver paid-for content to customers such as sports scores, logos and ringtones.
- Direct marketing messages can be sent – e.g. advertising events.
- Automatic text reminders can be sent to customers, reminding them of appointments they have made.
- Orders placed by customers can be acknowledged by text message.

**Practice point**

In small groups you should discuss creative ways in which businesses could use SMS services. Select your three favourite ideas and explain them to the rest of the class.

**Take it further**

Using a good search engine such as google.co.uk or altavista.co.uk, search the Internet for further examples of business use of SMS.

## www (worldwide web)

Undoubtedly one of the biggest changes in the company/customer relationship in recent years has been the increasing use of the Internet to both boost sales and to strengthen relationships with existing and potential customers. E-business has helped to bring businesses and their potential customers much closer and it has improved communication considerably.

### Widening target market

Businesses which have an online presence, and sell over the worldwide web, can access and communicate with a much wider customer base. A traditional business may only sell in its locality but e-business allows firms to access customers worldwide, so the target market is much larger. At the same time Internet trading conquers the problem of time differences, as an e-commerce presence can be available to customers round the clock.

### Communicating change

The Internet allows businesses to quickly change what products they offer to customers or to revise the pricing of products offered if circumstances change. Instead of having to reprint advertising materials, a 'brochureware' site can be quickly and cheaply updated, which means organisations can be very responsive to market changes.

### Providing information

Providing information to customers is significantly easier through the worldwide web. In the past organisations might have relied upon methods such as brochures, leaflets and catalogues being sent through the post, a system which took time and was relatively inefficient; today it is easier and more efficient to provide detailed information via a company website.

### Individualisation of products

It can be a major advantage to a business to be able to offer a more personalised product in a competitive market, and a well-designed website can enable an organisation to do this. Many websites will now allow the customer not only to choose a product to buy but also to choose extra features, colours and designs. Look at www.evesham.com, the website for Evesham Technology which makes and sell PCs. After choosing a particular model to buy you can then choose from a wide range of additional hardware and software options so you can design a product to meet your personal requirements.

## Real lives

**Internet research**

The Audi website, www.audi.co.uk, contains the Audi Configurator, which allows you to select the interior and exterior colours for your new car, and you can see exactly what your chosen combinations will look like on screen.

1. Search the Internet and see what other examples you can find of businesses offering individualised products to customers via their websites. ✓
2. Working with a partner you should decide on a product or service that could be offered over the Internet which would benefit from being sold on an individualised basis. Draw up a list of features that you could offer customers on this basis. ✓✓
3. Use flip chart paper to sketch out the web page that you would use to sell your product or service in this way and explain to your group the importance of these features. ✓✓✓

### ■ Targeted direct marketing

Websites can also be used to make very precise direct marketing suggestions to customers when they visit the site. If you visit the Amazon site (www.amazon.co.uk) for example, it recognises you when you return (by means of a small bit of computer code called a cookie that it places on the hard drive of your machine) and the site knows what products you might be interested in. It monitors all of the pages that you view and records the purchases that you make; this way it can select very precisely any new products in which you may be interested. The site will then suggest the products to you as a series of recommendations, and these will be different each time you visit. This is clearly much more likely to produce results than a system of randomly generated marketing suggestions.

### Gathering information

The Internet also offers the opportunity for customers to give direct feedback about products and services through email, chatrooms and message boards. These can prove to be valuable information sources, which is why so many organisations now include them on their sites.

Of course, the Internet is also a great way of keeping an eye on the competition. It is easy to find out what products and services competitors are offering, what prices they are charging and any special deals that are currently on offer.

# Methods of non-written communication

### Telephone call

Telephone calls are still very useful for fast communication, enabling quick feedback and discussion. Modern telephone facilities can allow conference facilities so that a number of people can be involved in the same conversation.

### Video conferencing

**Video conferencing** involves conducting meetings or conversations through computer screens. It allows people to speak face to face with colleagues who are many miles apart, even across the world. Such systems used to be the province of businesses with lots of money to invest in video conferencing suites and fast telephone lines, but today the investment required is minimal. With a simple webcam, broadband Internet connection and video conferencing software (which is often free, such as Skype, www.skype.com, or Microsoft's Windows Live Messenger) any company can set up video conferencing facilities.

### Key Terms

**Video conferencing** Video and audio communication through computer or TV screens between two or more parties usually over a broadband Internet connection using webcams.

# Technologies

Much communication happens today using different types of technology.

## Computers and the Internet

Using the Internet, email, instant messaging, broadband telephony and other software applications, computers are essential in business today.

## Touch screens

Touch screens are an adaptation of computer technology; instead of interacting with the machine using a keyboard or mouse we can touch certain areas of the screen.

Touch screens are used for many purposes in business:

- Displaying information – tourist information offices, for example, use screens to enable visitors to quickly access information that they require, without the need for an assistant to help them.
- Self-service tills – supermarkets and catalogue shops (such as Argos) employ touch screen technology to allow customers to select and purchase goods.
- Training – many businesses now offer training to employees via touch screen training packages.

▲ Touch screens can speed up the buying process

## Digital broadcasting

Digital TV viewers and radio audiences can now communicate with the broadcast provider via interactive services. Email can be accessed, products purchased, opinions expressed and choices made at the touch of a button.

## DVD (Digital Versatile/Video Disc)

DVD is now the video medium of choice for organisations today and the old VHS tape is becoming obsolete. The improved picture and sound quality means most businesses use DVD for all their video needs today. However the advent of High Definition, (HD) TV and DVD could mean that the days of the standard DVD system are also numbered. The improved quality picture offered by HD technology requires far more storage space than regular DVD so manufacturers will be persuading us, and businesses, to upgrade TV sets and DVD players to take advantage of these new developments.

## Mobile phones

It is surprising to think that most people have only been using mobile phone technology for about 20 years. It has so quickly become embedded into our lives that most of us cannot imagine how we would manage without it today. Businesses have also been enthusiastic users of mobile phones and much business communication now takes place using this method. As the range of services available on mobile phones expands it is likely that this use will increase further.

## WAP (Wireless Application Protocol)

**WAP** is the technology used by portable communication devices, such as mobile phones and PDAs (Personal Digital Assistants), for accessing the Internet, checking email, accessing newsgroups, using instant messaging and even buying products. Initially WAP was a little slow to get off the ground. The content available was not very comprehensive, screens were hard to read and were only in black and white; consequently some doubted its long-term potential. Modern phones, however, are now making WAP a much more attractive and useful tool, with a wide range of content available. For a great demonstration of the potential of WAP services, visit the following BBC site: www.bbc.co.uk/mobile/web/emulator.shtml.

## Key Terms

**WAP** The technology used by mobile phones and PDAs for accessing the Internet.

## Outcome activity 4.2

The Outcome activity requires you to investigate the main employability, personal and communication skills required when applying for a specific job role.

### Pass

First, obtain copies of recent newspapers or trade journals that contain job advertisements. Look through them and choose at least three jobs that you are interested in investigating. You will only need to investigate one job for this assignment; however, you may not get responses from all your chosen companies, so it would be a good idea to select at least three at this stage.

1. Using the instructions given in the job advertisement obtain application forms and job descriptions for each of the jobs chosen.
2. Once you have received all three job descriptions/ application forms you will need to choose one of them to focus on.
3. Examine the job description and application form in detail. Draw up a list of skills that you feel would be necessary in order to be able to do this job effectively. You should list these under the three key headings.
   - Employability skills
   - Personal skills
   - Communication skills.
4. Now compare yourself against each of the required skills for your chosen job. You will need to consider if you have each of the skills and what evidence you could give to demonstrate them.
5. Put your findings for tasks 1 to 4 together in a formal report. The report should be addressed to your tutor.

### Credit

To achieve this criteria you will need to extend the report written for P1. You will need to analyse the skills required to perform your chosen job. To do this you should complete the following.

1. Give a detailed explanation of the nature of each skill that you have identified as necessary for your chosen job.
2. Give a detailed explanation of why each is necessary to the successful performance of the job in question.
3. You will need to join with a partner to prepare and perform a short role play that illustrates how necessary some of the skills are that you have identified. You should do a role play set in a business context, such as a team meeting, appraisal, interview or staff briefing, which should be designed to illustrate some of the potential pitfalls if the member of staff does not have the required skills. Aim to include at least four skills on your role play.

### Distinction

This criteria requires you to examine the importance of good communication skills in the staff of a firm. You should write a document that covers the following:

1. Outline the benefits to a firm of good information handling and communication skills amongst their staff.
2. Outline the potential dangers to a firm of having staff who are poor at information handling and communicating.
3. Consider the firm that you have examined in P1 and M1. Outline the mission of the company and its principal objectives. Evaluate how important good information handling and communication skills are to achieving the mission and objectives. You should also consider the importance of customer feedback in this context.

## Grading tips

**Pass** p2

1. Before you contact your chosen companies for task 1 ask you tutor to check what you are sending (whether it be a letter or email) to make sure it gives the right impression about you.
2. Sometimes companies are slow to respond to requests so have a couple of other jobs you could enquire about if you have trouble obtaining responses.
3. Task 3 could be completed as a table which could later be included in your report.
   Your report should follow the following structure:

   *1.0 Terms of Reference*
   Say what your report is intended to cover.

   *2.0 Procedure*
   Outline the methods you used to obtain the information from companies.

   *3.0 Findings*
   This should contain your answers to tasks 3 and 4.

   *4.0 Conclusions*
   Summarise how suitable you think you would be for your chosen job.

   *5.0 Recommendations*
   Outline how you might obtain the skills and experiences you lack if you were to apply for the job.

   *Appendices*
   Attach the relevant job description and application form.

**Merit** m1

Analysis involves breaking something down and examining each part in detail, so you will only achieve this criteria if you extend your report significantly. Try to break down each skill you are examining and illustrate its importance by suggesting work contexts in which it will be crucial.

Although there is a serious intent in the role play there is an opportunity for some humour in your script, so use your creativity when making your preparation. Make sure you rehearse the role play before you perform it.

**Distinction** d1

Evaluation is about considering in detail the advantages and disadvantages of something, and coming to conclusions as a result of this analysis.

# 4.3 Different types of information and how it can be processed

Information helps people to understand the world; however, too much information or the wrong type of information is simply a source of confusion. Information must be collected from the correct sources, organised and presented in ways that are helpful to the user, or the message will not be clear. Therefore for anyone hoping to communicate in business it is essential to be able to process information clearly.

## Types of information

Information comes from a wide variety of sources and an effective business person will research information from a range of sources before making decisions. Researched information could be:

- **verbal** – the thoughts and opinions of interviewees, or someone presenting information orally to you

▲ Processing information is vital

- **written** – from a wide variety of sources including newspapers, books, trade journals and government publications
- **on-screen** or **multimedia** – through TV and CD-ROMs that combine text, graphics, animation, audio and video
- **web-based** – much interactive multimedia content is now delivered via the Internet.

### Key Terms

**Multimedia** Communication involving a variety of media such as text slides, photographs, images, video, sounds, music and links to Internet sites.

## Features of information

### Internal and external information

Information can be found inside an organisation (**internal information**) or outside the organisation (**external information**).

### Key Terms

**Internal information** Information found inside the organisation.

**External information** Information found outside an organisation.

Internal information could come from a variety of sources within the organisation. Some of the main ones include:

- Accounts department – this will have a range of figures relating to company performance, such as profit figures and the costs of each company department.
- Sales department – this will store details of previous sales records for different products or services sold by the organisation. Interviewing the sales staff will give you an idea about the prospects for sales in the future, but be careful. Sales staff are notoriously optimistic about the possibilities for future sales, so try to verify their estimates by comparing them with past sales figures. Many sales staff love to use the 'hockey stick' prediction method – see the illustration on page 181.

▲ The 'hockey stick' method

- Production department – this will be able to give you details of production costs along with past and possible future levels of production.
- Human resources department – this can provide information about staff turnover rates, numbers of employees and the skills they have, training needs and the types and numbers of employees that will be required in the future.
- Marketing department – this can give information about the success of previous marketing campaigns and promotional activities.
- Customer services department: this can tell you what customers are saying about the company's quality of service or products, and their reactions to new ideas.

Much useful information can also be gathered outside an organisation, either by interviewing customers or examining published information. This is known as primary and secondary research. We can classify the sources of market information under two headings – **primary sources** and **secondary sources**.

## Key Terms

**Primary source** Original information that you have researched yourself.

**Secondary source** Information found from previously published or written sources either within or outside the organisation.

### Primary sources

Any original information is referred to as primary information or a primary source. It is conducted by or on behalf of the organisation, is specific to its needs and will involve methods such as questionnaires, observation, group discussions and interviewing.

### Secondary sources

There are two types of secondary research – desk research and external information. Any information obtained from sources internal to the organisation, such as accounting records, stock records or sales sheets, is described as desk research. External information is when organisations make use of published research that was not carried out specifically for that company but which is available and can be used by the organisation. It may involve searching through publications by the government, trade associations, media, trade directories and others. It can also be obtained from websites or from sources such as the market research company Mintel.

### Currency and life expectancy of information

We live in an ever-changing world, and what is current and correct today may be outdated very quickly. Many industries develop extremely fast. For example, the computer technology and communications industries have changed almost beyond recognition in the last 20 years. We must therefore recognise that the currency of our research information – i.e. how up to date it is – is vital for conclusions that are true and valid. So it is essential to ensure that the information we acquire is as current as possible by checking publication dates on books, newspapers and journals, and also 'last updated' dates on websites.

### Validity of information

Once information has been gathered, it is important to try and determine how valid the information is – in other words, is it accurate, relevant and truthful?

An important question to ask in determining the validity of your research information is 'Who wrote this information and what were their motivations in writing it?' Much of the information that you find may well be valid, but some may be misleading. Some sources are clearly more reputable than others. If you read a political article in the *Daily Sport*, is it likely to be as reliable as one

## Case study

**Website validity**

Imagine that you have been given the task of researching the environmental impact of industry; it is possible that you might arrive at this site – www.dhmo.org. Look now at its home page. The site purports to discuss the dangers of the chemical dihydrogen monoxide and it appears to be quite plausible. Click on the 'Environmental Impact' button and read the information.

It sounds like a pretty problematic substance and you can imagine a student finding this site and cutting and pasting sections of this into their work. But have you spotted the clue yet to the fact that this is a bogus site? If not, think carefully about the name of the substance: dihydrogen monoxide. Dihydrogen means two hydrogen molecules; monoxide means one oxygen molecule. Two hydrogen, one oxygen – does that remind you of anything? $H_2O$? It's water! Now read the page again. You will see that none of the statements are untrue when related to water, but water isn't a problem – in fact we cannot live without it. One page, outlining the dangers of DHMO says 'For those who have become dependent, DHMO withdrawal means certain death.' You can't argue with that!

That was a spoof website but what about more serious inaccuracies or political censorship? Discuss with a friend and make notes about to what extent you believe the governments of different countries should regulate the content of websites. Consider the following questions.

1. Do you think that governments should interfere with what people want to put on websites? If so, what types of site/content should or should not be allowed? ✓
2. What steps might a government take to ensure the accuracy and validity of web pages? ✓✓
3. What are the dangers for individuals, businesses and researchers of there being no regulation of web page content? ✓✓✓

written in *The Times*? Quality newspapers are generally well researched and their published articles are more likely to be reliable (bearing in mind that each will have its own editorial or political slant). However, the same cannot be said of all of the popular dailies, some of which seem to aim to shock, titillate and entertain rather than presenting an objective and well-informed article.

This problem is much worse on the Internet. There is no regulation of content on the worldwide web, so you have to be very critical about what you read on websites. Clearly information from reputable known providers, such as www.bbc.co.uk or www.telegraph.co.uk, is to be trusted, but many others contain inaccurate information. (How far do you think you can trust the Wikipedia website?) Some are even deliberately set up to deceive the reader or aim to fool you into reading someone else's opinion. Some of the spoof sites are set up for a joke, but it may not be easy to detect this immediately, and it would be possible to believe that they give accurate information.

So when you are researching on the Internet, take care, because not everything you read will be true. Remember that much of what you read is opinion, and opinions are not facts. You should be critical when you look at different sites in order to identify those that are out to fool you.

# Purpose of information

Reliable and valid information is essential to all businesses and organisations. An organisation without information is like someone wandering around in the dark: they don't know where they are going and if they get to where they want to be it is more by luck than good planning.

Organisations use information for a variety of purposes, as outlined below.

## Updating knowledge

Information is required so that businesses know how their markets are developing, how labour markets are changing, what the economy is doing, what new laws are being passed that might affect the way they operate, and so on. All of this information helps organisations to make accurate decisions based on full knowledge – incorrect decisions are likely to be the result of inadequate information.

## Informing future developments

A business that does not adapt, develop and grow will quickly find itself left behind by the competition. But developments need to be based on informed decisions. A business will not launch a new product, for example, unless it has ample evidence that it is likely to sell. For example, Panasonic and NEC would not have launched the first 3G phones without clear research to suggest that they were likely to sell well; nor would Apple have developed the iPod if research had not indicated its likely success.

## Offering competitive insight

Monitoring and analysing the behaviour of competitors is essential for many businesses in competitive markets. Regular research and communication should help a business to assess its competitors' sales, marketing and development activities. It will keep a business alert to new product ideas being developed, new marketing strategies being used and new markets into which competitors may be moving. Some large businesses may employ Competitive Insight Managers to inform their strategic planning; alternatively, market research companies will undertake this sort of research on behalf of an organisation.

## Communicating sales promotions

In order to promote products and services effectively, organisations need to have some insight into their customers. Good market research information will offer an insight into the behaviour patterns of customers and their buying motivations. Information can therefore help businesses to promote their goods and services and so to sell more effectively.

## Inviting support for activities

You will need to communicate with different people in your organisation (or even outside it) in order to complete certain tasks. For example, you may need to enlist the support of staff members in a new sales drive, or you may be looking for them to suggest ideas for moving the business forward. If the activity that you are considering involves a lot of expenditure, you may contact external organisations to request sponsorship support. This happens frequently in the sports world, where many events would never take place without the financial backing of sponsors. Sponsorship can only be gained following extensive communication.

# Information gathering

## Information sources

It is essential to use a wide range of sources when gathering information for business purposes. This will be equally true for your assignment work, so there are some important lessons to be learned here for assignment preparation. You should also use a wide variety of sources; too many students assume that the Internet is the first and last word when it comes to gathering information, but if you are to create a complete and accurate picture you should employ as many methods as possible. The following is an outline of the range of sources available.

## Primary sources

Getting first-hand information by conducting questionnaires, observations, focus groups and interviews will give an up-to-date picture of how potential customers feel. Carefully targeted primary research should yield new ideas and opinions that you cannot obtain any other way. It can be time-consuming (and sometimes you may find it a little embarrassing), but it is usually well worth the effort.

Visiting organisations to interview members of staff can give you first-hand opinions of recent developments and what is happening in a market. Don't under-estimate the value of personal contacts when doing such research. If you have parents, brothers, sisters, friends or relations that work in a relevant occupation, take the opportunity to interview them, preferably at their workplaces. Personal contacts are more likely to be responsive to your approaches; they will usually help you to speak to the relevant people and make time to deal with your questions.

## Worldwide web using search engines

The worldwide web is a mine of information, covering every topic you could think of. It is relatively easy to find information on any topic today using one of the many search engines available; however, Internet researching is not always straightforward. Students often say, 'I can't find anything on the Internet on that subject' which generally means that they have tried a couple of queries on a search engine and not found anything relevant

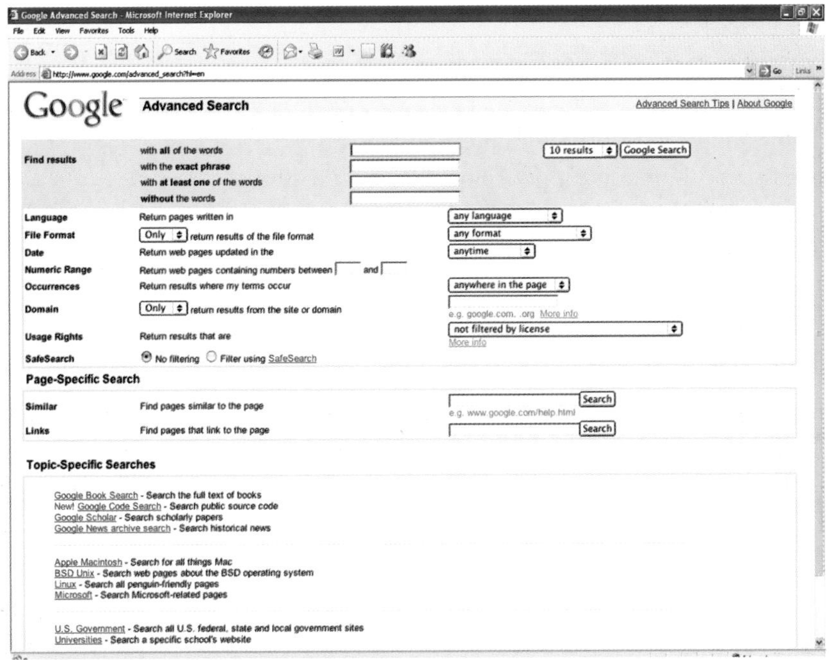


▲ Google offers an advanced search engine

immediately. Good research on the web requires logic and patience. Google is believed to have the largest search index on the web, so to find exactly what you want first time is never going to be easy.

So how can you improve your Internet researching skills? Here are a few handy tips:

- Use a variety of search engines. Different search engines will yield different results, so if you can't find what you want using one, then try another. Some of the best search engines include www.google.co.uk, www.altavista.co.uk, and www.lycos.co.uk. But there are many others, so try various search engines before you give up.
- Be specific with the words you use in your search. If you are researching sales trends in the cosmetics industry, for example, don't just put in the word *cosmetics* or *lipstick – sales trends cosmetics* is far more likely to give you something useful. Note that you don't need to type in very common words such as *in* or *the* as search engines will ignore them anyway.
- Use the '+' symbol to indicate specific words that must appear in your results. Going back to the previous example, the search 'sales trends cosmetics' gives lots of pages that only contain one of these words. If you only want results for sites that contain all of the words you enter, add a plus before each word. '+sales +trends +cosmetics' will only yield sites that contain all three of those words.
- Use the '–' (minus) symbol to indicate topics that should be omitted from search results. So if you wanted to eliminate references to Clarins Cosmetics from the above search you might search under '+sales +trends +cosmetics –Clarins'.

### Practice point

Use the techniques described above to find suitable information to help you plan a trip to London. Your planning should take in:

- the major sights
- accommodation
- some ideas of where to eat
- a show.

## Business communications

Businesses communicate constantly through advertisements, brochures, press releases, websites and also annually through their Company Report and Accounts.

Each year, every public limited company publishes a Company Report and Accounts. These documents are primarily intended to give the company's financial position and their pages contain details of company balance sheets and cash flow statements; however, they also contain many other useful nuggets of information. Details of new product launches, reviews of the market including the position of the business within that market, descriptions of the company's products and marketing campaigns may all be found in these documents, and they are usually presented in an attractive and accessible manner. The website www.carol.co.uk is an excellent source for such reports. You can search by company name to obtain copies of their latest reports on your computer screen, and it is all free.

## Government statistical sources

The UK government produces a vast amount of statistics that can be highly relevant to business investigations. Much of this is published in the form of booklets that are held in most libraries. However the website of the Central Statistical Office is now very comprehensive and should cater for most needs. The site can be found at www.statistics.gov.uk.

## News sources

For up-to-date information on the changing business environment and events that will affect businesses, there is no better source than the broadsheet newspapers and TV news. Most TV news programmes have articles on business related topics: BBC News 24 has Business News Reports, Channel 4 and Sky News have good coverage and BBC2 has a programme called *Working Lunch* every day that can be very useful.

There are also useful podcasts that can keep you up to date with business developments. A podcast can be downloaded to your computer or MP3 player and you can listen to it at your convenience; the service is usually free. A particularly good one is 'Wake up to Money' which can be found on the BBC Five Live website.

Newspapers still tend to be the very best source for business news; all of the quality papers have separate business sections that cover the latest events. Today it is not even necessary to buy the paper, as most of the newspapers have websites that you can access for free. The *Daily Telegraph* site at www.telegraph.co.uk has great coverage in the Business News section, but even more useful than this is the Search function that allows you to search for previous articles over the last few years. *The Times* site is also very good at www.timesonline.co.uk.

### Practice point

Search the web for podcasts on business news. Select one and subscribe to it (this should be free). Listen to the podcast for a week and then write a short summary of the most interesting business-related story of the week. You should read out your favourite story to your class or group and ask them to comment on the significance of the story.

### Trade journals

For the latest thinking from people on the inside of different industries, trade journals are a very useful resource. These are published by leaders in industries for the people working in that industry, but they also make excellent research materials. Magazines such as:

- *Marketing* published by Haymarket Publications offers insight into up to-date-developments. *Marketing* tells of the latest ad campaigns, branding methods and which advertisements are making the most impact with consumers.
- *Marketing Week* also covers the marketing industry, featuring in-depth articles outlining the latest techniques of marketers in the UK and abroad.
- *Supply Management* is published by the Chartered Institute of Purchasing and Supply and is aimed at company buyers and contract negotiators. It contains the latest information about buying in both retail and manufacturing environments.
- *Management Today* looks at employment law and different issues related to the management of people.

## Adherence to legislation

When using information that you have researched you should be aware that there are certain laws and codes of conduct surrounding what you can and cannot do with your results. Outlined below are some of the most important ones to consider.

### Intellectual property – copyright, designs and patents

**Intellectual property** is anything that someone has invented, designed, written or composed and which has some commercial value. Any original work of literature, art, music, computer software, sound recording, film or broadcast is subject to **copyright** law. This means that the original creator of the work has control over people using and making copies of their work. In the business world this also extends to product names, logos and the trade name of the organisation.

The researcher must be sure therefore that material they find and use is given due credit in their work. You must give full details of sources used and quoted in any assignment or presentation that you do. You are not allowed to copy or use substantial sections of someone else's work unless you get their express permission. Note that copyright law extends to material that is available on the Internet: just because it is freely accessible does not mean that you are free to use it without permission. The main legislation covering this area in the UK is the Copyright, Designs and **Patents** Act 1988.

It is important that you give due credit to the original writers of work that you have used in compiling your research; the details of references you have used should be listed using the **Harvard referencing system**. The following summarises the most commonly used entries for a Harvard system:

In the Harvard system, the references are listed in alphabetical order of authors' surnames.

**Reference to a book**

Author's surname, initials, year of publication, title (in *italics*), edition (if not the first), place of publication: Publisher. For example:

Needham, D., Dransfield, R., Guy, P. and Dooley, D., 2000. *Marketing for Higher Awards* London: Heinemann

**Reference to a journal article**

Author's surname and initials (or title of newspaper), year of publication, title of article, title of journal (in *italics*), volume number (and part number), page numbers of contribution. For example:

Page, W. P., 1999, Economies of Scale. *Economics Today*, 9 (3), 19–23

**Reference to a newspaper article**

Author's surname, initials, year of publication, title of article, title of newspaper (in *italics*), day and month, page number/s and column number. For example:

*The Times*, 2003. Growth or Bust. *The Times*, 8 June, p.15a.

**Reference to a government publication**

Name of issuing body, year of publication, title of publication (in *italics*), place of publication: publisher, report number (where relevant). For example:

Office for National Statistics, 2002. *Labour Market Trends*. London: ONS, ONS/3303/227.

**Reference to web pages**

Author/editor (Year). *Title* [online]. (edition), place of publication, publisher (if ascertainable). Available from: URL [accessed date]. For example:

Brown, J. (2001). *Business Report* [online]. Nottingham, New College Nottingham. Available from: www.ncn.ac.uk/reports/businessreport.htm [Accessed 21 June 2006].

## Key Terms

**Copyright** Law which states that the original creator of a work has control over people using and making copies of their work.

**Patent** If you invent something, registering a patent will give you the right to stop others from making it without your permission for a certain period of time.

**Harvard referencing system** A commonly accepted format for detailing the sources you have used in compiling your research.

**Intellectual property** Any original work of literature, art, music, computer software, sound recording, film or broadcast that has some commercial value.

## w3c (Worldwide Web Consortium)

The Worldwide Web Consortium is an organisation run by Tim Berners-Lee, the man who invented the worldwide web, and it has drawn up a code of practice which the majority of web developers now abide by. The Consortium is made up of a wide range of member companies that are involved in or rely on the Internet, such as Adobe Systems, British Telecom and Nokia, along with different web development companies, universities and other interested parties and organisations. Together they aim to develop standards and guidelines for all web designers and users to follow. Many of these recommendations set standards to be used when coding websites using HTML, XML and Cascading Style Sheets. By following their recommendations companies can ensure that websites are usable by as wide a range of people and companies as possible. Their recommendations are therefore now adopted by most web developers.

## Disability discrimination

The Disability Discrimination Act 1995 was introduced to remove the discrimination faced by many people with disabilities. It provides rights in a number of areas, in particular employment. The Act requires that a disabled person should not be treated any less favourably than others and requires that organisations make reasonable adjustments to working practices or premises to accommodate people with disabilities (unless there is reasonable justification for not doing so). Adjustments could involve wheelchair ramps or flexitime to allow for treatment. When engaging in business communication it is necessary to make sure that disabled people have equal access to the premises in which a presentation is delivered, and that a person with disabilities can receive the message as easily as anyone else.

## Equal opportunities

The Sex Discrimination Act 1975 and the Race Relations Act 1976 were passed to encourage people to treat others as individuals and to respect differences. The European Union Equal Treatment Directive now makes it unlawful to discriminate not only on existing grounds of sex, race and disability but also on grounds of sexual orientation and religion or other belief. From October 2006, age discrimination has also been unlawful. It is therefore essential that in business we respect these differences and communicate in a way that does not display prejudice.

### Practice point

You should work with a partner on this task. Assume that you are preparing to give a presentation on a new product or service that your company is preparing to launch (you can choose the type of product or service). Consider the principles of disability discrimination and equal opportunities. Make a list of the steps you would take to ensure that you do not contravene these principles.

### Take it further

Using Internet sources, make notes on the rules for avoiding discrimination in the workplace. You can use a range of websites, but a good place to start is the Business Link site at www.businesslink.gov.uk. What are the main laws/regulations that must be abided by? Produce a brief summary of their requirements.

## Outcome activity 4.3

In this Outcome activity you will be examining both electronic and non-electric methods of communicating in business. This task follows on from the scenario in Outcome activity 4.1. As a new entrepreneur you need to produce some information to use in the training of your new staff. You have observed that some staff are unclear about which methods of communication are suitable for different situations at work. You therefore decide to produce a guide to help new recruits to your business.

**Pass**

To achieve this criteria your guide should include two tables as follows: 

- A table listing and describing all electronic methods of communication available in business. You should also include examples of recipients that each method would be suitable for.
- A table listing and describing all non-electronic methods of communication available in business. You should also include examples of recipients that each method would be suitable for.

**Merit**

To achieve this criteria you should complete your guide by writing some notes to explain your table. These notes should discuss each of the methods listed in the tables and should explain in detail the reasons why each method is appropriate for the users that you have listed. m2

## Grading tips

**Pass** 

Your tables can use the following layout:

| Electronic methods of communication in business | |
|---|---|
| **Method** | **Suitable recipients** |
| Email (a system for sending messages electronically over a computer network) | Examples of recipients that would find this method helpful are ... |

**Merit** m2

A good way to explain the suitability of each method would be to give some examples of situations in which the method would be most suitable for the particular recipients you have named.

# 4.4 Present information effectively

The most skilled communicators are those people who:

- understand the message that is to be communicated
- think carefully about the audience that will receive it
- choose methods which are most appropriate for the audience
- use those methods effectively.

These are the skills that you will need to demonstrate – both to pass this unit and to be successful in your future professional careers. When choosing appropriate communication methods for your audience bear in mind that a variety of methods is often better than just one. This is especially true when delivering information to a number of people as not everyone receives messages in the same way, therefore it is important to meet a range of needs.

## Presentation methods to meet the needs of the user

Outlined below is a range of methods to consider when preparing to deliver your information:

### Documents

A variety of written documents have already been considered in this unit. Written documents are useful because they provide a lasting record of the communication that has taken place and they allow the receiver to re-read the information as often as necessary to gain a good understanding of the material; this can be vital if the information is technical and/or lengthy. Written documents can therefore be appropriate for the receiver of the message when:

- a record of the communication must be kept
- the receiver is likely to need to go through the information several times to fully understand it.

Different styles of document are useful in different circumstances and it is important to use the right method at the right time:

- letters, memoranda, reports and invoices – these methods were all described earlier in this unit
- agendas – these are used to outline the proposed items to be discussed during a forthcoming meeting
- minutes – these are used to detail the discussions and decisions made during a meeting.

## Grading tips

**Pass** 

Ensure that your information gathering allows you to collect a range of statistics about the market.

**Pass** 

Make sure you have accurately quoted the sources that you have used in collecting your information.

**Merit** 

You must ensure that you give a polished performance so make sure that you rehearse beforehand, preferably in front of a friend who can give you feedback.

**Distinction** 

This task requires you to explain why each method you used is helpful to the people you identified in the table you produced in P4. Since this is a Distinction criteria this explanation should be in considerable detail. You should also suggest suitable alternative methods that could be used for each of the people identified in your table.

## End of unit test

1. What is meant by staff retention?
2. How is staff turnover calculated?
3. What is the difference between expressed terms and implied terms in a contract of employment?
4. What is meant by 'employability skills'?
5. Name five employability skills and rank them in what you consider to be their order of importance. Explain your decisions.
6. Explain three business situations in which good listening skills would be vital.
7. Explain the difference between internal and external research information. Give examples to support your explanations.
8. Find out what 4G technologies are. In what ways might businesses make use of these in the future?
9. Some researchers believe that you should do secondary research before primary research. Explain the benefits of this approach.
10. What advantages do focus groups have over other primary information methods?
11. How can we check the currency of the information that we are gathering? Think of at least four different information sources, and explain how you would check the currency of each.
12. Outline an appropriate structure for a business letter of complaint.
13. 'Telephone technology is so good these days that we don't really need to produce written business correspondence any more.' Do you agree with this statement? Give reasons for your answer.
14. 'Patents and copyright rules are an incentive to innovators.' Explain why you think that these laws are necessary.
15. In what ways is PowerPoint a superior medium for delivering presentations? What limitations does it have?

## Grading tips

**Pass** 

Your tables can use the following layout:

| Electronic methods of communication in business | |
|---|---|
| **Method** | **Suitable recipients** |
| Email (a system for sending messages electronically over a computer network) | Examples of recipients that would find this method helpful are ... |

**Merit** m2

A good way to explain the suitability of each method would be to give some examples of situations in which the method would be most suitable for the particular recipients you have named.

# 4.4 Present information effectively

The most skilled communicators are those people who:

- understand the message that is to be communicated
- think carefully about the audience that will receive it
- choose methods which are most appropriate for the audience
- use those methods effectively.

These are the skills that you will need to demonstrate – both to pass this unit and to be successful in your future professional careers. When choosing appropriate communication methods for your audience bear in mind that a variety of methods is often better than just one. This is especially true when delivering information to a number of people as not everyone receives messages in the same way, therefore it is important to meet a range of needs.

## Presentation methods to meet the needs of the user

Outlined below is a range of methods to consider when preparing to deliver your information:

### Documents

A variety of written documents have already been considered in this unit. Written documents are useful because they provide a lasting record of the communication that has taken place and they allow the receiver to re-read the information as often as necessary to gain a good understanding of the material; this can be vital if the information is technical and/or lengthy. Written documents can therefore be appropriate for the receiver of the message when:

- a record of the communication must be kept
- the receiver is likely to need to go through the information several times to fully understand it.

Different styles of document are useful in different circumstances and it is important to use the right method at the right time:

- letters, memoranda, reports and invoices – these methods were all described earlier in this unit
- agendas – these are used to outline the proposed items to be discussed during a forthcoming meeting
- minutes – these are used to detail the discussions and decisions made during a meeting.

## Verbal presentations

Verbal explanations can often be helpful as you get the opportunity to explain things in more than one way if your audience does not understand immediately. This method is also very useful if immediate feedback or two-way communication is needed. Perhaps your audience will need to ask questions, offer ideas or seek clarification; in which case this is likely to be a good method to use.

▲ **Explaining ideas verbally can aid understanding**

## Role plays

Role play involves setting up a simulation of a situation that can be acted out in front of or even involving the audience. Although role plays can take a great deal of setting up and rehearsal, they can be a very effective way of delivering a message to an audience. Role plays can be both dramatic and entertaining, and as a result an audience tends to remember more of something that is demonstrated to them than something that is just talked about.

Role plays are used extensively by organisations training staff to deal with customers, interview clients or sell products. Role plays are effective because they can also be used to give the audience or receiver the opportunity to try out new ideas and skills that have been discussed. This can be a vital method for making sure the message is fully understood.

## On-screen multimedia presentation

A multimedia presentation is often one that is presented using a laptop and projector and would involve a variety of media such as text slides (possibly using a program such as PowerPoint), photographs, images, video, sounds, music and links to Internet sites. Such a presentation contains variety as well as both visual and aural impact, which is likely to keep your audience interested. The different media used make it easier to illustrate, demonstrate and explain points that need to be understood by the audience.

Such a presentation could be delivered by a person at the front of an audience or, alternatively, if the information is compiled onto a CD or DVD, the receiver could play it for themselves on their own computer at their own pace. This gives the advantage of being able to recap sections that the viewer needs to see more than once. This method also gives the opportunity to build in features that will be useful to people who are visually impaired or have hearing problems. An audio description that describes the images or video shown on the screen can help those who cannot see, and closed captions (text display of dialogue and sounds) make the information accessible to those who cannot hear well.

## Web-based presentation

Web-based presentations display many of the benefits of multimedia presentations described above. Using today's fast broadband connections it is possible to stream sophisticated content to a computer anywhere in the world. This is an advantage for many people as the message can be received wherever and whenever it is convenient for them, which can be a crucial factor for a busy executive.

## Use of images

We remember more of what we see than what we simply hear, so showing images can be the best way to help an audience remember the message. Images with impact can:

- gain the audience's attention
- illustrate the point being made
- explain something clearly
- make a point very strongly.

When you use images you should consider the resolution of image required; for more information see 'Output requirement' on page 192.

## Multilingual support

It is possible that in a presentation some members of the audience could be non-English speakers, i.e. people who speak English as an additional language. In such circumstances you might think about the following:

- Ask those members of the audience if they would like you to make special arrangements for them.
- Have paper copies of PowerPoint slides prepared in their native language for them to read during your presentation.
- Prepare translations of handouts to be used or reports that you have written.
- Organise an interpreter or English language support worker.
- Speak at a moderate pace and ensure that you pronounce your words carefully if they wish to follow the presentation in English.
- Offer to send a transcript of your talk in their native language before the presentation.

## Practice point

The table below lists a number of situations in which you will need to communicate. Complete the table by deciding the method you would use and justify your choice of method, i.e. explain why that is the best method.

| | Method chosen | Justification |
|---|---|---|
| You have to give a formal warning to a staff member about poor work. | | |
| You need to reply to a letter of complaint received today. | | |
| You must discuss a new sales strategy with your fellow directors in Glasgow, Cardiff and Basle. | | |
| You wish to show proposed new TV ads and website design to your salespeople to obtain their feedback. | | |
| You have to announce that the organisation is to make redundancies and you are looking for volunteers. | | |
| You need to check the date and time of a training course that you enrolled for some months ago. | | |
| You have to enlist the help of the staff in achieving the new branch sales targets. | | |
| You need to explain a complicated procedure to a new employee. This procedure is one they are likely to have to use repeatedly over the next few months. | | |
| You want to query your latest salary slip which is £500 short. | | |

# Output requirement

We have considered some different techniques you can use to make your message easier for your audience to understand. Here are a few further suggestions to think about. Each of these can make your final product more attractive to the eye or easier to use.

## Resolution of images

Images come in various **resolutions** and generally the higher the resolution you use, the more detailed and high definition your picture will be. However, there is a trade-off here. A high resolution image may look great, but if you put a few high resolution images into a Word document the file size soon starts to become quite big. You would soon fill an average-sized memory stick or CD, and large files also take longer to load into a computer. The bigger the file size, the more memory the computer needs to handle it and older machines with slower processors will find it a problem if you are using many high resolution images.

Therefore you should consider how high your definition needs to be. Take care when shooting with digital cameras or scanning pictures. If you choose a very high resolution setting, it will not only take a long time to scan the image or take the picture, the file size may be unmanageable. An A4 colour page scanned at just 300 dpi will create a file over 10MB big, which is too large for most uses. When you consider that many images on the worldwide web are very clear yet are only a few kilobytes big, you can see how little resolution you may really need.

Therefore, when scanning images or using a digital camera, a low resolution is going to be fine for most uses. The only time you will notice any dip in quality is if you want to greatly enlarge the image, but even for use on a PowerPoint data projector, images need to be no bigger than 300KB.

## Key Terms

**Resolution** The amount of fine detail in a picture. Photographs normally require much finer detail than simple drawings. On a computer, picture detail is measured in dpi or dots per inch.

## Text formatting

At the top of the screen in Microsoft Word are different options for altering the formatting of your text. Clicking on the menu options 'Format' and 'Font' will give you options for altering the text style, colour and size, as well as some specialised styles such as 'superscript', 'strikethrough' and 'shadow', and a number of others.

There are also four buttons for justifying the text. Highlight some text and click on the first one and it will all line up down the left side of the page (Left Justifying). The second button centres text, the third lines it up to the right of the page (Right Justifying). The fourth button fully justifies text; it creates text that lines up on both left and right sides of the column. This style is often used in newspapers.

## Page layout

Some elements of your page layouts should stay the same in your document. Your main font style and size should not alter throughout the text, and your headings should be of consistent styles too. Microsoft Word helps with this as it has a number of built-in heading and body text styles; sticking to these will give your documents consistency. However, offering some other variety in your pages can make life easier for your reader. Inserting images in your page can give some relief from endless text and, if they are well chosen, they can also aid understanding. Images can look good also if they have text flowing around them.

It is usually best to produce mixed text and graphics pages in a desktop publishing program such as Microsoft Publisher, Aldus Pagemaker or Quark Xpress, but today Microsoft Word can also handle frames quite well. In Word you can create text boxes (use 'Insert' and 'Text Box') and you can then insert pictures or diagrams into the text box. These can be easily moved around the page to the position that suits you best.

## Practice point

Look carefully at different pages in this book. Make a list of the features of one page that contribute to the fact that it is well laid out and easy on the eye of the reader.

## Take it further

Using Microsoft Word or a DTP program create a page of your own which uses the good layout features that you have identified. The content of the page can be any subject that you are interested in, possibly a favourite band, sports team or a hobby or pastime in which you are interested. Make sure that your page contains at least one photographic image plus one that you have created yourself, like a drawing or a graph.

## Use of tables

Microsoft Word and other programs contain powerful table functions. Tables are an excellent way of lining up information in columns and rows, so that it is all grouped neatly and is easy for your reader to interpret. This is particularly useful for sets of figures.

Below is an example of tabulated information. Statistics are often much easier to understand when they are put in a table like this.

| | Population mid-2005 | Percentage of total UK population |
|---|---|---|
| England | 50,431,700 | 83.8 |
| Wales | 2,958,600 | 4.9 |
| Scotland | 5,094,800 | 8.5 |
| Northern Ireland | 1,724,400 | 2.9 |
| United Kingdom | 60,209,500 | |

*Source:* www.statistics.gov.uk

## Combining information from a range of applications

When you have collected information from various sources you will then have to arrange it into one document, maybe a report or PowerPoint slides ready for a presentation. Your computer will help you with this as it is easy to copy and paste different information from various electronic sources into one document.

### ■ Copy and paste from text documents

To copy from one document, first highlight the text and/or pictures that you want to copy, then click on 'Edit' and then 'Copy'. Now open up the document that you want to paste into and click on 'Edit' then 'Paste'. You can use this technique for any text, tables or pictures that you have.

### ■ Copy and paste from spreadsheets

You may find some statistical data in spreadsheets (such as Microsoft Excel). This may be in either raw figures or as a chart, but it can also be imported using the same process.

It is possible to paste charts into a different document but link them to the original spreadsheet, so that if you make amendments to the figures in the spreadsheet later it will automatically update the graph in your new document. To do this, go to the new document, select where you wish to paste the chart, and then click on 'Edit' and 'Paste Special'. Click on the 'Paste Link' radio button and then OK. Your chart will be pasted in but will be updated if you change the spreadsheet.

### ■ Copy and paste from the Internet

Text and figures can be copied and pasted from Internet pages in exactly the same way as described above. Images can be copied by pointing at the image and pressing the right-hand mouse button. You can now click on 'Copy' and then 'Paste' into your new document. Alternatively you could click on 'Save Picture As . . .' and save it to a disc for later use. You should be aware, however, that the majority of images on the Internet are copyright and therefore should only be used commercially with permission.

## Use of specialist software and hardware

There are several computer programs and pieces of specialist equipment that may help you to present information well. Microsoft Word is a very versatile program that will enable you to easily produce effective written business documents. If you wish to produce something more visually appealing then a desktop publishing program such as Microsoft Publisher, Aldus Pagemaker or Quark Xpress can help to give a professional result.

If you are doing an oral presentation there is a range of specialist equipment that may help you. Some ideas for using them well are on paage 194.

## ■ Flip charts

Flip charts are relatively simple to use and many students feel that they are a little outdated, but many professional presenters still use them extensively. Remember that not every venue will have technological equipment for you to use, so being able to use flip charts creatively may be important. A neatly written, colourful flip chart can have immediate visual appeal.

Make the words bold and tall (use a wide-tipped marker pen), about 5cm is a good size. Use good quality pens and paper so that they don't 'bleed' onto other sheets.

Leave plenty of space on the sheets. A crowded sheet is confusing and difficult to read for your audience. You should also avoid using light colours, like yellow or orange, as your audience may not be able to read them.

If you are going to write on the paper during your presentation, it would be worthwhile rehearsing it first to identify any potential problems early (like words you have trouble spelling, or simply running out of space on the sheet).

Use of flip charts can give you some advantages over other presentation methods. It allows for spontaneity, and you can get your audience involved by encouraging them to write on the sheets too. After a session putting ideas onto flip chart paper you can keep the final results for later analysis, unlike writing on a whiteboard. Also you don't need to worry about power cuts or whether your electricity extension lead will be long enough!

## ■ Overhead projectors

Overhead projectors are available at many venues and they can add impact to your presentation if used well. Unfortunately, it is just as easy to use them badly as use them well. Here are a few tips to make your presentation go smoothly:

Try using the projector before the actual presentation to save any potential embarrassment. Find out where the on/off switch is, how to focus it and make sure it is far enough back to make a big image.

Practise putting the slide onto the glass. If you put it on upside down during the presentation you will get flustered, so practise this beforehand.

Leave your slides on the screen long enough so that your audience can read them thoroughly or interpret any figures or graphs. Talk about your slides so your audience can take in the information.

Don't keep turning to the screen and turning your back on your audience. If you want to see what point comes next, look down at the transparency itself on the glass.

Turn the projector off when you have finished using it. Projectors are both noisy and hot and will interfere with what you are saying next.

The quality of your OHP use will very much depend on the quality of your slides. When producing slides, you should use the same criteria discussed earlier (see page 164, 'Audience requirement – legibility').

## ■ PowerPoint and presenter kits

PowerPoint is a program produced by Microsoft specifically to aid presentations. It is very simple to use and you will quickly be able to produce professional looking slides. If you have never used PowerPoint before, visit this link – www.microsoft.com/Education/PPTTutorial.mspx – as Microsoft have produced a very useful tutorial that will take you through the program.

PowerPoint (and other similar programs) allows you to put colourful and artistic backgrounds on your slides, to incorporate sounds, photographic images, animations, video and web links within your slides. A presenter kit will allow you to project your slides onto a screen so that they are very large, and suitable for big venues and audiences. As a result it is a very powerful tool, but once again, you must practise using such equipment in order to avoid looking foolish.

▲ It is easy to get in a mess even using simple technology

## Outcome activity 4.4

For this Outcome activity you will need to explore the importance of gathering and communicating relevant and accurate information.

You work for CJG Electronics plc in its marketing department. CJG has been producing successful electronic products for the last 30 years, and the company's range now includes PCs, hi-fi systems, radios, DVD players and personal stereo systems. At a recent Board of Directors meeting it was decided that the company should look into the possibility of producing a rival to the Apple iPod. The Board feels that the future of personal portable music probably lies in this direction, but the directors are concerned about the cost of the research and development required as well as potential significant changes required in the manufacturing plant. They need more market information to help them make their decisions as to the *features* required on a rival model as well as the potential *demand* for such a product. You have been asked to gather research information in preparation for a presentation to be given to the Board of Directors in the near future.

**Pass**

p4

1. You will research the current state of the MP3 player market using three sources as follows:
   - MINTEL or another source of secondary market research information
   - your own primary research using whatever method(s) you choose
   - at least one of the following: newspapers, trade journals, the Internet or magazines.
2. You will transfer your results into a spreadsheet such as Microsoft Excel and produce a series of charts to illustrate the figures you have collected.

**Pass**

You will now present the information that you gathered in P4 in three ways:

1. Design an oral presentation of your findings.
2. Compile a detailed summary of your findings into a formal business report.
3. Produce an A4 leaflet containing the highlights of the data that you collected.

Finally, you should compile a short table giving examples of the recipients who are likely to find each of the methods you have prepared helpful. You might like to refer to the table that you produced in Outcome activity 4.3 to help you with this.

**Merit**

To achieve this criteria you should now perform your presentation to your tutor who will adopt the role of the Board of Directors of CJG PLC. You should also assume that there is a member of your audience who is profoundly deaf. You will need to adapt your presentation style in a number of ways to ensure that this person gains maximum benefit from your performance. Consider the ways that you are going to do this and make the necessary changes.

Produce an email to your manager at CJG PLC, Mr S Wilson, outlining the following:

- Your justifications as to why the methods you have used to convey the information are suitable for a Board of Directors.
- A list of the adaptations that you have made for the profoundly deaf person and the reasons why you think they will be helpful. This should be handed to your tutor at the end of your presentation.

**Distinction**

Refer to your answer for P4 above. Prepare a written assessment of the effectiveness of the methods for communication and presenting information that you used in P4.

## Grading tips

**Pass** 

Ensure that your information gathering allows you to collect a range of statistics about the market.

**Pass** 

Make sure you have accurately quoted the sources that you have used in collecting your information.

**Merit** 

You must ensure that you give a polished performance so make sure that you rehearse beforehand, preferably in front of a friend who can give you feedback.

**Distinction** 

This task requires you to explain why each method you used is helpful to the people you identified in the table you produced in P4. Since this is a Distinction criteria this explanation should be in considerable detail. You should also suggest suitable alternative methods that could be used for each of the people identified in your table.

## End of unit test

1. What is meant by staff retention?
2. How is staff turnover calculated?
3. What is the difference between expressed terms and implied terms in a contract of employment?
4. What is meant by 'employability skills'?
5. Name five employability skills and rank them in what you consider to be their order of importance. Explain your decisions.
6. Explain three business situations in which good listening skills would be vital.
7. Explain the difference between internal and external research information. Give examples to support your explanations.
8. Find out what 4G technologies are. In what ways might businesses make use of these in the future?
9. Some researchers believe that you should do secondary research before primary research. Explain the benefits of this approach.
10. What advantages do focus groups have over other primary information methods?
11. How can we check the currency of the information that we are gathering? Think of at least four different information sources, and explain how you would check the currency of each.
12. Outline an appropriate structure for a business letter of complaint.
13. 'Telephone technology is so good these days that we don't really need to produce written business correspondence any more.' Do you agree with this statement? Give reasons for your answer.
14. 'Patents and copyright rules are an incentive to innovators.' Explain why you think that these laws are necessary.
15. In what ways is PowerPoint a superior medium for delivering presentations? What limitations does it have?

# Resources

www.lighthouse.org/print_leg.htm – Designing text for people with partial sight

www.webstyleguide.com/type/legible.html – Web style guide

www.smallbizpod.co.uk/ – Regular podcasts of business topics

www.businesslink.gov.uk – Business Link (advice for business managers and owners)

www.statistics.gov.uk – National Statistics

www.bized.ac.uk – Website for students and educators in business studies

www.learndirect.co.uk – Online courses

www.dfes.gov.uk – UK government Department for Education and Skills

www.4g.co.uk – 4g news and information

# Books


Bryman, A. and Bell, E. 2003 *Business Research Methods*, Oxford University Press

Carysforth, C. 1998 *Communication for Work*, Heinemann Educational Publishers

Matthews, I. and Davies, P. 2001 *The Born Presenter*, Thomson Learning

Morris, D. 1977 *Manwatching*, Triad/Panther Books

Parry, H. 1994 *Successful Business Presentations*, Croner

Yate, M. and Sander, P. 2003 *The Ultimate Business Presentations Book* London, Kogan Page


| Grading criteria | Outcome activity | Page number |
|---|---|---|
| To achieve a pass grade the evidence must show that the learner is able to: | | |
| P1 Describe the recruitment and retention process and documentation in a selected organisation | 4.1 | 162 |
| P2 Describe the main employability, personal and communication skills required when applying for a specific job role | 4.2 | 179 |
| P3 Outline electronic and non-electronic methods for communicating business information using examples for different types of audience | 4.3 | 188 |
| P4 Select information from three sources and manipulate it, adhering to legislation, for business purposes | 4.4 | 195 |
| P5 Present the information from P4 using three different methods | 4.4 | 195 |
| To achieve a merit grade the evidence must show that, in addition to the pass criteria, the learner is able to: | | |
| M1 Analyse the employability, communication and personal skills required when applying for a specific job role | 4.2 | 179 |
| M2 Justify the reasons for using different methods for communicating business information | 4.3 | 188 |
| M3 Demonstrate and justify the use of suitable presentation methods using information from three sources | 4.4 | 195 |
| To achieve a distinction grade the evidence must show that, in addition to the pass and merit criteria, the learner is able to: | | |
| D1 Evaluate the advantages to an organisation of employing suitable people to communicate information | 4.2 | 179 |
| D2 Assess the suitability of the three methods used for communicating and presenting information | 4.4 | 195 |

# Introduction to accounting

## Introduction

Q. *What did the accountant's husband say to his wife when he couldn't get to sleep?*

A. *Why don't you tell me about your work, dear?*

Is that your impression of accountancy: boring and a good remedy for lack of sleep? Or maybe you're the sort of person who runs a mile when accounts are mentioned. If I had £1 for every time a student said to me, 'I don't like accounts – I've never been good at maths,' I'd need an accountant to add up all my money!

Accounts and accountants always seem to suffer from bad press, but much of it is undeserved. First, accounts are a vital function of businesses – without a good accounting system a businessperson would never be able to assess the true performance of the business. Secondly, students often exaggerate the importance of maths in accounting. If you can add, subtract, multiply and divide you can do most of the maths an accountant requires.

So don't be afraid of accounts, they are really not so daunting. You should be content in knowing that accounting skills will help businesses to measure their success accurately and to expand prudently.

### What you need to learn

On completion of this unit you should:

1. Understand the purpose of accounting and the categorisation of business income and expenditure
2. Be able to prepare a cash flow forecast
3. Understand profit and loss accounts and balance sheets
4. Be able to review business performance using simple ratio analysis.

## Consider this

DAILY ECHO 18/10/2006

### Thousands face bleak Christmas following Farepak demise

Christmas hamper company Farepak went into administration today leaving thousands of savers stranded with no money for presents and Christmas dinner this year. Farepak, which has been trading since 1969, employed agents across the UK who collected money regularly from customers as a means of saving for Christmas. It was revealed today that the expected payouts of food and vouchers would not take place this year as, following a detailed examination of its accounts, the firm's administrators confirmed that the company was unable to honour its financial commitments.

Customers, some of whom have lost hundreds of pounds, were said to be distraught about the prospect of an impoverished Christmas. The company's whole workforce have lost their jobs and agents operating for the firm were left shocked, confused and embarrassed at having to explain the problems to their customers.

Although many agents claimed that the collapse was totally unexpected, financial experts were saying that the company's parent firm EHR had seen their shares suspended back in August when they had financial problems.

The accounts of a business are of interest to many different stakeholders in the company. Consider the example above and think how this event might have affected the following stakeholder groups in the company:

- owners/shareholders
- customers
- UK government
- employees
- bankers
- local communities
- competitors.

Do you still think company accounts have little relevance?

# 5.1 Purpose of accounting and categorisation of business income and expenditure

Accounting has been described as 'the language of business'. You would not try to run a business in a country where you could not speak the language and communicate with customers and suppliers, so how can you hope to run a business well if you cannot understand the vital messages that the figures can give you? Understanding accounts is absolutely necessary to the success of any business.

## Purpose of accounting

There are several reasons why accounting is necessary to a business:

### Recording transactions

Accurate records are essential: if documents are lost the business may forget to demand payment for some jobs that have been done or may forget to pay bills that become due. This must be avoided at all costs because not paying your debts promptly is technically an act of bankruptcy.

### Monitoring activity and controlling the business

Sound record keeping allows the managers of the organisation to keep track of orders, sales and bills, which means they should have a good idea of how well the business is doing.

### Helping the management of the business

Financial information should also inform the management of the business and help the board to make better decisions. Well-prepared accounting statements will inform planning decisions and allow the directors and managers to monitor the progress of the company and to keep better control over its activities.

### Measuring the financial performance of the business

Profit is the lifeblood of the company and good accounting records will enable managers to assess accurately the levels of profit that are being achieved. Good records will also give clues about strategies that could improve the profitability of the business. The accounting documents that we will consider in this unit will reveal a number of key figures:

- **gross profit** – this is the difference between a company's total revenue and how much it cost to make the product or buy products in
- net profit – this is the gross profit minus the general expenses of the firm
- value owed to the business – this is the amount the business can expect to receive from customers in the near future
- value owed by the business – this is the amount that the business owes to suppliers and other people or companies from which it has bought products or services.

### Key Terms

**Gross profit** The profit figure at the end of the **trading account;** it is the difference between a company's total revenue and how much it cost to make the product or buy products in. Gross profit does not include the general expenses of the business.

**Trading account** The first of the set of final accounts, this account shows how profitably the firm makes goods or processes them for sale to customers. The trading account calculates the gross profit earned by the business.

As you will see later, a company's accounts are split into two main sections: income and expenditure. First, we will consider the types of income that may be included. Business income can be divided into two main types: capital income and revenue income.

## Case study

### Small business problems

Working with a friend, imagine that you run a small business together (you can decide what this business might be). A big problem for small businesses is managing their debtors, i.e. ensuring that they are paid promptly for work that they have done. As we will see later, poor management of monies owed can lead to the business having significant financial difficulties.

1. Together you should consider some practical suggestions to enable you, as owners of a small business, to ensure that you keep track of key financial documents and remember dates when important payments need to be paid or should be received. ✓
2. Produce a short leaflet with details of your suggestions. ✓✓
3. Draw up a list of strategies that other businesses could adopt to ensure that they get paid on time, and to chase up late payers. ✓✓

# Capital income

**Capital** is money or value contributed by the owner(s) of a business to get the business started or to buy equipment. For a sole trader there is just one owner so that one person has to raise all of the capital required, but limited companies may have many shareholders who all contribute. The figure for fixed capital may increase each year if profits are retained in the business. Additional capital can also be raised through share issue for a limited company or by a sole trader introducing additional money to the business.

## Key Terms

**Capital** Money put into the business by the owner(s) to get it started or to buy equipment.

### Sole traders

A sole trader is a person who owns a business on their own and who therefore needs to find all of the capital for the business themselves. If anything needs buying or paying for in the business the sole trader has to find the money. Sole traders will often use their own savings to get the business started, and may even put more of

Sole traders are responsible for all expenses themselves ▶

their own money into it later if they wish to expand the business. One of the problems for sole traders is that one person only has a limited amount of money, which can limit plans for the firm. Therefore sole traders are sometimes tempted to take on a partner.

## Partners

If a partner is introduced to the business that person should bring in some additional money to increase the amount of capital available.

## Shares

Limited companies are owned by shareholders, each of whom contributes some capital to the business. Shareholders receive a share certificate which details the amount of capital that they have contributed to the firm. Share capital is a good way to raise larger amounts of money for the business. There are different types of shares that may be held:

### Ordinary shares

These are the most common form of share and are often referred to as equity capital. Holders of ordinary shares become part owners of the company and they are therefore able to vote at general meetings of the firm. Ordinary shareholders are entitled to receive **dividends**, which are a share of the company profits each year. Since profits will vary from year to year, ordinary share dividends may rise and fall annually.

## Key Terms

**Dividend** This is a share of company profits received by shareholders each six months or annually. They appear in the appropriations section of the profit and loss account.

### Preference shares

These shares offer the holder a specific dividend, usually expressed as a percentage return. This is a fixed rate of return that will not change even if the business makes very high profits. Although preference shareholders are part owners of the company, they are not allowed to vote at meetings in the same way as ordinary shareholders can.

### Deferred shares

These are the same as ordinary shares except that the shareholders only receive dividends in certain circumstances, such as specific levels of profit being earned, or a particular date being reached. Sometimes the conditions of a **deferred share** require that dividends are only paid after certain amounts are paid out to ordinary shareholders.

## Thinking point

Having shareholders is a good way of raising more money for a business, but this method can also lead to some problems. With a friend you should consider the potential disadvantages to a sole trader or partners who are considering becoming a limited company and issuing shares. Make a list of the disadvantages to discuss with the rest of the class later.

## Key Terms

**Deferred shares** Similar to ordinary shares except that dividends are only paid in certain circumstances, such as a certain level of profit. They appear in the 'capital and reserves' or 'financed by' section of the balance sheet.

## Loans

Loans from banks are a flexible and accessible source of capital for most businesses, whether they are sole traders, partnerships or limited companies. Amounts available range from a few thousand pounds up to hundreds of thousands of pounds, depending on the project proposed and also the amount of security available to back the loan. Loans are usually granted for the purchase of capital items and they are often for extended periods. A typical business loan might be repaid over five years, but it is possible to negotiate longer periods depending upon the scale of the project. Personal loans to people are often unsecured, meaning that the borrower does not have to offer anything of value to the bank to cover the loan if they do not repay it; however very little business lending is done in this way. Most banks require the entrepreneur to offer some security for any loans they grant. This might be the entrepreneur's house, car, savings or any other valuable possessions they have. The borrower signs a legal document which gives the bank the power to seize the asset offered if the loan does not get repaid.

The financial services industry is extremely competitive, and a new entrepreneur would be well advised to shop around the various institutions to see which is offering the best deal before finalising a loan.

### Mortgages

A mortgage is a large loan, normally given for the purchase of property. A typical mortgage will last 25 years and they are always secured on the property that is being purchased. If a person or company owns a property that is mortgage-free, or if the mortgage is significantly less than the value of the property, a mortgage may be raised for purposes other than property purchase, such as starting up a new business.

## Revenue income

Revenue is income earned by the company by selling products or providing services. Outlined below are the main sources of revenue income.

### Sales

**Sales** can be for cash or as credit transactions. Cash sales are often best because the business receives the money for the sale immediately. However, businesses will often have to offer credit facilities to encourage growth in sales. Credit sales involve the organisation supplying the goods or service to the customer but allowing the customer time to pay for the item; typically this will be 28 days.

### Key Terms

**Sales (turnover)** The total amount of money received in sales for the year.

◀ Bank loans are a flexible form of finance for many businesses

## Thinking point

Imagine that a customer has approached you for credit on items that they intend to buy from you. What checks will you want to make before you agree to such an arrangement?

### Rent received

If a business owns property that it rents out to another company or person, the rental income received will be a source of revenue income for that business. Therefore if there are unused rooms in a company's premises, or buildings that they do not currently need, it makes sense to earn some income for the business by renting these out.

### Commission received

A business may sell products or services on behalf of another organisation and may then receive a commission for the work they have done. For example, when a mobile phone shop sells a contract to a customer it receives commission from the network operator, such as Orange or Vodafone, for completing the sale. This is an important form of revenue income for many businesses; indeed for some it may be their main source.

## Practice point

Consider the businesses that are local to your school or college and make a list of at least twenty. Now discuss these businesses with a friend and try to identify their sources of revenue income. Is it mainly sales income, rent received, commission received or a combination of all of them? You could draw up a table like the one below to collate your ideas.

| Company name | Sales income? | Rent received? | Commission received? |
|---|---|---|---|
| | | | |
| | | | |

**Take it further**

What conclusions can you draw from your table about the sources of revenue income for the businesses in your area?

# Capital expenditure

All businesses have different expenses to be paid. These can be divided into capital expenditure (which we will look at now) and revenue expenditure (see below). Capital expenditure is money used to acquire or improve the long-term **assets** of the business such as its property or equipment. It is shown on the balance sheet.

## Key Terms

**Assets** Items of value within an organisation. This could also include money owed to the business (debtors).

### Fixed assets

These are items of value which the organisation has bought and will use for an extended period of time, such as land and buildings, office equipment, machinery, motor vehicles, office furniture and fittings in the buildings such as carpets, shelving and curtains. Fixed assets are *tangible* items, meaning that they can be touched.

### Intangibles

A business may also pay for some things that cannot be touched, known as intangibles, which are not physical items yet still have considerable value for the business. Here are the most common intangibles you may come across:

#### Goodwill

When you buy an existing business you are also buying the reputation that the business has, the brand image of its products, the skills of the workforce and the customer base that has been built up. All of these factors contribute to the success of the business and it is not unreasonable to expect to pay for these when buying the business. When calculating the sale price, the owner of a business will often therefore add an amount on top of the actual value of the assets of the business to take account of these factors. This is known as goodwill and appears as an intangible asset in the accounts of the firm.

## Patents

A patent is a legal document that allows an inventor the exclusive rights to produce an invention. A company that owns the patent to an invention or idea clearly owns a valuable asset because it could lead to a unique product that will sell to customers. A business may buy a patent and this then becomes another intangible asset.

## Trademarks

A trademark is a name or a symbol that represents a company; a logo is a good example of this. These are powerful marketing tools; a strong brand name and logo can guarantee sales for a business since many people consistently buy products from names that they feel they can trust. This is another asset, but again an intangible one.

Logos have value as they are important marketing tools ▶

### Thinking point

If you were selling a successful business how would you go about deciding on an amount of goodwill to charge the buyer?

### Take it further

Using the Internet or textbooks find out the methods that accountants actually use to calculate the goodwill of a business.

# Revenue expenditure

You undoubtedly have expenses that you have to pay regularly and businesses are the same; any regular financial commitment is known as revenue expenditure and is shown on the profit and loss account. Below are the most common ones you may find in a company's accounts.

### Premises costs

Some regular bills are associated with the premises from which the business operates:

- Rent – if the business does not own the premises a regular payment of rent must be made to the owner.
- Rates – most businesses must pay business rates which are a form of tax paid to the local authority and which contribute to the services provided by that authority. The amount paid is assessed by the authority and depends on the nature of the business, where it is located, what the business does and how large it is.
- Heating and lighting – gas and electricity bills must be paid to the company supplying the service.
- Insurance – this is a legal requirement. The actual buildings themselves must be insured against perils such as fire and explosion and the contents must also be insured separately. Public liability insurance may also be payable.

### Practice point

The cost of premises and business rates can vary greatly. Using the Internet visit the websites of some local estate agents to determine typical costs for your area. Now do similar research in another area of the country, different from the one in which you live. How different are the figures?

### Administrative costs

These involve simple but important expenses on items such as telephone bills, postage, printing and stationery.

## Staff costs

Staff costs are often the biggest expense a business will have:

- Salaries – if employees are salaried they receive a set amount of money each week or month. You may see a job advertisement quoting a salary of £12,000, this means that, if the salary is paid monthly, the employee will receive £1000 every month (less tax, National Insurance, pension contributions, etc.).
- Wages – an employee who is waged will often be paid on an hourly basis or payment could be made according to how much the worker produces. Consequently a waged employee may earn more in some weeks than others, depending on how much work they do.

### Thinking point

Some businesses pay salaries while others pay wages; some will pay a salary to some workers and wages to others. What are the advantages and disadvantages of each method? Which would you prefer to receive – why?

### Take it further

Why might you want to use both methods in one business? In what circumstances might you recommend this and what problems might occur as a result of using both systems in one company?

- Training – training is essential but not cheap, especially if it is intended to deliver specialist skills. Simple part-time courses at a local college may cost several hundred pounds, and more specialist short courses run by consultants can cost £1000 per day to run. It is not surprising therefore that organisations will try to train their own employees whenever possible.
- Insurance – all employers must take out Employer's Liability Insurance. If an employee sustains an injury while working for you, this insurance protects you from any legal damage claims and court costs claimed against you or your company. Employers should also consider buying Public Liability Insurance. If a member of staff causes injury to a person or damage to property while at work this will insure the business owners against damages claims.
- Pensions – most businesses are required by law to provide some form of pension to their employees. There are many types of scheme; some of these involve contributions by both the employer and the employee, in this case the pension becomes another expense for the company.

## Selling and distribution costs

There is also a range of costs associated with selling the products or services which a business produces. The most common of these are:

- salaries – paid to sales staff
- carriage – the cost of delivering the product
- marketing – such as advertising and promotion costs.

## Finance costs

Very few businesses can operate without a bank account, but there are further expenses associated with this.

### Bank charges

These can become very expensive for business customers. Individuals generally benefit from free banking, meaning that as long as the account does not go overdrawn, all transactions are free; but this is not always the case for businesses. Many banks charge for every business transaction: every cheque that the business writes, each time cash is withdrawn, every cheque paid in, and every time cash and coins are paid in over the bank counter as well as all standing orders and direct debits the bank pays for the business. There is often a separate charge for each of these items and since large organisations carry out many transactions each day, and may pay in many cheques and/or lots of cash and coin most days, these charges can run into hundreds of pounds every month. It is wise therefore to 'shop around' the banks for the best deals to ensure that this expense is kept to a minimum.

### Overdraft, loan and mortgage interest

Any form of bank borrowing will also incur interest charges that must be paid; again the best advice is to compare the different deals offered by banks as some will cost more than others.

## Purchase of stock or raw materials

Businesses that sell products need stock to sell and this is invariably a large expense. When the business first starts up most of the payments for **stock** or raw materials will have to be made immediately; these are known as cash transactions. However once the firm has established a good reputation with suppliers it may be possible to negotiate some credit. Credit transactions mean the business receives the stock or raw materials but does not have to pay immediately for them. Typically 28 days' credit may be offered.

### Key Terms

**Stock** This is the total value of raw materials that will be made into goods for sale, partly manufactured items and also items that have been completely made or bought in by the business and are available for sale to customers.

### Thinking point

What are the advantages to a business of obtaining credit on the purchase of stock or raw materials? Are there any drawbacks to using this method of payment?

### Outcome activity 5.1

To achieve this first Outcome activity you should arrange to visit a local business owner. You should aim to establish the following information:

- whether the business is a sole trader, partnership or limited company
- the main items of expenditure the business owner incurred when setting up the business
- the methods the owner used to raise finance to pay for the set-up costs
- the main areas of regular expenditure for the business
- the main sources of income for the business
- the purpose and importance of keeping accounts for the business owner.

Once you have completed the interview you should prepare a short presentation to be delivered to your turor that covers the following areas.

**Pass**

A description of the purpose of accounting. You should relate this to the business you have investigated. 

Using examples drawn from your interview you should explain the difference between capital and revenue items of income and expenditure. 

### Grading tips

**Pass** P1

For a thorough answer you should ensure that you cover:

1. Why keeping accounts is necessary.
2. How the historical accounting records of the business enable the owners to check financial performance.
3. How accounting records help the business owner to plan effectively.

For a thorough answer you should ensure that you:

1. Define the four terms capital income, capital expenditure, revenue income and revenue expenditure.
2. Illustrate your definitions using examples from your research interview. Make sure you provide at least one example of each.

# 5.2 Preparing a cash flow forecast

Cash flow is one of the most important elements of management within a business. A business that can manage its cash will be able to invest, attract investment, pay for its expenses and hopefully make profits! However, if you don't anticipate cash flow problems, by the time you realise there is a problem it may be too late. The 'cash flow disease' can be terminal for many businesses, so treat it early and remember that 'Prevention is better than cure'. Some forethought will mean that you can anticipate and deal with the problems of cash flow.

A business needs enough money to pay for its outflows or it may become insolvent and ultimately go bankrupt. It is also important to make sure that outflows can be paid at the right time for both the business and its suppliers. If employees are not paid their wages, at the end of the week or month, they will not stay with the business for long and the same is true of suppliers. They want prompt and regular payment, especially if the supplier is a small business as it will be relying on the income.

## Cash flow forecast

### Structure and timescales of a cash flow forecast

A cash flow forecast is simply a statement of expected movements of cash into and out of the business. Predictions are normally done on a monthly basis and typically it will be prepared for a twelve-month period in the future. At the top of the forecast all of the income items are listed and the expenses come below.

Opposite is an example of a simple cash flow forecast. Beth's Garments is starting the New Year with £450 in the bank. Beth predicts sales for the first three months to be: January £2250, February £1000 and March £2400. Purchases will be: £900 in January, £400 in February and £960 in March. Wages are £1250 per month. The completed forecast looks like the example opposite.

The most significant figure on the forecast is the balance C/F (carried forward) as this shows what the projected bank balance is at the end of each month.

▲ Cash constantly flows in and out of the business

Total Receipts is all the Income items added together

Here is the £450 in the bank at the start of the year

Balance B/F is the same figure as the Balance C/F for the previous month

The Totals Column summarises all of the months shown on the forecast

The Balance B/F figure at the start of the forecast

| | January £ | February £ | March £ | Totals £ |
|---|---|---|---|---|
| **Balance B/F** | 450 | 550 | -100 | 450 |
| **Income** | | | | |
| **Sales** | 2250 | 1000 | 2400 | 5650 |
| **Total Receipts** | 2250 | 1000 | 2400 | 5650 |
| **Total Cash Available** | 2700 | 1550 | 2300 | 6100 |
| **Expenses** | | | | |
| **Purchases** | 900 | 400 | 960 | 2260 |
| **Wages** | 1250 | 1250 | 1250 | 3750 |
| **Total Payments** | 2150 | 1650 | 2210 | 6010 |
| **Balance C/F** | 550 | -100 | 90 | 90 |

Total Cash Available is Balance B/F plus Total Receipts

Total Payments is all the Expense items added together

Balance C/F is Total Cash Available minus Total Payments

These two figures should be the same. This shows that your forecast balances

▲ Cash flow forecast – example 1

If this figure is positive then the firm has money in the bank, if it is negative then the business will be overdrawn. In the above example the firm goes overdrawn by £100 in February, but the overdraft is cleared by the following month.

You should examine this example carefully until you are absolutely clear how all of the figures are calculated.

## Key Terms

**Purchases** For a manufacturing company this is the value of raw materials purchased; for a service business it would be the cost of items bought to sell to customers or used to provide a service to customers.

## Case study

### Josh

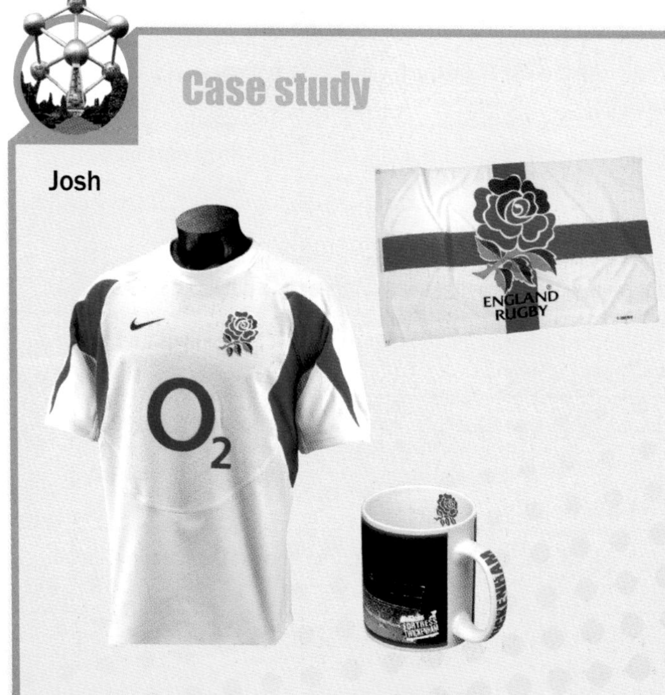


Josh has a business selling rugby and other sporting memorabilia. He is starting the New Year with £385 in the bank. He predicts sales for the first three months to be: January £3500, February £2625 and March £3060. Purchases will be: £1750 in January, £1300 in February and £1530 in March. Wages are £2100 per month.

1. Use the details above to compile a simple cash flow forecast for the first three months of next year. ✓
2. Josh is slightly concerned about his cash flow projections. What suggestions would you make to Josh that would improve his cash flow situation? ✓✓
3. Put your cash flow onto a spreadsheet and experiment with different figures for Josh's business. What do you see as the best way forward for him? ✓✓✓

## Receipts and payments

A full cash flow forecast will contain many more items of receipts and payments, but the process for constructing the forecast is just the same as our simple example above. The table below shows items you will typically find in a full forecast.

▼ What to look out for in a cash flow forecast

| **Receipts** | |
|---|---|
| Owner's capital | The amount that the owner(s) are putting in to get the business started. This will probably come from their own savings. |
| Bank loan | Sums borrowed from the bank, usually towards the purchase of fixed assets for the business. |
| Cash sales | Money received immediately from customers for goods or services purchased. |
| Credit sales (debtors) | Items sold on credit. The money is normally received one month after the original sale. |
| Rent received | Rent from property owned by the company. |
| Commission received | Fees paid for selling the products or services of another company. |
| **Payments** | |
| Initial stock purchases | When starting up a new business you will have to buy in items, especially if you are setting up a shop. This is a one-off expense when you first start trading. |
| Cash purchases | These are the purchases you make each month to replace items sold to customers or to replenish raw materials in a manufacturing firm. |
| Credit purchases | This is the same as cash purchases except payment does not need to be made until the following month. |
| Gas and electricity | Regular bills, normally paid either monthly or quarterly. |
| Fixtures and fittings | When setting up a new business you may need to put in shelving, cupboards, a counter, etc. This is a one-off expense when you first start trading. |
| Equipment | Items such as tools, computers, cash tills or machinery. This is a one-off expense when you first start trading. |
| Drawings | This is the salary you pay yourself for running the business. |
| Advertising | Another regular expense, but you will have to decide how frequently you need to publicise your business. |
| Insurance | A legal necessity. You will probably make monthly payments to cover at least your buildings and contents, and maybe also employer's and public liability insurance. |
| Rent and rates | Another monthly payment. City centres are more expensive than suburbs or the outskirts of towns. |
| Wages | You will have to pay any staff you employ on a monthly basis, even if you only give them the Minimum Wage. |
| Overdraft interest | If you go overdrawn one month the bank will charge you interest on that balance in the following month. If you do not go overdrawn you will avoid such charges. |
| Loan repayments | If you borrow money to get started or to buy capital equipment you will need to pay it back. This will be a regular monthly payment. |

Here is an example of a more complete cash flow forecast for the first four months for a new sole trader business:

| | January £ | February £ | March £ | April £ | Totals £ |
|---|---|---|---|---|---|
| **Balance B/F** | 0 | -240 | 218 | -162 | 0 |
| **Income** | | | | | |
| **Owner's Capital** | 4000 | | | | 4000 |
| **Bank Loan** | 3000 | | | | 3000 |
| **Cash Sales** | 2500 | 3500 | 2000 | 2500 | 10,500 |
| **Credit Sales** | | | | 1000 | 1000 |
| **Rent Received** | 1000 | 1000 | 1000 | 1000 | 4000 |
| **Total Receipts** | 10,500 | 4500 | 3000 | 4500 | 22,500 |
| **Total Cash Available** | 10,500 | 4260 | 3218 | 4338 | 22,500 |
| **Expenses** | | | | | |
| **Initial Stock Purchases** | 3500 | | | | 3500 |
| **Cash Purchases** | 750 | 1050 | 500 | 600 | 2900 |
| **Credit Purchases** | | | | 500 | 500 |
| **Gas and Electricity** | 97 | 97 | 97 | 97 | 388 |
| **Fixtures and Fittings** | 1500 | | | | 1500 |
| **Equipment** | 2000 | | | | 2000 |
| **Drawings** | 1250 | 1250 | 1250 | 1250 | 5000 |
| **Advertising** | 110 | 110 | | 75 | 295 |
| **Insurance** | 93 | 93 | 93 | 93 | 372 |
| **Rent and Rates** | 875 | 875 | 875 | 875 | 3500 |
| **Wages** | 490 | 490 | 490 | 490 | 1960 |
| **Overdraft Interest** | 0 | 2 | 0 | 2 | 4 |
| **Loan Repayments** | 75 | 75 | 75 | 75 | 300 |
| **Total Payments** | 10,740 | 4042 | 3380 | 4057 | 22,219 |
| **Balance C/F** | -240 | 218 | -162 | 281 | 281 |

Cash flow forecast – example 2 ▶

## Value Added Tax

A business will only need to register for VAT if it sells more than £61,000 of products per year (as at October 2006); but if it is registered, VAT receipts and payments must be included in a cash flow forecast. The current rate of VAT is 17.5% and this should be charged on top of the selling price of goods. Businesses that are registered must pay VAT received on goods and services sold to **HM Customs and Excise**, but they can also claim back any VAT paid. The cash flow forecast should therefore include two extra lines:

- Under 'Income' there should be a row entitled 'VAT received on sales'
- Under 'Expenses' should be a row entitled 'VAT on payments'.

## Key Terms

**HM Customs and Excise** The government tax office that deals with collecting VAT payments.

Sales income should now be broken down. For example, if the business sells a product for £10 + VAT the selling price will be £10 + £1.75, a total of £11.75. On the cash flow forecast under Receipts we should see the following:

| | April |
|---|---|
| **Receipts** | |
| Sales | £10.00 |
| VAT on sales | £1.75 |

Similarly purchases of items that carry VAT should also be broken down under the Expenses section. So an item bought for £47 including VAT should appear like this:

| | April |
|---|---|
| **Payments** | |
| Purchase | £40.00 |
| VAT on purchases | £7.00 |

Finally, once every three months, the business has to calculate whether it must pay net VAT to Customs and Excise, or whether it is entitled to claim any back. The process is simple in concept: the amount paid is deducted from the amount received and if the result is

## Case study

### Dhruv

Dhruv runs a small business selling mobile phone accessories. Sales and purchases for the 12 months will be as follows:

| | Total sales (£) | Purchases (£) |
|---|---|---|
| January | 5000 | 525 |
| February | 5000 | 525 |
| March | 5000 | 525 |
| April | 5250 | 525 |
| May | 5250 | 525 |
| June | 5250 | 525 |
| July | 5250 | 525 |
| August | 5250 | 525 |
| September | 5250 | 525 |
| October | 7600 | 700 |
| November | 7600 | 700 |
| December | 6500 | 700 |

In July Dhruv plans to purchase a new delivery vehicle and additional equipment for the store. He will be injecting £7000 of his own savings to the business and will be borrowing a further £8000 from the bank. Both of these amounts will enter the bank account in July, and in the same month the equipment will be paid for, costing £26,000.

The business mortgage on the shop costs £1000 per month, and business rates are £370 per month, payable in 10 monthly instalments beginning in March.

In April Dhruv plans to offer credit terms to one of his better customers. From April to September, £1750 worth of the sales made will be on 30 days credit. In October to December £2600 of the sales will be on 30 days credit.

Dhruv has some living accommodation above the shop that he rents out. The rent is £800 per month although this is due to rise to £860 per month in October. The wages bill will be £1600 per month. Dhruv's drawings will be £1500 per month and he will pay £45 per month on advertising. He will pay £190 per month insurance.

Overdraft interest will be charged at 10% per annum on a monthly basis. Interest will be paid monthly, based on the previous month's closing balance. Repayments on the new loan will begin in the month following the receipt of the loan money and will cost £200 per month.

1. Use a spreadsheet to create a cash flow forecast for Dhruv using this information. The opening balance of the forecast will be zero. ✓
2. Comment on Dhruv's cash flow situation. How good/bad is it? What is the effect of the purchase of equipment in July? ✓✓
3. Make at least two adjustments to the original spreadsheet, one to an income item and one to an expense; comment on the changes. ✓✓✓

a positive figure then this must be paid to HM Customs and Excise, but if it is a negative figure it can be claimed back from them.

Using the above examples, therefore: £1.75 has been received and £7 has been paid. £1.75 – £7 = –£5.25; this amount can therefore be claimed back.

Amounts of VAT claimed or paid will also appear as cash flow entries. If a refund is due, then in the Receipts section an additional row entitled 'VAT Refund' should appear containing the amount, but if a net payment of VAT is to be made then a row entitled 'VAT paid to C&E' should appear under 'Expenses'.

## Opening and closing cash/bank balances

These balance figures are significant. The first represents the balance in the bank account at the start of the forecast, so this may be ascertained fairly accurately. The second, the closing balance, which is the final balance carried forward at the end of the forecast, indicates what the bank balance will be at the end of the period covered on the forecast. This is of particular interest as it shows if the business is in credit at the end of the year, or whether it will be running an overdraft.

## Case study

### Gabriela's jewellery

Gabriela runs a business producing custom-made jewellery. Sales and purchases for the 12 months will be as follows:

| | Total sales (£) | Purchases (£) |
|---|---|---|
| January | 69,000 | 46,000 |
| February | 60,375 | 40,250 |
| March | 60,375 | 40,250 |
| April | 60,375 | 40,250 |
| May | 60,375 | 40,250 |
| June | 60,375 | 40,250 |
| July | 51,750 | 34,500 |
| August | 34,500 | 23,000 |
| September | 58,500 | 39,000 |
| October | 69,000 | 46,000 |
| November | 86,250 | 57,500 |
| December | 103,500 | 69,000 |

These sales and purchase figures do not include VAT, so you must also have rows for VAT on sales and VAT on purchases. VAT will added at 17.5%.

In April Gabriela plans to purchase a new delivery vehicle. She will be injecting £11,000 of her own savings to the business and will be borrowing a further £8000 from the bank. Both of these amounts will enter the bank account in April, and in the same month the vehicle will be paid for, costing £22,000. Repayments on the loan will begin the following month; the amounts will be £134 per month capital repayment and £66 per month interest. Gabriela has some living accommodation above the shop which she rents out. The rent is £520 per month.

The business mortgage on the shop costs £2800 per month, and business rates are £620 per month, which is payable in 10 monthly instalments beginning in March. Gabriela's drawings will be £2600 per month and she will pay £240 per month on advertising. The advertising bill rises to £450 per month for October, November and December. Insurance will be £165 per month.

The wages bill will be £12,600 per month rising to £13,800 per month in May. Overdraft interest will be charged at 10% per annum on a monthly basis. Interest will be paid monthly based on the previous month's closing balance.

The opening balance of the forecast will be £1312. Do not forget to claim back excess VAT paid or pay excess VAT collected on your forecast.

1. Use a spreadsheet to create a cash flow forecast for Gabriela using the details above. ✓
2. What comments would you make concerning Gabriela's bank balance over the twelve-month period? ✓✓
3. What advice would you give her? Explain your reasons. ✓✓✓

## Remember

The closing balance does not represent profit for the business, it is simply the amount of cash (or the size of the overdraft) sitting in the bank. It is entirely possible to have a negative closing balance while still trading profitably; equally a business could have a positive closing balance but not be making profits.

# Cash flow management

If a business has a lot of money left over at the end of a month because it has fewer outflows than inflows there are choices to be made about what to do with that money. The table below shows what the business could do with its money.

### Problems within the cash flow forecast

If a business has more outflows than inflows it will have a more serious problem and end up with a negative balance, meaning that it has insufficient cash to meet the payments that are due. Clearly it is essential to avoid this problem. It should not prove too difficult if the business owners have a thorough understanding of the cash flow cycle for their business, can anticipate problems and implement strategies to cope with the problems. The first thing to accept is that a business will not necessarily be in a positive cash position all the time. Because of seasonal fluctuations in business activity, sometimes the cash position will be positive and sometimes it will be negative. A cash flow cycle might look something like the diagram below.

A bank will usually be happy to provide assistance to help the business cope with negative periods of cash flow. A cycle like the one below is not a problem for either the business or the bank as the periods of overdraft are only temporary and the seasonal improvements at Easter and the approach to Christmas yield substantial positive cash balances.

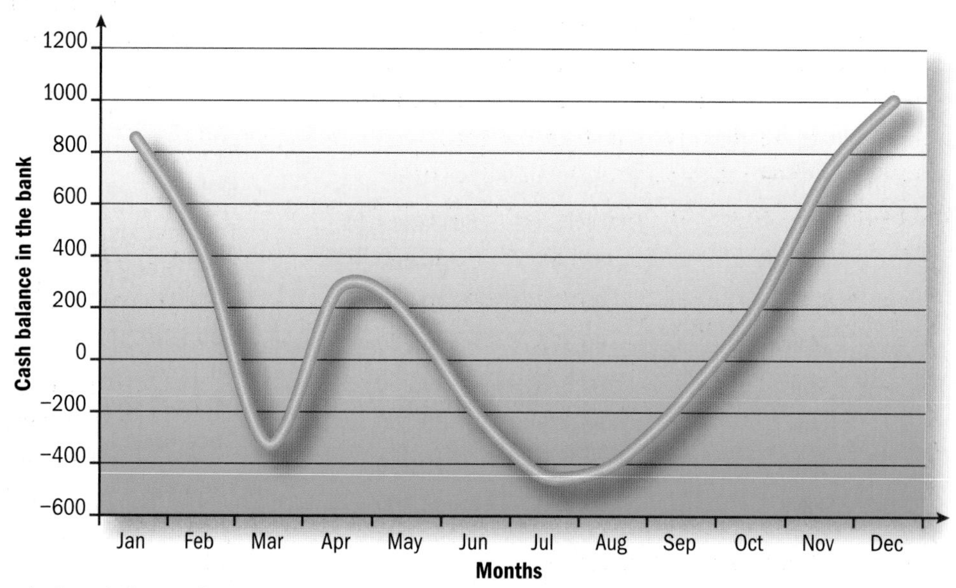


▲ A cash flow cycle

| What to do with the money? | Implications |
|---|---|
| Leave the money in its business account because there are some big expenses in the next month | The disadvantage of doing this is that the business will not make any extra interest on that money so this is a lost opportunity (opportunity cost). |
| Put the money on deposit | This means the business puts the money into a higher rate bank account to gain extra interest that can be used in the business later. It will be transferred back when it is needed. |
| Invest the money in the business | There may be other purchases that the business needs to make to improve how it works. |
| Pay some of its expenses early | The business could choose to pay some of its expenses earlier than normal. This would be unusual but if one of its suppliers was finding cash flow management difficult, it may be done as a goodwill gesture. |

▲ Managing a positive cash flow

## Solutions to cash flow problems

If you approach a bank for business overdraft facilities you will be asked how much you will need and you will then have to give some evidence that:

- the amount you have asked for will be sufficient
- the account will show cycles of balances with periods when the account is in credit.

The best evidence for this is a cash flow forecast, and this is what the bank will ask to see. Your Balance C/F figures could look like these (taken from the example on the previous page):

| Jan | Feb | Mar | Apr | May | June | July | Aug | Sept | Oct | Nov | Dec |
|---|---|---|---|---|---|---|---|---|---|---|---|
| 840 | 420 | -340 | 280 | 180 | -200 | -420 | -400 | -180 | 190 | 710 | 1000 |

This suggests that the business will need an overdraft facility of £420, but it also indicates that it will not be needed every month as the bank account will often be in credit. An overdraft is a short-term solution but interest rates on overdrafts are usually much higher than other sources of finance, such as a loan.

A pre-arranged overdraft facility is therefore a good way of overcoming short-term cash flow problems as it allows the firm to draw out more when necessary. Armed with a cash flow forecast, however, it is possible to consider other options for solving the problem, as shown in the table below:

Anticipating cash flow needs gives the managers of a business time to make these changes to their business plans. However, if managers do not plan and examine the finances carefully problems may occur which may then be much harder to solve.

### Practice point

Seasonal businesses face particular problems from a cash flow point of view. Working in small groups choose a product or service that you know will suffer from significant seasonal variations. Discuss the steps you might take to cope with these problems. Put your ideas on flip chart paper and be prepared to explain them to the class.

### Thinking point

We said earlier that the Balance C/F is not profit, just the bank balance. What are the differences between profit and the cash left in the bank?

| Dealing with cash flow problems | Implications |
|---|---|
| Obtaining credit from suppliers | Once a business has been trading for a little while, suppliers may be prepared to give credit, so that the business does not have to pay immediately for goods delivered. |
| Leasing | The business could lease capital items instead of buying them. This would avoid a big payment up front. |
| Rescheduling capital expenditure | The forecast may reveal that it is not possible to pay for fixed assets, in which case the managers may have to decide not to buy them but wait until the business is in a better cash position. |
| Increase prices | The additional revenue could avoid the need for an overdraft, as long as customers are willing to pay the increased prices. |
| Look for alternative suppliers | Can the business get gas and electricity cheaper elsewhere? Can advertising costs be reduced by using a different printer? |
| Move premises | A more long-term solution, but a cash flow forecast may indicate that the firm will not be able to afford its premises. Better to know this early and make alternative arrangements. |

## Outcome activity 5.2

**Pass**

You have been approached by Alan Hull who runs a small local business selling watches and other jewellery items. He has asked for your help in creating a 12-month cash flow forecast.

You should create it using the details given below.

Sales and purchases for the 12 months will be as follows:

| | Total sales | Purchases |
|---|---|---|
| January | 37,800 | 27,000 |
| February | 34,020 | 24,300 |
| March | 31,500 | 22,500 |
| April | 37,800 | 27,000 |
| May | 37,800 | 27,000 |
| June | 36,540 | 26,100 |
| July | 31,500 | 22,500 |
| August | 21,420 | 15,300 |
| September | 37,800 | 27,000 |
| October | 44,100 | 31,500 |
| November | 50,400 | 36,000 |
| December | 60,000 | 44,000 |

These sales and purchase figures do not include VAT, so you must also have rows for VAT on sales and VAT on purchases. VAT will added at 17.5%.

In March Alan plans to purchase a company vehicle. He will be injecting £5000 of his own savings to the business and will be borrowing a further £3000 from the bank. Both of these amounts will enter the bank account in March, and in the same month the vehicle will be paid for, costing £9000. Repayments on the loan will begin the following month, the amounts will be £50 per month capital repayment and £25 per month interest.

Alan has some living accommodation above the shop which he rents out. The rent is £250 per month. The business mortgage on the shop costs £950 per month. Business rates are likely to be £360 per month, which is payable in 10 monthly instalments beginning in March.

Alan's drawings will be £1700 per month and he will pay £175 per month on advertising. This is expected to rise to £300 in September and October and £450 in November and December in the run up to Christmas. Insurance will be £110 per month. The wages bill will be £7600 per month rising to £8000 per month in June. Alan is contemplating taking on another employee to help him as he has been very busy lately. If this happens, he would hope to take on someone in May or June, and it is likely that their wages would be an additional £750 per month.

Overdraft interest will be charged at 10% per annum on a monthly basis. Interest will be paid monthly based on the previous months closing balance. The opening balance of the forecast will be £1050. Do not forget to claim back excess VAT paid or pay excess VAT collected on your forecast.

**Merit**

Analyse the cash flow problems a business might experience.

**Distinction**

Recommend and justify actions a business might take when experiencing cash flow problems.

## Grading tips

**Pass** 

In order to do this task accurately you must ensure that you have included all of the items in the list. It is recommended that you deal with each item in turn and cross it out on the list as you include it on your forecast, so that it will be obvious if you miss any out.

**Merit** 

You should write a report to Alan detailing your analysis of his problems with cash flow over this six-month period. Analysing requires you to break the situation down and look in detail at all aspects. In this case you should look in detail at the closing balances, trends, the causes of any problems you identify and Alan's plans as suggested in the detail given above.

**Distinction** 

You should conclude your report begun in the previous task by recommending and justifying actions Alan might take to cope with the cash flow problems that you have predicted. You might support this by:

- projecting your six-month cash flow forward to cover a further six months to show Alan exactly how the position might develop, and/or
- producing a revised cash flow forecast to show Alan exactly how your suggestions will help.

Your report should also outline to Alan the potential dangers and costs to his business of poor financial planning.

# 5.3 Profit and loss accounts and balance sheets

'Business without profit is not business any more than a pickle is candy,' said Charles F. Abbott, the famous American lawyer, and he was right: a business without profit really is no business at all (although the directors of Eurotunnel might wish to argue that point).

One of the fundamental questions for any organisation is 'How profitable is the business?' There are many factors to take into account in determining this, and we look at these in this section. The profit and loss account is the first of the legally required financial statements for a business and it contains much vital information for the owners or shareholders. In essence, the profit and loss account simply calculates the total income for the firm and deducts from that its expenses to give a total profit figure. It is important that these documents are always prepared using the same layout and conventions so that a company's performance can be accurately assessed and compared with other businesses.

## Profit and loss account

### Purpose and use

Profit is clearly the lifeblood of any business and being able to assess it accurately is essential to any firm but not always easy. Some entrepreneurs make the mistake of assuming that money left in the bank must be profit, but the true picture is somewhat more complex. The profit and loss account makes an accurate calculation of the true profit made by the business.

## Trading account

Trading is the basic process of business. Manufacturing organisations, for example, buy in raw materials and use them to make products for sale; whereas retail businesses buy in finished goods for sale at a higher price. This is the basis of their trade.

The trading account shows how much profit the organisation makes by this basic business process, ignoring other expenses it may incur. It simply looks at how profitably the business makes goods or processes them for sale to customers. The profit earned by this process is known as the gross profit of the business.

## Components of the trading account

Here are the main entries that you will find in any trading account:

- Sales (or turnover) – receipts for sales for the year.
- Sales returns – amount paid back to customers when items are returned.
- Opening stock – value of stocks of finished products, work in progress (partially completed products) and raw materials held in the business at the start of the year.
- Purchases – for a manufacturing organisation this is the value of raw materials purchased; for a service business it would be the cost of items bought to sell to customers or used to provide a service to customers.
- Purchase returns – receipts to the organisation from suppliers when it returns items.
- **Closing stock** – value of stocks of finished products, work in progress (partially completed products) and raw materials held in the business at the end of the year.
- Gross profit – the difference between the organisation's total revenue and how much it costs to make the product or buy products in.
- Commission received and other non-operating receipts – some businesses may receive extra income other than normal sales income, which could include rent received or commission received.

## Key Terms

**Closing stock** The value of stocks of finished products held in the business at the end of the year.

## Calculation of gross profit using the trading account

The trading account is always laid out in the same way and gross profit is calculated as follows:

Sales/turnover *minus* Sales returns *equals* Net sales *minus* Cost of goods sold *equals* Gross profit

Cost of goods sold is calculated as follows:

Opening stock *plus* Purchases *minus* Purchase returns *minus* Closing stock *equals* Cost of goods sold

It is easier to see this in action rather than try to imagine this, so here is the full trading account for a sole trader called Steve Hackett who runs a business making high quality handcrafted guitars. From his records he has identified the following receipts and expenses that are relevant:

- Sales (or turnover) – he has sold £285,400 of instruments in the year.
- Sales returns – three guitars were returned to the company and refunds totalling £2960 were given.
- Opening stock – the value of stocks at the start of the year was £12,000.
- Purchases – £174,340 was spent on materials in the year.
- Purchase returns – £2504 worth of materials were returned to suppliers and refunds were received for these amounts.
- Closing stock – the value of stocks held in the business at the end of the year was £12,500.
- Commission received and other non-operating receipts – the business received rental income of £5750.

These details are combined into a trading account as follows:

## STEVE HACKETT

**Trading Account for Year Ended 31.3.07**

| | £000s | £000s | £000s |
|---|---|---|---|
| Sales | | | 285,400 |
| Less Sales Returns | | | 2960 |
| Net Sales (or Turnover) | | | 282,440 |
| **less Cost of Goods Sold** | | | |
| Opening Stock | | 12,000 | |
| Purchases | 174,340 | | |
| Less Purchase Returns | 2504 | | |
| Net Purchases | | 171,836 | |
| | | 183,836 | |
| less Closing Stock | | 12,500 | |
| Cost of Goods Sold | | | 171,336 |
| **GROSS PROFIT** | | | 111,104 |
| Non-Operating Receipts (Rental Income) | | | 5750 |
| | | | 116,854 |

Net Sales

minus Cost of Goods Sold

equals Gross Profit

Sales

minus Sales Returns

equals Net Sales

▲ Steve Hackett trading account

You should now spend some time studying this trading account. Check all of the calculations to make sure that you can see how the totals are arrived at.

### Practice point

Junaid runs a shop selling hi-fi equipment. Here are extracts from his accounts for the year ended 31.3.07:

Sales (or turnover) – £75,700

Sales returns – Nil

Opening stock – £3150

Purchases – £19,024

Purchase returns – £216

Closing stock – £3600

Commission received and other non-operating receipts – Nil

Using the figures above, prepare the trading account for Junaid.

## Calculation of net profit

The trading account shows us what the organisation has made from its basic line of business, but it does not reveal the true profit as it does not take into account any of the general expenses. The profit and loss account takes the gross profit figure and deducts all the expenses to get the final profit of the business for the year, known as the net profit.

### Expenses

These are amounts that the business has had to pay out, such as rent, wages, petrol and many others. Note that 'drawings' (amounts that a sole trader takes from the business for their personal use) and the cost of **fixed assets** are not classed as an expense and *do not* appear in the profit and loss account.

### Depreciation

Most of the capital assets of a business do not retain their value. Motor vehicles, for example, lose value each year; this reduction is known as **depreciation**. It is important to show this reduction in value in the accounts, otherwise

## Key Terms

**Depreciation** The loss in value of the assets of the business over time, due mainly to wear and tear.

**Fixed assets** Capital items of value which the business has bought and will use for an extended period of time, such as buildings, machinery, equipment and vehicles.

the final accounts will overstate the value of the business. Depreciation is an expense to the business (even though no money actually changes hands) and so it appears in the profit and loss account. There are two main methods of accounting for depreciation; either may be used:

**Straight line depreciation.** A fixed percentage of the original cost of the asset is taken off each year. This means that the amount of depreciation on a particular asset will be the same each year.

For example, a machine cost £80,000 to buy and is depreciated by 20% per year on a straight line basis. The amount per year is:

£80,000 × 20% = £16,000 per year for each of five years.

The number of years used will be based on an estimate of the useful working life of the asset. In the example above the business must consider that after five years the asset will be valueless and will probably look to replace it at that point.

However, most assets will have some value left at the end of their useful lives (known as the residual value of the asset), so the best way to calculate straight line depreciation is to use the following formula:

$$\frac{\text{Cost of asset} - \text{Residual value}}{\text{Number of years of expected useful life}}$$

Using the previous example, if we assume that after five years the asset will be worth £5000 to the company, the new calculation will be as follows:

$$\frac{80{,}000 - £5000}{5}$$

Depreciation = £15,000 each year.

**Reducing balance depreciation.** If the firm chooses to use this method a consistent percentage figure is used but it is applied to the reduced balance each year. Using the same example, a machine costs £80,000 to buy and is depreciated by 20% per year; using the reducing balance method the depreciation would be as follows on page 221.

## Case study

### Stephen Howe

Stephen Howe is a sole trader. He buys a machine worth £200,000 for his business. He expects depreciation on this asset to be 10% per year. Complete the following table showing the balance at the end of each subsequent year using the two different methods:

| | Straight line | Reducing balance |
|---|---|---|
| Initial cost | £200,000 | £200,000 |
| Value end Year 1 | | |
| Value end Year 2 | | |
| Value end Year 3 | | |
| Value end Year 4 | | |
| Value end Year 5 | | |

1. What is the residual value after five years using each of the two methods? ✓
2. What do you notice about the rate of depreciation using the two methods? ✓
3. The asset should depreciate to the same residual value whichever method is chosen. What does this tell you about the relative percentage rates required using each method to achieve the same residual value? ✓✓
4. What do you think of Stephen's method of deciding how much to charge for depreciation on this asset? ✓✓✓

| | |
|---|---|
| Original cost | £80,000 |
| Year 1 depreciation (£80,000 × 20%) = | £16,000 |
| Value at end of Year 1 (£80,000 – £16,000) = | £64,000 |

In year 2 it will be as follows:

| | |
|---|---|
| Value at end of Year 1 | £64,000 |
| Year 2 depreciation (£64,000 x 20%) = | £12,800 |
| Value at end of Year 2 (£64,000 – £12,800) = | £51,200 |

In year 3 it will be as follows:

| | |
|---|---|
| Value at end of Year 2 | £51,200 |
| Year 3 depreciation (£51,200 x 20%) = | £10,240 |
| Value at end of Year 3 (£51,200 – £10,240) = | £40,960 |

You can see, therefore, that with this method the amount of depreciation reduces each year.

## Calculation of net profit using the profit and loss account

The profit and loss account follows on from the trading account and simply deducts all of the expenses of a business from the gross profit; the resulting figure is the net profit.

Continuing the example of Steve Hackett, here is his trading and profit and loss account for the year ending 31.3.07. From his records he identifies that he has had Administration expenses of £69,804. These are shown towards the bottom of the profit and loss account.

### STEVE HACKETT

**Profit and Loss Account for Year Ended 31.3.07**

| | £000s | £000s | £000s |
|---|---|---|---|
| Sales | | | 285,400 |
| | | | 2960 |
| Net Sales (or Turnover) | | | 282,440 |
| **less Cost of Goods Sold** | | | |
| Opening Stock | | 12,000 | |
| Purchases | 174,340 | | |
| | 2504 | | |
| Net Purchases | | 171,836 | |
| | | 183,836 | |
| less Closing Stock | | 12,500 | |
| Cost of Goods Sold | | | 171,336 |
| **GROSS PROFIT** | | | 111,104 |
| Non-Operating Receipts (Rental Income) | | | 5750 |
| | | | 116,854 |
| **Less Expenses** | | | |
| Administration | | | |
| Rent & Rates | | 22,800 | |
| Wages & Salaries | | 42,000 | |
| Telephone & Postage | | 725 | |
| Motor Expenses | | 2250 | |
| Advertising | | 1800 | |
| Sundry Expenses | | 229 | |
| Depreciation | | | |
| Buildings | | 0 | |
| Equipment | | 14,700 | |
| Motor Vehicles | | 2185 | 86,689 |
| **Net Profit** | | | 30,165 |

This top section is the Trading Account (you should notice that this is the same as the one we looked at previously).

This bottom section is the Profit and Loss Account and it includes all of the expenses of the firm.

◄ Final accounts for sole trader Steve Hackett

Steve also has some fixed assets that will need depreciating. Equipment that originally cost £98,000 will be depreciated at 15% per year and a motor vehicle that originally cost £10,925 that will be depreciated at 20% per year, both using the straight line method.

Depreciation is calculated as follows:
Equipment: £98,000 x 15% = £14,700
Motor vehicle: £10,925 x 20% = £2185

These figures are included at the bottom of the profit and loss account.

This shows us that Steve has made a net profit for the year of £30,165 after accounting for all his business expenses.

You should now go back and check all of the figures in the profit and loss account so that you are clear where each of them comes from.

## Practice point

Continue the example of Junaid (see page 219) to compile his trading and profit and loss account for the year ending 31.3.07.

Junaid has identified the following expenses for the year:

| | |
|---|---|
| Rent & rates | £5440 |
| Wages & salaries | £13,500 |
| Telephone & postage | £180 |
| Motor expenses | £900 |
| Advertising | £90 |
| Sundry expenses | £80 |

Junaid also has some fixed assets that may need depreciating:

- buildings that originally cost £45,000
- equipment that originally cost £4500
- motor vehicle that originally cost £7200.

They will be depreciated as follows:

- equipment – 20% on cost
- motor vehicle – 20% on cost
- buildings – 0% on cost.

## Transfer of net profit to balance sheet

The net profit for the year is then transferred to a final document known as the **balance sheet** and we shall see how this is constructed in the next section. We have considered the example of Steve Hackett, who has a net profit of £30,165 to put into his balance sheet.

## Real lives

### Amazon

On 25 October 2006 Amazon.com announced its latest trading figures. These revealed that sales had risen by 24% to $2,250,000,000 ($2.25 billion) and that net profit had fallen from $30,000,000 ($30 million) to $19,000,000 ($19 million). What do you think this can tell us about Amazon.com's trading situation? Think about this in terms of the sales and costs of the business.

1. What might account for a 24% rise in sales coupled with a 37% fall in net profit? ✓
2. Do you think this statement describes a positive situation for the company or a negative one? ✓
3. How do you think the management of Amazon.com should respond to this news? Justify your answer. ✓✓
4. On the day of announcement the company's share price rose by 12%. Explain why you think this might have happened. ✓✓✓

## Key Terms

**Balance sheet** An overview of the financial position of a business on a particular date showing its total assets and liabilities (money it owes).

**Liabilities** Monies that the business owes.

# Balance sheet

## Purpose and use of balance sheet

The true value or worth of a business involves many factors, such as the things that it has bought, the things it has made, its regular customers and even the reputation of the business or its brand.

While the trading and profit and loss account shows the profit that a business has earned in a particular year, the balance sheet shows what the business is truly worth and what makes up its value. It starts with a comparison of the items of value within the business (its assets) and the money that it owes (its liabilities). The balance sheet is the last document in a set of final accounts and can be defined as an overview of a company's financial position on a particular date showing its total assets and **liabilities.**

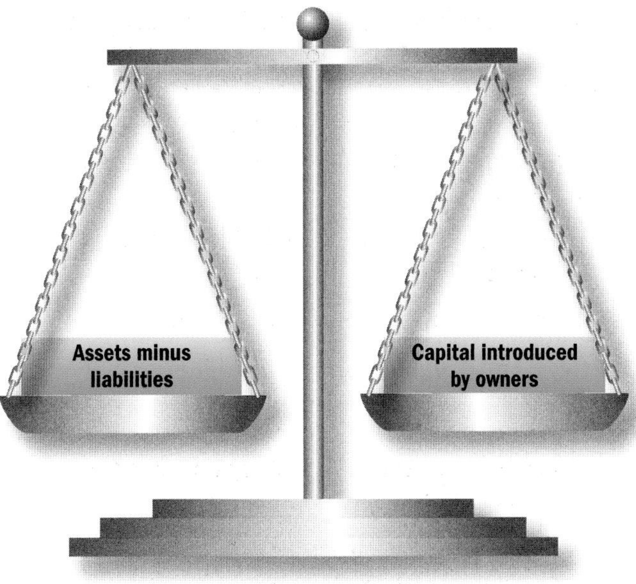


▲ Accounts in balance

## Vertical presentation

Sometimes a balance sheet is laid out in a horizontal format but it is more common these days to use the vertical format. This layout adopts the following basic pattern:

Intangible assets (such as goodwill)
\+ Fixed assets (such as premises and equipment)
\+ **Current assets** (such as cash and stocks)
– **Current liabilities** (such as amounts owed to **creditors** or overdrafts)
– **Long-term liabilities** (such as bank loans)
= Net assets

<u>Capital employed</u>
Opening capital (the amount the owner invested to start the business)
\+ Net profits (transferred from the profit and loss account)
= The same figure as net assets – *when these two figures are equal the accounts balance*

### Key Terms

**Current assets** Money that is readily available in the business for paying debts.

**Current liabilities** Amounts owed to suppliers or lenders which are due to be repaid fairly shortly (usually within one year).

**Creditors** People to whom the business owes money for goods or services it has received.

**Long-term liabilities** Sums that have to be paid for in more than one year's time, such as a mortgage on company property or a long-term bank loan.

## Fixed assets

The first section on a balance sheet details the fixed assets of the business, which comprise the capital items of value that the business has bought and will use for an extended period of time, such as buildings, machinery, equipment and vehicles. These are often referred to as tangible fixed assets. The fixed assets section of the balance sheet will show the original prices paid for these assets, the amounts by which their value has depreciated and the net current value of each of them (original price minus depreciation). Note that fixed assets are usually listed in **order of permanence**, meaning the most permanent assets are first followed by those that are more likely to deteriorate and depreciate. This normally means that land is listed first, then premises followed by equipment and then vehicles.

Fixed assets come in many forms ►

## Thinking point

To what extent should land and buildings be depreciated in a set of company accounts? Justify your response.

### Intangible assets

Occasionally you will see an item in the fixed assets section entitled 'Goodwill'. This is an example of an intangible fixed asset. Goodwill does not represent an item of value but arises when a new owner pays above the book value of the business for its good reputation.

### Current assets

This is the second section in the balance sheet and it contains assets that are readily available in the company for paying debts. This generally includes stocks, debtors, money in the bank and cash held on the premises.

### Current liabilities

The third section in the balance sheet contains amounts that are owed to suppliers or lenders which are due to be repaid fairly shortly (normally within one year); these are known as current liabilities. This will typically contain creditors, bank overdrafts, VAT and loans that are due to be repaid in less than one year.

### Working capital

**Working capital** (also known as net current assets or current capital) measures how much a business has available to pay bills. Working capital is calculated by deducting current liabilities (those debts to be paid shortly) from current assets (money that is readily available). The result should be a positive figure, otherwise the business may find it hard to meet its debts. You will find the figure for working capital at the heart of the balance sheet in the example on page 226.

## Key Terms

**Working capital** Money needed for the day-to-day running of the business. It is calculated by current assets minus current liabilities.

### Long-term liabilities

This section contains those debts that have to be paid for in more than one year's time, such as a mortgage on company property or a long-term bank loan.

## Net assets

This is the difference between the total assets of the business and its total liabilities. It is the figure to which the accounts should be balanced. As long as the final section (capital employed or financed by) of the accounts results in the same figure, then the accounts are deemed to balance.

## Capital employed or financed by

The final section of the balance sheet shows where the money came from to run the business; in the final accounts for a sole trader this will typically be **capital introduced** by the owner and **retained profits** from previous years of trading. The net profit figure from the profit and loss account is transferred into this section. For a sole trader account, this section will also include the amount that the owner has taken from the business for their own use; this is known as drawings.

## Key Terms

**Capital introduced** Money put into a business by the owners.

**Retained profit** Profits that have not been distributed to the shareholders but are saved to finance future expansion of the business. They appear in the appropriations section of the profit and loss account.

### Remember

You will know if the accounts balance by comparing the net assets figure with the final figure in the capital employed section – if they are the same then the accounts balance; if not you need to go back and check the workings, because something must have gone wrong!

## Balance sheet for a sole trader

This follows the example of Steve Hackett who we considered earlier in this unit. Look back at the trading and profit and loss account for Steve now to refresh your memory (see page 221). The following figures have also been extracted from Steve's records in order to complete the balance sheet:

| | |
|---|---|
| Debtors | £3970 |
| Bank | £0 |
| Cash | £275 |
| Creditors | £3200 |
| Overdraft | £3370 |
| Bank loan | £32,000 |
| Opening capital | £58,750 |
| Drawings | £18,700 |

Steve's balance sheet is shown on the next page.

You should study this balance sheet carefully so that you are sure where each of the entries comes from and how all of the calculations are done.

### Practice point

Use the trading and profit and loss account that you compiled for Junaid (page 222) to compile his balance sheet for the year ending 31.3.07. You will need the following additional figures to do this:

| | |
|---|---|
| Debtors | £0 |
| Bank | £0 |
| Cash | £0 |
| Creditors | £500 |
| Overdraft | £270 |
| Bank loan | £9000 |
| Opening capital | £40,000 |
| Drawings | £26,600 |

# STEVE HACKETT

**Balance Sheet as at 31.3.07**

| | Cost | Accumulated Depreciation | Net Book Value |
|---|---|---|---|
| | £ | £ | £ |
| **Fixed Assets** | | | |
| Buildings | 0 | 0 | 0 |
| Equipment | 98,000 | 14,700 | 83,300 |
| Motor Vehicles | 10,925 | 2185 | 8740 |
| | 108,925 | 16,885 | 92,040 |
| **Current Assets** | | | |
| Stock | | 12,500 | |
| Debtors | | 3970 | |
| Bank | | 0 | |
| Cash | | 275 | |
| | | 16,745 | |
| **Less Current Liabilities** | | | |
| Creditors | 3200 | | |
| Overdraft | 3370 | | |
| | | 6570 | |
| **Working Capital** | | | 10,175 |
| | | | 102,215 |
| **Less Long-Term Liabilities** | | | |
| Bank Loan | | | 32,000 |
| **NET ASSETS** | | | 70,215 |
| **FINANCED BY** | | | |
| **Capital** | | | |
| Opening Capital | | | 58,750 |
| Add Net Profit | | | 30,165 |
| | | | 88,915 |
| Less Drawings | | | 18,700 |
| | | | 70,215 |

**MOST IMPORTANT!**
These are the figures that MUST end up the same for the accounts to balance. If they don't, then you have done something wrong!

Original cost minus depreciation

Total value of current assets (£12,500 + £3970 + £275)

Total value of current liabilities (£3200 + £3370)

Current assets minus current liabilities (£16,745 – £6570)

Fixed assets **plus** working capital (£92,040 + £10,175)

£102,215 – £32,000

Capital originally put into the business by the owner

This comes from the bottom of the Profit and Loss Account

This is the amount the owner has paid him or herself

▲ Final accounts sole trader Steve Hackett

## Outcome activity 5.3

**Pass P4**

For the purposes of this assignment assume that you are working for the firm of accountants, Waters, Gilmour, Mason and Wright who are based at Floyd House, Grantchester Meadows, Oxford, OX3 5DS.

You have been approached by one of your clients, Mr Kong Han, who has a shop in your town selling collector's items of science fiction memorabilia. Mr Han has recently received his latest set of accounts from your company, the accounts are attached below:

### Kong Han

**Profit and Loss Account for Year Ended 31.3.07**

| | £000s | £000s | £000s |
|---|---|---|---|
| Sales | | | 63,850 |
| Less Sales Returns | | | 250 |
| Net Sales (or Turnover) | | | 63,600 |
| **less Cost of Goods Sold** | | | |
| Opening Stock | | 7700 | |
| Purchases | 35,700 | | |
| Less Purchase Returns | 0 | | |
| Net Purchases | | 35,700 | |
| | | 43,400 | |
| less Closing Stock | | 7400 | |
| Cost of Goods Sold | | | 36,000 |
| **GROSS PROFIT** | | | 27,600 |
| Non-Operating Receipts | | | 0 |
| | | | 27,600 |
| **Less Expenses** | | | |
| Administration | | | |
| Rent & Rates | | 6000 | |
| Wages & Salaries | | 3920 | |
| Telephone & Postage | | 190 | |
| Motor Expenses | | 1500 | |
| Advertising | | 1500 | |
| Sundry Expenses | | 240 | |
| Depreciation | | | |
| Buildings | | 0 | |
| Equipment | | 2325 | |
| Motor Vehicles | | 600 | 16,275 |
| **Net Profit** | | | 11,325 |

▲ Final accounts Kong Han – profit and loss account

## Kong Han

**Balance Sheet as at 31.3.07**

| | Cost | Accumulated Depreciation | Net Book Value |
|---|---|---|---|
| | £ | £ | £ |
| **Fixed Assets** | | | |
| Buildings | 0 | 0 | 0 |
| Equipment | 15,500 | 2325 | 13,175 |
| Motor Vehicles | 3000 | 600 | 2400 |
| | 18,500 | 2925 | 15,575 |
| **Current Assets** | | | |
| Stock | | 7400 | |
| Debtors | | 150 | |
| Bank | | 560 | |
| Cash | | 250 | |
| | | 8360 | |
| **Less Current Liabilities** | | | |
| Creditors | 1610 | | |
| Overdraft | 0 | | |
| | | 1610 | |
| **Working Capital** | | | 6750 |
| | | | 22,325 |
| **Less Long-Term Liabilities** | | | |
| Bank Loan | | | 10,000 |
| **NET ASSETS** | | | 12,325 |
| **FINANCED BY** | | | |
| **Capital** | | | |
| Opening Capital | | | 16,000 |
| Add Net Profit | | | 11,325 |
| | | | 27,325 |
| Less Drawings | | | 15,000 |
| | | | 12,325 |

▲ Final accounts Kong Han – balance sheet

Mr Han has been having great trouble understanding these accounts and he has asked for your help in understanding them.

Write a letter to Mr Han (his address is 32 Crookdale Lane, Ipswich, IP32 6TY), explaining all of the components of his profit and loss account and balance sheet.

## Grading tips

**Pass** 

You must include the following as a minimum in your letter:

- a description of the purpose and use of the trading, profit and loss account and balance sheet
- an explanation of the cost of goods sold section and the **overheads** section in the profit and loss account and a copy of the profit and loss account with these sections labelled clearly
- an explanation of how gross profit and net profit are calculated
- an explanation of the kinds of income and expenditure that are included in the accounts
- an explanation of each of the elements of the balance sheet
- a description of how to tell if the accounts balance.

## Key Terms

**Overheads** Costs that do not change when the business sells more products and which are not incurred by a specific department of the company, such as rent.

# 5.4 Review business performance using simple ratio analysis

You now know the structure of a set of accounts, but what do they actually tell us about the business? The accounts contain many messages for those who choose to read them, but these messages may not be completely clear at first. It is helpful to have a 'phrase book' or some tools to help us interpret the messages in a set of accounts.

Some messages are very straightforward; for example, you should now easily be able to identify the total profit made in a year by a business. But what if you wanted to know how good an investment a business had been for its shareholders? Or how efficient the business is in chasing customers who owe it money? Can the business keep its costs under control? Can you tell if the position of the business is improving or deteriorating? All of this information is available if you know how and where to look.

Ratio analysis is the accountant's phrase book. Armed with a number of simple tools we can make accurate judgements of an organisation's performance; so outlined below are some of the most important ratios that you could use. Remember that the accounts of a sole trader are private, so only the owner of the business and an appointed accountant will be able to make use of ratio analysis. However, if the business becomes a limited company – with shareholders – ratio analysis can be used by many of the stakeholders in the business, such as:

- owners – to inform them when they are looking to make decisions about the future of the business

▲ A phrase book can help us to interpret different accounts

- investors – to check that their investment is doing well and providing a fair return on their money
- suppliers – if they are owed money by the business then they will want to know if they are likely to get their money back; if they are approached to supply on credit they can use the accounts to see if the business is worthy of credit
- employees – individual employees or trade unions may check the accounts to monitor how profitable the business is and therefore whether they can request pay rises or improvements in their working conditions
- customers – to check that the business is likely to be financially healthy and therefore able to keep supplying them
- tax authorities – to check that the business is paying the correct amounts of tax
- creditors – such as the bank which may wish to check that the business is still in a position to make repayments on loans they have advanced.

## Profitability

A factor that is most important to the owners of a business is its profitability. The following ratios can help to monitor the company's profit performance.

### Gross profit percentage of sales

This is calculated using the following formula:

$$\frac{\text{Gross profit for year}}{\text{Sales for year}} \times 100$$

This ratio shows how much gross profit is being made compared with the sales made. For example, a gross profit percentage of 15% means that £1.50 gross profit is made by the business from every £10 of sales.

It is usual to compare these figures from one year to the next, and ideally the percentage will stay relatively stable – showing that the business is consistent in its trading. If it changes, especially if the percentage should fall, this should be investigated and the reasons determined. A deteriorating percentage, for example, could mean that purchase costs are increasing or that sales are falling.

## Net profit percentage of sales

This is calculated using the following formula:

$$\frac{\text{Net profit for year}}{\text{Sales for year}} \times 100$$

This ratio is similar to the gross profit percentage but this time shows how much net profit is being made compared with sales. For example, a net profit percentage of 5% means that 50p net profit is made by the business from every £10 of sales.

It is useful to compare the gross profit percentage with the net profit percentage as this shows how much of gross profit is being taken up by the expenses of the business, such as running its vehicles and paying wages and salaries. Ideally the gap between the two should decrease over the years, showing that the business was working well on controlling expenses.

A fall in net profit percentage would indicate that expenses were increasing and this should be examined to see where the problem is and what could be done to put it right.

## Return on capital employed (ROCE)

This is calculated using the following formula:

$$\frac{\text{Net profit for year before interest and tax}}{\text{Capital employed}} \times 100$$

$$= \text{percentage return}$$

The only difficulty with this ratio is defining the term 'capital employed' as a range of definitions is used by different accountants. For the purposes of our exercises we will take capital employed to be defined as: fixed assets plus current assets minus current liabilities. Be aware that some accountants will use different definitions to this.

This ratio shows us the percentage return that the investors have received on the capital that they invested. It is like the interest rate that you would receive on your building society account, and investors will often compare the return on capital employed to the current rates of interest being offered at building societies, to see if they are getting a better or worse deal.

## Case study

### Gross and net profit percentages

The gross profit percentage and net profit percentage for organisations in different industries will not be the same, so we should take care about comparing results. However, comparing the results for two companies in the same industry can be revealing. Consider the following extracts from the accounts of two companies for 2006:

| 2006 | Gross profit £ | Net profit £ | Sales £ |
|---|---|---|---|
| Emerson Ltd | 1000 | 600 | 8000 |
| Lake and Palmer Ltd | 1920 | 480 | 24,000 |

1. Calculate the gross profit percentage and net profit percentage for each of the organisations. What conclusions can you draw from your results? ✓

Here are the results for the same companies for the previous year:

| 2005 | Gross profit % | Net profit % |
|---|---|---|
| Emerson Ltd | 15% | 9% |
| Lake and Palmer Ltd | 7.9% | 2.1% |

2. What further conclusions can you draw when comparing the 2006 figures with the 2005 figures? ✓✓

Obtain a copy of the Report and Accounts from a company. Your teacher should be able to help you obtain these; alternatively you could visit this website: www.carol.co.uk. The CAROL website offers free access to the accounts of many publicly quoted companies in Europe and the USA.

3. Using the accounts you have obtained, try to calculate the gross and net profit percentage for the business. What conclusions can you draw from your calculations? ✓✓✓

## Case study

**ROCE**

The ROCE for a number of organisations is as follows:

- Page PLC 7%
- Plant PLC 3%
- Bonham PLC 1.5%
- Jones Ltd 19%

Using the Internet, check the current interest rates offered at two major building societies for accounts requiring a maximum of four weeks' notice.

1. Which of the above companies are offering attractive deals to their investors? ✓
2. What other factors would be important when deciding whether to invest in a building society or shares in a limited company? ✓✓
3. What problems might an investor encounter in trying to invest in Jones Ltd? ✓✓✓

# Liquidity

As we have seen, working capital is essential to the health of a business. The following ratios are commonly used to measure how **solvent** the firm is, i.e. how easily it can pay its debts.

## Key Terms

**Liquid assets/liquidity** Monies available to a company which are immediately available for business use.

### Current ratio

This is calculated using the following formula:

$$\frac{\text{Current assets}}{\text{Current liabilities}}$$

This ratio shows the proportion of current assets to current liabilities. It shows how easily the business could raise enough money to pay the debts that it has to pay in the near future. A result of 2:1 is usually considered to be adequate liquidity for most businesses, although a business dealing mainly in cash may well be able to survive with a lower ratio. If the ratio is 3:1 or more the business should query whether it is managing its current assets sufficiently well. Such a ratio implies that the business is holding too much in current assets. Perhaps it has too much stock, or maybe there are large sums of cash sitting idle in the business. If this is the case the business should consider finding a productive use for this cash, rather than leaving it sitting in the business or the bank account producing no revenue.

### Acid test ratio/liquidity ratio

This is calculated using the following formula:

$$\frac{\text{Current assets} - \text{Stock}}{\text{Current liabilities}}$$

This ratio is very similar to the current ratio, except that the stock figure is omitted. The reason for this is that sometimes it is difficult to sell stock quickly and for the anticipated price if the money is needed quickly. Consequently it may be unrealistic to rely on stocks to pay debts as they become due. This ratio therefore shows how much readily available assets the business could rely on if a creditor insisted on immediate payment. A result of 1:1 indicates that the business should not have a problem paying bills as they become due, but if it falls below 1:1, such as 0.9:1 the company has fewer liquid assets and this could cause problems. The lower the ratio, the more illiquid is the business and the closer it is to **insolvency**. If a business has a healthy current ratio but a poor **acid test ratio** it might be that the business is holding too much stock.

## Key Terms

**Solvency** How easily a business can pay its debts.

**Insolvency** Where a business is unable to pay debts when they become due for payment.

**Acid test ratio** Current assets minus stock divided by current liabilities. This ratio shows how well a business can meet its liabilities without having to sell stock.

▲ The acid test

## Case study

### Current ratio and acid test

Consider the following extract from a company's accounts:

| | 2005 £ | 2006 £ | 2007 £ |
|---|---|---|---|
| Current assets | 49,140 | 54,054 | 59,460 |
| Current liabilities | 23,664 | 26,830 | 29,782 |
| Stock | 22,464 | 25,834 | 29,991 |
| Current ratio | | | |
| Acid test | | | |

1. Complete the table by calculating the current ratio and acid test for the company for each of the three years. ✓
2. Comment on what your results show and on how the company's position might be improving or declining. ✓✓
3. Some businesses are able to trade quite happily on lower liquidity ratios than others. Consider the following business types. For each you should consider whether they would need to have a high degree of liquidity or whether they could operate with a relatively low liquidity ratio. Make sure you justify each of your answers. ✓✓✓
   - **a.** a public house
   - **b.** a construction company
   - **c.** a butcher
   - **d.** a car manufacturer.

# Efficiency

These ratios examine the productivity of a business. **Productivity** looks at how efficiently a company is using its factors of production to produce goods/services and profit.

## Key Terms

**Productivity** How efficiently a business can produce goods/services and profit.

### Debtors' payment period

This is calculated using the following formula:

$$\frac{\text{Debtors}}{\text{Credit sales for year}} \times 365$$

= debtor collection period in days

*Note:* If it is not clear how many sales were on credit then the sales figure from the profit and loss account should be used.

This ratio shows how long it takes on average for debtors to pay for goods bought on credit. This will be different for businesses in different industries as some sell on credit more than others. Shops, for example, do not sell on credit nearly as much as trade suppliers. You should compare this figure with that of previous years to make any sense of the result. If the number of days is increasing, then the company's procedures for chasing debtors should be examined as this is likely to be having an adverse effect on the company's cash flow. If it is stable, this suggests that debt collection is under control. It is also interesting to compare this ratio with the next one, the creditor payment period.

### Creditors' payment period

This is calculated using the following formula:

$$\frac{\text{Creditors}}{\text{Credit purchases for year}} \times 365$$

= creditor payment period in days

*Note:* If it is not clear how many purchases were on credit then the purchases figure from the profit and loss account should be used.

This ratio reveals how long the business is taking to pay for goods it has bought. If this period is increasing, it implies that the business is either negotiating better terms from its suppliers or it is having difficulty paying its bills. You may like to compare the creditor payment period with the debtor payment period.

If the creditor payment period is greater than the debtor payment period then the business is getting better terms for buying on credit than it is giving to its customers. This will clearly help cash flow as money will be received from purchases before bills have to be paid for supplies.

▲ Stock turnover rates vary from company to company

If the debtor payment period is greater than the creditor payment period then the situation is not so good as the firm is allowing longer periods for its customers buying on credit than it is receiving from its suppliers. This will clearly hinder cash flow as bills for supplies will need to be paid before money is received for sales.

## Practice point

Consider the following extract from a company's accounts:

| | 2005 £ | 2006 £ | 2007 £ |
|---|---|---|---|
| Debtors | 18,900 | 20,790 | 22,870 |
| Creditors | 16,380 | 17,198 | 18,059 |
| Credit sales for the year | 17,1600 | 180,180 | 189,190 |
| Credit purchases for the year | 120,000 | 132,000 | 145,200 |
| Debtor collection period | | | |
| Creditor collection period | | | |

Complete the table by calculating the debtor collection period and the creditor collection period for the company for each of the three years. What do you results show? How the do you think the company's position might be improving or declining?

## Rate of stock turnover

This is calculated using the following formula:

$$\frac{\text{Average stock}}{\text{Cost of goods sold}} \times 365 = \text{stock turnover in days}$$

*Note:* Average stock is calculated by adding opening stock to closing stock and dividing by two.

This ratio returns the number of days that an average item of stock is held at the business, in other words how long it takes to sell the item. It is difficult to determine what a good rate of **stock turnover** might be for a business, as the situation is different for companies in different industries. For example, a manufacturer of electrical goods may hold stock for several weeks before it leaves for a retailer; however a supermarket would expect a much shorter turnover as food items perish quickly.

## Key Terms

**Stock turnover** The measurement of how quickly the business has sold the value of its stock. The higher the turnover, the quicker the business is selling its stock. This is very important in a business where goods are updated quickly or are perishable.

In general terms, however, businesses will be looking to reduce the number of stock days wherever possible. The important points to consider are as follows:

- How does the company's ratio compare with those of other similar businesses in the industry?
- How does the ratio compare with this time last year? A shorter period than last year indicates that the company is becoming more efficient; one that is longer implies that the business needs to determine why and correct the trend.

## Outcome activity 5.4

For the purposes of this assignment assume that you are still working for accountants, Waters, Gilmour, Mason and Wright as in Outcome Activity 5.3, and you are continuing work on Mr Han's accounts. Mr Han has asked you to help him analyse his organisation's financial position.

### Pass

Write a further letter to Mr Han explaining how ratio analysis can be used to measure the profitability, liquidity and efficiency of his business. Using the trading and profit and loss account and balance sheet earlier in this unit, complete the table below by calculating Mr Han's ratios for the year ended March 2007.

### Merit

Analyse the performance of a business using suitable ratios.

You should now continue the letter begun for P5 by analysing the performance of Mr Han's business using the ratios that you explained and calculated earlier for P5.

### Distinction

This final task will be performed in a group of three or four students. Using the results of your calculations for M2 you should now evaluate the financial performance and position of Mr Han's business using ratio analysis.

Assuming that you are still working for accountants, Waters, Gilmour, Mason and Wright, you will individually prepare and deliver a presentation of your findings to Mr Han that uses PowerPoint or OHTs to explain your analysis. Your analysis should take account of the following statistics:

| | Mr Han's business year ending March 2005 | Mr Han's business year ending March 2006 | Industry averages | Mr Han's business year ending March 2007 |
|---|---|---|---|---|
| Return on capital employed | 41% | 45% | 37% | |
| Gross profit percentage | 44% | 45% | 39% | |
| Net profit percentage | 28% | 27% | 30% | |
| Stock turnover | 44 days | 56 days | 62 days | |
| Debtor payment period | 0.89 days | 0.88 days | 0.9 days | |
| Creditor payment period | 5.7 days | 13 days | 12 days | |
| Current ratio | 4.8:1 | 4.9:1 | 4.5:1 | |
| Acid test | 1.1:1 | 0.89:1 | 1:1 | |

## Grading tips

**Pass** 

To succeed in this task you should outline clearly what is meant by the terms profitability, liquidity and efficiency. The letter will also include details of each of the ratios that can be used to assess these areas. You should detail the meaning and relevance of each of the ratios.

**Merit** 

This task will require you to do the following as a minimum:

1. Calculate each of ratios accurately.
2. Explain what each result tells you about the state of Mr Han's business. Remember to relate these results to the three themes of profitability, liquidity and efficiency.

**Distinction** 

Evaluation is about considering in detail the positives and negatives of something, in this case the strengths and weaknesses of Mr Han's business. You should consider each ratio in turn and make an assessment of the strength or weakness of his business demonstrated by the year-on-year comparison, as well as that with the industry averages. Remember that you must come to an overall conclusion about the health of his business; it is important that this is clearly a result of your analysis.

## End of unit test

1. What is the purpose of accounting?
2. What is the difference between capital income and revenue income? Give two examples of each.
3. What is the difference between capital expenditure and revenue expenditure? Give two examples of each.
4. What is goodwill? Why should someone purchasing a business be charged for this?
5. Name and explain two other possible intangible assets of a firm.
6. What is the difference between debtors and creditors?
7. Give two suggestions for solving cash flow problems.
8. Why is the totals column in a cash flow forecast useful?
9. What is fixed capital and what is working capital? How do you work out the working capital of a business?
10. What is a trading account and how is it constructed?
11. What is the difference between gross profit and net profit? Where would you find each of these figures in a set of final accounts?
12. State the two main methods used to depreciate the fixed assets of a company and, using examples, explain how each of them works.
13. What is the difference between a firm's assets and its liabilities? Give examples of each.
14. What are liquid assets? Give examples of them.
15. What is the difference between the current and acid test ratios and why are they useful to a business?

# Resources

http://www.bbc.co.uk/schools/gcsebitesize/business/finance/accountsrev2.shtml – BBC Bitesize Accounts Revision

http://www.bized.ac.uk/learn/business/accounting/busaccounts/notes/pl.htm – Bized, and databank of knowledge for business students

www.londonstockexchange.com – The London Stock Exchange

www.accountancymagazine.com – Magazine for professional accountants containing professional updates and information

www.accountingweb.co.uk – The latest accountancy news

http://www.staffs.ac.uk/schools/business/bsadmin/staff/s5/mscproj/defn.htm – Staffordshire University, explanations of accounting terms

www.carol.co.uk – Company Annual Reports On-Line. A great source for online sets of final accounts for UK companies

http://www.businesslink.gov.uk – Businesslink, a government initiative to support small businesses

www.statistics.gov.uk – National Statistics

# Books


Allin, M. 1998 *Painless Business Finance*, David Grant Publishing

Cox, D. 1999 *Business Accounts*, Osborne Books

St John Price, A. 1999 *Understand Your Accounts* (4th edition), Kogan Page

Watts, B. 1991 *Business Financial Management* (6th edition), MacDonald and Evans


| Grading criteria | Outcome activity | Page number |
|---|---|---|
| To achieve a pass grade the evidence must show that the learner is able to: | | |
| **P1** Describe the purpose of accounting | 5.1 | 207 |
| **P2** Explain the difference between capital and revenue items of expenditure and income | 5.1 | 207 |
| **P3** Prepare a twelve-month cash flow forecast to enable an organisation to manage its cash | 5.2 | 216 |
| **P4** Explain the component parts of a profit and loss account and balance sheet in a given organisation | 5.3 | 227 |
| **P5** Perform ratio analysis to measure the profitability, liquidity and efficiency of a given organisation | 5.4 | 235 |
| To achieve a merit grade the evidence must show that, in addition to the pass criteria, the learner is able to: | | |
| **M1** Analyse the cash flow problems a business might experience | 5.2 | 216 |
| **M2** Analyse the performance of a business using suitable ratios | 5.4 | 235 |
| To achieve a distinction grade the evidence must show that, in addition to the pass and merit criteria, the learner is able to: | | |
| **D1** Recommend and justify actions a business might take when experiencing cash flow problems | 5.2 | 216 |
| **D2** Evaluate the financial performance and position of a business using ratio analysis | 5.4 | 235 |

# Exploring creative product promotion

## Introduction

This unit considers all the aspects of marketing that contribute to effective promotional campaigns. Promotion is something we are all exposed to every day of the week. Even the best product, sold in the appropriate places at the right price, may experience poor sales if the promotional support is ineffective.

An understanding of customer behaviour helps produce effective promotional activity which contributes to the organisation achieving its business objectives. The use of new technology is providing marketing managers with new and innovative ways to deliver the promotional message. The unit considers these developments alongside the traditional promotional methods that organisations have been successfully using for many years.

The unit explains how advertising agencies can make a very significant contribution to the effectiveness of a campaign. As well as developing relevant messages, agencies can advise organisations about which media to use and how often it should be used.

The final part allows for the creation and justification of a local promotional campaign for a medium-sized organisation. It will show that effective promotion can be achieved by local small- and medium-sized organisations with modest budgets. The final part of the unit is also an opportunity to produce some promotional materials showing your flair for marketing.

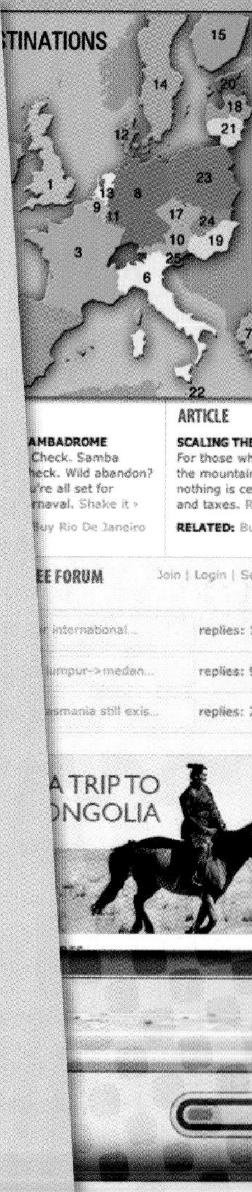

### What you need to learn

On completion of this unit you should:

1. Know the constituents of the promotional mix
2. Understand the role of promotion within the marketing mix
3. Understand the role of advertising agencies and the media
4. Be able to create a simple promotional campaign.

## Consider this

You are in a senior management meeting where the design department reveals its latest new product idea, which it has spent five years developing. The managing director suggests that the success of the product depends on the promotional campaign informing the customer about the key product benefits and then persuading them to buy the product.

Obviously it will not be long before competitors launch their version of the product and it is essential that your organisation establishes its product first and generates significant sales in the short term. Product life cycles are becoming shorter and shorter all the time.

The managing director suggests that sales could be expected to be over £4 million within twelve months, making it the organisation's most successful product. This will require a massive investment in promotion. However, you know that the advertising agency used by the organisation has a proven record of success in developing campaigns to launch new products. You are delighted that the nature of the product will allow you to use some of the promotional techniques that new technology is making more available such as 'animatronic' robotic human and animal puppets.

What would you write on your blog about this exciting challenge?

# Promotional mix

## Purpose and objectives

The purpose of advertising is to create awareness, persuade and inform consumers about a product while pointing out the superior features compared with competitive products. These purposes can be expressed as objectives such as:

- increasing sales and acquiring a greater **market share**
- showing the product features which outperform competition
- educating the market to the benefits of acquiring the product
- explaining the number of potential uses of the product
- conveying the **brand image** of the product or organisation
- promoting the new and improved features of an established product.

The tools available to achieve these objectives include advertising, publicity and public relations, sponsorship, personal selling, direct marketing and corporate image development. These options have to be blended together to ensure the maximum number of consumers are exposed to the promotional message at the lowest cost.

## Key Terms

**Market share** The sales of a product by a company expressed as a percentage of total sales in a market. If a company sells 20,000 products and the total number of those products sold overall is 200,000 then that company has a market share of 10%.

**Brand image** The set of views and opinions consumers hold about a product.

## Products and services

Much product promotion is straightforward when the features of the goods can be touched, smelt and seen. However, conveying benefits can be more challenging when customers, for example, buy for emotional reasons.

Promoting services presents some special issues because the communication is about something intangible, something you cannot touch, smell or see. This makes the promotional task more difficult. Providers of financial services, for example, have the problem of communicating a range of product benefits to potential customers where some of the benefits are complex, difficult to understand and only likely to be needed sometime in the distant future.

▲ The promotional mix

## Advertising

**Advertising** is when an organisation promotes a product using paid-for **media** such as television. Advertising must speak to its target audience and should draw attention to the characteristics of the product which will appeal to the needs or wants of the potential consumer.

If the product does not have a distinguishing feature – referred to as a unique selling proposition (USP) – uniqueness can be promoted by brand image. The ultimate purpose of advertising is to improve potential buyers' reactions to its products by channelling desires and supplying reasons for consumers to prefer one product over its competitors.

### Key Terms

**Advertising media** Communication channels, including print media (newspapers, magazines, direct mail letters); broadcast media (radio, television); display media (billboards, signs, posters) and the Internet (pod-casting).

**Blog** A frequently updated online diary, with links to other blogs or websites.

## Publicity and public relations

In marketing terms, publicity and public relations are two separate activities. Publicity is any activity aimed at the media (television and radio as well as newspapers and magazines) and undertaken in order to generate news or information about an organisation or its products. The aim is for the news to be broadcast or published at no charge. Publicity can be generated through **press releases**, news conferences, interviews with the media and articles in appropriate publications.

### Key Terms

**Press releases** Brief news items or information given to newspapers and magazines.

Public relations can be defined as the development and maintenance of positive relationships between an organisation and its public – employees, local community, customers, suppliers, media – through activities designed to create understanding and goodwill. These activities can include, for example, organising conferences, open days, hospitality events and award celebrations.

### Case study

**Pod-casting holds key message for smaller firms**

Many large organisations are using **blogs** (online diaries) and pod-casts (downloadable audio or visual web recordings) already. Microsoft uses blogs to disseminate information about its applications and upgrades, while IBM uses pod-casts to update staff, investors and the media on business developments. Yet some innovative small businesses are also experimenting with how to benefit from this technology.

Fisher Jones Greenwood, a Colchester-based firm of solicitors, recently started www.i-legal.info, a website offering pod-casts on legal matters, such as wills. Tony Fisher, a senior partner at the firm, says: 'Few people are prepared to spend time reading through a turgid legal guide online, but if you present it well they will listen to a pod-cast. About 2000 of our guides are being downloaded each month which is helping to gain new business for the partnership.'

Karen Ainley, the director of Mosiac Publicity, a company that offers audio training, says: 'To make a good pod-cast, you really have to think about what it is you have to say and how to say it. It is not worth doing boring monologues, nobody will listen. Sound effects and music help, and encourage people to come back for more.'

1. What might be some of the other benefits of blogs in addition to promoting an organisation? ✓
2. What sort of companies may find pod-casts inappropriate? ✓✓
3. What problems might be associated with this type of promotional activity? What could an organisation do to prevent such issues arising? ✓✓✓

## Thinking point

Press releases can be produced whenever a newsworthy event occurs in an organisation such as a large order received, a new product launched or new senior staff appointment. They need to be written in the style of a newspaper article – as they would be used in a local paper or during a TV news programme.

In order to increase the chances of a press release news story being used, follow the tips in the example below.

### Sponsorship

Sports sponsorship is undoubtedly the most common form of sponsorship, and can range in scale from international and national down to regional and local events. It is a specialised form of promotion where an

▼ **An example of a press release**

Organisations generally produce special headed paper for press releases

The headline needs to attract the attention of the publication's editor

The first paragraph should summarise the story in about 20 words – the editor may only read this much before making a decision on whether to publish the story

Double spacing is preferred so the editor can make notes for colleagues

Wide margins are preferred so the editor has the space to make notes for colleagues

Include a quotation – preferably from someone not attached to your organisation – as it adds personal interest as well as reinforcing the point of your story

Journalists may want to find out more – make the contact information accurate as they may try only once

A photograph will improve the chances of publication; include a caption explaining the content of the photograph

NEWS FROM BUSINESS COLLEGE 

**Students find just the jobs they were seeking**

Twelve students who successfully passed their BTEC National in Business this summer at Business College have already found the jobs they wanted.

Local organisations have been quick to spot the capabilities of the Business students. They have obtained jobs in marketing, sales, finance, human resources and quality control. Without doubt the topics studied on the BTEC National course are highly relevant to the needs of businesses in the local area.

Wesley Bradshaw, the recruitment officer for SW Digital Stores, said: 'I was very impressed with their knowledge of how business works and the number of skills they already possess that can be useful immediately in our organisation. We will certainly be looking to recruit students from next year's classes.'

Students who are thinking of enrolling on the programme need to apply shortly to guarantee a place on this increasingly popular programme.

-End-

Susan Davies
Press Officer
Telephone 0112 598 1316
E-mail: susan.davies@bc.ac.uk

Notes for editors: The photograph shows the students celebrating their successful job applications.

organisation helps to fund an event or support a group or venture in return for publicity.

Sponsorship does not always have to be financial – in many cases it takes the form of providing equipment, facilities or services. It is this flexibility that helps sport sponsorship gain the largest part of the sponsorship market. Sponsorship of the arts also offers a wide range of opportunities, including the performing arts such as opera, concerts and the theatre.

Other forms of sponsorship include education sponsorship, where companies offer scholarships at universities or finance research projects; and media sponsorship, with the sponsoring of programmes; for example ITV drama has been sponsored by the supermarket Sainsbury's.

## Sales promotions

Much money is spent on sales promotion activity which can be aimed at the consumer (such as three items for the price of two) or the trade buyer (free point of sale material with an order).

The 'buy one get one free' (or BOGOF), buy two products and get a third free and extra points on your loyalty card are known to be effective ways of prompting purchase, especially by heavy users. Free samples, however, are probably more effective where the marketing manager wishes to encourage brand switching or trying of a new product.

Unfortunately for companies, in many markets customers have come to expect special promotional offers to accompany the brands they purchase and they will not buy or switch if these expected promotional offers are not available. The dilemma for the marketing manager, therefore, is that in some ways sales promotion can over time lose its ability to achieve the sales and marketing objectives set out for it. There is also the concern with regular sales promotions for a brand that it becomes 'devalued' to some extent in the mind of the customer with the image of the brand being cheapened. However, generally customer perception of sales promotions are favourable in as much as they are seen as offering value for money and strong incentives to purchase.

## Personal selling

Some people may not immediately identify personal selling (selling through a team of sales representatives) as a promotional tool, but in many markets it is the major tool of promotion. It is a high cost method of promotion. The aim of the sales team is to inform customers about products, to demonstrate products and ensure their effective display where appropriate. In addition, the sales team is expected in many cases to provide after-sales service and even training in the use of products. Personal selling allows the organisation to develop good customer relationships, and is used for example by drug companies selling to GPs.

Personal selling has some disadvantages. The cost of customer contact is high and a substantial amount of training may be required to ensure that sales staff are operating effectively.

## Exhibitions

Exhibitions are organised so that manufacturers (such as car producers) and suppliers of services (such as couriers) can promote their products to potential buyers.

For an exhibition to be successful, both exhibitors and visitors must be attracted in sufficient numbers. Organisations may decide to exhibit at an event in order to display new or existing products, or to meet with existing or potential new customers. Usually the aim is to generate business, but it is also an opportunity to see what the competition is doing.

## Direct marketing

In its most common forms, direct marketing includes sending direct mail letters and making telephone calls (or telemarketing) . However, leaflet dropping and even handing out flyers in the street all fit this category of promotion. The objectives of such a campaign can range from promoting special offers to offering the opportunity to try new products.

Many direct mail letters are of no interest to the recipient and are dismissed as 'junk mail' – usually because they are wrongly targeted or poorly produced.

## Case study

### Putting on a good show

Obtaining the attention of everyone even before they have stepped inside an exhibition is a smart way of making the most of the event. It is also a reminder that to exhibit your products well you must start a long time in advance.

Tim Etchells of Single Market Events says, 'Identify your aims before you book your space. Is it about obtaining orders or demonstrating your new product? The space you take and the way you use it should be defined by your aims.

'Don't just sit back and hope it happens on the day. Tie your key customers to appointments. Most buyers are busy people who want to make the most of their time. They will be happy to set up an appointment.

'Set a budget for the stand and remember a third of the money is likely to be accounted for by space costs. Then display your corporate logo, website and telephone number prominently. Think about access, lighting, the use of graphics and sound. It can be a good idea to introduce some kind of movement – it helps draw the eye and attract people. Even a small LCD panel can achieve this effect.'

There are other important questions to be asked: will your customers spend a long time talking to you? Will you need comfortable furniture? How will you keep the stand tidy?

1. Write a short brief to a designer about a stand which your school or college needs to attract students for sixth form studies. ✓
2. What should you do with any leads – people that show an interest in your product – you acquire at the show? ✓✓
3. What would you talk about when you are briefing the sales team about the exhibition? ✓✓✓
4. What else could you do to make the exhibition a success? ✓✓✓

If a direct mail letter is to succeed it must stimulate interest with good design and appropriate content. The successful direct-mail letter depends on a well-researched and properly constructed mailing list. A mailing list contains the names and addresses of potential customers who have been identified as possibly having an interest in the product or service.

Telemarketing is direct marketing by telephone. It is often used to find sales leads (details of potential customers) which are passed on to specialist sales staff to convert into a sale. Good telemarketing requires excellent 'people' skills, a sound knowledge of the organisation's products and services and good administrative abilities to deal with such matters as processing orders and collecting customer details.

### Corporate image

Organisations often carry out activities to 'sell' the organisation itself. Organisation marketing consists of activities aiming to create, maintain or change the attitudes and behaviour of target consumers towards an organisation.

Both profit-making and non-profit organisations practise organisation marketing. For example, IBM wants to establish itself as the company to turn to for 'e-business solutions'. Similarly, non-profit organisations such as churches, colleges, charities, museums and performing arts groups market their organisations in order to raise funds and attract supporters.

# Decisions about appropriate mix

With so many different promotional options available, the marketing manager needs to carefully choose the methods which are best suited to the situation. Outlined over the next few pages are a variety of situations and the factors that should be considered when making decisions about which methods to use.

## Case study

### Head girls wooed by record bosses

They are the thoroughly sensible role models for all good pupils. But now head girls are to become record industry tastemakers. Jamie Cullum, the jazz musician, sent a copy of his new album to the head girl at every all-girls school in Britain. A mail-out of 430 state and independent schools included postcards and stickers, which was followed up by a copy of the CD.

▲ Jamie Cullum in concert

Universal is unapologetic about targeting schoolchildren, arguing that a jazz-based performer such as Cullum struggles to get airplay on teenage-focused radio stations and music channels. A spokesperson for some independent schools said, 'We are surprised that he is not sending it to boys' schools since they would enjoy his music as well.'

This is not the first time such a campaign has been tried. For Busted and McFly, Europe's biggest record company, Universal, signed up a teenage army. They put up posters in schools and urged fellow pupils to vote for the bands in polls and email DJs with requests. The 'chairmen' of each school army received free merchandise and a promise of a telephone call from the bands.

1. Describe the promotional mix being used by Universal to promote Cullum. ✓
2. What other promotional mix activities would you use to support the activity in schools? ✓✓
3. Can you think of a campaign, similar in nature, to promote BTEC National Business in schools? Who might be an excellent choice of business celebrity to spearhead the promotion? ✓✓✓

## Cost versus benefits

Promotional activity does not always pay for itself immediately. Advertising around Christmas time for toy producers, and in the summer for soft drinks producers, usually generates immediate short-term sales and perhaps improved market share.

However, sometimes organisations need to take a long-term view. The cost of the campaign to obtain new customers may look expensive for the organisation until the lifetime value of the customer is taken into consideration. A bank, for instance, may promote its savings accounts realising that account holders in the long term will want a mortgage, some loans and maybe a pension.

## Target market and exposure to media

The costs of the various promotional methods vary enormously. National TV advertising is significantly more costly than a local neighbourhood leaflet campaign. Sometimes the costs influence marketing managers when they are choosing methods – picking the low cost option rather than the most effective method. This can mean that the people who should see the promotional activity do not, while others to whom it is irrelevant are subjected to unnecessary messages. The methods chosen should be those the target market will see and notice.

## Case study

### Skoda – changing perceptions

The launch of the Octavia, a new car produced by Skoda, into the most competitive part of the car market in the UK, would have a huge impact on the brand image of Skoda – banishing forever the jokes that shaped its brand image in the 1970s.

This was the opportunity to create positive perceptions towards the brand and the company – the main objective of Skoda's marketing team. Skoda had a number of key messages which its promotional campaign had to deliver.

- The Octavia was a completely new and modern car extending the appeal of the Skoda brand to younger people, family men and working women who were more highly qualified – working in professional occupations – than current Skoda owners.
- Skoda owners receive much more for their money compared with competitive models.
- The Octavia was designed to the same quality standards as any Volkswagen Group product.
- The Octavia experience is the Skoda experience.

▲ **The Skoda Octavia**

A variety of promotional activities were undertaken including:

- exhibiting the product in shopping centres and other busy venues
- test drive campaigns
- 'the Skoda challenge' – a test drive at dealerships where customers could drive both the Octavia and competitive models
- local and national press advertisements
- public relations activity with newspapers, magazines and television
- local sponsorship activity.
- allowing local dealers to use national campaign materials locally to ensure a consistent message was conveyed to the consumer.

The promotional message was straightforward – 'the way things should be' – showing the car's design and specification features. The theme was carried through press, poster and TV advertising. Unfolding alongside this programme was a campaign to ensure the powerful car press appreciated the changes that the brand was undergoing – otherwise the company risked all its good work being undermined through negative press or maybe just a lukewarm reception to the car and what it represented. The company began to build links with the press through press releases, press product launches, regional press tours, factory visits to the Czech Republic factories and briefings with journalists.

The focus of the message was how Skoda had changed though Volkswagen's involvement and investment in new products, new factories and new manufacturing techniques.

1. Describe the role of corporate image within the promotional mix. ✓
2. Evaluate the promotional mix used by Skoda. ✓✓
3. Make some recommendations as to how it could be improved. ✓✓✓
4. Describe your perception of the Skoda brand – is it still a joking matter? Justify your answer. ✓✓✓

## Type of market

There are two types of market: business to business (B2B) and business to consumer (B2C), and the approach to these two types of market can be quite different. B2B customers are often subjected to promotional activity which includes personal selling, public relations activity in trade journals and invitations to exhibitions. They are concerned with the profitability of the products they stock. This type of approach, where traders are encouraged to order stock, is called the push method – as stock is being forced into the distribution channels.

However, B2C customers are likely to experience advertising (such as on TV), direct marketing and sales promotions designed to encourage repeat purchases. Customers are concerned about the benefits of the product. This method, which encourages customer demand, is called the pull method – as consumers ask traders (such as retailers) for a particular product.

## Rapidly changing or relatively stable market

Rapidly changing markets require an approach which allows organisations to take advantage of the opportunities as they occur. Some promotional methods need some time to be prepared – you cannot make a TV commercial quickly. In those circumstances a high profile public relations campaign could be used because it can be organised quickly. Rapidly changing markets may also require new methods (such as SMS promotional messages) to be used as different sorts of customers begin to buy the product.

Promotional activity for relatively stable markets, that behave in a similar manner year after year, has the advantage of consistently using the same promotional methods even using the same materials each year. When the materials do need updating (such as a more topical magazine advertisement) the changes can be planned well in advance, so minimising cost.

## Budget requirements

Organisations use a variety of techniques to set the promotional budget. These include using a percentage of the previous year's sales, the expected sales for the next twelve months or last year's profit. Alternatively organisations use the amount spent by competitors as a guide.

These methods do not necessarily take into account what the promotional activity for the year is being asked to accomplish, therefore the preferred method by marketing managers is the 'objective and task' method. The marketing objectives for the year are established and the budget is calculated to achieve the objectives.

One of the problems associated with promotional activity is that the costs are all too obvious but the gains not very clear. The result of this tends to mean that promotional activity is seen as a cost rather than an investment for the organisation. Consequently marketing can find it hard to obtain the money needed to develop brands and products properly. Regardless of how the budget is determined the money allocated will have a direct impact on promotional activity levels.

## Timing requirements

Some products experience sales increases at certain times in the year. For example, holidaymakers start to think about booking their summer holidays just after Christmas, yet TV air time needs to be booked perhaps eight weeks ahead of the date of transmission. Consequently holiday companies need to organise their TV advertising in the October prior to the new year.

Other examples of where timing is important would be exhibitions where space has to be reserved and stands designed well in advance of the event. Sponsorship deals can also take some time to negotiate.

Sales people for personal selling cannot generally be recruited and trained in the space of a few days. But they need to be ready to cope with demand when it occurs.

Other promotional methods can be organised and implemented fairly quickly and easily, such as public relations, and some direct marketing activity like household leaflet distribution.

# Communications model

Communication models can help marketing managers develop successful promotional messages because they focus on all the elements that need to be considered. The well-known model at the foot of the page illustrates the point very effectively.

Communication can be subject to a wide range of factors which interfere with the effective transmission of the message from sender to receiver. These factors are often known by the collective term 'noise'. They include technical interference, such as a poor phone line or poorly printed advertisement, or sources of misunderstanding, such as emotion, prejudice and differences in perception. Only by seeking feedback can the sender trust that the message has been both received and understood.

In the context of promotional activity feedback can take a number of forms:

- an order or an offer below the asking price
- request for further details
- a question about, for example, delivery or payment options
- notification that they have bought the product somewhere else.

# Consumer response hierarchy

Consumer response hierarchy theory suggests that customers pass through a sequence of steps, which include awareness, knowledge, liking, preference and conviction, before finally making a purchase. The most widely known is the AIDA model.

## AIDA (attention, interest, desire, action)

The AIDA model is a simple framework, which usefully suggests the desirable qualities of an effective promotional message.

| | |
|---|---|
| **Attention** | An effective message will gain the attention of the target audience. It must have sufficient sensory (visual, audible) impact to be noticed. |
| **Interest** | An effective message will hold the interest of the target audience. It must be sufficiently relevant to engage the customer. |
| **Desire** | An effective message will arouse desire in the target audience. It must offer to satisfy a need or want or solve a problem. |
| **Action** | An effective message will obtain a response from the target audience. It must describe how the product or service can be bought. |

## Thinking point

Posters are a popular form of advertising. They can be large ones that appear on massive billboards on busy roads to small-scale ones placed on notice boards in libraries or schools. The example poster on the next page should help you see how the AIDA model works to produce an effective design.

| Sender | Encoding | Medium | Decoding | Receiver |
|---|---|---|---|---|
| Private company. Public organisation (such as university). Government dept (Ofsted – school inspectorate). Voluntary organisation (such as a charity). | Creating message that suits the audience and achieves promotional objectives (see AIDA on page 249). | Advertising, public relations and publicity, personal selling, sponsorship, direct marketing, sales promotions, corporate image and exhibitions. | Receiver interprets message through its tone, style, design, content and purpose. | Individuals (B2C). Businesses (B2B). |

▲ A well-known communications model

The first words should attract the **attention** of the customer and convey the major benefit of the product

Use images to attract **attention**, communicate key benefits, create an atmosphere and encourage customers to read the text

Build **interest** by highlighting other features and benefits relevant to the customer

Encourage **desire** by reminding customers what they might be missing or could be enjoying if they bought the product

Provide customers with all the details they need in order to take **action** and buy the product

# ENTER UNIVERSITY IN ONLY ONE YEAR

- This pre-degree programme is a one-year qualification for international students who want to study at a British university.
- The syllabus closely follows the topics that most management and business first degrees require. You will study economics, marketing, information technology, law, management and finance.
- You will write an assignment for each topic and sit an end-of-year examination.
- The course includes specialist classes in writing academic English to help students write essays at university.
- The programme uses the teaching and learning methods students will experience at university.

**Enrol today and receive a FREE textbook worth £24.99**

CONTACT
International Office – Monday to Friday 8.30 to 4.30
Maria Gomez – International Student Officer, Business College, Commerce Avenue
Cardiff CF2 3ER

Telephone (+44) 112 598 1315; Fax (+44) 112 598 1314
E-mail: maria.gomez@bc.ac.uk; website www.bc.ac.uk

▲ 'The perfect poster'

| | |
|---|---|
| **Attention** | Advertising on television, radio and billboards with bold headlines.<br>Sponsorship and corporate image programmes can keep a brand or product in the public's mind. |
| **Interest** | Advertising, such as newspapers, magazines and leaflets can explain product benefits.<br>Public relations and publicity can highlight product features.<br>Exhibitions allow customers to view product.<br>Personal selling and direct marketing (such as direct mail letters) can explain the product features. |
| **Desire** | Advertising such as brochures can show the product in use or being enjoyed.<br>Personal selling can explain the product benefits and special deals.<br>Exhibitions allow customers to see demonstrations.<br>Direct marketing such as telemarketing and direct mail letters can emphasise the product benefits.<br>Sales promotions can encourage purchase with special offers. |
| **Action** | Advertising in newspapers and brochures can give store opening times, payment options – everything a customer needs to know to make a purchase.<br>Personal selling can inform a customer how they can buy a product.<br>Sales promotions can help to convince the buyer to make a decision. |

▲ Promotional methods used within the AIDA model

## Different promotional methods at different stages

The various promotional methods can play different roles within the AIDA model, as shown in the model above.

### Outcome activity 9.1

**Pass**

Read the case studies about Universal Records (page 245) and Skoda (page 246).

Describe the promotional mix used by these organisations.

### Grading tips

**Pass** P1

List all the elements of the promotional mix and, using a column for each, describe the mix being used by Universal Records and Skoda.

# 9.2 Role of promotion within marketing mix

Promotion is an important marketing activity – it is part of the marketing mix. The marketing mix for a physical product describes the combination of product, price, place (sometimes called distribution), promotion and packaging offered by an organisation to potential consumers. When the product is a service, then the people delivering the service, the processes which the consumer experiences while buying it and the physical evidence (such as a programme at a concert) which accompanies the service are also important.

### Remember

Even the best product, sold in the appropriate places at the right price may experience poor sales if the promotional support is ineffective. In many markets where competition is intense, high levels of promotional support are sometimes necessary if a product is to succeed.

The marketing mix ▶

What is perhaps special about promotion is that the promotional approach can be heavily influenced by the other elements of the marketing mix. The features and benefits of the product have to be included in any promotional activity. Product features, such as a car having leather seats, can be easily conveyed. Promotional activity may also have to convey the point that ownership of such a car shows a person has been successful in life – and these aspects are more difficult to convey.

The price of a product may have been chosen to help convey the message of quality. The promotional campaign must not contradict such a message and this may exclude some types of promotional activity, such as leaflet drops through letterboxes.

The decision about where to place the product for the consumer to buy it may have a significant impact on promotional activity. If a business chooses to deal directly with its consumers then promotional activity is the sole responsibility of the producer. If an organisation decides to use retailers, then it can rely on them undertaking some of the promotional support required.

### Remember

Direct marketing occurs when producers approach their customers directly using a combination of personalised letters, magazine advertisements, telephone selling and the Internet to obtain sales.

# Products and services

## Product range

Very few businesses sell just one product. Most organisations offer a range of different products and perhaps a number of variations of each individual product, designed to meet the needs of different market segments. Car companies clearly do this, producing different models of car to suit different price expectations, different power and performance requirements and different usage conditions – from the long-distance sales representatives to the family wanting a car largely for short journeys in busy streets. The key role of promotion is to convey to customers the features and benefits of a product or service. This is particularly important for new products because the customer will need education about its features and benefits.

## New product development, product testing and market trials

Undertaking new product development can be a costly exercise for an organisation and in order to reduce the risk of failure organisations try to establish which products are most likely to succeed. Promotion is involved in several ways on a product's journey to what is termed 'commercialisation' – the establishment of the product successfully in the market.

Many organisations take the opportunity to test market their product in order to fine-tune it to the needs of the potential customers. Test marketing is when a product and marketing programme, including the proposed promotional mix, is tested in realistic market conditions. For example, the product can be tested in a particular region of a country before it is launched nationwide. The aim of test marketing is to finalise plans and determine changes that need to be made before incurring the cost of full-scale production. This would include making changes to the proposed promotional mix.

## Product features and variations

Sometimes a product may not have a strong set of features or product variations to truly set it apart from competition. In such circumstances the promotional activity has to create and establish a unique selling proposition (USP) for the product. Advertising agencies can play an important role in this process.

It has to be decided whether to promote a single product or a product range. The success of using a name – such as Dove – across a range of products

## Case study

### Dove – a leading global brand

Unilever is one of the world's leading producers of household products including margarine, ice cream, tea, deodorants, fragrances, personal washing and cleaning products. Among its leading brands are Flora margarine, Persil detergents, Birds Eye frozen foods, PG Tips tea and Walls ice cream.

The company has decided to focus on 400 of its key products and gradually scrap the other 1200 it had previously tried to support. The company expects the greater brand focus to reduce complexity and increase the cost-effectiveness of its marketing activity. Dove is expected to be a brand which will benefit significantly from this decision.

In 1991 Dove was sold in thirteen countries. Nowadays it is available in 75 countries, expanding from soap into skin care, hair care and deodorant lines, and has become the leading cleansing brand in the world. Unilever is committed to expanding its key brands into new product areas when appropriate. The investment in building these few key brands can then spread over a range of products sold under the same brand name rather than spending large amounts of promotional money in developing a lot of smaller brands. Every pound spent promoting Dove soap is now also enhancing Dove hair and skin care products. It is anticipated that new products launched under the umbrella of an established brand will be readily accepted by the consumer. They will benefit from the brand values that have already been established.

▲ Dove products

The company should benefit from lower marketing costs as they operate a few brands across many products and many national borders. Most importantly this strategy obeys a key marketing principle of building on your strengths rather than being sidetracked by your weaknesses.

1. What other products might benefit from being marketed using the Dove brand name? ✓
2. Which elements of the marketing mix are crucial to the success of Dove? ✓✓
3. What are the advantages of a strategy which sees organisations concentrate on a few key brands? ✓✓✓
4. Consider any disadvantages that might result as a consequence of this strategy. ✓✓✓

depends on the power of the brand name. The advantage is that products can be promoted cheaply and effectively. It can work where the success of previous products have been based on values such as quality and value-for-money. As long as these qualities remain constant across the other products, promoting a range can be effective. In contrast, multi-branding involves the introduction of a number of products and brands which are targeted at a particular market segment. For example Kellogg's promotes a vast number of different brands, each targeted at a particular market segment in the cereal market.

## Quantity and timing of promotional activity

Once the product design, brand name and unique selling point(s) have been agreed, the quantity and timing of promotional activity is considered. For some products, such as washing-up liquid, the timing of the launch and the promotional activity may not matter. But the sales of many products are influenced by events during the year, such as Valentine's Day or Halloween products and Christmas gifts.

The quantity of promotional activity depends on the amount of the product the organisation is expecting to sell over a particular period. If an organisation has the objective of achieving a 2% market share within two years, the promotional activity may be modest. Compare that with a business which decides to dominate a market quickly and sets itself the task of capturing a 15% market share within six months. The investment in promotional support will need to be much, much larger.

## The role of quality, style and associated services in promotion

Many organisations emphasise the quality and style of their products in their promotional activity. Yet quality seems to have a number of meanings. It is not always clear which meaning of quality an organisation is referring to in its promotional activity. In its simplest form, a quality product is one that meets the needs of the consumer well. But quality can involve one or more of the following points:

- Performance – what the product can actually do. A power drill with a variable speed of 3000 rpm might be perceived as high quality because it has the ability to tackle any job. Promotional activity could highlight the superior performance.
- Durability – the expected life of a product. Some customers are prepared to pay more for a product that is likely to have a long useful life.
- Reliability and maintenance – many consumers are concerned that a product might break down and the cost of repairs could be high and inconvenient. Organisations use guarantees and comprehensive customer-care support to reassure customers about these aspects of a product. These associated services and benefits, which might also include delivery and installation services, can feature prominently in promotional activity.
- Design and style – the visual aspects of a product may influence perceptions of its quality. Packaging, such as that for Ferrero Rocher, can enhance a quality image. The implication that by buying a certain product you will be perceived as being stylish is often a characteristic of promotional activity.
- Corporate image and reputation – if customers are still uncertain about the quality of competing products, they may fall back on their **perceptions** of the organisation. For example, some may feel that Dell is a well established and familiar name. They may have had other Dell products which served them well in the past. They may decide to buy on the basis of image and reputation.

## Key Terms

**Perception** The process by which people select, organise and interpret information to form a 'picture' of a product in their mind.

### Remember

Marketers recognise that quality and style in the marketplace is often a matter of perception rather than technical specification and consequently promotional activity can have a major impact.

# Price

Unlike the other marketing mix elements, pricing decisions affect profits through their impact on revenue rather than on costs. Pricing is, of course, the only element of the marketing mix which generates revenue rather than costs. It is a key function of any promotional activity to inform customers of the prices being charged for products and services.

## Importance of price and its influence on promotion

Price has an important role to play in creating an overall image for a product. No organisation can hope to offer a high quality product with a low price – the price must be consistent with the overall image. In a similar way, the promotional activity must reflect the pricing – nobody would contemplate using leaflets pushed through household letter boxes to promote designer clothes.

### Remember

The ultimate objective of pricing, as with the other elements of the marketing mix, is to produce the required level of sales so that the organisation can achieve its objectives. It is good **customer value** which attracts customers and generates sales.

If you look on eBay you will find plenty of examples of products where the original selling price was based on its cost but which are now selling for very much more. Basing prices on costs has clearly failed in these instances. Look at DJ Mr Scuff's New Year Gig CD – one recently sold for £14 on eBay.

### Key Terms

**Customer value** The difference between the value the customer gains from owning and using a product and the cost (price) of obtaining the product.

## Factors affecting prices and pricing strategies

The prices set by an organisation are determined by managers, and different groups of managers are likely to set different prices for the same product. There are three factors which influence prices – cost, competitors and demand.

### ■ Costs

In practice, cost is the most important influence on price. Many businesses base prices on simple cost-plus guidelines. Costs are calculated and then a profit margin is added in order to determine the price. For example, if an item costs £10 to make and the profit margin is set at 25%, then the selling price will be £10 + £2.50 = £12.50. The cost plus approach leads to price stability with prices changing only to reflect cost changes. This approach provides an understandable, practical and popular solution to pricing issues.

### ■ Competitors

Prices are set on the basis of what competitors are charging. This method is used mostly by organisations facing fierce competition. Generally if there are many organisations in a market selling a similar product then the tendency will be towards competitor-based pricing.

'Going-rate pricing' is where a business examines competitors' prices and chooses a price broadly in line with them.

'Close-bid pricing' occurs when organisations have to submit prices, generally called bids, for a project by a particular day, and all the bids are opened at the same time under strict rules and procedures. The organisation submitting the lowest credible bid secures the order. This is the procedure normally undertaken if a new hospital has to be built by a health authority. Organisations therefore have to anticipate the price that competitors might bid.

### ■ Demand

'Demand pricing' considers the conditions prevailing in the market before setting prices. For example, a business might look at the amount of **disposable income** the potential customers have, or whether it is becoming socially important to own a particular product. A popular method is to charge 'what the market will bear'. This means setting prices depending on what the consumer is prepared to pay. The pricing of DVDs is an excellent example of this approach.

A number of options are open to an organisation adopting a demand-pricing policy. 'Skim pricing' can be used when a market contains relatively little competition. It means setting a high initial price in order to make maximum revenue from the product quickly; exploiting the fact that some customers will pay a high price to be one of the first with a new product. Later the price is reduced to attract fresh customers. This approach to pricing is often found in the market for computer games.

'Penetration pricing' means setting a low price to establish a product. The firm may even make a loss initially, but once it is established the price is raised to maximise profits. Multi-part magazines are often priced in this way. The first issue may cost you 99p with a free binder, but once you're hooked the price goes up.

## Key Terms

**Disposable income** Money that is left to an individual once taxes, such as income tax, are deducted and the household bills, mortgage/rent, etc. are paid.

All profit-making and many non-profit-making organisations face the task of setting prices. Prices can go by many names, such as fares, tuition fees and rent. Historically, price was the key marketing decision but the importance of the other marketing mix elements has now been accepted and it is no longer considered the key factor. Marketing managers now respond to competition by trying to satisfy consumer wants and needs better, by introducing new products or skilfully modifying existing products. The once common reaction of reducing prices is now not so common.

# Place

'Place' describes the marketing decisions which are involved in ensuring that products are available where the consumer would expect to buy them. Organisations can decide to sell their products through wholesalers, retailers, via vending machines, directly to consumers or using a combination of all these. Promotion has the key role of informing the customers where to buy a product.

However, organisations who decide to offer their products through wholesalers and retailers can rely on them to make a significant contribution to any promotional activity. Organisations that decide to deal directly with consumers through, for example, the Internet will have to undertake all the promotional activity themselves. Decisions about place will therefore have an important impact on promotional activity.

### Wholesale

Wholesalers stock a comprehensive range of goods. They sell these products to other organisations such as retailers, who intend to resell them. They may provide a range of services for their customers including **breaking bulk**, packing and labelling, supplying promotional materials and quick delivery.

## Key Terms

**Breaking bulk** Breaking into smaller amounts. This is an important part of a retailer's function – buying large quantities from a producer or wholesaler and offering smaller quantities to consumers.

The most recent development in this area has been the growth of 'cash and carry' units such as Makro. Retailers who buy from this type of organisation are responsible for transporting the stock and paying in cash, but prices are lower than those obtainable generally at the traditional wholesaler. Cash and carry outlets undertake a great deal of promotion themselves.

## Retail

Wholesalers break bulk supplies from producers, and retailers then cut the bulk again so individual consumers can buy the quantity they require – very often a single item. The term 'retail' comes from the French, meaning 'to cut again'. There are several categories of retailer, as shown in the table below.

| Type of retailer | Example | Promotional activity |
|---|---|---|
| Small, family owned | Londis, Spar | Rely on producers to promote the goods they sell |
| Multiple chains | Matalan, W.H. Smith | Produce own catalogues, use special-point-of-sale material |
| Supermarkets | Morrison's, Sainsbury's | Use many promotional methods - they are some of the biggest advertisers nationally |
| Department stores | House of Fraser, John Lewis | Use a variety of promotional methods |
| Catalogue stores | Argos | Produce their own catalogue twice a year which they promote widely |
| Discount stores | Curry's, Superdrug | Use a variety of promotional methods to convey a 'price' message |

## Direct selling

More and more organisations are using direct selling methods to sell their products to consumers, as shown in the table below. Direct selling methods allow producers to deal directly with their customers. Not many years ago the local insurance broker would find out the requirements of a consumer and then contact a variety of insurance companies on his or her behalf. Nowadays many people deal directly with insurance companies themselves and will shop around, using the Internet or by phone, to get the best deal.

| Selling method | Products/service |
|---|---|
| Door-to-door | Used for example by energy suppliers to gain customers |
| Telemarketing | Replacement windows, conservatories, financial services |
| Vending machines | Wide variety of food products now on offer, such as drinks, sandwiches and chocolate |
| E-commerce | Virtually any product can be bought over the Internet |

### Key Terms

**E-commerce** Buying and selling conducted electronically over the Internet.

### Remember

All the direct sales methods – television, factory, telephone, door-to-door, vending machines and e-commerce – require the producer to undertake the promotional activity.

## Role of intermediaries

Traditionally, producers would involve a number of other organisations in the process of delivering the product to the final customer. For example, a producer of software in the Far East would appoint a UK distributor to whom the goods were shipped. The distributor would then sell the goods to wholesalers which showed an interest. The wholesaler in turn would supply the retail stores which sold the product to the end user. The organisations between the producer and the customer – distributor, wholesaler and retailer – are called intermediaries.

Consequently many organisations have found themselves at a distance from their consumer. Their success can be very much determined by the attitude of an intermediary to their product. A major retailer, such as Argos, which chooses not to stock a certain product will adversely affect the performance of the producer. Sometimes producers seek to make it very difficult for organisations such as Argos not to stock the product.

– colour, sound, tone of voice, language, image, and light – to develop a special atmosphere for the customer that can be featured in promotional activity.

Colour and lights are important elements in developing a welcoming atmosphere. Warm colours, such as yellow and orange, and bright lights can be used for entrances and windows as they make customer areas look bright and welcoming from the outside. Cool colours, such as blue and purple, are appropriate where customers need to think about the purchase.

Sound, such as pre-selected music that is likely to appeal to customers, creates a relaxing environment. The tone of voice and the language used by staff when answering the telephone and greeting and dealing with customers plays a key role in building a welcoming customer environment.

# Promotional objectives

## Supporting business aims and objectives

It is important to remember that for promotional activity to be effective it must support the overall business aims. It is then likely that the promotional activity will complement rather than compete with the other organisational activities. The transformation of business aims and objectives into marketing objectives and then promotional objectives is shown in the table:

| Planning level | Content |
|---|---|
| Corporate mission statement | Overall vision, e.g. to be known for innovation |
| Business aim and objective | What has to be achieved to deliver the vision? E.g. to launch technologically advanced products |
| Marketing objectives | Marketing contribution to the corporate objectives, e.g. to offer products using mobile technology |
| Promotional objective | Promotional tactics to be used, e.g. to have well-known celebrities using and endorsing the products |

## Raising awareness

Promotional activity can raise the awareness of a product or an organisation in the consumer's mind. Strong awareness can translate into improved sales because when customers think of a particular product the one with the better awareness will be the one which springs to mind.

▲ Business and promotional objectives

## Increasing market share

Promotional activity can help capture a greater market share of an established market for a company and as a consequence increase an organisation's sales. Improvements in market share can therefore generate more profit or market leadership status.

## Creating distinctive market presence

There are very few really unique products or organisations nowadays so businesses try to create a distinct market presence for themselves to help them stand out from the crowd. For example, B&Q supports local community groups by providing employee action teams to help renovate and decorate community amenities to enhance their image of being a caring and responsible organisation. Other organisations have tried to present themselves as designers of innovative products (for example, the Hewlett-Packard 'invent' advertisement). Not surprisingly, promotional activity plays a key role in this process.

## Target relevant audience

In order to be effective, promotional activity needs to be directed to the customers who are going to respond to the messages. Organisations cannot generally satisfy all customers in a given market. At least they cannot satisfy all customers in the same way: there are too many different kinds of customers with too many different needs. Also some organisations are in a better position to serve certain parts of the market than others.

## Atttitudes, interests, opinions, aspirations and demographics

Promotional activity needs to respond to the attitudes, interests, opinions and demographics of the customer.

| | Implications for promotional objectives |
|---|---|
| Interests | Discuss the concerns of customers and things they enjoy doing |
| Opinions | Reflect the beliefs of the customer |
| Aspirations | Refer to their personal goals |
| Demographics | Respond to the age and gender of customers |
| Attitudes | Be sensitive to the way customers feel and think |

## Business to business (B2B) and business to consumer (B2C) promotions

It is important to realise that promotional activity is not just aimed at consumers (B2C) but significant amounts of activity are targeted at businesses by other businesses (B2B). The process of segmentation, targeting and positioning is relevant in business to business markets, just as are all the other promotional tools including advertising and personal selling. The key difference between these two sectors is the possible complexity of the business to business buying decision.

- Personal selling is very important for explaining, demonstrating and following up matters discussed during the selling interview.
- Promotional activity tends to focus on helping the sales team become more effective.
- It is important to identify the people who can influence the decision in an organisation, such as users, and target promotion towards them. This can sometimes be a very small number of potential customers.
- Specialist B2B media are used, such as exhibitions and specialist trade publications. Public relations can be very effective in this market.
- Promotional budgets tend to be small.

## Segmentation, branding and brand loyalty

The process of segmentation normally requires products to be positioned to reflect the buying motives of the customer. Different segments may require different sorts of positioning; it is the role of promotion to establish and maintain the product positioning.

- Segmentation – segmentation techniques use marketing research to help identify groups of consumers who will respond to marketing activity in the same way, e.g. first-time buyers of houses.
- Targeting – research can help select the groups whose needs and wants can be best met by the organisation.
- Positioning – research can help discover why customers are likely to buy a product (e.g. because it is exciting) – enabling organisations to develop brands and brand loyalty.

### Remember

Segmentation is the dividing of a market into groups who have the same characteristics. Each individual group would be subjected to a unique package of marketing activities.

Branding is the usual way to position a product. A brand can be a name, a symbol or a design used to identify a product and make it different from its competitors. Clearly the establishment of a brand can be a significant promotional objective. Branding can convey facts about a product or an organisation. The more similar a product is to competing goods, the more branding is necessary to create a separate product identity. People respond or connect to the brand values being promoted, which results in strong loyalty to particular products.

When brand loyalty is established, a price increase may not have a marked influence on overall sales. Brand loyalty exists when consumers tend to re-purchase a product even though there are many alternatives. This reduces the importance of price differences between products, allowing organisations to have more control over price. If they do not have to compete in the market simply on the basis of price, profits can rise.

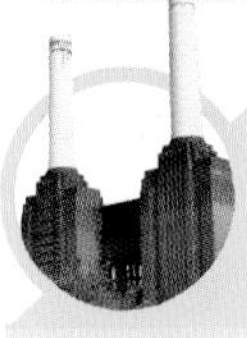

## Outcome activity 9.2

Walkers, the producer of Britain's best-selling crisps, has cut unsaturated fats in its products by more than 70% amid rising concerns about the health risks from snack foods high in salt and fat.

A £20 million campaign to promote the new crisps will be headed by Gary Lineker, the former England footballer who is now a BBC sports presenter. Nutritional experts said the decision was a step in the right direction. However, they noted that such snacks were still more than 30% fat and should be eaten only occasionally. A packet of cheese and onion crisps has 11.4 grams of fat and 3.5 grams of unsaturated fat. The saturated fat has been cut to 0.9 grams in the new product, but the overall fat content and the number of calories remain the same.

Consumer taste tests suggested that nobody could taste the difference, with some saying they would now start eating this new healthier option. Walkers say the launch is a response to consumer demand for healthier products. But Walkers has been one of the companies targeted by food campaigners who want to improve the nation's diet. Ofcom, the broadcasting regulator, is currently considering whether advertisements for fatty snack foods should be banned from children's television.

**Pass**

Using Walkers crisps as an example, describe the role of promotion within the marketing mix.

**Merit**

Explain how the promotional aspect is integrated and used with the whole marketing mix to achieve its business aims and objectives.

**Distinction**

Evaluate and justify the use of an appropriate promotional mix with respect to business and marketing objectives.

## Grading tips

**Pass** 

Consider and discuss which aspects of the marketing mix are currently really important to Walkers.

**Merit** 

Explain how promotion is used by Walkers to help it achieve its business aims and objectives. This discussion should consider when promotion has the crucial role to play in ensuring Walkers achieves its business aims.

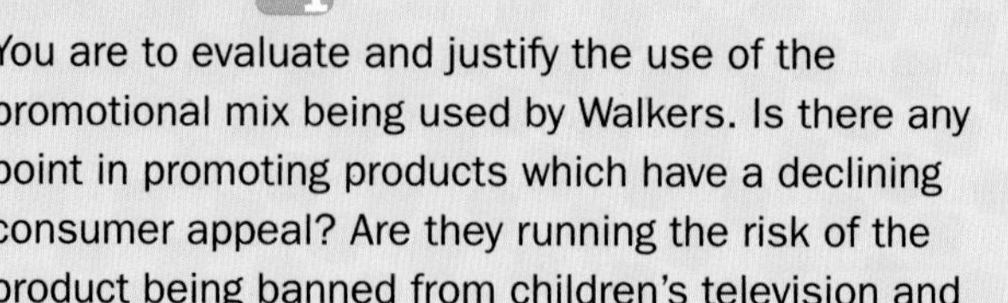

**Distinction** d1

You are to evaluate and justify the use of the promotional mix being used by Walkers. Is there any point in promoting products which have a declining consumer appeal? Are they running the risk of the product being banned from children's television and should celebrities be used to endorse such products?

# 9.3 Role of advertising agencies and the media

## Roles of advertising agencies

There are two ways in which an organisation can organise its promotional activity: **outsourcing** or in-house. Businesses which regard promotion as important to their success can outsource the work to an advertising agency to help them develop effective promotional campaigns. Other organisations adopt an in-house approach, where employees do the promotional activity.

### Key Terms

**Outsourcing** Appointing another company or business to do some work for an organisation.

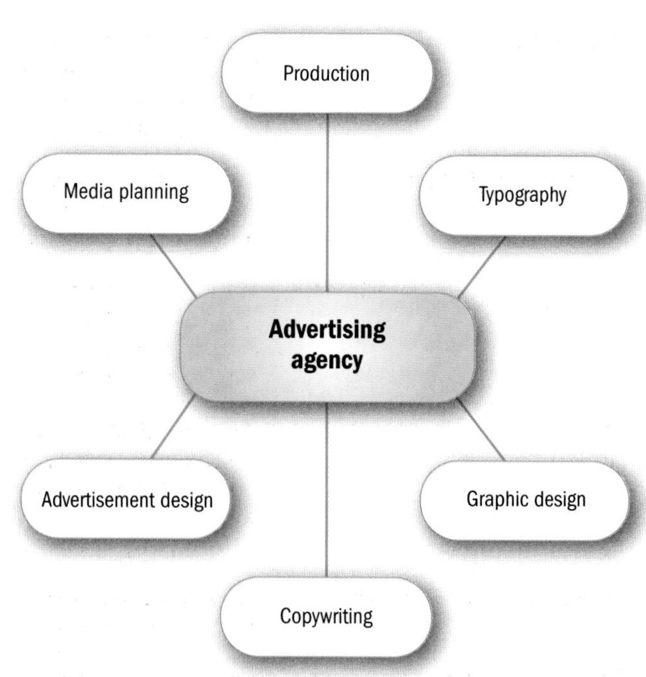


▲ An advertising agency will create and implement effective promotional activity for an organisation

## Services offered

One outsourcing option is to appoint a full-service agency to provide a complete range of services as shown below. They are probably the most popular choice of organisations and include well-known agencies such as Ogilvy & Mather and Saatchi & Saatchi. Organisations which use this type of agency tend to be those with significant amounts of money to spend on promotion but which have few internal resources to develop and implement promotional activity. Using a full-service agency means an organisation can be confident that all the elements of the promotional activity are coordinated, ensuring a consistent approach and consequently more effective activity. A simple example would be the consistent approach to the positioning and use of the organisation's slogan, such as Hewlett Packard's 'invent'.

Another outsourcing option is to use limited-service agencies. These tend to specialise in a particular aspect of promotional activity. An agency might specialise in media buying, buying exactly the right media to target an audience and obtaining extra discounts through bulk buying so helping with the client's budget. Other agencies may concentrate on developing sales promotion ideas, or designing and printing brochures.

Using this approach, clients can find the best in a particular field. It also gives scope for doing some work in-house and going to a limited-service agency for particular expertise. However, an organisation then has to spend more time coordinating activity and ensuring a consistent message is conveyed to the consumer by all the people involved in the project.

Regardless of whether they are full service or limited service, agencies can enhance promotional activity through, for example, imaginative creative ideas that make a memorable commercial. A good example is Nationwide's 'brand new customers only' series of commercials.

## Cost and other options

Not every organisation chooses to use agencies for any of its work. They may choose to do the work themselves – to work 'in-house'. Organisations will consider a range

▼ Services provided by full-service agnecies

| Service | What it is and who provides it |
|---|---|
| Media planning | The media planning team decides where the advertisements should be shown and buys the media time on radio or television, or space in magazines or newspapers. The team's aim is to reach the target audience in a cost-effective manner and their knowledge of the media enables them to do this. They know, for instance, that the average reader of the magazine *Just 17* is a female aged 14. |
| Designing the advertisements | The creative department develops promotional ideas through effective copywriting (writing the words used in an advertisement), distinctive typography (type style and layout) and attractive graphic designs (e.g. the Adidas three strips). |
| Producing the advertisements | Production has the task, for example, of producing a TV commercial or a full page magazine advert. They know a range of people who can provide recording studios, compose jingles, generate computer animation, design imaginative props (e.g. Churchill the dog) and draw illustrations to produce a 30-second commercial. |
| Help in identifying the target audience | The planning team helps determine the type of consumer at which to target the promotion. Vodafone was advised to target young people with their mobile camera phones, using David Beckham as a model. This was an inspired decision which produced brilliant results for the company. Planning teams sometimes use marketing research to discover more about the consumer, or test proposed ideas before making the final decision. |
| Providing public relations activity | Some full-service agencies also include a public relations service which writes press releases and organises conferences and exhibitions. |
| Providing direct marketing support | Some agencies also have a direct marketing team which advises clients on how to use direct personalised mail, direct response advertising in publications such as the Sunday newspaper magazines, telemarketing and the Internet. |

of issues when deciding whether to employ an agency or to have an in-house team do the work.

- Cost – it might be simply cheaper to keep the work inside the organisation. There must, of course, be enough work to keep the team busy. Outside agencies are expensive to use – even a small local agency may charge £400 per day so it is not surprising that some companies decide to have an in-house team.
- Confidentiality – a company working on innovative products may want to limit the number of people who are aware of such projects.
- Commitment – it is rare for an agency to have only one customer (or client), and as a result conflicting demands are likely to be made. This may persuade an organisation to undertake the work in-house, where employees will be fully committed to the products.
- Accessibility – a major advantage of using in-house facilities is ease of working with the promotional team – who may be in the office next door!
- Expertise – a business may feel that the nature of the market is too complex for an agency to understand. Or it may believe it will take an agency too long to learn about it.
- Results – senior management may feel that because an employee's job depends on the company's success, they will be more concerned about achieving the right result from a campaign than an outside agency. Agencies that fail for one business can still generally find new clients.
- Speed of delivery – most promotional activity can be planned in advance, but there are situations which require an organisation to respond quickly to unforeseen circumstances. For example, a sports team sponsored by a company may produce an unexpected spectacular result, providing an opportunity for the company to publicise itself through a press release describing how it helped. In-house teams may be more willing to respond quickly – an agency would at the very least be likely to charge a high price for a quick response.

However, an in-house team may find it difficult to keep generating creative ideas. They may simply run out of effective advertising ideas and if an in-house team fails to produce the desired results, it is difficult to dismiss them all. Agencies generally have a number of groups in their creative team and consequently every time a new approach is needed a new team, with a fresh outlook, can be asked to develop the advertising.

## Types of media

Advertising agencies will have a variety of projects to undertake, sometimes involving local media and at other times international media. For example, the agency acting for the retailer Boots may include among its projects:

- The opening of a new store using local media such as free newspapers, local radio, leafleting households and advertising on local buses and billboards.
- The extension of Internet shopping to a new region, using regional newspapers, magazines, television and in-store, point-of-purchase materials such as posters.
- The national launch of a new service in store, such as cholesterol level testing, using media such as national television, national newspapers, billboards and in-store, point-of-purchase materials.
- An international campaign to launch a Boots product, such as Ibuprofen, using satellite television, the sponsorship of an international event, such as the European Athletics Championships, and the launch of an Internet site.

The different media and their characteristics are outlined in the table opposite.

## Criteria for media selection

### Promotional objectives

Different media will be used for different types of promotional campaigns and will depend on the objectives. If the promotional campaign needs the product to be demonstrated it is likely that the media choice will be television. If the consumer needs a detailed explanation of the product features and benefits, then print media probably offer the best option. If the purpose of the activity is to put a brand name in the consumer's mind, posters may fulfil the

▼ **Characteristics of the media**

| Type of media | Example | Advantages | Disadvantages |
|---|---|---|---|
| Local | Newspapers (e.g. *Metro* in London)<br>Magazines (e.g. parish magazine)<br>Radio (e.g. Radio Trent in Nottingham)<br>Billboards and posters<br>Transport – buses/taxis | Can reach local target market<br>Reasonable costs<br>Message can make reference to local area or characteristics (e.g. local saying or well known landmark)<br>Can reinforce a national or even international campaign locally | Difficult to make an impact with so many advertisements being presented to consumers – not just local advertisements<br>Not easy to pick a medium that speaks to a particular audience<br>Television is usually not an option for local advertisers because of its cost |
| Regional | Newspapers (e.g. *The Western Mail* in Wales and south-west England)<br>Magazines (e.g. *Lincolnshire Life*)<br>Radio (e.g. BRMB in the West Midlands)<br>Billboards and posters | Can reach a regional market<br>Reasonable costs<br>Can provide effective support for a regional TV campaign | Not easy to pick a medium that speaks to a particular audience, e.g. young people |
| National | Newspapers (e.g. *The Mirror*)<br>Magazines (e.g. *Hello*)<br>Radio (e.g. Classic FM)<br>Billboards and posters | Covers a big audience<br>Builds quality brands through use of quality media such as television<br>Proven record of success | Expensive to buy space and air time |
| International | Newspapers (e.g. the *Financial Times*)<br>Magazines (e.g. *The Economist*) | One advert can cover several international markets | Not many media options available<br>Tend to be English language publications |
| Terrestrial television | Includes ITV, Channel 5 and cable companies like Virgin Media | Large number of target audiences can be reached<br>High proportion of a target audience is likely to see the advert<br>Uses colour, movement and sound to create impact<br>Relatively low cost per audience member because large number of consumers can be reached | Message is very short (e.g. 30 seconds) so has to be repeated often<br>High absolute cost – both advertisement production costs and air time<br>Difficult for advertisement to be noticed with so many other commercials |
| Satellite television | Sky | Large number of channels to help target the right audience<br>Can be seen across international borders | Many commercial breaks<br>May need to use a large number of channels to reach the target audience |
| Digital | Press the red button on your remote control | Can order brochures or test drives<br>Can view products in action<br>Encourages action immediately after the viewing of an advertisement | Only available to viewers with digital TV services |
| Worldwide web | www.hof.co.uk (House of Fraser) – some sites do not allow any purchases and are simply for promotional purposes | Can interact with consumer through site<br>Low costs – although updating costs can be high<br>Site content can attract a particular audience | Media full of adverts, which makes it difficult to be noticed – and some irritate consumers<br>High costs to start with<br>Needs to be updated and refreshed at regular intervals |
| Specialist media | Magazines and newspapers published for specialist sectors (e.g. *The Grocer*) | A small circulation but can reach decision makers in an industry<br>Reasonable costs<br>While circulation might seem low, it may have wide readership in an industry | Possibly need a series of advertisements to create impact<br>Some industries have little choice of publications to use<br>May take some time to circulate through an organisation – so always out of date for some employees |

Issues involved in making the right media choice for a promotional campaign ▶

requirement. The choice of media revolves around three main issues – the interaction of coverage, frequency and media impact.

- Coverage is the percentage of people within the target audience (such as young adults) who might see the promotional message during a certain time period.
- Frequency is the number of times people within the target audience will see the message in a certain time period.
- Media impact involves conveying the product characteristics effectively – the message should be seen when the target audience is open to persuasion.

## Target audience, timing, cost and coverage

To achieve a high coverage of the target audience and ensure they see an advert a significant number of times would require a very large budget. Usually a compromise has to be reached between two options:

- a campaign that maximises coverage but provides limited opportunities for the target audience to see or hear the message
- a campaign which reduces the coverage but increases the frequency of the message being seen or heard.

### ■ Timescales

Although a great deal of work has been done to determine the appropriate balance of coverage and frequency, there are no definite answers. In some instances, in order to achieve the maximum level of impact, media expenditure will be concentrated into a relatively short period. These 'burst campaigns', as they are called, are associated with building product or brand awareness. A good example of this is when Argos publishes a new catalogue which it promotes heavily for a short period after launch. After the 'burst', there is usually a relative long period of little media activity.

An alternative approach, generally associated with reminder campaigns, is to extend the timescale of the promotional message over a long period. This is called a 'drip' campaign. An example would be the approach that Kellogg's use with corn flakes.

The compromise between the two is the 'pulsing campaign'. These campaigns have a low level of media activity over long periods, with increases coinciding with greater buyer activity, such as before Christmas. A good example of this would be After Eight mints.

A campaign is said to have impact when the effectiveness is greater than the frequency and coverage would predict. It usually occurs because the way the message is conveyed captures the imagination of the audience. A clever advertisement can generate an effective campaign even with low levels of coverage and inadequate frequency. This also means effective campaigns can be developed without spending a great deal of money.

It is easy for small businesses to think that marketing is something which only big companies can afford to do. But promotion can be about creativity and not about spending lots of money. This is important because marketing is not an optional extra. There is absolutely no point in having the best product unless you go out and sell it to someone.

Cost in itself is not a helpful basis for selection unless it rules out certain media types because the agreed budget would be exceeded. Advertisers need to know how much of the target audience will see the advert, how many times they will see it and how much such a campaign will cost.

## Readership and circulation

Cost per thousand is a common measuring device. It tells an organisation how much it costs to reach 1000 readers, viewers and so on. However, it is only a crude measure which does not take some important points into consideration. If an advertisement in a magazine with a circulation of 500,000 costs £2500 then the cost per thousand is £5. Some publications have an extended readership, however, meaning that more than one person reads each copy of the newspaper or magazine. Consequently the cost per thousand may under-estimate the impact of a publication.

No media schedule is ever perfect. There are more media to choose from nowadays, so media planning is becoming a specialist area. While the choice of media makes the planning more difficult, the result can be a well-targeted and effective campaign.

## Real lives

### Make a big splash with a small budget

Smyle is an events company run by Rick Stainton. When he started the business he identified the 500 richest people in the UK and sent them a letter containing a £20 note. This ensured that the personal assistant did not redirect the letter into the litter bin. It was a brave tactic costing £10,000. The accompanying letter, which explained the company's expertise, was printed on top-quality paper but the envelopes were handwritten. Over 70% responded, with half returning the £20 to donate to Inspire (the spinal injuries charity). Because of this innovative mailshot, Stainton was asked to organise three events generating £250,000 of business.

The online law firm, Lawyers Direct, decided to draw attention to the fact that it can provide high-quality lawyers at a fraction of the usual cost because of its lower overheads. It did this by filling the goody bags at a Department of Trade and Industry awards ceremony with 1000 bags of peanuts with the Lawyers Direct logo and the slogan: 'These days you have to be nuts to pay for overheads.' At a cost of £1 a bag, the activity cost less than £1000. The ploy worked very well. In the weeks after the ceremony, Lawyers Direct gained seven new clients who had been at the event and liked the firm's unconventional approach.

So clever promotional ideas can reap enormous rewards for an organisation, no matter what its size – and in most cases it need not cost a fortune.

1. Describe some advertising that in your view was rather unusual or clever. ✓
2. What do you consider to be the characteristics of clever promotional activity? ✓✓
3. Agreeing to some clever promotional activity can sometimes be uncomfortable for a marketing manager – can you suggest why that might be the case? ✓✓✓
4. Have you any ideas on how your school or college could advertise in a 'clever' manner? ✓✓✓

## Practice point

Advertising costs in different national press media are as follows:

| | Cost per colour page | Readership (all adults) | Cost per 1000 readers |
|---|---|---|---|
| *Daily Telegraph* Magazine | £22,575 | 2,063,786 | £10.94 |
| *Guardian* Magazine | £9,000 | 1,210,581 | |
| *Sun* TV Magazine | £31,000 | 7,207,013 | £4.30 |
| *News of the World* Magazine | £31,500 | 7,113,750 | |
| *Vogue* | £21,300 | 1,055,477 | |
| *Tatler* | £9,850 | 178,067 | £55.32 |
| *Cosmopolitan* | £18,296 | 1,769,096 | |

*Source*: BRAD, February 2007

Calculate the cost per 1000 readers for *The Guardian*, *News of the World*, *Vogue* and *Cosmopolitan* magazines. Now choose three of the publications and describe how the cost per thousand might not reflect the true value of advertising in these publications.

### Focus of appeal

When customers have a genuine interest in a product the promotional messages tend to be rational or information-based, proclaiming product benefits and the key attributes. Where the audience is not really so interested the focus of the promotional appeal can be emotional, empathetic or intellectual, as shown in the table below. The focus of the appeal will have an impact on the media chosen.

# Role of the Internet

### Disintermediation

Traditionally, the producers of goods have used organisations known as intermediaries (such as retailers and wholesalers) to sell their products to customers. But the Internet is encouraging producers to sell directly to customers using websites – this is a form of direct marketing. This process whereby organisations such as retailers are no longer involved in marketing products to customers is called disintermediation. Retailers such as HMV are already feeling the impact of disintermediation as customers download their music from organisations such as iTunes.

### Direct marketing

While direct marketing via the Internet is gaining in popularity with both producers and consumers, this approach has several implications – especially for promotional activity.

#### Implications for promotion

The process of disintermediation has a number of implications for promotion.

- Producers can make larger profits while offering lower prices – because the intermediary's profits are eliminated.
- Producers can build databases which may be used to send promotional material to customers who may well have agreed to receive it – making them more receptive to the message.

| Focus of appeal | Promotional message |
|---|---|
| Emotional | Images of people starving or having lost their homes are commonly featured in messages from charities such as World Vision. The media used for this is often TV with dramatic images and harrowing commentaries. |
| Empathetic | Allows the audience to identify with the characters and a common problem. The brand is then perceived as a suitable solution, such as breakdown rescue, nicotine patches and insurance services. Radio and TV is used to involve the audience in the story as it unfolds. |
| Intellectual | Promotional messages convey the good sense of taking a particular course of action, such as starting pension payments early. The media choice tends to be newspapers, magazines and brochures where the arguments can be clearly explained. |

- Websites have the capacity to contain large amounts of product information – far more than a sales person could remember.
- Smaller producers can have a web presence which is just as impressive and effective as the largest international brand as long as their prices and deliveries are customer-focused.
- International markets can be accessed through multi-language sites.
- Producers become solely responsible for promotional activity, not just in terms of informing customers about their products but also encouraging surfers to visit their site.

## One-to-one communications

Powerful databases are able to undertake one-to-one promotional communications, sometimes referred to as micro-marketing. This means that they can match new products and new offers to customers who are likely to be interested. For example, Amazon notes the books which customers have previously bought and alerts them when a similar title is published.

Nowadays the Internet and mobile phones are working together to produce personalised promotional communications. Mobile phones can now easily connect to the Internet. Some websites ask surfers to register to access special areas. This can involve giving some key details, including areas of interest, which are then used to communicate with that customer through their mobile phone. This is called 'permission marketing' and is considered a more effective way to deal with a customer because they have actively asked you to send them certain sorts of information to which they are more likely to respond. As a consequence, the messages sent are individual to that customer.

Organisations can attempt to re-activate customers by providing something special to regain their custom. Databases can be used to send out materials just before a lapsed customer is about to purchase that product, such as insurance, again.

## Outcome activity 9.3

Erin O'Connor's military jacket, Twiggy's cardigan and Laura Bailey's culottes sold out across Britain as shoppers snapped up the trendy fashion items featured in Marks & Spencer's latest advertisements. Even the website had sold out just a fortnight after the television and print advertising campaign was launched. This was achieved while other clothing retailers were experiencing falling sales.

Marks & Spencer were thought to have sold 12,000 pieces of each item and raced to replenish stock. This was Marks & Spencer's first clothing campaign since its ridiculed 'I'm normal' advert five years ago, which featured a naked woman running around the countryside. The 'Twiggy' adverts followed the highly successful food campaign, which was thought to have increased sales of a featured chocolate pudding by 3000 per cent.

City analysts have commented that, 'Marks & Spencer are now more competitive on price, its product offer is stronger and it has communicated this effectively to customers through a thoughtful advertising campaign.'

**Pass**

Describe the role of advertising agencies and the media in the development of this successful promotional campaign.

**Merit**

Explain the relative merits of using professional agencies in ensuring promotional success.

## Grading tips

**Pass** P3

Describe the role Marks & Spencer's advertising agency would have played in the creation of the 'Twiggy' campaign. Use the table on page 263 to help you.

**Merit** 

Use a table to distinguish between the advantages and disadvantages of using a professional agency as against an in-house team. What aspects of the 'Twiggy' adverts do you think were included through the special contribution of the Marks & Spencer advertising agency?

# 9.4 Create a simple promotional campaign

## Campaign brief

An advertising campaign is usually organised with the services of an advertising agency. The company employing the agency must provide clear guidelines on how the campaign should be developed.

The campaign brief is likely to contain the following sections:

1. The background to the proposed campaign. This will include comments about the market and the organisation's current objectives. Why is there a need for some promotional activity, and how is it expected to contribute to the overall aims of the organisation?
2. The objectives of the promotional activity, along with any marketing aims it is designed to support. The objectives should be clear and measurable and given a timescale.
3. The target market/audience. These are the people the promotional activity is intended to influence. As much detail as possible is required – age, gender, income, ethnic background, where they live, jobs they do and how they enjoy themselves. Alongside this information, the **consumer benefits** of the product should be included and any details of the competition.

### Key Terms

**Consumer benefit** What the consumer will gain if they buy the product, e.g. buyers of iPods can enjoy the music of their favourite artists virtually anywhere.

4. As much detail as possible about the product to be featured. The agency should understand the processes involved in its production and how it is different from competition.
5. The budget. Setting a budget is very difficult, since there is not always an obvious direct link between promotion and sales.
6. The timescale of the campaign. The advertising may need to be timed to coincide with a particular event or date, such as summer or Valentine's Day.

### Budget

As mentioned above, it is not easy to set an advertising budget. But methods of determining an advertising campaign budget can include the following:

- the 'objective and task' approach calculates the costs of the activities considered necessary to achieve the objective

## CAMPAIGN BRIEF
## Big Lick – the tastiest ice cream

1. **Background**
   Big Lick is an ice cream company that has decided to launch one of its internationally successful brands in the UK. The company, because it uses others to actually produce the ice cream, is able to exploit any emerging or established consumer preference. The market is growing strongly because of the hotter summers and because consumers have more money than ever for indulgences.
2. **Campaign objectives**
   The promotional activity should encourage consumers to sample the tastes of the Big Lick range of flavoured ices, while supporting the marketing aim of beginning to establish the brand characteristics of the Big Lick brand. The activity should aim to provide 1.5 million sampling opportunities during July and August, while having 20% of the consumers who try the product recalling several characteristics of the Big Lick brand.
3. **Target market**
   The main consumers for Big Lick are expected to be young adults enjoying the reward of a Big Lick product. The product has a universal appeal in terms of gender and ethnicity, and attracts successful although not necessarily loud people.

   It has a range of unique exotic flavours, is low-calorie - very low in sugar - and has generally healthy ingredients.

   The main competitors in the market are considered to be Walls and Mars.
4. **Product details**
   Big Lick has a range of unique flavours which makes it different from other leading brands.

   The product is available in singles (original £0.99; deluxe £1.35), multi-packs of 12 (£10.99) and 24 (£19.99).

   It is expected to be stocked by all the leading supermarkets and at all leading leisure attractions in the UK. Distribution in vending machines and convenience stores is expected to be slower.
5. **Budget**
   The budget is £1million (excluding advertisement production costs). This is based on the knowledge that Mars spent such an amount when launching their range of ice creams.
6. **Timescale**
   The activity should start in May as the better weather approaches and climax in July and August during the summer holidays.

▲ Campaign brief for Big Lick – the tastiest ice cream

- the 'competition matching' approach encourages organisations to spend a similar amount to their main competitors
- the 'percentage of sales revenue' approach allocates say 5% of revenue for advertising. If sales are £500,000 then the advertising budget is £25,000.

Alternatively, an arbitrary decision may be made by a senior executive. This relies on individual judgement, but is quick.

# Creative brief

A creative brief outlines possible ideas and media plans which need to be explored to enable the campaign brief's objectives to be achieved.

Once the brief has been agreed, the agency must be allowed to develop detailed creative solutions (such as memorable advertising ideas) and media plans without interference from the client company.

## CREATIVE BRIEF
## Big Lick – the tastiest ice cream

1. **Background**
   Big Lick is an ice cream company that has decided to launch one of its internationally successful brands in the UK. The company is capable of exploiting any emerging or established consumer preference. The market is growing strongly because of the hotter summers and because consumers have the income to indulge themselves.
2. **Advertising objectives and target market**
   The promotional activity should generate sales of £0.5 million in the first 12 months of the product being available.

   The main consumers for Big Lick are young adults enjoying the reward of a Big Lick product. The product has a universal appeal in terms of gender and ethnicity and attracts successful although not necessarily loud people.
3. **Advertising proposition or brand promise**
   It is an 'indulgence' – a reward for hard and long working days or for helping a friend or acquaintance.
4. **Brand promise support**
   New product development in this market is about developing ice creams with personalities, such as Magnum.

   Marketing research in a number of international markets has confirmed the ice cream is seen as the perfect reward.

   The exotic tastes appear to enhance the brand image of 'something special for someone special'. It is a low-calorie, healthy ice cream with low sugar content.

   Competitors are Walls and Mars.
5. **Tone of voice**
   The advertising approach should show people enjoying their indulgence. Music, locations and the actors should reinforce this image. Big Lick should be shown in a variety of situations which deserve an ice cream as a reward, such as solving a problem or helping a friend.
6. **Budget**
   The budget for producing the adverts is between £45,000 and £75,000. This excludes money which has to be spent on media air time.
7. **Other points**
   The organisation's logo and the product as it would be seen in store should appear in the advertisement.

Creative brief for Big Lick – the tastiest ice cream ▶

## Case study

### A campaign brief in action

An advertising whiz-kid, five models and a London bus driver are on an industrial estate in Wimbledon early on a bright April morning. They are all involved in the shoot for the Gossard lingerie brand's new TV commercial. This is part of Gossard's quest to double its market share in six months from 3% to 6% of the UK lingerie market.

Nine months after the campaign brief was developed the commercial was broadcast for the first time. This was the timescale:

- September: the campaign brief. The new marketing director for Gossard believes there is significant growth potential for its coordinates range – matching pants and bras.
- October: the research. The advertising agency's job is to create a new image to capture the attention of consumers. Several focus groups are held with women to investigate the market.
- November: the creative brief. The agency TBWA suggests a new name – Altogether. It recommends the advertising plays on women's embarrassment at being caught in public with mismatching underwear. 'Get yourself Altogether, woman' will be the message of the advertisement.
- January: the script. The advert will show a young woman who has been hit by a bus suffering the humiliation of being 'criminally uncoordinated' – shocking the medical staff with her badly mismatched bra and pants. The final few seconds feature a group of models draped over the bus, with the line 'Altogether with Gossard'.
- February: the director. A top-class director can be very expensive – up to £10,000 a day. In this case Frank Budgen has agreed to take on the project, and he is one of the hottest directors around.
- March: the casting. Casting the actress who will star in the commercial proves difficult. Gossard's marketing director, the commercial's director and the script writer all have to agree. They watch a series of potential candidates on videotape in their offices. They settle on a particular actress who is fashionable rather than glamorous.
- April: the shoot. Everything is agreed before the two-day shoot begins in a disused hospital in south London. The production cost is around £200,000 on top of the £5 million being spent on buying TV airtime to broadcast the commercial. The shoot goes well and everybody seems happy.
- May: the final edit. The final touches are made to the commercial. A music track is added a week before it is due on screen.
- June: the broadcast. The first showing is on Channel 4 – appropriately, in a break during the hospital drama ER.

1. Comment on the sort of media that might be used to support the television advertising campaign. ✓
2. Discuss whether it would increase coverage, improve frequency or enhance the impact of the promotional campaign. ✓✓
3. How would you effectively include the Internet in such a campaign? ✓✓✓
4. Explain whether you think the message of this commercial had an emotional, empathetic or intellectual appeal. ✓✓✓

# Selection of content

## Communicating the promotional message

The agency has the task of deciding how to convey the message required in order to achieve the campaign objectives and marketing aims. The content used to convey the brand promise can take one of the following approaches.

- **Superior features** – the product has some features that make it better than others on the market. For example, a car insurance policy may include breakdown recovery anywhere in Europe at a small additional cost.

- **Excellent performance** – the product is better than competitors in key areas. An example might be a savings account that has a high rate of interest.
- **Benefits** – what the consumer gains when they buy the product. This is illustrated in airline commercials showing passengers enjoying comfortable seats, tasty meals and with cabin staff responding to their every request.
- **Quality** – products have special features which are not found in ordinary products. Car adverts emphasising the leather seats, walnut trimming and alloy wheels, and showing that the ride inside is smooth and noiseless, are designed to show the superior quality of the vehicle.
- **Reliability** – the product just keeps on working day after day. Examples are watches that keep excellent time and bus services that promote a bus every five or six minutes on major routes.

### Practice point

Read the Big Lick campaign brief on page 271 and in small groups develop a creative brief of your own. Ask your tutor to select a brief from amongst those produced, and justify their choice.

## Campaign tactics

You may think of promotional campaigns in terms of advertising on television, the radio, in the cinema, and in newspapers and magazines. However, a promotional campaign can also (or only) include other activities such as public relations, exhibition attendance, sponsorship, personal selling, direct marketing and deployment of point-of-purchase material in-store.

### Target audience and media

The use of a TV commercial or radio advertisement to promote a particular product is determined by whether the target audience (consumers who buy the product frequently) watch or listen. Once the media has been selected, effective advertisements have to be designed. They should follow the AIDA framework: attention, interest, desire, action.

- **Attention** – the first words spoken or printed in an advertisement should concentrate on the major benefit the product offers; for example, 'the lightest MP3 player on the market'.
- **Interest** – the key to building consumer interest in a product is to highlight the other features and the benefits relevant to the potential consumer; for example as shown in the table below showing features and benefits for a MP3 player.

| Feature | Benefit |
|---|---|
| Long-life battery | Listen all day without worrying |
| Downloading software | Everything a person might need to download their favourite tunes |
| Special carry case | Always have it handy wherever you are – clips on belt, rucksack and coat |

- **Desire** – the consumer is reminded of what they might miss or could be enjoying to create desire for the product; for example, 'Buy today and receive a *free* accessory' or '*Book now* and guarantee the holiday hotel of your choice'.
- **Action** – all the details a consumer would need in order to buy the product. This might include:
  - the organisation's name, address, telephone and fax number, email and website details
  - the opening times, payments options and credit terms offered
  - installation, repair and refund arrangements, delivery options.

### Focus groups

Focus groups can be used to test the likely effectiveness of promotional activity. Focus groups consist of six to ten people (chosen as likely to belong to the target market) who are invited to look at promotional material and discuss the issues, led by an interviewer. The main benefit of such groups is that ideas and opinions can be discussed with representatives of the target market, allowing marketers to develop an idea, perhaps even finding a common view emerging from the group.

## Guidelines for designing promotional materials

1. Every advertisement should embody a clear, straightforward proposition – the consumer should be offered one clear reason to buy the product. This is sometimes called the unique selling proposition (USP). For example:
   'Gain a BTEC National for a university place'
2. Say what you have to say in as few words as possible – with headlines, this should be in five to eight words.
3. Give the consumer credit for intelligence – never speak down to consumers or insult them. You can, however, flatter, congratulate and encourage them. For example:
   'Gain a professional qualification and become a chartered marketer'
4. Be original – this attracts attention: A 'Mini' adventure.

## Advertising in newspapers and magazines

Clients are usually presented with a drawn illustration of how the advertisement is expected to look in the chosen media. This is called a mock-up. Before a printed advertisement is finally produced, clients receive proofs – these have to be 'signed off' as acceptable by the client. This is the last chance to correct any errors or omissions. Changes can still be made at this stage, but they are expensive to undertake. The 'signing off' process makes everybody check the material carefully, and it helps minimise disputes between printer, agency and client.

## Developing TV and cinema advertisements

Agencies use storyboards to show clients how they expect a TV commercial to unfold. Eight or more drawn pictures will be pasted on a board with the words of the commentary set out beneath. Information will be given about the type of actors required, the locations to be used, and the overall effect.

## Images and promotional objectives

The creative use of images within promotional materials can achieve several objectives:

- It can attract the attention of the target audience.
- It can communicate product features and/or benefits.
- It can create an atmosphere through lighting, colour and texture of the image – for example tenderness and romance.
- It can encourage people to read the text through creating curiosity and interest among consumers.

The impact of images can be influenced through three main factors – size, colour and medium. The impact of size is probably overstated, as it is the meaning of the image that is crucial – does it have a clear message? Colour is essential for some products, such as decorative items, and in other cases colour can be used to emphasise a feature. The medium – such as cartoons, photography, computer graphics – is an important decision. Photographs can add an element of credibility, and emphasise detail while some think they prompt better recall of a product than drawn illustrations.

### Practice point

Use the annotated example opposite to help you construct your own effective direct mail letter.

### Remember

A consumer benefit is what the consumer will gain if they buy the product.

## Text and script

A direct mail letter incorporates many of the points concerning the production of effective promotional material. It is also potentially another piece of promotional material you could produce for assessment outcome 9.4.

# Developing a promotional plan

This involves a number of factors, such as choosing the promotion mix, timing and frequency, costs, mix of media and possibly use of the Internet. These are outlined in the steps below.

## Steps in developing a promotional plan

### ■ Outline the objectives in the campaign brief

The objectives of the campaign must be clearly established, preferably expressed as a numerical target (such as to raise brand awareness by 15%) and to be achieved by a certain time (such as December). Without such information, it will be impossible to judge whether an organisation has achieved its objectives. This information is in the campaign brief.

BUSINESS COLLEGE, COMMERCE AVENUE, CARDIFF CF2 3ER

Sara Khan
45 St James's Drive
Penarth
CF29 4JQ

Direct mail letters are generally personalised

Dear Ms Khan

Highlight the main benefit of the product in the title

**Obtain that job you have always dreamed about**

The BTEC National Diploma in Business provides young people with the skills and knowledge that organisations are looking for locally and nationally.

Explain other important product benefits in the next paragraph

You will be able to study without the worry of having to pass examinations, and benefit from Business College's team of experienced teachers, many of whom have worked in important positions in a variety of business organisations.

Tell customers exactly what they will receive if they buy the product

Enjoy studying marketing and management. Learn how to present business information and manage teams. Find out about the potential of e-commerce and how functions and departments work together to achieve business aims and objectives.

Insert a quotation from a satisfied customer to add credibility to your comments

Luke Harding (from the Class of 2004) said: 'Since I started working I have realised that the BTEC National in Business has given me skills that I am using already in my job. I would recommend the programme to anybody.'

Build desire by pointing out what they might miss if they fail to act

If you enrol before the end of the school year you will receive on joining the programme a **FREE** BTEC National textbook.

Give all the details necessary for a customer to obtain the product

Include a postcard consumers can return indicating what they would like to happen next, e.g. arrange an interview

To enrol or organise an interview with the course leader complete the return postcard, telephone 0112 598 1315 or e-mail tutor@bn.ac.uk

Yours sincerely

*Jane Griffiths*

Jane Griffiths
BTEC National Programme Leader

▲ An effective direct mail letter

## ■ Identify the target audience in the campaign brief

Who should hear the organisation's message? In most cases it will be customers, but it can also include, for example, shareholders and employees. Target audiences are people who are classified or grouped together by a factor that makes them behave in a similar fashion. For example, some consumers are referred to as being 'cash rich but time poor'. They lead busy lives and need products which allow them to save time or use it effectively. Buying wine on the Internet would be a typical time-saving activity of such a group.

## ■ Detail the promotional message in the creative brief

The promotional message will be determined by the objective of the campaign, which could range from increasing sales to altering the perceptions of a brand. Skoda used to be a brand associated with poor quality vehicles. They were bought by people with small budgets who wanted a new car. After a few years under Volkswagen ownership the product has been transformed and recent promotional campaigns have transformed the customer's perception of the brand. Their cars are still budget priced but the quality standard is excellent.

## ■ Establish a promotional budget or cost

Having identified the intended message, the organisation should establish the finances available before it considers the type of marketing activities it might undertake. A limited budget may restrict the options available.

## ■ Choose the promotion and media mix

In many markets promotion is central to success – you have to promote toys heavily at Christmas because of the wide choice available to consumers. Once the total amount of money is allocated for promotion it needs to be divided between the elements of the promotion mix – advertising, personal selling, sales promotions, publicity, public relations and corporate image enhancement.

The final task would be to decide which advertising media to use – local, regional, national, international, terrestrial television, satellite television, the Internet and/or specialist media. In some cases the type of message selected may also affect the media used – print may be used for delivering detailed information, for example on a pensions product.

The Internet has added an interesting media option which marketing managers need to consider utilising in their plans. One of the main attractions of this option is its low cost. Detailed below are two of the ways of using the Internet within the promotional mix.

- Banner advertising, which can be static or animated, is usually placed across the top of a web page. Banners are very effective because they can be placed on relevant sites.
- Links with other sites – this is a relatively straightforward promotional method which ensures a site has links to it from as many other sites as possible. The site benefiting from the links can then display links to the sites cooperating. This can be achieved at very low cost.

## ■ Schedule the frequency and timing of the promotion

A promotional campaign should not be restricted to one short period, but should be considered as a continuous activity which runs throughout the product's life.

In the short term, bursts of promotional activity may be undertaken, as opposed to a constant drip of promotional activity over a longer period.

In the long term, messages must be repeated continually because the target audience may miss a message the first time it appears. It is likely that several elements of the promotional mix will need to be used simultaneously to deliver an effective campaign. In other words, personal selling and advertising can be used together. Advertising will stimulate demand and personal selling secure the order.

Running the campaign at the right time is important – it must be when consumers are in a suitable frame of mind to purchase. Holidays are traditionally promoted immediately after Christmas, as this is the time a pleasant summer break is in the consumer's mind.

▲ Running a promotional campaign must be timed accurately

## ■ Using the promotion plan

A campaign can only be considered successful if it achieves the objectives stated at the beginning. In many cases, objectives may be measured in the sales or profit generated for the company. However, it is almost impossible to directly measure the effect on sales and profits – any increases may simply be due to the market growing. Promotional activities cannot be viewed in isolation since the organisation does not act alone in the market and other factors, such as competitors' actions and relative price changes, can affect the outcome of all promotional activity.

Nevertheless the promotion plan is useful for evaluation purposes and improving performance next time. For example, an evaluation of the promotion plan can include the following sections:

- the strengths and weaknesses of the campaign
- how the campaign's effectiveness in meeting the aims and objectives of the organisation could have been improved.

In conclusion, promotion is a question of faith – it is based on the belief that increased awareness and positive attitudes towards the organisation and its products will eventually result in higher sales and thereby increase profits.

## Outcome activity 9.4

A chain of health and fitness clubs is opening a new branch in the area. It has to attract a large number of new members who are prepared to sign a one-year contract. The club is aiming to have similar numbers of men and women. The available budget is £20,000 for a two-month pre-launch promotion.

**Pass**

Design a promotional campaign for the health club which meets the needs of the campaign/creative brief. 

**Merit**

Provide a rationale for the promotional campaign and make recommendations for improvement. 

## Grading tips

**Pass** 

Use a combination of local media and strive to produce promotion materials which have genuine impact.

**Merit** 

Take each element of your campaign and explain and justify its role. If this proves difficult remove it from the campaign.

## End of unit test

1. Explain the difference between publicity and public relations.
2. Why does sport obtain such significant amounts of sponsorship?
3. Name the six parts of the communications model.
4. Describe the four parts of AIDA.
5. Describe the various meanings of the word 'quality' as used in advertising.
6. Name the elements of the marketing mix which are especially important for services.
7. Describe three promotional objectives.
8. What are the special features of B2B promotional activity?
9. Explain the role of advertisement production in an advertising agency.
10. Name two disadvantages of local media.
11. Explain the terms coverage, frequency and impact.
12. Explain the meaning of a 'drip campaign'.
13. What are the sections of a campaign brief?
14. Why do advertising agencies produce 'mock-ups'?
15. What are the elements in the promotion mix?

# Resources

www.adassoc.org.uk/ – The Advertising Association

www.rab.co.uk – Radio Advertising Bureau

www.transad.net – Poster advertising company

www.the-dma.org.uk – Direct Mail Association

www.ipr.org.uk/ – Institute of Public Relations

www.asa.org.uk – Advertising Standards Authority

# Books

Smith, C. and Hiam, A. 2006 *Marketing for Dummies*, Wiley

| Grading criteria | Outcome activity | Page number |
|---|---|---|
| To achieve a pass grade the evidence must show that the learner is able to: | | |
| P1 Describe the promotional mix used by two selected organisations for a selected product/service | 9.1 | 250 |
| P2 Describe the role of promotion within the marketing mix for a selected product/service | 9.2 | 261 |
| P3 Describe the role of advertising agencies and the media in the development of a successful promotional campaign | 9.3 | 269 |
| P4 Design a promotional campaign for a given product/service to meet the needs of a given campaign/creative brief | 9.4 | 278 |
| To achieve a merit grade the evidence must show that, in addition to the pass criteria, the learner is able to: | | |
| M1 Explain how the promotional aspect is integrated and used with the whole marketing mix of a selected organisation to achieve its business aims and objectives | 9.2 | 261 |
| M2 Explain the relative merits of using professional agencies in ensuring promotional success | 9.3 | 269 |
| M3 Provide a rationale for a promotional campaign and make recommendations for improvement | 9.4 | 278 |
| To achieve a distinction grade the evidence must show that, in addition to the pass and merit criteria, the learner is able to: | | |
| D1 Evaluate and justify the use of an appropriate promotional mix with respect to business and marketing objectives for the selected organisation | 9.2 | 261 |

# Introduction to marketing research

## Introduction

This unit explores how marketing research can contribute to the key marketing decisions an organisation needs to take. It builds on the work in Unit 3 Introduction to Marketing. It reviews the marketing research methods that can be used to gather the information required and the stages to be followed to ensure the research is a success.

The unit then explains the planning which has to be undertaken to achieve the objectives of the marketing research. The third section considers how to implement the research plan, including deciding who to interview and how to design an effective questionnaire. The final part examines how to analyse and present the information before concluding with a reminder that research does have its limitations.

### What you need to learn

On completion of this unit you should:

1. Understand the main types of marketing research and how it is used to make marketing decisions
2. Be able to plan simple research
3. Be able to carry out simple research
4. Be able to interpret research findings.

## Consider this

Imagine the design team present you with a new product idea and you have to recommend whether it should be further developed. You feel that the senior managers in your organisation are not in touch with the fast-changing nature of the market so you recommend that some marketing research is undertaken. A Google search reveals plenty of information about similar products but there is not enough detail for you to recommend that the product idea should be developed.

You decide to undertake some new research using a model of the product, although this will be costly, and two groups of consumers meet for 90 minutes one evening to discuss the product. However, the results are very encouraging, so you have to present the findings to your senior managers.

The presentation is a great success and the product gets the go-ahead. When the sales team hit their target five weeks ahead of schedule you are convinced that marketing research is essential to business success. The sales team have a lot of views about the market but you are unsure that they are relaying the views of the customers accurately. Should you now spend more money to speak directly to the customers themselves?

# 10.1 Types of marketing research used to make marketing decisions

The purpose of marketing research is to help organisations make effective decisions by providing information on consumers, competitors and the market. The two main types of marketing research are primary and secondary research.

Primary research obtains new information. Secondary research makes use of research already carried out by someone else for another project. An organisation wanting to gauge the reaction to a proposed new advertising idea would not be able to find the answer from existing research sources and would therefore have to carry out some primary research.

## Primary research methods

Primary research can be costly to undertake and can take a considerable amount of time to complete. There are different methods which can be used.

### Observation

Observation is a data gathering approach where information is collected without any questions being asked of the participants. The researcher is the witness of behaviour and events. Observation cannot explain the underlying reasons for the behaviour it records, so observation is therefore often combined with other research methods.

The major advantage of observation research is that the information collected does not have distortions or inaccuracies as a result of memory error or socially desirable answers. In other words the research process itself does not influence the behaviour of the individual. For behaviour that the individual feels reflects badly on them, such as smoking or drinking, observation may give a more accurate picture than personal interviewing. For example, doctors believe that patient estimates of drinking and smoking are underestimated by 100%. Observation data records the actual behaviour that takes place.

Another aspect of observation is when retailers send out employees, called mystery shoppers, to visit their own and competitors' stores. They are required to observe store layouts, displays, store traffic and special promotions. Some organisations even send out specially trained staff to their own stores to pose as customers. They are generally concerned with the standard of customer service.

Are you a mystery shopper in disguise? ▶

## Case study

### I spy with my little eye!

DVD players are used for an average of seven hours per week according to a study by AGB Research. This result was obtained from the first DVD player study using AGB's FingerPrinting technology. AGB attached a small device to a DVD player that automatically measures playing. This information is useful to organisations such as Blockbuster, which markets DVDs for home entertainment, education and a variety of other purposes.

Mystery shopping, or mystery customer research, is a well-established technique, involving observers contacting or visiting sellers of goods and services as if they were real customers. It has been extensively applied by retailers, travel agents, restaurant chains, car dealers and financial services companies amongst others, to assess the performance of staff and measure it against competition.

London Underground, with the help of AGB Research, has been running an extensive programme of mystery shopping for several years, with investigators making frequent visits to tube stations to report on the quality of service ranging from courtesy of the staff to cleanliness of stations. Research Manager, Justin Gutmann, is using the information, for example, to ensure staff training focuses on the key issues and cleaning schedules are sufficient to keep the stations clean.

1. Apart from recording how long DVD players are used during a week what other information might usefully be collected by the technology? ✓
2. What competitors would you send your mystery customers to visit if you were Research Manager of London Underground? ✓✓
3. What might be the limitations of the DVD player information gathered by the technology? ✓✓✓
4. What else could be observed at London Underground stations to help understand customer behaviour? ✓✓✓

## Surveys

Surveys are used to collect marketing research data from a carefully chosen group of consumers. Those who take part are called **respondents**. There are several different methods of conducting surveys, which are outlined below.

## Key Terms

**Respondent** Somebody who is asked and agrees to participate in a marketing research project.

### Telephone surveys

Telephone interviews are used for business-to-business and consumer research. They are ideal when a national, regional or even international survey is required. Telephone interviews are generally computer controlled. Each question appears on the interviewer's screen and they read the question exactly as it appears. Generally questions are short-answer questions, where the respondents are limited to a choice of possibilities. Answers are immediately entered into the computer for analysis.

| Advantages of telephone interviews | Limitations of telephone interviews |
|---|---|
| People usually answer the telephone.<br>Good coverage is gained as 95% of UK households have telephones – including people normally difficult to contact.<br>Very high response rate.<br>No travel involved – so saving time and costs.<br>Question order can be changed by the computer to eliminate the bias of last and first responses being favoured choices.<br>Data can be analysed almost immediately. | Telephone number list can be outdated.<br>A telephone interview can generally be no longer than 15 minutes.<br>No way to use visual aids.<br>Sometimes used to disguise a selling approach.<br>Cannot ask complex questions.<br>Telephone ownership not so widespread in some developing nations. |

## Postal surveys

In postal surveys, questionnaires are mailed to pre-selected respondents along with a return envelope, a covering letter and possibly an incentive. The respondents complete and return the questionnaire. Although postal surveys have been around for many years their importance has grown as a result of the availability of customer databases and the need to measure customer satisfaction.

Postal surveys can look an attractive proposition because they have low costs, but unfortunately they tend also to have low response rates. It is not uncommon for surveys to experience response rates as low as 20%.

| Advantages of postal surveys | Limitations of postal surveys |
|---|---|
| National and international areas can be covered.<br>Data can be obtain from people who are normally difficult to interview (such as carers).<br>Responses can be obtained on sensitive issues such as personal hygiene and income.<br>They are low cost – telephone surveys can be three times more expensive and face-to-face interviews nine times.<br>They can be completed when it is convenient for the respondent. | Low response rate.<br>Questionnaires are often not fully completed.<br>They may not be completed by right person.<br>Those who respond may not be representative of the people mailed – just people with time on their hands.<br>They are only suitable for tick box questions.<br>The return of questionnaires can be spread over several weeks. |

## Email surveys

Email surveys involve delivering a questionnaire through desk-based PCs but also through digital television and mobile phones. They are essentially postal surveys delivered electronically.

This type of research tends to be cheaper and faster to implement than postal surveys. Respondents may also give more detailed responses to open-ended questions than is the case with postal surveys as they have a keyboard in front of them and are used to producing short responses using email.

The amount of junk mail 'spam' being sent to computer users is growing, which may make it more difficult to succeed with email surveys. It is considered a good idea to ask people to participate rather than simply to send them an unexpected questionnaire. Some respondents may be concerned about the confidentiality as the returned questionnaire will have the respondent's email address attached.

## Face-to-face surveys

Personal interviews involve respondent and researcher speaking face-to-face. At one time it was a very popular way of conducting surveys, particularly in home interviews for consumer products such as televisions and food. However, face-to-face interviews are expensive and generate low response rates unless a great deal of time is spent in revisiting people. Nowadays fewer people are at home when interviewers are most likely to want to call so personal interviews are now largely conducted in shopping centres. Personal interviews may also be conducted at businesses and other types of organisation.

### Remember

If a researcher asks for personal details such as a telephone number it is a strong indicator that the data is being collected for selling purposes.

▲ Face-to-face interviews can take place in shopping centres or at home

| Advantages of face-to-face interviews | Limitations of face-to-face interviews |
|---|---|
| Little of the researcher's time wasted.<br>Possible to use illustrative materials during interview (such as new packaging).<br>Possible to motivate respondent to take part.<br>Possible to check respondent is of the type being sought before interview is conducted.<br>Respondent can be convinced that the researcher and research is genuine. | People in a hurry are difficult to question.<br>Interviews have to be done in clusters (for example in the city centre) to keep costs under control.<br>Sometimes difficult to control interviewer **bias** – interviewers may pick friendly looking people and those who appear not to be in a hurry.<br>Interview cost is the highest of any method.<br>Refusal rates are high – between 5% and 30%. |

## Key Terms

**Bias** The difference between the answer given by respondents and the truth.

## Thinking point

Look at the tables describing the advantages and limitations of face-to-face interviews, telephone interviews and postal surveys. Convert the tables into points ranked in order of importance.

## E-marketing research

Web surveys generally appear in two forms: the standard questionnaire format and the interactive questionnaire. The standard questionnaire format appears as it would on paper. The respondent scrolls down the page, answering each question. The interactive questionnaire has questions appearing on the screen one at a time. The respondent submits an answer and then the computer selects a new question according to the answer to the previous question.

## Case study

### More muscle from microchips

Multimedia notebook computers are not only used by researchers to record responses from people, but also to present TV advertisements and other material in their home. The market research company BMRB has around half of its 500 researchers using the notebook computers. Clips from TV commercials can be shown on screen and followed with an on-screen questionnaire, to which the respondent answers by clicking on the relevant box or, where an opinion is being sought, into the notebook microphone. The spoken answers are saved and can be downloaded into an audio tape, so that other researchers can listen to them at a later date.

'Previously we would have summarised the answers in a report, but it's got so much more impact with the original intonation. You can see the force with which it was said. Hearing customers talk about a brand like this is very, very powerful,' says BMRB director Graham Wilkinson.

The system is not limited to showing TV advertisement clips, it can also be used to show different packaging options, a proposed poster or magazine advertisement, alongside competitor's material. Notebook computers can also help interviewers overcome language barriers. The questionnaire can be translated beforehand into any language and played back to the respondent.

1. What is a major advantage of the respondents' answers being recorded by the computer? ✓
2. What are advantages of this type of face-to-face interview compared with a postal survey? ✓✓
3. What else could be effectively researched using the multimedia capabilities of the notebook computers? ✓✓✓
4. Discuss whether you think Internet-based surveys will eventually replace face-to-face interviews. ✓✓✓

Web surveys are currently useful for monitoring web usage and attitudes towards websites, as well as feedback on computers and technology in general. It can be anticipated that in the future web-based surveys will replace a significant number of postal surveys.

## Focus groups

Focus groups are in-depth interviews undertaken with a group of about eight to twelve people. They involve interaction between the participants. The aim of focus group research is to learn and understand what people think about a topic at length and in detail.

Focus groups provide a rich and detailed source of information. The purpose is to discover how they feel about a product, concept, idea or organisation. The views of one person may become the stimulus for another's ideas or may start a useful discussion. People tend to be encouraged to talk when they realise that others have similar experiences and attitudes.

## Panels

A panel is a form of survey that collects data from people over an extended period of time. They provide a measurement of change over time. Panels can consist of households, organisations and individuals. They are useful for a variety of purposes, such as:

- identifying broad trends in a market, for example are consumers buying healthier products?
- investigating consumer behaviour, for example are consumers influenced by sales promotions?
- discovering consumer attitudes or reactions to a product, such as a new style of packaging.

Information may be gathered by questionnaire, telephone interview, diaries (booklets where respondents record their behaviour and purchases over a period such as a month) or through the Internet. The best known examples of panel research are the consumer purchase panels monitoring individual or household buyer behaviour in the areas of food and drink. There are some important organisational issues when using panel surveys:

- It can be quite difficult to retain panel members for the entire task.
- For consistency, there is a need to replace people who leave with similar people.
- There is a need to check that panellists are completing recording procedures correctly.
- It is difficult to obtain a representative group of people, as the only people who participate may be those who have a deep interest in the product.
- There is a need to ensure people do not change their behaviour because they know their actions are being recorded, for example they might stop buying convenience meals.

## Field trials and piloting

Some products need to be tested over a period of time, such as microwaves in the home, scooters on the road and copiers in the office. This process is called field-testing.

Pilot testing involves administering a questionnaire to a limited number of potential respondents in order to identify and correct design flaws.

| Technique | Appropriateness | Limitations |
|---|---|---|
| Field trials | When the consumer has to undertake some preparation or installation.<br>When a long period of consumer use is required to fully appreciate a product's strengths and weaknesses.<br>The method has been used by confectionery and food companies prior to a national launch. | They can be expensive to organise and undertake as sufficient numbers of products in their finished format need to be produced for testing. People tend to drop out of the process before the tests are complete, either because they do not like the product or they simply lose interest in the activity. |
| Piloting | Used with a questionnaire when there are concerns over the format of questions, the time needed to complete the questionnaire and how respondents may react to certain questions, especially ones of a personal nature. | Pilot and full surveys must be conducted with the same type of respondents.<br>Pilots must be undertaken with a relatively small number of people who reflect the views of the whole group. |

## Case study

### In-store radio advertisements

The Northern Pharmacy Company conducted an experiment to examine the effectiveness of in-store radio commercials to encourage customers to buy. Twenty similar stores were selected based on size, location, customer flow and age. Half were randomly selected as test stores, and the other half served as control stores. The test stores aired the radio advertisements, whereas the control stores had their radio system removed. A variety of products were studied from inexpensive items to small kitchen appliances. Results indicated that sales of the advertised products in the test stores at least doubled. Based on this evidence the retailer concluded that in-store radio advertising was highly effective.

1. Would you measure the sales in the test period against sales from previous weeks or from the same weeks last year? ✓
2. What other factors might have influenced the sales in the test stores? ✓✓
3. What might be the next experiment to try to improve the effectiveness of in-store radio advertising? ✓✓✓
4. How could observation be used to further help the company understand the impact of in-store radio advertising? ✓✓✓

### Experimentation

Experimental research allows the researcher to change one aspect of an offer (such as price) and observe the impact on another aspect of the same offer (such as sales). All the other aspects of the offer remain the same – product, promotion, packaging and shelf display. For example, when launching the round teabag, Lyons Tetley experimented by analysing purchasing behaviour while altering the shape of the teabag; all other aspects of the offer were kept constant.

# Appropriateness of each method

The different primary research methods can be summarised as shown in the table overleaf.

# Secondary research

Secondary research is useful because it:

- may answer some of the organisation's research needs – for example identifying trends in the market
- could assist in the design of a research project – for example finding out where to conduct research interviews
- should enable researchers to interpret primary research data better, allowing them to truly understand the broader picture
- could provide a source of comparative data to help check results
- may provide data that cannot be collected in any other way, such as government spending.

### Internal sources of secondary research

Internal data is information held inside the organisation conducting the research. The different sources of internal data are discussed below.

### ■ EPOS (electronic point of sale)

EPOS systems are mainly used by businesses that have a large number of regular sales, such as retail stores and hotels. An EPOS terminal linked to a back-office computer handles payments quickly, updates stock lists and provides instant information.

| | Observation | Experimentation | Surveys | Focus groups | Field trials |
|---|---|---|---|---|---|
| Fitness for purpose | Useful for quantitative data. | Provides quantitative data. | Provides both qualitative and quantitative data. | Provides detailed qualitative data. | Provides both qualitative and quantitative data. |
| Cost | Low – once technology bought and installed (such as CCTV in store). | High – time-consuming, needs careful organising, monitoring and analysis. | Low – although face-to-face interviews can be expensive. | High – may need to conduct several groups before common views emerge. | High – recruitment of participants costly, need to check records being kept properly. |
| Accuracy | Good – records exactly what happens. | Maybe difficult to identify the factors that are really influencing consumers. They may alter their behaviour because they know their actions are being analysed. | Depends on the quality of the sample. Sample determines whether appropriate people participate. | May follow views of most vocal participant. May give socially acceptable answers. | Behaviour might change because records being kept. Other factors may influence results. |
| Time | May require a considerable amount of time to organise, complete observation and then to review tapes several times to identify behaviour. | May take considerable length of time before researchers can be certain change is permanent. | Can take a long time for all face-to-face interviews to be completed or for postal surveys to be returned. | Takes time to recruit, organise group discussion and analyse comments. | This method is generally designed for long-term projects. |
| Validity | See what is happening – but researcher interpretation may be inaccurate. | False situation – people start acting differently. | Can produce invalid answers because people have poor memories or do not understand the questions. | Good moderator can ensure all key issues are explored fully. | Excellent if recording done properly – records what is happening. |
| Response | Not an issue – may not even realise participating. | May be difficult to recruit participants and retain them for period of experiment. | Generally poor, especially postal surveys. | Once recruited tend to talk freely in group. | Participants can become bored or lose interest. |

▲ Appropriateness of each method of research

## Remember

Secondary research makes use of research already carried out by someone else for another reason. Primary research obtains new information.

EPOS software can provide a business with data about individual store sales, product sales by region, product sales by department or by a product category, such as clothing. It can also reveal changing consumer buying behaviour, such as a move towards credit card transactions.

### ■ Loyalty schemes

Loyalty cards, such as the Advantage card offered by Boots or Tesco Clubcard, record details of every individual purchase made by a cardholder.

Consequently the card issuers have customer details on:

- the frequency they visit stores

- the range of products they purchase
- the consistency with which they buy particular brands
- the extent to which they will try new products
- whether advertising influences their purchasing patterns.

The fact that organisations such as Tesco and Boots, and Sainsbury's with its Nectar card, are willing to invest a lot of money in these schemes shows how much they value the information gathered.

## Sales figures

Businesses generally have a lot of sales data at their fingertips. It needs to be reported in an efficient manner so it can become important marketing research data. This usually involves summarising the sales from individual customers into useful categories. The case study opposite shows the same sales data summarised and presented in two different ways for Power Drills Ltd.

## Website monitoring

It is possible for web-based traders to monitor the number of times different pages on their site are accessed, what search engines brought people to the site and track the peak times at which people access the site. A web trader can identify when users revisit the site and the sections of the site that they visit. For example, an organisation, such as HMV (www.hmv.co.uk), can monitor the type of music particular customers are interested in and whether they listen to excerpts or consider alternatives. Web-based traders have an advantage over traditional retailers as they can obtain information on browsers (the equivalent of window shoppers) as well as customers.

## Case study

**Power Drills Ltd – Sales by product category, January to March**

| Product description | Invoice price £ | Unit sales | Total revenue £ |
|---|---|---|---|
| Super 50 | 100 | 9500 | 950,000 |
| Super 100 | 125 | 7500 | 937,500 |
| Super 150 | 150 | 5000 | 750,000 |
| Super 200 | 175 | 2000 | 350,000 |
| Super Deluxe | 200 | 750 | 150,000 |
| Category total | | 24,750 | 3,137,500 |

**Power Drills Ltd – Sales by channel of distribution, January to March**

| Channel of distribution | Unit sales |
|---|---|
| Hardware stores | 12,500 |
| DIY warehouses | 2250 |
| Builder's merchants | 6500 |
| Others | 3500 |
| Total | 24,750 |

1. How might the sales team wish to see the information presented? ✓
2. What other information could transform this data into even more useful marketing research data? ✓✓
3. How might the information be used by the organisation? ✓✓✓

Web traders gain valuable market information by monitoring website traffic ▶

## E-transactions

More importantly, web-based traders can use sophisticated software products to keep a database of customers, which can be used to email information about special products and offers tailored to their past store-browsing patterns. For example, when a consumer enters www.amazon.com the store greets them with a personalised greeting and some purchase recommendations based on previous purchases.

## Data records

Organisations hold all sorts of data records some of which might contain valuable market research data. A good example would be records held in the sales office.

| Information discovered | Uses of information |
|---|---|
| Geographical location of customers | Ask sales team to seek new customers in areas where few customers located. |
| What products are purchased | Devised a sales promotion to boost sale of products which should be selling better. |
| When products are bought | Advertise best-selling products when demand peaks. |
| When the product was last bought | Send a direct mail letter suggesting they consider upgrading to latest model. |
| Average order value | Revise the discount scheme to encourage customers to increase their order value. |

## Accounting records and production records

An indication of a product's popularity may be its production output figures. However, production may simply have been transferred into the warehouse, so it is sales to consumers that are the important figures. The accounts department will also have records which may be of interest to a researcher. They may know the payment method customers are using – credit or debit card, cheque with banker's card, loans or simply cash. This sort of information contributes to building a comprehensive picture of the organisation's customers.

## Sales personnel

The management of many organisations is dependent on their sales personnel for marketing information. Sales people commonly discover information on the following:

- Promotional activity of competitors. Competitors are likely to be actively offering special deals. The impact of offering free installation at home for computers can be useful information, for example.
- Price offers that may indicate a competitor is struggling to meet sales targets or holding too much stock. It might be a sign about the replacement of a range and the imminent launch of new products.
- Competition data such as the announcement of a national advertising campaign, changes in delivery arrangements and improvements in after-sales service.
- Market trends, such as a shift to healthy foods or a shift to a new holiday destination.

Sales personnel might gain this data from speaking to consumers, reading sales brochures from competitors, speaking to contacts involved in the industry or attending exhibitions and conferences.

## Delphi technique

The Delphi method can be used with experts from within the organisation to help develop a picture of how the future might unfold for the business. A panel of experts is recruited but they never meet together – to remove the possibility that panel members might influence each other. The method works as follows:

- Each member of the panel gives their opinion without consulting other panel members.
- A nominated person gathers together all the opinions. At this stage any extreme views are discarded and the general view of the panel is established.
- This view is then described to each panel member for further thought. The members will have the opportunity to amend their views.
- Over time, a general agreement emerges about the future from the experts.

The table opposite shows the type of people who might make up a Delphi panel and what sort of topics might be suitable for discussion.

| Delphi panel members | Topics for potential discussion |
|---|---|
| Marketing director<br>Research & Development manager<br>International sales manager<br>Customer care coordinator | The growth in the number of consumers over the age of 65.<br>The impact of increasing levels of traffic congestion on shopping.<br>The continuing reduction in the birth rate in the UK. |

The conclusions from this type of activity are normally used to develop future plans for the organisation. In other words, a number of 'futures' are considered. Regardless of which one proves the most accurate, at least the organisation will have spent some time considering the implications.

## Practice point

Describe three of the internal sources of secondary data from the table below.

Consider the examples of decisions internal secondary research data can help make and add some of your own thoughts to the list.

| Internal research data | How useful in making marketing decisions? |
|---|---|
| Sales team market reports | Altering sales promotion plans |
| e-transaction data | Highlights how people choose to pay for products |
| Production records | Possibly highlights most popular products |
| Product sales records | Suggests areas for further new product development |
| Delphi 'futures' | Helps design team develop innovative ideas |
| Accounting records | Identifies most important customers |

## Take it further

Can you think of any limitations surrounding internal secondary data? Select and justify the internal secondary research sources you believe are really useful.

## External sources of secondary data

External data is that which is available outside the organisation conducting the research.

### Internet

A large amount of secondary data is now available in electronic format. Even if the information itself is unavailable electronically, the sources of data available can frequently be identified by electronic means. It is becoming a very useful and important source of marketing research information.

If you do not know the location of the information you are seeking, you can use a search engine. This allows you to enter one or more key words relating to a product, market, country or company and in return the search engine displays a list of sites that has information relating to those key words. Some popular search engines are shown in the table below.

| Search engine | Web address | Comments |
|---|---|---|
| Ask Jeeves | www.ask.com | Simply input a question |
| Google | www.google.com | Examines over two billion web pages |
| Yahoo! | www.yahoo.com | Has local country-based versions |

There are also many useful business sites, listed here are some which students have often found useful:

http://education.ntu.ac.uk/resources/BusEd.html – links to business related sites

http://www.bized.ac.uk – lots of business information

http://europa.eu.int/comm/index_en.htm – the European Commission home page

### Government statistics

The government regularly analyses business activity and publishes in reference books the results that are often available in college or university learning centres. Increasingly this information is available through government reports that can be downloaded from the Internet. Many such reports can be found on the website for National Statistics: www.statistics.gov.uk.

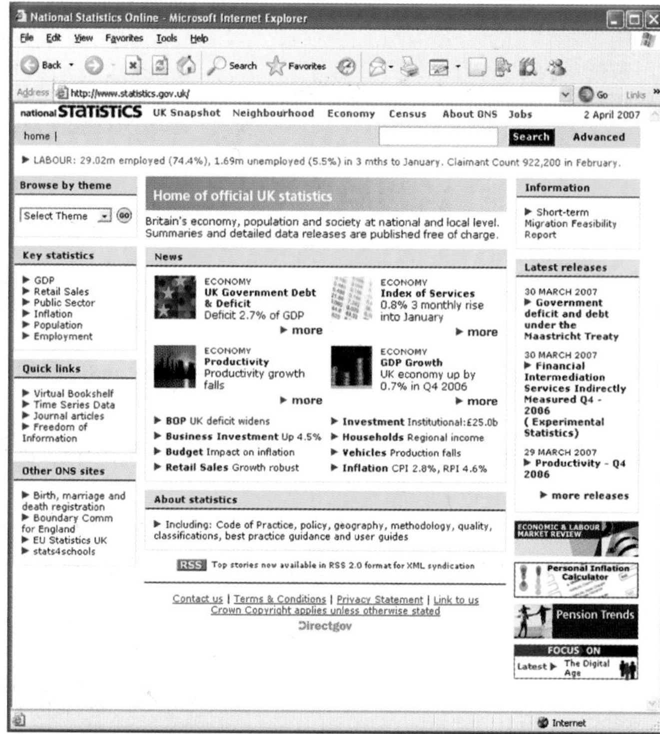


▲ **The home page of National Statistics (ONS)**

These government reports can include:

- *Social Trends* – draws together social and economic data from a wide range of government departments and other organisations. It paints a broad picture of Britain and how it is changing.
- *Annual Abstract of Statistics* – covers population, social conditions, production prices and employment.
- *Expenditure and Food Survey* – provides information on spending patterns in these key areas.
- *Regional Trends* – includes economic regional profiles, details of households, labour market facts and indicators of living standards.

### Thinking point

Use the 2005 *Annual Abstract of Statistics* and look at Table 21.16 Estimated household food consumption. Consider the changing pattern of drink consumption – tea, instant coffee, milk (various varieties) and fruit juice. Think of some reasons for the changes you have observed.

- *Labour Market Trends* – provides, amongst other facts, detailed statistics showing employment in different industries, levels of unemployment and wage rates.
- *Monthly Digest of Statistics* – summarises information on monthly economic trends.

## Libraries

Libraries generally contain the following essential sources of information:

- business information, including UK and international telephone directories
- foreign newspapers and company reports
- financial and statistical company information
- market research reports
- company databases with contact names and addresses
- reference books on business topics.

## Universities

In addition to holding sources found in most libraries, universities also have journals which provide a rich source of information because the journal articles are themselves pieces of research. The university will also publish the research work of its own academic staff. For example, Nottingham University researches into issues important to the insurance industry; consequently companies in that industry may be especially interested to view the research work of the university.

## Company reports

Company reports are useful when compiling a competitor analysis report, since they contain information such as sales and profit figures. This information may be provided for the last five years. Some contain statements from key directors about the previous trading period and the prospects for the future.

It is possible nowadays to order company reports over the Internet from www.hemscott.net or www.ftannualreports.com. Companies are obliged to send their accounts annually to Companies House, which can therefore provide copies of the accounts. Use www.companieshouse.gov.uk to review the complete range of services they offer the researcher.

## Reports by specialist agencies

Market research companies produce reports on markets and products and then offer them to organisations with an interest in that particular market – producers, retailers and suppliers. The reports are expensive to buy.

Mintel produces a wide variety of reports covering market size, market segments, levels of advertising, factors determining market growth and future forecasts. They are also available online at www.mintel.com.

Thomson Financial (www.thomson.com) produces DataStream, a valuable source of current financial data including stock market share prices, historical economic data, economic forecasts and exchange rate information.

Dun & Bradstreet (www.dab.com) publishes, for example, comprehensive financial reports on companies and on the trading prospects in a particular industry. Other Dun & Bradstreet reports, using the name MarketLine, can be accessed online from http://dbic.datamonitor.com on industries, companies and countries.

Economic forecasts and changes in market information can be obtained from the Investors Chronicle (www.investorschronicle.com.uk) or (www.bloomberg.com).

### Trade journals

Trade journals contain much valuable information. They discuss key trends and developments in an industry and are published by people who work in the industry. They provide information on new products and services. Trade journals often carry profiles on successful companies and examine the prospects for important product categories. A list of trade journals can be found on Yahoo! at Directory>business and economy>business-to-business>news and media>magazines>trade magazines.

### Criteria for selection

Just because data has been found which appears to answer or contribute to the questions being investigated by the research project that does not mean it is accurate, reliable and useful. The flow chart below describes how to decide whether the source is valid.

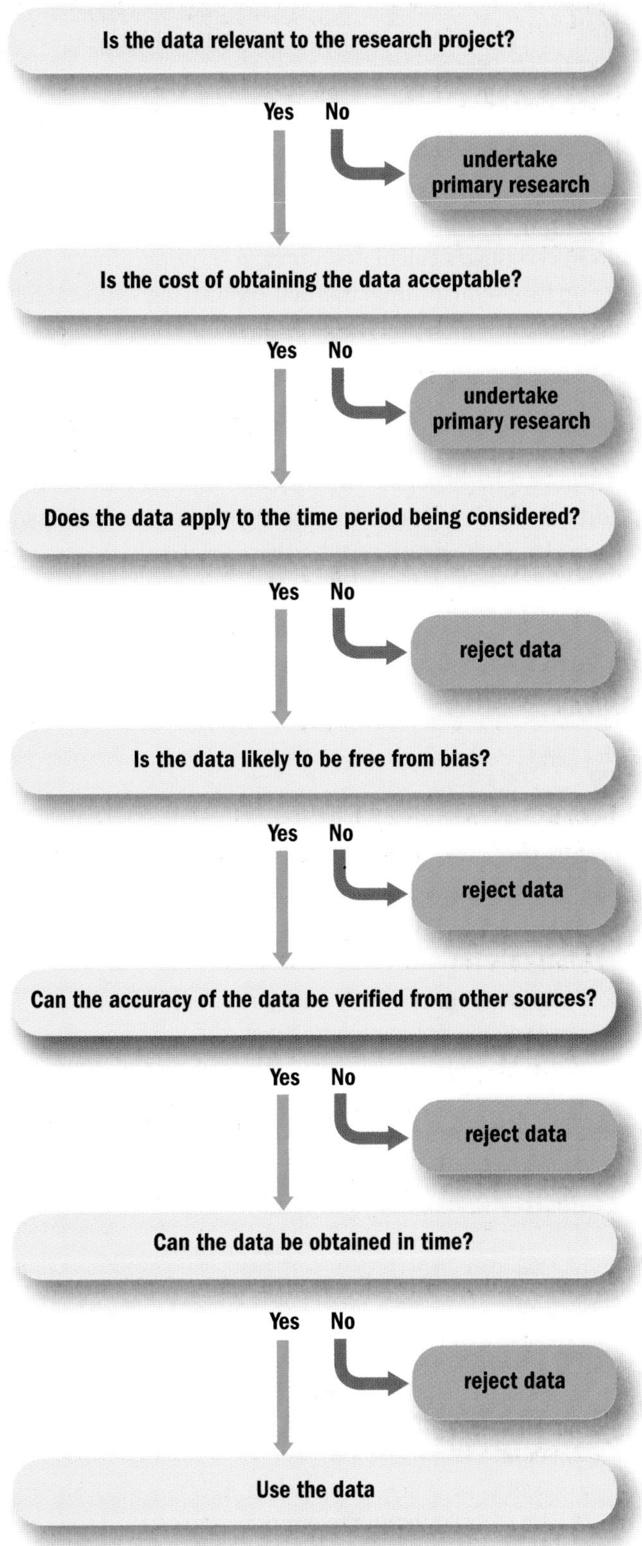


▲ Criteria for selecting secondary data

## Use of ICT applications in handling data

Before the widespread use of computers, when surveys involved relatively small numbers of questionnaires, data processing was carried out by hand. Simple counts were made of the answers given to questions with numbers and percentages calculated for each response. Apart from being time-consuming, manual analysis also prevented any complex interpretation of the data.

The development of 'data warehouses' able to store vast amounts of data from a variety of sources has been a major advance for data processing and marketing research. The storage is organised to make it easy to find and use the data. It can be updated using the scanning of barcodes at checkouts and loyalty card data.

Data mining is the technique which describes the process of exploring these large amounts of data with the objective of revealing hidden relationships or patterns which provide an insight into customer behaviour.

### Case study

**How the data mountain became a mountain of information!**

ResearchPlus operates a large tracking data base covering the entire grocery purchasing of more than 7000 households on a daily basis. It revealed that many shoppers using Sainsbury's for their main purchases were buying their ready-to-eat cereals – Cornflakes, Weetabix, Rice Crispies – from Tesco. But they were buying Tesco own-branded options.

Although the results of the data mining program itself could not answer all the questions this finding prompted, it did ensure the right questions were asked.

1. What is it about Tesco's branded cereals that attracts Sainsbury's shoppers? ✓
2. What else might they be buying during those visits? ✓✓
3. How could these shoppers be persuaded to return to Sainsbury's? ✓✓
4. Can you think of an unusual combination of products you purchase that might only be revealed through data mining? ✓✓✓

# Qualitative and quantitative research

## Importance and uses

Primary and secondary research can be either qualitative or quantitative in its nature. Quantitative research produces numbers and figures, such as the size of a market in terms of unit sales. Quantitative research can therefore be used to:

- show the pattern of sales over a year
- track market shares of major brands
- calculate the number of stores in a region stocking a product
- list the amount of advertising money being spent on a product range.

Qualitative research, on the other hand, provides data on why people buy, what motivates them to buy and their impression of products, services or advertisements. Qualitative research can therefore be used to:

- investigate customer reaction to a new advertising idea
- find out consumer views about a potential new product
- ascertain information about consumer preferences, lifestyles and aspirations.

## Triangulation

This is when different marketing research methods are used to research the same issue. It allows the results to be cross-checked, increasing the reliability of the results.

# Marketing research strategies and activities

## Strategic research

Strategic research delivers the knowledge needed to guide decisions that are likely to have long-term implications for the organisation.

▲ Data mining is used on large amount of data to reveal hidden paterns

### Technical research

Technical research helps an organisation understand the impact of such things as competitor activity or adjustments in prices.

### Databank research

Databank research involves the collection and updating of all relevant market information held by an organisation.

### Ad hoc research

Ad hoc or 'one-off' research meets information needs that cannot be identified far in advance. For example, a new opportunity may present itself to the organisation or some newly emerging problem needs to be explored.

### Continuous research

Any type of research may be organised so as to produce a continuous stream of data. The advantage of doing this is that it indicates trends and measures performance over time. This is particularly valuable in enabling an organisation to spot changes in the market before they become serious problems.

| | Strategic research | Technical Research | Databank Research |
|---|---|---|---|
| Continuous | Assessing new geographical markets. | Monitoring the effectiveness of advertising. | Updating figures for market size and market share. |
| Ad hoc | Assessing the potential of a new product idea. | Testing the impact of new advertising. | Reporting on a newly emerging competitor. |

▲ Types of research – the options matrix

## Purpose of research objectives

Marketing research can cover a wide range of objectives from trying to understand customer behaviour to looking at the activities of competitors. The table on page 296 shows some possible objectives.

| Research objectives | Research content |
|---|---|
| Customer behaviour | What sort of prices do customers expect to pay?<br>How important is personal selling to the purchaser?<br>What sort of after-sales care is required? |
| Buying patterns | When are the main sales periods?<br>How sensitive is buying to sales promotion activity?<br>Do different international markets have different buying patterns? |
| Consumer preferences | Which flavours do consumers prefer?<br>What are the most popular price points?<br>Which information sources do consumers prefer? |
| Customer satisfaction | Are the product features the ones consumers want?<br>Do consumers receive satisfactory after-sales service?<br>Is the promotional activity explaining the product benefits effectively? |
| Sales trends | Which products are experiencing falling sales?<br>Which stores are recording rising consumer sales?<br>How have products been selling in the south of the country? |
| Marketing mix changes | What has been the impact of introducing a super deluxe product option?<br>Is the new delivery procedure working effectively?<br>What is the potential for making sales using a catalogue delivered to households? |
| Brand awareness | Do consumers recall the brand unprompted?<br>What values does the brand have in the customer's mind?<br>Do product prices reflect the brand image? |
| Advertising awareness | Are consumers aware of the product options available?<br>Do consumers understand the key features of a product?<br>Is the advertising message understood by customers? |
| Product development success | Which new products have failed to reach their sales targets?<br>What products have competitors successfully launched recently?<br>How well have the new products been accepted in international markets? |
| New product opportunities | Would further multi-pack options increase sales?<br>What new consumer preferences might require some products to be modified?<br>What new products might be needed to achieve international success? |
| Changes in the market | How could a product be redesigned to take account of changing consumer tastes?<br>Should staff wear uniforms to emphasise the importance the organisation gives customer care?<br>How acceptable would be sending email messages to promote a service? |
| Emergence of new markets | What products are likely to have appeal in this new market?<br>Where would consumers expect to buy this type of product?<br>What type of promotional activity will be effective in these markets? |
| Competitor activities | What is the financial situation of the organisation?<br>Does the product range have genuine customer appeal?<br>How effective is their marketing activity?<br>Is the company well organised to respond to changing market conditions? |

▲ Marketing research objectives

## Practice point

Marketing research can often have the objective of helping develop an organisation's PESTLE analysis. Here are some examples of the questions the research might help answer:

- Political factors – what government ideas might affect the organisation or its market (such as further enlargement of the European Union)?
- Economic factors – will the economy continue to flourish, maintaining demand for an organisation's products (such as new houses)?
- Environmental factors – what is the attitude of consumers to current packaging styles (such as replacing polystyrene cartons with recycled cardboard cartons)?

Marketing managers use PESTLE analysis to investigate the environment in which an organisation is operating. See page 129 in Unit 3 Introduction to Marketing.

1. Using the information above for inspiration list some social, technological and legal developments which might help the gaming industry in the UK.
2. Which of the points you have mentioned would you consider to be the most significant?
3. On balance, do you think organisations involved in the gaming industry can look forward to a period of growth, stability or decline?

## Thinking point

Produce a mind map to investigate marketing research objectives. Start with local, national and global companies, and then add branches for their products, before identifying marketing research objectives that you might want to investigate in respect of those products. Try to add further branches by highlighting the information you could collect about those objectives. Finally, add the primary and secondary research methods you might recommend to obtain the information. Information on how to produce a mind map can be found at www.mind-map.com.

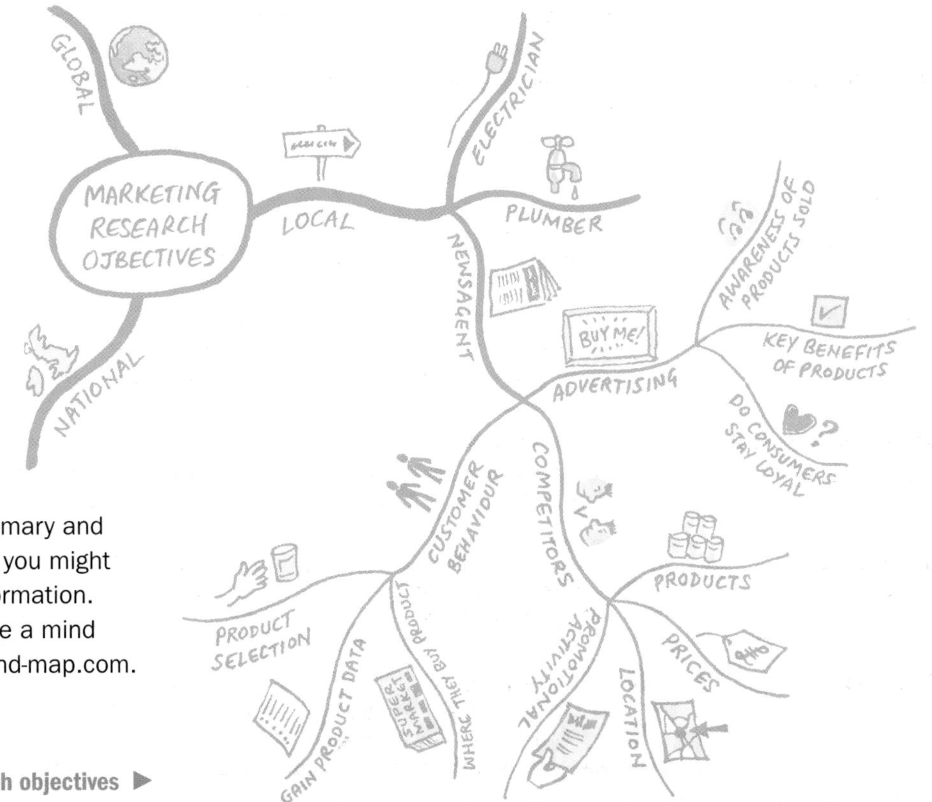


Mind map – marketing research objectives ▶

## Outcome activity 10.1

A key marketing research activity for Greggs plc is carrying out taste tests on potential new products. It also uses a range of other marketing research techniques, such as surveys and interviewing, to investigate other aspects of new product development, such as product names, appearance, price options and in-store display ideas. Reports from organisations such as Mintel are used to keep up to date with overall market developments.

Taste testing is a quantitative marketing research technique in which interviewers recruit people on the street and invite them to take part in the research. These tests can be used for tracking views on a product over time, assessing changes or improvements made to a product or gauging reaction to a new product. Participants are unaware of the identity of the brand being tested. People are then not influenced by their previous views on a brand. Participants are only asked to taste three products to ensure their taste buds are not overloaded.

**Pass**

Using the case study above, describe the main types of marketing research and how they have been used to make a marketing decision.

**Merit**

Explain the context in which different marketing research methods are appropriate.

## Grading tips

**Pass**

Describe the primary research methods and secondary research sources used by Greggs in their new product development programmes.

**Merit**

m1

Produce a table listing the majority of primary research methods and secondary research sources and the sort of marketing decisions for which they might provide useful data. See the table 'Marketing research objectives' on page 296 as a source of ideas.

## Planning stages

Professionally organised marketing research projects follow a number of stages. In order to ensure that a project is successful the following research stages should be followed.

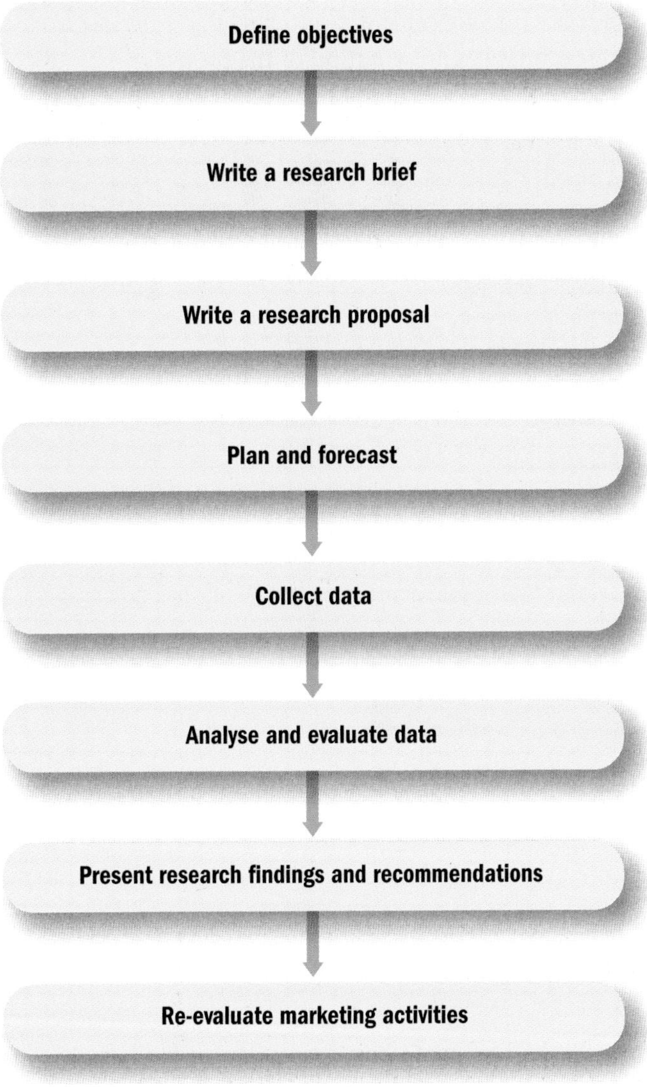


▲ Flow diagram to show planning stages for research

### Defining the issue and setting objectives

A vast number of marketing research objectives is possible. Defining the issue accurately is a very important step because organisations must guard against collecting inappropriate data. For example, a business may be experiencing falling sales but fail to notice there is a general fall in the demand for the product, and that this is the important issue. Instead it may believe that competitor activity is to blame and consequently make an investigation of the competition the objective of its marketing research. What it should have explored were the reasons for the overall market decline, and how the company could improve or introduce new products to stop the decline.

### The brief – planning data, types and target population

Once the marketing research objectives have been correctly determined then a research brief should be written. A written brief:

- provides a check that the data is genuinely needed
- checks the information collected will be useful for the decisions being considered
- ensures that the results of the project will be available when the key decisions have to be made.

During this stage an investigation should be undertaken to check whether the information is already available in the organisation. It often seems more exciting and interesting to develop new information than to delve through old files and reports. This stage also includes deciding details of the target population, planning the data to be collected – what and how it is to be collected – and the timings involved.

### Research brief

The format of a typical brief is shown below.

1. Background to organisation:
   Its products and its markets.
2. The project:
   The reason for the project being required (such as a need to evaluate new advertising idea)
   Decisions to be influenced by project results (such as whether to use magazines or radio in the promotional campaign)

3. Objectives:

   The precise information required (such as which idea is likely to be the most effective)

   Outline of the approach to be taken (such as whether to have a qualitative focus on a small number of people; or a quantitative focus on a large number of people)

4. Possible research methods:

   For example, whether a secondary research project, such as reading existing research reports, should be undertaken before deciding to authorise more expensive primary research such as focus groups

   The sampling options that could be used to ensure reliable and valid data will be collected; sampling (discussed in more detail later in this unit, see page 304) is concerned with how to select the people involved in the research project; it is not simply a case of interviewing people as they come along

5. Reporting and presentation requirements:

   Whether written or verbal reports are needed, and if any progress meetings are required during the project

6. Timing:

   The timescales for submission of the proposal and completion of the research

   The budget available for the project is rarely included within the brief. This is to ensure that the research is designed to meet the information needs of the organisation rather than the size of the budget available. However, it is probably sensible to indicate a maximum budget that the researcher should keep in mind when designing the research.

## Research proposal

The research manager should produce a research proposal to respond to the research brief. A fully completed proposal appears on page 302.

## Objectives, planning and forecasting

Several management tools can be used for planning and forecasting the research project. The most popular methods are Gantt charts and the critical path method (CPM). CPM is an approach that involves dividing the research project into parts and forecasting the time required to complete each activity. A Gantt chart is a form of table or flow chart that provides a diagrammatic representation of the project.

| Task | Week 1 | Week 2 | Week 3 | Week 4 | Week 5 | Week 6 |
|---|---|---|---|---|---|---|
| Plan project | | | | | | |
| Recruit consumers to be interviewed in their homes | | | | | | |
| Undertake interviews | | | | | | |
| Analyse data | | | | | | |
| Present information | | | | | | |

▲ Gantt chart used for planning and forecasting purposes

## Collection of data

Research projects generally collect both primary and secondary research, which may be internal as well as external.

## Analysis and evaluation of data

The analysis of qualitative data is conveyed typically through consumer comments and the thoughts of the researcher in a written or verbal format. It should not be presented in a statistical format.

Quantitative data produces statistics to describe trends and factors such as competition, market structure and consumer habits. It is normally presented using tables, charts and graphs produced using software such as Microsoft Excel.

## Presentation of research findings and recommendations

Most projects involve an oral presentation and written report. The quality of these is crucial as it is difficult for the organisation benefiting from the research to take the findings seriously if they are confusing, inaccurate or lack relevance to the key marketing decisions. A format for the written report can be viewed in the final section of this unit page 318.

### Practice point

Here are some findings from a research conducted on the MP3 player market. Draw up a list of recommendations you would make to a company thinking of entering the market. Is this a market which you would recommend a business enter?

| Marketing mix | Findings |
|---|---|
| Product | Current products – battery life too short<br>Screens scratch too easily<br>Very much a fashion accessory<br>Apple, Sony and Creative leading brands |
| Price | Most popular price points are around £80 and £150 |
| Place | Internet very popular place to purchase product<br>Discount retailers like Comet have significant sales |
| Promotion | Internet used to acquire information<br>Innovative promotion a key method of attracting attention of consumer<br>Word-of-mouth recommendation very important |

### Take it further

Design some PowerPoint slides to convey your ideas with prompt card notes.

Include your decision about whether or not you would recommend a company consider entering this market.

## Re-evaluation of marketing activities

In the light of the findings, the organisation benefiting from the research should re-evaluate the marketing activity it is currently undertaking and make considered changes. See the table below for examples of this.

| Research finding | Current activity | Revised activity |
|---|---|---|
| Promotional effectiveness could be improved | Using newspapers such as *The Mirror* | Use magazines such as *Hello* |
| Product looking old fashioned | Offering original size only | Introduce mini-sized version |
| Prices are too high | £1.75 each | Offer 15% extra free |
| Products are not widely available | Available in discount stores | Make available on Internet and in supermarkets |

# Research stages

On the following page is a fully completed research proposal which illustrates the stages of a marketing research project.

# RESEARCH PROPOSAL: Big Lick – An approach to entering the UK ice cream market

1. **Background to organisation**
   Big Lick is an ice cream company that has decided to launch one of its internationally successful brands in the UK. It does not have any production units of its own, but instead uses contract producers to make products it feels would have market appeal. This provides the company with the ability to satisfy consumer tastes and preferences whatever they might turn out to be.
2. **The project**
   Big Lick wants to gain a thorough understanding of the current trends in the UK ice cream market and the strengths and weaknesses of competition. It also needs a clear idea of what new products to consider introducing.
3. **Target Audience**
   Everybody enjoys ice cream and therefore every group in the population should be included in this project.
4. **Objectives and data to be collected**
   - Provide market size data for last five years in both terms of amount eaten and value of consumption.
   - Provide market share data for past three years showing and explaining shifting patterns.
   - Provide figure for the value of sales by category in recent years, including a forecast of likely consumption patterns.
   - Identify main competitors and provide an analysis of their approach to the marketing mix.
   - Provide a list of possible ice creams that would have appeal to UK consumers.
5. **Research methods and timing**
   - Undertake secondary, quantitative, external research to ascertain market size, market share, category sales and competition profiles by referring to company reports.
   - Undertake secondary, qualitative, external research to ascertain consumer opinions on ice cream by consulting market reports from organisations such as Mintel.
   - Explore further consumer tastes (such as flavours) and preferences (such as sizes) through qualitative primary research using focus groups and face-to-face interviews.
   - Respondents to be selected using the judgement sampling technique.*
6. **Reporting and presentation requirements**
   - Progress meeting 10.30am on 7 January at Big Lick main offices.
   - Preliminary results to be presented verbally 9.30am on Tuesday 4 February at Rapid Research Ltd, 45 Dovecote Lane, Beeston, Nottingham NG9 1HR.
   - Written report (six copies) to be delivered to Big Lick by 18 February.
7. **Fees**
   - Face-to-face interviews – 12 @ £450 each
   - Focus groups – two @ £1250 each
   - Mintel report purchase – Ice Creams - £4500
   - Internet searches – four hours @ £120 per hour
   - Company report appraisal – four hours @ £120 per hour
   - Other expenses including hotel accommodation and travel £1640
   - Total budget requirement £15,000
8. **Researchers**
   - Donna Hudson – worked for Rapid Research for three years; has been involved in work for Mars Confectionery and Crown paints.
   - Carlos Perreira – worked for Rapid Research for eight years completing research for organisations such as Citroën Cars and Holmes Place Leisure Centres.
9. **Contract terms and other points**
   - Payment seven days after receipt of written reports.
   - Research team only to discuss content or findings of project with Big Lick staff.

▲ Research proposal for Big Lick: an approach to entering the UK ice cream market

*Sampling is discussed on page 305

## Outcome activity 10.2

You work for Personal Portable Music in its Marketing Department. PPM has been producing successful electronic products for the last thirty years, including PCs, hi-fi's, radios, DVD players and personal stereo systems. At a recent board meeting it was decided that the company should look into the possibility of producing an MP3 player. The board feels that the future of personal portable music probably lies in this direction. It needs more market information to help the directors make their decisions. You have selected a marketing research company – Rapid Research – to help you complete the project.

**Pass**

Select an appropriate method of data collection and plan research for PPM. 

**Merit**

Explain the reasons for selecting the particular method of data collection. 

## Grading tips

**Pass** 

Write a research brief to help you clarify exactly what information you are hoping to obtain. Then write a research proposal which should show how the required information will be obtained. Guidance in writing both documents is provided in this section.

**Merit** m2

Use a table like the one below to match the research methods to the information requirements. Summarise your reasons for choosing these methods.

| Research method | Information to be obtained |
|---|---|
| Secondary (external) - Mintel Report | Estimates of market size and market share over last three years. Forecast sales by product category for next three years. |

# 10.3 Carry out simple research

This section explains how you can carry out some simple marketing research.

## Census or sample

Research involving everybody in a particular population is called a census. This is seldom possible because of the expense; they are only used when a market is very small, which can be a characteristic of some industrial markets. Consequently, samples are usually used when researching. In marketing terms, a sample means a small number of individuals who can give an insight into the views of a whole group.

### Sample size

There are three ways of determining sample size: by the budget available, by choosing the sample sizes used in previous studies or using a statistical method.

Frequently the sample size is determined by the amount of money that is available for the project. A marketing manager may declare that £17,500 is available to investigate a particular issue. After deducting the costs for such things as questionnaire design, and analysing the data, an amount would remain which could be spent on interviews. This is perhaps how a large number of research projects determine their sample sizes.

Many researchers will rely on past experience to determine an appropriate sample size. Previous studies investigating similar research objectives may guide the researcher.

The final method to determine a sample is to use a statistical technique. Statistical methods are only used to calculate the sample sizes for probability sampling methods. Statistical methods allow researchers to have confidence in the fact that results from a randomly selected sample are truly representative of the population being studied. The researcher can actually calculate the degree of confidence that can be applied to the results and the accuracy of the results can be expressed as a likely deviation from the final figure. For example, the researcher might have a high degree of confidence (such as 99%) in the result that showed the average young person eats 12 packets of crisps a week with an accuracy of plus or minus three packets.

The degree of confidence required from a sample and the level of accuracy thought appropriate can all be decided prior to the start of the research and the calculation of the required sample size.

## Choosing the sample

There are several ways of selecting a sample. Sampling methods can be grouped under two headings – probability and non-probability sampling. A respondent is somebody who is asked to participate in a marketing research project.

## Probability sampling

This method systematically selects people; the chances of somebody being selected could be expressed as a mathematical probability.

### Random sampling

Random sampling means all members of a population have a known and equal chance of being included in the sample. For example, the names of every household in a community could be written on slips of paper and the slips deposited in a box. The box could then be shaken so that the slips of paper become thoroughly mixed. Someone drawing out successive slips of paper would be taking a random sample of the households in that community.

The technique works well for small groups, but for larger ones the method is not appropriate, since it is difficult to obtain a list of all the members of the group.

### Systematic random sampling

Systematic sampling produces samples that are almost identical to those generated by simple random sampling. However, it is considered easier to implement, as it does not need to identify every member of the population individually. A random starting point may be generated, possibly by computer, and after that people are selected at regular intervals, say, every twenty-fifth person in the population. This method does require a full listing of the population in an appropriate random order, such as an alphabetic list.

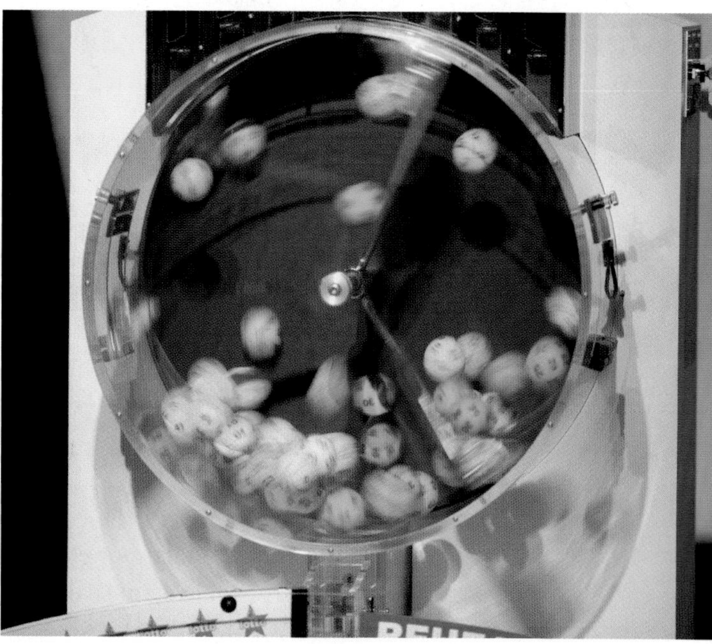

▲ Every number has an equal chance of selection

If the number of students in a class is 30 in total and it is decided to select every fifth student starting from the random number of 5 then students 5, 10, 15, 20, 25 and 30 would be selected for the sample.

## ■ Stratified random sampling

Stratified sampling takes into account that some customers are more important than others. It therefore weights the sample on the basis of the importance of each group of customers in the market.

If a business has 10,000 small users of products, accounting for sales of £1 million, 8000 medium users, accounting for £1 million, and 1000 large users, accounting for £2 million, a random sample of 200 would not be representative of the whole market. To make the sample representative, the large users should be allocated half of the sample because they make up half of the sales. A quarter of the sample should be allocated to medium and small user groups. The stratified random sample would have 100 large users, 50 medium users and 50 small users all randomly chosen from their respective categories.

## ■ Cluster sampling

Cluster sampling involves dividing the total population into separate groups that represent the population in microcosm; in other words, the cluster has the same characteristics as the total population. This means that each cluster group is the same, which is different from stratified groups where each group is very different. Once the clusters have been identified, then they are sampled in a random manner. Area sampling is a common use of this technique: areas are selected that possibly represent a region. The results would be expected to mirror the views of the whole nation.

## ■ Multi-stage sampling

Multi-stage sampling is used to reduce the cost of random sampling without losing the element of randomness. In the case of sampling UK households, at the first stage of the process a simple random sample may be taken of all parliamentary constituencies in the UK. For the constituencies selected, a list of wards is compiled and a simple random sample selected of wards within each constituency. At the third stage each ward could be divided into groups of streets known as polling areas, and a simple random sample taken of these streets. This means that there is no need for a complete list of everybody in the population. Another advantage of this method is that interviewing generally takes place in a confined geographical area. This reduces administration and travelling costs when the fieldwork is undertaken.

# Non-probability sampling

Probability sampling, if properly conducted, generally produces the best results; but it can be costly and time-consuming and in some situations it is difficult to identify a random sample. Under these circumstances non-probability sampling is used.

## ■ Quota sampling

This ensures that the proportions in a sample reflect the whole market. Quotas are identified on the basis of known features of the market under investigation. Dividing a market into age groups is a popular way to ensure that the characteristics of the sample reflect the features of the whole group. This prevents particular groups, such as older or younger people, from dominating a sample.

Because quotas can be selected from a relatively small geographical area they are cost-effective in gathering data. Anyone who refuses to participate can be replaced by someone else who fits the quota characteristics.

## ■ Judgement sampling

This involves researchers selecting the sample based on who they think will most likely reflect the views of the group to be interviewed. This method is used in research where a few large businesses dominate a market. All the major companies in a sector might be included, plus a sample of the smaller ones. The purpose is to weight the results with the views of the important members of the sample. For example, an investigation into the do-it-yourself retail market might include B&Q, Homebase and Wickes, plus a sample of all the smaller companies.

## ■ Convenience sampling

This uses no sample design. For example, when an interviewer questions people on the street, choice is left entirely to the interviewer. The sample is chosen on the basis of who can be contacted easily. Another example might be a business producing a prototype vacuum cleaner and asking some of its employees to test it in their own homes. Such a sample provides useful information as long as the sample seems to be reasonably representative of the likely customer. For example, asking pensioners about their holiday habits would not shed light on the habits of the nation.

## Implications of different methods

A comparison of sampling methods is shown in the table below.

| Probability sampling | Non-probability sampling |
|---|---|
| Results can be projected to represent the total population.<br>Results are clear and not in doubt.<br>Researchers can be sure of obtaining information from a representative group of the population being investigated.<br>Respondent selection and sample design significantly increase the cost and time. | Cost is significantly lower than probability sampling.<br>Sample sizes tend to be smaller.<br>Researchers can target important respondents.<br>The results reveal likely views.<br>Researcher does not know how representative the sample is of the population being investigated. |

### Cost and accuracy of information

The different sampling methods may be summarised regarding their accuracy and cost as shown in the following table.

| Sample selection method | Cost | Accuracy | Comments |
|---|---|---|---|
| Probability – random | Very high | Excellent | |
| Systematic random | High | Excellent | |
| Stratified | High | Good | |
| Multi-stage | Lower | Good | Cost-effective |
| Cluster | Lower | Good | Cost-effective |
| Quota | Lower | Good | Very popular method |
| Judgement | Lower | Reasonable | Appropriate for some markets |
| Convenience | Low | Questionable | |

### Practice point

Your school or college has decided to conduct a research project across the school or college. It wants all the groups that make up the education community to be involved. Explain three sampling methods which could be used.

### Take it further

Describe the strengths and limitations of the selected methods. Then recommend and justify the use of one method.

# Questionnaire

Questionnaires are used in a variety of contexts in marketing research. They can be the format used for conducting surveys including mail surveys, telephone interviews and formal structured personal interviews. The ways in which the questionnaire is constructed are broadly similar.

### Remember

A questionnaire is a data-collecting device. It formally sets out the way research questions should be asked.

### Design

Even the simplest questionnaires need careful wording and organisation to produce accurate information. Consideration needs to be given to the content, the phrasing of questions, the type of questions to be used, the layout and the sequence. Questionnaires should be tested – this is called piloting – before they are used. Effective questionnaires generally have the following design characteristics:

- They start with a statement about the reason for the survey, to put respondents at ease and reassure people it is not a selling activity.

- They provide example questions and answers at the beginning to show how the questionnaire should be completed.
- They avoid the use of jargon (such as 'cookie'), acronyms (such as 'BTEC') or complex language.
- Questions are phrased precisely.
- Questions do not ask for information outside the objectives of the research project.

## Questions to be asked

Three types of information can be gathered using questionnaires – facts, opinions and motives.

- Factual data can include information about age, gender or geographical location.
- Data about opinions can be very useful to decision-makers. It provides them with information about beliefs, attitudes, feelings and knowledge but the answers have to be treated with some caution as they will not be as reliable as factual data.
- Knowing people's motives for a particular action can be important to those wishing to influence them, such as advertisers. Analysis is inevitably **subjective** and can only deliver an impression rather than certainty about people's real motives.

### Key Terms

**Subjectivity** A feature of qualitative data analysis that means the research findings and conclusions are only the opinions that the researchers formed from the research.

## Types of questions

### Sequencing

The **sequencing** of questions is important. The early questions should attempt to create respondent interest, so that the respondent will continue. The questions should follow a logical order. Overall the questions should move from the general to the more detailed, and there should be a logical flow from question to question and from topic to topic. All questions relating to a particular topic should be asked before moving on to another topic. Questionnaires should be easy to use and encourage the user to answer the questions posed. Any potentially embarrassing or personal questions should be left until later in the questionnaire.

### Key Terms

**Sequencing** The careful ordering of questions to reduce the impact of bias as well as putting questions into a logical order to encourage completion.

### Dichotomous questions

Dichotomous questions are the simplest form of closed question as the respondent is limited to two fixed alternatives, as in the example below:

Have you downloaded music from iTunes? Yes/No

These sorts of questions do not provide much detail but are useful as screening questions to determine whether a respondent should be asked further questions on a particular subject

### Multiple-choice questions

Multiple-choice questions provide respondents with a choice of potential responses. The respondents are normally asked to tick one alternative that best matches their views. Such questions are difficult to design because the designer needs to know all the potential answers; however, other options can be accommodated by inserting 'Others (please specify)' as one of the options.

### Scaled questions

It is sometimes necessary to judge the strength of feeling about a topic. This requires the use of a rating or response scale question. There are various types; Likert scales, for example, show how strongly a respondent agrees or disagrees with a statement.

Semantic differential scales, as illustrated in question 3 of the sample questionnaire on the following page, use two key words describing the opposite ends of a scale, with a series of points highlighted between. Respondents are asked where on the scale their opinion lies.

# TELL US ABOUT YOUR PROGRAMME AND COLLEGE

This questionnaire will only take a few moments to complete

**Return to Student Services, Business College, Cardiff**

1 Please tick which compulsory unit is your favourite on the BTEC National Business programme:

Exploring business activity ☐

Effective people, communication and information ☐

Introduction to marketing ☐

Investigating business resources ☐

2 We would like to know your opinions on the following topics.

| | Strongly agree | Agree | Neither agree nor disagree | Disagree | Strongly disagree |
|---|---|---|---|---|---|
| This course has prepared me well for work | | | | | |
| Teachers prepared interesting lessons | | | | | |
| I was well prepared for my assignments | | | | | |
| The refectory food is good | | | | | |

3 Finally, tell us a little more about the refectory food. Place a circle on the scale below to express your views on the food in the refectory.

| | | | | | | |
|---|---|---|---|---|---|---|
| Good value | 1 | 2 | 3 | 4 | 5 | Poor value |
| Tasty | 1 | 2 | 3 | 4 | 5 | Tasteless |
| Plenty of choice | 1 | 2 | 3 | 4 | 5 | Limited choice |
| Satisfying | 1 | 2 | 3 | 4 | 5 | Unsatisfying |

▲ An example of a questionnaire

## Open-ended questions

Open questions invite respondents to offer their opinions and allow them to express themselves freely, possibly at length. They can lead to a wide variety of replies and can therefore be difficult to interpret. Such questions are simple to design and are often used where the researcher is not sure what the response is likely to be. An example of an open-ended question is:

What do you think about students having to pay university tuition fees?

### Length of questionnaire

If the topic being investigated is of genuine interest to the respondent they may well be prepared to complete a lengthy questionnaire. Postal surveys, where there is nobody encouraging completion, have to cover less ground. Good sequencing and easy-to-follow instructions will help.

Questionnaires should contain no more than 40 questions, but should be as short as practically possible. Questions towards the end of a survey may provoke hasty answers, producing inaccurate information. The use of **skip questioning**, where respondents are asked to skip certain questions on the basis of previous answers, can reduce the length of the questionnaire as it ensures people are asked only relevant questions.

## Key Terms

**Skip questions** These direct respondents to the questions they should answer.

## Practice point

Students are seen as important customers nowadays and are consequently asked about their learning experience and environment so it can be improved. Use the sample questionnaire on page 308 and pilot it with eight to ten students. Review the questionnaire and recommend any improvements based on the pilot.

## Take it further

Pick a question and rewrite it using another question method. Can you think of any additional questions which you feel could be included?

### Bias

Bias is defined as the difference between the answer obtained from respondents and the truth. The ordering of potential responses in a multiple-choice question is important as it can influence a respondent's choice, especially when they are slightly unsure of the answer. Research has shown that respondents are more likely to choose the answers at the beginning or end of a list rather than from the middle. To reduce the impact of this interviewers are asked to frequently rotate the sequence of questions.

Questions that may reveal the respondent in a poor light should be avoided, as many people will give an answer that they think will gain approval rather than the truthful answer. Questions that require an explanation also run the risk of introducing bias into the survey.

### Relevance

It is important that respondents are only asked questions that are relevant to them. Early questions may use the skip questions technique, determining which questions need to be answered by a respondent further into the questionnaire. If a viewer only has terrestrial television, skip questions can prevent them being asked about satellite channels. On completion of a skip question, respondents will typically be directed, for example: 'If you answered *no* go to Question 6. If you answered *yes* go to Question 7.'

### Encouraging response

Response rate is the number who participated in a research project compared with the total number of people approached. Answering a questionnaire requires a respondent to give time, attention and thought to a subject that, although of interest to the researcher, may not be of much interest to the respondent. The length should be kept to a minimum, although some topics will themselves maintain the respondent's interest longer than others.

Questions should be as easy for the respondent to understand and answer as possible: an uncertain respondent is more likely to terminate the interview. Explanations should be included to bridge any changes of question topic. A respondent who feels the overall content makes no sense is again more likely to cease cooperating. As far as possible, the format and type of question used should be made varied and interesting for the respondent.

A covering letter introducing and explaining the purpose of the questionnaire can influence the rate of response to postal surveys. Reminder letters to non-respondents can also gain more responses. Small incentives such as free entry to a prize draw often improve response rates.

### Pilot stage

If time and costs allow, questionnaires should be piloted with some respondents. Using the questionnaires with ten or twelve respondents should reveal any major problems. A pilot will help identify errors in the order of questions or the questions themselves. It will also indicate whether the questionnaire will meet the research objectives.

### Practice point

Design a questionnaire which your school or college could use to investigate what students think of the organisation. Try to use a variety of question types while also making it easy to analyse the answers. Remember to pilot the questionnaire with a few students.

### Take it further

Review the questions making appropriate changes. Adopting the judgement sampling method, use the questionnaire with 20 students and attempt some straightforward analysis.

▼ Piloting a quesionnaire will reveal any defects

## Outcome activity 10.3

Continue the assignment concerning Personal Portable Music Ltd from Outcome activity 10.2. You have been asked to gather the necessary information and present it verbally to the board.

**Pass**

Conduct both primary and secondary research using the sampling method mentioned in the research proposal.

**Distinction**

Evaluate the application of your selected research method and plan, make and justify recommendations for improvement.

## Grading tips

**Pass** p3

You will need to design a questionnaire if you are undertaking surveys such as telephone, postal, email or face-to-face interviews. Remember to pilot the questionnaire using the sample method outlined in your research proposal.

Review your marketing research proposal. You might alter the methods used – but remember to discuss the benefits of any recommendations. Then consider how you actually applied the proposal. For example, did the questionnaire work effectively and was the sampling method implemented properly? You should then make and justify some recommendations for improvement.

# 10.4 Interpret research findings

The communication of the research findings in the form of a written report or a verbal presentation is the culmination of the research project. This step is particularly important, as the clarity and the relevance of the findings are critical to the client's satisfaction with the marketing research project. A manager may question the overall value and accuracy of the research if it is presented in a confusing or hesitant manner.

## Statistical procedures

A variety of statistical procedures are available to help researchers draw conclusions from the findings of the research they have undertaken.

### Arithmetic mean

It is often useful to talk about an average, such as the number of customers served in a day or the average distanced travelled to deliver a product. The mean is the most commonly used average. To find the mean of a set of numbers, add them up and divide by the number of values in the set.

*Example:*
The number of customers visiting a store over 15 days was as follows (in units):
5, 6, 7, 9, 10, 5, 15, 7, 16, 10, 6, 9, 15, 8, 7.

$$\frac{\text{Sum of demand}}{\text{Number of days}} = \frac{135}{15} = 9$$

The mean daily demand is for 9 units.

## Median

The median is the middle value in a set of numbers. To find the median, place the numbers in order and find the middle value. This average has the advantage of not being affected by extreme numbers at either end of a set of numbers. It may be a more appropriate measure of an average where a few extreme values may impact adversely on the calculation of an arithmetic mean.

*Example:*
To find the median of the following values using the same store data:
5, 6, 7, 9, 10, 5, 15, 7, 16, 10, 6, 9, 15, 8, 7.

First put the values in order:
5, 5, 6, 6, 7, 7, 7, 8, 9, 9, 10, 10, 15, 15, 16.

Now select the middle value, in this case the eighth value. The median is 8.

## Mode

The mode is the value that occurs most frequently in a set of numbers. The mode has the unique characteristic for an average in that there can be any number of modes. If the price of a range of products is being examined, it is perfectly possible for a number of price points to be very popular with customers, such as £1.99, £3.99 and £9.99. The mode would highlight these important prices which both the mean and the median may fail to reveal.

*Example:*
Using the same store data the mode can be identified:

| Number of visitors | Number of days |
|---|---|
| 5 | 2 |
| 6 | 2 |
| 7 | 3 |
| 8 | 1 |
| 9 | 2 |
| 10 | 2 |
| 15 | 2 |
| 16 | 1 |

The mode is 7 visitors, because it is the value that occurs most frequently.

You might have noticed that, even though the same data has been used throughout the examples, on two occasions the average was 8 and on one it was 9.

## Range

It is sometimes useful to examine how spread out a set of numbers is. Identifying the range is probably the simplest measure, and is found by calculating the difference between the largest and smallest values in a range of numbers.

The extreme numbers in a set directly affect the range. The method could, for example, help to establish the price difference between the basic product and the super deluxe option – the difference between a standard class rail and a first-class rail ticket.

### Practice point

Find the mean, median, mode and range of the following numbers: 3, 4, 7, 7, 9, 12, 13, 16, and 31.

## Inter-quartile range

The inter-quartile range reduces the impact of any extreme values. It divides the data into quarters and disregards the lower and the highest quartiles. Therefore it only looks at the two central quartiles, which account for 50% of the values being analysed.

This can be shown by plotting a cumulative frequency distribution chart on a graph. The curve will always be 'S' shaped. The data is divided into quarters before calculating the inter-quartile range. This technique might be useful to analyse the amount of money spent by customers in a single transaction.

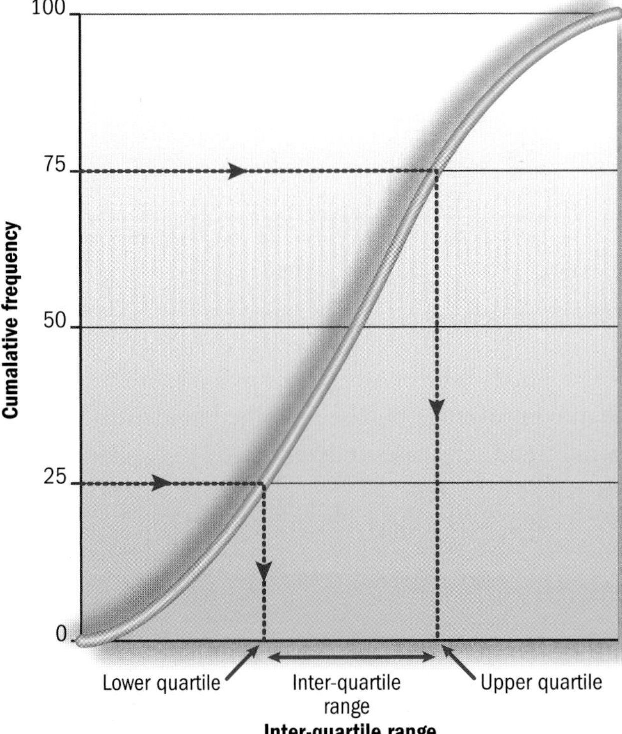


▲ Inter-quartile range

## Scatter diagrams

Scatter diagrams plot the **dependent variable** (such as sales) on the horizontal y-axis and the **independent variable** (such as advertising) on the vertical x-axis.

### Key Terms

**Dependent variable** Responds to the change in the other variable.

**Independent variable** Causes the change in the other variable.

Correlation refers to situations in which there is a relationship between the behaviour of two variables. When both variables are moving consistently in the same direction – for example, sales increase when more sales people are employed – there is a positive correlation.

When one variable moves consistently in the opposite direction to the other variable, so that as one falls the other rises, there is said to be a negative correlation. For example, as more shelf fillers are employed, the number of out-of-stock products reduces.

When there is no pattern to the relationship between two variables, there is said to be no correlation. This might occur, for example, if complaints were plotted against the number of customer care counters in a store.

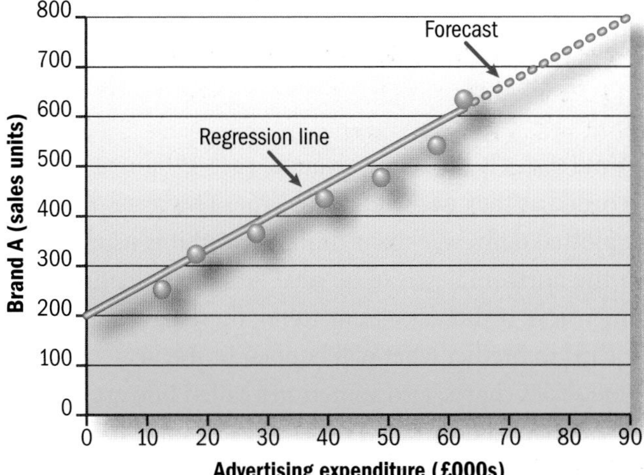


**1** Scatter diagram showing a positive correlation between advertising and brand sales

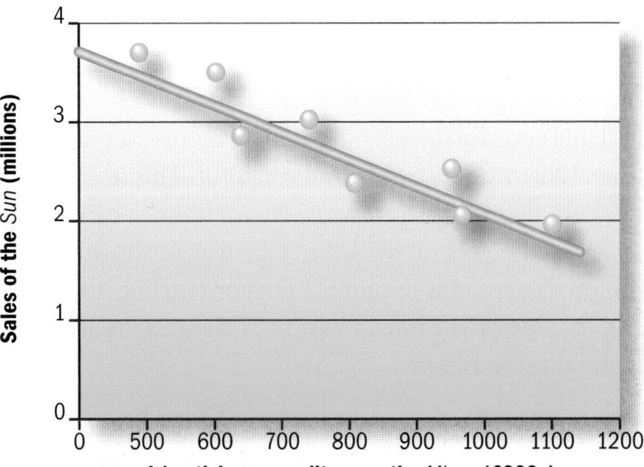


**2** Scatter diagram showing a negative correlation between advertising expenditure on the *Mirror* and sales of the *Sun*

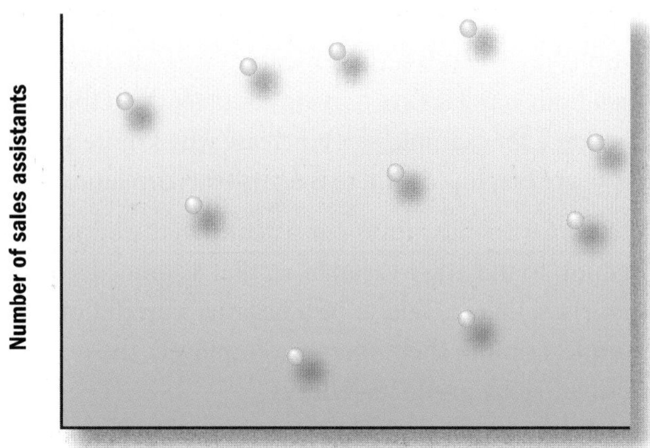

**3** Scatter diagram showing no correlation between complaints and number of sales assistants

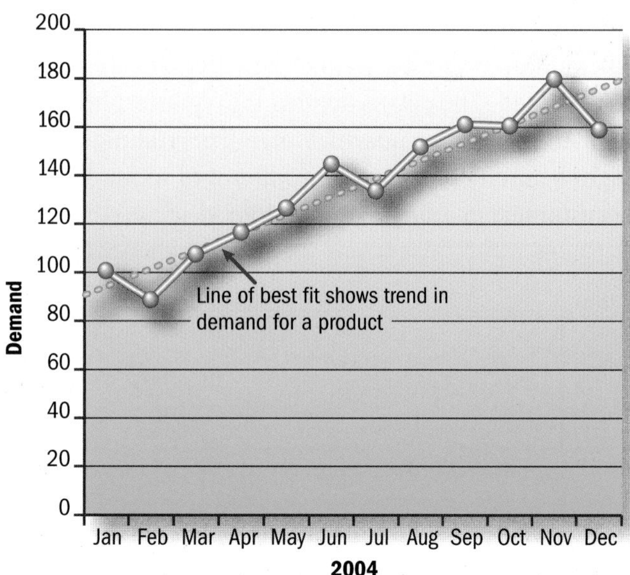

▲ **The trend in the demand for a product**

## Time series

A time series is the name given to a set of figures recorded as they occur through time. The series may be plotted daily, weekly or monthly, and it is usual for the horizontal axis to be used to denote the time dimension. If there is a clear trend, these figures can be used to predict what will happen in the near future. Time series charts, also sometimes called line graphs, can be used to illustrate a wide range of topics, such as change in incomes, interest rates, retail prices, growth of the economy and population.

## Trends

A trend is a general direction or tendency whereby a variable appears to rise, fall or fluctuate over a period of time. Illustrating a trend can be helpful. This involves smoothing out the short-term fluctuations in order to show a more general tendency. One way of showing the underlying trend is to plot the data onto a line graph and then draw 'the line of best fit'. This straight line highlights the trend.

This works well when sales are not affected by seasonal factors, as would be the case with toys where sales occur mainly in the last three months of the year. Sales that are affected by seasonal variations can, by calculating the moving average, still be examined to identify the overall trend. The case study on page 315 explains how this can be achieved.

## Use of spreadsheets for analysis

Microsoft Excel enables managers to quickly illustrate business trends diagrammatically. For example, if managers want to make a comparison between the market shares of different supermarket chains, this can be achieved graphically by using pie charts and bar charts.

In a pie chart each slice of the pie represents a component's contribution to the total amount. The 360° of the circle is divided up in proportion to the figures obtained. For example, if two firms have 50% of the market each, this would be represented in a pie chart by each firm's market share being allocated half of the pie, or 180°. An example can be seen later on page 320.

Bar charts are an easily understood way of presenting information that can be used to good effect in business. Bar charts are drawn against a horizontal 'y' axis describing the variables and a vertical 'x' axis showing value. The height of each bar corresponds to the value for each variable. An example can be seen on page 321.

## Case study

### Geezer Gas Ltd

A firm supplying gas for central heating faces high demand in autumn and winter and lower demand in spring and summer. In order to find out the long-term trend in demand for its product, the business needs to eliminate the seasonal variation from its demand. It does this by creating a moving average which smooths out demand for the four seasons of the year.

The first step is to calculate the average for the first group of four seasons. Then an average is taken for a second group of four seasons, starting with spring, and so on. The demand patterns and resulting moving averages are shown below.

| Year | Seasons | Demand for gas ($m^3$) | Moving average ($m^3$) |
|---|---|---|---|
| 2005 | Winter | 100 | |
| | Spring | 80 | |
| | Summer | 70 | |
| | Autumn | 90 | 85 |
| 2006 | Winter | 110 | 87.5 |
| | Spring | 90 | 90 |
| | Summer | 80 | 92.5 |
| | Autumn | 100 | 95 |

To identify the trend it is necessary to convert the moving averages to a trend value. This is created by calculating the centre value for the moving average of the first set of four values and the moving average for the second, third, fourth and fifth values as shown in the table below.

| Year | Seasons | Demand for gas ($m^3$) | Moving average ($m^3$) | Trend – centre of moving averages ($m^3$) |
|---|---|---|---|---|
| 2005 | Winter | 100 | | |
| | Spring | 80 | | |
| | Summer | 70 | | |
| | Autumn | 90 | 85 | |
| 2006 | Winter | 110 | 87.5 | 86.25 |
| | Spring | 90 | 90 | 88.75 |
| | Summer | 80 | 92.5 | 91.25 |
| | Autumn | 100 | 95 | 93.75 |

1. What is happening to the demand for gas? ✓
2. How would you react to this finding if you were the manager of Geezer Gas Ltd. ✓✓
3. What might you consider if the supply of the gas was limited? ✓✓✓
4. Make a prediction for sales over the next four seasons. ✓✓✓

## Practice point

Microsoft Excel can be used to analyse the market shares of soft drink categories:

- Click on the Microsoft Excel programme.
- A series of rows and columns will appear.
- Put in the heading, starting in cell 1A, 'Market shares of soft drink sectors – 2006'.
- Fill in the name of the sectors in the first column – Carbonates, Juice & juice drinks, Bottled water, Sports drinks, Energy and smoothies drinks.
- In the second column enter these figures: 54.5%, 19.8%, 19.4%, 3.1% and 3.2%.
- Now highlight this area of the table and using the mouse, go to the top of your window where you can see an icon that looks like a bar chart. Click on this to give you a list of options of different charts.
- Select pie chart and the type of pie chart that you want to illustrate. Print off the pie chart.
- Repeat the process, selecting bar chart and the type of bar chart that you want. Then print the bar chart.

Study the charts and list some market research findings.

## Appropriate uses of statistical procedures

The table shows how the different statistical procedures which we have considered might be used in business.

| Statistical procedure | Use |
|---|---|
| Mean | How much prices have been increased by competitors.<br>How many complaints are received in a week.<br>How many credit card transactions are processed each day. |
| Median | Same uses as above, but with any high and low numbers eliminated. |
| Mode | Identifying the most popular price points for a range of products.<br>The amount of money generally spent by consumers.<br>For forecasting sales in future weeks. |
| Range | Difference between the prices for standard and best seats at a concert.<br>Time spent by consumers shopping in a shopping mall.<br>Difference between best and weakest sales person. |
| Inter-quartile range | Time taken for customer to be served.<br>Days taken to resolve customer complaints.<br>Amount of money spent by the majority of consumers on their store cards during a year. |
| Scatter diagram | Response of sales to amount of shelf space allocated to a product.<br>Changes in demand to alterations in credit card interest rates.<br>Impact on sales as customer incomes rise or fall. |
| Time series and trends | To help determine products that should be dropped from range.<br>To set targets for the sales team over the coming month.<br>To suggest products that would benefit from promotional activity. |

# Presentation of findings

You will have to undertake a verbal presentation as part of your assignment. This section will provide valuable advice about presentations and general methods of presenting findings.

## Oral reports

Making an effective oral presentation is sometimes seen as more difficult than writing a report because of the direct interaction with the audience. Therefore it is essential to plan carefully for an oral presentation.

The basic structure for a presentation should be as follows:

1. Introduction
   Thank the audience for attending.
   Introduce the people involved in the presentation.
   Explain the format and structure of the presentation.
   Explain the reason for the study and the objectives of the project.
2. Methodology
   Give a brief description of the methodology including the data collection method, sampling technique used and timescales.
3. Key findings
   Give a brief description of the findings that are relevant to the objectives of the study, supported by graphs and tables.
   Organise the material into sections, perhaps reflecting the research objectives, to make it easier for the audience to absorb the information.
4. Conclusions and recommendations
   Emphasise the key points to emerge from the

research and their implications for decision-making. Highlight any recommendations.

5. Questions
   Invite questions and comments from the audience.

A wide range of software packages, such as Microsoft's PowerPoint, are now available to enable researchers to make high-quality, computer-aided presentations or professional-quality overheads.

A number of basic guidelines should be followed when giving an oral report:

- Check the facilities available for the presentation beforehand.
- Whatever technology and software packages are being used, always ensure that the facilities and layout of the room are compatible with them.
- Maintain eye contact with the audience and do not simply read notes or stare at a screen.
- Keep the attention of the audience by ensuring there is variety in terms of the tone and pitch of your voice, visual aids and activities.
- Keep the message simple – use visuals aids as prompts and not as a substitute for the researcher's script.
- Check understanding throughout the presentation, perhaps using question and answer sessions – finding out at the end that the audience has misunderstood is too late.
- Provide handouts to save the audience taking notes, which also allows them to pay attention and to participate fully.
- Stay calm and act naturally – this will give the impression of confidence and trustworthiness.
- Rehearse to check the timings of the presentation and practise speaking effectively.
- Clarify questions before answering them.

### Thinking point

You have been asked to present a verbal marketing research report to a new client at a hotel near their head office. Produce a checklist you can use when you visit the hotel to review the facilities available.

▼ Keep your message simple, otherwise you risk boring the audience

## The research report

**Title page**
Title, client, research organisation, date

**List of contents**
A detailed, numbered guide to the report sections, followed by a list of graphs and statistical tables

**Preface**
An outline of agreed research brief, followed by a statement of objectives and methods of research undertaken

**Summary of conclusions and recommendations**
A summary of main findings, sometimes accompanied by some creative interpretation in the form of recommendations

**Research method**
Procedures used to collect information – where, how and from whom, and techniques used in analysis; the characteristics and size of the sample should be recorded

**Research findings**
The main body of the report, commenting on the findings in detail; emphasis should be on ease of understanding and logical presentation for the reader

**Conclusions**
Even though the findings may speak for themselves, it is helpful to bring them together in a conclusion relating them to the objectives of the research

**Appendices**
Any detailed or technical matter that is essential to a full understanding of the research report, for example a copy of the questionnaire used

### Written reports – formal and informal

Above is a typical format for a formal written research report.

Informal reports tend to have fewer sections and generally only include the sections – introduction, findings and conclusions. They will normally be shorter, and must be concise and precise. They might well be used to publish preliminary results for a research project or for a progress report during a lengthy programme of research activity.

### Visual aids

In both oral presentations and written reports, computer graphics, graphs and charts can help understanding by communicating information in a very succinct and effective manner. They can also maintain the interest of the audience by providing breaks from blocks of text or speech.

Too many visual aids, however, can become distracting and often boring. They should therefore only be used to clarify and reinforce a point, when they can serve a real and necessary purpose. There are numerous ways that computer graphics, graphs and charts can be produced and used, while graphical presentation can also be combined with text detailing key points.

### Conclusions and recommendations

The presentation of the conclusions and recommendations drawn by the researcher from the research results, within a written report or a verbal presentation, is the culmination of the research project. This step is particularly important, as the clarity and the relevance of the conclusions and recommendations provide a lasting impression of the quality of the research long after the project is finished.

### Audience

When presenting the report the researcher should remember the following points:

- The report should be of a suitable length, clear and relevant to the research objectives.

- The research findings should be related to the marketing decisions being considered.
- The audience will be interested in the implications of the findings for their own organisation.
- The audience will need to be convinced that the information being presented is accurate. They will want to see charts, tables and actual respondent quotes that support the findings. Researchers should think about the likely questions from the audience and answer them before they are even asked.
- Irrespective of the length of the presentation or report, there should be a summary of the key points.
- The conclusion needs to suggest what should happen next and any issues that demand further investigation.

Managers may return to read the report at a later date, so the report needs to be easily understood months later; and the findings and recommendations need to be understood by people who had no previous connection with the report.

### Effectiveness and quality of information

A number of issues may compromise the quality of the information being given to the audience and the effectiveness of a report or presentation. For example:

- Some researchers present tables and graphs with very little commentary on how the figures should be interpreted. The researcher may simply display the data and repeat the numbers shown. It can be very tedious for an audience to see page after page of data without any explanation of what the figures mean.
- Exceedingly long reports or presentations can mean key points get lost in the detail and the results are devalued.
- Unrealistic recommendations, for example ones that are beyond the financial capabilities of the client or do not fit with their overall corporate objectives, will be of no use to the client.
- Charts for an oral presentation that are very eye catching and colourful may fail to communicate information because clients may get distracted by the visual aspects and so miss the key points.

Therefore care must be taken so that the message of the research does not get obscured by the means of presentation.

## Diagrammatic analysis and presentation

Graphs and charts can help understanding by communicating information in a very succinct and effective manner. They can also maintain the interest of the audience by providing breaks from blocks of text or speech. This section considers a number of popular diagrammatical techniques.

### Pictograms

A pictogram is a special type of bar chart that uses pictures of the items it is connected with, such as boats, tickets or money, rather than bars (see the diagram on page 320).

### Pie chart

Pie charts show a total figure split into various categories (see the diagram on page 320). For example, if we wished to show how different market segments share total sales, the whole pie would represent total sales and each segment would show how much of the total was sold in each market segment.

### Bar chart

A bar chart consists of a series of bars, positioned horizontally or vertically, to represent the values of a variety of items (see the diagram on page 321).

Bar charts are used to compare data totals. A multiple bar chart shows different data side by side. For example, if you wanted to compare sales for different years, a multiple bar chart would be a good way.

A stacked bar chart shows the data stacked on top of each other. The advantage of this is that you can see the relevant total (for example sales) by noting the height of each bar. The sections that make up a stacked bar are normally shaded so that each individual section can be identified easily.

## Practice point

Urban Headgear Ltd produces beanie hats, baseball caps and sun hats. The sales team are competing for a special bonus based on the number of products sold during a month. The pictogram below shows the performance of the sales team after two weeks.

1. Which member of the team looks likely to win the special bonus?
2. Which member of the team perhaps needs more training?

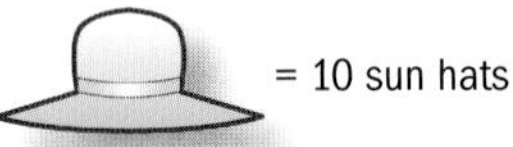

= 10 sun hats

= 10 beanie hats

= 10 baseball caps

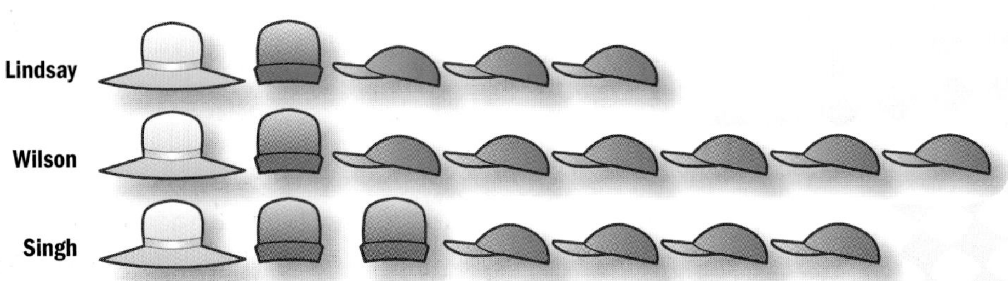


▲ Pictogram to show the performance of the sales team after two weeks

## Practice point

The pie chart shows the proportion of sales accounted for by beanie hats, sunhats and baseball caps for Urban Headgear Ltd.

1. Which product type would you select for further new product development? Explain your selection.
2. Which product type would you select for a discount promotion? Why?

Sun hats 15%

Baseball caps 65%

Beanie hats 20%

Pie chart to show sales of beanie hats, baseball caps and sun hats ▶

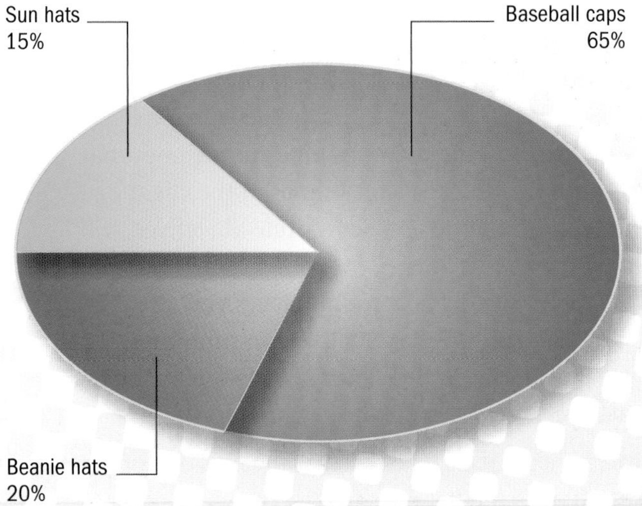

## Practice point

The bar chart below shows how many of each product each sales person has sold.

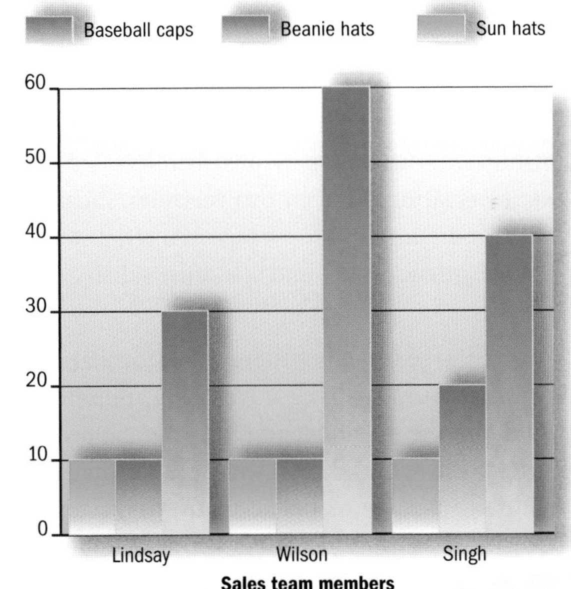


▲ Bar chart to show sales by sales team member and by product

1. Which member of the sales team may require further training in baseball cap product features?
2. Which member of the team has been the most successful in selling sun hats?

## Frequency curves and histograms

The table below shows the size of hat orders, in units, taken by the Urban Headgear Ltd sales team, expressed in a frequency distribution table.

| Order size | Frequency |
|---|---|
| Less than 5 | 1 |
| 5 and less than 10 | 10 |
| 10 and less than 15 | 25 |
| 15 and less than 20 | 16 |
| 20 and less than 25 | 5 |
| 25 and less than 30 | 1 |

A histogram is a graphical representation of a frequency distribution table. The graph below shows the 'size of hat orders' frequency distribution table expressed as a histogram.

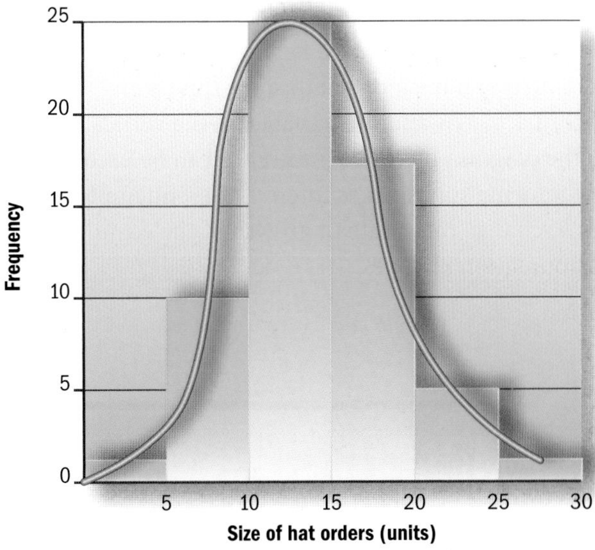


▲ Frequency distribution table expressed as a histogram

A curve joining the mid-points of the tops of the rectangles of a histogram is called the frequency curve.

## Thinking point

Consider the information on hat orders above. If you showed the diagram at a sales meeting, what order size might management wish to encourage through offering a special discount?

## Remember

Bar charts and histograms can look very similar, however they do have quite different features.

| Bar charts | Histograms |
|---|---|
| Gaps between bars | No gaps between bars |
| Bars are of equal width | Width of bars can vary |
| **Length** of bar represents frequency | **Area** of bar represents frequency |
| Separate categories on horizontal axis (e.g. countries, products) | Continuous scale on horizontal axis (e.g. age, opening hours) |

## Line graphs

Line graphs are particularly useful in showing how values or quantities rise and fall over a period of time. On a line graph it is normal to show time along the horizontal 'y' axis and the variable on the vertical 'x' axis (see the diagram below). Line graphs can be used to show information, such as interest rates, unemployment rates, exchange rates, rate of growth of the economy and population changes.

### Remember

Line graphs are sometimes also called time series charts.

Line graphs can also be used to make comparisons between two or more sets of observations. They are particularly useful for identifying patterns and trends in data such as seasonal effects (more sales in winter) and turning points (when sales growth weakens).

## Scatter diagrms

Scatter diagrams are useful for examining statistical relationships. Marketers are frequently interested in the degree of association between two variables, such as advertising and sales, square footage of a retail store and sales, average queue length and customer satisfaction levels.

If you wanted to see whether there was a correlation between the amount spent on advertising and sales, you would plot the data on a graph. If there appears to be a strong positive correlation we could say that there appears to be a strong link between advertising and sales – the more we advertise the more we sell.

### Practice point

The line graph shows the sales of each product over the month of a promotion.

1. What change of approach did the sales team adopt near to the end of the promotion?
2. What changes should the sales manager have considered after week 2 of the promotion?

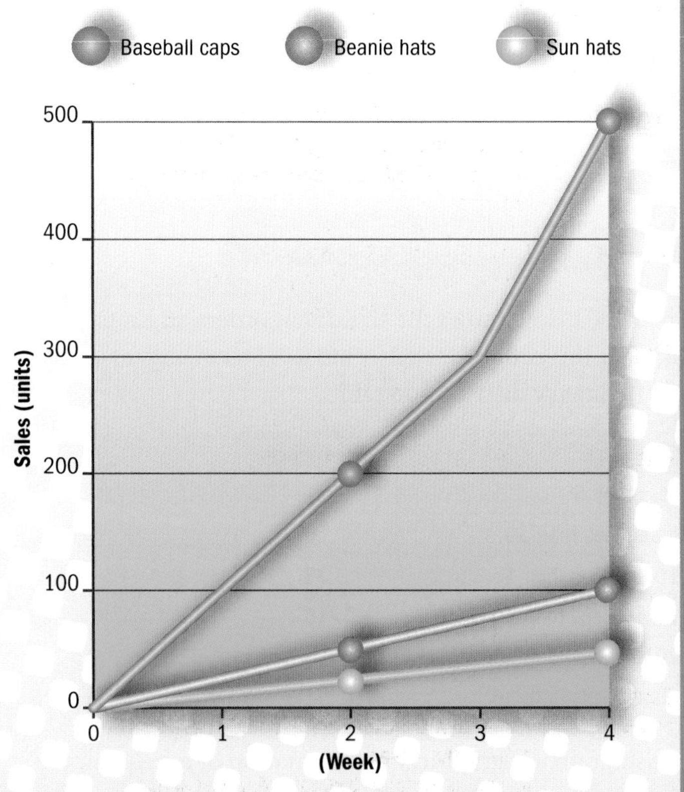


Line graph to show sales by product over the period of a special bonus ▶

## Practice point

The scatter diagram plots sales of sunhats and hours of daily sunshine.

1. What is this correlation called?
2. What are the implications of this data for a marketing manager contemplating using further special bonus schemes to boost the sales team's performance?

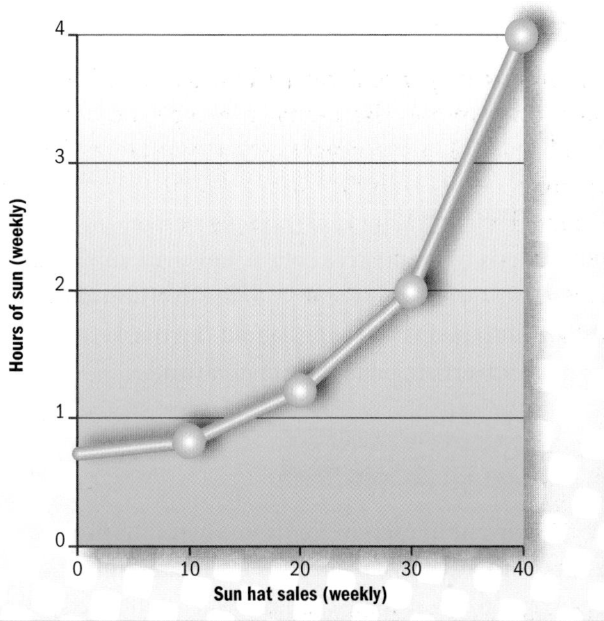


Scatter diagram to show sales of sunhats plotted against hours of daily sunshine ▶

## Appropriate use of techniques

The following table lists the different methods of diagrammatic analysis and presentation, and shows examples for each technique.

| Techniques | Appropriate uses |
|---|---|
| Pie chart | Market shares of major competitors<br>Sales from different regions of the country<br>Orders received from different international markets |
| Bar chart | Sales in a market by segment<br>Orders received for most popular products<br>Number of stores by size |
| Frequency curves | Value of purchases by customer<br>Time spent in store by consumers<br>Delivery distances of customer orders |
| Histogram | Sales analysed by opening hours<br>Number of customers moving through checkout each hour<br>Number of purchases by price ranges |
| Line graph | Sales over five years<br>Advertising money spent over twelve months<br>Average order value over two years |
| Scatter diagrams | Response of sales to advertising expenditure<br>Lengths of checkout queues and customer satisfaction levels<br>Impact of temperature on swimwear sales |

## Thinking point

Marketing research presentations can also incorporate the diagrams associated with marketing analytical techniques such as the product life cycle, Boston Consulting Group matrix and Porter's Five Forces. These techniques were discussed in some detail in Unit 3 Introduction to Marketing. What might be the advantages and disadvantages of using such diagrams in a presentation?

## Interpretation of results

The interpretation of quantitative data involves examining statistics. Interpretation should draw out the implications of the data for management. While the underlying statistics are not open to subjective interpretation, the conclusions and implications for management could be.

The first step in interpreting results is to go through the evidence presented, looking at the statistics. What do the statistics indicate about the characteristics of the market?

The purpose of the analysis is to uncover the relevance and significance of the data. For example, there may be trends or new factors in the competition (such as a new newspaper being launched like *Metro*), market structure (such as growth in daily free newspapers) and consumer habits (such as the growth in consumption of convenience meals).

The analysis of qualitative data is, however, subjective and impressionistic. It conveys to the decision-maker insights into people's feelings about the market, the product, advertising and customer attitudes

## Limitations of research

It is important to exercise caution when interpreting results and drawing conclusions from data, since they relate only to the sample. The more carefully the sample size and composition have been selected, the more valuable the final data; but the results can only ever be used as a guide for decision-making. There will be a certain amount of statistical error in any results and therefore in the conclusions drawn from those results. However, as long as marketing managers use their common sense, valuable messages can still be drawn from marketing research.

## Customer databases

In the past, managers often had difficulty in gathering sufficient information to make sound decisions. Today's problems relate more to the filtering of relevant data from the explosion of information which is available in a wide range of formats from a wide range of sources. These sources may be internal to the organisation, coming from customer databases and electronic barcode scanning devices, or external – from the Internet or marketing research sources.

More information does not always mean better decision-making. It is important that the amount of information presented to the decision-maker is kept to a manageable scale. Therefore managers need to be specific about the information they need. The fact that market researchers can draw information from a number of sources does mean, however, that the reliability of the data can be confirmed by reference to other sources.

## E-business feedback

Nearly all Internet selling sites offer the consumer the chance to contact the organisation generally by email. This has resulted in organisations receiving vast amounts of information from customers as organisations have become more accessible. Customer comments, complaints or simple enquiries, were traditionally considered to be a valuable source of marketing research data; but the volume of data now being generated is proving difficult to cope with, process and analyse. The electronic collection of data through loyalty cards and the use of computers has enabled organisations to analyse vast amounts of consumer data. However, managers have reported that decisions are being delayed as a result of the huge amount of information available to them. In addition, a substantial amount of time is being wasted collecting and searching for relevant information.

## Reliability of sample and accuracy

Any sample must be as representative as possible of the group being investigated. It must also be chosen in such a way as to minimise the risk of sampling error.

The sampling error of a statistic is the difference between the figure arrived at from the sample and the figure for the whole population. So if we were seeking the average loan taken out by customers, the sampling error would be the difference between the average loan of the sample and the average loan for all customers.

Some samples will only have a small sampling error – in other words they will produce an estimate close to the population average. Other samples will show a large sampling error, and it is therefore important to realise that even when the best sampling methods are used, there will always be the potential for error.

## Bias

Interviewer bias can be a problem if interviewers are allowed to influence answers. This can happen when questions have to be explained to the respondent, as the interviewer will be offering an interpretation. It can be an issue when controversial topics are being investigated; it is now common practice to screen interviewers to ensure they do not hold strong views concerning the issue being researched, such as smoking, drinking and moral conduct.

Bias can also arise when interviewers are asked to approach potential respondents of a particular age group. For example, in a quota of 20- to 30-year-old women there will be a disproportionate number of 24- to 26-year-olds, because it is more difficult to judge the age of those close to either 20 or 30. There is also a tendency to approach friendly, happy-looking, attractive people, who may have different views and opinions from others.

Questionnaire bias can be minimised by paying particular attention to the sequence and the wording of questions. The questionnaire should make it easy for the respondent to answer truthfully and care must be taken to avoid questions or words that may lead the respondent into giving answers that do not reflect their true opinions.

## Subjectivity

Group discussions and face-to-face interviews are the most common ways to collect qualitative data. In each case it is normally the person who was responsible for the collection of the information, the interviewer, who carries out the analysis. The analysis of qualitative data is subjective and impressionistic. How good the analysis and interpretation of qualitative data is depends on the individual who undertakes both the conduct of the research and the analysis.

Quantitative data may be less liable to the problems of subjectivity, but interpretation still needs to draw out the impact of the data for the organisation. So, while the underlying statistics are not open to subjective interpretation, the conclusions and implications drawn from them might be.

## Outcome activity 10.4

Continue the assignment concerning Personal Portable Music Ltd from Outcome activities 10.2 and 10.3.

**Pass**

Interpret the findings from your research and present them clearly in an appropriate format.

**Merit**

Analyse your own research and findings and make recommendations on how marketing strategies could be adapted.

**Distinction**

Evaluate the findings from the research undertaken.

## Grading tips

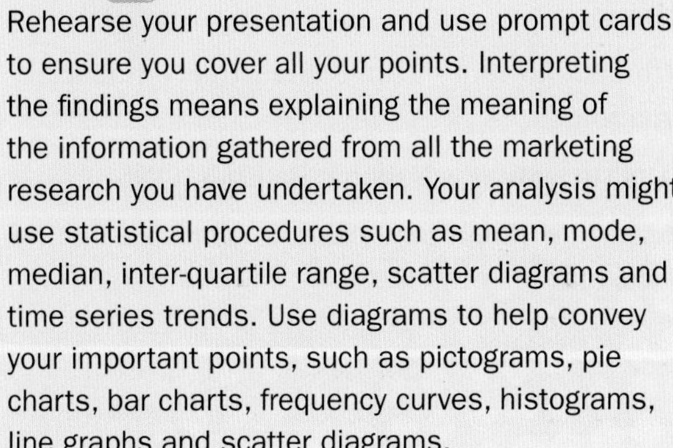

**Pass** p4

Rehearse your presentation and use prompt cards to ensure you cover all your points. Interpreting the findings means explaining the meaning of the information gathered from all the marketing research you have undertaken. Your analysis might use statistical procedures such as mean, mode, median, inter-quartile range, scatter diagrams and time series trends. Use diagrams to help convey your important points, such as pictograms, pie charts, bar charts, frequency curves, histograms, line graphs and scatter diagrams.

**Merit** m3

To obtain a merit grade you need to present a number of findings with comments on their implications for Personal Portable Music Ltd.

**Distinction** 

Refer to your research proposal. How well did the research address the project objectives and how well did it help in the development of a future strategy?

## End of unit test

1. What is the purpose of marketing research?
2. Explain the difference between primary and secondary research?
3. Describe three advantages of face-to-face interviews.
4. When can secondary research be very useful?
5. What sort of topics can be effectively explored using the Delphi technique?
6. Explain the difference between quantitative and qualitative research.
7. Draw a flow diagram to show the marketing research stages.
8. Describe the sections of a marketing research proposal.
9. Describe three features of probability sampling.
10. Design a scaled question to investigate people's opinions of the local bus service.
11. Explain the unique characteristic of the mode.
12. What is the advantage of using diagrams in a presentation?
13. What can a line graph be used to illustrate?
14. Describe the basic structure of an oral presentation.
15. Produce a list of guidelines to follow when giving an oral presentation

# Resources

www.mintel.com – Mintel market research reports

www.thomson.com – DataStream – company financial information

http://bduk.dnb.com – Dun & Bradstreet – financial information

www.statistics.gov.uk – National Statistics (ONS)

www.europa.eu.int/comm/eurostat – European Union statistical office

www.carol.co.uk – Company annual reports online

www.keynote.co.uk – market research reports

www.datamonitor.com – Datamonitor – business intelligence

# Books

Proctor, T. 2005 *Essentials of Marketing Research,* FT Research Hall

| Grading criteria | Outcome activity | Page number |
|---|---|---|
| To achieve a pass grade the evidence must show that the learner is able to: | | |
| **P1** Describe the main types of marketing research and how they have been used to make a marketing decision in a given situation | 10.1 | 298 |
| **P2** Select an appropriate method of data collection and plan research for a selected product/service | 10.2 | 303 |
| **P3** Conduct primary and secondary research, making use of an identifiable sampling method | 10.3 | 311 |
| **P4** Interpret findings from the research and present them clearly in an appropriate format | 10.4 | 325 |
| To achieve a merit grade the evidence must show that, in addition to the pass criteria, the learner is able to: | | |
| **M1** Explain the context in which different marketing research methods are appropriate | 10.1 | 298 |
| **M2** Explain the reasons for selecting the particular method of data collection for a selected product/service | 10.2 | 303 |
| **M3** Analyse own research and findings and make recommendations on how marketing strategies could be adapted | 10.4 | 325 |
| To achieve a distinction grade the evidence must show that, in addition to the pass and merit criteria, the learner is able to: | | |
| **D1** Evaluate the application of a selected research method and plan, make and justify recommendations for improvement | 10.3 | 311 |
| **D2** Evaluate the findings from the research undertaken | 10.4 | 325 |

# 13 Investigating recruitment and selection

## Introduction

Recruitment and selection describes the process that organisations follow to attract people to work for them so they can choose the best person for the job. It is important that a business gets this right so that they employ people who will be happy and work hard.

This unit goes through the stages of recruitment and selection. You will learn about the processes involved before a vacancy is advertised and the reasons why a business might need to recruit additional staff. You will learn the difference between vacancies that are advertised inside the business and those outside the business. As part of this process you will become familiar with the different paperwork that is involved in the process and how the selection of candidates happens at each stage, from the application form through to a selection interview where the successful person is offered the job.

Recruitment and selection must comply with legislation from the UK and EU so you need to be aware of different laws that have been brought into force and the effect they have on recruitment, for example equal opportunities and the minimum wage. You will be given an insight into some of the ethical issues that relate to recruitment and selection, such as making sure every candidate is asked the same questions to ensure that everyone is treated equally.

### What you need to learn

On completion of this unit you should:

1. Understand the processes involved in recruitment planning
2. Know the documentation involved in the recruitment process
3. Be able to participate in a selection interview
4. Understand the implications of the regulatory framework on the process of recruitment and selection.

## Consider this

Think about how you have found and applied for part-time jobs or work experience placements: maybe through a friend, an advert in a shop window, the local paper or online. Consider how you actually sent the information to the employer – did you go in person, send a letter or an application form or apply online?

What happened next? How did you communicate with the employer – was the interview by phone or in person, did you have to do any tests or other activities? What happened in the interview situation – what sort of questions did you have to answer, how long did it last, was there more than one? Finally, how did you find out the result? How long was it from when the process began until you started the job?

Draw the process that you followed as a flow chart or diagram and in small groups compare your results. Then add time labels to your diagram showing the number of days for each stage of the process. Which vacancies took longest to recruit for?

- Are there things that are the same in all of the processes?
- Are there any differences?
- Why are they different?
- Is there a minimum number of processes that must take place?

Keep your flow chart or diagram until you have finished the unit.

The first stage of recruitment that you may be aware of is as an **applicant**. This is after the organisation has placed the advertisement (and you have applied for it) but a lot of work happens before this stage. Part of recruitment planning involves the organisation working out if they need to recruit anyone at all. There may be lots of reasons why an organisation may think about recruiting. The organisation will then need to consider whether to **recruit internally** or **externally** and how that process is going to take place. You will need to be aware of the different possible methods and influences on which choices an organisation makes.

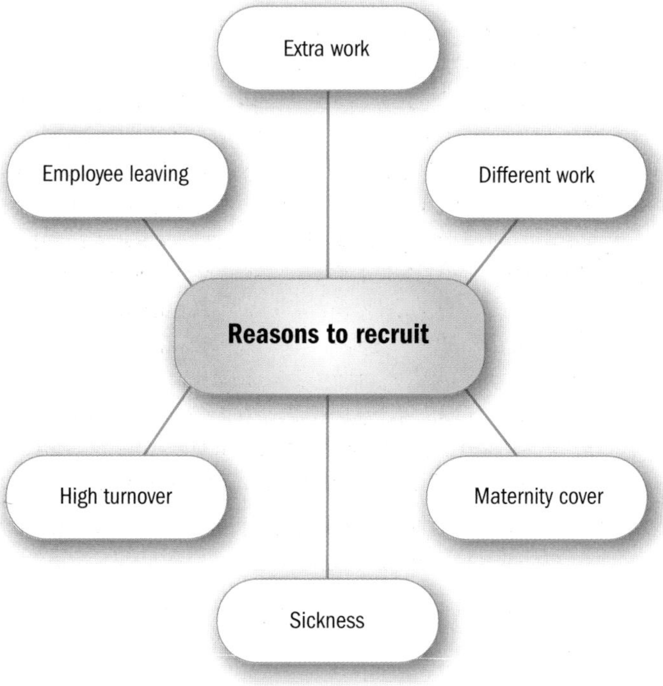

### Key Terms

**Applicant** The person applying for a job.

**External recruitment** Recruiting outside the business.

**Internal recruitment** Recruiting someone who already works for the business to do a different job.

Reasons to recruit

- Extra work
- Employee leaving
- Different work
- High turnover
- Maternity cover
- Sickness

▲ Different reasons to recruit

## Recruitment planning

There are many different reasons for an organisation to recruit someone. One of the most common reasons is that an employee is leaving to go and work for another organisation and their position needs to be filled. There are many other reasons and these are shown in the diagram.

### Key Terms

**Temporary** For a limited amount of time specified, e.g. a month or a year.

**Permanent** The person is to be employed until that person decides to leave or the job ceases to exist.

### Reasons for a vacancy

As you have seen there are many reasons why there might be a vacancy, including that an employee is leaving and must be replaced. The person being recruited for the vacancy may be needed to work on a **temporary** or **permanent** basis. Also, a person may be recruited to cover another employee when they go on maternity leave, or if they are ill for a long time, and their work needs to be done by someone else. This work would be as part of a temporary contract. Sometimes vacancies happen because the business has more work or is expanding, perhaps to another country or area. The organisation would require additional employees and would have to provide resources and training for them.

## Case study

### Jet2.com

Jet2 is an expanding airline business in the north east of England. It was voted Best Short Haul Airline in the Guardian and Observer Travel Awards 2006. As a result of increasing the number of flights and destinations, Jet2 needed to recruit an additional 200 staff during Spring 2007. Jet2 was flying to more destinations in Spain as well as maintaining its existing flights to countries such as Poland and Holland. These employees were used to help look after extra customers flying on extra planes purchased by the company. Newcastle Airport was servicing some of these additional flights to offer more choice to people flying from the local area, so may also need to recruit additional staff as well to cope with the increasing demand for airport services in the future.

1. Which types of vacancy might Jet2 recruit for as a result of the expansion? ✓

▲ Jet 2 is expanding

2. What might happen to Jet2 if it could not recruit the right people? ✓
3. What effect did Jet2 have on Newcastle Airport? ✓
4. What are the advantages and disadvantages of Jet2's recruitment for the people of Newcastle? ✓✓
5. Discuss the effects of this recruitment on the local area. ✓✓✓

Organisations are changing as well as expanding so, although the volume of work may not be going up, the type of work that is needed may be changing which means new staff have to be recruited. For example, in supermarkets customers are able to self-scan and self-pay for their shopping. This means fewer staff working on the tills. In contrast, many more people are ordering their shopping online so extra delivery drivers and staff to pack the shopping are required. This means that additional staff may need to be recruited for some jobs while for others a vacancy no longer exists.

Vacancies can be permanent or temporary. Some organisations will need to recruit to cover their female staff if they take maternity leave. From April 2007 mothers are entitled to up to nine months' maternity pay and leave, so employers will take on temporary staff as cover. Sometimes employees are ill and employers also need to cover for illness. The length of time for cover will depend on how long the person is going to be off work. Other employees may be able to cope with extra work for a week or so, but if the situation lasts for weeks or months another person may need to be employed on a temporary basis.

## Decision to recruit

Before an organisation does recruit a new person it will make sure that this is really necessary on a permanent basis and that the work cannot be done by somebody else. You may have heard of organisations being 'restructured'. This is when a business has looked at its employees and decided that, rather than recruiting someone into the same job, it will look at the organisation as a whole and re-divide the work.

The organisation may also consider how productive its employees are, i.e. how much work they are producing per person. It may be decided that some people have the capacity to do extra work and it is not necessary to recruit a new person to cover the difference. In order to be competitive, businesses have to be very careful about how they spend their money and therefore will save money on staff costs whenever possible. A further issue to consider is whether the vacancy is going to exist in the future or if technology might make the job redundant. Many organisations increasingly work online so staff in shops or branches may not be needed, but staff in call centres or operating online services may have to be increased. Once the decision has been made about whether to recruit, the next stage is to consider how to recruit and whether or not the person chosen should come from inside or outside the organisation.

## Internal recruitment

Internal recruitment is when the person recruited to do the job comes from inside the organisation. This means that the person will already know the organisation that they are working for and the skills required. Sometimes this type of recruitment can give current employees the chance for promotion or additional responsibility so it can be motivating for them.

Organisations will sometimes decide to advertise a vacancy internally first, then if no suitable employees are found will advertise outside as well. Of course, if a vacancy is advertised internally and a person is found for the position then somebody new may also be needed to replace them! This can extend the recruitment process and may be a problem for the organisation if it needs to recruit quickly.

Some of the key advantages and disadvantages of recruiting internally are shown in the table below.

| Advantages | Disadvantages |
|---|---|
| Cheap to advertise<br>All candidates known<br>Candidates already know the organisation<br>More likely to have smaller number of applicants<br>Can encourage career progression | Limited choice of candidates<br>May cause problems among employees due to the change<br>Employees may be stuck in their ways<br>May not generate new ideas<br>The person applying for the job will need to be replaced so another recruitment plan will need to be put into place |

## External recruitment

External recruitment is when the new worker comes from outside the organisation. There are different ways this can be done, which include: the organisation doing the recruiting itself, making use of job centres, consultants and recruitment agencies.

| Advantages | Disadvantages |
|---|---|
| More candidates to choose from<br>Candidates may have new ideas<br>Potential for new skills to be brought into the organisation | Takes longer<br>Person appointed may not be as good as they appear<br>More expensive to advertise |

Organisations recruiting new employees externally themselves will need to manage every part of the recruitment process from deciding the type of skills and salary needed for that employee to where it is best to advertise the vacancy to get the right type of applicants. There is more about advertising on page 334.

If an organisation is not able to manage the process of recruiting, because it is too busy or does not feel able to do it, it may decide to use other agencies. Job centres are popular places for employers to advertise vacancies as this is where people go to get advice on different jobs and benefits to which they may be entitled. Job centres work with employers to provide additional training and support to local areas so that employees can be found to fill vacancies that are needed. More than five million job vacancies are available for people looking for work to view (www.jobcentreplus.co.uk) so it is a popular method of recruitment. Job centres are also able to offer employers extra training and support and can give advice on recruitment from other countries within the EU or how to manage vacancies.

Some employers prefer to work with consultants to manage their vacancies. Specialist consultants can give advice and work with employers to give suggestions about where and how to recruit. Consultants may also work with prospective applicants to find out whether or not they would be suited to a particular organisation or job vacancy. They will then match the applicant to the right organisation for a fee. This means that the organisation will only receive applications from individuals that it is looking for and will not have to spend time considering unsuitable people.

Recruitment agencies work in a similar way to consultants in that they provide employers with details about potential applicants. Often recruitment agencies will provide staff on a temporary or permanent basis, which means that an employer can see how an employee is likely to work out by putting them on to a three-, six- or twelve-month contract first. This can be a cost-effective option for employers, particularly if their business changes rapidly and they may not need to keep staff permanently.

| Benefits of using an agency or consultant | Disadvantages of using an agency or consultant |
|---|---|
| The organisation can concentrate on running the business and not looking for new employees.<br>The organisation does not have to employ a recruitment team.<br>They have access to many different people and will screen out those unsuitable.<br>They will not tell competitor organisations that you are recruiting but your own advertisements will.<br>They can offer specialist support or people for the area needing recruitment.<br>They can offer advice about what is happening in the employment area. | Cost! The organisation must pay the agent and the new employee.<br>They may not find the right person for the job as the agent does not work within the organisation.<br>They may not care as much about employing the right person for the job as someone working for the organisation. |

## Case study

### Jefferson Maguire

Jefferson Maguire is a headhunting agency based in Hampshire. It recruits employees for leading companies including Marks & Spencer, Harrods, Littlewoods and Thorntons. Its activities include targeting high achievers, presenting candidates to clients, interviewing candidates and helping candidates to resign from their current employer. Jefferson Maguire also conducts assessment days so that employers can be given details about applicants' previous knowledge, experience and ability before the recruitment process starts.

1. What is a recruitment agency? ✓
2. What are the advantages to businesses of using headhunters to recruit new members of staff? ✓✓
3. Are there any disadvantages? ✓✓
4. 'Headhunters are only useful to recruit the most senior employees.' Discuss the extent to which you agree with this view. ✓✓✓

## Cost and time considerations of external sourcing

External sourcing of applicants means the process of finding employees from outside the organisation. Recruiting new employees – whether it is being done directly or through an agency – takes a long time and can take a lot of money. This is because time is needed both to outline the vacancy, the type of person required, the advertising and then there is the selection process itself. Each of these stages takes time and if an applicant is already working for another organisation they will have to work their notice. The **notice period** required will depend on the type of job, but it could be anything from one week to six months. If it is not possible to fill a vacancy when the current employee leaves it may cause a problem for an organisation and so damage its customer service, its reputation or results. If an employee is recruited from within the organisation this is less likely to happen and they may be able to move more quickly to their new post.

Cost is another factor when considering external sourcing. The cost of recruitment should be measured in two ways: the cost of advertising, or the fee that must be paid to an agency for recommending an employee, and also the opportunity cost. Money that is spent on external recruitment cannot be spent elsewhere in the business so this is an **opportunity cost** for that organisation.

## Key Terms

**Notice period** The time an employee must work for their current employer before they are allowed to leave.

**Opportunity cost** The cost to an organisation of making one decision over another – the cost of the lost opportunity.

# Recruitment advertising

Once the decision to recruit and whether or not the vacancy should be advertised internally or externally has been made, the process of getting the advertisement into circulation needs to take place.

### Internal advertising

Internal advertising is simpler than external advertising. This is because it only needs to be shown to employees who currently work for the organisation. It can be done through: the staff notice board, email, web page, company magazine or staff meeting. The details of the job must be given, together with any increase in pay or responsibilities. These should be made available to all members of staff so they can decide whether or not they want to apply. Organisations sometimes ask employees to provide a 'declaration of interest' for a vacancy. This means that they write a letter to their employer or speak to their employer about why they are interested in a particular job. The employer can then see how many people might apply for an advertised job and could decide whether or not this is the best way to recruit.

### External advertising

External advertising is more complicated than internal as it can be achieved in a number of different ways. Some organisations use newspapers or radio, others a poster in a window; some businesses now keep an up-to-date list of interested people to email and others rely on industry-related magazines. Online advertising through websites is becoming increasingly popular. The most suitable place to advertise a post is where potential applicants will read it! Advertising may, of course, also be done by using an agency or job centre.

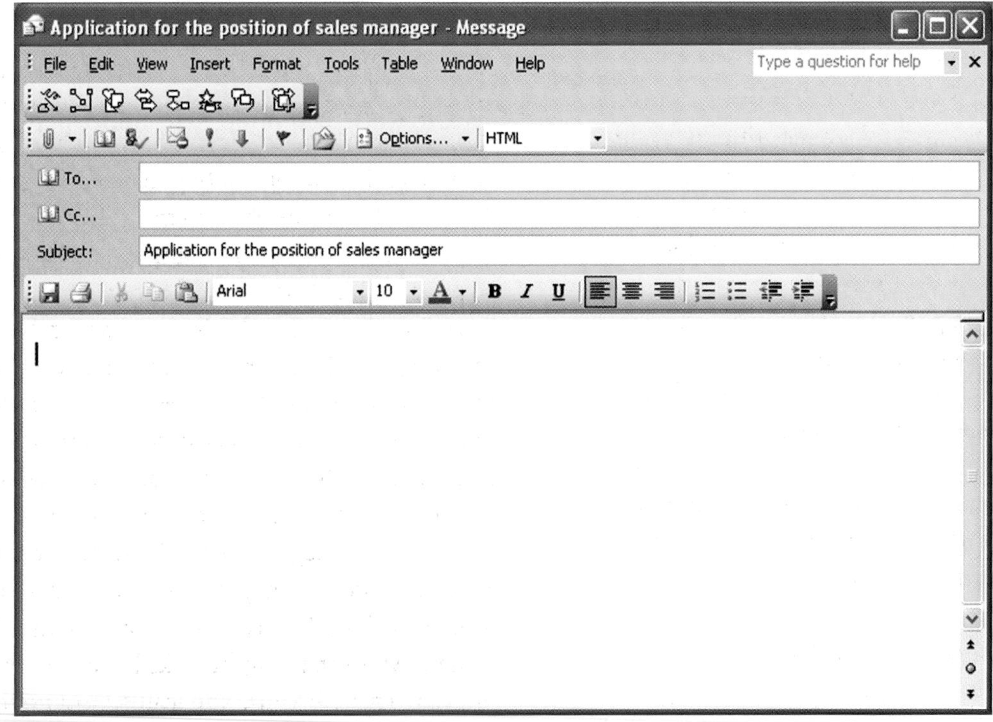


▲ Internal advertising is often completed by email

One of the cheapest methods of advertising a position is a poster in the window of a business or on a notice board. You may have seen this type of notice when you were looking for a part-time job. An employer will put it in the window so anyone in the local area may see it. Any applicants will already know a bit of information about the company. However, although it is cheap, this type of advertising limits the number of potential applicants because only those who have been past or into the organisation will see it.

Online advertising is also becoming a popular method of recruiting new employees. Many employers have a section of their website devoted to giving details about possible vacancies. This means that access to vacancies is possible from outside the country and 24-hours per day which makes it very time-effective. If the advertisement is hosted on the organisation's own website it may also be free. The problem with using this method of advertising is that applicants need to keep going back to the site to see if there are any vacancies or applicants who may not really be interested might apply to see how they would get on. To avoid this problem some organisations use an external agency to host the advertisement for them. One such online recruitment agency is www.fish4.co.uk which advertises vacancies on behalf of employers and agencies in one place so that potential applicants can source them. Potential employees are also able to advertise their skills and CV on the site so they can be seen by employers.

As well as advertising online with a recruitment agency, many organisations still make use of recruitment agencies to advertise their vacancies both online and offline. Some agencies have posters in the window advertising new jobs. Using the local and national newspaper is also still a popular way for both agencies and individual organisations to recruit. Many newspapers offer employers the opportunity to have their advertisement seen in print and online so they have access to two potential audiences. Radio is also used if employers are looking to recruit a number of people at the same time and want to interview them as a large group at an event like a recruitment fair.

## ■ Format and type of advert

Advertising can be very expensive and take a lot of time. The cost will depend on where the vacancy is advertised. Many organisations have a 'house style' for their advertisements, which means that they will use the same layout for every vacancy. This is very important for external advertising as it makes it easy for potential applicants to recognise a job opportunity with the organisation; for example, the advertisement would have the company logo on it or be printed in a particular text or on a particular colour. The size of the advertisement will also be important as employers or agencies pay per column centimetre in a printed newspaper. Many organisations choose to advertise all their vacancies in one place so it makes it easier for people to see how many vacancies they have at one time. Other organisations, for cost reasons, use smaller advertisements without their logo or further information.

The type of advertisement will depend on the job. The advertisement will be based on the job description and person specification already produced. Vacancies for some jobs may include a lot of information including pay and conditions written into the advertisement itself whereas senior managerial jobs may have pay and conditions negotiable.

## ■ Legal considerations

A further consideration of advertising externally is that employers must make sure that they take into account the legal implications of recruitment advertising. There is more on legislation relating to recruitment on page 361. In order to comply with the law, external advertising must be fair and not discriminate. This means that advertising which stops equal access for everyone must be avoided – whether this is on the grounds of age, sex, race, sexual orientation and so on. Making sure that an advertisement complies with legislation is very important. Mistakes can be costly if employers are fined as a result of it being proven that their advertisements were discriminatory. As a result of the Employment Equality (Age) Regulations 2006 that came into force on 1 October 2006 employers now also need to be careful when wording advertisements to ensure that they do not contain words that may be linked to age, such as mature or lively. This is because applicants must not be treated any differently because of their age.

## Case study

### Comparing job adverts

Making sure that the right information is provided within an advertisement is critical for online recruitment because it is the only opportunity that an employer has to help someone to decide whether or not to apply for the job.

Compare the two advertisements for the job of accountant below.

1. What do the two vacancies have in common? ✓
2. What is different about them? ✓
3. Which one would you apply for and why? ✓✓
4. Discuss the extent to which a job advertisement is critical in the recruitment process. ✓✓
5. Produce a guide for employers detailing the critical information that is needed within any recruitment advertisement, with your justification for those choices. ✓✓✓

**Job title:** Accountant
**Location:** Belvedere, Greater London
**Salary:** POA
**Working options:** Permanent

**FINANCIAL ACCOUNTANT**

Established damp proof and timber preservation company requires suitably experienced person to maintain financial data and records. Reporting directly to the Directors, the successful candidate will be responsible for the financial records, including the sales ledger, purchase ledger and nominal ledger. The role includes raising invoices and the weekly maintenance of payroll records for both employees and subcontractors. You will be responsible for all month-end routines, including the preparation of accurate monthly accounts for management use and for all accounting administration. Hands-on experience of Sage Line 50 and Sage Payroll is required, as well as knowledge of the Construction Industry Scheme, cards, certificates and vouchers. 9am–5.30pm, Monday–Friday. Vacancy to commence next January.

**Apply with CV to:** Mr L J Singh, Human Resources Manager.

**Job title:** ACCOUNTANT
**Location:** Liverpool, Merseyside
**Salary:** £18,000
**Job sector:** Accountancy

**Description:**
**ASSISTANT ACCOUNTANT**

Wirral-based company is seeking an experienced person to assist in preparation of monthly accounts, bank reconciliations, cash flow forecasting, VAT returns, etc. Salary is £18K to £19K. Call the Blue Agency.

## Practice point

Read the recruitment advertisement that appeared in your local paper.

What information is missing from this advertisement?

What are the advantages and disadvantages of using the local paper to advertise for vacancies externally?

To what extent does the quality of the advertisement affect the number of people applying for the job?

WANTED

Part-time
Administration Asssistant

£200 per week
39 hours per week

Please write or fone for more infomation to
C Wythe
Enterprising Solutions Ltd
Tickleton Road Lorrencester R4 8PQ

## Methods of application

When an advertisement is published, the employer must clearly outline how people should apply. There are three main methods that are used now: letter, online and telephone.

### ■ Letter

This is the traditional method of application. A letter is requested to be sent in with either an application form or curriculum vitae (see page 343). Letters make use of traditional post so the time taken to send the application in has to be considered when drafting the advertisement. The time needed to send out an information pack to potential applicants also means that the process can take a long time.

### ■ Online

Online applications are becoming increasingly popular. They take two main forms: the email application and the online application form. Email applications are very similar to the letter application but take less time as the information is emailed in rather than sent through the post. Some employers will ask applicants to send their CV by email or to download and fill in an application form that can be sent as an attachment by email. This saves time and postage costs for both the employer and prospective employee.

Many employers have also moved to complete online applications. This means that rather than filling in an application that is sent in, the application is directly online so the information is sent to the employer and can be immediately stored within an online database. This method of application is very cost-effective for employers as data can be sorted before the employer needs to sift through an application to reduce processing costs. An example of this might be an employer asking that potential applicants have a double Merit for BTEC National Business. When the online application reaches the online database those details will be checked for. If the candidate has a double Merit, their application will go through but if they do not it will be immediately discounted.

### ■ Telephone

Employers are also increasingly using the telephone to help with applications. This means that applicants telephone a recruitment number and are often screened by being asked a series of questions. If their responses are good, they will be put through to the next stage of the process; if they are not good they will be unable to go forward. Large employers, including Barclays Bank and Marks & Spencer, both use this form of application. Smaller employers can also use the telephone as part of the application process as prospective employees may be asked to telephone for an information pack or application form. This way the employer can get an idea of how successful their advertisement has been and, as a result of it, how many people have applied.

▼ **Advantages and disadvantages of the three methods of application**

| Method | Purpose | Advantages | Disadvantages |
|---|---|---|---|
| By letter | Applicants write a letter about their suitability for a job and send it in to the organisation by post or fax. | Gives the organisation the ability to compare. Allows applicants to demonstrate their suitability for the job. | Applicants are likely to only show their strengths and not weaknesses. Not in a standard format. The post may take a long time or get lost. A fax can be read by others so may not be kept confidential. |
| Online | Email allows applicants to send letters and CVs direct to organisations and online application forms are growing more common. | Organisations can advertise job vacancies themselves on their website for free. Can increase the number of candidates which is very useful for specialist employers. Data can be sent into the organisation very quickly. Data is sent directly into the organisation and needs little processing. Can happen 24 hours a day, 7 days per week. People looking at company information may see the job on the off chance and apply for it. Can be accessed by people with disabilities on an equal basis. | Technical problems, e.g. the website or email not working. Jobs advertised on the Internet may receive too many applicants so employers take a long time to choose candidates. Not everyone has access to the Internet so it may reduce the number of possible applicants and may not be accessible to certain groups of people. It may be difficult to prove where the information has come from; electronic signatures can be used but are not used widely at the moment. |
| Telephone | Applicants call a number and notes are made about them. Sometimes tests are also done on the applicants to try to work out their personality type. | Can be used for large numbers of applicants as the information can be put into a database and can be sorted. Allows the applicant to speak to someone from the organisation and ask questions. | The telephone may be busy or engaged and good applicants never get through. It may involve using an automated service so applicants may be put off or it may not operate outside office hours. |

## Case study

### Marks & Spencer

Marks & Spencer uses telephone interviewing as part of its recruitment and selection. The purpose of this is to make sure that fewer unsuitable applicants are put through for interview. By asking a series of specific questions, Marks & Spencer is able to select applicants with certain personality and occupational traits by asking specific questions to go through to the next stage. The software used to do this is known as the 'Talent Screener'. Talent Screener ensures that only suitable applicants are then interviewed. This means that unsuitable applicants are withdrawn from the process before time and costs are allocated to them when they are interviewed face to face. As a result of introducing this extra step into the process, Marks & Spencer has had more suitable applicants for jobs and also more applicants have then gone on to be offered jobs and have accepted them.

**Why do organisations use telephone interviewing?** ▶

1. Why does Marks & Spencer use telephone interviewing? ✓
2. What advantages and disadvantages might there be for using such screening? ✓✓
3. To what extent can telephone interviewing as part of the interview process help to reduce unsuitable applications? ✓✓✓

## Outcome activity 13.1

P1

Using the case study on Jet2 on page 331, and your own school or college, produce a report giving details of how these two different organisations plan their recruitment. Throughout your report you should consider issues such as the potential choice of candidates, costs involved, and make sure you include all the different stages necessary.

## Grading tips

**Pass** P1

To produce the report you must consider:

- the reason for the vacancy
- why the business has taken the decision to recruit
- the internal aspects of recruitment planning, including advertising internally, promotion and succession planning
- the external planning aspects of recruitment, including using agencies, and advertising locally and nationally.

To find out the information you need to complete the report, you may find it useful to:

- interview the human resource manager or another member of staff and ask them questions about vacancies and why they chose to recruit
- go to www.jet2careers.com to see Jet2's current vacancies
- complete a search in www.google.com looking for recruitment agencies in your area and considering costs
- consider using websites such as www.tes.co.uk in order to gain information on your school's or college's recruitment planning
- find out information on your area and the local job market by entering your postcode at www.neighbourhood.statistics.gov.uk.

# 13.2 Documentation involved in the recruitment process

You have learned about the process of planning to recruit and about how different organisations choose to recruit, but you also need to understand and be familiar with the paperwork that is used to support the process. The key documents here are the job description and the person specification.

## Job description

The purpose of the job description is to give information to prospective employees about what the job involves. It explains the purpose of the job and the type of responsibilities and duties that will be expected as part of that job. Different organisations will have their own particular information that they will include but the key elements that are always required are shown in the following table:

| | |
|---|---|
| **Title of the job** | This is essential as it gives an idea of what the job involves and the rough level of responsibility, e.g. Finance Manager. |
| **Department and location** | A job description will be written for a particular department in an organisation especially if the organisation is very large. |
| **Broad terms** | This gives a very rough idea of what is involved in the post. Many job vacancies have **open-ended terms**, which means that they can change slightly to take into account the needs of the business or employee. |
| **Responsible to whom** | This tells the employee who they must report to with any problems or queries. |
| **Responsibilities** | This tells the employee about any people or resources they are responsible for. |
| **Scope of post** | This gives guidance on how far-reaching the post is, for example whether or not they have the possibility to supervise others or can make management changes. |
| **Education and qualifications** | Some organisations will also include details about the level of qualifications and experience that the job requires, e.g. graduate. Such information may also be included in the person specification. |
| **Name of compiler and approver** | This is the person who designed and agreed the job. |
| **Date of issue** | This is when the description was issued. In a fast-changing business world, it is important to know when the last changes were made to the job. |

An example of a job description ►

**MONEY MANAGEMENT**
LIMITED

**Job Description**

| | |
|---|---|
| Job Title | Finance Assistant |
| Department | Accounts |
| Responsible to | Sarah Pearson |
| Scope of the post | The Finance Assistant's main role is to assist the Finance Manager |
| Responsibilities | The post holder is expected to help with company accounts using Sage Accounting Software. This requires preparation of accounts for budgets within the organisation and assistance in the production of annual accounts for external agencies. Duties performed by the post holder include<br>• Reconciliation of accounts and problem solving of any variances<br>• Preparation of invoices<br>• Raising orders<br>• General office duties such as travel claim processing<br>• Ad hoc reports as and when required<br>• Any other duties as commensurate with the post |
| Compiled by | C Taylor |
| Date | 8 March |

## Practice point

In pairs, write a job description for the position of classroom assistant. Using the table on page 339 and the example to help you, write something for each of the areas. You may need to interview a member of staff to complete this activity.

Compare your job description with others in your class to find the similarities and differences.

What are the benefits and issues of producing a job description?

To what extent is an accurate job description essential to recruitment and selection?

## Key Terms

**Open-ended terms** Terms that are written much more vaguely than others. This allows the employer and employee some flexibility about what they actually require. Sometimes an employer might write into the job description a statement that covers 'any other reasonable duties as required by the post'.

# Person specification

The job description essentially concentrates on providing information about the job. The **person specification** is a direct contrast; it provides information about the type of person that the organisation is looking for to do the job.

The person specification gives a list of requirements, but these relate to the person doing the job. It will have an introduction at the start of the person specification giving details about the job such as job title, post reference number and management responsibilities (including who the employee needs to report to and is responsible for). It will then detail attributes that the organisation wants that person to have, for example their type of personality or intelligence level.

Attributes are the characteristics that someone has, for example their type of personality such as outgoing or conscientious. The type of attributes needed will change depending on the type and level of the job.

## Key Terms

**Person specification** Attributes needed by the person to perform a job, such as personality type or experience.

**Personal specification**

Post Title: Finance and Administrative Officer

Grade: Clerical 3/4

| Criteria | Essential | Desirable |
|---|---|---|
| Qualifications/ Knowledge: | BTEC National Diploma in Business GCSEs in Maths and English plus 3 others at Grade C or above or equivalent IT skills, particularly spreadsheets and database | |
| Work Related Experience: | ½ year general office and/or financial experience<br>Good level of numeracy | Experience in higher education |
| Skills/Abilities & Special Attributes | Good organisational skills<br>Able to prioritise workloads<br>Good communication Skills<br>Team-working ability | Previous experience or willingness to work in an open-plan environment |

An example of a mini person specification ▶

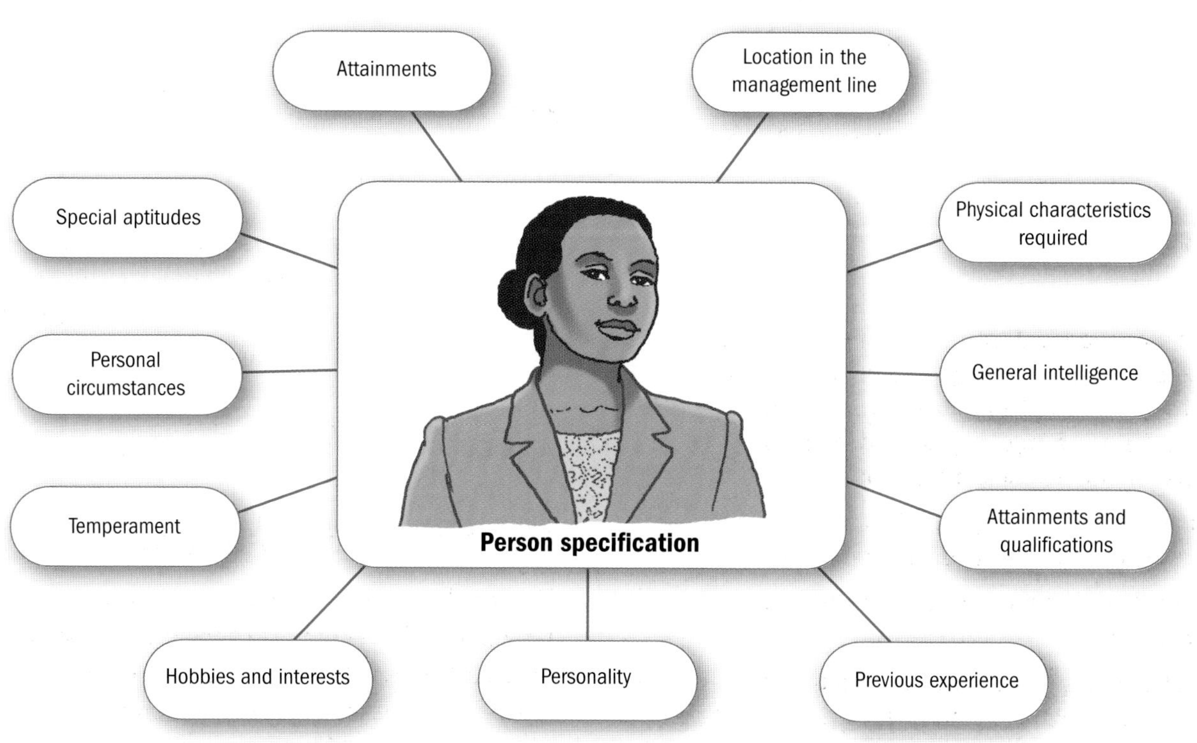

## Practice point

Write a person specification for the job of BTEC Business Student! Using each of the categories given above, describe what is needed and then rate how important that attribute is. An example is started below to help you.

| | |
|---|---|
| Previous experience | 3 |
| Able to work to deadlines | 1 |

Previous experience was rated a 3 because it is not essential but useful to have studied business before to do the BTEC course. Working to deadlines is given a 1 because it is essential to get work in on time.

When you have finished your person specification, compare it with others in your class. How can a person specification help an employer to choose the right person for the job?

'A person specification may limit an organisation's ability to get a range of applicants for a job.' Discuss this view.

Some organisations will also use ratings in their specification. This means that they will rate how important a part of the person specification is to a job with 1 meaning that this attribute is very important and 4 not important.

# Application documentation

The main documents used as part of the application are the letter, application form and curriculum vitae (CV).

### ■ Letter

A letter of application should highlight all the positive aspects of the applicant and the special skills that they have.

Letters are used by applicants to outline why they are suitable for a job. Applicants can use a letter to highlight special skills they may have and attributes that they feel they have that make them suitable for the job. Applicants should use the job description and person specification when highlighting their particular strengths so that an employer can match them to the job.

### ■ Application form

Application forms are another way of gaining information in a standard format that makes it easier for employers to actually compare applicants. They can be completed online or in paper form. The information in the questions can be directly related to the individual business needs.

Application forms ask for a standard set of questions and boxes to be completed. This makes it easy for the organisation to compare candidates. Application forms will only ask questions and information that the organisation asks for and therefore will avoid the employer having to read information that they don't need. Paper-based forms may take time and money to be sent out and then will need to be processed and put into a system to compare them. This may take a long time. Online forms have the advantage of doing this automatically. Care should be taken with online application forms to ensure that they are completed using appropriate English and not 'text language' as this might not give the right impression of an applicant to an employer.

### ■ Curriculum vitae (CV)

Applicants write all their details including education and history on a two-page sheet including referees. The organisation can see in one go everything about an applicant. CVs only focus on positive aspects of an applicant so it may be difficult to compare candidates. CVs may also have been used to apply for lots of jobs so may not be specific to a particular role. It is important to review CVs regularly or to write them for each individual job if an applicant really wants that job.

38 Thornton Lane
Teeton
TR8 7PU

18 December

Money Management Ltd
8 Marks Square
Teeton
TR7 8NK

Dear Mr Halford

**Application for the post of Finance Assistant**

I am writing to apply for the position of Finance Assistant as advertised in 'The Local Paper' on 16 December.

I have spent the past two years working for Smart Money Finances in Teeton. As part of my role I am required to process invoices and enter them on to the computer. I also type letters as required for clients and answer the telephone. Within my role I work with two other Finance Assistants, so I am used to working as part of a team. I really like working in this way and would like to do so in the future.

I am a well-organised person with good communication skills and believe that I would make an excellent employee for your organisation. I developed my skills whilst I was studying BTEC National Business at Teeton College. This course gave me excellent knowledge of business, and finance in particular, so I have been able to use these skills at work.

In my personal life I am a keen football player and have represented the county on more than one occasion. I am also interested in travelling and have visited many different European countries, including Spain, France and Italy.

I believe I would be a very useful addition to your team. I am a hardworking and very conscientious employee and would be pleased to bring my skills and experience to your company. I am enclosing my Curriculum Vitae for your information and would be available for interview at your convenience.

Yours sincerely

J Cheng

Enc.

**Letter of application ▲**

## Curriculum Vitae

**Personal Details**

| | |
|---|---|
| Name | Shannon McIntyre |
| Address | 18 Hill Lane<br>Southampton<br>SO15 5RL |
| Telephone | 023 80511822 |
| Date of Birth | 2.2.88 |

**Education**

| | |
|---|---|
| 2005 – 2007 | Topton College |
| 2000 – 2005 | Besthampton School |

**Academic Qualifications**

| | |
|---|---|
| BTEC National Diploma in Business | MMP awarded |
| Eight GCSEs | including Maths and English |

**Work Experience**

| | |
|---|---|
| 2005 - 2007 | Part-time employment at HMV using the till, pricing stock and stock management as well as dealing with customers |

**Personal Statement**

I am a really outgoing person who likes to play sport. I am a member of the Rugby Team at College and also play at the weekend for my local team. I enjoy computing and am able to use a number of different software packages, including Microsoft Office XP. I am hard working and am always on time.

**Referee**

Kate Sharp
76 Laxford Avenue
Southampton
SO26 8PU
02380 876233

**A CV ▶**

# Employment Application Form

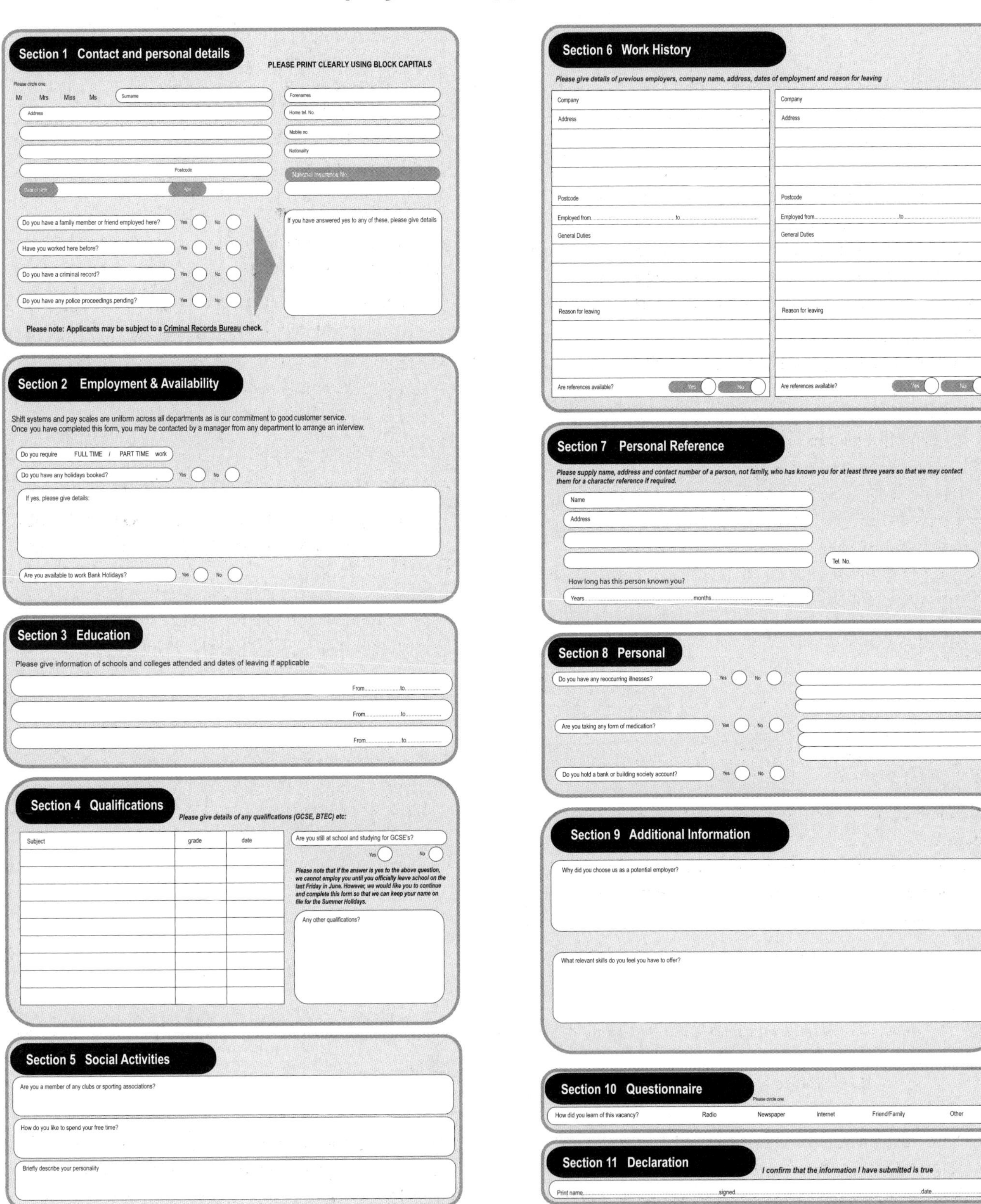

**Section 1 Contact and personal details**

PLEASE PRINT CLEARLY USING BLOCK CAPITALS

Please circle one:

Mr Mrs Miss Ms

Surname

Forenames

Address

Home tel. No.

Mobile no.

Nationality

Postcode

National Insurance No.

Date of birth

Age

Do you have a family member or friend employed here? Yes No

Have you worked here before? Yes No

Do you have a criminal record? Yes No

Do you have any police proceedings pending? Yes No

If you have answered yes to any of these, please give details

Please note: Applicants may be subject to a Criminal Records Bureau check.

**Section 2 Employment & Availability**

Shift systems and pay scales are uniform across all departments as is our commitment to good customer service.
Once you have completed this form, you may be contacted by a manager from any department to arrange an interview.

Do you require FULL TIME / PART TIME work

Do you have any holidays booked? Yes No

If yes, please give details:

Are you available to work Bank Holidays? Yes No

**Section 3 Education**

Please give information of schools and colleges attended and dates of leaving if applicable

From.................to.................

From.................to.................

From.................to.................

**Section 4 Qualifications**

*Please give details of any qualifications (GCSE, BTEC) etc:*

| Subject | grade | date |
|---|---|---|
| | | |
| | | |
| | | |
| | | |
| | | |
| | | |
| | | |
| | | |
| | | |

Are you still at school and studying for GCSE's? Yes No

***Please note that if the answer is yes to the above question, we cannot employ you until you officially leave school on the last Friday in June. However, we would like you to continue and complete this form so that we can keep your name on file for the Summer Holidays.***

Any other qualifications?

**Section 5 Social Activities**

Are you a member of any clubs or sporting associations?

How do you like to spend your free time?

Briefly describe your personality

**Section 6 Work History**

*Please give details of previous employers, company name, address, dates of employment and reason for leaving*

Company

Address

Postcode

Employed from.................to.................

General Duties

Reason for leaving

Are references available? Yes No

Company

Address

Postcode

Employed from.................to.................

General Duties

Reason for leaving

Are references available? Yes No

**Section 7 Personal Reference**

*Please supply name, address and contact number of a person, not family, who has known you for at least three years so that we may contact them for a character reference if required.*

Name

Address

Tel. No.

How long has this person known you?

Years.................months.................

**Section 8 Personal**

Do you have any reoccurring illnesses? Yes No

Are you taking any form of medication? Yes No

Do you hold a bank or building society account? Yes No

**Section 9 Additional Information**

Why did you choose us as a potential employer?

What relevant skills do you feel you have to offer?

**Section 10 Questionnaire**

Please circle one

How did you learn of this vacancy? Radio Newspaper Internet Friend/Family Other

**Section 11 Declaration**

*I confirm that the information I have submitted is true*

Print name.................signed.................date.................

▲ **Sample application form**

## Case study

### Debenhams

Debenhams uses its website to provide information for applicants. The site uses drop-down boxes to help potential applicants search for job vacancies that might be relevant to them. They then give their email address to Debenhams and start the online application. This means that Debenhams has contact information from the earliest part of the recruitment stage and can monitor who is interested in its vacancies.

Debenhams uses an online application form to screen any applications by asking questions about the applicant's:

- age
- previous criminal convictions
- hours they can work per week
- relationships with others at Debenhams
- previous employment with the company
- hours available to work
- equal opportunities information, e.g. marital status, religion, ethnic group
- customer service experience
- skills and qualities
- interests and hobbies
- occupational skills
- second job working arrangements
- absence record
- gaps in employment history
- data protection information.

All of this information is collected easily online and then can be sent to the store to be processed.

1. How does Debenhams use online applications as part of recruitment? ✓
2. What are the advantages of using such a system? ✓✓
3. What might any possible issues be? ✓✓
4. 'Online applicants ensure that unsuitable applicants do not get through the recruitment process.' Discuss this view. ✓✓✓

## Thinking point

Compare and contrast the online application process for three different organisations that you are aware of. To what extent are common features contained within these processes? How important is conformity in recruitment?

## Thinking point

As a result of the new Employment Equality (Age) Regulations 2006 employers are no longer allowed to ask for dates of birth or dates of education on application forms or CVs.

How will this affect the recruitment process? What positive and negative effects do you think it will have? To what extent do you think this will avoid age discrimination in recruitment?

## Outcome activity 13.2

You are going to prepare a research pack of information including the documents needed to recruit an employee for the post of an Office Administrator for one of the organisations that you have already used for Outcome activity 13.1 or one that you are familiar with. This could be your part-time job or work experience employer.

**Pass**

Prepare the advertising, job description and person specification required to recruit an employee for a specific role. 

Apply for a job by completing the application documentation. 

## Grading tips

**Pass** P2

Use the templates on pages 336, 340 and 341 to help you with the outline of how an advertisement, job description and person specification should look. Make sure you check your spelling and content to include everything that is needed for each.

Complete a standard application form (available by searching online or from your teacher) to apply for the job and produce a curriculum vitae and covering letter. An example of an application form is on page 344. P3

Completing an application form:

- Make sure you read and understand what the question is asking you to provide before you answer it.
- Check your spelling for online and paper forms.
- Photocopy or print out the paper version and practise your answers before you write or type them up.
- Proof read your work for spelling and grammar problems.
- Make sure your writing is as neat as possible and use the right ink colour, e.g. black if the form asks for it.
- Use full sentences not bullet points and make sure you write in appropriate English – not as if you were sending a text or email.
- Complete it in plenty of time before the application date.
- If a section does not apply to you write N/A (Not Applicable) in it.
- Relate your answers to the person specification and the job description.
- Use full examples to answer the questions, showing what you did, where and when.
- Provide full details of referees, including name, address, telephone and email (if possible).

Producing your curriculum vitae (CV) and covering letter:

- Make sure you include a suitable amount of 'white space' around the sections so that it looks neat.
- Adjust your margins so that it fits onto a maximum of two pages.
- Keep all your headings the same and use the tab key on your keyboard to line up your work neatly.
- Put the information in reverse order so what you are doing now comes first and then go back through information to your schools and previous qualifications.
- Don't use too many bullet points; it may be better to write your skills and work experience as paragraphs.
- Adapt your CV for the job that you are applying for – you should make these adjustments for each and every application.
- Make clear links between your CV and the covering letter highlighting the skills, attributes or qualifications that you think are most important for the job.
- Use the appropriate start and end to a formal letter, e.g. 'Dear Mrs Brown' and 'Yours sincerely' or 'Dear Sir' and 'Yours faithfully'.
- Use blocked paragraphs with a line between to improve your letter layout.
- Don't forget to include your address, the company's address and a date on the covering letter including when you would be available for interview.

Once the job description and person specifications are written, including details of how the application process is going to take place, the next stage is the application process itself – including any tests or additional documents that need to be taken or provided before the interview. This stage is known as pre-interview.

## Pre-interview

In order to decide who to ask for interview employers need to look carefully through the application information that has already been sent to them. The type of information provided will depend on whether the organisation has used application forms or curriculum vitae. The organisation will look at:

- experience
- qualifications
- skills
- references
- and the quality of the documents themselves (including typing or handwriting)

to decide which applicants they should invite in for interview and the type of interview that is needed for the job.

### Selection criteria for short-listing

Applicants know that employers use the person specification as the primary method for short-listing by matching the skills and attributes required against those of the applicants. Applicants should try to match their experience as closely and clearly as they possibly can.

Employers may use a form to make comparison easier by making notes on each individual applicant and then looking at them altogether. An example of a simplified form is shown here.

An alternative short-listing grid may also be used by writing the selection criteria next to each application so that each area can be ticked or crossed. Again this makes comparison much easier.

It is important at every stage of selection that reasons are clearly outlined why an applicant has been chosen to go forward and why another has been rejected. This is to avoid discrimination. If an applicant wishes to find out why their application was rejected they are entitled to do so and an employer will need to have clear reasons to feed back to them. Employers must also only use the information that they have been given in front of them and not make any assumptions about candidates, to avoid stereotyping and discrimination.

### Application packs and information for candidates

In order to help candidates understand the selection process, employers send out application packs with more information – including details of the process that is going to happen.

| Candidate | Communication Skills | Qualifications | Ability to work as part of a team | Shortlist |
|---|---|---|---|---|
| 1 | No evidence provided | 5 GCSEs at C grade | No evidence provided | No |
| 2 | Evidence of telephone skills and good standard of report writing | BTEC National Diploma (Distinction) | Working in a bank for the past two years in a team | Yes |
| 3 | Typing skills (30wpm) Reception skills | A Levels in Spanish, French and English | No evidence | No |
| 4 | No evidence provided | 3 GCSEs in Art, Geography and Music | No evidence | No |
| 5 | Reception skills, typing (60wpm) | BTEC National Diploma (Merit) | Part-time restaurant supervisor of a small team | Yes |

▲ A short-listing form

The application pack often includes additional information about the organisation they are applying to and the structure of the day(s) that they need to take part in, including any tests or additional tasks to be undertaken. This information is important for candidates as it may help them to decide whether or not they actually want to go through the recruitment process.

## References

References are written statements that an employer, college or personal friend supplies in support of an application. It is usual to have an educational and employment reference as part of the process. The reference usually contains information about the applicant's employment history, timekeeping, sickness record and relevant experience to help the organisation to make judgements about whether to employ that person.

References are a very important element of the recruitment process. It is common for references to be taken before the process starts if the job involves working with young people or vulnerable groups. References can indicate whether or not someone is likely to be suitable for a job. They should be written very carefully as they must be factually correct and give opinions that present the candidate in a reasonable way. Former employers have to be very careful about how they write a reference because an inaccurate reference could lead to legal action; for example, if a reference is written in a way that is too negative and leads to the withdrawal of a job offer, the person may be able to sue them if it is inaccurate.

Employers should:

- make sure opinions are reasonable and that only facts are expressed
- make sure that the reference does not give an unfair impression
- make it clear if they are only able to offer a limited opinion of an applicant.

Employers should not:

- give misleading information
- provide a reference if they do not wish to; there are few legal obligations for an employer to provide a reference
- provide a reference that they do not wish the job applicant to see (the person about whom the reference is written has a right to see the reference as part of the Data Protection Act).

## Types of interviews

The employer will need to decide which method of interview is to be used as part of the selection process. There are six main methods of interview that can be used: group, individual, team, panel, telephone and multi-stage.

### ■ Group

Group interviews are held if large numbers of staff are needed by an organisation. A number of candidates are invited to receive a presentation from the recruiting organisation, to talk to other candidates and ask questions about the job. Group interviews may be used as the first stage of the process to select candidates who seem more interested in the job or who ask suitable questions. It can be a good opportunity for a candidate to decide whether or not they wish to go forward with their application and for an employer to get a first impression of the candidates. However, in a group interview it is important for candidates to 'stand out' from the rest of the people and this may be difficult. Employers may give candidates a task to complete as part of a smaller group to monitor how well they work with each other.

### ■ Individual

This type of interview is very intense as the candidates are expected to meet in a one-to-one situation to talk about why they want the job. This type of interviewing is expensive as it requires each candidate to be spoken to individually. It is likely that only very promising candidates will be picked to go through to this stage.

## Team

Team interviews are those conducted by a team of personnel who will be asking different questions of candidates. These are normally taken from a number of different areas within the organisation, such as finance, personnel or marketing. Each person brings a different set of skills to the interview so will be looking for different features in the candidates. Usually each member of the interview team will have equal weighting of their opinion. This means that each person's view will be taken into account as important.

## Panel

Panel interviews are similar to team interviews in that a group of people are brought together to interview the candidates. A chairperson is appointed and each member of the panel is given the opportunity to ask questions as directed by that chairperson. Each member of the panel will have their questions ready to ask. This type of interview is often used in public sector organisations; organisations such as hospitals or colleges. Panel interviews often ask the same questions of all candidates to make effective comparisons.

▲ Panel interview

## Telephone

Telephone interviews are often conducted with candidates who are applying to work in a customer service environment, such as in a retail store or in a call centre. The telephone interview can take place at any time and requires the interviewer to talk to the candidate over the phone to judge whether or not they have the right skills to work for their organisation. The interviewer may ask questions about organisational skills or ask for any other information in order to make decisions about the suitability of the candidate. Telephone interviews can be a useful way of screening out unsuitable candidates at an early stage as they do not require the candidates to travel to a location. This cuts out time and costs for both parties. As telephone interviewers often have a set of standardised questions, the process may be completed by less experienced interviewers and therefore be more cost effective for the organisation. As part of the interview, candidates may be asked different sorts of questions – including calculations – so they should be prepared for this.

## Multi-stage

Multi-stage interviews mean that more than one interview takes place in order for a candidate to be chosen. Different types of interview may be used and candidates must go through each stage successfully to eventually get the job. The first interviews might be less formal, for example an informal chat with some members of staff from a relevant department. The next stage might be a more formal interview with a manager or human resources employee. The final stage could be a panel interview with the senior management team. Candidates must pass through each interview stage to get the job so it can be a good way of seeing how candidates perform at different levels and in a variety of situations.

## Tasks and tests used to complement the interview process

Different tasks and tests may be used as part of the interview process and these are categorised into four main areas: occupational preference tests, attainment tests, aptitude tests and psychometric tests.

▲ Aptitude tests may be used to help with the process

### ■ Occupational preference tests

These are tests that measure skills which are important for the job, for example if a person needs to be very customer-focused the test will measure this. A role play may be used where a candidate is asked to deal with an 'angry customer'.

### ■ Attainment tests

Attainment may be measured by observing candidates performing in a group to see which level they are working at. It shows the level at which candidates work within a group, such as high or low achiever.

### ■ Aptitude tests

These assessments try to measure suitability for a job and may be more practical, such as putting tasks into priority order or demonstrating the management of a small group.

### ■ Psychometric tests

Psychometric tests aim to measure intelligence or personality type to assess how good a person will be at a job. These may be multiple-choice, paper-based tests or completed online.

## Case study

**Links of London**

Links of London is a luxury jewellery company, trading across the world in locations that include London, New York and Hong Kong. Links employs more than 250 staff and uses psychometric testing to identify the skills and attributes needed for its store managers. Links has assessed that there are some skills or personality traits which a store manager needs to have and it uses psychometric testing to work out the extent to which an applicant matches this profile. The tests are complex and measure a person's emotional tendencies, their energy levels, whether they are shy or extrovert and their confidence. By measuring the characteristics of current managers, as well as new applicants, Links can also work out the training and development needs of its current staff. Links is growing and doing well within its market so it would seem likely that the strategy of using testing in the recruitment process for store managers is working well.

1. What are psychometric tests? ✓
2. What kind of traits can they measure? ✓
3. How might psychometric tests limit the number of applicants for a job? ✓✓
4. How could psychometric tests be used with existing staff and what might the issues with this be? ✓✓
5. 'Psychometric testing can lead to the best applicants being put forward for the job.' To what extent do you agree with this view? ✓✓✓

### Thinking point

Find out about the use of psychometric testing in your area. You may wish to conduct online research or interviews/questionnaires to gather this information. Which companies are using it? How are they using it? How do you think they benefit from it?

### Use of specialists in the interview

It is important that specialists are present at an interview so that accurate judgements can be made and the appropriate processes followed. This will often be a member of the human resources team who can process all the paperwork and keep to UK and EU legislation. Specialists may also be used to give advice and guidance to the interviewer or interview team. These people may advise on the results of any tests that have been given or can give an opinion on the expertise of an individual. Advisers may be brought in for short-term projects to help businesses recruit the right individuals.

### Interview questions

Interview questions are critical to the success of any interview. If candidates are not asked the right questions it is difficult to assess whether or not they are suitable for the job. It is also important to ask all candidates the same questions to make sure the process is fair. There are some personal issues that a business should never ask about – shown below – and to do so will break the law. Questions must not be asked about:

- race
- colour
- sex
- religion
- nationality
- birthplace
- age
- disability
- marital status
- children
- sexual orientation.

Questions that are good to ask an employee relate to things they feel they have done well in the past, any relevant experience they have highlighted in their application and how they would approach a particular role.

### Procedure for informing candidates on interview decisions

Candidates are told what is going to happen during and after the interview, so they will know when they are going to be informed about the outcome of the interview, for example by the end of the day, next day or week. This is important as it helps the candidates to know how long it might be before they are informed about their performance.

## Interview

The process of interviewing is complex as there are agreed rules about what happens within the interview situation and what happens to the information that is created as part of the process during and after it has taken place. Body language as well as the spoken word is important so you need to understand the impact of these different areas on the interview itself.

### Interview protocol

Interviews need to follow what is called interview protocol. Interview protocols are accepted rules and guidelines that are not written down but which the candidate(s) and the interviewer(s) are expected to follow. These may be such things as:

- candidates arriving at the interview early
- the need to dress smartly with clean and tidy appearance
- the interviewer(s) shaking hands with candidates when they enter the room
- the candidate will speak highly of their last or current employer and not say bad things about them
- that candidates do not chew gum
- at the end of the interview the candidate should thank the employer for the interview.

▲ Wearing a suit is part of interview protocol

Human resources departments deal with the management of policies and procedures relating to the people who work for an organisation. They cover areas including payroll, sickness monitoring, grievance and disciplinary procedures. Making sure that information is correctly stored and processed is usually the responsibility of someone from the human resources department.

### Thinking point

Can you think of any interview protocols that are not listed here for an interview to join your school or college as a student or as an employee?

### Confidentiality

Candidates will also be told what will happen to their personal information if they are not successful. It may be destroyed or some organisations will ask candidates if they may keep the information for another six months so that, if a job should be advertised again, the candidate will be considered. Keeping this information secure is part of the organisation's responsibility to maintain **confidentiality**.

## Key Terms

**Confidentiality** Keeping information secure and only allowing it to be given to people with permission to see it.

### Fairness

You will learn more about fairness when you consider the ethics and legal aspects of the interview process. It is important that all candidates are treated fairly in terms of their seating arrangements, the questions used, the information about the process and so on. This means that all interviewees can be compared equally. It also includes making sure that every candidate is allocated the same amount of interview time and receives the same information.

### Interview environment

The interview environment should be made as comfortable as possible, taking into account any health and safety issues. Candidates should have equal access to any relevant equipment. Distractions or interruptions should be avoided so that each candidate is given the time and space to perform to the best of their ability.

### Agreed questions

As mentioned above, agreeing appropriate questions is a key part of the process to make sure that the interview is conducted fairly. The same questions should be asked of each of the candidates and these should be agreed before the interview starts. Often where there is more than one interviewer, the interviewers will agree which questions they will each ask, focusing on their own area of expertise.

## Checking of personal information

Checking personal information is also an important part of the process. This may take place in the information stage of the process, for example where a member of the human resources team photocopies the candidate's certificates or other personal information, such as birth certificate or driving licence. During the interview a verbal check of that information takes place using the application form or CV to help the interviewer.

## Interview checklist

Many interviewers will use an interview checklist. This is particularly helpful if there is more than one stage to the process. Some organisations will include both formal and informal interviews to help them make decisions. A checklist helps the organisation to ensure that all questions have been asked and responses noted.

Candidates may also use a checklist to help them prepare for the interview and during the interview they may use their own checklist to ask any questions of their own. It is important that the checklist is not used too much by candidates in the interview as it may not give the employer a good impression of the candidate if they keep needing to refer back to their information rather than answering questions directly.

## Control of interview

To control the whole interview process, a member of that team will need to coordinate the questions to make the interview flow well. Candidates also need preparation and some control. Candidates often feel under pressure in interview situations and will therefore need to control themselves mentally (by giving focused and well thought-out answers) and physically (by giving good eye contact and body posture). They are usually given an outline of the format of the interview, for example how long it will last and the type of questions that they will be asked. This allows them to try to do their best. It is important that appropriate and fair questions are asked of candidates so that each person has an equal chance of getting the job.

## Decision criteria and documentation

It is important through every stage of the process that the correct decision criteria are used to help decide which candidate should receive the job offer. Documentation should also be kept with notes about the candidates to help with this decision making. A comparison chart, like the one used in the selection of candidates on page 347, may be used to help employers make effective comparisons between candidates. This may also make it possible to give a rank number to candidates to indicate who is best for the job.

## Communicating the decision to candidates

During the interview candidates will usually be told when and how they will be informed about who has got the job. It is usual for all candidates to have completed their interviews and then for the employer to telephone them later that day or the next day. Sometimes interviews may need to take place over more than one day so it is important to communicate this to candidates.

## Communication and listening skills

Communication skills are necessary for both the interviewer and the candidate during an interview situation. The ability to communicate clearly what you mean and being able to listen to answers is extremely important. Questioning techniques and the type of questions are important but so are listening skills in order to really hear what people are saying and whether or not they would be suited to a particular employer or job. The interview might be by phone, face to face or by video conference, but listening and analytical skills are required. Listening is very important for the interviewer so that they can really hear what the candidate can offer the organisation and make a decision to employ the right person.

Sometimes interviewers will use summarising skills to help them. Summarising is a form of recapping, or going over, what has been said before. If a statement is made the interviewer may start by saying, 'I think you are saying . . . is that correct?' Summarising allows the interviewer to confirm their understanding and show the candidate that they are listening.

## Body language

Body language is very important. Eye contact and smiling can help to communicate that you are open and trustworthy. A firm handshake can show that you are confident and a suitable person for the job; but being over-confident is as counter-productive as being shy and nervous because it may make the interviewer perceive you as big-headed. The way you sit in the interview chair can also give signals to the interviewer. If you slouch backwards during the interview, cross your arms defensively or tap your foot you may appear to not be interested in the position.

There are other non-verbal barriers that may affect how you communicate. Dress is an extremely important issue within recruitment and selection. The way in which you dress for the interview will communicate to your interviewer something about whether or not you will fit in to the organisation. It is usual within the business world to wear smart clothes in an interview, such as a suit, and for men a tie. Your choice of dress may be a barrier to communication if you dress in a way that the interviewer does not expect. Wearing smart, clean clothing, being washed and well groomed with combed hair and appropriate general body hygiene also influences the interviewer subconsciously. A person who smells too much of after-shave or perfume can often create a negative impression as much as someone who has body odour – so this needs to be managed carefully!

## Questioning techniques

The use of effective questioning techniques is also very important. Asking the right questions will help the candidate to give the right answers!

### Open questions

These are questions that give the candidate the opportunity to give an open answer, such as: 'What is your greatest strength?' or 'How would you deal with this problem?' They may also be used to check information given.

### Closed questions

These are questions that only allow a candidate to give a short and defined, closed answer, such as: 'How long did you work at ABC Ltd? or 'How many GCSE's do you have?'

Using a variety of types of question will allow the interviewer to get a good idea about the candidate so it is essential that the questions are prepared well before the interview, especially if the interview is going to be done by a team or panel.

Questions must be fair and appropriate!

**Body language is important in an interview as it shows how interested an applicant is in the job**

## Practice point

Look at the questions below and decide which are closed and which are open questions. Check your answers with someone in your class.

1. Which skills do you think are needed for this job?
2. Do you have a BTEC National Business qualification?
3. Can you type?
4. How long did you work for your last company?
5. What do you think is your biggest weakness?
6. What do you know about our organisation?
7. Is your name Sam Brown?

Imagine you are one of the people asked to interview candidates for the position of sales assistant in a shop. The sales assistant is responsible for customer service, taking money, dealing with the till and filling shelves. Produce a list of closed and open questions that you could ask and practise using them by doing a role play in pairs.

## Barriers to communication

Overcoming barriers to communication is about ensuring the recruitment process is made available in the right places to attract the widest range of candidates possible. Examples of this include: jobs being advertised in Welsh and English for vacancies in Welsh-speaking parts of Wales to promote bi-lingualism amongst the workforce; or advertising vacancies for jobs where women or ethnic groups are under-represented in cultural or single-sex magazines, such as *Cosmopolitan* magazine having job advertisements encouraging women to join the police. New methods of encouraging variety in terms of numbers and types of candidates also include online applications and text messaging information services.

In addition, most organisations have an equal opportunities policy that states how they work to maintain equality of opportunity within their organisation. Equal opportunity policies are designed to

## Case study

**BT plc**

Below is an extract from BT's Equal Opportunity Policy.

> BT is an equal opportunity employer and it is the aim of this policy that all persons, wherever they are in the world, should have equal opportunity for employment and advancement on the basis of their ability, qualifications and suitability for the work.
>
> It is BT's policy that no job applicant or employee receive less favourable treatment in any aspect of employment on racial grounds, or on grounds of gender, religion, disability, marital status, age or sexual orientation, gender status or caring responsibilities, or be disadvantaged by conditions or requirements which cannot be shown to be justifiable. To this end our policies will become the global benchmark, reflecting sensitively the particular circumstances and local cultures of each country and community in which we operate.
>
> There must be no unlawful discrimination; direct, indirect or institutional, against any person whether in recruitment, selection, training, promotion or in any aspect of employment. Harassment of any form at work is also a form of discrimination and will be treated as such under the terms of this policy. No form of harassment or bullying, including derogatory remarks at work, will be tolerated. Cases will be dealt with under the BT Harassment and Bullying Policy.

(*Source:* www.btplc.com)

1. What is the purpose of BT's Harassment and Bullying Policy? ✓
2. What do you think is the difference between indirect and direct discrimination? ✓
3. What benefits do you think BT gains by having an equal opportunity policy? ✓✓
4. How could BT try to measure if its policy is working or not? ✓✓
5. To what extent can organisations remove both indirect and direct discrimination from their organisations? ✓✓✓

encourage candidates to apply for jobs that they may not have considered before. They also give the organisation good publicity as they are seen as being fair.

### Analysing and summarising

Analysing answers and making sense of them may lead to further questions, so it is important that the interviewer has good listening and analytical skills in order to probe the candidate on their suitability for the post in a fair and controlled manner. This may be the only chance the interviewer has to ask questions and compare candidates before deciding who will be chosen for the job. It is crucial that the interviewer can analyse and judge the answers in order to make a decision. One way to do this is by summarising what a candidate has said and checking it back to ensure that what the interviewer thinks is being said is really being said.

## Post-interview

When all the candidates have been interviewed, the job of choosing the best candidate must be carried out. This can be done in many ways but a popular method is to rate the candidates against criteria with a score. The individual scores are then added up and the totals compared. The candidate with the highest score is the one that gets the job. The aim of this is to make the process fairer and more objective. It is important to recognise that the candidate with the highest score will not necessarily be the one with the most qualifications or experience to do the job. It is the person who is 'best' for the job.

### Informing candidates

Once the candidates have been rated and the person chosen for the job, the next stage is to write down any other relevant information on the applicants and why they have not been chosen for the job. This is needed for several reasons but the four main ones are to:

- feedback the information to candidates so they can improve in their next job application
- keep notes on why the person was not suitable for the job for the organisation's own records
- monitor equal opportunities, looking at all the different types of people who applied for the job and did not get it; this demonstrates that the organisation carried out the process fairly and legally
- keep candidates' notes on record, with the candidates' permission, for consideration of other possible vacancies.

### Practice point

To see how a simplified rating system works, rate two candidates based on their histories. Discuss in small groups which of the two would get the job and why!

The job is for a hairdressing junior in a salon with the possibility of training in the future. The pay is minimum wage and the hours are 35 per week. Using the information given, rate the candidates on each of the criteria and give them an overall total.

| Gemma Smith | Zinat Uddin |
| --- | --- |
| Has 3 years full-time work experience in a hairdressing salon but gave up salon but gave up to go and work in an office after a disagreement with the owner.<br>NVQ2 Hairdressing completed. | Has been working on Saturdays for six months in a hairdressing salon while at full-time college doing beauty therapy exams.<br>Has no formal qualifications in hairdressing but has a customer service qualification.<br>Willing to learn new skills. |

| Rating | Gemma | Zinat |
| --- | --- | --- |
| Qualifications required: none essential but NVQ 1 desirable | | |
| Demonstrates good customer service skills | | |
| Able to respond to, and follow instructions | | |
| Well organised and adaptable to change | | |
| Able to work under pressure | | |

## Making a job offer

The successful candidate receives a job offer at this stage. It is usual for the successful candidate to receive communication first so that if they decide not to take the job, the other candidates could be contacted afterwards.

### Verbal/non-verbal offers

A verbal offer is usually the first way of offering the job and commonly this is done by telephone or face to face. In jobs where the candidates have been through one or two days of recruitment interviews this is usually done in the evening after consideration by the interviewer(s). The candidate accepts or declines the job verbally. If they accept, a written offer letter is sent to them to confirm the offer with them.

### Contents of job offer

The written offer letter gives details of all the relevant information that the employee may wish to know, including the start date, salary or wages, hours of work or holiday entitlements. This makes the offer very clear to the candidate. An example of an offer letter is shown opposite (top).

### Other conditions

Sometimes employers will want to make the offer subject to additional conditions such as the taking up of references from previous employers, medical or health checks or the achievement of qualifications. This is known as a conditional offer. An example of this is given opposite (lower).

## Expense claims

Often candidates are able to claim expenses for travel, hotels or meals – this is very important if they have travelled a long way. They must either give their receipts to the organisation on the day of the interview or afterwards by post. It is important that they are given

An offer letter ▶

**BARNACLES LTD**
17 EAST STREET BROMPTON BR9 8KU

Dear Kalpesh

**Job Offer for the Post of Finance Assistant**

Further to your interview of 18 October, I am pleased to offer you the position of Finance Assistant. The post will commence on 1 January. The starting salary is £16,000 per annum. Your working hours will be from 8.30am until 4.30pm, Monday to Friday and you will be entitled to six weeks' holiday per year.

Please could you send written confirmation that you wish to accept this job offer as soon as possible.

Yours sincerely

J Crabb

Mr Crabb
Managing Director

**BARNACLES LTD**
17 EAST STREET BROMPTON BR9 8KU

Dear Kalpesh

**Job Offer for the Post of Finance Assistant**

Further to your interview of 18 July, I am pleased to offer you the position of Finance Assistant. The post will commence on 1 September. The starting salary is £16,000 per annum. Your working hours will be from 8.30am until 4.30pm, Monday to Friday and you will be entitled to six weeks' holiday per year.

This offer is subject to a health check with our medical team and you passing your BTEC National Certificate with Double Merit

We will also be taking up references at this stage.

Please could you send written confirmation that you wish to accept this job offer as soon as possible subject to these conditions.

Yours sincerely

J Crabb

Mr Crabb
Managing Director

▲ A letter containing a conditional job offer

this information at the start of the recruitment process so they are aware of what they need to do. Offering expenses is a good way to attract applicants who are out of the immediate area and so can mean a wider range of candidates to choose from.

## Candidates' feedback

Candidate feedback is also important at the end or after the interview has finished. This may be to gain extra information about candidates or ways that the interview process could be improved the next time. Gaining information from candidates can also be a good way of finding out what they thought of the organisation and if they would apply again. If candidates go away with a negative impression of an organisation they may not apply for other jobs in the future.

## Taking up and checking references

The taking up and checking of references is a critical stage of the recruitment process. It is important because it can confirm where a candidate has worked before and any relevant experience or details from that employer. Some employers will ask for references to be taken up before interview so that a quick decision can be made; other employers will take up references after the interview.

## Police and/or medical checks

Police checks are conducted by the Criminal Records Bureau (CRB). These are particularly important if the job involves working with young or vulnerable people. The candidate will complete an application form that the organisation will then send to the CRB to be checked to see if the person has a criminal record. The organisation needs to pay for this but it ensures that young and vulnerable people are not put in the care of unsuitable employees.

Medical checks can be completed in two ways: either by the employee going to the workplace and having a medical completed or by the organisation writing to the candidate's doctor. If the organisation chooses to use the first method, the candidate must go into the organisation and have a medical examination completed. They must be told why the examination is needed and what is being looked for. If a health issue is then highlighted, reasonable steps should be taken to help that employee do the job in order to comply with the Disability Discrimination Act.

If the organisation uses the doctor to complete a medical check, they must make sure that the information they ask for does not discriminate against the candidate due to disability. The information must also comply with legislation: the Access to Medical Records Act and the Data Protection Act. This means that the candidate must be aware that this information is being collected and written permission given.

▼ **Taking up references**

| Before the interview | After the interview |
|---|---|
| Employers will have all the relevant information before they interview the candidates. | References will only be taken up from the successful candidate so this takes a shorter amount of time.<br>References will not be taken for somebody who is going to turn down the job offer if they have been asked whether they would like the job in interview. |
| References will be taken for candidates who will not be offered the job and this takes a long time.<br>Employees may not wish their current employer to know that they have applied for a job unless they are successful. | The candidate has already been chosen by the organisation and a negative reference at the final stage may mean that the employer needs to rethink the whole job offer. |

### Rejection of unsuccessful candidates

Often employers will decide not to reject unsuccessful candidates until they are certain that their preferred candidate has accepted the job. It is important that decisions and information about why they were unsuccessful is noted so that they can be given feedback to help them with future applications. This should make the reasons for the appointment and non-appointment very clear. It is important that the reasons for someone not being employed are kept in case they ask for further verbal or written feedback. This should avoid any suggestion that the reason they were not appointed was discriminatory, e.g. due to sex, race or age.

## Outcome activity 13.3

To complete this task you will need to take part in a role play demonstrating the interview process. This will include the documentation that is needed before, during and after the interview as part of the selection process. You should use the documents that you prepared for Outcome activities 13.1 and 13.2. A witness statement is provided as an example for you to work with at the end of this Outcome activity.

**Pass**

Take part in a mock interview for the post of Office Administrator as an interviewer or interviewee. 

**Merit**

Compare the purposes of the different documents used in the three stages of the selection process. 

Analyse your contribution to the selection process for the position of Office Administrator. 

**Distinction**

Evaluate the usefulness of the documents in the interview pack in facilitating the interview process. 

Evaluate your experience of planning and participating in the recruitment and selection process. 

## Grading tips

**Pass** 

You should show that you are prepared for the interview and have the necessary documentation for the process including:

- advertisement
- job description
- person specification
- application form or CV and letter of application
- short-listing documentation
- interview checklist including questions.

Your tutor or assessor will complete a witness statement giving details of how you have performed using the witness statement form overleaf. Use the template to help you work on areas that you need to think about when you are performing in the interview.

**Merit** 

Identify all the documents used in the three stages of the selection process. You should explain the purpose of each of the documents and the purpose of the information that the completed documents will provide for the interviewers. You should then draw comparisons between the purposes of those documents, for example showing what they have in common and what is different.

You will be assessed as part of the witness statement below for Merit work. You should demonstrate that:

- you are organised
- the interview has been conducted in a professional manner
- you show suitable preparation
- that appropriate questions are asked
- you show good listening skills
- you show good interviewing skills.

Using your interview pack, make judgements about the usefulness of each of the documents you have produced. How do they help the organisation, management and conduct of the interview and final selection process? How are they limited as part of the selection process?

You should use the information contained within this unit to consider how they help. You may wish to use tools such as SWOT to consider the strengths and weaknesses of the process.

Write a report to evaluate your experience throughout the selection process, including planning, pre-interview, interview and post-interview work. You should consider what went well – the strengths of the process including documentation used in the role plays. You should then consider what did not go so well – the weaknesses of the process.

Make sure you link your evaluation back to the witness statement(s) produced by your assessor and any issues or strengths raised.

| Aspect | Comments |
|---|---|
| Preparation of documentation in advance | |
| Organisation of interview including opening of interview | |
| Checking back of information from application documentation | |
| Professionalism within the interview situation | |
| Quality and appropriateness of questions and questioning techniques | |
| Listening skills | |
| Tone of voice | |
| Body language | |
| Analysing and summarising skills | |
| Closing of interview | |

▲ Witness statement

# 13.4 Implications of the regulatory framework on the process of recruitment and selection

Recruitment and selection is a very important part of any organisation so there is a lot of legislation that must be complied with. This is to ensure that the process is fair and that everyone can get equal access to job vacancies.

## Current UK and EU legislation

The UK is governed by two key areas of legislation: laws passed within the UK and laws passed within the European Union. The EU consists of the 27 European States of Europe which have joined together to become integrated and have free movement of people, goods and services across them. The European Parliament is responsible for passing legislation that affects all the states of the EU. The EU also brings into force directives such as the Equal Pay Directive (75/117) that stops discrimination on the grounds of sex in relation to pay. Each of the main pieces of legislation which currently affect the UK as part of the EU are briefly outlined for you in this section of the unit. You will need to check government websites and publications for the latest information when you are working on your assignment. This is because the law is changing all the time and you need to be aware of the latest changes and their possible effects on recruitment and selection.

### Sex Discrimination Act 1995/97

These Acts make it law that men and women are treated equally. People must not be discriminated against because of their marital status, sex or if they have had their gender reassigned. Indirect and direction discrimination are both unlawful according to the Sex Discrimination Acts.

Direct discrimination means a less qualified man could not be given a job over a more qualified woman.

Indirect discrimination is when a job has requirements that one sex is unable to fulfil compared to the other, e.g. 'must be 6 foot tall' – very few women are this tall.

Sometimes jobs do not have to apply with the Sex Discrimination Acts if they must be carried out by a particular sex, such as a youth worker specialising in helping young women may have to be female. If a particular group is under-represented positive steps can be made to encourage that group, such as offering free management courses to women in a particular organisation because there were not enough.

### Race Relations Act 1992

This Act makes it unlawful for anyone to be discriminated against on the grounds of race, colour, nationality, ethnic origin or national origin. Employees must be protected from discrimination, victimisation and harassment and can use an industrial tribunal to force employers to change the way they operate or to seek compensation. Indirect and direct discrimination can also be applied to the Race Relations Act.

Direct discrimination would be a job being advertised as only suitable for someone of black skin so it would discriminate against anyone with white skin.

Indirect discrimination would be when a job requires someone to only be fair haired so it would be discriminating against non-Caucasians.

### Equal Pay Act 1970

This Act forces employers to pay men and women equally for equal work. This includes all aspects of pay including benefits, childcare allowances, sickness benefits and car allowances. When the Act was brought into force, the gap between the pay of men and women was 37% (Women and Equality Unit). This Act makes

## Case study

**Lorell Garages Ltd**

1. How does this job discriminate directly and indirectly? ✓
2. Rewrite the job advertisement in a more suitable format. ✓
3. To what extent can a fair job advertisement prevent discrimination in the workplace? ✓✓✓

**Blonde-haired person wanted for car technician post in local garage. Must be physically fit and at least 6' 2" tall. No previous experience necessary but should be willing to learn and be prepared to get dirty. Pay subject to negotiation.**

**Closing date: 26 June**

sure that men and women are paid the same amount of money when they are doing:

- the same jobs
- equivalent jobs
- jobs of an equal value.

In April 2003 the Equal Pay Questionnaire was brought into force to help employees to make a complaint if they felt they were receiving unfair pay. The questionnaire is completed by the employee and then by the employer. This makes it easier for both parties to see if there is an issue to be investigated before any proceedings go forward.

### Disability Discrimination Acts 1995 and 2005

The Disability Discrimination Act (DDA) makes it unlawful for a disabled person to be treated less favourably because they are disabled unless there are very good reasons. Reasonable adjustments must be made to premises so that applicants or workers with a disability are not put at a substantial disadvantage. Making reasonable adjustments might include adding handrails for wheelchair access or a hearing loop for a person with a hearing impairment. In April 2005 the new Disability Discrimination Act 2005 was passed, which came fully into force from December 2006. It amended or extended the provision of the DDA 1995. This makes it:

- unlawful for operators of transport vehicles to discriminate against disabled people
- easier for disabled people to rent property and for tenants to make disability-related adaptations
- unlawful for private clubs with 25 or more members to keep disabled people out, just because they have a disability
- include protection for people who have HIV, cancer and multiple sclerosis from the moment they are diagnosed
- ensure that discrimination law covers all the activities of the public sector
- a requirement for public bodies to promote equality of opportunity for disabled people.

### European Working Time Directive

This directive introduced the idea of a maximum working week of 48 hours to be maintained over a period of 17 weeks, 26 weeks or 52 weeks by workforce agreement. It also provides restrictions on the maximum length of nightshifts, provides rest periods and annual leave of four weeks. Employers have to keep records of how many hours an employee has worked to avoid any disputes.

▲ The European Working Time Directive provides guidance on the hours an employee can work

## Employment Act 2002 and Work and Families Act 2006

The Employment Act 2002 covers a number of areas within employment law, including the following:

- it gives mothers the right to 26 weeks' paid maternity leave and 26 weeks unpaid
- it gives two weeks' paternity leave for working fathers and 26 weeks for adoptive parents
- fathers and mothers can ask for flexible working arrangements if they have children under 6 or disabled children under 18
- the Act tries to finish disputes more quickly by introducing grievance and disciplinary procedures into the workplace
- it gives rights to people who are on fixed term contracts
- it helps to monitor equal opportunities through a questionnaire
- it gives members of a trade union paid time off to attend meetings and training.

The Work and Families Act 2006 has extended some aspects of the Employment Act 2002 by offering enhanced legislation for employees and families. The main changes are:

- extended maternity pay from six months to nine months for babies born after 1 April 2007
- extended rights for carers of adults to have flexible working hours
- up to 26 weeks' paternity leave for fathers (with or without pay depending on the mother's situation)
- the introduction of better planning and other measures for employers to deal with planned leave
- improved communication between employers and employees during maternity leave.

## National Minimum Wage

The National Minimum Wage is the amount of money set by the government as recommended by the Low Pay Commission. Each year the amount goes up but it is the minimum amount that workers aged 16 or over must be paid for doing a job of work. There are very few exceptions to this amount and specific rates are given for workers aged 16 and 17 as well as 18 to 21 years and 22 or over. These amounts are the minimum rates that must be paid but of course employers can choose to pay more if they wish.

In October 2006 the rates were:

- adults (people aged 22 and over) receive the full rate of £5.35 an hour
- a 'development rate' of £4.45 an hour is paid to workers aged 18 to 21 inclusive
- young people (those older than school-leaving age and younger than 18) receive £3.30 an hour.

(*Source* www.direct.gov.uk)

If employees are not being paid the minimum wage they can ring a helpline operated by National Minimum Wage Compliance Officers to report their employer either by giving their name or anonymously.

### Data Protection Act 1998

The Data Protection Act 1998 came into force in 2000 and aims to protect an individual's right to privacy in relation to their personal data. Personal data does not just mean personal details such as medical information, it means any data relating to a living person. This includes information about current employees and anyone who applies for a job such as their address, pay, bank details, date of birth, training record or references.

This information can only be kept if a person has consented to it being stored or if it is necessary for the performance of the person's job. The Data Protection Act seeks to provide a balance between the interests of an organisation that holds data and the individual. It gives individuals the rights to:

- access the information
- stop information being held about them
- prevent the information being passed on for marketing purposes
- compensation and the ability to ask the data controller to rectify errors.

## Ethical issues

The final aspect of the recruitment and selection process that you should consider are the related ethical issues.

### Asking candidates the same qquestions

The first ethical issue that has already been outlined is asking the candidates the same questions. This makes it fairer for everyone as their answers can be compared more easily. It is only discriminatory to ask different questions of candidates if they are unfair to those candidates so this is not a legal obligation but an ethical one.

### Interviewers not related to candidates

It is not ethical for a member of staff to interview candidates if they are related to them by marriage or if they are directly related. This is because there may be a conflict of interest as the member of staff wants to give a job to their relative. Interviewers may also let their employer know they cannot interview if they are friends or former colleagues of a person and therefore may be biased. This can avoid the suggestion that a candidate only got the job because of who they were related to or who they were friends with. This makes the process more open and fair. Many application forms now ask applicants to make it clear if they have personal links with any member of the senior management team or other significant individuals within the institution.

### Gender and ethnic balance on panels

It is also important from an ethical perspective to make sure that the interview process, including the interview panel, reflects a balance of employees or managers of both sexes, male and female, and different ethnic groups, e.g. white, black or Asian. This is important because different ethnic group members might provide a more balanced judgement of a candidate and have different qualities that they think are important in an employee. This rounded judgement should ensure that the right candidate is chosen to fit in with everyone.

## Outcome activity 13.4

**Pass**

Refer back to Outcome 13.3 which involved a mock interview for the post of Office Administrator. Design a concise briefing sheet for the interviewer to guide them on the regulatory requirements of recruitment and selection practice. P5

## Grading tips

**Pass** P5

- You should include information on the legislation included within this unit and the impact of that legislation on recruitment.
- Make sure you add appropriate headings and keep your briefing sheet clear.
- You may wish to use images or charts to enhance your work.
- Include a bibliography of sources of useful information from your research.

## End of unit test

1. Describe three reasons why an organisation may wish to recruit.
2. Name two benefits of externally recruiting.
3. Name two benefits of internally recruiting.
4. What is the difference between a job description and a person specification?
5. Name two types of information usually given on a job description.
6. Describe one advantage of using CVs as part of the application process.
7. Describe one disadvantage of using the telephone as part of the application process.
8. Give two advantages of online recruitment.
9. Give two disadvantages of online recruitment.
10. What does compliance mean?
11. What is the purpose of a selection centre?
12. What are psychometric tests?
13. Describe the difference between open and closed questions.
14. What does candidate rating involve?
15. What does outsourcing involve?
16. Name and describe four different pieces of legislation that must be followed in the recruitment and selection process.

## Resources

www.cipd.co.uk – Chartered Institute of Personnel and Development website with lots of information on all types of recruitment and advertising activity

www.direct.gov.uk/Homepage/fs/en – Government website with information on public services and including information on legislation such as the Disability Discrimination Acts

www.ico.gov.uk – Information Commissioner's website providing information about the Data Protection Act and other information issues

www.lawontheweb.co.uk – 'Law on the Web' site with information on law relating to all aspects of recruitment including discrimination

www.dti.gov.uk – Department of Trade and Industry with information on recruitment and training processes

www.jobcentreplus.gov.uk – Job centre website with links and information about current vacancies

## Books

Bartol, K. M. and Martin, D. C. 2001 *Management*, Irwin

Bratton, J. and Gold, J. 2003 *Human Resource Management: Theory and Practice*, Palgrave Macmillan

Cuming, M. W. 1993 *The Theory and Practice of Personnel Management*, Butterworth-Heinemann

Edenborough, R. 2002 *Effective Interviewing: A Handbook of Skills and Techniques*, Kogan Page

Fowler, A. 2000 *Writing Job Descriptions (Management Shapers)*, Chartered Institute of Personnel and Development

Gillespie, A. 2002 *Business in Action*, Hodder Arnold

Grout J. and Perrin, S. 2002 *Recruiting Excellence: An Insider's Guide to Sourcing TopTalent*, McGraw Hill

Martin, M. and Jackson, T. 2002 *Personnel Practice (People and Organizations)*, Chartered Institute of Personnel and Development

## Journals

*Personnel Today*
*Personnel Review*
*Personnel Management*

| Grading criteria | Outcome activity | Page number |
|---|---|---|
| To achieve a pass grade the evidence must show that the learner is able to: | | |
| P1 Identify how two organisations plan recruitment using internal and external sources | 13.1 | 339 |
| P2 Prepare the advertising, job description and person specification required to recruit an employee for a specific role in a selected organisation | 13.2 | 346 |
| P3 Apply for a job by completing the application documentation | 13.2 | 346 |
| P4 Participate in a selection interview | 13.3 | 359 |
| P5 Design a concise briefing sheet for a selection panel to guide them on the regulatory requirements of recruitment and selection practice | 13.4 | 365 |
| To achieve a merit grade the evidence must show that, in addition to the pass criteria, the learner is able to: | | |
| M1 Compare the purposes of the different documents used in the selection process of a given organisation | 13.3 | 359 |
| M2 Analyse your contribution to the selection process in a given situation | 13.3 | 359 |
| To achieve a distinction grade the evidence must show that, in addition to the pass and merit criteria, the learner is able to: | | |
| D1 Evaluate the usefulness of the documents in the interview pack of a given organisation in facilitating the interview process | 13.3 | 359 |
| D2 Evaluate your experience of planning and participating in the recruitment and selection process | 13.3 | 359 |

# Exploring team development

## Introduction

Modern workplaces are typically characterised by teamwork, whether this is working in a McDonald's crew or in the customer service team at a large insurance company or bank. Increasingly, individuals working in teams are asked to take on more responsibility, so that most young team members get some experience of supervising others.

Teams typically work together towards the achievement of organisational objectives. It is essential therefore to develop an understanding of the processes involved in effective teamwork and the contribution that individuals can make to creating high-performance teams. This unit explores important issues in the management of teams: including how teams are formed, the ingredients of effective teamwork, contributions made by individuals towards achieving team objectives, and how to create a high-performance team. You will need to identify your own strengths which will enable you to make a positive contribution to teamwork. You will also be given opportunities to identify the strengths that you will need to develop to become an even better team member.

### What you need to learn

On completion of this unit you should:

1. Understand the importance of teams
2. Understand team development
3. Know how teamwork supports organisational performance
4. Be able to work as a team member.

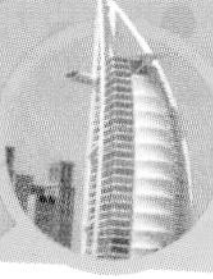

## Consider this

The photograph shows a team in action – working to put out a fire. You will be able to think of many other examples of teamwork – caring for others, achieving sales objectives, coming up with creative ideas and so on.

1. What sorts of qualities do you think that team members generally need to have to be able to make a good contribution to the well being and success of the team?
2. What specific skills might individual members of a team need to have?
3. What sorts of teamwork skills do you possess which would help you to make a contribution to a team?

# 19.1 Importance of teams

## Practice point

Try the following activity. First you must work on your own to answer the questions in the box. You have three minutes to do this. Next you can work with two or three other students to answer the questions. You have an additional three minutes to do this. You can then calculate the difference in performance by counting up:

- The total score of individuals working on their own.
- The total score of the group members when working together.

**Questions:**

1. What countries are the following the capitals of?
   a. Nairobi b. Brussels c. Tel Aviv d. Madrid
   e. New Delhi f. Warsaw g. Manila h. Christchurch
2. Which football teams play at the following grounds?
   a. Oakwell b. Old Trafford c. Ninian Park d. Anfield
   e. Hillsborough h. The Emirates Stadium i. Ewood Park
3. What clothing items do you associate with these brands?
   a. Jimmy Choo and Tods
   b. Mulberry and Fendi
   c. gent Provocateur and Triumph
   d. Burberry
   e. Speedo.

(Answers to these questions can be found at the end of the unit on page 398.)

This practice point should illustrate for you one of the most important benefits of teams. A team typically has considerably more combined knowledge than the individuals that make up the team have on their own. Teams benefit by pooling knowledge, information, skills, and ideas.

## Types of team

A team is a collection of people with a shared purpose and a commitment to working together.

- A **formal team** is one that is created for a specific purpose – for example a Premier League football team or the management team of a company. A formal team is recognised as being 'official' and will normally be set up to perform a set task or group of tasks.
- An **informal team** develops in a less structured way. For example, a group of students might start a discussion in the canteen about something they are not happy with and then agree to do something about it together, or a collection of people kicking a football around in the local park might decide to split into teams to play a game.

Formal teams have more rules, and clearer expectations about the parts that team members should play. For example, a committee will have roles such as chair, secretary, treasurer and so on. The team may have written rules.

## Thinking point

What formal or informal teams have you been part of recently? Were they small or large? Were they permanent groupings, or temporary project teams? Compare your answers with those of others in your group.

Some teams are very small, such as two or three students working together on an assignment; whereas others may be much larger, consisting of hundreds – for example a team of volunteers searching for a missing child.

## Size

The size of a team needs to be appropriate to the mix of individuals needed in the team, the task in hand, and the speed with which decisions are to be made. If an important decision needs to be made by tomorrow, there is little point in having a very large team to discuss the problem – this will only slow down the decision-making process.

It has been suggested that the optimum team size is five people, because:

- the odd number will prevent a deadlock in decision making
- the team is sufficiently large to avoid the mistakes that result from insufficient information, or the power of one individual with an entrenched view
- the group is small enough to involve everyone.

Others argue that a modern team should include between five and 15 members. The team will be large enough to provide sufficient resources, but small enough to function efficiently. If the size of the team grows too big, it will be as difficult for the members to manage themselves successfully as it would be for a traditional supervisor to manage them.

### Thinking point

1. Think of your own experience of working in teams on project-based work for this course. What was the best size of team, and why?
2. Contrast this with another activity you have been involved with, where a different team size was more effective. Why is the size of team that you have mentioned more appropriate in this other situation?

## Temporary and permanent teams

Temporary project or task teams are set up for a relatively short period of time to complete a task. They come together to agree on a team plan, and they split up when the project is completed. For example, a property development team may come together to renovate and sell an old house. The project team might include an architect, interior designers, and building contractors. In modern organisations, teams will frequently be assembled to work on shared projects, such as advertising campaigns for different products. Individuals will frequently work for several teams at the same time.

In contrast, a permanent team is one that works together continuously. Their work is frequently ongoing. For example, a group of business lecturers may work together in a business team for years, although they may also be part of other project teams.

### Thinking point

Identify one project team and one permanent team that you have been a member of. Which team stayed together longer? How did the nature of the work in the two teams differ? Was there a definite start and end to the work of the teams?

## Project and task teams

It is also possible to classify teams according to how they work, and what types of people they usually consist of. For example:

- management teams are made up of managers representing various functions, and coordinating other teams
- problem-solving teams work together to resolve a particular problem
- work teams undertake the daily work of the organisation
- **quality circles** are teams who work together to resolve work-based problems
- virtual teams interact and communicate through the Internet.

### Key Terms

**Quality circle** A study group of volunteers (typically five to 15 people) who meet regularly to discuss and work on a variety of work-related problems and to put solutions in place.

## Practice point

For this activity you will need to work in a discussion group made up of an odd number of students, e.g. three, five or seven. You are part of a project team working to complete an advertising campaign for a well-known business producing a health food product. It is essential that the project is completed on time and it requires clear leadership. For the project you have been offered some expert advice from one of the following:

- Jade Goody of *Big Brother* fame
- Ruth Badger from *The Apprentice*
- Laurence Llewlyn Bowen from *Changing Rooms*.

As a group you need to decide which of the above you would want to take advice from:

a. If your team was to operate as a formal team, and

b. If your team was to operate as an informal team.

# Benefits of teams

Teamwork can make a major contribution to departmental and organisational productivity and effectiveness. Project teams can be formed to enable organisations to meet goals at key levels – for example at departmental level. So in an insurance company, employees who deal with customers are the 'front-line troops'. In dealing with insurance claims involving car accidents a front-line team may consist of a customer service team made up of claims managers and damage assessors, and clerical support staff responsible for dealing with compensation payments or customer repayment for losses (indemnity). This team and many others will help to deliver the company's aims of putting the customer first.

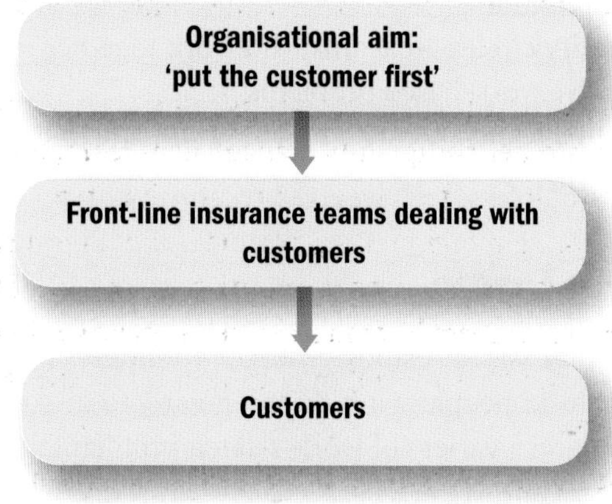


▲ Putting the customer first

Working together, the team creates a positive **synergy**; in other words team members are able to do more together than they could do if they were to work as individuals.

### Key Terms

**Synergy** Sometimes described as the 2 + 2 = 5 effect, i.e. the combination of individual efforts leading to greater efficiency, because the combined effort is greater than the sum of the individual efforts.

## Accountability

Accountability involves making sure that the team takes on responsibility for meeting team goals, while at the same time individuals play their required roles. Creating a team makes it possible to identify within the organisation the human resource (employee) contribution to meeting organisational objectives. It is easier to identify how many people are needed and what skills they should have. This is particularly important today because in many service organisations the human resource is much more important than other resources – for example in hairdressing, financial services and insurance. The table shows some examples of accountable teams in service organisations.

| Industry | Team | Accountability of the team |
|---|---|---|
| Hairdressing | Receptionist, hair washer, technician, stylist | To provide client satisfaction with the salon experience |
| Football | Manager, coach, goalkeeper, defence, midfield, attack | To play interesting football and win games |
| Air travel | Ground staff, cabin crew, pilot, other staff | To provide a smooth, relaxing, safe and punctual travel experience |

## Thinking point

Identify three teams in other service areas. Identify the sector, the team, and the accountability of the team.

Teams frequently consist of employees from different levels within the organisation and with different specialisms. For example, a multi-level, multi-specialism team in an advertising agency may consist of:

- senior advertising account managers as well as junior trainees, such as recently employed graphic artists
- individuals with a range of specialist skills, for example selling to clients or financial management, as well as creative people such as artists, computer animation specialists, and so on.

### Task and process

There are two main elements to working in a team: the task and the process. The task is what needs to be done and the process is the way in which the team works together. For example, in an Argos store, customer orders are taken and money is paid at the reception area. The orders are then electronically communicated to the warehouse area, from where items are collected by a team of staff who bring them to the collection area for customers to pick up. For the collection team, the task involves examining a customer's order and bringing out the item or items they have ordered. The process includes the way in which the employee interacts with other members of their team and with the customer. Both the task and the process are important; if the task is done badly, the wrong items may be brought out, and if th poor, employees may not work well togethe customers properly.

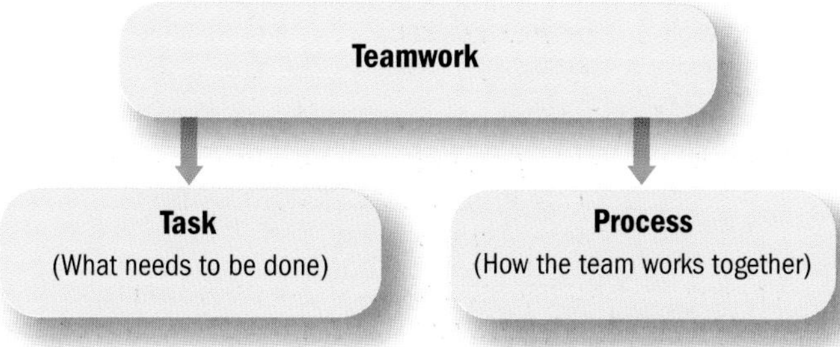


▲ Task and process are important elements in teamwork

Other requirements for an effective team which relate to the task and the process include the following.

- Task-relevant experience – if team members have had experience of carrying out a particular task before, they can usually make a better team contribution. A supermarket restaurant worker who is used to dealing with customer complaints can help new trainees in the team when dealing with an angry customer.
- Definitions of responsibility within and between teams – in a hockey team, you wouldn't want your goalkeeper rushing up the field to try to join the attack. People need to have clear team roles, such as team leader or note-taker, so that individuals know where they stand. It is also important to avoid an unplanned overlap between the work of two teams, where they duplicate each other's work or get in each other's way.
- Feeling of interdependence – if they are to believe in the effectiveness of their team, members need to know their work will contribute to the work of other team members, and vice versa.
- Feeling of involvement – someone who is left out of the task or the process will not be an effective member of the team.
- Mutual respect and support – teams need cohesion, which is like an invisible glue that helps to create team synergy. Respecting and supporting each other will produce this.
- Responsibility for individual development – if individuals' development needs are ignored, they won't feel that the team has their interests at heart, and will lose motivation.
- Opportunities to take responsibility and ownership – a customer complaints management team, for example, needs to be given responsibility for handling individual complaints using their own skills and discretion (given appropriate training). If the team members have to refer to a supervisor in every instance, they are not operating as a self-managing team.
- Flexibility – team members need to be willing to adapt to meet changing needs and circumstances.

▲ People need to have clear team roles

## Thinking point

Think of a team you were a member of which worked well together and which was part of a larger organisation. What were the benefits of that team to the organisation it was associated with?

## Case study

### Production teams at Jaguar

The Jaguar plant at Castle Bromwich near Birmingham is one of the most productive car-producing units in Europe. At Castle Bromwich, employees work in teams known as quality circles alongside the production line. Each team has a team leader who is an expert in all of the processes involved at a particular stage of production. The team has its own rest and discussion area alongside its work area, with comfortable chairs, tables and a display area.

The team can take time out from production to discuss work-related problems – with the aim of identifying improvements in working methods so that they can work smarter rather than harder. The team uses a 'five-minute management' approach, through which they create simple charts and posters setting out work problems and solutions to these problems. The idea is that an outsider can examine these posters, which are displayed on boards, and within five minutes understand what is going on in that work area.

In team discussions everyone is equal and is encouraged to voice an opinion. All views and opinions are listened to before the team suggests work improvements.

1. What are the benefits to Jaguar of employing the teamwork approach described above? ✓
2. What are the benefits to employees? ✓✓
3. How might the Jaguar approach outlined above lead to better results for Jaguar customers? ✓✓✓
4. How could the approach outlined for team working at Jaguar be applied to another teamworking situation with which you are familiar? ✓✓✓

The Jaguar example helps us to appreciate some of the benefits of teamworking, as shown below.

## Contribution to productivity

Teamwork can contribute greatly to departmental and organisational productivity as we have seen with the Jaguar case study. Having a team to contribute ideas and work together also reduces over-reliance on key individuals. This is particularly important at points of pressure in working situations, in which a solution to a problem may be required quickly and key individuals need some help in thinking things through. An example might be an engineering problem, or in a service industry how to deal with a difficult customer. Teamwork situations also provide scope for deputising. Because team members develop a familiarity with the roles of others, they are often able to stand in for or replace key individuals when required.

## Reducing alienation

Everyone has a part to play in a team and this helps motivation, because not only do individuals feel that they have a stake in the decisions made but also they can feel proud of their contributions as they feel part of a team. This helps to reduce **alienation**. In addition, team members are able to learn from each other and develop increased respect for each other, because they are able to see that others sometimes come up with suggestions and approaches that they would not have thought of themselves.

## Fostering innovation

Teamwork approaches also encourage innovation (the generation of new ideas) because people feel empowered to be creative. They know that if their ideas are exciting, other team members will be enthusiastic; but if their ideas are not appropriate someone else in the team will modify them.

### Key Terms

**Alienation** Situation in which individuals do not feel as if they belong to a unit or business. Teamwork helps to reduce alienation by creating a feeling of belonging to the team.

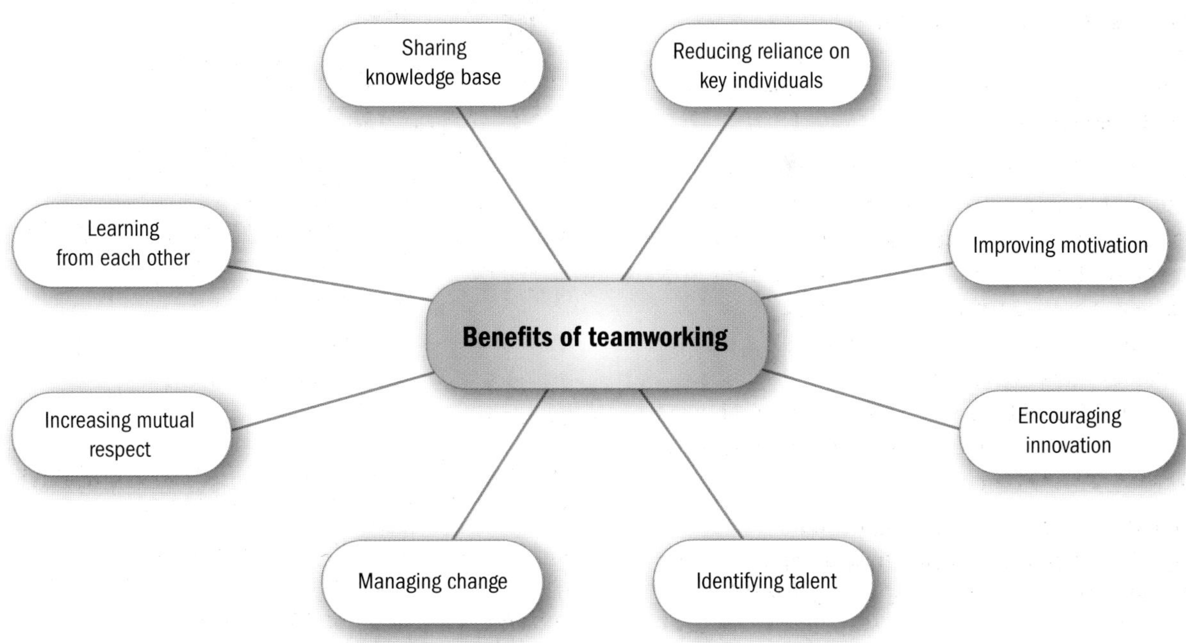


▲ There are many benefits to teamworking

## Sharing expertise

It is possible to share the knowledge base of team members – everyone can contribute ideas. In this way it is possible to share expertise. For example, in a sports team, one member may be able to advise others on how to make the defence work better together. Another may be able to give some useful tips about attacking moves. Another may have played for a rival team and so can tell the others about what playing patterns to expect from the rival outfit. In a similar way, in a management team, one person may have expertise of marketing or sales, another of finance and accounts, another may have worked for a competitor etc.

## Implementing change

Teamwork provides an ideal vehicle for managing change in the organisation. Employees can be resistant to change if it is forced on them from above with little explanation. Introducing change through teams involves considerable shared involvement with and discussion of change processes, leading to a greater sense of ownership of the change.

## Identifying and developing talent

An effective team needs to be made up of people with different skills and abilities to contribute to the team. For example Robert Belbin (see page 379) carried out research in which he identified a number of team roles that help a team to work well. Some of his roles included people who make sure that a task gets completed; other team roles related to making sure that the views of everyone in the team are listened to. One of the important roles of a team leader is to make sure that the team recruits people with the full range of skills required so that a team works well. Just as a sports team manager will need players who perform different roles, e.g. defending the goal or attacking the goal, the team leader of any team needs specialists that are appropriate to the team.

Teamwork also provides an opportunity for managers and supervisors to identify talent within their team, and to provide the development and training opportunities to build on that talent.

## Outcome activity 19.1

Working in a team, you have been assigned the task of identifying various types of teams that exist in a particular organisation, e.g. college, school, workplace or another organisation that team members belong to. Identify the types of teams, e.g. formal, informal, small, large, project or permanent team, etc. Identify the benefits resulting from these teams in various situations within the organisation. It will be easier if you focus this activity on teamwork in a specific workplace which could include your college, school, or other workplace that you have access to. What sorts of functions within the organisation lend themselves to teamwork? For example, you could consider selling and the sales team, or organising and displaying stock. How can teamwork help these functions to be carried out more effectively?

The goal of the team is to produce an interesting and attractive presentation using eight PowerPoint slides or other visuals to identify the benefits of teamwork.

You should then produce a short written report outlining ways in which you contributed to the success of the teamwork project described above. What were your main strengths and weaknesses as a team member?

**Pass**

Describe types of teams and their associated benefits.

**Merit**

In addition to the criteria for P1 compare the roles of the different members of a team.

**Distinction**

In addition to the above, evaluate your own performance as a team worker.

## Grading tips

**Pass** 

Describe teams that exist in an organisation that you are familiar with. What types of team are they? For example, are they formal or informal teams? What is the purpose of each team? Is it a permanent team or one that just comes together for meetings, and irregular events? Give as much information about the team as possible and show how it fits into specific organisational functions, e.g. is it an administrative team, a marketing team? Describe at least three team structures.

**Merit** 

How is the team organised, e.g. does it have a team leader, are there various roles and responsibilities in the team? What does each member do in the team? Perhaps you could set out a questionnaire for team members, asking them to identify which of Belbin's roles they see themselves as playing.

**Distinction** 

To do this you could create a questionnaire for other members of your team asking them to identify the teamwork style that most closely fits the way you operate. Describe the strengths and weaknesses that you have as a teamworker. Identify aspects of teamwork where you need to make improvements. Explain ways in which you could improve your skills as a member of a team.

# 19.2 Team development

## Team building

Since good teamwork is a key feature of a successful organisation, it is important to study team building. Teamwork is most likely to be successful when it operates in a supportive environment. Senior managers and team leaders play an important role in creating high-performance teams. However, it is also important to have team members with complementary skills – as outlined by Belbin and others.

Team building starts with recruiting the right mix of team members and then coaching and mentoring members to create a high-performance team. This can be represented in an input, processes and output diagram, as shown here.

**Input**
Recruiting and selecting people who will be good team players

↓

**Processes**
Training them, providing mentoring and coaching, to help them perform better in the team

↓

**Output**
Creates your high-performance team

▲ The process of team building

## Recruitment

One of the key responsibilities in managing and supervising people at work is managing the flow of new people into the organisation and retaining those who are already there. Team managers and supervisors therefore have considerable responsibility for overseeing the successful running of a series of integrated activities involved in team building, as shown in the flowchart below.

The recruitment process involves identifying the skills and competences that will be required in new team members. This is referred to as job analysis, and from this a person specification can be drawn up setting out all the qualifications and qualities that a new team member would be expected to have.

### Practice point

Set out a person specification for the recruitment of a new team member who would be expected to act as a finisher/completer in a project team brought together to create a new advertising campaign for a cereal bar.

## Induction and training

An induction programme is a series of activities designed to introduce new employees to an organisation, its members, and its working practices. Research has shown that tailor-made induction programmes improve staff retention. The induction period is the time when individuals are introduced to their team. It should be seen as an opportunity for team building.

A good induction programme should include the following:

1. Describing where the facilities are, e.g. toilets, canteen, etc.
2. Showing how the new employee fits into the team.
3. Health and safety information – this is a legal requirement.
4. Explanation of working terms and conditions.
5. Details of the organisation's history, its products and services, and its values. An important value to stress is that of team work.
6. A clear outline of the job role/requirements. The requirements of the job and the job role should be explained in terms of how it fits into the team structure.

There are two broad approaches to training people in teamworking: experiential learning and counselling.

- Experiential learning is learning by carrying out real or simulated tasks. This may involve analysing case studies. More often it involves carrying out a number of brief tasks which can be completed successfully with the necessary team skills. After each task, the team, with the guidance of the trainer, analyses the lessons learned from the exercise. In a teamwork situation experiential learning would involve some form of team simulation or real teamwork exercise. For example, this might include some form of problem-solving activity that has to be carried out in a team structure.
- A counselling approach is usually more appropriate with management teams. The trainer is a consultant and adviser and works both with the team and with its individual members.

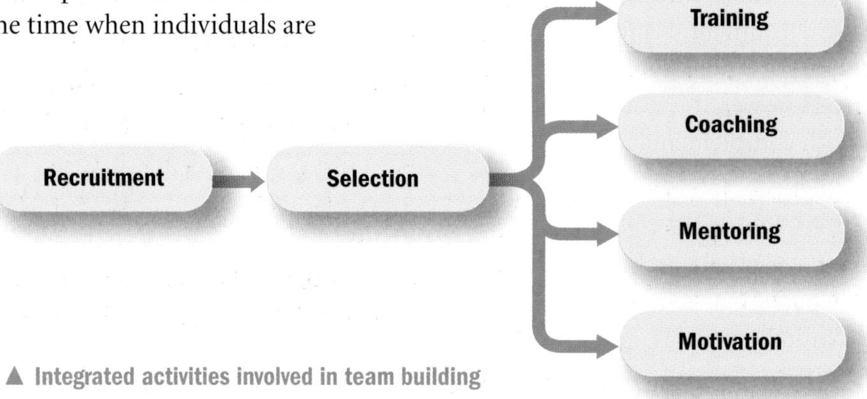


▲ Integrated activities involved in team building

## Coaching and mentoring

Both coaching and mentoring involve an experienced person helping a learner to become more effective. However, there are four key differences between mentoring and coaching:

- Mentoring is a long, if intermittent, relationship; coaching can cover a long time span, but it can also be limited to a single session.
- Coaching is a valuable skill for line managers and supervisors; the mentoring role, by contrast, is separate from that of line manager and the same person should not carry out both.
- The mentoring relationship is less concerned with day-to-day work than with longer-term issues such as working relationships and career paths.
- Coaching can be public – groups of people can be coached – but mentoring is conducted in confidence on a one-to-one basis.

## Motivation

Motivation is an important part of supervising and managing team members. It involves making sure that everyone feels part of a team, and that they are given the right training and development opportunities to contribute to the team. Mentoring and coaching can be used to encourage team members, and to provide targets for them to achieve that are manageable, rewarding and motivating.

## Team knowledge and team roles

Team selection involves identifying potential team members with a specific contribution to make to the team. Team selection will be concerned with identifying a range of personality traits, such as the ability to listen to others, to encourage others to share their ideas, to help the team to move forward, and to make a contribution to a shared decision-making process. Managers will also need to have an awareness of team members' strengths. An understanding of Belbin's roles helps in the selection of team members. Team members can be selected to fill the appropriate roles.

### ■ Belbin's team roles

Dr R. Meredith Belbin identified ways in which people behave when put into syndicates or teams. He identified eight major roles, and argued that teams work particularly effectively when they consist of members who are able to play all of these eight roles. An individual may play more than one role. The important thing is to have all of the eight roles covered.

## Case study

### Coaching to secure change

An international pharmaceutical company has used coaching in recent times as part of a programme of change designed to get the organisation closer to its customers. Managers have had to change the way they operate, from the old-fashioned way of telling employees what to do – to encouraging them to make decisions for themselves working in teams.

Each manager has been assigned a coach. Each pair has between six and eight one-to-one sessions, each two or three hours long, over a six-month period. The manager sets the goals, but it is up to the coach to guide the process. After each session the manager works on the subject covered, and reports on progress next time. One subject covered was coaching skills. Success was measured by feedback from those who worked in teams responsible to the managers.

1. What sort of person would make a good coach? ✓
2. In what ways is the coaching described above different from mentoring? ✓✓
3. Why did the managers need to change from their previous approach of telling employees what to do? ✓✓✓
4. How do you think the employees might have felt about this new approach? ✓✓✓

The different roles are:

1. The chair – who coordinates the team efforts and ensures all resources are used effectively in achieving goals.
2. The shaper – who sets the objectives and priorities and guides the team towards completion of the task.
3. The plant – the creative 'ideas' person.
4. The monitor evaluator – someone who is shrewd and analytical, who can analyse problems and evaluate progress.
5. The resource investigator – is extrovert and good at making outside contacts and reporting developments outside the organisation.
6. The company worker – practical, loyal and task orientated.
7. The teamworker – caring and very person orientated. Keeps the team together and improves communications within the team.
8. The finisher – maintains momentum and ensures the completion of the task.

## Team development

Staff development is an important role for team leaders and supervisory managers. Planned staff development is the process of identifying development opportunities that meet the needs of individuals in your team – which new skills they can learn that will help them with their work. For example, there may be learning opportunities for new IT packages such as presentation software and spreadsheet packages.

### Tuckman and the creation of the high performance team

Tuckman's study of the development of teams is helpful in showing how groups can be developed into real teams given the right sort of support. This is illustrated in a diagram with two dimensions – group effectiveness and time.

## Case study

### Team work assignment

A group of students was working as a team to complete an assignment looking at the value of working in teams.

Sanjay paid particular attention to making sure that the team was focused on getting the task completed on time. When others were slacking he set out to remind them of goals and priorities.

Sumita felt that if the team was going to work well then it would be essential to involve everyone. She spent a lot of time talking to and encouraging others in order to make everyone feel part of the team.

Lloyd felt the team would only work well if it had clear direction. He saw himself as a leader, pulling together the various components of the teamwork and making sure that each of the components of the team had the necessary resources.

Mohammad realised that if the group was going to get high marks then it would be necessary to tackle the project in unconventional ways. He therefore sought out exciting new methods of working and new ideas to give his team an edge over rivals.

Sandrine was good at looking at what had been achieved and weighing up progress in order to inform other members of the team about what remained to be done. She was good at analysing information and building it into reports.

Sylvester saw himself as a 'mover and shaker', with lots of contacts that he could draw on for advice and information. He was able to use these contacts to benefit the team project.

1. Can you identify the nature of each of the roles described in terms of Belbin's teamwork roles? ✓
2. Which of these roles are more concerned with building the processes of team working and which are more concerned with completing the task? ✓✓
3. What roles appear to be missing in terms of creating an effective team? ✓✓
4. Describe two or three individuals who could complete the team by filling the missing roles. ✓✓✓

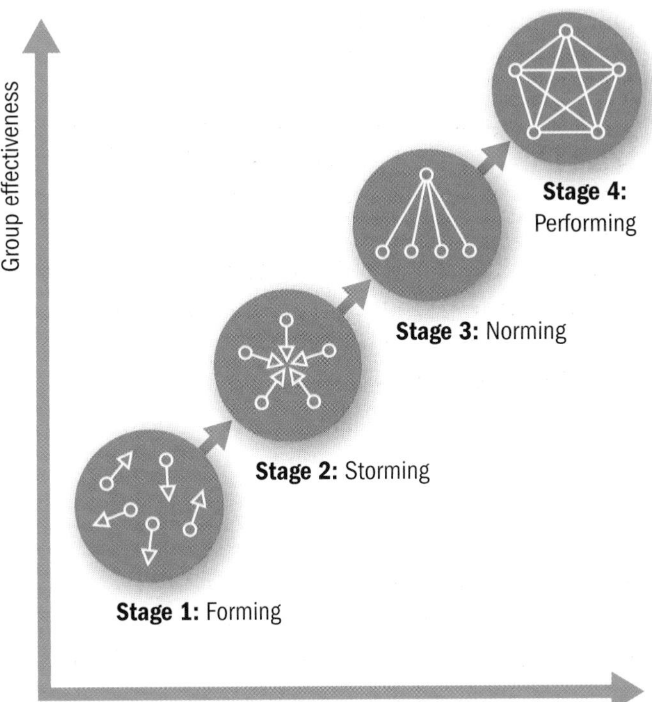


▲ Stages of small group development

Tuckman identifies four stages:

1. **Forming** – a number of individuals come together. They are simply that – a loose collection with no clear sense of purpose.
2. **Storming** – the group begins to exchange ideas, but there is as yet little structure to the group, and there are no clear plans to take the group forward.
3. **Norming** – the group beings to share ideas – a team begins to form. A leadership pattern may begin to emerge, and the group starts to conform to a given set of ideas. Decisions begin to be formulated.
4. **Performing** – this is where the group is transformed into a high-performance team. A clear organisational pattern is formed, based on mutual respect, the sharing of ideas and the drawing out of plans and proposals from all members of the team. Every member of the team is therefore able to make the best possible contribution to the group process.

## Supporting team members

Team leaders have an important responsibility for helping to build team morale by supporting and encouraging their team members. Good team leaders are aware of the strengths, weaknesses and sensitivities of team members and make it their business to try to support all team members. The team leader who motivates the team and makes them feel valued is able to retain valued employees (enabling the organisation to be more effective and to reduce costs). Good team leaders also know when to delegate. You don't have to do everything yourself; you need to know when to trust other team members. Trusted team members are typically the most committed ones.

## Understanding weaknesses and sensitivities

Good team leaders and team developers understand the strengths and weaknesses of their team members. For example, some team members are good at coming up with ideas, others are good at the process side of things, i.e. making people feel comfortable within the team. Good team leadership and team membership involves being sensitive to the skills and abilities of others. For example, if someone has good ideas it helps if others are encouraged to listen to these ideas. If someone is good at finishing and completing a project then they can be given more responsibility in the later stages of the project.

### Thinking point

The following have been identified as the qualities of a successful teamworker:

- has good listening skills
- has good persuasive communication skills
- able to express technical ideas lucidly to persuade other people
- receptive to new ideas
- not afraid to look foolish by airing new or unconventional ideas
- understands and is committed to the team's objectives
- can give and take constructive criticism
- trusts and is trusted by fellow team members
- expresses feelings honestly and openly
- does not claim personal credit for a team success.

Which of the above characteristics do you honestly believe you have recently shown in team situations?

# Team performance

Business organisations place a strong emphasis on performance. There are four main ways of measuring team performance:

1. Individual's contribution to the team – this can be measured by how the individual works with other team members. For example, this could be shown by the extent to which they contribute to team meetings, whether they volunteer for team projects, how they communicate with others (e.g. supportive or threatening way).
2. In terms of individual results from teamwork. The work carried out by a team member that contributes to the final team product could be assessed.
3. Measuring the team performance. This could involve looking at team dynamics; for example, how well the team works together, the effectiveness of team meetings, the ability of the team to achieve agreement, etc.
4. Team results. The team performance could be measured in terms of its work results, e.g. number of cases or products completed, the use and acceptance of the team's report, etc.

You can see therefore that there are different ways in which the performance of the team can be measured. In judging team performance you need to decide on which measures to use – probably a combination of several of them.

## Performance indicators

In business it is good practice to create performance indicators (PIs). A performance indicator helps to measure the extent to which an individual or team meets targets.

Team performance indicators (TPIs) can be set out in terms of processes or in terms of products or outputs. For example, a team effectiveness process indicator might be that 90% of team members attend team meetings, and that teams agree to arrive at a consensus view by voting on issues where there is disagreement.

Output/product indicators are measured in terms of the results of team activities. For example, you could measure the effectiveness of a sales team in terms of the number of sales that the team makes.

## Target setting

These TPIs act as targets for teamwork activity. Examples might include:

- that the team will meet at regular weekly intervals
- everyone in the team will have the chance at some stage to chair a team meeting
- the team will set out to make sure that the views of all participants are listened to.

In addition the team might set work-based targets, for example:

- as a team to increase output by 5% per month
- that individuals in the team will each increase their output by 5% per month.

It is then a fairly straightforward task to monitor the success of the team in meeting its targets. Regular checks need to be carried out to check that performance is on track. For example, in a student project targets are set that in two weeks time Davinder will have researched the topic, Mohammad will have prepared a PowerPoint presentation, Claire will have interviewed the managing director of a company, etc. A review can then be carried out to check that these individual targets have been met so that the team is on track to complete the project.

## Monitoring and review of performance against targets

It is then possible to measure each individual's performance and the team's performance against these targets. It is possible that certain team members have fallen behind. This indicates that they may need extra support and encouragement. For example, Mohammad may not have completed the PowerPoint presentation because he lacks the right sort of skills or because Claire has not given him the information to put into some of the slides.

## Support and development of team members

Sometimes team members will require additional support to make up for current weaknesses. For example, Mohammad's team leader might put his name forward to go on a training course to further develop his Information Technology skills. The training and development manager in an organisation will liaise closely with team leaders to try to identify training and development needs of individual employees. A TDNA (Training and Development Needs Analysis) can be used to identify areas of weakness in an employee. Using this analysis it is possible to identify the types of training programmes that enable individuals and teams to perform better.

An improvement cycle for team performance is shown below.

### Practice point

For a team project that you are currently working on, decide what the best individual and team performance indicators are. Create measurable targets. Then, once the team project is underway, set a date/dates at which performance will be monitored. Carry out a review. Decide how support will be provided for individuals and the team if the project falls behind plan.

# Team cohesion

The word 'cohesive' means 'sticking together'. In cohesive teams some team members tend to concentrate on task functions while others focus on process maintenance roles.

Task functions help the team to get the task done. They include:

- proposing objectives
- clarifying goals
- seeking information and opinions
- keeping the group on track
- summarising ideas
- suggesting ways forward
- evaluating contributions.

Process maintenance roles include:

- supporting other group members
- ensuring all members of the group are included
- reconciling disagreements and reducing tension
- making suggestions for compromise
- monitoring the group.

### Thinking point

In team situations, do you tend to concentrate on task functions or maintenance roles?

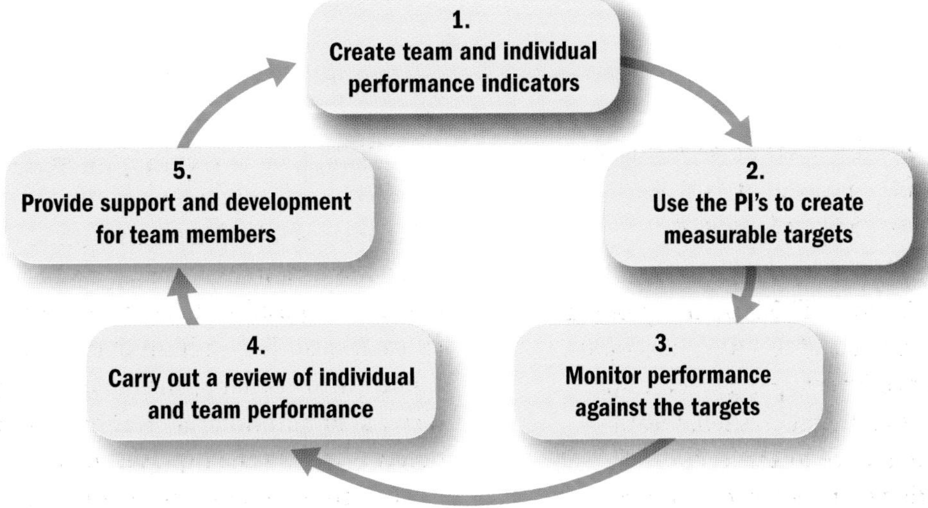


▲ Improvement cycle for team performance

## Case study

### Belbin's other team members

We saw above that Belbin identified eight roles that are required for effective team work. However, Belbin neglected to mention some of the other players that you are likely to come across in teamwork situations. These include:

9. The clueless one, who has no idea about team goals and confuses everyone by identifying irrelevant issues which bear no relation to team goals.
10. The idler, who promises to do all sorts of things by given deadlines, but the work never materialises so the rest of the team becomes disenchanted and demotivated.
11. The critic, who knocks down everyone else's ideas but comes up with nothing practical or realistic to replace them.
12. The rude one, who offends and intimidates other members of the team, so that they are discouraged from contributing.
13. The apathetic one, who doesn't join in and looks disenchanted.
14. The 'doesn't-turn-upper', who isn't there, doesn't want to get involved and hasn't done the required work in any case.

1. Which of the above do you find the most frustrating to have to work with? ✓
2. Have you ever played one of the roles described above? If so, what sort of impact do you think you had on team motivation and performance? ✓✓
3. Which of the above is most likely to spoil group cohesion? What sort of conflict is likely to arise? ✓✓✓
4. What sorts of strategies could be applied by a team leader to deal with the conflict you mentioned in point 3 above? ✓

▲ The 'doesn't turn up' type of team member can threaten team cohesion and effectiveness

## Problems with cohesion

Lack of cohesion in teams can occur for the following reasons.

- Team goals are poorly defined. If you don't know what the goal is, how do you expect to achieve it? How can people pull in the same direction, if they don't know what that direction is?
- High turnover of team members. There is no continuity or stability. What the team previously agreed on may be disputed by new members. High turnover is typically a sign of poor motivation.
- Little opportunity for career progression. Commitment to the team will be limited because most people want opportunities for personal development and career progression.
- Contributions are not recognised or rewarded. People will be less inclined to contribute next time. They don't like being taken for granted or having the credit for their work taken by someone else. They feel cheated.
- Weak or authoritarian team leadership. Under weak leadership a team quickly loses direction. Under an authoritarian leader team members are frightened to voice their ideas and innovation is stifled.

- Internal challenges to team leadership. This can lead to disputes, disagreements and lack of focus on team goals. Both the process and the task performance begin to lack clarity. This is also the case when actual or potential conflict between members exists. In these situations individuals concentrate on individual differences rather than team goals.
- The team is unable to **self-manage**. In the absence of the team leader or supervisor the ongoing effectiveness of the team suffers.
- Particular members are not suited to the nature of the work. For example, a team leader in a situation requiring democratic discussion may be too used to operating in an autocratic way.
- Personal problems. Members' personal problems may prevent them from concentrating on their work.
- Frequent resort to crisis management. Rather than planning ahead, and deciding on priorities and ways of tackling problems when they arise, teams may be faced by problem after problem, all of which need to be resolved immediately, and have no clear framework for dealing with them.

In the event of team under-achievement, corrective measures will need to be applied. Many of these will relate to the process, and some will relate to both the task and process. For example, in situations where the team leader may be away on important business, the team needs to be **empowered** to operate as a self-managing team, making decisions for itself, with appropriate structures for working independently without supervision.

## Key Terms

**Self-managing team** Team that has had the training and developed the skills to work on its own to solve work-related issues.

**Empowerment** The process of spreading power and decision-making responsibility across the organisation and within teams, rather than a few key individuals retaining it.

In order to create team cohesion it is essential to develop a number of team management strategies to avoid the problems noted above.

### Definition of team goals

From the outset it is essential to set out clear team goals. What is it that the team is seeking to achieve? For example, if the goal is to play entertaining football then this is quite difficult from the goal of trying not to lose a match. In the former the team could legitimately concentrate on attack, in the latter the emphasis might be more on defence. If team members are clear about their goals they are more likely to concentrate effectively on them.

### Management of group conflict

It is very important to develop strategies for managing conflict. Actual conflict occurs when there are obvious disagreements. Different team members want things to be done in different ways. Team managers can also anticipate potential conflict. For example, in a team with an ideas person who is a poor finisher others may be frustrated by the inability of the ideas person to complete tasks. It is therefore essential to be aware of this potential difficulty, perhaps by allowing the ideas person to generate ideas but not have responsibility for task completion.

### Management of group turnover

Group turnover is another major issue in business. New people come into the team while others leave to work elsewhere. This can be harmful if a key member of a team leaves at a crucial time. Ways of dealing with this include preparing succession management, i.e. training someone to take over the role of the person who is leaving – before they go. In preparation for the rugby World Cup in 2007 the New Zealand rugby management made sure that they had two people to fill every position on the field – just in case of injury. Other ways of reducing turnover include providing incentives for people to stay in the team. A good way of doing this is to offer opportunities for career progression at work. A team member does not have to leave because they can be promoted within the team – so they have no cause to go elsewhere. Other strategies involve recognising the contributions of team members; make them feel good about what they are doing – so they feel that they are valued members of the team.

### Team leadership

Weak leadership can be another reason why teams lack cohesion. Teams need to have some sort of direction. However, it is important to have the right leadership for the team. It is helpful to recognise different leadership styles.

- An authoritarian leadership style is one where a particular individual is controlling and likes to make most of the decisions. This works in teams where the rest of the team is happy to be told what to do. However, many people resent authoritarian styles.
- A consultative style is where a leader consults with other team members asking them for advice before coming to a decision for the team. Team members feel more involved although ultimate direction is with the team leader.
- A democratic style is opposite to an authoritarian one. Here there are lots of leaders. Everyone is listened to and plays a part in team decision making.

## Outcome activity 19.2

To carry out this activity you will need to be working as part of a team of students with the responsibility for creating a PowerPoint presentation which sets out:

- the characteristics of a high-performance team
- obstacles in the way of creating a high-performance team
- ways in which these obstacles can be overcome through effective team management
- a description of the way in which your student team has set out to overcome any obstacles to your team development, and how you have created a high-performance team.

**Pass**

Describe ways how to build cohesive teams that perform well.

## Thinking point

Which of the styles outlined above would you prefer to work with in teamwork situations? Which of the leadership styles do you tend to adopt? Can you think of situations in which each of the styles described would be most appropriate?

## Practice point

What corrective measures can you suggest for the following situations? An example is given to get you started.

| Situation | Solution |
|---|---|
| Lack of recognition of members' contributions | Articles in company newsletter naming individuals and their good ideas; bonuses for particularly good ideas |
| Persistent reliance on crisis management | |
| Poor definition of team goals | |
| Weak team leadership | |

## Grading tips

**Pass** 

You need to be able to describe in your presentation how to build a cohesive team that performs well. One way of doing this is to examine the characteristics of high-performance teams and then to use examples of successful teams and show how these examples fit with the theory that you have outlined. You could also give illustrations of obstacles to high team performance by quoting examples, e.g. a well-known example of a team that suffered because one of the members made life difficult for others. Use the example of your own student team to outline ways in which high-performance processes may or may not be achieved.

## Target setting

All organisations have targets that they want to achieve. For example, the England women's rugby team has set itself the target of winning the next World Cup in 2010. Cadbury-Schweppes has set itself the target of being the number one global player in the confectionery, soft drinks and chewing gum markets. The Labour Party has set itself the target of winning the next general election.

The women's rugby football union is made up of several teams – the playing team, the management team, the young player development team, the marketing team and so on. In a similar way, the Cadbury-Schweppes business is made up of finance, marketing, sales and other teams. The Labour Party too has campaign teams, policy development teams and so on.

Teams establish team targets. These team targets are aligned to organisational targets. At the same time the individuals who make up the teams have personal targets which are aligned to team targets. For example, individual players in the England women's rugby team have training and fitness plans to enable them to play at optimum level.

Target setting involves a cycle of objectives, strategies and evaluation that is illustrated below.

Objectives set out what we want to achieve, e.g. for our business to be the market leader. Strategies set out how we are going to achieve these objectives, e.g. by creating quality circles in production, high-quality sales teams, and customer-focused marketing teams. We can then review performance against objectives. If we are not achieving our targets then it may be necessary to revise our objectives or our strategies or both.

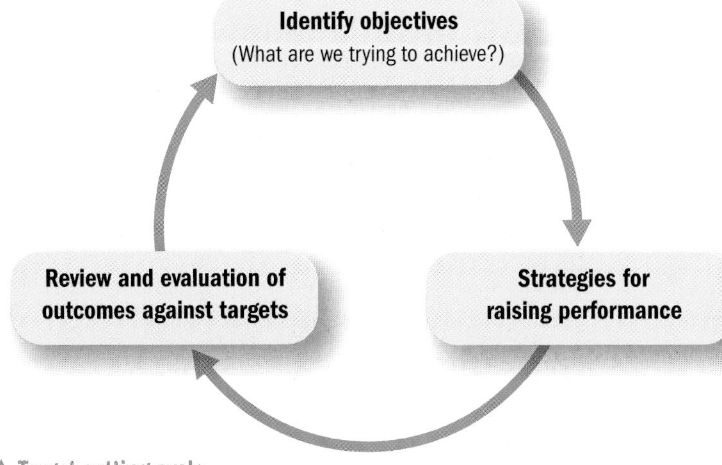


▲ Target setting cycle

▲ Teams and organisations all have targets to aim for

Team leaders and supervisors carry out a number of activities in setting targets, including:

- planning of objectives, targets, and activity schedules
- structuring the way in which the team will be organised to meet its targets, such as who will work with whom, and how relationships will be managed
- organising and scheduling work, taking a lead role in managing the task activities of the team
- prioritising activities – so that the team focuses on essentials, rather than wasting time on less important activities
- controlling the work of the team in order to meet targets – changing the team and teamwork schedules if necessary in order to improve performance
- dealing with contingencies or emergencies – being able to come up with Plan B if Plan A is failing, and being able to intervene in a crisis to successfully steer the team through an emergency

- coordinating the various activities which the team is involved in, for example by establishing schedules so that activities A and B are completed successfully on time for C to start, and making sure that resources such as materials arrive when and where required.

## Identifying objectives

The identification and clarification of team objectives is always an important starting point. In the bustle of everyday working activity, some members of the team can lose sight of the objectives – for example, the football player who gets involved in a fight with a member of the opposing team and is sent off has forgotten that the objective is to win the game! The role of the supervisor or team leader is to keep the team focused on the objectives, and to remind the team of how well they are performing.

## Strategies for raising achievement

The team leader can use a number of approaches and strategies for raising achievement, including:

- continually encouraging the team and getting to know about them as individuals
- being able to model good practice to the rest of the team, perhaps having the ability to do all or most of the team jobs if required
- helping to establish ambitious yet achievable goals and schedules
- encouraging participation in agreeing and setting objectives and targets
- making sure that the reward system (pay, bonuses and so on) reflects effort and achievement
- rotating work within the team, to maintain interest and involvement
- identifying the development needs of team members, and seeing that these are met
- identifying factors holding back achievement and making sure that something is done about them.

## Review and evaluation of outcomes against targets

The team leader and the team will continually need to review progress. For example, in a hairdressing salon, one hair stylist may be slower than others and may need to be scheduled to work with fewer clients. Another stylist may become careless in their work and need help to improve performance.

Evaluation of the process involves weighing up what went badly and what went well over a period of time, in order to make future improvements. Often this leads to a reallocation of tasks. So, for example, a trainee hairdresser, who previously only washed clients' hair, may be promoted to a fully fledged stylist after undergoing suitable training.

## Planning

Managers play a key role in making sure that organisations meet their objectives. Teams can be seen as the front line troops that enable managers to achieve organisational objectives.

A starting point is to create plans. Plans are set out on paper (or in electronic format) and show the various steps and activities that are required to achieve company objectives. At the top level within an organisation there will be a strategic plan for a three- to five-year time period covering the whole organisation. This is then broken down into plans for different parts of the organisation – right down to team action plans which cover a shorter period of time. Clear plans help team members to know where they are going and how their efforts contribute to the achievement of the team's goals.

## Organising and structuring

Another important aspect of management is to create organisational structures. Structures are the patterns of relationships that exist within an organisation. Today many organisations are **flatter** and more **democratic** than in the past.

### Key Terms

**Flat organisation** An organisation with only limited numbers of layers of command. The distance between grassroots employees and senior managers is relatively small.

**Democratic** Organisations in which grassroots employees are involved in decision making.

In teamwork-focused organisations small customer-facing teams deal directly with groups of customers. Employees are given training in customer service but often have considerable freedom in how they deal with customers. Of course, in some environments, such as call centres, their interactions with customers can also be monitored, e.g. through telephone monitoring.

### Prioritising

Team leaders and supervisors are responsible for prioritising work within a team. The role of the team leader may be to allocate teamwork tasks amongst team members so that the team is most effective in managing its workload and hence in meeting company objectives.

### Controlling

Control is an important management or supervisory role. Control is all about setting goals and standards and then taking control actions to make sure that performance meets these goals and standards. Team leaders may have an important role in monitoring team performance, highlighting variances from expected performance and then taking control actions to put the team back on track. For example, in a modern Japanese car factory a team leader can stop the production line at any stage if they feel that the team is falling behind in the completion of a process. Control actions can then be taken to make sure that all the necessary processes are completed before the line is started up again.

### Scheduling of work

A schedule is an action plan setting out when given actions will be taken, and often by whom. For example, a team responsible for displaying fruit and vegetables may be given a daily schedule for setting out how many items will be put on display and in what locations, as well as how stock will be checked at the end of the day to see what has been sold. A team of hairdressers will be given a schedule of client appointments that they need to attend to.

Supervisors play an important role in monitoring this work – checking that it is being done on time, by the right people and to the right quality standards. From time to time the supervisor may need to intervene, for example by shifting an employee to wash or colour a different client's hair than was originally scheduled because 'bottlenecks' are occurring in the scheme of work. Intervention therefore requires thinking on your feet.

### Thinking point

From your own experience of working in a team:

1. Identify ways in which supervisors have intervened and reallocated tasks in an existing work schedule. Why did they make these changes?
2. Explain how you would reallocate work tasks in order to improve the performance of your team.

## Monitoring progress

Team leaders and supervisors have plenty to do in monitoring the progress of their team. A supervisory role involves making sure that the team has clear objectives, that its activities are carefully planned, and that the team has all the necessary support and encouragement

▲ How might scheduling be important in this situation?

required to operate efficiently. Because team objectives are tied to company objectives, the team leader is effectively enabling the organisation to stay on track.

## Practice point

Interview someone who has had team leadership or supervisory experience. Ask them what is involved in monitoring progress at work.

Create a poster entitled 'The role of the team leader in monitoring the work of a team.' Add a photograph of the team leader at the centre if possible, and create a spider diagram illustrating the activities they have to carry out in monitoring team progress.

A number of 'tools' can be used by team leaders to keep the team on track and these are outlined below.

### Milestones

Milestones are markers which show how much distance you have travelled in moving towards your destination. They show you how far you have to go to meet your targets. Milestones are very useful as communication tools because they help to break down an overall target into sub-targets that need to be reached.

For example, where an organisation has set itself the target of becoming the market leader, important milestones along the way may be when it makes its millionth sale or when it becomes the third and then the second biggest business in the market.

### Responsibilities

Allocating responsibilities within a team makes it possible to find out who should be responsible for what. Creating responsibilities breaks down the overall responsibility for meeting organisational and team goals into discrete individual responsibilities.

### Accountability

Accountability means that individuals and teams have to take on responsibility for delivering given results and achievements. They are accountable for their actions and for their results. Usually performance indicators (see above, page 382) are tied to accountability so that it is possible to identify who is doing well and who is not doing so well.

### Renegotiating/rescheduling

Monitoring of team and organisational performance makes it possible to identify where targets are and are not being met. The team leader and relevant managers are then able to renegotiate and reschedule objectives. For example, if performance indicators show that targets have not been met then it might be possible to allocate some of the work to another team, or to create a new schedule with a different time frame.

Renegotiating and rescheduling team objectives and target dates where necessary, requires a flexible approach. It may also be necessary to reschedule patterns of working and timings to accommodate absences, so that work carries on as smoothly as possible.

### Maintaining team focus

Maintaining team focus involves keeping the team on task and aware of team objectives. Monitoring team performance also makes it possible to identify when the team is losing its focus. If this happens then it is helpful to take remedial action such as:

- clarifying the nature of the team's objectives
- engaging in team building and other motivational activities to pick up the focus.

### Review and evaluation

Once a team has been set up then it is important to maintain the momentum of that team. Team leaders and team builders have a key role to play in making sure that the team continues to be a high-performance team. Review and evaluation of team working are therefore essential. Important questions to ask include:

- How well is the team working?
- What steps can be taken to help the team to work better?
- What additional support can be given to the teamwork process?

Analysis and review of the team at work is therefore crucial to keep up the dynamism of any work team. A key aspect of this review is to examine the roles that individuals are playing in the team:

- Does the team consist of people with all of the required skills?
- Are they able to perform the necessary roles?
- Do some individuals need further training in team work skills?

## Practice point

Once your team has been up and running for a few weeks carry out a review to consider:

- Is team momentum being maintained?
- Are the key milestones established for the team being met?
- Does the team consist of people with the required blend of roles?
- Are team targets clear?
- Is everyone pulling in the same direction?
- What improvements can be made to the team dynamic?
- How could these improvements be introduced?

## Revision of individual responsibilities

At times it may be necessary to look at individual responsibilities within a team, particularly if there are problems. The team leader must be aware of and deal effectively with under-performance rather than pretending it doesn't happen. For example, an individual employee may be letting the team down and will have to be given an initial informal warning about behaviour. Another cause of under-performance could be lack of resources or perhaps poor training of team members. A team leader needs to bring this to the attention of more senior managers within the organisation, rather than making do with inferior resources.

## Outcome activity 19.3

To achieve the outcomes for this part of the unit you will need to produce a short team presentation outlining ways in which teamwork supports organisational performance in a specific organisation. Clearly the organisation must be one that involves a number of teams. It may be helpful to focus on the activities of just one of these teams.

**Pass**

Explain how targets are set and team performance is monitored. 

In your team presentation:

- Explain what are the key organisational targets. Show how team work targets are aligned to organisational targets.
- Explain how team performance is monitored within your chosen organisation.

**Merit**

Assess the value of different methods of monitoring the performance of a team. 

## Grading tips

**Pass** 

Find out what the key organisational targets are and how they are set – for example, who is responsible for setting them. How are team targets aligned with organisational targets?

**Merit** 

Once the team is up and running how is its performance monitored? What checks are made on team performance? Typical ways of assessing individual and team performance include the creation of Team Performance Indicators. Now evaluate the effectiveness of different methods. For example, one method might be to look at the extent to which the team meets its work targets. However, another way is to look at team processes, i.e. how well people within the team work together, and how happy and motivated they are. You should compare these or other methods.

# 19.4 Working as a team member

What type of skills do you need to make an effective team member? The next section identifies two main characteristics of effective team skills: communication skills and personal organisation.

## Communication skills

The key communication skills of an effective team worker are shown in the diagram below. Good communication skills are essential in making an important contribution to a team. Different elements of these are outlined below.

### Articulation of ideas

To speak clearly and with confidence you need to feel sure that your ideas are worth sharing. Focus on the key message that you want to get across, and avoid getting sidetracked into irrelevant issues. Avoid long pauses and 'ers' and 'ums' that break up the flow of your message.

### Self-presentation

A good upright body posture is helpful in enabling you to communicate your message in a confident way. So, for example, avoid crossing your arms into a defensive position. You also need to look the part, so follow the dress code for your team – whether this is formal or smart/casual. Give feedback to others when working in a team work situation. When you are listening to someone else, you might nod every now and then to show that you understand. At appropriate points you may also wish to smile, frown, laugh, or be silent.

### Building morale/confidence

Good team players support others. They look on the positive side and are typically encouraging. When reviewing progress you should focus more on what went well, although you need to identify weaknesses in a fair way. You can build morale by pointing to successes, identifying who did what well, etc. You should also identify the benefits of taking particular courses of action. Make other members of your team feel that they are doing a good job and that they have useful skills.

### Questioning

It is useful to be able to ask appropriate questions. You should help to clarify issues in a team, and show you are aware of areas that need clearing up. If you don't ask questions you are more likely to make a mistake. If you are not sure about something then ask a polite question. The chances are that someone else in your team is also not sure but was too polite or scared to ask.

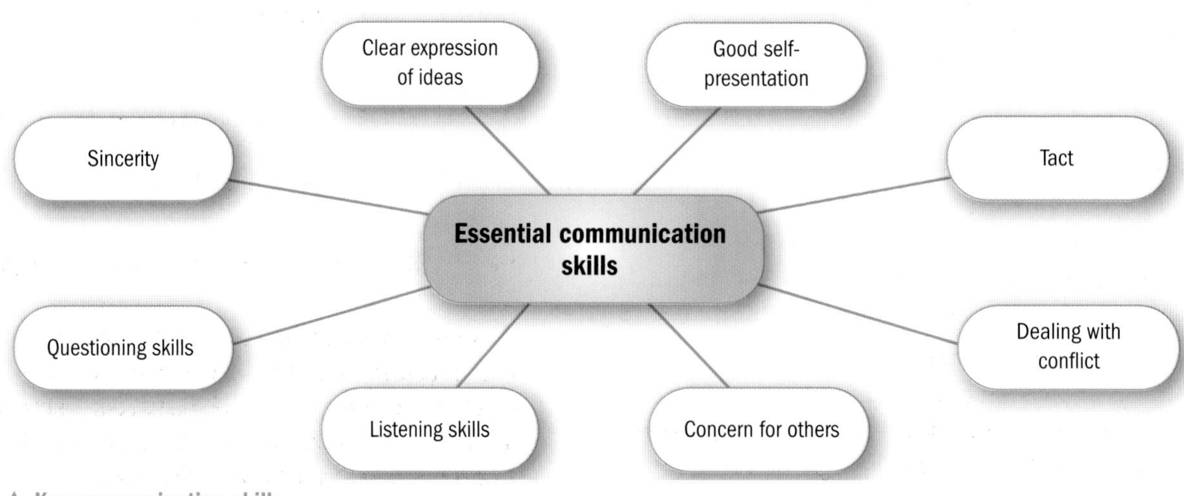


▲ Key communication skills

## Defusing and resolving conflict

The defusion and resolution of conflict is important in reducing tension in a team and raising team morale. You can resolve conflict by stepping in when there is a disagreement. One way is to try to identify the positives in both positions; make it a 'win-win' situation.

It is even better if you can try to anticipate conflict. Conflict will occur when people have different ways of working, different characters, or give different values to their own contribution to the team. Try to anticipate where this is likely to occur and take actions to prevent conflict from occurring. For example, if you think that one person is likely to try to force their view on others without listening to alternatives – then encourage others to put forward their views first.

## Tact

Tact is a very important teamwork skill. Being tactful involves having respect for others and their ideas. Don't be abrupt or cut other people off while they are still trying to say something. Everyone in the team is important and deserves respect, so listen to their ideas and value their contributions. If you have to disagree (and this is not a bad thing) do so in a sensitive and tactful way.

## Sincerity

Sincerity is important. We all want to work with people who are sincere and honest rather than superficial. One of the main criticisms of team members is that they are 'two faced' or 'insincere'. Teams are built on trust. Put forward your ideas and contribute to the team in a sincere and open way and you will help to build a powerful team.

## Effective listening

The unfortunate truth is that many of us pay little attention to the quality of our listening, leaving a gap between hearing others and really listening to what they have to say. Real listening involves three steps:

1. Hearing – listening hard enough to catch what the speaker has to say. For example, if the speaker is talking about team roles and says that it is important to have a leader. You hear just enough to repeat this fact – then you have heard what was said.
2. Understanding – you take in what has been said and understand it in your own way. When you heard the speaker say that it is important to have a leader then you understand that the speaker could be suggesting that the team should have a leader.
3. Judging – if you understand what the speaker has said you will want to judge whether it makes sense. Has the speaker put forward a good case for having a leader? What were the arguments put forward – were they sound arguments? To get to stage three then you really need to listen carefully.

So you have to listen attentively and get to the end of what the speaker has to say. Try not to start dismissing the idea before the speaker has finished getting their point across. If you can do this then you will be a good team listener – someone who is willing to see that the sum of the team is greater than the individual parts. You will see that other people have good ideas which may be better than your own.

## Concern for team members

Earlier we saw that the difference between a group and a team is that the team is all about shared responsibility in achieving goals. We also saw that there are two main elements of team work – concern to complete the task, and concern to support the process. Concern for team members is an important process skill. Tasks are completed better when everyone is pulling in the same direction. A united team is a motivated team. If you can show that you have a genuine concern for others, they will typically reciprocate; more than that, the team will perform at a much higher level.

### Thinking point

The following advice is important in developing good listening skills:

- Let the speaker finish before you start to talk.
- Let yourself finish listening before you speak!

What do you see as being the distinction between the two pieces of advice given above? Try them out next time you listen in a teamwork situation.

## Practice point

Set out a self-assessment chart for your communication skills, using the following format. Tick the relevant boxes. In the final column cite a piece of evidence showing that you are good at or poor at the relevant skill. Then set out a list of action points that you need to take to improve those skills you are not good at.

| Skill | Good? | Poor? | Evidence |
|---|---|---|---|
| Articulation of ideas | | | |
| Self-presentation | | | |
| Ability to encourage and build morale | | | |
| Appropriate questions | | | |
| Defusing and resolving conflict | | | |
| Being tactful | | | |
| Being sincere | | | |
| Effective listening | | | |
| Concern for team members | | | |

## Case study

### Communication at the Whale Rescue Team

The following account is taken from the Whale Rescue Team (WRT) in Los Angeles 2003 Report.

'One memorable rescue happened this spring. This rescue is a good example of how the WRT works. On Sunday, May 26, the WRT received a call from County Lifeguard personnel about a sea lion suffering from poisoning on the rocks, just in front of the Lifeguard's Venice Headquarters. Upon arrival, I was shocked to see this already distressed animal – weakened by poisoning – wedged into the bottom of the jetty, trapped and struggling to raise her nose, up to her forehead out of the water in an attempt to gasp for air.

There was no time to waste. So we immediately went into action. Los Angeles County Lifeguard, Chris Staffield, had kept a close eye on the animal so the rescue attempt would not be delayed. Captain Tom Seth attached a Lifeguard flotation device around my waist which was tethered to him by a rope line. Tom and I entered the surf. Tom kept tension on the line which kept me from washing into the rocks too violently. Brent Katz provided critical support from the rocks above. We had a very difficult time evaluating just what was obstructing the 150 pound sea lion's movement. If it was the rocks, there was nothing we could have done. Time was running out. I reached below the surface to see if I could feel what was obstructing her release. I took this action having complete confidence that Tom and Brent were watching out for my safety. My face was inches away from the sea lion's face, knowing very well she could turn and bite me out of fear. I held my breath and hoped for the best. Then, with my hand I felt the obstruction. I felt a rope line putting great pressure across the animal's chest. That must be what was keeping her stuck in her potential tomb. Brent secured a knife from an LAPD Officer who was also at the scene and passed the knife to me. Waiting for the right moment, I reached down and cut the rope line. It worked. This animal that I thought had no chance at all for survival was free.'

1. What part did communication play within the rescue of the sea lion? ✓
2. What particular communication skills would the team have needed to employ? ✓✓
3. Do you believe that you have the communication skills that would have enabled you to operate effectively as part of the team described? ✓✓✓
4. What communication skills would you like to develop further and why? ✓✓✓

# Personal organisation

Are you an organised type of person? If you want to be a good member of a team then you will probably need to be better organised. Areas to work on will include the following.

## Preparation for meetings

It is important to be effectively prepared for meetings: Make sure you arrive on time and have done the appropriate background work. For example, if the meeting is to discuss an action plan, you need to make sure that you have completed all the actions required from the last meeting. If there is an agenda for the meeting, have you read it before arriving? Make sure that you have organised the required information prior to the meeting. If you are being asked to present information you should ensure that it is set out in a summary paper that is clear and easy to understand.

Make sure you put the dates of meetings and other important team activities into your diary and that you haven't double booked meetings on your calendar. Why not keep a desktop calendar on your computer? They are very easy to set up.

## Identification of issues

As a team member it is important that you are able to identify key issues facing your team. Think about what these issues are and then about the best ways of presenting them to your team. For example, an issue might be that the team is falling behind in meeting targets. Perhaps a team meeting would be required to resolve this issue. Having identified what the root causes of these issues are it will be necessary to broach them in a tactful and sensitive way.

▲ It is important to arrive on time and well prepared for meetings

## Scheduling activities

Teams need to create schedules setting out when activities have to be carried out. Most team work activities involve targets and deadlines. Scheduling involves identifying the key stages and processes that need to be completed. Dates should be attached to the completion of these activities and team members allocated responsibilities on a clear schedule.

### Practice point

As a team, agree a schedule for some of the key activities that your team needs to complete in carrying out a specific project.

An important element of scheduling activities at the personal level is effective time-management. In order to develop this skill it is necessary to allocate time in a well-organised way. By focusing on one activity at a time it is possible to maximise attention on that activity, before moving onto another prioritised area.

One way of allocating time to make sure that tasks are completed within their deadlines is called ABC analysis, which is a value analysis of time.

- 'A' activities are those that are ranked as very important. They can be effectively carried out only by the person involved or by a team working with that person.
- 'B' activities are important but can be delegated.
- 'C' activities are less important, but usually represent the lion's share of the work. They include routine tasks such as paperwork and telephone calls.

In order to meet deadlines, concentrate on the most important 'A' tasks. Complete one or two 'A' tasks each day, earmark a further two to three 'B' tasks, and set aside some time for 'C' tasks.

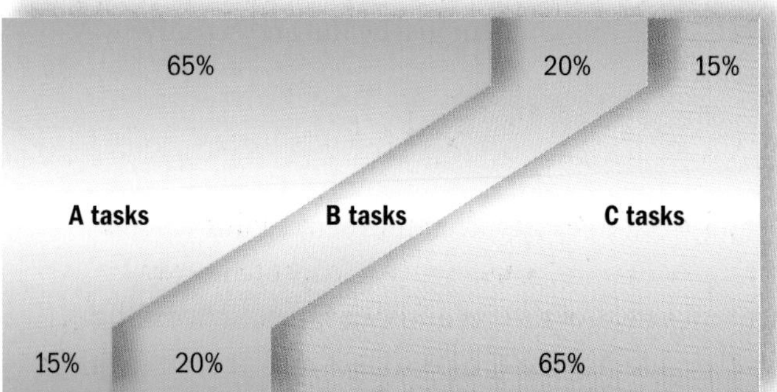


▲ ABC value analysis of the use of time

You are most likely to complete tasks on schedule when you carefully prioritise activities and give appropriate time to the most important ones.

## Responsibility

Allocating responsibility is important in team work. At the end of the day the team needs to take responsibility for getting team tasks completed to an appropriate standard on time. However, within the team it is important to allocate responsibilities to individuals. An important teamwork skill therefore involves taking on responsibility.

Self-management means that you are able to manage yourself effectively in your interactions with others. This is very important, because as people are asked to take on more responsibility in organisations it can lead to increasing levels of stress and frustration if others do not accept their responsibilities.

## Accountability

A typical dictionary definition of accountability is 'subject to having to report, explain or justify; being answerable, responsible'. However, this definition takes a rather negative aspect of accountability. It indicates that you are responsible to someone or to a team or organisation.

By way of contrast it is possible to take a more positive view. An alternative definition of accountability is: an individual team member's choice to rise above their circumstances and demonstrate the ownership necessary for achieving desired results; to see it, take responsibility for it, solve it and do it.

Here the suggestion is that you take responsibility for the part you play in a team. Rather than having accountability forced upon you, you create your own accountability. In this way you can show your commitment to the team. If all members of the team take this approach then everyone will feel responsible for the success or failure of the team.

## Responsiveness

Good team workers are responsive to the needs of their team and to the needs of other team members. They respond to emails, they respond to other forms of communication, and they respond to the challenges of creating a great team. A responsive team member rises to any team challenge that comes their way.

## Adaptability

Team workers need to be able to adapt to changing situations. Modern organisations are characterised by change, and teamworkers are frequently asked to adjust to changing situations by:

- making decisions for themselves when dealing with customers
- taking on more responsibility
- dealing with situations they have never faced before
- taking on new team roles – perhaps roles that they have not played before, e.g. to chair a team meeting.

### Thinking point

Think of an example of a situation in which you needed to be adaptable when working in a team. What evidence would you cite to prove that you are adaptable? If you were told that there is an additional short task that you need to complete for an assignment to be handed in tomorrow, how would you respond?

### Consideration of options

In most problem-solving and decision-making situations there are options to choose from. Teams are likely to generate more options than individuals working alone. A good team member will seek to find out as many different options as possible. They will then consider the options and help the team come up with a decision to choose the best option. A poor team worker will only consider one option – their own.

The Japanese are renowned for being slow in making team decisions. This is because they listen to all views and opinions before making a decision. However, in working like this they often arrive at the best decision.

### Maintaining focus

People tend to be only able to concentrate on tasks for a relatively short period of time. Then they lose focus. This means that a team project can get off to a good start before losing momentum. Just before the deadline date people regain focus – but often it is too late.

Maintaining focus involves helping your team to concentrate on the end goals and the most effective processes throughout the lifespan of a team project.

### Openness to criticism

We all need to learn to be open to criticism. Good criticism should focus on processes rather than judgements about people. For example, if something is not going particularly well then it is helpful to make criticisms such as 'that didn't work particularly well – perhaps we could try doing this an alternative way'. This is helpful or positive criticism which helps the team to move forward. If providing criticism is focused on processes then we should accept it in good spirit. Process criticism helps us to make improvements to our practice.

## Outcome activity 19.4

For this Outcome activity you will need to consider a team you are working in at the moment or a team that you have been a part of in the past. If you wish you can focus on the team that you set up for Outcome activity 19.2.

**Pass** P4
Describe the communication skills and personal organisation used when working in a team.

**Merit** 
Compare the contribution of different skills used in team working.

**Distinction** 
Evaluate the effectiveness of interpersonal skills in a given team situation.

## Grading tips

**Pass** 
Don't just list the skills. Explain how you and others are able to use these skills to make the team work more effectively.

**Merit** 
Focus your explanations on particular team members who are able to use communication and organisation skills to help the team work effectively. What do they do and how do they act? What particular aspects of communication and personal organisation are they good at?

**Distinction** 
Getting on with others requires a lot of sensitive interpersonal skills. Weigh up the contributions of the individual team members. Give examples of the way that their actions and what they said and did (or did not say or do) added to team cohesion and performance.

## End of unit test

1. How would you distinguish between a group and a team?
2. What is the appropriate size for a team?
3. List four benefits of organising employees in a hairdressing salon into teams.
4. What are the main ingredients of a high-performance team?
5. Why is it helpful to regularly monitor team performance against targets?
6. What are the drawbacks of high team-member turnover?
7. Describe one corrective measure that could be taken in response to poor team performance.
8. What is a quality circle?
9. Describe three features that you might find in an under-performing team.
10. Which two of Belbin's team members do you see as being most influential in helping to create a successful team?
11. What is the difference between 'storming' and 'norming'? What needs to be done to take 'norming' through to 'performing'?
12. What do you consider to be the most important communication skills required in teamwork?
13. How could you measure team performance? What steps could be taken to use these measures to improve team performance?
14. What personal organisation skills are required by team members? Describe three of these in detail.
15. What part should induction play in helping new members of an organisation to feel that they are part of a team?

# Resources

Websites related to Belbin:

www.belbin.com/belbin-team-roles.htm – What are team roles?

www.belbin.com/onlinetest.htm – Online Belbin questionnaire

www.chimaeraconsulting.com/tuckman.htm – Related to Bruce Tuckman

www.reviewing.co.uk/toolkit/teams-and-teamwork.htm – Site giving links about teamwork

# Books


Belbin, M. 1981 *Management teams: why they succeed or fail*, Heinemann

Dransfield, R. 2000 *Human Resource Management* (especially Chapters 6 and 8), Heinemann

Foot, M. and Hook, C. 2002 *Introducing Human Resource Management* (especially Chapter 9), Longman

Schermerhorn, J. R. *et al* 2006 *Managing Organisational Behaviour*, John Wiley


Answers to questions on page 370:

1. a. Kenya b. Belgium c. Israel d. Spain e. India f. Poland g. The Philippines h. New Zealand
2. a. Barnsley b. Manchester United c. Cardiff City d. Liverpool e. Sheffield Wednesday f. Arsenal g. Blackburn Rovers
3. a. Shoes b. Bags c. Bras d. Coats e. Swimming gear

| Grading criteria | Outcome activity | Page number |
|---|---|---|
| To achieve a pass grade the evidence must show that the learner is able to: | | |
| P1 Describe the types of team and their associated benefits | 19.1 | 376 |
| P2 Describe how to build cohesive teams that perform well | 19.2 | 386 |
| P3 Explain how targets are set and team performance is monitored | 19.3 | 391 |
| P4 Describe the communication skills and personal organisation used when working in a team | 19.4 | 397 |
| To achieve a merit grade the evidence must show that, in addition to the pass criteria, the learner is able to: | | |
| M1 Compare the roles of the different members of a team | 19.1 | 376 |
| M2 Assess the value of different methods of monitoring the performance of a team | 19.3 | 391 |
| M3 Compare the contribution of different skills used in team working | 19.4 | 397 |
| To achieve a distinction grade the evidence must show that, in addition to the pass and merit criteria, the learner is able to: | | |
| D1 Evaluate own performance as a team worker | 19.1 | 376 |
| D2 Evaluate the effectiveness of interpersonal skills in a given team situation | 19.4 | 397 |

# 29 Introduction to the Internet and e-business

## Introduction

Internet technology is more than fifty years old. The worldwide web is not yet twenty. Together they are a business-, life- and world-changing force. This unit is important in understanding business today. It takes you through some history of the Internet and the web. It covers a range of ways in which the Internet can be brought to use by businesses; and outlines some of the latest networking technologies. Then it deals with one or two possible pitfalls and problems, before outlining some of the benefits – for both businesses and customers – that can be the result of good online business. Finally, the unit covers some of the ways in which businesses and individuals can plan and prepare for a world in which we all benefit by doing 'digital business'.

### What you need to learn

On completion of this unit you should:

1. Understand how the Internet operates and the facilities available
2. Understand how the Internet and related technology can be used for a range of business activities
3. Be able to explain the trends in the use of e-business
4. Understand the key features of planning for the increased use of e-business at national, organisational and individual level.

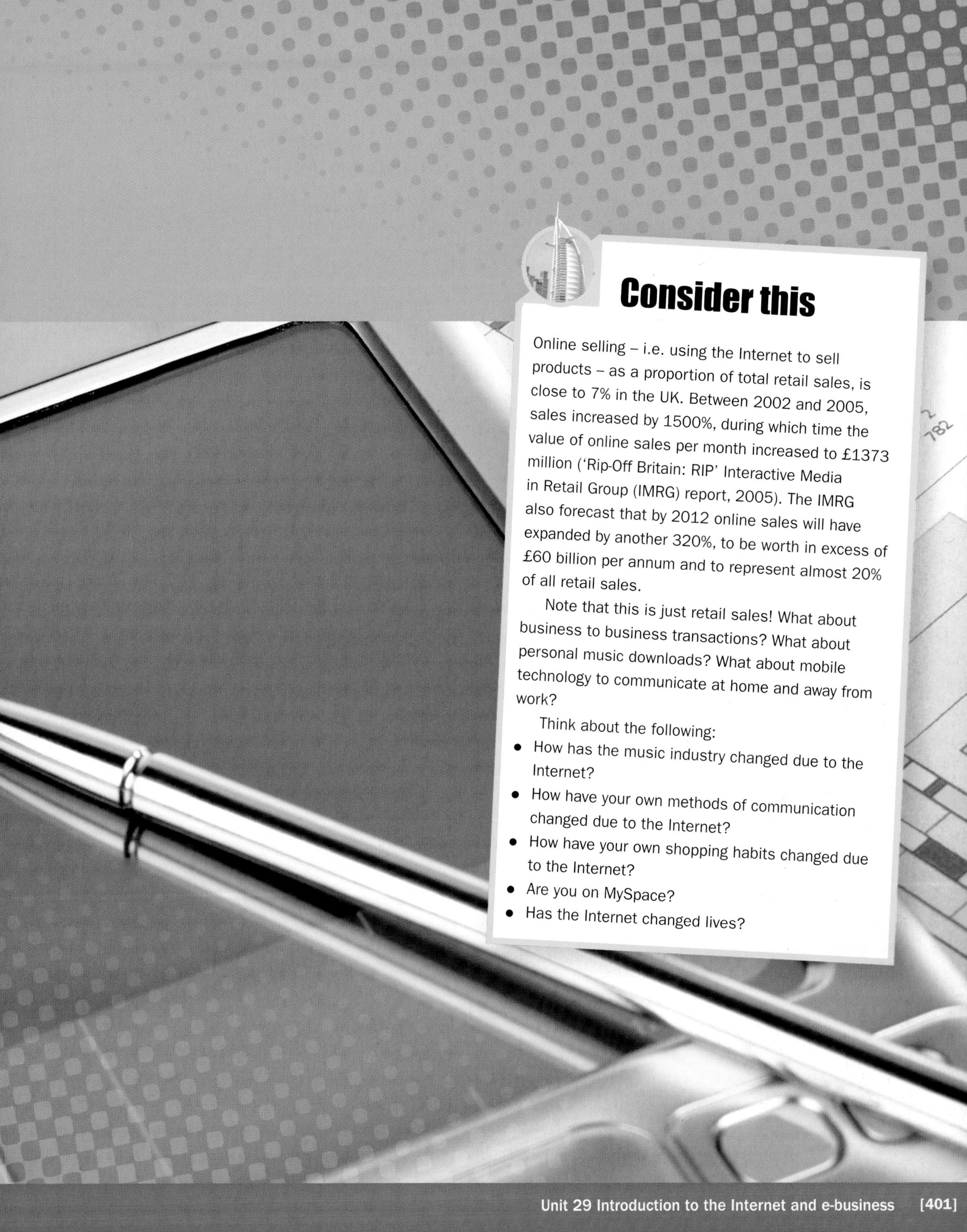

## Consider this

Online selling – i.e. using the Internet to sell products – as a proportion of total retail sales, is close to 7% in the UK. Between 2002 and 2005, sales increased by 1500%, during which time the value of online sales per month increased to £1373 million ('Rip-Off Britain: RIP' Interactive Media in Retail Group (IMRG) report, 2005). The IMRG also forecast that by 2012 online sales will have expanded by another 320%, to be worth in excess of £60 billion per annum and to represent almost 20% of all retail sales.

Note that this is just retail sales! What about business to business transactions? What about personal music downloads? What about mobile technology to communicate at home and away from work?

Think about the following:

- How has the music industry changed due to the Internet?
- How have your own methods of communication changed due to the Internet?
- How have your own shopping habits changed due to the Internet?
- Are you on MySpace?
- Has the Internet changed lives?

# 29.1 How the Internet operates and the facilities available

## How the Internet works

### The Internet and the worldwide web

It is a common mistake but try not to confuse the worldwide web (www) and the Internet. Technically, they are not the same thing; the Internet has existed for over fifty years, long before the web. While it is the 'web' that has made the Internet such a vital part of our lives today, without the basic techniques that enable computers to talk to each other, the web would be useless.

The 'Internet' refers to the massive network of connected computers stretching all over the world. In fact, the word Internet comes from the two words, *inter*connected and *net*works. The Internet is a linked network of computer networks.

This in itself does not quite explain how so many PCs are able to connect together and exchange information. Computers on the Internet do not all link to the same central 'mega-computer' that holds all of the information or services we need. Within each sub-network on the Internet, some PCs hold the information we need and others just access the information. This arrangement is known as 'client-server' architecture.

### Servers and clients

The Internet works on the basis that some computers act as '**servers**'. These computers offer services for other computers that are accessing or requesting information; these are known as 'clients'.

So, sitting in your room at home, or your school or college computer workshop, you are able to access the Internet because the PC you are using has a connection to a server. Your PC will have a piece of software loaded on it called a browser. This software (often Internet Explorer, but possibly Netscape or Mozilla Firefox) takes your request for Internet access and services and then displays the results on your PC. To do this, your browser mainly reads Hypertext Mark-up Language (HTML); this is the simple code created by Tim Berners-Lee.

You might require different types of information or services from the Internet. You might want a written document from a website; or a catalogue, a multimedia presentation, a photograph, a video, a piece of music or an email. Different kinds of servers can deliver different services. So, you have, amongst others:

- web servers
- email servers
- application servers.

### Key Terms

**Server** A higher capacity computer that offers services to client computers that can connect to it.

### Remember

The worldwide web and the Internet refer to two different things that evolved at different times. The Internet has existed since the 1960s. However, without the worldwide web, there would be limited use for it.

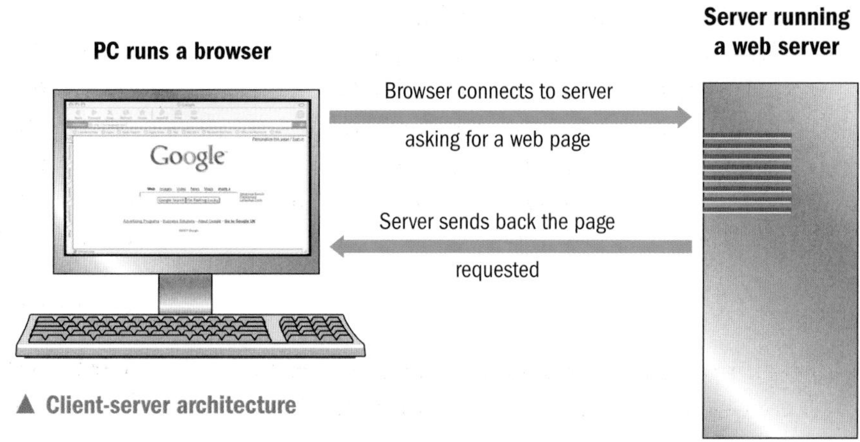


▲ Client-server architecture

## Types of connections to the Internet

There are different ways of connecting to the Internet. This includes the speed with which you can connect and get access to services – a very important consideration for most users. A 56K modem (modem meaning **mo**dulator **dem**odulator) uses an analogue connection using the phone lines. Every time you need access to the Internet, analogue or ISDN modems must dial a number to secure a connection. (The modem's job is to convert analogue signals received into digital format so your PC can understand it.)

A growing trend is for more and more Internet users to switch to 'broadband' connection. Broadband gives permanent, 'always on' connectivity, so there is no need to dial a number. DSL and cable are types of broadband connection; these are much faster than analogue or ISDN links. Broadband connection (as the name '**broad**band' suggests), carries more data, at a faster rate, than dial-up. Because of this it is becoming more popular both for home and business use.

## Internet service providers (ISPs)

An Internet service provider is a business that offers Internet access services for both businesses and individuals. The main function of an ISP is to provide a link to the worldwide web. Many ISPs these days also host websites and offer email services. Examples of ISPs are Wanadoo, BTInternet, Tiscali and Pipex.

## Protocols

A '**protocol**' is a particular way of doing something. When the Internet was first being developed by computer scientists in America there had to be common agreement about how computers would 'speak' to each other. What has emerged is a set of protocols that everyone using the Internet must follow. There are several important ones.

### Internet Protocol (IP)

This is the **protocol** that establishes a unique name for every computer on the Internet. This is a twelve digit number, e.g. 216.24.62.133; each number separated by the point is called an 'octet'. This identifies every network, host and organisation on the Internet.

**Remember**

Computers are able to speak to each other because of a series of protocols that everyone agrees to follow.

**Key Terms**

**Internet protocols** Agreed ways of doing things so that everyone on the Internet connects in the same way.

### Transmission Control Protocol (TCP)

IP addresses let the Internet find the right route for messages, so that they get to where you want them to go ('get me in touch with Yahoo! please'). But it is Transmission Control Protocol (TCP) that takes the overall piece of data (whatever it is), breaks it down into 'packets' and checks for errors, reassembles the packets at the other end and re-sends anything that gets lost.

Imagine yourself in New York and you want to send a message home. All you have is four postcards, each with space for only one word. You write 'Hello' on one, 'Having' on the next, 'Nice' on the next and 'Time' on the last. You stick these in the post and hope for the best. At home your folks receive, Time, Hello, Having and Nice – eventually. It does not make much sense. TCP is the transport system of the Internet which sorts this out. It does its best to ensure delivery of sensible data across the inter-network. TCP takes each of your 'packets' of messages and puts them in proper order at the other end and checks that each packet has been received. Together, the TCP/IP protocols make the Internet work.

### HTTP protocol

The Hypertext Transfer Protocol (HTTP) was created by Tim Berners-Lee while working for CERN (a research centre based in Geneva, Switzerland) in 1991. Berners-Lee is therefore correctly regarded as the creator of the worldwide web. The function of HTTP is to specify the way in which browsers and web servers transmit data to each other.

The essence of the 'protocol' is to establish which computer speaks first, how they then speak in turn and the format of the data they exchange, which is HTML. Without HTTP, the Internet would be a vast network of variable networks, all struggling to speak with each other – very limited indeed. It would not be a worldwide web.

### Domain names

The IP addresses containing twelve digit numbers could never be remembered by people. So web servers hold lists of human readable names (sometimes called 'symbolic names') called domain names.

Unlike IP addresses, you will probably know many domain names by heart, e.g. www.yahoo.com; www.google.co.uk; www.msn.com.

### Worldwide Web Consortium (W3C)

Although no one actually owns the worldwide web, there are leading bodies which try to ensure it develops in an open and accessible way, so that it will benefit as many people as possible. A major contributor is the Worldwide Web Consortium (known as W3C) and they amongst others attempt to define web standards.

A web standard is made up of elements and structures. The purpose of developing a core of web standards is to ensure as far as possible that web based content is designed and structured in such a way that the greatest benefit will be gained by the greatest number of web users – see www.webstandards.org.

### Internet Society

The Internet Society is a global voluntary group that works to coordinate and develop an accessible Internet and its underlying technology. It was founded in 1992 and is based in Virginia, USA.

## Networking of computers

Computer networks have spread fast. They have revolutionised the way we live and do business. As we shall see, networking technology (how we create networks) is improving. The Internet is one huge network of computers.

### Networks and wireless networks

But what is a network?

Imagine a fishing net and you picture a series of connected fine ropes forming see-through squares. Each of the corners of the squares is knotted and has ropes shooting off in four different directions.

Now think of these corners of the 'net' as being formed of PCs. Each PC is linked using cables/lines to form a virtual 'net'; some points in the net have bigger computers feeding the others. This is the basic structure of a computer 'network'. These days, however, some networks are 'wireless' and therefore do not have cables.

Networks can be confined to an organisation; this is known as an '**intranet**'. Your school or college probably has its own intranet. Some organisations open up their intranet to some outside partners. Entry is protected by passwords; this creates an '**extranet**'. On the biggest scale is the global network, the Internet, connecting all computer networks together.

### Key Terms

**Intranet** Restricted computer network confined to a specific organisation.

**Extranet** Restricted network that extends outside an organisation to include other computers.

### Current related technology

There are different technologies forming computer networks. These are developing all the time. Outlined below are a few of the emerging network technologies.

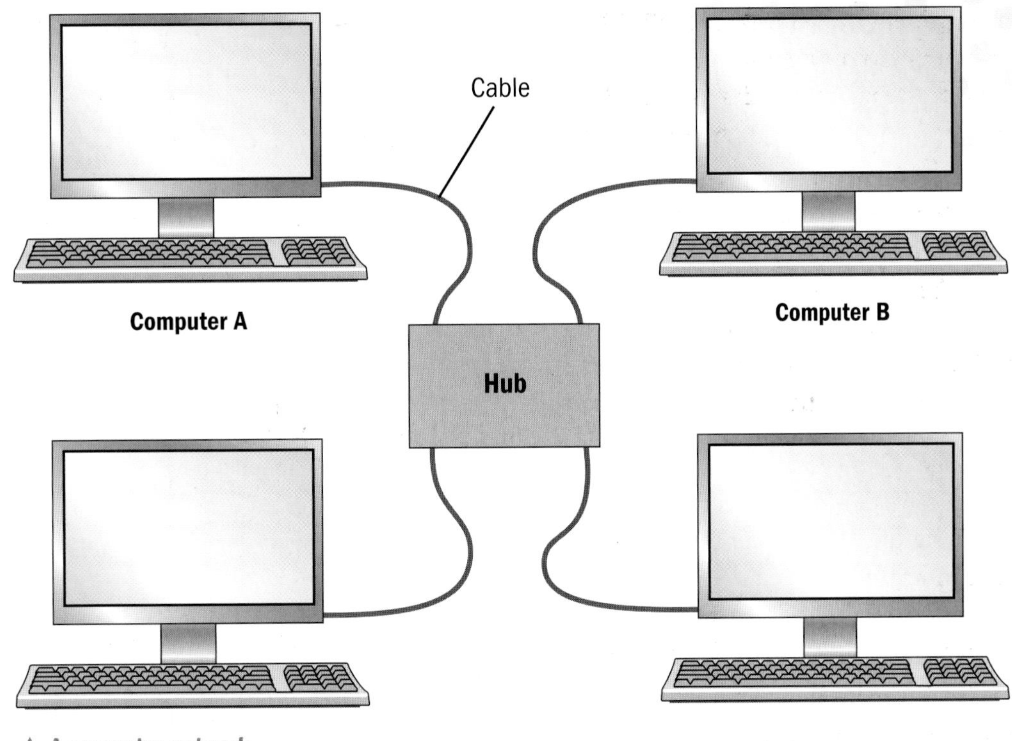


▲ A computer network

## ■ Wi-fi

It is now possible to connect computers without the use of physical wires – a wireless connection. **Wi-fi** (**w**ireless **fi**delity) uses specified radio frequencies to send and receive data. More and more wireless laptops are being used. These devices have to be connected and enabled to work with wi-fi. A wireless-enabled laptop contains a wireless access card that is able to connect to other cards on other laptops directly, creating a 'point to point' connection. More likely, the laptop and any other client device will connect to a router to join a much larger network.

Wi-fi is now becoming more popular in home computing. (Who wants to network devices at home using cables dragged under carpets?) In business, more staff carry their own laptops while away from the office.

## Key Terms

**Wi-fi** A way of connecting to the Internet without physical wires.

## ■ Bluetooth

This is a low-speed, short-range wireless protocol designed to allow a variety of enabled 'gadgets' to connect. (Do you exchange ringtones using bluetooth?) Once a device fitted with a bluetooth chip is within a 10-metre range of other bluetooth devices, it can connect by using a small, 'personal area network' (known as a piconet).

Once connected, each device announces its presence on the piconet and it can then pair off with others. Devices can be phones, laptops, printers, fridges, freezers or anything fitted with the chip.

## Remember

The Internet consists of a global network of connected computer networks. People and businesses can connect to these using either cables or wireless connections.

## Other ways of connecting

A report in September 2006, by Informa Telecoms and Media, predicted that by the end of 2006 there would be 2.1 billion mobile subscribers. Mobile web communication is going to be big business. A range of technologies is used.

## 3G mobile phones

This is the 'third generation' of mobile phones. These devices use WAP (wireless application protocol) technology to offer 'always on' connection to data services as well as a range of other features. These phones can send and receive data by connecting to the Internet, albeit at a significantly slower rate than modern broadband connections.

## Personal Digital Assistant (PDA)

A PDA is a handheld computer that runs a reduced version of standard software. A PDA comes with personal information management software and can be used as an organiser or a diary planner that is portable and capable of connecting, using bluetooth or wi-fi, to a PC. It is capable of connecting to the Internet; it can act as a global positioning system (GPS) and run multimedia software.

▲ A PDA

## Smartphones

A smartphone is either a PDA that has mobile phone capabilities, or a mobile phone with PDA features. A smartphone therefore combines the features of both.

### Thinking point

A typical small- to medium-sized business might use a number of travelling sales people. Think about ways in which specific devices and technologies may be able to help.

## Uses of the Internet and worldwide web by business organisations

The web is now a key aspect of business life for a growing number of businesses. Nevertheless, there are still some large businesses today that do not have a website; they could be called 'siteless' or 'sightless' if you prefer. Eventually, all business will be on the Internet. They will all have a 'web presence'. In just about every case, their websites will be interactive, meaning that visitors can make use of the information, change it and get something back.

We saw earlier that the Internet is a lot older than the worldwide web. However, it is the 'web' that has made the Internet such a valuable tool for business. This is because businesses can do many things using the Internet and the worldwide web.

## Procurement

This means buying. Businesses that are seeking to make profits have to 'procure' the things they need to pursue their activities. Some need raw materials for a production process; others have to buy finished products to re-sell in their stores.

## Case study

### E-procurement

Large companies have achieved some excellent savings using e-procurement software available on the Internet:

- Compaq – achieved a 50 per cent reduction in process costs and a direct saving on purchased goods and services of over £30 million
- Boeing – achieved similar cost savings but also reduced their supplier base by over 80 per cent in some commodity areas; and,
- Xerox – predicted that it would save in excess of $10 million per annum through the introduction of e-procurement.

(*Source:* Business Gateway, www.bgateway.com)

1. These savings appear impressive. However, are there any extra costs involved in adopting an e-procurement system? ✓
2. How does e-procurement lead to cost savings? ✓✓
3. In your view, is an e-procurement system a good thing to adopt? Why? ✓✓✓

Every public sector organisation, such as your local authority, has to buy things: stationery, desks, furniture, road materials and so on. Primary Care Trusts on behalf of NHS hospitals have to buy drugs, equipment, scanners and cleaning materials.

## Research

Businesses need to be aware of things that are happening around them. Modern business managers are under increasing pressure to provide everything that customers need or want. They have to be competitive in their market; otherwise they risk being overtaken by events.

The Internet offers all sorts of opportunities to research market developments and keep in touch with the wider world. Businesses can investigate their own markets, they can investigate industrial trends through participating in industrial portals, and they can keep in touch with sales trends in a locality far away from their headquarters. The web is a rich source of business intelligence.

## Developing an online presence for sales

After the 'dot com bubble' of the late 1990s many people were far too quick to dismiss the Internet as a passing fad that would blow away. How wrong they were. In fact, what has happened is that many long-established businesses have added an online sales channel to their existing business. Big organisations like Tesco (www.Tesco.com ), Sainsbury (www.Sainsbury.co.uk), Next (www.next.co.uk) and B&Q (www.diy.com) all offer home shopping. There are so many that some people are now complaining that online shopping is killing the high street!

## Promotion

In the first six months of 2006, online advertising in the US rose 37% to $8 billion. Businesses have increased spending on Internet advertising, particularly using banner ads (described later) and pop-ups. The newer mobile channels are a big potential advertising opportunity too, with some new techniques employed to persuade people to look at the ads.

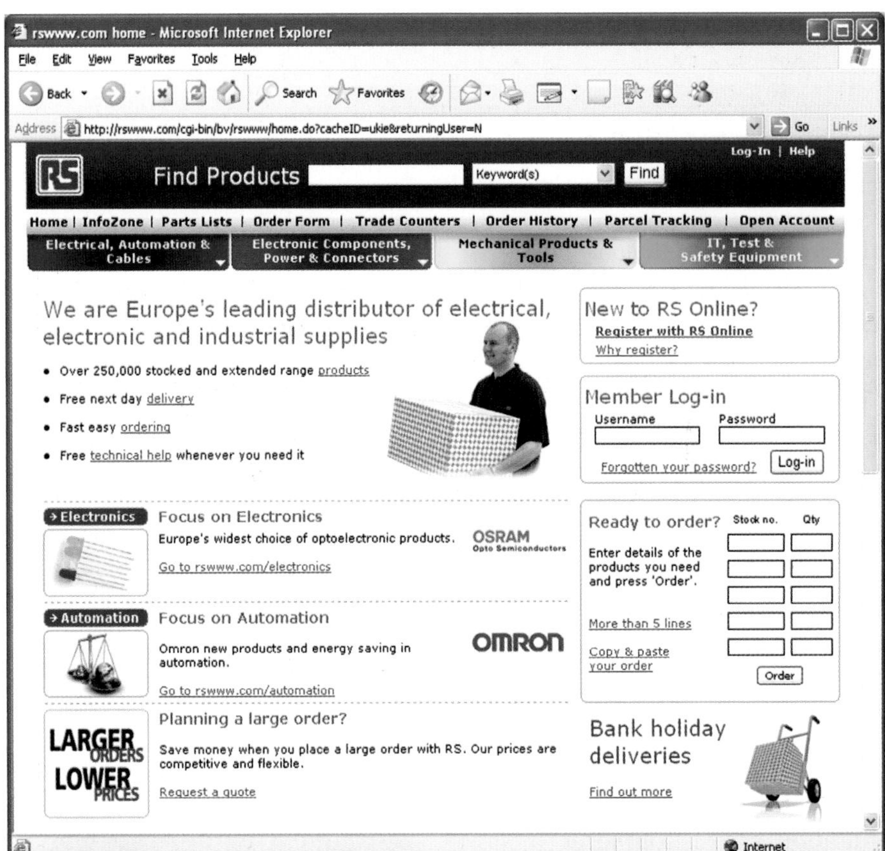


◀ **RS Components offers procurement on the web**

## Case study

**'Watch ads, get free calls' says Virgin Mobile US**

'Virgin Mobile USA is giving hard-up youngsters the chance to make free phone calls in return for watching ads. The 'yoof-oriented' cellco has hooked up with ad outfit Ultramercial to launch the ad-for-airtime service called 'SugarMama'.

'Punters interested in SugarMama must first fill out a 'demographic profile' before confirming that that they are at least 13 years old. Once the administration has been done, they can watch a streaming video ad. Customers get free airtime depending on the number of correct questions they can answer about the ad. Alternatively, they can respond to text-based ads to earn free minutes.

'Either way, the suits behind the scheme are looking to generate revenue from mobile advertising. For advertisers, it's yet another way to get their brand or product across to this hard-to-reach youth audience. 'Everyone is racing to shove ads into the mobile channel,' said Howard Handler, top marketing bod at Virgin Mobile USA. 'But the last thing young people want is spam on their phones.'

'Earlier this year mobile marketing firm I-movo began recruiting punters to test a new service that offers mobile phone users in the UK the chance to send text messages for free, in return for viewing ads on their phones.'

(*Source*: from an article by Tim Richardson in *The Register* www.theregister.co.uk © The Register)

1. This is an innovative way of getting young people to take notice of the advertisements on their mobiles. How would you justify it as a possible promotional strategy for a business? ✓
2. How would you 'sell' this form of promotion to a business entrepreneur? What do you feel are its major selling points? ✓ ✓
3. What drawbacks, if any, can you see in this form of promotion? Justify your points. ✓ ✓ ✓

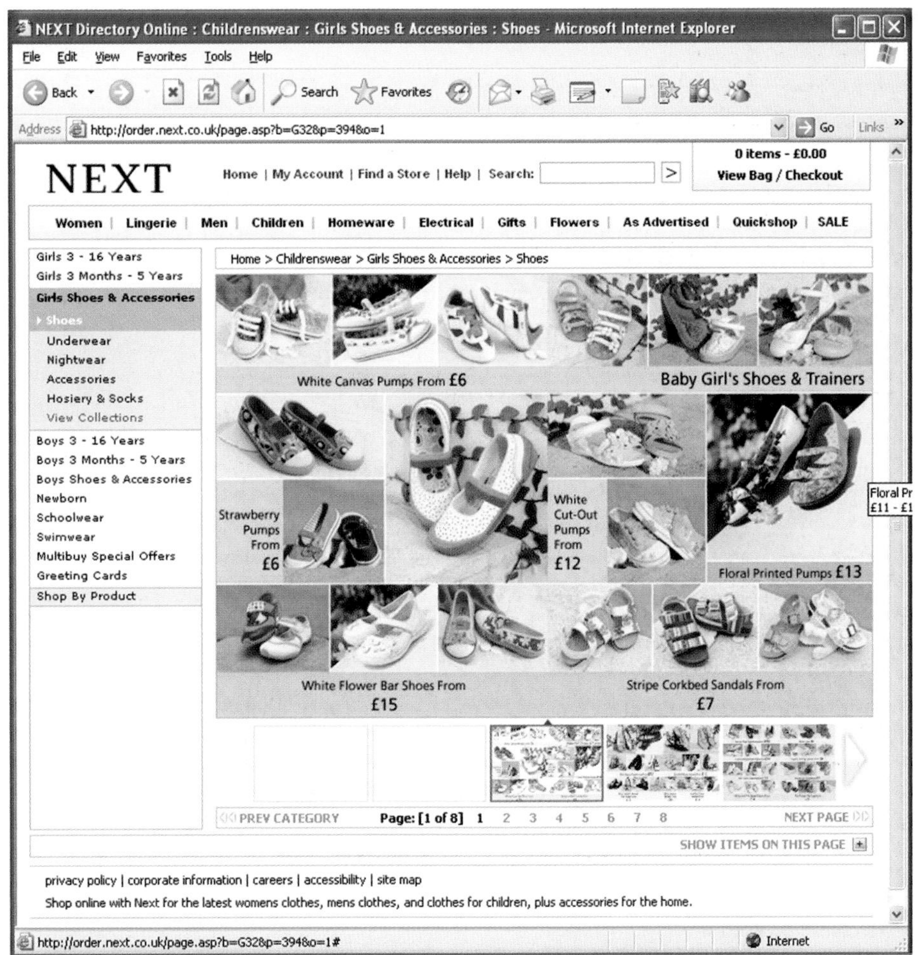


◄ Next sells a variety of products and services online

## Customer service

Customer service is about meeting the needs and requirements of every single customer. Businesses may have exactly the same products that do exactly the same thing, so how do we choose one rather than another? The answer lies in customer service. By offering excellence in service, businesses compete better. How can the Internet help in this?

Today there is software that can offer businesses templates and techniques for offering excellent customer service on the Internet. People who shop online expect the very highest standards in care. Delivery, product descriptions, FAQs (frequency asked questions), catalogues, images and added design services are all features of the web. 'Contact us' pages can also help. In a last resort, telephone contact can be made with the online business.

## Public relations

Public relations (PR) is about giving out a good message about a business and its activities. A website allows businesses to state loudly and clearly what they do and what they do well. The Co-operative Bank is an ethically aware business that takes great care to say clearly what it does.

## Providing information

Every web page gives us information. Local councils and government departments increasingly use the power of the Internet to give information that will be useful to citizens. Private businesses, large and small, can give out information to potential customers and stakeholders. As the case study on 'Product information' shows, online shoppers want good product information before they buy.

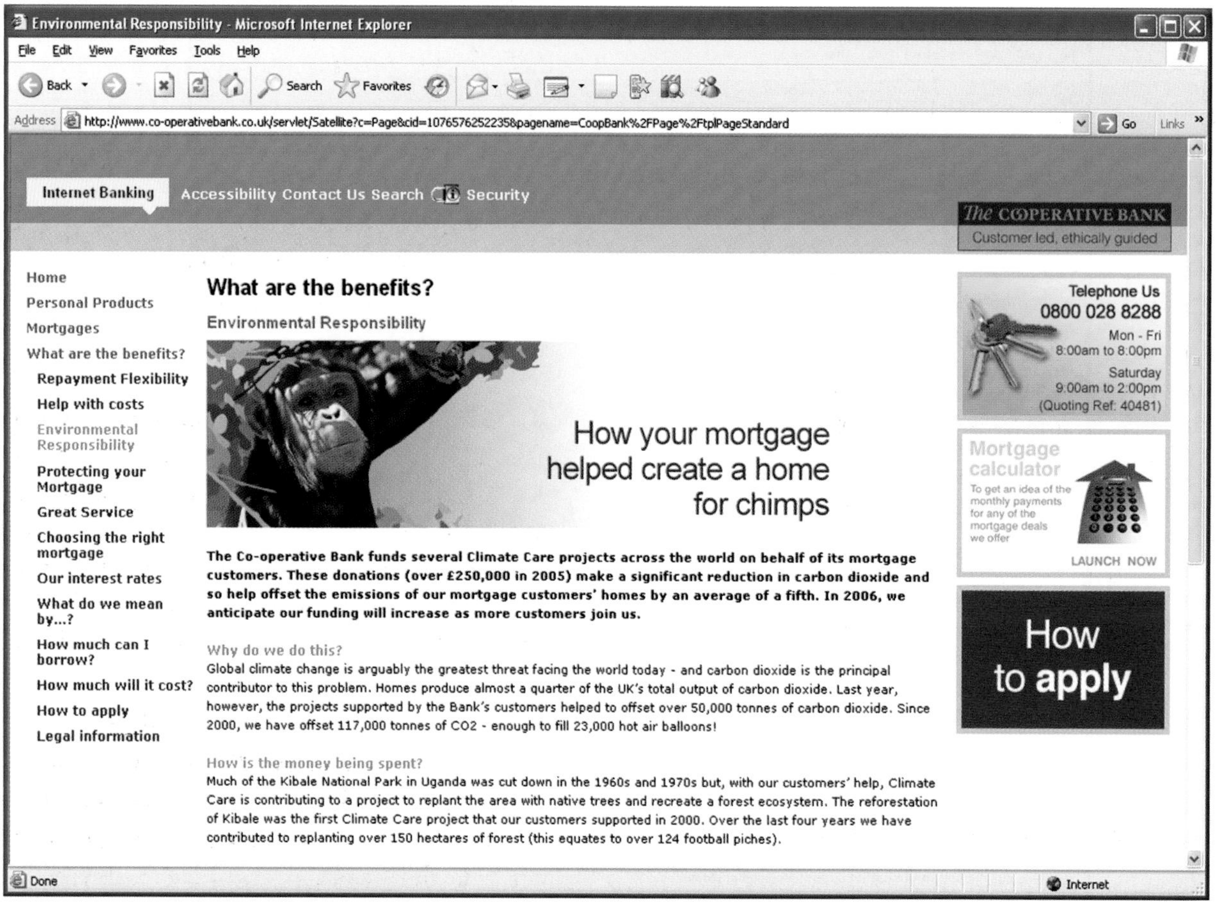

▲ The Co-op Bank uses the Internet for PR

## Case study

### Product information

E-Commerce sites lose as many as 67% of consumers; many abandon their shopping carts due to a lack of product information. The 'Online Merchandising Survey' research brief released by Allurent details consumer perception on online shopping.

Increased interactive elements and innovative ways to display and purchase products would encourage Internet purchasing for 83% of survey respondents.

Enhanced features that would help could include mix and match outfits where shoppers can put together an entire outfit on screen (44%); 360-degree product views (78%); side-by-side comparisons (63%) and personalisation or customisable products (53%).

(*Source*: Adapted from an article by Enid Burns: www.clickz.com, 'Shoppers Seek Web 2.0 E-Commerce', October 2006)

1. How might this survey be used by a possible online retail business? ✓
2. Using your own experience of interactivity on websites, make recommendations for an online clothes retailer as to how the business could improve its online customer experience. ✓✓
3. What other 'innovative' aspects could you suggest an online fashion retailer might adopt on a website? ✓✓✓

## Influencing others

Because the web is full of information, and can be used as a powerful tool for research, it can also be used to try to influence others. This can happen in a number of ways.

Many websites allow discussion forums where site users can leave comment. There was a problem with an initial batch of the Apple iPod Nano when the screens cracked after only a short period of use. Apple's initial refusal to deal with the problem was overcome when an aggrieved customer set up a website. The fear of bad publicity across the Internet forced Apple into action.

Pressure groups such as Friends of the Earth, Greenpeace, Corporate Watch and others can use the global spread of the Internet to try to change people's views.

### Practice point

Investigate three websites that in your view set out to 'influence others'. Prepare a short presentation saying how they attempt to influence and whether in your opinion they might succeed.

## Communications – emails, intranets and extranets

We know that computer networks make up the Internet. The crucial thing for business organisations is that this enables rapid communications beyond and within a business. People can work remotely, either at home or on the move, by connecting to an intranet or extranet using a password and username. It is possible today to email from a range of portable devices such as your phone or a handheld PDA.

The Internet phone revolution is well underway, and many companies are now taking advantage of free telephone services through online providers. Now that ADSL has become widely available across Europe so Internet phone services have become a compelling new way to communicate and to reduce costs.

### Remember

Businesses can connect to the Internet for a number of reasons. They can buy and sell, they can advertise and promote, they can tell the world about themselves and they can communicate.

Skype (www.skype.com) is free technology. Anyone with an Internet connection can use the system to speak with anyone else who is also registered, and so far Skype has more than 287 million users around the world. The most useful function is being able to speak, for free, from computer to computer; but Skype is also built to allow calls to landlines, although to use this feature there is a small charge.

In order to use Skype, a user must either have a microphone and speakers activated on a computer, or an Internet telephone handset. These are widely available and have the advantage of being more private than using the speakers in a PC. Skype also works as an instant messaging system in a very similar way to MSN Messenger.

## Uses of related mobile technology

The beauty of **mobile technology** is that it allows people to use information technology without being tied to the office. Many organisations have staff that work away from their office. The availability of wi-fi, 3G mobiles and PDAs (see above) has enabled fast communication of data, images and audio in a much more flexible way.

### Key Terms

**Mobile technology** Portable devices that can connect to the worldwide web.

Mobile technology can improve the speed of service that can be offered to clients. For instance, a carpet fitter can come to your house, measure the areas to be carpeted, store these digitally using a laptop and send the estimate to the store. This way, the carpets can be cut more quickly because information transfer is speeded up. In another business, situation sales staff can give presentations or store appointments on a handheld computer.

### Thinking point

What kinds of business situation could benefit most from mobile communications technology?

### Voice over Internet Protocol (VoIP)

Mobile technology such as VoIP allows you to call anyone in the world and talk for as long as you wish. This, together with all the other portable devices with connection ability, gives much greater flexibility to business practices. More and more people today have the flexibility to work from home thanks to these developments.

### Thinking point

Mobile technology could mean that the days of working nine till five are over. What do you think about this?

## Trends in Internet developments

### Increasing penetration and speed

The Internet is a global phenomenon and the numbers of people using it grows day by day. The increase in availability and access to the Internet is a major trend that encourages businesses to get online. However, there are still parts of the world where Internet 'penetration' – i.e. the percentage of the population who have regular Internet access – is low, as can be seen in the table below.

| | |
|---|---|
| UK | 62.9% |
| USA | 68.6% |
| Australia | 68.4% |
| Canada | 67.9% |
| India | 4.5% |
| China | 8.5% |
| Papua New Guinea | 2.8% |
| Madagascar | 0.5% |

(*Source*: ClickZ.com)

### Thinking point

The figures for global Internet penetration are growing. Do you think that this presents business opportunities? How?

Connection speeds are increasing as technology improves, which makes it even more desirable for businesses and individuals.

### Falling costs

Other factors can encourage greater access and use of the Internet. The cost of broadband connection is falling, which encourages more people and businesses to use the web and get more from it.

As businesses see opportunities and realise that greater numbers of people are accessing the web, and as costs, speed and reliability continue to improve (as they are) the Internet evolution is likely to accelerate.

### Remember

The Internet has taken off. It will continue to grow because of cheaper, faster access.

## Outcome activity 29.1

**Pass**

As a consultant advising a local entrepreneur, create a set of presentation slides and notes to describe how the Internet operates. Give eight examples of how it is used by at least two contrasting organisations.

## Grading tips

**Pass** 

A structured set of slides, with notes, should describe the early Internet at first, then the 1992 beginnings of the worldwide web; the rapid growth of web pages throughout the 1990s until today; finally describing the growth of online business and web-based commerce, explaining how the Internet operates. The two business examples might contrast one simple web presence, used for PR only, and a full e-commerce site.

# 29.2 Using the Internet and related technology for a range of bussiness activities

Business activity is increasingly taking place on the Internet. Businesses can buy and sell from each other – known as B2B transactions – as well as selling to people like us, private consumers; these are known as B2C transactions.

The number of B2C transactions on the Internet far outweighs B2B, yet in money terms it is the B2B business that has the greater value. Consumers will frequently purchase fairly low value items, such as a book or a CD. However, less frequently, a big business might purchase a high value piece of equipment. These opportunities will be discussed later.

When a businesses wishes to alter its strategy and open up an online presence, it has a number of things to consider. One of the most basic of these is the question of capacity to meet increased demand. Can the business cope with a potential global interest in its products? This is all part of the business planning process. If management decides that an online sales channel is potentially of benefit, then it must consider a number of issues as outlined below.

## Setting up an Internet-linked computer

### Equipment requirements and cost

To make use of the Internet, a business must invest. First of all, obviously, there will need to be hardware in the shape of PCs that connect to the web, using either cabling or wireless technology. The costs of these are falling and if a business buys in bulk then the costs can be reduced further. In addition to the PCs there are the costs of cabling, modems or routers, and printers as well as the software.

To connect effectively to the Internet for business purposes, there must be a 'host' for your website. This means that the site will be placed on a server (see above), with its domain name (see above) and there will be costs associated with this. The price of a domain name is quite low; hosting services will depend on the

▲ The price of PCs is falling

kind of website it is. The average cost of a website in 2003 was quoted as £3000 (Chaffey, Mayer, Johnston & Ellis-Chadwick *Internet Marketing*, Prentice Hall).

## Risks of an Internet connection

A business with only physical premises to look after still needs to consider security; a business that presents itself on the Internet immediately has many other forms of threat.

When a business begins the process of transferring much of its operations online, it tends also to computerise most of its internal functions. This means that sales figures, staff details, financial performance and much other confidential information is at risk. In this situation, a fully fledged 'e-business' (i.e. one that uses digital data extensively) must take steps to protect the business.

### Key Terms

**E-business** A business that has digitised many of its internal functions by using computer systems. These are often connected to the web.

There are some annoying issues that can affect an online business at any time and these must be considered and monitored at the outset. These include:

- **spam** – unrequested rubbish or junk mail, which can be blocked through easily installed filters on email accounts
- **spyware** – 'aggressive commercial' software that uses various methods to get installed on your PC and attempt to sell you things or, in some cases, scam money from you by stealing your passwords or card numbers. Avoid spyware by setting 'Internet options'> 'Tools'> 'Security options' to medium or high
- **adware** – irksome advertising and snooping software
- **scams** – for example, phishing, where users are taken to spoof websites pretending to be legitimate businesses, where they are asked to 're-register' – don't ever do this! Newer browsers have an anti-phishing scanning feature to counteract this.

## Viruses, Trojans aand worms

The term 'computer virus' has come to be a catch-all means of referring to any sort of malicious code introduced unwittingly, or deliberately, into a computer. There are three main variants:

- viruses
- Trojans
- worms.

Software programs consist of hundreds of thousands of lines of code that act as individual instructions for the computer. A 'virus' is a small piece of program code that is designed to enter computer systems and which then spreads to infect more and more files and systems. The virus spreads from computer to computer, carried by any sort of file that is transferred by portable disc or email attachment. Increasingly, in these days of global inter-connectedness, viruses spread very rapidly across the Internet.

Some viruses enter systems having been set to wait until something triggers its infection. This could be a date (e.g. the Michaelangelo virus was set to infect on 6 March, the date of his birth) or a particular time. The deletion of someone's payroll number from a database has been used to trigger a virus. Other viruses just attack immediately on introduction.

## Sub-types of virus

There are several sub-types of virus. One of the more serious is a **boot sector virus**. The boot sector is a small area on the computer hard drive or disc where information about the drive or disc structure is stored. Whenever the computer is started (booted up), the virus is loaded into memory. This could mean that every time you start up the machine, all files and removable media such as floppies, are infected as well. In some of the worst cases, these viruses can recognise anti-virus software programs and delete them before they run. A boot sector virus often sends error messages on start up or refuses to boot at all.

**Program infector viruses** attach themselves to the exe files of programs so that each time you run a particular application, such as Word, the virus loads itself into the system. Every other program that is started after that is also infected. Programs infected with this sort of virus tend not to run as they should. Warnings are therefore given quite early on that infection has occurred.

**Macro viruses** work by infecting files from other programs that run macros; a 'macro' is a prescribed sequence of actions. A common example would be where a spreadsheet is designed to carry out a calculation at a certain point, or a Word program checks for spelling errors. Macro viruses can spread quite easily because they infect files rather than programs. They are platform independent so can easily spread from one operating system to another.

A **Trojan** is a piece of programming language that works by appearing to be something else. It is disguised as either something useful or entertaining, or perhaps something mysterious. These are often attachments to emails, or they may be downloaded from the Internet. A Trojan will enter a system and then wait until it is ready to strike. Trojans can sometimes simply be destructive and ruin files, more commonly they are used to create back door entrances into systems so that intruders can access data, or gain control of computers.

A '**worm**' is a rapidly self replicating (re-creating) program that does not necessarily infect other programs. Instead it spreads across networks and the web. (Sometimes this can happen extremely quickly – the 'Slammer Worm' propagated at a rate in which during the first minute of its release it doubled in size every eight seconds – infecting millions of users.) Worms work in hidden parts of a system and like other virus forms can simply be a nuisance slowly undermining and destroying a system, or they can be dangerously sinister by creating weaknesses and entry points for later access to data within systems.

▲ Computer viruses can spread rapidly

## Case study

### Melissa

In 1999 a macro virus known as 'Melissa' was discovered. An email was headed 'Important Message From....' Within the text body were the words, 'Here is the document you asked for, don't show anyone else ;-)'. A Word document was attached called List.doc that contained a list of the URLs for 50 pornographic websites.

The Word document attached to the email contained a macro which was executed once the document was opened. Written in Visual Basic, a powerful and simple way to create macros, this one accessed as many email directories as it could within Microsoft Outlook mailing lists, pulling 50 addresses from each one and sending the document with your name on it to these people. Microsoft was forced to close down its mailing services for a while in order to get rid of the virus.

1. In view of the situation that occurred with Melissa; what general advice would you give to staff in a new e-business? ✓
2. Offer a summary of the main anti-virus software that a business might consider. ✓✓
3. As a manager in an online business, what precautions would you require staff to take relating to various computer threats? ✓✓✓

### ■ Blended threats'

So called 'blended' **threats** combine the characteristics of worms, viruses and Trojans to cause widespread damage. They propagate rapidly by a range of methods, embedding themselves into html code within files on a server; sending unauthorised emails with a worm attachment, infecting visitors to a website (seriously compromising to an e-commerce site). Blended threats often exploit known vulnerabilities in operating systems to gain access points by scanning the Internet for servers to attack.

## Key Terms

**Security threats** Openings in the software or networking arrangements of an e-business that allow intrusion, data theft or virus infections.

## Practice point

In pairs, investigate reports of at least three computer viruses, describing their scope, effect and impact.

## Loss of data

E-businesses are seriously vulnerable to security breaches. This vulnerability can come as much from perception (how things are seen) as from reality. Whatever kind of business is under discussion, wrongful access to information, falsely transferring funds, destruction of data, or other malicious attacks can happen in a number of ways; some of these are external threats and some can come from inside. We will examine a number of threats.

### ■ Software problems

More than 1400 new software vulnerabilities are reportedly discovered every week.

Businesses usually do not have the staff resources to develop their own applications software and therefore tend to purchase well-established packages or acquire 'open source' programs from outside. These programs sometimes introduce 'bugs' that can create serious security loopholes. A 'bug' in software terms is an unintended problem caused by the program. These can have the effect of creating an undesirable 'doorway' into a computer system and its data. This can be used by malicious hackers to extract private information, or introduce further unwanted programming code that corrupts data in a system.

As an illustration, in February 2004, Microsoft was forced to issue a 'critical security alert' because of the discovery that some of their programs were vulnerable to a problem called 'buffer overflow'. A buffer is a piece of memory in a computer that can store a set amount of data. Sometimes, usually because of a software bug, more data is sent to the buffer than it can hold, causing it to overflow into the next piece of buffer memory. This makes a computer vulnerable to hackers because, by deliberately causing buffer overflow, they can force the machine to execute their own illegal code. Hackers insert malicious program instructions into areas of memory that should contain only authentic data; the computer is then made to execute the hacker code. In this way anyone's private data – stored in a Microsoft operating system – could potentially be either corrupted or stolen.

It is obviously in the interests of Microsoft, as well as anyone using its software, to eliminate these bugs as and when they are discovered. Microsoft has a policy of investigating and fixing bugs as soon as it is alerted about them. This is done by issuing downloadable software 'patches' that have the effect of closing security loopholes.

Software design is crucial in helping to create computer system security. An e-business by its nature is Internet-facing. The business has to be part of the open web to be part of the online community. This means that any weaknesses in software design can have the effect of allowing dangerous unauthorised access to all sorts of data. Software design should, for example, ensure correct user validation (the user is who they say they are) and a program should flow in ways that are in line with business intentions. The latter problem in programming tends to be referred to as a 'logic error'. This occurs where the program flow can be manipulated or changed by a hacker so as to gain access into the system. In extreme cases a hacker can gain total control of an operating system.

In some instances it is neither software bugs nor software design that causes a security threat. Incorrect configuration of some software (such as a firewall setup) may inadvertently allow hackers to read corporate data. The applications software might be fine, but the security setup is wrong.

### Practice point

Investigate the question of 'software bugs' Write a simple explanation – in plain English – of how these might introduce vulnerabilities into a computer system.

## ■ Theft of identity

This is sometimes called 'spoofing'. It occurs when a hacker pretends to be someone else and thereby gain access to data. One method of spoofing is by pretending to be a certain IP address. Many web facing computer systems are restricted to a limited set of IP addresses. Hackers can gain access to the system and gain an entry point that will disclose other more sensitive data.

## ■ Physical insecurities

Business managers need to be aware of simple poor practice that can have dramatic effects on data security. By carelessly discarding old media, such as floppy discs or CDs, data that can allow access to a system can be picked up by outsiders. Just by picking through a rubbish bin, people can gain all sorts of sensitive information, including passwords, code numbers or access information. No amount of technical security can overcome this sort of oversight. Similarly, technical steps are no match for physical intrusion into a building or office.

## ■ Internal security threats

Many security problems do not come from outside, they come from within the organisation. Statistically, most (80%) threats come from inside – mainly from untrustworthy employees. Usually, the aim of unauthorised intrusion is to gain information from databases, to access research data, to view sales reports, view marketing statistics or human resources records. Information can be valuable to others and is sold; occasionally data can be tampered with and corrupted.

A 'root password' is the main means of authorised entrance to a full system. The trusted individuals with access to this password will have full rights to do virtually anything with the system and therefore its data. If this password is carelessly issued, or communicated using unprotected methods, damage can deliberately or mistakenly be done to a system.

## ■ 'Cracking', 'hacking' and 'bombing'

Computing terminology is evolving and different computer interest groups worldwide have different preferences. Not so long ago 'hacking' would be taken to refer to unauthorised access and tinkering with computer systems for fun, in order to satisfy pure intellectual curiosity. But now a whole underground of hacker groups exists; some of them intending to do malicious damage, some merely in it for bravado and the technical buzz. Many hacker groups claim to operate for legal purposes, some even claim to be a force for good. These groups prefer the term 'hacker' to be seen as respectable, whereas a 'cracker' is the criminal.

'Bombing' is an activity in which large amounts of email are sent to an individual or organisation with the aim of completely filling the recipient's hard disc with immense, useless files. This causes at best irritation and at worst complete system failure.

### Practice point

Research and find out the various categories of 'hacker'. Produce a clearly sectioned poster, designed to warn of the different kinds of threat.

## Measures to reduce risks

To help reduce the risk to computer security, organisations can implement sensible procedural precautions, such as IT technicians switching off features that automatically open attachments to emails, ensuring that operating system updates are always installed and instructing staff about the dangers of opening email attachments from unknown senders. In addition to this, anti-virus software is also required.

## ■ Anti-virus software

Anti-virus software is essential protection for any business organisation that is connected to the Internet. This software needs to be applied not only to single PCs but to the network as a whole. This should ensure that viruses carried by floppy or zip discs or any other removable media are stopped. Additionally, anti-virus software should be able to scan incoming mail.

Many software vendors offer anti-virus products. Most of them are similar in terms of what they do. The most effective are those that offer an updating of virus definitions as part of their service. Updates are usually available on demand or are sent out automatically via email. Typical of this sort is Norton Anti-virus (see www.norton.com); also see www.drsolomons.com; or www.Mcafee.com.

Good anti-virus packages tend to offer three components as part of their service:

1. They **scan** all files on local or hard discs, floppies or network drives.
2. They **shield** automatically in the background, looking out for viruses while downloading takes place or a floppy disc is put into a PC.
3. They **clean** a file system or disc of viruses once they have been found. This is done by scanning a database for established remedies. Most anti-virus solutions erase a virus immediately and it is expected that the recipient of a virus informs the sender straightaway so that the source can be eliminated.

### Practice point

Investigate two anti-virus software packages. Create a display showing their main features and comparing what they offer.

## Firewalls

A firewall is a security system implemented in software or hardware that is used to prevent unauthorised access to or from an intranet (private network). Firewalls are frequently used.

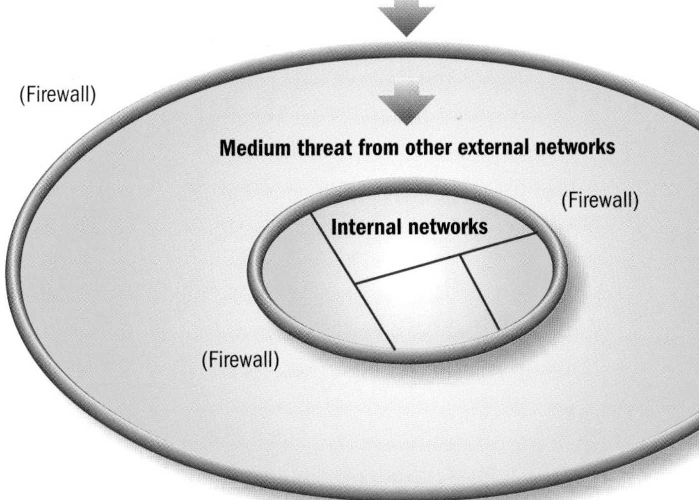


▲ Threats to private networks

A good illustration of how this works is the medieval castle. In the diagram above, we can see that the 'treasures' of the internal networks are all hidden behind a high external firewall, which itself hides another security firewall. Each level of security – from the inside out – gets progressively more robust and strong. Internally, less security (but still good security) is required because the outer layers are strong. Firewalls can work by filtering 'packets' of data as they enter or leave a network – on the basis of pre-configured rules; alternatively, they apply security to particular applications. Firewalls are the first line of defence for networks.

### Remember

Any computer connected to the Internet can be subject to attack from elsewhere on the web. Everyone should take steps to protect their PC.

## Information technology policies

When an organisation uses a computer network it tends to have computerised systems across all its internal functions. This means that finance, human resources, sales, production and other specialisms, all depend on digital data. The security methods outlined will offer good protection from external threats, but internal threats also exist. Poor staff practices, and inappropriate Internet use, can cause damage to a business.

A business therefore needs to have a set of IT policies (see below). These will establish the 'ground rules' for all staff to follow. Such measures as passwords, authentication, firewalls and restrictions will all have to be implemented.

### *An Internet policy for your employees*

*Access rules*

Give employees proper training before they use the Internet. This should cover:

- How to use your Internet software.
- Your Internet policy, and how it works.
- Efficient use of the Internet.

Make sure employees follow your access procedures:

Configure software to maximise security. Do not allow employees to change settings or use other software.

Depending on the nature of your connection, employees may need to disconnect once they have finished using the Internet. You can set your Internet connection to close down after a specified time if it is not being used.

Only give employees remote access (e.g. using a laptop) to your network or Internet connection when it is absolutely necessary.

(*Source:* Sample taken from The KnowledgeNetwork – HSBC, www.knowledge.hsbc.co.uk)

▲ Sample Internet Policy Information from THE HSBC KNOWLEDGE NETWORK

### Backing up data

A simple security measure that is advisable for individuals as well as businesses is to 'back up' the data that is stored on computer. A business that uses an intranet will have a lot of crucial data on file. Malicious hacking or loss of data can be very harmful to the organisation. Computer systems are often configured to automatically back up all data. This means creating an additional copy of all files and storing this separately.

For individuals, backing up important data on CDs, or other portable media such as a data stick, is good practice.

## Use of the Internet for business research

All businesses have to take account of their external environment. They need to be aware of things that are going on and be aware of the forces that could affect their own performance. The web offers many opportunities for research. The ability and the willingness of an organisation to use these opportunities is governed by the degree to which a business has embraced digital media.

There are different levels of Internet business. As we saw above, some businesses have no website of their own and simply place an entry on a business listing (e.g. www.yell.co.uk); others have a basic site that provides information about the company and products. The next stage is a more interactive site allowing users to query the information and search the site. Finally, a growing number of businesses have fully interactive sites where people can make purchases and where the site contains the full range of marketing functions.

### Types of data

E-business has generated a new type of research. When a business goes fully online and uses the Internet extensively, there is often a great deal of investment involved. '**Web analytics**' refers to a series of methods by which the contribution and performance of a website can be measured. How many people visit the site? How long do they stay? Where do they 'click through' to? What do they purchase? WebTrends at www.webtrends.com offers this service.

The web also offers a series of specialist services that can be of use to a business.

#### Key Terms

**Web analytics** Software services that can track users of websites, measure click through patterns and provide data to assist in web strategic planning.

### Demographics

Population statistics and trends have an obvious influence on the online business. How many people are online, where are they, what are the trends? There are some useful online services provided by specialist sites such as ClickZStats (at www.clickz.com) or www.demographicsnow.uk where business managers can analyse what is happening and take more informed decisions.

### Competitor analysis

A well-formulated business strategy takes account of all external forces. Among these, it is very important to be aware of what competitors are doing.

On its financial pages, Yahoo! (http://finance.yahoo.com) offers information about many firms around the world and Dun and Bradstreet (www.dunandbrad.co.uk) has data on millions of worldwide companies.

### Environmental analysis

All businesses function within their industrial environment. Increasingly, we live and work in a global economy. This means that many different environmental factors will have an impact upon the performance of a UK-based business. To take an obvious one, the price of fuel affects business; so does the price of commodities.

The Internet makes the world a much smaller place. The availability of instant communications helps to keep a business in touch with what is happening.

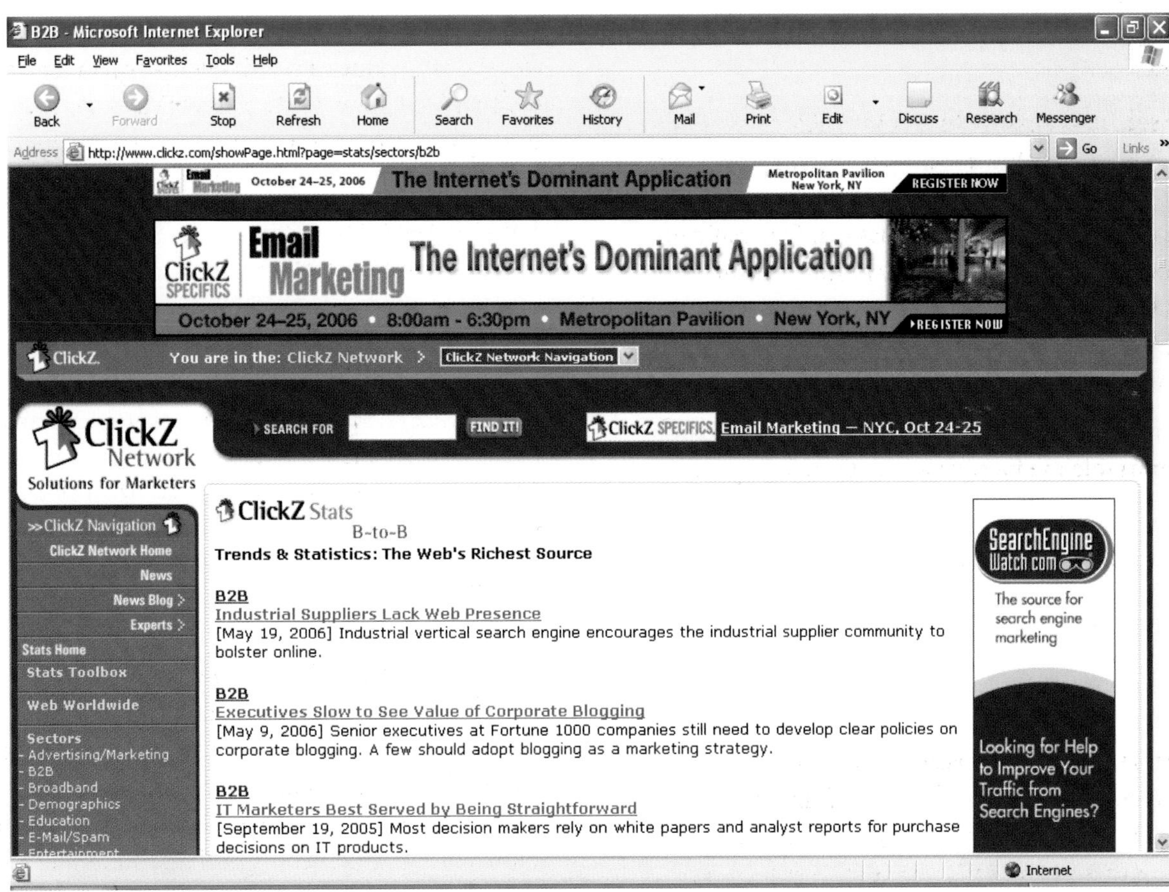


▲ The ClickZStats website

### Thinking point

You own a café selling high-quality coffee and related products. In what ways will the web offer you a chance to stay in touch with your business environment?

### Thinking point

Global terrorism is a big threat not only to individuals, but to big business interests too. In your view, which industrial sectors are most vulnerable to the threat of terrorist attack?

## Legislation and specialist sites

In general, weather conditions, climate change, global population trends, political change in a region, and the threat of global terrorism, are all of importance to some very significant industries. Businesses will also use specialist sites to find out technical information as well as data on legislation that will affect them, transport information and so on.

### Efficient use of search engines

Search engines are directories that list everything on the web. There are hundreds of them. The most popular for personal users may not be the most suitable for professional or business users. For general use, here is a selection:

- www.google.com
- www.excite.co.uk
- www.ask.co.uk
- www.yahoo.com

## Case study

**'Industrial Suppliers Lack Web Presence'**

Buyers of industrial equipment and services look to the Web to source goods, but the distributors they want to locate are slow to build an online presence. That's according to a survey conducted by GlobalSpec, a vertical search engine for the engineering, industrial and technical communities.

'Today, you find far fewer companies that don't have a website, it's really more about how they've embraced the Internet and online,' said Chris Chariton, VP of marketing at GlobalSpec. 'It takes them out of their comfort space a little bit.'

Traditional means of sourcing new suppliers, trade shows, sales calls and catalogues, are being replaced by web searches. Seventy-three per cent of buyers of industrial equipment look for new sources on search engines and online directories. Search engines are the first place to query for new vendors, online industrial directories account for 21% of first searches. Online sources exceed initial searches through traditional channels like recommendations from colleagues, manufacturer sales calls, trade magazines, and direct mail.

'The audience has moved online, and the first place they're going to look for new sources is the Internet,' said Chariton. 'From a time savings standpoint, the engineering and tech audience really embraces the Internet as a place to find information and news sources.'

When finding a source on the Web, up-to-date content and technical specifications are the most important functions of a site.

(*Source:* From an article by Enid Burns, 19 May 2006: www.clickz.com)

If you were an 'industrial buyer', you would be responsible for the purchase of many thousands, perhaps millions of pounds worth of materials and equipment.

1. What does the article by Enid Burns tell you about the uses of the Internet for buying? ✓
2. Is this information of use to business planners? ✓✓
3. What points would you make to the management of a small- or medium-sized business to encourage them to take up Internet opportunities? ✓✓✓

For a business user, Copernic is an automatic search of other search engines. A query raised on Copernic can be sent to multiple search engines simultaneously.

### Different types of search

For a business (and a student!), using better search techniques can improve the chances of finding useful information.

**Example – Refining a search**

A manager wishes to search for 'printers'. A Google search might return 124 million entries. If this is refined by entering 'inkjet printers' the return falls to 4,800,000 entries. By enclosing inkjet printers within "quote marks", the search result drops still further to 1,380,000.

Some search engines allow a user to use some special commands to get more precision. Using the '+' in search engines before the word, means that it must be included in the matched page. Placing a '- ' before the word means that it must not be included in the matched pages.

For business users of the web, there are many directories and newsgroups that are also of use. A list of all UK newsgroups can be found at www.usenet.org.uk.

### Bookmarking sites

When a website resource is discovered that offers useful information or resources, it is possible to 'bookmark' the site in the Netscape browser, or 'Add to Favourites' in Internet Explorer. This means the site web address is stored ready for quick access the next time it is required.

▲ **Copernic – a searching agent**

## Filtering sites

Business organisations as well as home users will seek at times to block certain websites that do not fall into the useful category. By using filtering software, web sites containing distasteful or inappropriate content can be filtered out and blocked.

## Validity of data sources

The Internet offers the capability to conduct extensive secondary research and extract detailed primary data; we looked above at the technique known as 'Web Analytics'. A business using the web can analyse how a site is being used.

A recent report, Marketing Sherpa's 'Buyer's Guide to Web Analytics' described more than 50 different tools for measuring website traffic – and said there were at least 50 others. The report didn't include companies that provide traffic measurement services using panels of web users (such as comScore Media Metrix and Nielsen//NetRatings) or those that collect behavioural information from users via telephone or online surveys.

While site administrators are awash in data, many have found that the numbers generate as much confusion as understanding.

## Case study

### Making sense of data

Greg Swanson, director of Internet sales for Lee Enterprises, just wanted to know two things. How many people were visiting the websites of his company's 44 newspapers? And how often did they visit? The problem was, the answers Swanson got didn't make sense to him. In Montana, for instance, the *Billings Gazette* had a Sunday readership of about 52,000 people, but the website had almost 10 times that many visitors in a month and the average site user was visiting the site just one or two times per month.

'We had unbelievably large reach – which in some months exceeded the entire population of the state of Montana. Huge reach, but incredibly low frequency,' Swanson said. 'For advertisers, it was as if we were putting a message on the side of a bus and driving though a crowded downtown area once a month.'

Swanson would ultimately conclude that the problem stemmed from the inaccuracy of the tools his company was using to measure website usage. At newspaper websites, he is one of many people who have been frustrated by the difficulty in getting answers to seemingly simple questions about their online audiences.

(*Source*: From Rich Gordon: The DigitalEdge.com © 2005 Newspaper Association of America)

1. How would you describe 'web analytics' to a new e-business? ✓
2. Do you think this case study shows that web analytics do not work? Why? ✓✓

# Use of Internet for procurement

To 'procure' something means to buy it. Every business organisation has to buy things. Business could, in fact, be summed up as just that – buying and selling. The trick for a private sector business is to buy things at a low cost, add value and sell them for more. For a public sector organisation, 'efficiency' is vital because it is spending tax payers' money. 'Procurement' is, therefore, crucial to the success of any organisation.

## Selection of suitable sites

The Internet can offer a range of 'procurement services' and there are web services specially tailored for both private businesses and public bodies. There are several advantages in using the web for procurement purposes. For example:

- Comprehensive purchasing intelligence – some web-based services offer analytical applications ranging from simple Internet reports to data warehouse-based workbooks. This helps a business to measure performance and identify the most significant opportunities to save money.
- Self-service purchasing – provides purchasing activities which reduces irresponsible spending by staff and speeds up the buying process.
- Self-guiding catalogue – enables users to find catalogue items quickly using a powerful text-based search engine.
- Supplier collaboration – web-based applications can link suppliers and partners together and integrate the supply chain.
- Global solution – web-based services can support dealings in multiple languages and currencies for businesses of all sizes, with services and support offered around the clock and around the globe.
- All products and services – manage procurement for any type of goods or service, whether in production or administrative support.

## Intermediary sites

Procurement services are also offered via so-called 'intermediary sites'. These are websites that exist between buyers and sellers and bring them together. The web offers access to a number of business directories; these allow managers to check things out in their own markets and specialist areas.

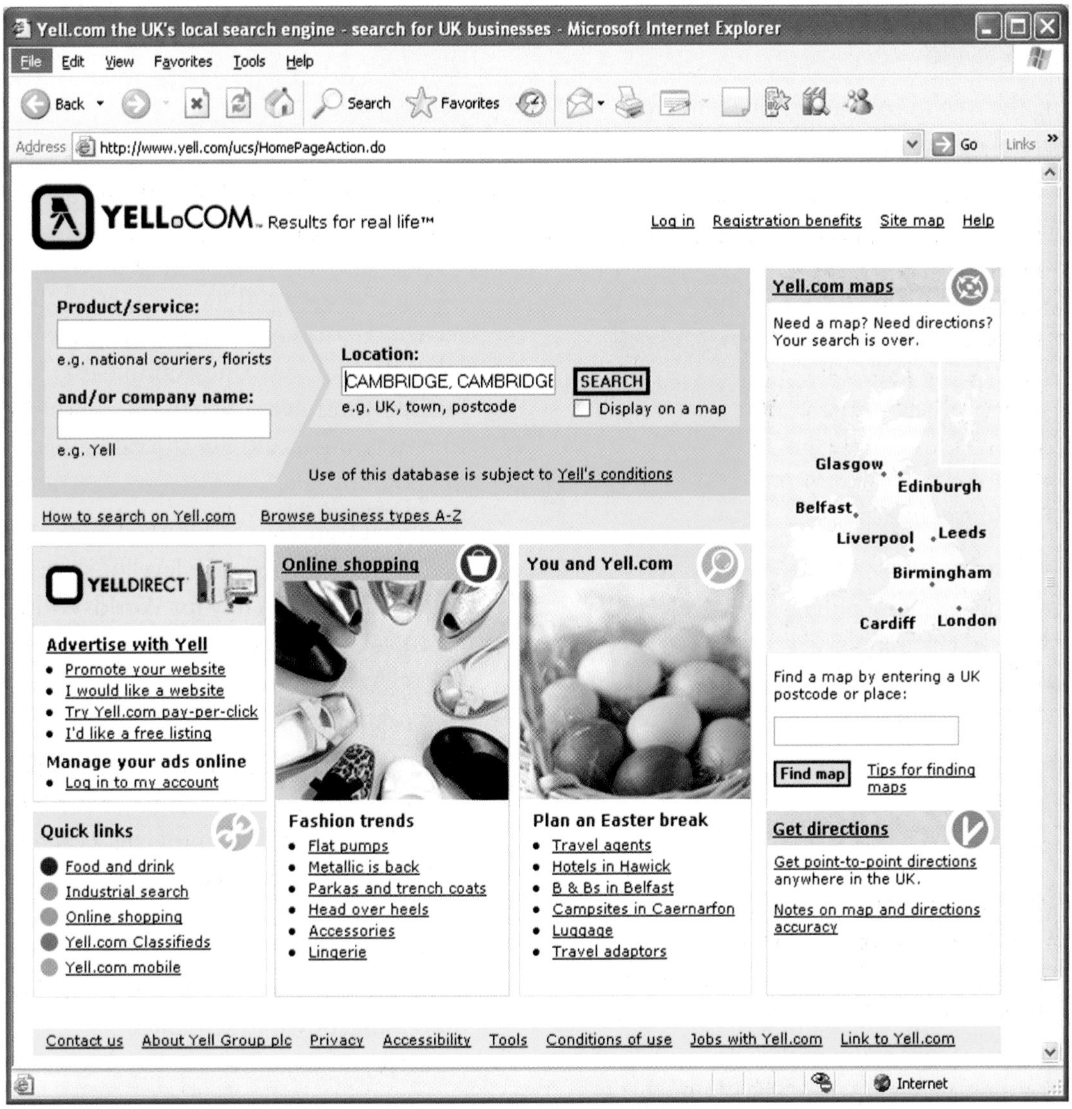

Yell.com the UK's local search engine - search for UK businesses - Microsoft Internet Explorer

File Edit View Favorites Tools Help

Back Search Favorites

Address http://www.yell.com/ucs/HomePageAction.do Go Links

YELL.COM Results for real life™

Log in Registration benefits Site map Help

Product/service:

e.g. national couriers, florists

and/or company name:

e.g. Yell

Location:

CAMBRIDGE, CAMBRIDGE SEARCH

e.g. UK, town, postcode

Display on a map

Use of this database is subject to Yell's conditions

How to search on Yell.com Browse business types A-Z

Yell.com maps

Need a map? Need directions? Your search is over.

Glasgow Edinburgh Belfast Liverpool Leeds Birmingham Cardiff London

Find a map by entering a UK postcode or place:

Find map Tips for finding maps

YELLDIRECT

Advertise with Yell

- Promote your website
- I would like a website
- Try Yell.com pay-per-click
- I'd like a free listing

Manage your ads online

- Log in to my account

Online shopping

Fashion trends

- Flat pumps
- Metallic is back
- Parkas and trench coats
- Head over heels
- Accessories
- Lingerie

You and Yell.com

Plan an Easter break

- Travel agents
- Hotels in Hawick
- B & Bs in Belfast
- Campsites in Caernarfon
- Luggage
- Travel adaptors

Quick links

- Food and drink
- Industrial search
- Online shopping
- Yell.com Classifieds
- Yell.com mobile

Get directions

Get point-to-point directions anywhere in the UK.

Notes on map and directions accuracy

Contact us About Yell Group plc Privacy Accessibility Tools Conditions of use Jobs with Yell.com Link to Yell.com

Internet

▲ Yell brings buyers and sellers together online

## Practice point

Look at business directory websites, such as www.yell.com, www.scoot.co.uk, and www.uktradeinvest.gov.uk. As a small-business adviser, draft a report specifying how these online directories could help a small- to medium-sized enterprise to develop its e-business.

## Remember

The Internet helps to bring partner businesses together so that they can share information and act more quickly in buying and selling.

## Security symbol

Anyone using the web to conduct business must consider the level of security. It is wise to look at the security setting shown by the browser and to set the level appropriately. This is displayed by a security symbol that appears on the browser.

▲ The security symbol

### Remember

Always check the level of your browser security by looking at the security symbol.

## Secure payment methods

A business that opens up an online channel will obviously hope to take credit card payments. In doing this there are natural fears about security from all parties. Two web standards have been designed to try to make credit card payments secure on the Internet.

The first of these, SSL or Secure Sockets Layer, acts by encrypting (i.e. rendering non-readable) traffic between a web server and a web browser – in the payments context this means the consumer's computer (the client) and the online seller's computer (the server).

The SET standard (Secure Electronic Transactions), unlike SSL, was designed exclusively for Internet financial transactions. The SET standard goes further than SSL and offers more protection for e-businesses. Using 'digital certificates', each participant within a transaction can be verified and authenticated and each message can be checked for alteration. This means that no one can legitimately deny later that they placed an order, because all orders have to be digitally signed and a digital signature cannot be forged. SET defines the way a transaction flows, the formats of messages and the forms of encryption used. The confidentiality and integrity of SET-based financial transactions is said to be high.

### Remember

Customers thinking of buying online want to be reassured that their card details are secure.

Many software vendors are entering the payments security market and offering packages that build upon security standards; one example is FraudShield, created by ClearCommerce, which sets up rules so that any transaction is automatically validated and checked at the point of sale.

Financial transactions between banks have for several years been digitised. The level of security has necessarily been high. The Society for World-Wide Interbank Financial Telecommunications (SWIFT) is a private intranet that is used by financial organisations to exchange funds between them (see www.swift.com).

Further means of **securing the payments network** are available from Verisign (www.Verisign.org ) which adopts a policy based upon checks across the whole process of an electronic transaction. The Verisign approach is that a transaction is capable of being monitored along its entire 'lifecycle'; in other words, from first customer payment effort, through initial processing, down to settlement.

### Key Terms

**Secure payments** Payments system on a website that offers security to customers who know that credit or debit card details cannot be stolen.

## Online services and ways to reduce risks

Many online users now like to use the Internet for purchasing music or software. In fact, the web offers free downloads of software (freeware) and music sharing packages are now well established (e.g. Limewire and AllofMP3). Online banking has also become more popular as a convenient way of managing personal finances. However, all of these services should only be used in the context of anti-virus software and with Internet security browser settings set to at least 'medium'. In this way, the risks of infection to a PC are reduced.

### Legal protection and limitations

A business advertising goods or services via a website, interactive TV or mobile phone must comply with the E-Commerce Regulations 2002. Anyone selling anything online is certainly affected. The UK's E-Commerce Regulations 2002 came into force on 21 August 2002.

At the heart of the regulations there are new information requirements:

- Adverts online must provide the full name of the business and contact details including geographic address.
- Prices must also give details of any associated taxes or delivery charges.
- If online activities are subject to VAT, the VAT number must be shown.
- Details of association with a trade or professional body must be shown.

If email campaigns are used to promote goods or services, the regulations mean that the following must be observed:

- Make it unambiguous who the email is being sent by, or on behalf of.
- Any description of discounts or promotional offers must set out all the qualifying conditions.
- If email is unsolicited, it needs to be clear to the recipient that it is unsolicited without the recipient having to open the email.

If customers can place orders online, there are some further things to do:

- It must be clear at what point in the ordering process a customer has committed themselves.
- Users must be able to view, store and print business terms and conditions.
- The business must acknowledge receipt of orders electronically and without undue delay.

**Remember**

Using the Internet to set up an extra online sales channel can provide tremendous opportunities for a business; however the E-Commerce Regulations set out important rules that protect the consumer. These must be followed.

## Use of the Internet for promotion

To 'promote' a business can involve all sorts of techniques; some paid-for, others free (PR). Paid advertisements traditionally used the printed media, the radio or TV. The Internet has offered new forms of advertising and has become a multi-million-dollar industry.

### Websites

Some businesses simply wish to promote their activities on the Internet. They have no interest, or no scope, to actually 'transact' on the web. There are many businesses where having at least this basic level of web presence can contribute to their aims.

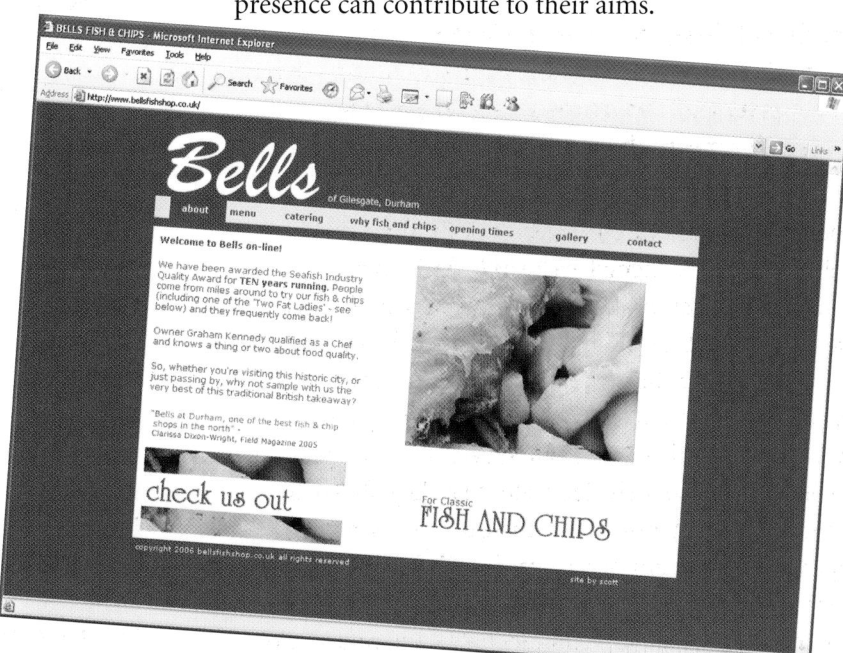


▲ A fish and chip shop promoting online

## Banner advertising

A space across the top of a web page, usually with animated content, advertising products or services from another business, is known as a 'banner'. A click on the banner by a visitor to a site leads to a referral through to the site of the advertising business. This is known as a 'click-through'.

▲ Banner ad space

The choice of which sites to place the banner on will be considered by marketing specialists and there are several specialist sites offering services to help in placing, or targeting, banners. Banner ads can be exchanged between sites offering complementary products or services, or they can be specifically targeted onto sites where it is felt that the audience will be appropriate.

### Case study

**Online advertising**

An online advertising forecast, at the Search Engine Strategies Conference & Expo 2005, claimed that in 2010 the global online advertising market will be worth $18.9bn, compared to $9.3bn at the end of 2004. It is thought that by 2010 the keyword search ads segment of the market will generate more revenue and will grow twice as fast as the banner ads segment, which has been the industry's staple ad format for years.

(*Source*: quoted in The Register 2005 © ElectricNews.net)

1. What are the trends in relation to banner ads? ✓
2. What form of online advertisement would you recommend for a local business? ✓✓
3. Make a justified recommendation to the management of a local business as to how it might best make use of the Internet for promotional purposes. ✓✓✓

Banner ads can be accurately targeted onto sites that are likely to have the audience a business is hoping to attract. For example, in consumer markets a business selling gardening products can target an online gardening publication and have their banner placed in a prominent page. Retired people can be targeted through sites geared towards the elderly.

### Thinking point

You have a business selling designer knitted sweaters. On which websites might you consider placing a banner advert?

## Link registration

Once a business has a website up and running then it is important to register the site with the search engines. Search engines are extremely important for the promotion of a website. Over 80% of web users are known to use them and if a business has not bothered to register with the search engines then they are unlikely to be found unless they have an extremely well-known brand name.

### Remember

A business setting up a new website should register with one of the well-known search engines. This is free and easy to do.

We saw earlier that a vague search by a user can throw up literally millions of websites. Even a carefully refined search possibly offers thousands of websites containing at least some reference to what is being looked for. How does a business make sure that its website has a good chance of coming up in a search engine? The answer is it must register with the search engine and ensure that the 'keywords' in the site header are relevant.

### Direct emails

It seems the easiest thing in the world to send out hundreds, even thousands of emails, to unsuspecting people. The trouble is that sending out 10,000 emails might get 50 people interested in whatever product a business has to offer and 9950 people thoroughly annoyed. The practice of sending out unrequested email is known as 'spamming', the term spam is said to mean Sending Persistent Annoying (e)Mail, sometimes known as 'junk'. If PR is the effort to promote an effective and positive image on the Internet, spamming tends to have the opposite effect. Maturing Internet users are simply learning to delete spam.

If Internet marketers are going to tap into the potential benefits of email, they need to consider ways of by passing any accusations of spamming. To do this they might use **'opt-in' emailing**. This means that, before sending anyone any mail they seek permission first, hence the sometimes used term, 'permission marketing'. Users must actively check a box giving the organisation permission to mail them in future.

#### Key Terms

**'Opt-in' emailing** Collecting permissions from customers to send them emails detailing future services or promotions.

The benefits of permission-based emailing are considerable, according to a survey quoted in eMarketer. The survey, by Quris, found that 67% of consumers believed that the quality of opt-in emails positively influenced their opinions about the companies sending them and 53% said that such emails had an influence on what they purchased.

Marketers must be extremely careful when considering both emailing and PR on the Internet. Because the Internet is a network, the effect is that news travels very fast. Internet marketers can and do use this effect to the benefit of their businesses, but they must be aware of the negative effects of bad mailing practice or bad PR. '**Viral marketing**' is the term used to describe the way in which marketing messages can be rapidly spread around the Internet through word being passed on, either through emailing, (virtual word of mouth) or real world word of mouth.

#### Key Terms

**Viral marketing** Marketing through word of mouth on the web, i.e. very rapidly indeed; whether the news is good or bad.

#### Remember

Direct emailing can access millions of potential consumers; however, 'spamming' carries the danger of getting a business a bad name. It is better to seek permission before mailing people.

## Use of the Internet for business communication

Businesses can profit from the increased speed and efficiency of Internet communications. However, they have to be careful about how they use the technology.

### Email

The speed with which computer networks can now connect means that documents and messages can move rapidly around them. Within most modern organisations there are intranets; email has become the norm in business internal communications.

Emails can be addressed to single individuals using an organisational email account, or they can be globally addressed to all staff. By using the 'cc' facility, a copy of a mail is sent to further email addresses.

It is possible to use another facility in email services such as Outlook, which allows an email sender to send multiple copies to many recipients, but not show this to the individuals. These are 'hidden (or blind) CCs; they avoid the irritating situation for some people who do not appreciate being one of many recipients.

Using email in an organisation is today the norm for just about everyone. All businesses have company policies on emails. Staff are expected to use email professionally and sensitively. Any abusive content or inappropriate content, can be traced and action taken.

### Thinking point

There is so much email today that people are becoming immune to it. How would you advise a business manager to think carefully about an email strategy?

A corporate business strategy for email must include security practices. This will ensure that attachments – always a dangerous source of possible viruses – can be scanned and appropriate warnings given before they are opened.

Other important aspects of email include tone and style within emails. It can be easy to offend via email. Users should always ensure that they use correct grammar, a suitably professional tone and are careful about emailed data. Remember that emails can be a permanent record. They may be quick to write but they need to be produced with care.

## Digital cameras and video images

The web is a quick and convenient way of sending digital photographs and video images. While these are very useful facilities, especially for businesses such as estate agencies, users need to treat digital cameras and the use of digital images with care.

## Voice over Internet Protocol

Technology known as Voice over Internet Protocol (VoIP) allows users to make phone calls over a computer network. Once they have the specialist handsets needed to convert voice data into computer data, businesses with a broadband connection can make free calls (including international calls) to other broadband users with VoIP equipment. All the users pay for is their Internet connection.

According to a survey by Inclarity of 500 small-business managers, while only 12% of firms made phone calls over the Internet, those that did saw their telephone bill drop by 23% and IT costs fall by 13%.

## Video conferencing

Video conferencing involves a range of technologies used in a wide range of situations. Sometimes it is not just video and audio being transmitted, but also data, allowing a business with multi-site operations the chance for collaborative working though shared applications.

▲ **Business video conference**

Video conferencing may be used in:

- one-to-one meetings, also known as point-to-point communications, involving full two-way audio and video
- one-to-many involving full audio and video broadcast from the main site, where other sites may be able to send audio
- many-to-many, known as multi-point communication, providing audio and video between more than two sites. With most multi-point systems only one site in a conference can be seen at time, with switching between sites either controlled manually or voice activated (i.e. the loudest site is on screen).

For a business to set up video conferencing, the basic hardware components are:

- camera, usually attached to the top of the monitor
- microphone
- speakers – even where speakers are built into a workstation, external ones will provide better quality audio. Alternatively, headphones may be useful, particularly in a shared office
- video board – to capture the signal from the camera and convert it to digital form
- network card – usually an Ethernet card for connection to the LAN, or an ISDN card.

## Remember

Video conferencing can allow a business with separate operations located geographically far apart, to engage in video, audio discussion and instant data transfer.

## Outcome activity 29.2

You are advising a small- to medium-sized business which is considering getting a fully transactional website. It has already commissioned web designers and is pleased with the 'look and feel' of the site as it is emerging in design. Now your client wants to know more about how the web can help the business.

**Pass**

Describe how the Internet can be used for different types of business activity, taking actions to reduce the inherent risks to security and reliability. **P2**

*Task 1*

Visit www.nielsen-netratings.com and look for the 'solutions and products' panel on the left of the home page. Click on 'read more' under 'customise analysis and surveys'. Draft a short report on the kind of data that this service can bring for a newly web-based business.

Carry out research using a search engine such as www.google.co.uk.

You are required to discover a full range of prices and product comparisons for laser printers suitable for business use. Create a written summary for the business explaining how you searched for the information.

Report to the business owner giving them the following information from the web:

- population statistics for EU countries
- Internet penetration for South America
- any other business-related data that you feel will help them understand how web-based information can help a growing business.

The business owner is convinced about the information available and how the Internet can be used; however, now they are asking about security.

*Task 2*

You must demonstrate how to download two important security measures for the business:

- firewall protection
- anti-virus protection.

Access http://www.personalfirewall.comodo.com/ and demonstrate, using a download, how to create a firewall protection for a network.

Look up a freely downloadable anti-virus software package, such as AVG. Demonstrate how to download the package and show evidence that you can do so. Produce a short explanation to the business of why such measures are important.

**Merit**

Demonstrate how to solve problems in Internet use for four different types of business activity.

Having demonstrated how to take protective measures; draft an outline 'staff policy on Internet use' that can be issued to the staff of the newly online business.

## Grading tips

**Pass** 

Pass level work is thorough and will offer a full description, or demonstration, of each category of information required and each security measure. Clear presentation is required.

**Merit** m 1

For Merit, you need to carefully analyse how worries/problems about web trading can be reduced. Note that you are asked to think about 'four different types of business activity'.

# 29.3 Trends in the use of e-business

A survey in 2006 on e-business trends in manufacturing by SVM showed that:

- 78% of manufacturers intended to increase spending on their website
- 60% intended to increase investment in email marketing
- 48% were boosting spending on search engine marketing
- 25% were reducing spending on magazine advertising
- 17% were reducing spending on trade shows.

The evidence is strong that businesses are taking up Internet opportunities in many sectors. As the SVM survey clearly shows, one of the key areas of take-up is in marketing.

### Marketing benefits

The Internet helps businesses to acquire a good knowledge of customers because it is a way of connecting everyone who is online. Millions of pounds, dollars, euros and many other currencies pass through wires linking computers all over the world. According to ClickZstats (www.clickz.com) the worldwide Internet population in 2005 was 1.08 billion.

Of course, eventually growth will slow down, but it will not stop completely, as more and more of the newly developing world (China, Russia, Eastern bloc countries and perhaps even the 'third world') come online. The number of users will continue to grow and more importantly so will the frequency of use and the time spent online. Technological improvements and increasing use of broadband will almost guarantee this.

**Remember**

China has a population of 1.3 billion and only 5.5% of these people are online. Imagine the growth of the Internet population when China begins to approach the levels of nations like Canada (60%).

Not only will more people be online, but the comfort and ease with which they use the Internet will improve and fears about security issues will diminish.

### Re-formulating the marketing mix

Traditional marketing uses tactics based on the 'marketing mix': product, price, place and promotion. Internet marketing specialists refer to a 'remix' of these, so that traditional marketing is re-applied in different ways in the online world. This **e-marketing remix** changes the traditional marketing tools and adds one or two new ingredients designed specifically for the online community.

To make visitors want to 'stick' around, a website has to offer something that is of value to a visitor. This is an **online value proposition** (OVP) and it is a similar concept to the 'unique selling proposition' (USP) commonly referred to in traditional marketing. In the case of the USP, marketers are trying to communicate something unique about a physical product that will make people want to buy it more than others. Similarly, the OVP is the special set of characteristics about a website that will make people want to stick around on the site and make a purchase.

## Key Terms

**E-marketing remix** New marketing tactics designed to market a web-based business.

**Online value proposition** Characteristics about a website that make people want to use it.



▲ Implementing the marketing remix online

## 24-hour global presence and flexible location

The use of the Internet in marketing means that products may be displayed and offered online 24 hours a day, all over the world. Catalogues can be made available showing images and giving full details. Promotion can happen 24 hours a day using Search Engine Marketing (SEM) and banners. Prices are competitive because of lower overheads. Prices can also be dynamic; they change according to market conditions and feedback from customers. Products (non-digital) can be made available (place) anywhere, because there is the possibility of flexible location; digital products download immediately. People can staff contact centres, or email. Finally, processes, e.g. easyJet flight bookings, are simple.

## Personalisation and feedback

One of the longest participating online businesses is Amazon. Anyone who registers with Amazon (www.amazon.co.uk) and makes a purchase will find that the next time they visit the site they have 'personalised' recommendations. Amazon's web software remembers what customers have ordered and promotes similar products – from books to cameras and PC games. There is also the opportunity to gain valuable feedback from customers through the use of interactive websites.

## Key Terms

**Personalisation** Where a web page is presented in such a way that it offers personal messages based on an individual's tastes and preferences.

## Opportunities for competitor analysis

The Internet offers the opportunity to do careful and accurate analysis of what competitors are doing online. Each company that goes online immediately becomes open and transparent as it does so. By its nature, the Internet is open and everyone can view its content. Marketing activities have to include keeping a close eye on the tactics, the ideas and offerings of competitor businesses. The websites themselves can be looked at and are a primary source of information.

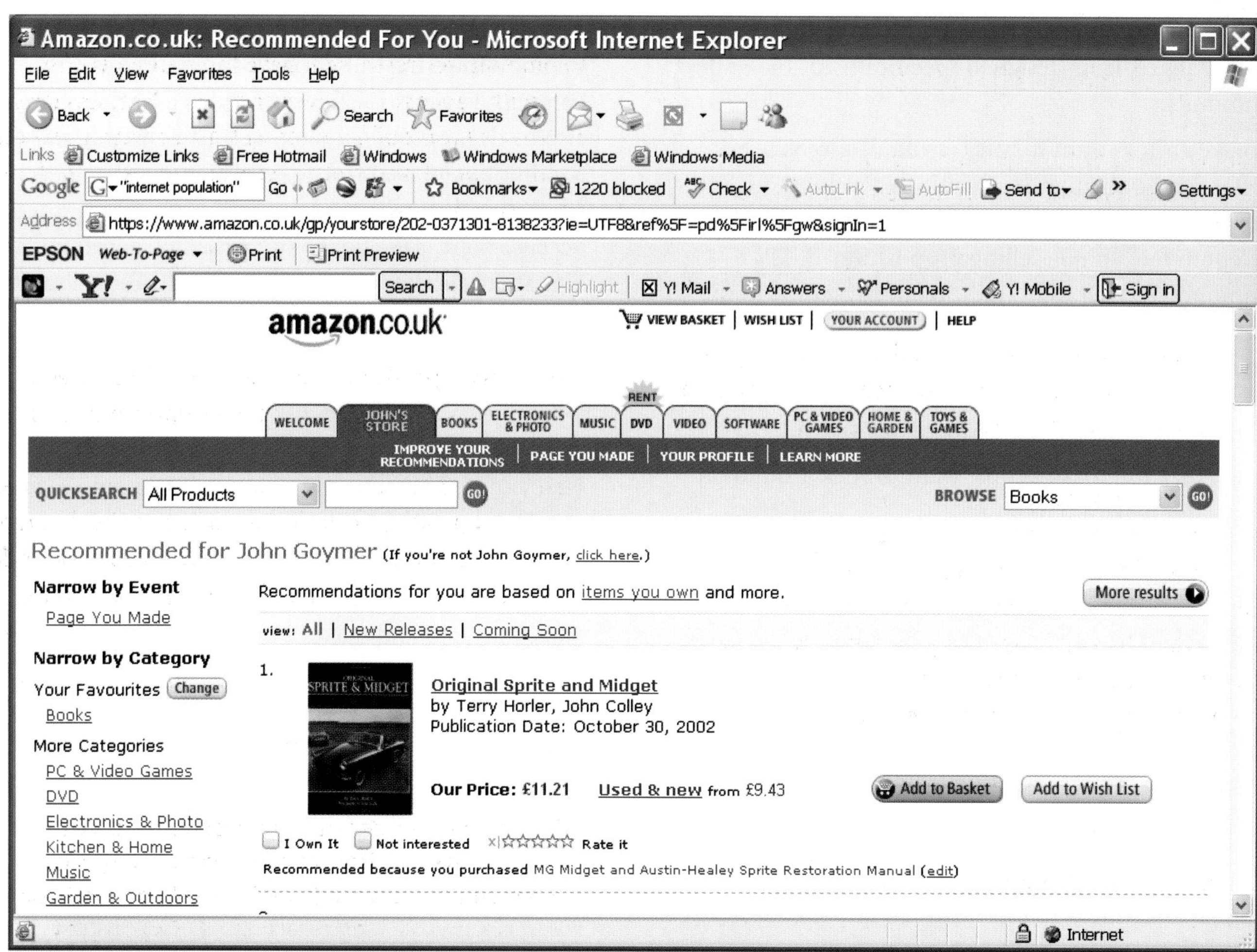


▲ **Personalising a web offer – Amazon**

Marketing specialists look for new ideas, for offers and tactical manoeuvres, particularly from organisations competing for the same segment of the market. The idea is not to copy a website but to gain an insight into competitor strategy. As we saw earlier, there are organisations offering this kind of intelligence as a service on the web (e.g. www.finance.yahoo.com and www.dunandbrad.co.uk).

### Opportunities to communicate with customers

The web allows a business to capture contact details of customers through registration. Again, this also can mean better customer feedback. Communication is made through opt-in email or regular email news bulletins. Some software, known as 'customer relationship management' (CRM), can automate communications and keep detailed records of important staff in B2B contexts.

## Cost benefits

### Premises and location

The Internet gives immediate geographic spread, without the need for relocation. A business considering growth through expansion could consider the web option as a way of saving on capital costs. Customers target the business online, rather than a business having to seek out customers.

### Thinking point

What is meant by the phrase 'the customer targets the businesses' online? How is this the case? Do you agree?

Because an online business is virtual, dealing in digital information, there is no immediate need for investment in physical premises. These could if necessary be confined to third party distributors, depending on the nature of the product sold. In addition, the positioning of premises can be an important factor when an organisation does business online. For example, some retailers can sell their products, using the Internet, from a base in the Channel Islands to gain tax advantages for themselves and so offer lower prices to their customers – gaining an edge over their competitors.

## Reduced staffing costs

The potential for cutting staff costs is strong for businesses that begin to use the web for e-transactions. In a traditional business, there is an enormous amount of paperwork and records that need to be kept, such as invoices, orders, delivery notes, credit notes and so on. Administrative staff have to be employed to deal with paperwork. However, when a business uses electronic means of conducting transactions it reduces the need for administrative records and also therefore administrative staff.

## Cash flow advantages

A business depends on good cash flow. Cash flow refers to the stream of revenue that comes into a business from sales activities so that working capital can be maintained. This allows it to pay for wages and salaries as well as operating costs. Many businesses fail because of poor cash flow. By opening up a new web-based sales channel, there is an opportunity to improve income.

### Remember

The Internet can generate impressive increases in sales revenue. For example, the following was reported by SHL group (an HR consultancy) in 2005: '40% increase in web revenue to £14.6m (2004: £10.4m).'

### Case study

**Ebookers**

'Online travel agent Ebookers cut its losses in the third quarter thanks to a lower wage bill arising from job cuts. The firm said it is still in discussions about a possible sale and "a further announcement will be made in due course".

'Ebookers has cut £1.3m from its annual wage bill. It has moved more sales online. In the third quarter of this year 62 per cent of sales were made online compared to 46 per cent in the third quarter of 2003.'

(*Source*: from article by John Oates in *The Register* 2004 © The Register)

1. How did Ebookers save on staff costs by moving sales online? ✓
2. In what ways would you say that Ebookers was responding to competitive forces by moving sales online? ✓✓
3. Prepare a case for a business that evaluates the costs and benefits of moving sales online. ✓✓✓

## Disintermediation of the supply chain

Everything has to come from somewhere. A business that makes railway carriages depends on other businesses that produce the parts that go into railway carriages. The parts that go into railway carriages are themselves made from raw materials or other component parts. The supply chain refers to the way in which raw materials and parts find their way eventually to the customer.

A chain consists of many links. The supply chain can consist of many links too. Once raw material (e.g. timber) is sourced, it is then transported to a merchant. The merchant may alter the raw material in some way before selling to a customer for use. The transport, the merchant, or distributors are all 'intermediaries'. This means they work in between. The web is capable of cutting out these intermediaries – a process known as **disintermediation**; this of course helps to cut costs.

### Key Terms

**Disintermediation** Where the intermediaries in a supply chain are eliminated because they are no longer required on the web.

### Thinking point

Can you think of particular products where there is now no need for an intermediary thanks to the web?

# Benefits to customers

The Internet offers a vast range of products and services to customers. These products and services are accessible 24 hours a day, from anywhere. Customers are now able to choose products from a wider range of businesses, irrespective of their location.

A new type of intermediary has grown up on the web. Traditionally, wholesalers and distributors were the intermediaries between manufacturers and retailers – and then consumers. Today 'infomediaries' provide consumers with the ability to compare prices and quality of service. One of these is Kelkoo at www.kelkoo.co.uk.

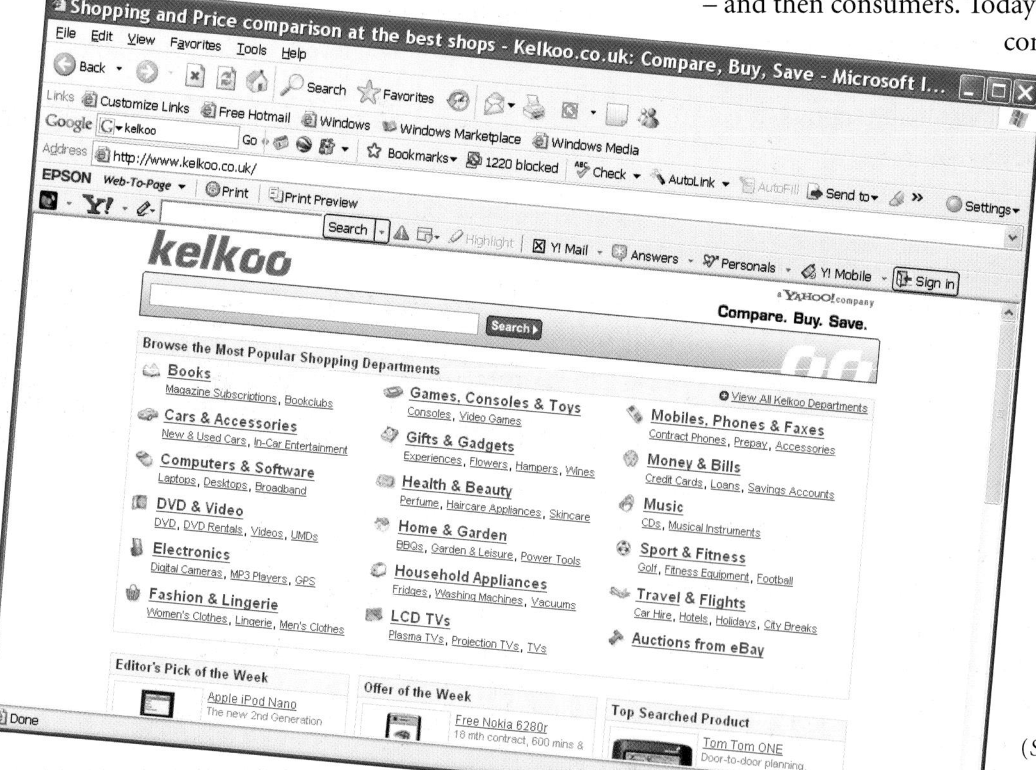


▲ The price comparison service from Kelkoo

(*Source*: Reproduced with permission of Yahoo! Inc. ©2007 by Yahoo! Inc.)

### Personalised offers

We saw above how a website can offer a personalised page that suits the personal preferences of a visitor. Amazon does this very effectively and so do the supermarkets – remembering your shopping list favourites week after week when you do your grocery shopping online.

## Operational implications of trends

A number of factors deserve consideration before a business sets up a transactional (buy and sell) website. These factors all affect the way an organisation works. The day-to-day running of a business is known as 'operational management'. There can be a number of operational implications for a business that starts to trade online.

### Expectations and product fulfilment

Having a quality website can give an organisation real advantage over rivals. However, it is crucial that the operational implications are considered. For instance, does the business organisation have the background systems and processes that can meet an increase in demand, possibly from a worldwide customer base? This means there must be stock available at all times and online orders have to be fulfilled.

### Customer expectations

Consumers who shop online are quite demanding. They have expectations that a website will be quick to load up in a browser. They will want all site links to work and for the site to have a minimum of annoying 'pop ups'. References to products in catalogues should be up to date and accurate. Prices should be easily available along with terms and conditions. The web shopper also requires a chance to give feedback or view a FAQ (frequently asked questions) page. Finally, the online shopper expects privacy and complete security.

### Increased competition

A business that opens up online immediately opens itself up to increased competition. Competitors can see the entire product range; they can see promotional offers and prices changes. The online business will be subject to online price comparisons. Certainly, offline businesses will be attempting to meet and better prices and services.

### New providers of old services

In some business organisations there has been a change caused by the fact that the business is now operating in new markets on the web. Tesco.com now offers music downloads from its website.

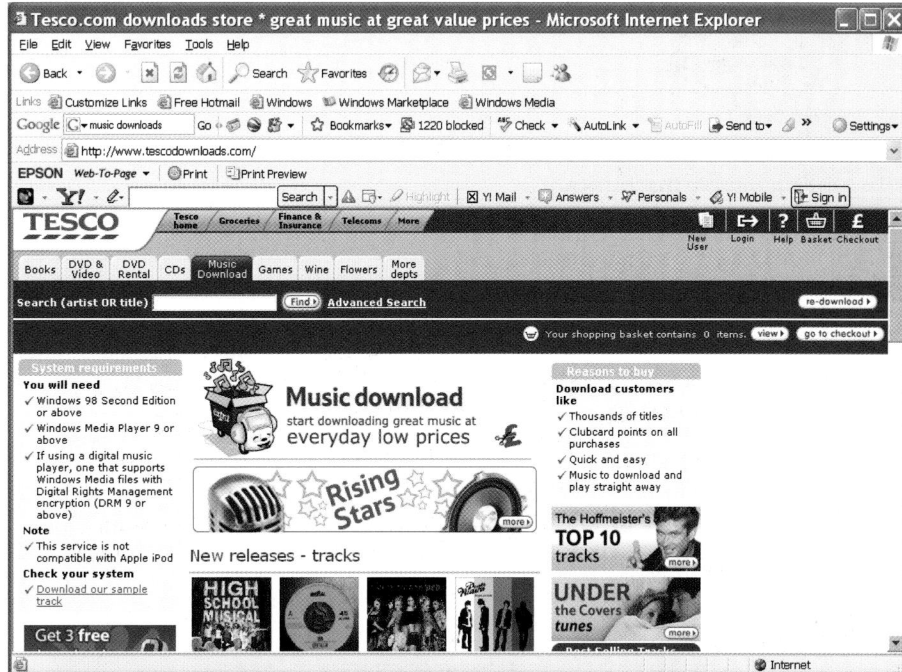

▲ Tesco now offers a music download service

Further examples of this include new telecommunications services offered through VoIP (considered above on page 430) and the huge growth of online shopping for everything from lingerie to household groceries.

# Strategic implications of trends on organisations

The general direction a business takes involves the bigger issues. These things are not about whether for example to buy paper from one source rather than another, they are about whether to enter new markets, produce new things, open or close premises, relocate or trade online. However, before opening up a new web presence, a business has to consider certain strategic implications. In other words, what will be the effect of a big change in direction on the business?

## Competitive pressures

The growing volume of online trading, and the increasing tendency for businesses to use web-based information technology, is increasing competitive pressures. Competition online can increase in a number of areas, as outlined below.

### Prices

The web-based business is faced with very competitive pricing. A recent survey by Sage showed that in 2005 most businesses expected a squeeze on profits caused by increased price competition. Businesses deciding to trade online are often obliged to publish lists of their prices. These lists are then quoted by price comparison services such as Kelkoo or Dealtime. This is known as 'price transparency'.

### Recruitment

When it comes to competitive pressures on business, access to quality staff is still top of the list according to the Sage report. The web creates a fiercely competitive recruitment environment.

## Case study

**Pricing on the Internet**

The following is adapted from an article by Lester Haines in *The Channel Register*, November 2005 (www.channelregister.co.uk):

'Sony and other manufacturers have been accused of asking online retailers for 10–15 per cent more for wholesale electronic goods than they charge their traditional counterparts,' *The Times* reports.

'This "dual pricing" strategy – designed to narrow the price differential between net and high street – was allegedly initiated by Sony and quickly adopted by other suppliers. Big-name retail chains have exerted pressure on the electrical giants at a time of falling high street sales in the face of cut-price Internet offers.

'"The cost of distribution through the Internet is about 20% of sales, compared with 45% of sales for a bricks-and-mortar store, and consumers have greatly benefited as a result of online operations," argues retail management consultant Edward Whitfield.'
© The Register

1. What is meant by 'dual pricing?' ✓
2. What is a 'bricks and mortar' store? ✓✓
3. If you were advising a high street store selling mainly electrical goods, how would you suggest that it improved its preparation to meet growing Internet competition? ✓✓✓

## Thinking point

What other competitive pressures do you think are brought to a business by the Internet?

## Relocations, take-overs, closures and mergers

We saw at the beginning of the unit how Internet shopping is growing in popularity and looks set to continue to grow at a rapid rate. This has caused particular pressure on the retail sector. When firms face declining market share, and are unable to compete, there is a tendency to look for ways of strengthening the position. This can include relocations and sometimes take-overs by or of another business. The extreme response is to close an outlet altogether; alternatively, mergers with other firms can sometimes create a stronger business, better able to compete.

The implications of a decision to close down a business operation can be immense for a region or a community. Jobs are lost that will affect families. This loss of jobs can have a knock-on effect on other businesses in the area. The whole effect can snowball.

## Refocusing business

Some business activities have been completely changed in order to take up Internet opportunities, as can be seen in the case study below.

## Case study

### Save and Drive

Save and Drive (www.saveanddrive.co.uk) is a 'clicks and mortar' motor accessories supplier – this means there is a physical store and web-based transactional website. It is based in the City of Sunderland, in north-east England. The business began as a Motorist Discount Centre, selling car accessories in 1977. In those days there was a strong market for car parts and accessories.

By the 1990s the market for car parts was in decline. Cars had become much more reliable. Design improvements meant that many replaceable components were obsolete; engines had evolved into 'black boxes' that were computer managed. Modules could be unplugged and replaced. It was now the era of the 'throw away car'. People had stopped coming into the Motorist Discount Centres for do-it-yourself car maintenance and repair.

Save and Drive had to refocus its business or close down. The owners decided to set up a website that promoted their full range of accessories. They found, for instance, that there was a market for roof boxes and that these could be marketed online. Indeed the whole range of accessories could be offered online.

Today Save and Drive uses a promotional and e-commerce website. People can purchase online in a secure payments system. All of the information a customer needs is available from the site. If not, staff are available to give advice and personal assistance.

One of the dangers of adopting an online strategy such as this is that local customers will stop visiting the physical store. In fact, Save and Drive has succeeded in keeping local people interested in the physical range of products while at the same time extending its market reach online.

1. Describe how Save and Drive has changed its business. Do you think that new skills would have been needed? ✓
2. Explain how far you think that the owners of Save and Drive have 'refocused' their business. ✓✓
3. Could it be argued that Save and Drive has not 'refocused' at all; it has just opened up a new sales channel? Explain and justify your answer. ✓✓✓
4. What would a business have to do to completely refocus its activities? ✓✓✓

# Implications of trends on customers

The Internet offers great opportunities for those who have the skills and understanding, or the cash, to be able to take advantage. For those who do not have such opportunities, there is disadvantage. Many people, mostly those already poor or socially disadvantaged in some other way, cannot or do not have access to the new technologies and the opportunities they bring. These people – the 'socially excluded' – are said to be on the wrong side of the 'digital divide' because they lack the technical literacy skills to access the range of full digital services available to others.

Income, education and age are the biggest factors in creating the digital divide, according to a European Union report ('e-Inclusion revisited: the local dimension of the Information Society'). It reveals that women are taking to technology in greater numbers than ever, and the over-55s are also gaining computer skills. But poor, badly educated people are still lagging behind.

### Practice point

Research the report 'e-Inclusion revisited: the local dimension of the Information Society'. Summarise its findings and write a report offering your own conclusions.

Those who do not have Internet access are the ones with the most to lose if high street businesses are forced out of business. We saw earlier that the retail sector is under pressure. The loss of physical outlets or services will hit these people harder, increasing social disadvantage.

### Thinking point

'Poorly educated people have no chance of accessing the Internet properly' – do you agree? Explain your response.

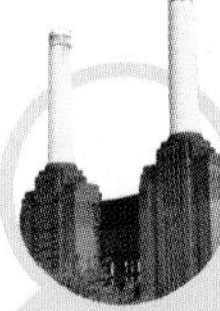

### Outcome activity 29.3

You have been asked to help local business leaders who are experiencing a downturn in their businesses.

**Pass**

Describe the competitive forces that apply to two contrasting organisations to develop or update their use of e-business. P3

**Merit**

Explain, using two contrasting organisations, how they have responded to the competitive forces that have caused them to update or develop their use of e-business and give reasons for their responses. M2

◄ More and more older people are gaining computer skills

## Grading tips

**Pass** 

You need to take two businesses, so your work will have two sections. Then look at the various competitive forces and create headings for each one. Say how these forces might cause each business to think about using the Internet to compete more strongly.

**Merit** 

Merit grades are awarded for analytical work. In this context you need to take two organisations using the web and then relate the various competitive forces to what they are actually doing. Explain how external forces might have obliged them to take up the Internet opportunity. For example, did they see an opportunity for more sales to keep up market share?

# 29.4 Key features of planning for an increased use of e-business

## Government support

The Internet does not belong to any one country; it is a 'stateless' phenomenon that crosses national and international boundaries. Both the UK and the European Union – of which we are a part – have adopted policies designed to encourage both private and business Internet use. The UK government has had a policy to make the UK 'the best place in which to do e-business'. The European Union has a stated aim of creating an 'information society' amongst all member states.

### Legislative framework

#### ■ E-Commerce Regulations 2002

In 2002, the EU issued instructions to all member states to implement the E-Commerce Regulations. These must be taken into account by any business intending to trade online. The key features of the Electronic Commerce (EC Directive) Regulations 2002 are as follows:

- Online selling and advertising is subject to the laws of the UK if the trader is established in the UK. Online services provided from other Member States may not be restricted. There are exceptions, particularly for contracts with consumers and the freedom of parties to choose the applicable law.
- Recipients of online services must be given clearly defined information about the trader, the nature of commercial communications (i.e. emails) and how to complete an online transaction.
- Online service providers are exempt from liability for the content that they convey or store in specified circumstances.
- Changes to the powers of enforcement authorities, such as Trading Standards Departments and the Office of Fair Trading.

The purpose of the directive (and the Regulations) is to ensure the free movement of 'information society services' across the European Community and to encourage greater use of e-commerce by breaking down barriers across Europe.

## ■ Consumer Protection Distance Selling Regulations

Distance selling means selling and buying by phone, mail order, via the Internet or digital TV. Such transactions are covered generally by normal buying and selling legislation, but they are also covered by special Distance Selling Regulations.

Distance Selling Regulations give protection to consumers who shop by phone, mail order, via the Internet or digital TV. This protection includes:

- the right to receive clear information about goods and services before deciding to buy
- confirmation of this information in writing
- a cooling-off period of seven working days in which the consumer can withdraw from the contract
- protection from credit card fraud.

## ■ Data Protection Act

The Data Protection Act 1998 is the law that governs the processing of personal information held on living, identifiable individuals. Businesses must comply with the Act if they process personal information about people.

The Act requires that a business is open about the use of information and follows certain principles for processing that information. These principles are known as the eight data protection principles. The Act also provides individuals with certain rights, including the right of subject access.

### Practice point

What are the eight data protection principles? Do you think these are important to a business? Why?

### Business support and education

The UK government offers free training and advice for businesses that are considering adopting a strategy of e-commerce. The website at www.businesslink.gov.uk gives advice on training, grants and support schemes. The Department of Trade and Industry (DTI) attempts to promote e-commerce through its innovation advice programme and has tried to encourage a nationwide knowledge network (see www.dti.gov.uk). The DTI also promotes a 'digital content forum' that specifically looks at the needs of the digital media industries.

# Organisational level

### Strategic level decisions

Strategic decisions at organisational level have a big impact on which direction a business takes and, of course, on whether it succeeds or fails in its marketplace. The Leeds business Card Corporation took a strategy decision based on e-commerce that intended to make full use of Internet technology (see the 'Real Lives' feature).

### Location of manufacture and service provision

The Card Corporation website illustrates another aspect of the Internet. Because it is a stateless media, people can access data and interact with designs from a distance. This means that the potential for online collaboration is significant – irrespective of location.

In manufacturing, global businesses are increasingly giving consideration as to where is the best location to carry out production activities. It is often felt that these businesses will relocate only in areas where labour is cheap.

One of the major business functions capable of relocation is customer services. A big incentive to do this is the availability of a large local supply of personnel. The mobile telecoms company, 'three network' offers its customer service provision from India.

Some businesses have adopted an e-commerce website and 'outsourced' their customer service function. The Kingfisher Group's DIY.com outsourced product enquiries and customer service to another company called Spark Response, at Follingsby Park, Gateshead.

## Real lives

### Card Corporation

Card Corporation (www.cardcorp.co.uk)was founded in 1988 by Ivor Jacobs. The business set out to plug a market gap by producing short-run print items such as business stationery. It could only achieve its aim by being a 'seamless' end-to-end e-business – internally integrated and open to its supply chain partners. Its own systems needed to focus on providing a cost-effective, high-quality service, eliminating many of the costs and delays associated with traditional communication and the transfer of information.

An integrated approach to technology has given the company a single system that offers:

- online ordering, design, approval, dispatch and order tracking
- automatic data capture
- the conversion of designs from low resolution (on the website) to high resolution (in print)
- the rendering of material into a press-ready format
- digital printing
- automated guillotining and finishing.

Having built its own technology infrastructure, the company was also well placed to amend its processes in response to customer requests. 'Whenever a customer or supplier comes to us and says they'd like a certain feature to be added, we go back and write it in. They're the people who are using it, so we have to take their suggestions on board,' says Ivor.

Because it integrated technology from the start, many of the traditional measures of success, such as cost savings or increased sales, don't apply to Card Corporation. The benefits are more straightforward – web technology made the company possible. It enabled the company to meet an unanswered demand and to do so very profitably.

Card Corporation has very few direct competitors and, with sales snowballing, turnover is increasing at an annual rate of 80–90%. Its pioneering role in the industry has also allowed Card Corporation to grow through word of mouth, rather than through extensive marketing campaigns. 'People tell other people about our site because they've had such a good experience from it,' says Ivor. 'Other people's take-up of faster bandwidths and general misunderstanding of what technology is all about is a barrier,' he admits.

As an early adopter of an e-business strategy, Card Corporation's response is to help move its trading partners forward as well. It does this by building simple but powerful features into its system that will provide demonstrable benefits to clients. For example, the company has set up an automated online approval tool and has built sufficient flexibility into its system that it can develop new offerings in response to client requests. This adaptability helps clients see the benefits of technology and encourages them to e-enable their own businesses.

Although cost is a major consideration for all businesses, Ivor feels that you have to be patient about when you will see a return on your investment: 'You have to be persistent and push through any financial obstacles.' Ivor sees consumer adoption of broadband as the next significant step for the growth of the company and for e-business generally. 'We're hoping that more customers embrace broadband – as we do a lot of image swapping, broadband would speed up the process markedly for us,' he explains.

Read the information above and research the www.cardcorps.co.uk website.

1. Describe the company's e-commerce strategy. Why do you think it appears to be succeeding? ✓
2. Do you think that the Internet has allowed Card Corporation to offer a better service to clients? How? ✓✓
3. What is meant by 'seamless end to end e-business'? Prepare a summary of what this is in relation to Card Corporation. ✓✓✓

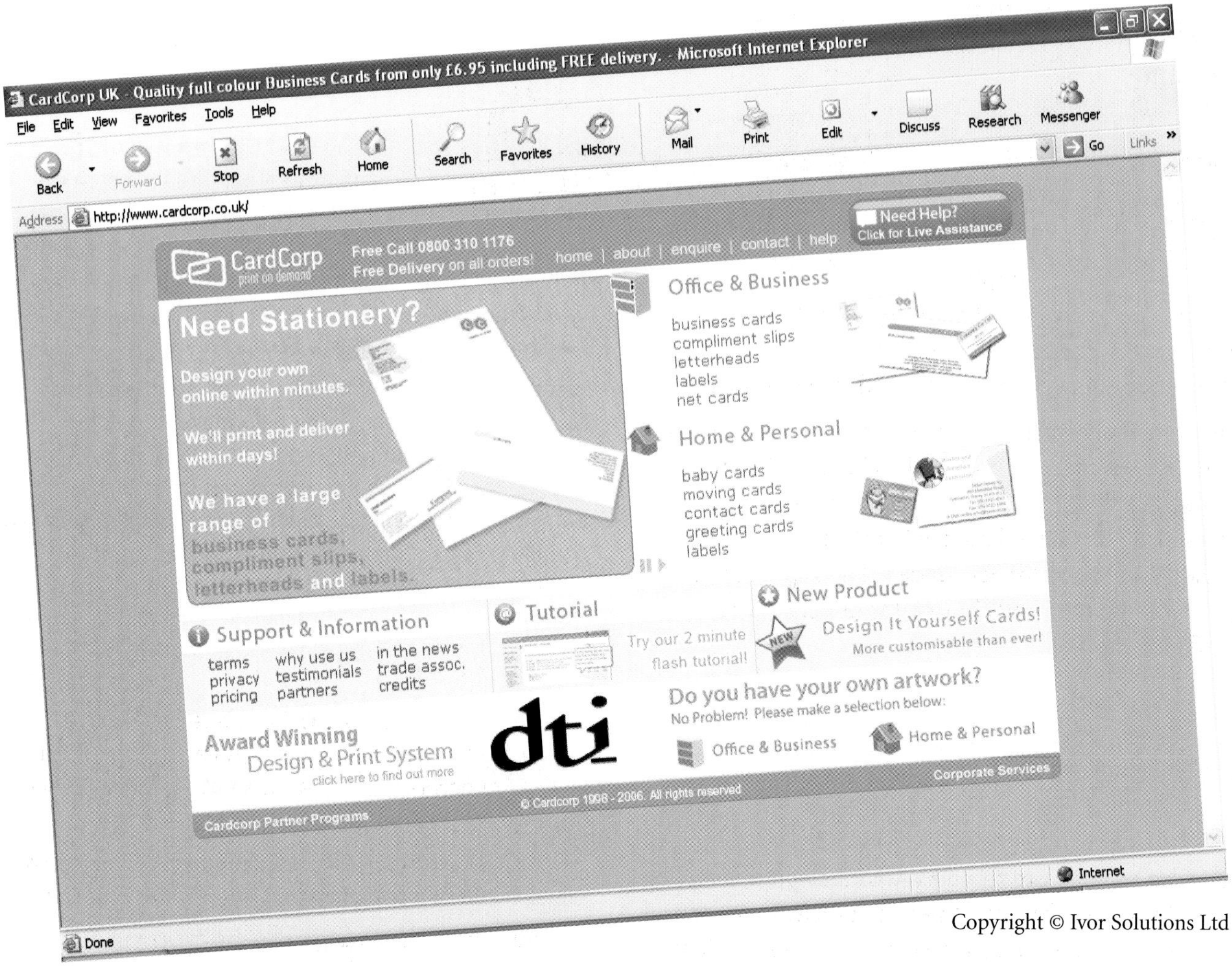

▲ **Card Corporation website – an e-business strategy**

Customers surfing to www.diy.com placed an order, made an enquiry or a request and all of these were dealt with by SparkResponse personnel, albeit with B&Q managers on site.

## Re-engineering of business processes

The 're-engineering' of business processes is a systematic method of examining everything a business does, from top to bottom. Why are particular processes done? What is the reason for them? Are they still needed?

A business that adopts an e-business strategy will need to look again at all of its 'functional areas' to see how they integrate with the whole business. There is no place for separate 'silos' of data that are used only by one specialist function. All data within the organisation is related to the whole purpose – everyone must base their day-to-day activities, their planning, and their objectives upon the same sets of data.

This reinforces the need for a high quality, secure, network that is accessible to all decision makers.

### Remember

An e-business must have processes that make use of digital data. Process re-engineering checks all processes (ordering, stock taking, selling, manufacturing, quality controls) to make sure they are contributing to the organisation's objectives.

## Redefining the supply chain

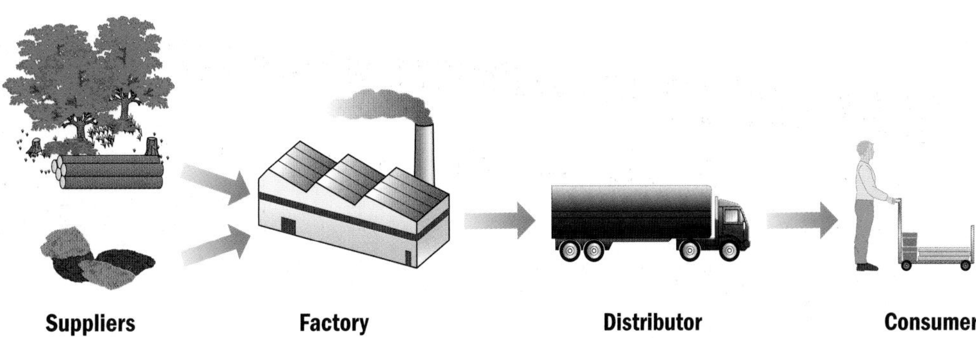


▲ The supply chain

What is a supply chain?

A supply chain for the factory in the diagram consists on one side of a network of suppliers that the business deals with and on the other side a network of customers. Supply chains differ for different products.

The Internet allows firms working together in a supply chain the chance to become much closer in the ways they work. As has been described, there can be a process of 'disintermediation' where 'distributors' or 'wholesalers' are no longer needed. The supply chain becomes integrated and shorter. Ideally, customers benefit.

## Investment in information technology

Obviously, businesses must invest in IT if they are to succeed in making productive use of the opportunities from e-business. This investment can include: hardware and software requirements; security issues to consider; website design and maintenance; and network technologies to weigh up.

From a strategic view, the question is, whether a business should 'outsource' the IT function. This means that the installation and maintenance of IT becomes subject to an external contract with another business. The internal operation of IT systems remains with the organisation's own staff.

## Acquisition and development of appropriaate skills

Basic IT skills are becoming essential for staff in all organisations. If a business is to go ahead with an 'e' strategy it is even more important that its employees are IT literate. Many employees can learn 'on the job' by training at their desk. Often, IT contractors can train staff as part of the initial contract and this has the advantage that they are most familiar with the software and the systems that they have been responsible for implementing. Ideally, in such a situation, the IT contractor will have consulted with staff users before a computer system is implemented.

Alternatively, staff can be trained by external IT trainers 'in house' or off the premises. The ECDL (European Computer Driving Licence) has become the recognised measure of computer literacy.

### Case study

**Business link**

The government's own business link service offers practical business advice about selecting IT suppliers from its website at www.businesslink.gov.uk.

1. What sort of advice is given to businesses on the site about 'choosing an IT supplier'? ✓
2. Write a summary of the advice for people considering an e-business strategy. ✓✓
3. Do you think that businesses need the kind of advice service offered by Business Link? Why? ✓✓✓

### Remember

Staff training is essential if a business is to make effective use of IT. Staff should be aware of the implications of IT and know how it will affect their jobs.

# Individual level

## Growth of home computing

In 1981 IBM launched the first home computer, the IBM 5051. At today's prices the machine would cost you £2500. In 1982, a British entrepreneur, Sir Clive Sinclair, launched a mass market ZX Spectrum machine which cost just £125 (about £307 at today's prices). The ZX held only 16K of memory. (PCs today are said to give 11,000% extra capacity!)

However, it was the start of home computing. Before then computers were confined to large obscure rooms usually located in basements within workplaces. Since 2001, the market for home computing has grown by 52%. More than 6.5 million home computers will be sold in the UK in 2006 and according to Jupiter, the research company, 70% of UK homes have a PC.

This means that home computing is continuing to grow. Computers are becoming the central entertainment area in households. More and more families are connecting their computers to TV flat panels; the TV screen becomes the computer screen.

### Remember

Home computing continues to grow. Technology gets better; devices converge and more and more can network. The opportunities for web-based businesses to communicate are potentially great.

The computer has evolved into the home entertainment centre rather than being the thing that produces spreadsheets.

## Employability and ICT skills

Individuals increasingly have to consider their personal level of ICT skill. Employers can offer IT training, as we saw earlier. However, for those who are out of work or considering a career change, it is essential that they possess at least the basics in computer literacy. The British Computer Society's European Computer Driving Licence (ECDL) has been used by 1.5 million people in the UK to acquire the basics.

If the UK is to compete successfully in the wider European knowledge economy, the ICT skills of the entire workforce need to be improved, according to IT trade body Intellect.

### Thinking point

Investigate the 'Home Computing Initiative' (HCI). What is it? What did it intend to do? Do you feel that it is a good thing?

## Increase in flexible working models

Some organisations today employ only a reduced full-time permanent 'core' of multi-skilled staff. There is an increase in secondments, part-time or flexible working patterns, and work being contracted-out to freelance or self-employed individuals. Because information technology allows novel forms of communication between individuals and organisations, people can adopt more flexible work patterns.

From an individual staff viewpoint, there is the likelihood that at some point in their working life they will need to change job roles and get new skills. Lifelong careers have been replaced by lifelong learning.

## Real lives

**Woolley & Co. Solicitors (www.business-lawfirm.co.uk)**

'We run as a virtual firm, all our lawyers and typists/ support staff work from home on total flexi-time and flexi-holidays. We have no offices.

'We get incredibly high quality lawyers from top firms joining us because of the lifestyle they can achieve. We would never attract those lawyers to a small firm like ours without this flexibility. We have never had any issue with trust or how long people have worked, etc. Good professional people know what hours to work and don't need it enforced.'

1. Describe what is meant by flexible working. ✓
2. Do you think that flexible working depends on IT skills? ✓✓

## Outcome activity 29.4

Continuing your work as an advising business consultant, you have been asked to prepare some further information for local business in various sectors, considering opting for an online sales channel based on network computer systems.

**Pass**

Prepare a presentation that describes (using examples) how the various stakeholders in an e-business strategy can plan effectively for the growing use of e-business. You must cover: the government, business organisations and individuals.

**Distinction**

For a particular business showing especially keen interest in a new e-business strategy, prepare a written report making justified recommendations as to how it may improve its preparation for the growing use of the Internet by all business organisations. Produce an appendix to the report, outlining how individuals can improve their own preparation.

## Grading tips

**Pass** 

This descriptive presentation falls into three sections. You should look at government initiatives such as Business Link or the DTI website to describe the UK government approach to helping businesses compete online. There are also EU measures. For business organisations, describe training, the nature of their product, cost factors and supply chain considerations. Finally, individuals have to think about skills, job security and career planning.

**Distinction** 

Distinction grade work (the best!) has to demonstrate an evaluation of things based on the evidence you have seen or researched. In this context, you have to consider the ways in which a particular business can prepare for e-business. For instance, the government has introduced regulations; can the organisation meet these? Staff and an employer must think about their skills; the business must think about its internal systems. At this level, work must be based on your own evaluation of the facts.

## End of unit test

1. How would you distinguish between the 'Internet' and the worldwide web?
2. What is a 'wireless network'?
3. Describe how a business might make use of a range of mobile devices for Internet access.
4. What is e-procurement and what are its advantages?
5. How could a business make use of the Internet for promotional purposes?
6. How could a business conduct research on the Internet?
7. What are the main security issues for a business considering doing online business?
8. Describe the following protective measures that a business can take when it plans to go online:
   - firewall
   - password
   - authentication
   - organisational policies
   - payment methods.
9. What is meant by 'competitive forces'? How can the following potential advantages of e-business assist a business to meet them?
   - increased sales
   - cost savings
   - wider market reach
   - better marketing opportunities.
10. What is the 'supply chain' and how does the Internet help?
11. What are the main legal considerations for a possible e-business?
12. How could a business plan for developing an online business strategy?
13. What sources of advice would you recommend for a possible e-business and why?
14. What is meant by 'process re-engineering' and why might it be needed for a newly developing e-business?

# Resources

www.clickz.com – Click Zstats, specialist online service

http://searchenginewatch.com – Search engine marketing

www.statistics.gov.uk – National Statistics (ONS)

http://www.theregister.co.uk/ – The Register

www.norton.com – Norton Anti-virus

www.businesslink.gov.uk – Business Link

www.dti.gov.uk – Department of Trade and Industry

www.saveanddrive.co.uk – Save and Drive, motor accessories supplier

www.webstandards.org – Web Standards Project

www.usenet.org.uk – News groups site

# Books

Amor, D. 2002 *The e-business (r)evolution,* Prentice Hall

Chaffey, D., Mayer, Johnston and Ellis-Chadwick, F. 2003 *Internet Marketing* (second edition), Prentice Hall

Goymer, J. 2004 *BTEC National e-Business Book 1,* Heinemann

| Grading criteria | Outcome activity | Page number |
|---|---|---|
| To achieve a pass grade the evidence must show that the learner is able to: | | |
| P1 Describe how the Internet operates and give eight examples of how it is used by selected contrasting business organisations | 29.1 | 413 |
| P2 Describe how the Internet can be used for different types of business activity, taking actions to reduce the inherent risks to security and reliability | 29.2 | 431 |
| P3 Describe the competitive forces on two selected contrasting business organisations to develop or update their use of e-business | 29.3 | 440 |
| P4 Describe (using examples) how the government, business organisations and individuals plan for the growing use of e-business | 29.4 | 447 |
| To achieve a merit grade the evidence must show that, in addition to the pass criteria, the learner is able to: | | |
| M1 Demonstrate how to solve problems in Internet use for four different types of business activity | 29.2 | 431 |
| M2 Explain how two selected contrasting business organisations have responded to the competitive forces to develop or update their use of e-business and give reasons for their responses | 29.3 | 440 |
| To achieve a distinction grade the evidence must show that, in addition to the pass and merit criteria, the learner is able to: | | |
| D1 Make justified recommendations as to how a selected business organisation and an individual could improve their preparation for the growing use of the Internet by business organisations | 29.4 | 447 |

# Glossary

**Accessibility** Methods used to make business communications (and all aspects of everyday life) accessible to people with disabilities.

**Acid test ratio** Current assets minus stock/current liabilities. This ratio shows how well a business can meet its liabilities without having to sell stock.

**Advertising media** Communication channels, including print media (newspapers, magazines, direct mail letters); broadcast media (radio, television,); display media (billboards, signs, posters) and the Internet (pod-casting).

**Aesthetically pleasing** When a building is designed and decorated to look attractive to the eye.

**Alienation** Situation in which individuals do not feel as if they belong to a unit or business. Teamwork helps to reduce alienation by creating a feeling of belonging to the team.

**Applicant** The person applying for a job.

**Assets** Items of value within an organisation. This could also include money owed to the business (debtors).

**Auction** Selling items to the highest bidder.

**Average cost per item** The typical cost of making or selling an item. These costs are separate from overheads.

**Average stock** This is opening stock plus closing stock divided by two.

**B2B** Business-to-business markets.

**B2C** Business-to-consumer markets.

**Balance sheet** An overview of the financial position of a business on a particular date showing its total assets and liabilities (money it owes).

**Bespoke** When something is specially made for an individual or organisation.

**Bias** The difference between the answer given by respondents and the truth.

**Body language** Gestures, expressions and movements that a person subconsciously uses to communicate.

**Blog** A frequently updated online diary, with links to other blogs or websites.

**Brand image** The set of views and opinions consumers hold about a product.

**Breaking bulk** Breaking into smaller amounts. This is an important part of a retailer's function – buying large quantities from a producer or wholesaler and offering smaller quantities to consumers.

**Capital** Money put into the business by the owner(s) to get it started or to buy equipment.

**Cascading training** The process when someone gives training to others. They pass on skills that they might have gained from doing the job or after completing a training course.

**Closing stock** The value of stocks of finished products held in the business at the end of the year.

**Common law** Developed through the courts, this is based on previous decisions. Precedent, as it is called, requires the courts to follow past decisions in cases with similar facts and covering the same points of law.

**Confidentiality** Keeping information secure and only allowing it to be given to people with permission to see it.

**Consumer benefit** What the consumer will gain if they buy the product, e.g. buyers of iPods can enjoy the music of their favourite artists virtually anywhere.

**Continuous improvement (Kaizen)** The ability across the organisation to make improvements to the way things are done, including working practices and customer service. Each employee is responsible for their own small set of changes that builds up a culture of improvement.

**Contribution** The financial contribution that each unit of an item sold makes towards paying off the fixed costs of a business. For example if the variable cost of producing a biro is 10p and the biro is sold for 40p, each biro is contributing 30p (revenue minus variable cost = 40 – 10 = 30).

**Copyright** Law which states that the original creator of a work has control over people using and making copies of their work.

**Corporate image** The characteristics an organisation seeks to establish for itself in the minds of the public.

**Credit** Involves receiving a good or service now and paying for some or all of it over a period of time.

**Creditors** People to whom the business owes money for goods or services it has received.

**Current assets** Money that is readily available in the business for paying debts.

**Current liabilities** Amounts owed to suppliers or lenders which are due to be repaid fairly shortly (usually within one year).

**Customer value** The difference between the value the customer gains from owning and using a product and the cost (price) of obtaining the product.

## D

**Debtors** People that owe the business money for goods or services they have received.

**Deferred shares** Similar to ordinary shares except that dividends are only paid in certain circumstances, such as a certain level of profit. They appear in the 'capital and reserves' or 'financed by' section of the balance sheet.

**Demand** Exists when consumers have wants and needs backed up by the purchasing power to buy the products they desire.

**Democratic** Organisations in which grassroots employees are involved in decision making.

**Dependent variable** Responds to the change in the other variable.

**Depreciation** The loss in value of the assets of the business over time, due mainly to wear and tear.

**Disintermediation** Where the intermediaries in a supply chain are eliminated because they are no longer required on the web.

**Displacement activities** Involuntary movements that indicate a degree of nervousness in a person.

**Disposable income** Money that is left to an individual once taxes, such as income tax, are deducted and the household bills, mortgage/rent etc. are paid.

**Distribution network** Support structure and businesses that help goods to be moved from where they are made to the customers who buy them.

**Dividend** This is a share of company profits received by shareholders each six months or annually. They appear in the appropriations section of the profit and loss account.

## E

**E-business** A business that has digitised many of its internal functions by using computer systems. These are often connected to the web.

**E-commerce** Buying and selling conducted electronically over the Internet.

**Economies of scale** The cost to do a job or make a product reduces as more are made, for example through bulk buying or expertise within the company.

**E-marketing remix** New marketing tactics designed to market a web-based business.

**Empathy** Understand the problems, opinions and feelings of other people and imagining clearly what it would be like to be in their position.

**Employability skills** A range of skills that will allow a person to perform different jobs well.

**Empowerment** The process of spreading power and decision-making responsibility across the organisation and within teams, rather than a few key individuals retaining it.

**Extended marketing mix** The normal elements of product, price, promotion, packaging and place plus another 3Ps (often referred to as the 7Ps) associated with marketing services: people, process and physical evidence.

**External information** Information found outside an organisation.

**External recruitment** Recruiting outside the business.

**External research data** This is secondary data that is available outside an organisation, such as government statistics.

**Extranet** Restricted network that extends outside an organisation to include other computers.

**Fixed assets** Capital items of value which the business has bought and will use for an extended period of time, such as buildings, machinery, equipment and vehicles.

**Fixed costs** Costs which the firm has to pay, regardless of how much they make or sell. For example, the sandwich shops would have to pay out rent, rates and electricity charges whatever their level of sales.

**Flat organisation** An organisation with only limited numbers of layers of command. The distance between grassroots employees and senior managers is relatively small.

**Flow chart** Diagram illustrating a process that involves a number of steps and a series of decisions.

**Flow production** Manufacturing where goods move through a continuous line of different stages until the goods are finished e.g. canned foods.

**Franchise** Granting another individual or business the right to set up or trade using your name, and to provide the service that you provide or the product that you supply.

**Government regulations** Rules set out by the government that businesses need to go by.

**Gross profit** The profit figure at the end of the trading account; it is the difference between a company's total revenue and how much it cost to make the product or buy products in. Gross profit does not include the general expenses of the business.

**Hacking** Breaking into an electronic computer system and trying to access data illegally.

**Hardware** The physical parts of an IT system such as the keyboard or screen.

**Harvard referencing system** A commonly accepted format for detailing the sources you have used in compiling your research.

**HM Customs and Excise** The government tax office that deals with collecting VAT payments.

**Incentive** Something that is used to encourage people to work harder.

**Independent variable** Causes the change in the other variable.

**In-house** Employees within the organisation carry out the work.

**Insolvency** Where a business is unable to pay debts when they become due for payment.

**Intellectual property** Any original work of literature, art, music, computer software, sound recording, film or broadcast that has some commercial value.

**Intention movements** Involuntary gestures that indicate people's intentions.

**Internal information** Information found inside the organisation.

**Internal recruitment** Recruiting someone who already works for the business to do a different job.

**Internal research data** This is secondary information held inside an organisation, such as sales records and customer complaint reports.

**Internet protocols** Agreed ways of doing things so that everyone on the Internet connects in the same way.

**Interpersonal skills** Skills that enable us to get on with other people and promote positive relationships in the workplace.

**Intranet** Restricted computer network confined to a specific organisation.

**Invoice** A demand for payment sent to the customer once the goods (or services) have been sent to the customer.

**Job description** This is the list of working conditions that come with a job, for example pay, hours and duties.

**Leasing** Paying to use a factory or machine for an agreed amount of time.

**Legibility** How easy a document is for your audience to read, its 'readability'.

**Liabilities** Monies that the business owes.

**Liquidity** The ability of a business to change its assets or stock into cash to be able to pay its bills.

**Long-term liabilities** Sums that have to be paid for in more than one year's time, such as a mortgage on company property or a long-term bank loan.

**Manufacturing** Making things (in the secondary sector).

**Marketing mix** The combination of product, price, place (sometimes called distribution), promotion, people, processes and physical evidence offered by an organisation to potential consumers.

**Market share** The sales of a product by a company expressed as a percentage of total sales in a market. If a company sells 20,000 products and the total number of those products sold overall is 200,000 then that company has a market share of 10%.

**Mobile technology** Portable devices that can connect to the worldwide web.

**Multimedia** Communication involving a variety of media such as text slides, photographs, images, video, sounds, music and links to Internet sites.

**Net profit** The gross profit less the other costs of the business that are needed to run it, e.g. rent or staff wages.

**Non-probability sampling** This relies on the judgement of the researcher in terms of selecting respondents.

**Notice period** The time an employee must work for their current employer before they are allowed to leave.

**Online value proposition** Characteristics about a website that make people want to use it.

**Open-ended terms** Terms that are written much more vaguely than others. This allows the employer and employee some flexibility about what they actually require. Sometimes an employer might write into the job description a statement that covers 'any other reasonable duties as required by the post'.

**Opportunity cost** The cost to an organisation of making one decision over another – the cost of the lost opportunity.

**'Opt-in' emailing** Collecting permissions from customers to send them emails detailing future services or promotions.

**Outsourcing** Paying for outside contractors to do some of the work rather than doing it yourself. You buy in services from outside sources.

**Overheads** Costs that do not change when the business sells more products and which are not incurred by a specific department of the company, such as rent.

**Patent** If you invent something, registering a patent will give you the right to stop others from making it without your permission for a certain period of time.

**Perception** The process by which people select, organise and interpret information to form a 'picture' of a product in their mind.

**Perishable** Goods that are perishable are likely to spoil or go off, for example food items with limited dates on them.

**Permanent** The person is to be employed until that person decides to leave or the job ceases to exist.

**Personalisation** Where a web page is presented in such a way that it offers personal messages based on an individual's tastes and preferences.

**Person specification** Attributes needed by the person to perform a job, such as personality type or experience.

**Plant** The factory or base where the machinery is located; may also refer to mobile machinery and equipment.

**PowerPoint** Applications software produced by Microsoft that allows you to produce professional and versatile slides for display using a computer during a presentation.

**Press releases** Brief news items or information given to newspapers and magazines.

**Primary research** Carried out to find new information required for a marketing research project, which has never previously been collected.

**Primary sector** Extracting raw products from nature.

**Primary source** Original information that you have researched for yourself.

**Privatisation** Transferring the ownership of a business from the government to private owners.

**Proactive** When someone is seeking out problems or issues and trying to resolve them before they are actually formally presented to them.

**Probability sampling** This means that everybody in the population has the same chance of being selected, just as in the Lottery draw every ball has an equal chance of being selected at any time. This requires everybody in the population to be known and allocated a number.

**Productivity** How efficiently a business can produce goods/services and profit.

**Profit** Difference between money coming in (revenue) and costs paid out.

**Publicity material** Publications produced by an organisation that are intended to attract attention and promote sales.

**Purchases** For a manufacturing company this is the value of raw materials purchased; for a service business it would be the cost of items bought to sell to customers or used to provide a service to customers.

**Quality circle** A study group of volunteers (typically 5 to15 people) who meet regularly to discuss and work on a variety of work-related problems and to put solutions in place.

**Qualitative research** Provides information of a qualitative nature, such as about why people buy, what motivates them to buy or their impression of, for example, products and advertisements.

**Quantitative research** Produces numbers and figures, such as the number and percentage of consumers who are aware of a brand.

**Recruitment** Taking on employees

**Resolution** The amount of fine detail in a picture. Photographs normally require much finer detail than simple drawings. On a computer, picture detail is measured in dpi or dots per inch.

**Respondent** A person who is asked and agrees to participate in a marketing research project.

**Retailing** Selling things in small quantities (shops in the tertiary sector).

**Retained profit** Profits that have not been distributed to the shareholders but are saved to finance future expansion of the business. They appear in the appropriations section of the profit and loss account.

**Retention** Keeping employees at the workplace for as long as possible to benefit from their experience.

**Sales revenue** Number of sales multiplied by average price per item sold.

**Secondary research** Makes use of work already carried out by someone else for some other marketing project or other purpose.

**Secondary sector** Transforming those raw products into finished and part-finished goods.

**Secondary source** Information found from previously published or written sources either within or outside the organisation.

**Secure payments** Payments system on a website that offers security to customers who know that credit or debit card details cannot be stolen.

**Security threats** Openings in the software or networking arrangements of an e-business that allow intrusion, data theft or virus infections.

**Self-managing team** Team that has had the training and developed the skills to work on its own to solve work-related issues.

**Sequencing** The careful ordering of questions to reduce the impact of bias as well as putting questions into a logical order to encourage completion.

**Server** A higher capacity computer that offers services to client computers that can connect to it.

**Skip questions** These direct respondents to the questions they should answer.

**Software** The packages that make the computer work, e.g. Microsoft Windows or Vista or applications packages to be used on the computer such as Microsoft Word or Excel

**Sole trader** A person who owns and runs their own business.

**Solvency** An organisation is able to pay its expenses as it has money available within the business.

**Statutory law** This is created when Parliament passes new legislation through an Act of Parliament.

**Stock** This is the total value of raw materials that will be made into goods for sale, partly manufactured items and also items that have been completely made or bought in by the business and are available for sale to customers.

**Stock turnover** The measurement of how quickly the business has sold the value of its stock. The higher the turnover, the quicker the business is selling its stock. This is very important in a business where goods are updated quickly or are perishable.

**Strategy** The business plan.

**Subjectivity** A feature of qualitative data analysis that means the research findings and conclusions are only the opinions that the researchers formed from the research.

**Synergy** Sometimes described as the 2 + 2 = 5 effect, i.e. the combination of individual efforts leading to greater efficiency, because the combined effort is greater than the sum of the individual efforts.

**Temporary** For a limited amount of time specified, e.g. a month or a year.

**Tertiary sector** Providing services to individuals and businesses.

**Trading account** The first of the set of final accounts, this account shows how profitably the firm makes goods or processes them for sale to customers. The trading account calculates the gross profit earned by the business.

**Turnover** This is another term describing sales revenue.

**Variable cost** A cost that increases with the level of output or sales, e.g. the cost of ingredients in producing smoothies.

## D

## E

## F

## G

## H

## I



## J



## L

## M

## Q

## R



## S

## T



## U



## V